SPRINGER PUBLISHING

MW01487110

GET THE MOST FROM YOUR BOOK

 SPRINGER PUBLISHING
CONNECT™

VOUCHER CODE:

4YY04YMV

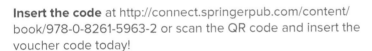

Online Access

Your print purchase of *Fundamentals of Case and Caseload Management: Skills for Rehabilitation Practice*, includes **online access via Springer Publishing Connect**™ to increase accessibility, portability, and searchability.

Insert the code at http://connect.springerpub.com/content/book/978-0-8261-5963-2 or scan the QR code and insert the voucher code today!

Having trouble? Contact our customer service department at cs@springerpub.com

Instructor Resource Access for Adopters

Let us do some of the heavy lifting to create an engaging classroom experience with a variety of instructor resources included in most textbooks SUCH AS:

INSTRUCTOR MANUAL

POWERPOINTS

TEST BANK

Visit **https://connect.springerpub.com/** and look for the **"Show Supplementary"** button on your **book homepage** to see what is available to instructors! First time using Springer Publishing Connect?

Email **textbook@springerpub.com** to create an account and start unlocking valuable resources.

Fundamentals of
Case and Caseload
Management

Lee Ann Rawlins Williams, PhD, CRC, CFLE, currently serves as a Clinical Assistant Professor within the Education, Health, and Behavior Studies Department at the University of North Dakota. In her role, she not only serves as the Program Director for the Undergraduate Rehabilitation and Human Services Program but also as a faculty resource within the Counseling program, specifically concentrating on rehabilitation counselor education. With a rich academic background, Dr. Williams possesses extensive experience collaborating with programs centered around disability and rehabilitation across various educational institutions. Her professional journey encompasses active involvement in the field of rehabilitation, spanning domains such as blindness and low vision, general rehabilitation counseling, and human resource training and development, as well as contributions to the former Regional Rehabilitation Continuing Education Programs (RRCEP), now known as the Technical Assistance Continuing Education (TACE) centers. Drawing from her previous experience as a rehabilitation counselor, Dr. Williams possesses a profound appreciation for the significance of delivering high-quality services to a diverse continuum of individuals with varying disabilities. Her insights are informed not just by theoretical knowledge but also by hands-on involvement in the field. Furthermore, Dr. Williams has assumed multiple leadership roles, operating at local, state, regional, national, and international levels within professional rehabilitation associations. She has contributed to the body of research in rehabilitation sciences through publications in peer-reviewed journals demonstrating her commitment to advancing the field. Moreover, she has co-authored a book examining the complexities of caseload management.

Gina Oswald, PhD, CRC, LPC, is a senior extension associate at Cornell University. She serves as the principal investigator (PI) on the Vocational Rehabilitation-Training, Education, and Development (VR-TED) and the New York State Consortium for Advancing and Supporting Employment (NYS-CASE) projects, in addition to supporting other training contracts and state needs assessments. Previously, she was an associate professor and coordinator for the Center for Assistive Technology (AT) at the University of Maine at Farmington. Most recently she served as the PI on the multiyear *ME-MADE: Maine-Makerspaces for Abilities Driving Entrepreneurship* grant, a project designed to promote accessible makerspace technologies for persons with disabilities, and a National Science Foundation (NSF) INCLUDES Planning Grant designed to broaden the participation of rural students with disabilities into science, technology, engineering, and mathematics (STEM) educational opportunities and career pathways. As a past vocational rehabilitation counselor, she is particularly familiar with providing case management services to individuals from marginalized rural communities, transition youth, and individuals with a broad range of disability types. In her past roles as professor, program director (rehabilitation services, transition-to-work, veteran services, and disability studies programs), and faculty director of the Center for Teaching and Learning at Wright State University, Dr. Oswald was responsible for the coordination, evaluation, and promotion of accessibility, educational training, and collaborative research efforts. She also has extensive experience in facilitating work groups at the national and local levels, developing training opportunities and presenting on universal design and transition for persons with disabilities, writing and managing grants, and hosting conferences.

Fundamentals of Case and Caseload Management

Skills for Rehabilitation Practice

Lee Ann Rawlins Williams, PhD, CRC, CFLE

Gina Oswald, PhD, CRC, LPC

 SPRINGER PUBLISHING

Springer Publishing Company, LLC
902 Carnegie Center/Suite 140, Princeton, NJ 08540
www.springerpub.com
connect.springerpub.com

Acquisitions Editor: Mindy Okura-Marszycki
Compositor: S4Carlisle Publishing Services
Production Editor: Dennis Troutman

ISBN: 978-0-8261-5962-5
ebook ISBN: 978-0-8261-5963-2
DOI: 10.1891/9780826159632

SUPPLEMENTS:

 SPRINGER PUBLISHING CONNECT™ | A robust set of instructor resources designed to supplement this text is located at **http://connect.springerpub.com/content/book/978-0-8261-5963-2**. Qualifying instructors may request access by emailing **textbook@springerpub.com**.

Instructor Materials:
LMS Common Cartridge With All Instructor Resources ISBN: 978-0-8261-5967-0
Instructor Manual ISBN: 978-0-8261-5964-9
Instructor Test Bank ISBN: 978-0-8261-5965-6
Instructor PowerPoints: 978-0-8261-5966-3

24 25 26 27 / 5 4 3 2 1

The author and the publisher of this Work have made every effort to use sources believed to be reliable to provide information that is accurate and compatible with the standards generally accepted at the time of publication. Because medical science is continually advancing, our knowledge base continues to expand. Therefore, as new information becomes available, changes in procedures become necessary. We recommend that the reader always consult current research and specific institutional policies before performing any clinical procedure or delivering any medication. The author and publisher shall not be liable for any special, consequential, or exemplary damages resulting, in whole or in part, from the readers' use of, or reliance on, the information contained in this book. The publisher has no responsibility for the persistence or accuracy of URLs for external or third-party Internet websites referred to in this publication and does not guarantee that any content on such websites is, or will remain, accurate or appropriate.

Library of Congress Cataloging-in-Publication Data

Names: Rawlins Williams, Lee Ann, author. | Oswald, Gina, author.
Title: Fundamentals of case and caseload management : skills for
    rehabilitation practice / Lee Ann Rawlins Williams, Gina Oswald.
Identifiers: LCCN 2023051852 (print) | LCCN 2023051853 (ebook) | ISBN
    9780826159625 (paperback) | ISBN 9780826159632 (ebook)
Subjects: LCSH: Rehabilitation counseling—Management. | Supervision of
    vocational rehabilitation.
Classification: LCC HD7255.5 .R33 2024 (print) | LCC HD7255.5 (ebook) |
    DDC 362.17/86068—dc23/eng/20240116
LC record available at https://lccn.loc.gov/2023051852
LC ebook record available at https://lccn.loc.gov/2023051853

Contact sales@springerpub.com to receive discount rates on bulk purchases.

Publisher's Note: New and used products purchased from third-party sellers are not guaranteed for quality, authenticity, or access to any included digital components.

Printed in the United States of America by Hatteras, Inc.

To my husband, Treyton, for his love, patience, extraordinary support, and lifting my wings allowing me to soar; to my daughter, Jessie, who is a constant inspiration and source of joy, laughter, and fun; and in loving memory of my mother, Dr. Richa Cox Russell, who accompanied me on this journey but couldn't witness its conclusion. Her unwavering support enabled me to achieve far more in life than I could have ever imagined. Finally, I extend my heartfelt gratitude to my co-author and dear friend, Dr. Gina Oswald. Her invaluable contributions played a crucial role in the realization of this project. The dedication, time, and effort she invested were instrumental in bringing this endeavor to life. I feel privileged to have collaborated with her, side by side, as we crafted something that will undoubtedly bolster our profession for years to come.

—Dr. Lee Ann Rawlins Williams

To my family who, through their love, understanding, and persistent encouragement, provided a solid foundation and consistent support system that gave me the courage to grow into the professional I am today. They had faith in me especially when I didn't. To my loved ones, friends, and colleagues over the years, thank you for always appreciating the work I do, even if you may still not have a firm grasp on what I do, and refraining from making me feel bad for every time I chose work or a project over "quality time." You allow me to be me, and I couldn't ask for better people by my side. Finally, I am humbled and honored by Dr. Lee Ann Rawlins Williams who entrusted me with assisting her in such a worthy and monumental project. I am proud to offer this small contribution to her efforts to enhance the future of the field and improve the lives of people with disabilities.

—Dr. Gina Oswald

Contents

Preface

Caseload management is…work. More specifically, it is the work of caseload managers in the public and private rehabilitation sectors. Caseload management is not merely relying on intuitive strategies, but rather, it is the disciplined application of skills, tools, and techniques that facilitate positive movement toward a desired, successful, productive outcome. It is the skilled interaction of managers and management constructs that create responsible performance. Such achievement is a positive alternative to random behaviors, confusion, and inappropriate decision-making in rehabilitation caseload functions and practice.

The field of rehabilitation counseling has evolved significantly in recent years, highlighting the critical role of rehabilitation counseling professionals. This book explores the dynamic domain of case and caseload management, tailored for contemporary rehabilitation counseling practitioners. Rehabilitation counseling professionals are no longer solitary, but integral components of a diverse network that includes clinicians, therapists, educators, and other specialists. Efficiently managing cases and caseloads is pivotal in achieving optimal outcomes for clients. This requires an in-depth understanding of clients' needs and effective communication within a collaborative context.

This book is meticulously crafted for rehabilitation counseling professionals navigating today's healthcare landscape. Recognition is apparent of the expanded responsibilities that transcend traditional boundaries, demanding mastery of case management principles, and resonate within the field. Within these pages, a comprehensive exploration of case and caseload management will be found, uniquely tailored to the realm of rehabilitation counseling. The authors delve into strategies empowering professionals to coordinate plans, collaborate effectively with diverse professionals, and align efforts with rehabilitation objectives. Anchored in real-world practice, best practices, and current research, this book is equipped with practical tools to lead, communicate, and excel in this evolving field. Our goal is to offer a pragmatic resource that strengthens your daily rehabilitation counseling practice. Whether you're a seasoned professional honing interprofessional skills or a newcomer beginning this fulfilling journey, this book provides actionable guidance. It transcends being a mere manual—it becomes a companion helping you navigate the intricacies of case and caseload management, nurturing meaningful partnerships, and delivering exceptional care.

As the scope of rehabilitation counseling expands, the significance of your role becomes more pronounced. We invite you to immerse yourself in these pages, embrace the insights within, and embark on a voyage of enriched understanding and empowered case and caseload management. Your dedication to providing comprehensive services in the field of rehabilitation is commendable, and we stand alongside you as you navigate this ever-evolving landscape.

This book has been developed with consideration for two groups of individuals. The first group is students involved in academic programs. For educators, this text fills a void in academic courses and training seminars/workshops. Educators will find that the rational and conceptual framework provides a solid foundation for teaching managerial principles and skills to complement the aspiring students' professional program.

The second group is the numerous rehabilitation professionals who could refresh and/or learn principles of management for application to existing cases and/or caseloads.

xiv | PREFACE

It is evident that even the most counseling-oriented rehabilitation practitioner cannot survive without the implementation of at least minimal skills in management. In fact, because of the managerial focus of this text, its utility as a "desk reference" would expand beyond public and private rehabilitation caseload management situations.

In this textbook, you will encounter the term "client," which forms one part of the three-pronged perspective alongside "counselor" and "organization." This utilization should consistently be perceived in a positive light. Although more recent language options have introduced "consumer" and "customer" as relevant role designations within this trio, it is crucial to recognize that "client" was chosen as the fitting term. This choice is rooted in the substantial influence that clients hold over the management of rehabilitation caseloads. Our utmost objective remains centered on prioritizing the client and delivering high-quality services to enhance professional case and caseload management practice.

Lee Ann Rawlins Williams, PhD, CRC, CFLE
Gina Oswald, PhD, CRC, LPC

Acknowledgments

Decades ago, Drs. Jack L. Cassell and S. Wayne Mulkey embarked on a journey that would shape the landscape of rehabilitation caseload management. Their unwavering dedication to this field laid the foundation for the principles and practices discussed within these pages. As we navigate the contents of this book, we remember Drs. Cassell and Mulkey with gratitude and admiration. Their tireless pursuit of excellence and their dedication to advancing rehabilitation caseload management have left an enduring legacy. Moreover, the development of this textbook was greatly enriched by the contributions of Georgia Oswald, Kelly Hackett, and Savannah Williams. Mrs. Oswald provided editorial support for content and continuity, ensuring the material would be understandable and appropriate to novice professionals. Additionally, Mrs. Hackett played a pivotal role in expanding instructional design and refining language, particularly in her support for the creation of tables and figures across the entire text. Furthermore, Ms. Williams played a crucial part in elevating the instructional and supplementary materials integrated into the textbook resources. Clearly, their support was a very valuable influence in bringing a functional book to fruition. Additionally, thanks to the numerous professionals in the field who encouraged and supported the need for this text as a guide for professional practice. We are thrilled this resource will be provided to new and existing professionals looking to support individuals with disabilities at all levels into the future.

Springer Publishing Resources

 A robust set of instructor resources designed to supplement this text is located at http://connect.springerpub.com/content/book/978-0-8261-5963-2. Qualifying instructors may request access by emailing textbook@springerpub.com.

- **LMS Common Cartridge With All Instructor Resources**
- **Instructor Manual**
  - Chapter Overviews
  - Learning Objectives
  - Additional Discussion Questions
  - Review Questions With Rationales and Guidance
- **Test Bank** With 150 Multiple-Choice Questions Including Full Rationales
- **Instructor PowerPoint Presentations** Providing Overviews of All Chapters

Visit https://connect.springerpub.com/ and look for the "**Show Supplementary**" button on the **book homepage.**

PART I

Introduction to Case and Caseload Management

CHAPTER 1

Case Management and Rehabilitation

LEARNING OBJECTIVES

By the end of this chapter, learners will be able to:

- Understand the historical context of case management and its evolution within the field of rehabilitation counseling.
- Describe the functions, tasks, and responsibilities of case management, providing an overview of facilitating comprehensive services and support for clients.
- Examine the overall process of case management, including the stages of assessment, goal setting, plan development, implementation, and evaluation, to gain a comprehensive understanding of its sequential nature.
- Explain the importance of specific case management tasks and responsibilities, such as monitoring client progress, ensuring confidentiality, and providing counseling, in supporting the overall success of the case management process.
- Discuss the impact of the functions, tasks, and responsibilities of case management on its practice, including their influence on client outcomes, service coordination, and the overall effectiveness of the case management approach.
- Analyze the ethical considerations and legal obligations associated with case management tasks and responsibilities, recognizing the importance of upholding professional standards and safeguarding client rights.
- Explore the multidisciplinary nature of case management and the collaborative partnerships required to effectively fulfill case management functions and responsibilities.
- Recognize the significance of cultural competence and sensitivity in case management practice, emphasizing the need for diverse perspectives and tailored interventions that respect the uniqueness of each client.
- Understand the impact of technological advancements on case management functions and responsibilities, such as the use of electronic records, telehealth, and data analytics, and their potential to enhance the efficiency and effectiveness of the case management process.
- Evaluate the importance of continuous professional development and self-reflection in enhancing case management skills, competencies, and the ability to adapt to evolving client needs and best practices.

INTRODUCTION

Case management in the context of rehabilitation is a collaborative process that involves the assessment, planning, coordination, implementation, and evaluation of services to support individuals with disabilities or chronic health conditions to achieve professional and personal goals while improving their quality of life (Browning et al., 2013). The primary goal of case management in rehabilitation is to promote self-determination and independence by helping individuals access appropriate care, services, and support to address client need, including medical treatment, rehabilitation services, independent living, and community resources (Browning et al., 2013). Case management in rehabilitation is noted as a flexible and patient-centered approach that takes into account the unique characteristics and preferences of each individual and may involve interprofessional collaboration, including other areas of the profession in rehabilitative health sciences, occupational therapy, physical therapy, social worker, and therapeutic counseling.

CASE MANAGEMENT DEFINED

The definition of case management has evolved over time, reflecting the vibrant and modernized standards of professional practice (Case Management Society of America [CMSA], 2017). According to Tahan and Treiger (2017), the basic concepts of case management involve timely coordination of quality services in a cost-effective way that promotes positive outcomes. Browning et al. (2013) reflect on **case managers** in rehabilitation settings, where it is noted that case management definitions reflect working closely with individuals with disabilities to assess needs, develop personalized care plans, monitor their progress, and adjust their rehabilitation plans. Also, practitioners serve as advocates for clients, helping to navigate the healthcare system and access valued resources needed to achieve independence and life goals (Maki & Tarvydas, 2012). By providing comprehensive, coordinated care, case management can make a difference in the quality of service provision, reduce costs, and improve overall client satisfaction.

The *role* of case managers, which is often referred to as coordinator of services, is to synchronize care across different settings and providers, thereby helping clients navigate the healthcare system, while advocating for their preferences and needs (CMSA, 2021). Case managers work closely with clients and their families to assess their individual needs, develop personalized *care plans*, monitor progress, and adjust plans when needed or determined necessary (CMSA, 2021). By providing holistic, patient-centered care, case management can improve the health outcomes of individuals with complex healthcare needs and reduce healthcare costs (Cesta & Flanagan, 2019; Frankel et al., 2019).

One of the key components of case management is **assessment**, which involves gathering information about the client's medical, social, and psychological needs. This information is used to develop a personalized care plan that addresses the client's unique needs and goals. The care plan is developed in collaboration with the client and their family, and it outlines the specific services and resources that the client needs to achieve their goals. A study published in the *Journal of Gerontological Nursing* found that a comprehensive assessment is essential for effective case management and that it leads to improved outcomes for clients (Schober et al., 2018).

Another critical component of case management is **treatment planning**. Once the client's needs have been assessed, a treatment plan is developed that outlines the specific services and resources that the client needs to achieve their goals. The treatment plan is developed in collaboration with the client and their family, and it is regularly reviewed and updated to ensure that it remains appropriate and effective. A study published in the *Journal of the American Medical Directors Association* found that a comprehensive treatment plan leads to improved outcomes for clients, including reduced hospitalizations and improved quality of life (Nakamura et al., 2020).

Rehabilitation case management is a specialized form of case management that focuses on providing coordinated and integrated services to individuals with disabilities or chronic health conditions. It involves working with clients to identify their needs, goals, and barriers to achieving those goals and developing a personalized plan to help them achieve maximum independence and functioning. The rehabilitation case manager acts as an advocate and liaison between the client, their family, and other service providers to ensure that the plan of care is implemented effectively and that the client receives the services and resources they need to achieve their goals.

Case management is a critical component of rehabilitation and healthcare delivery that seeks to provide comprehensive, coordinated, and patient-centered care to individuals with complex healthcare needs. It involves the assessment, planning, coordination, and **monitoring** of services and resources to meet the client's unique needs and goals. The continued growth and development of case management services are necessary to meet the evolving healthcare needs of the population and to achieve the goal of a high-performing healthcare system.

CASE MANAGEMENT FUNCTIONS

Case management is a critical process for providing high-quality care to individuals with complex healthcare needs. Case management *functions* include outreach to clients, assessment of needs, treatment planning, and linking for appropriate services. *Outreach* is an essential component of case management, as it enables case managers to identify individuals who may benefit from case management services. A study conducted by the American Public Health Association found that outreach interventions for individuals with chronic conditions were effective in improving health outcomes, reducing hospitalization rates, and increasing adherence to care plans (Brown et al., 2003).

Assessment of needs is another vital function of case management. It involves identifying the client's unique health, social, and economic needs, as well as their strengths and abilities. A comprehensive assessment of needs is crucial for developing a personalized plan of care that meets the client's specific needs and goals. A study published in the *BMC Geriatrics* found that a comprehensive assessment of needs for older adults led to better health outcomes, increased adherence to care plans, and reduced healthcare costs (Wong et al., 2022).

Treatment planning is a critical component of case management that involves developing a plan of care based on the client's needs and goals. Treatment plans typically include specific interventions, such as medications, therapies, and social support services. Case managers work closely with clients and their families to develop a personalized plan that addresses their unique needs and goals. A study conducted by the *Journal of General Internal Medicine* found that comprehensive treatment plans led to improved patient outcomes, reduced healthcare costs, and increased patient satisfaction (Tang et al., 2017).

Finally, *linking for appropriate services* is a crucial function of case management that involves connecting clients with appropriate resources and services. Case managers work closely with community organizations, healthcare providers, and social service agencies to ensure that clients have access to the services they need to achieve their goals. A study conducted by the *Worldviews on Evidence-Based Nursing* found that linking for appropriate services led to improved patient outcomes, increased adherence to care plans, and reduced healthcare costs (Connor et al., 2023).

In conclusion, case management functions play a crucial role in ensuring that individuals with complex healthcare needs receive high-quality, comprehensive care. Outreach to clients, assessment of needs, treatment planning, and linking for appropriate services are all essential components of case management that help to improve health outcomes, reduce healthcare costs, and increase patient satisfaction (see **Figure 1.1**).

Outreach to Clients

Outreach is a critical component of effective case management. Outreach refers to the process of identifying and engaging individuals who may benefit from case management services. According to the Substance Abuse and Mental Health Services Administration (SAMHSA), outreach can involve a variety of activities, such as conducting community presentations, distributing information, and conducting screening and assessment activities (SAMHSA, 2017). Outreach is essential for identifying and engaging individuals who may be reluctant to seek services on their own, such as those who are homeless, who have a mental health disorder, or are involved in the criminal justice system.

Successful case management and outreach require a collaborative and client-centered approach. According to the CMSA, effective case management involves building a trusting relationship with the client, engaging them in the process, and empowering them to take an active role in their care (Morley, 2023). Outreach efforts must also be tailored to meet the unique needs and circumstances of the target population. By working collaboratively with clients and tailoring outreach efforts to meet their needs, case managers can help individuals access the resources and support they need to achieve their goals and improve their overall well-being.

Outreach and rehabilitation are complex processes that involve a wide range of services and resources. Case management is a critical function in rehabilitation, helping to ensure that individuals with disabilities or injuries receive the appropriate care and support they need to achieve their goals. Outreach to clients is an essential aspect of case management in rehabilitation, as it helps to identify individuals who need services and engage them in the process of care. Rehabilitation counselors and case managers may use a variety of outreach strategies, including community events, advertising, and targeted referrals, to connect with individuals and families who may benefit from their services (National Rehabilitation Association, 2015).

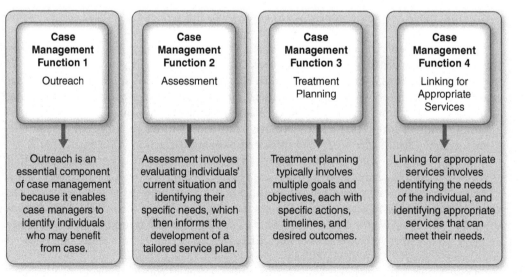

FIGURE 1.1 Case management functions.

Outreach to clients is particularly important in rehabilitation because many individuals with disabilities or injuries may be hesitant to seek out services. They may feel stigmatized or embarrassed about their condition, or they may not know where to turn for help. Rehabilitation counselors and case managers can play a critical role in reaching out to these individuals, building trust and rapport, and providing them with the support they need to overcome their barriers and achieve their goals (Tennant et al., 2015). Additionally, outreach helps to identify individuals who may benefit from rehabilitation services and connect them with appropriate resources. Rehabilitation counselors are often responsible for conducting outreach activities to raise awareness of the availability of rehabilitation services and educate individuals about the benefits of rehabilitation. By reaching out to clients in need, rehabilitation counselors and case managers can help ensure that clients receive the care and support they need to achieve their goals and improve their quality of life (Roessler et al., 2018).

Rehabilitation counselors also play a critical role in building relationships with clients and establishing trust, which can help to improve client engagement and adherence to treatment plans. By working collaboratively with clients to develop personalized plans of care, rehabilitation counselors can help clients feel empowered and invested in their own recovery. Case managers can then support these efforts by linking clients to appropriate services and resources and providing ongoing support and communication. By building strong relationships with clients and ensuring that they receive comprehensive and coordinated care, rehabilitation counselors and case managers can help clients improve independence.

Cultural competence and sensitivity are also essential for effective outreach, ensuring that all individuals have access to the care and support they need to achieve their goals and improve their quality of life. Effective outreach to clients requires cultural competence and sensitivity to the unique needs and experiences of different populations. Rehabilitation counselors and case managers must be aware of cultural, linguistic, and socioeconomic barriers that may prevent individuals from accessing rehabilitation services and work to address these barriers in their outreach efforts. By providing outreach that is inclusive and accessible to all individuals, regardless of their background, rehabilitation counselors and case managers can help ensure that everyone has the opportunity to benefit from rehabilitation services and support (Leahy et al., 2019; Mullahy, 2010).

In summary, rehabilitation counselors play a critical role in providing outreach to clients, working to identify individuals who may benefit from rehabilitation services, and connecting them with appropriate resources. By building relationships with clients, establishing trust, and working collaboratively to develop personalized plans of care, rehabilitation counselors can improve client engagement and adherence to treatment plans. Case managers can support these efforts by linking clients to appropriate services and resources and providing ongoing support and communication while working with other service providers, such as physical therapists, occupational therapists, and physicians, to develop and implement care plans that address the individual's needs and goals. Also, they may provide education and support to individuals and families, empowering them to take an active role in their own care. By performing these functions, case managers in rehabilitation can support individuals with disabilities or injuries to achieve optimal outcomes and improve their quality of life (Brown & Jason, 2017; Fadyl & McPherson, 2009; O'Connor & Gardner, 2019; Vos et al., 2019).

Assessment of Needs

Assessment of needs is a crucial aspect of case management. It involves evaluating an individual's current situation and identifying their specific needs, which can then inform the development of a tailored service plan. Chan and Leahy (2013) outline assessment as the first step in case management, and it involves gathering and analyzing information to identify the individual's strengths, challenges, and resources. The assessment process may involve various methods such as observation, interviews, and standardized assessments.

Assessment of needs helps case managers to better understand the client's unique circumstances and develop an appropriate service plan. According to the American Public Human Services Association (APHSA), the assessment process involves gathering information about the client's physical, emotional, social, and economic needs, as well as their strengths and resources (APHSA, 2013). This information can help case managers identify potential barriers to care and develop a plan that addresses the client's needs and goals.

Case managers can use various assessment tools to identify a client's needs. For example, the SAMHSA recommends using standardized assessments to identify behavioral health needs, such as mental health and substance use disorders (SAMHSA, 2017). Standardized assessments are structured questionnaires that help to identify specific problems, symptoms, or behaviors that may indicate the need for further assessment or treatment.

The assessment process also involves identifying the client's strengths and resources. According to various authors, identifying and building on client strengths is an essential component of effective case management (Bond et al., 2012; Lashley, 2018; Rap et al., 2010). This involves looking beyond the client's challenges and identifying their unique abilities and resources that can be leveraged to support their care. Identifying client strengths can help to build a positive relationship between the client and case manager and increase the client's motivation to engage in the **case management process**.

Assessment of needs occurs throughout the case management process and is a critical component to successful rehabilitation outcomes. The assessment of needs in rehabilitation involves a holistic approach that considers all aspects of the individual's well-being. Rehabilitation professionals may use a variety of assessment tools, including standardized tests, clinical evaluations, and interviews, to evaluate an individual's needs and develop a personalized plan of care. The assessment process helps to identify the individual's strengths and limitations and develop an integrated care plan that addresses all aspects of their needs. This approach ensures that the individual receives comprehensive and coordinated care that supports their recovery and maximizes their potential for independence and success (Hagar, 2013; Haggans, 2023).

Rehabilitation case managers work with other healthcare providers, including physicians, physical therapists, and occupational therapists, to gather information about the individual's condition and develop an integrated care plan to ensure that the individual receives the appropriate interventions and services to support their recovery and improve their overall quality of life (Lamper et al., 2021). This interdisciplinary approach helps ensure that the individual receives comprehensive and coordinated care that addresses all aspects of their needs (American Counseling Association, 2014; O'Connor & Gardner, 2019).

Case management in rehabilitation counseling also involves ongoing assessment and modification of the **care plan** as the individual progresses, as client's needs may change over time. Rehabilitation counselors and case managers ongoingly evaluate the individual's progress and modify the care plan when needed to ensure appropriate services and support goal achievement.

In conclusion, the assessment of needs is a critical component of case management that helps to identify the client's specific needs, strengths, and resources. By identifying the client's needs and resources, case managers can develop tailored service plans that address the client's goals and barriers to care. Assessment occurs throughout the case management process, and case managers should regularly review and adjust the service plan to ensure that it remains appropriate for the client's needs.

Treatment Planning

Case management is a critical aspect of healthcare that involves coordinating care and services for individuals with complex medical and social needs. One of the essential functions of case management is developing a **treatment plan** that addresses the client's specific needs and goals. The National Association of Social Workers (NASW) identifies *treatment planning* as a critical component of case management, and it involves developing a plan that is tailored to the individual's unique needs and preferences (NASW, 2018).

The treatment planning process in rehabilitation counseling involves a person-centered approach that considers the individual's preferences, strengths, and limitations. Rehabilitation counselors work with the individual to identify their goals and develop a plan of care that addresses their needs and preferences. The plan outlines interventions and services that the individual will receive and identifies the goals and objectives of treatment. Additionally, the plan typically involves multiple goals and objectives, each with specific actions, timelines, and desired outcomes. According to Grubbs et al. (2006), a good treatment plan should be "**SMART**"—Specific, Measurable, Attainable, Relevant, and Time-scheduled. This helps to ensure that the treatment plan is achievable, realistic, and aligned with the client's needs and goals.

In addition to identifying appropriate interventions and services, treatment planning also involves coordinating care and services across multiple providers and settings. The case manager is responsible for coordinating the delivery of services, monitoring the individual's progress, and modifying the care plan as needed. By performing these functions, case managers in rehabilitation can support individuals with disabilities or injuries achieve optimal outcomes and improve their quality of life. (Grubbs et al., 2006; Higginbotham & Hundley, 2019; Iwanaga & Chan, 2017; Roessler et al., 2018; Simon, 2014). According to the American Case Management Association (ACMA), care coordination is a critical function of case management, and it involves linking the client with appropriate services, providers, and resources (ACMA, 2017). Effective care coordination requires collaboration and communication among providers, including physicians, nurses, social workers, and other healthcare professionals.

Treatment planning also involves regular monitoring and evaluation of the client's progress. The importance of ongoing assessment and modification of the care plan in case management has been highlighted in the literature. According to Minkoff and Cline (2004), ongoing assessment is necessary to ensure that the individual receives appropriate services and support to achieve their goals and improve their quality of life. This is in line with the National Council for Behavioral Health's recommendation that the treatment plan should be reviewed and updated regularly (National Council for Behavioral Health, 2020). This may involve regularly measuring and evaluating the client's outcomes, adjusting interventions and services as needed, and communicating with the client and their caregivers to ensure that the treatment plan remains appropriate.

Moreover, ongoing assessment is also essential to identify potential issues and address them before they become significant problems. As noted by Allen and Petr (1996), regular assessment can help to identify changes in the client's needs, preferences, and circumstances, which may require modifications to the treatment plan. Furthermore, ongoing assessment can also help to ensure that the client's goals are still relevant and achievable. As noted by O'Donnell and Gordon (2011), ongoing assessment can help to identify changes in the client's circumstances or preferences that may require a revision of their goals or the development of new ones. This is also supported by the Commission on Rehabilitation Counselor Certification's Code of Professional Ethics, which states that rehabilitation counselors should work collaboratively with clients to set appropriate goals and regularly assess their progress toward achieving them (Commission on Rehabilitation Counselor Certification, 2017).

In conclusion, treatment planning is a critical component of case management that involves developing a tailored plan that addresses the client's specific needs and goals. Treatment planning includes identifying appropriate interventions and services, coordinating care and services across multiple providers and settings, and regularly monitoring and evaluating the client's progress. By developing a comprehensive treatment plan, case managers can help ensure that clients receive the right care and services to achieve their goals and improve their health outcomes.

Linking or Referring for Appropriate Services

Linking or referring individuals to appropriate services is an essential function in counseling, healthcare and other human services. This involves identifying the needs of the individual, assessing their strengths and limitations, and identifying appropriate services that can meet their needs. For example, a case manager working with an individual with a mental health diagnosis may create a referral to a therapist or psychiatrist for treatment (National Council for Behavioral Health, 2018).

In addition to linking or referring individuals to appropriate services, case managers also play a crucial role in monitoring the quality and effectiveness of these services. This involves regular check-ins with the individual to ensure that they are receiving the services they need and that these services are meeting their needs. Case managers may also coordinate services and communicate with other service providers to ensure that care is comprehensive and consistent (National Council on Aging, 2015).

Another important function of case management is advocating for the individual. Case managers serve as the voice of the individual, ensuring that their needs and goals are being heard and addressed. They may work with other service providers to ensure that the individual's rights are being respected and that they are receiving appropriate care. This advocacy role is essential for vulnerable populations, such as children, elderly individuals, and individuals with disabilities (Mauk, 2018).

Rehabilitation professionals utilize a *variety of referral resources* when linking individuals with individualized services. Also, case managers provide education, training, and support to individuals and families, empowering them to take an active role in their own care. They may provide information regarding available services and community resources, educate individuals on how to access these resources, and provide support as individuals navigate the healthcare and social service systems (Schuck et al., 2023). The case manager is responsible for coordinating the delivery of services from community rehabilitation providers, monitoring the individual's progress, and modifying the care plan as needed in collaboration with the referral source. By working collaboratively with other healthcare providers and community rehabilitation providers/organizations, case managers in rehabilitation can ensure that the individual with a disability or co-occurring condition receives comprehensive care that supports and maximizes their potential for independence and success (Anastasi & Zammit, 2022; Crawford et al., 2012; Rapp et al., 2010).

Rehabilitation counselors use a variety of counseling and psychotherapeutic techniques to help individuals with disabilities or injuries achieve their goals and improve their quality of life. These techniques may include vocational counseling, cognitive behavioral therapy, psychoeducation and medical services, vocational services, or community-based services to support rehabilitation and improve outcomes. Rehabilitation counselors may also provide education and support to the individual and their family, empowering them to take an active role in their own care. The case manager is responsible for coordinating the delivery of services and linking the individual to appropriate resources, such as vocational rehabilitation services, job training programs, or community-based services. By working collaboratively with other healthcare providers and community organizations, case managers and rehabilitation counselors can ensure that the individual receives comprehensive and coordinated care that supports their recovery and maximizes their potential for independence and success (O'Connor & Gardner, 2019).

Finally, case management involves *documentation and record-keeping*. Case managers must maintain accurate and up-to-date records of the individual's care and progress. Documentation is essential for ensuring that the individual receives appropriate care, for communicating with other service providers, and for billing and reimbursement purposes (Mullahy, 2010). This area of coordination will be explored more extensively in Chapter 8, with emphasis placed on aspects such as recording for effective and professional practice.

CASE MANAGEMENT TASKS AND RESPONSIBILITIES

Case management is a complex process that involves a variety of **tasks** and **responsibilities** to help individuals navigate the healthcare system and access the resources they need to achieve their goals. Some of the key tasks and responsibilities of case management include *assessment of needs, treatment planning, linking individuals to appropriate services and resources, monitoring progress, and advocacy* (Browning et al., 2013). Case managers may also be responsible for coordinating care between different healthcare providers, managing medication regimens, connecting with community rehabilitation providers, and providing support and counseling to individuals and their families (Browning et al., 2013).

Case management is a **collaborative process** that helps individuals access necessary resources and services to achieve their goals. The case manager is responsible for performing a range of tasks that support the individual's care, including assessment, planning, linking to services, monitoring progress, and advocacy (CMSA, 2017). Effective case management requires a deep understanding of an individual's needs, goals, and limitations, as well as the ability to navigate complex systems to obtain necessary services.

In addition to these clinical tasks, case management may also involve **administrative responsibilities**, such as maintaining records and documentation, coordinating referrals, and managing budgets and resources (Miller, 2013). Case managers may also be responsible for ensuring compliance with relevant laws and regulations, such as Health Insurance Portability and Accountability Act (HIPAA) and Medicaid (Miller, 2013). Effective case management requires a high level of organizational and communication skills, as well as the ability to work collaboratively with a variety of stakeholders, including healthcare providers, social service agencies, and insurance companies (Rawlins-Alderman & Dunn, 2015).

Overall, case management is a **multifaceted process** that involves a variety of tasks and responsibilities to support individuals with a wide range of needs (see **Figure 1.2**). By providing comprehensive, coordinated care, case management can help individuals achieve their goals and improve their quality of life. However, effective case management requires a high level of skill and expertise, as well as a commitment to working collaboratively with individuals, families, and other stakeholders to ensure that they receive the care and support they need.

Monitoring

Monitoring is an essential component of effective case management, as it ensures that the care plan remains relevant and effective over time. The case manager must remain vigilant to the individual's changing needs, adjusting the care plan as necessary to ensure that it continues to meet their goals and objectives (Morrison et al., 2017). Monitoring may involve regular check-ins with the individual, ongoing communication with service providers, and tracking the individual's progress over time.

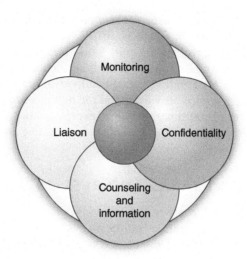

FIGURE 1.2 Case management as a multifaceted process.

One of the primary responsibilities of the case manager is to advocate for the individual, ensuring that they receive the necessary services and support to achieve their goals. Advocacy can take many forms, from navigating complex systems, to obtaining necessary services, to ensuring that the individual's rights are protected (CMSA, 2017). Monitoring and advocacy are closely related, as effective monitoring often requires the case manager to be an effective advocate for the individual. For example, if the individual's needs are not being met or their progress is stalling, the case manager may need to intervene on their behalf, advocating for additional services or resources to support the individual's progress (Morrison et al., 2017). Effective monitoring and advocacy are critical to the success of the case management process, as they help ensure that the individual receives the necessary support and services to achieve their goals.

The case manager must be an effective communicator, able to articulate the individual's needs and goals to service providers, healthcare professionals, and other stakeholders. Therefore, it is crucial for healthcare providers and policy makers to invest in case management monitoring and rehabilitation programs to improve the health outcomes and quality of life of clients.

Confidentiality

Maintaining **confidentiality** is an essential component of case management, as it ensures that the individual's privacy and personal information are protected. The case manager must ensure that all personal information is kept confidential and that only authorized individuals have access to the individual's records (CMSA, 2017). Confidentiality is critical to establishing and maintaining trust between the individual and the case manager and is essential for effective communication and collaboration. Case management confidentiality is a crucial aspect of the rehabilitation process to ensure that the client's personal and health-related information remains private and secure. Case managers must adhere to strict confidentiality policies and procedures, including obtaining written consent from the client before disclosing any information. The confidentiality of client information helps to build trust and maintain a positive therapeutic relationship between the client and case manager. It also ensures that the client's personal information is not disclosed to unauthorized individuals or third parties, which can potentially harm the client's reputation or lead to discrimination. Therefore, it is essential for case managers to uphold strict confidentiality standards to protect the privacy and dignity of their clients.

Confidentiality also plays a role in ensuring that the individual's needs are met. By maintaining the confidentiality of the individual's information, the case manager can work with service providers and healthcare professionals to develop a comprehensive care plan that takes into account the individual's unique needs and circumstances (Morrison et al., 2017). The case manager must ensure that all service providers are aware of and committed to maintaining confidentiality and that all necessary steps are taken to protect the individual's personal information.

According to the National Council on Disability (2012), confidentiality is a critical component of case management for individuals with disabilities. The council emphasizes the importance of informing clients about their rights to privacy and ensuring that any information obtained during the rehabilitation process is used only for the purposes of providing quality care. The council also recommends that case managers undergo regular training on confidentiality and privacy laws to stay up-to-date with current policies and procedures. Overall, maintaining confidentiality in case management is crucial to ensuring that clients receive the best possible care without the fear of their personal and health-related information being disclosed without their permission.

Confidentiality is a critical aspect of healthcare that ensures the privacy and protection of patients' personal and health-related information. In rehabilitation, confidentiality is essential to establish trust and maintain a positive therapeutic relationship between the client and healthcare provider. Clients need to feel that they can trust their healthcare provider with their sensitive information without the fear of it being disclosed to unauthorized individuals or third parties. When confidentiality is maintained, patients are more likely to share accurate and complete information, leading to better diagnoses, treatment, and outcomes.

The importance of confidentiality in rehabilitation is highlighted in several laws and regulations, such as the HIPAA and the Americans with Disabilities Act (ADA). These laws mandate that healthcare providers protect the confidentiality of patient information and disclose it only when necessary or with the patient's consent. Additionally, professional organizations, such as the American Psychological Association (APA) and the NASW, have ethical codes that require their members to uphold confidentiality standards. Therefore, healthcare providers must be aware of these laws and ethical codes and take appropriate measures to protect their patients' confidentiality. However, it is also critical to remember that there are situations in which confidentiality must be breached, such as when the individual is at risk of harm or when required by law. In these situations, the case manager must carefully balance the individual's right to privacy with their duty to protect the individual and others from harm (CMSA, 2017). The case manager must be familiar with the legal and ethical guidelines for confidentiality and be able to make informed decisions that prioritize the individual's safety and well-being.

Counseling and Information

Counseling and provision of information are key tasks in case management that aim to provide clients with emotional and psychological support to help them cope with challenges and achieve their goals. General counseling can take many forms, including individual therapy, group therapy, and family therapy. Additionally, counseling involves providing emotional and psychological support to clients who may be struggling with mental health issues or coping with a traumatic event. Case managers help clients identify their strengths and weaknesses, set realistic goals, and develop strategies to overcome any barriers to their rehabilitation. Providing information is also a crucial task in case management, as clients may require information about available services, community resources, and their legal rights. Case managers must provide clients with accurate and up-to-date information to help them make informed decisions about their healthcare and rehabilitation. Case managers who provide counseling must have strong communication and interpersonal skills to build trust and rapport with clients. They must also have a solid understanding of various counseling techniques and modalities to tailor the counseling to the client's unique needs.

Studies have shown that counseling can be an effective component of case management, leading to better mental health outcomes and improved rehabilitation outcomes. For example, a study by Berger et al. (2011) found that counseling and support services provided by case managers improved the mental health and well-being of clients with chronic illness. The study showed that clients who received counseling had better symptom control, fewer hospitalizations, and improved quality of life. Similarly, various studies found that counseling and support services provided by case managers improved the physical and mental health of clients with chronic conditions, demonstrating that clients who received counseling had better medication adherence, improved health status, and higher levels of satisfaction with their care (Bickman et al., 2010; Herman et al., 2016; Levit et al., 2017).

Counseling and information are critical tasks in case management that help clients access the necessary resources and support to achieve their rehabilitation goals. Providing emotional and psychological support, as well as accurate and timely information, are essential to building a positive therapeutic relationship between the client and case manager. By providing these services, case managers can help clients overcome barriers to their rehabilitation and achieve better health outcomes.

In conclusion, counseling and the provision of information are important tasks in case management that can lead to better mental health outcomes and improved rehabilitation outcomes. Case managers who provide counseling must have strong communication and interpersonal skills and a solid understanding of various counseling techniques and modalities. By providing emotional and psychological support, case managers can help clients cope with challenges and achieve their goals.

Liaison

As a **liaison,** case managers play a critical role in facilitating communication and collaboration between clients and various service providers. They act as *advocates* for their clients and work to ensure that their needs and preferences are considered in the care planning process. Case managers must have strong interpersonal skills to build trust and rapport with clients and be able to communicate effectively with a wide range of stakeholders, including healthcare providers, social workers, and family members.

Studies have shown that the role of the case manager as a liaison is critical to the success of the rehabilitation process. For example, a study by Quanbeck et al. (2013) found that case managers who acted as liaisons between clients and healthcare providers were more effective in promoting medication adherence and improving treatment outcomes for clients with mental health conditions. The study showed that clients who received care from case managers who acted as liaisons had better medication adherence, fewer hospitalizations, and improved quality of life. Further, studies have shown that the role of the case manager as a liaison is associated with improved rehabilitation outcomes for clients. For example, a study by Guo et al. (2021) found that case managers who acted as liaisons between clients and healthcare providers were effective in improving physical and psychological rehabilitation outcomes for clients with spinal cord injury. The study showed that clients who received care from case managers who acted as liaisons had improved functional ability, better mental health outcomes, and increased satisfaction with their care.

Additionally, the role of the case manager as a liaison can also help to reduce healthcare costs by ensuring that clients receive the appropriate level of care at the right time.

A study by Scanlon et al. (2016) found that case managers who acted as liaisons between clients and healthcare providers were able to reduce hospital readmissions and emergency department visits for clients with chronic conditions. The study showed that clients who received care from case managers who acted as liaisons had lower healthcare costs and improved health outcomes.

In conclusion, the role of the case manager as a liaison is critical to the success of the rehabilitation process. Case managers who act as liaisons can improve communication and collaboration between clients and service providers, promote better rehabilitation outcomes, and reduce healthcare costs. The case manager's ability to serve as a liaison is a vital component of effective rehabilitation and critical to the success of the overall rehabilitation process.

THE CASE MANAGEMENT PROCESS

The **case management process** is a *collaborative approach* to the coordination and delivery of services to individuals who require assistance in accessing a range of social, health, and other community services. The overall process involves building rapport with the client, assessing their needs, developing and implementing a care plan, monitoring and evaluating the plan's effectiveness, and making adjustments as necessary. The process also includes communication and coordination with multiple service providers and stakeholders to ensure that the client's needs are met. Additionally, the process involves termination and follow-up or referral to ensure the client's continued success.

Stages in the Case Management Process

Building **rapport** is the first step in the case management process. It is important to establish a relationship of trust and respect with the client to ensure effective communication and collaboration. A positive rapport with the client helps to ensure the feeling of being heard and understood, which promotes overall engagement in the process.

The next step in the case management process is problem assessment, which involves gathering information about the client's situation, including their physical, emotional, and social needs. This information is then used to develop a care plan that addresses the client's specific needs and goals. Goal setting is an important component of this process, as it helps to establish clear objectives for the client to work toward.

After the care plan is developed, the case manager helps to implement the plan by *coordinating services* and *supports* for the client. This involves communication and coordination with various service providers, such as healthcare professionals, social workers, and community organizations. The case manager may also assist the client in accessing financial and other resources to support their care plan. As the plan is implemented, the case manager monitors the client's progress and evaluates the plan's effectiveness. Adjustments may be made to the plan as necessary to ensure that the client's needs are being met and that their goals are being achieved. Additionally, the case manager may provide termination and follow-up or referral to ensure the client's continued success.

The case management process is a collaborative approach to the delivery of services to individuals with disabilities requiring assistance in accessing a range of social, health, rehabilitation, and other community services. The process involves building rapport with the client, assessing their needs, developing and implementing a care plan, monitoring and evaluating the plan's effectiveness, and making adjustments as necessary. Further, the process includes termination and follow-up or referral to ensure the client's continued success. Communication and coordination with multiple service providers and stakeholders are critical to ensuring that the client's needs are met and that their goals are achieved (**Table 1.1**).

TABLE 1.1 THE CASE MANAGEMENT PROCESS

STAGES	PROCESS NAME	FOCUS
1	Building Relationship and Rapport	Communications
2	Problem Assessment	Needs and Challenges
3	Goal Setting	Priorities
4	Development/Implementation of Services	Plan of Action
5	Evaluation	Effectiveness
6	Termination	Goals Achievement
7	Follow-Up or Referral	Future Services Needed

BUILDING RELATIONSHIP AND RAPPORT

Building a positive relationship and rapport with clients is a key component of effective case management. This is particularly important when working with vulnerable populations who may have experienced trauma, such as individuals seeking rehabilitation services. Establishing trust and respect with the client can promote their engagement in the case management process and increase the likelihood of success. The case manager should approach the client with empathy, active listening, and cultural sensitivity. The professional should also demonstrate a willingness to understand the client's perspective, needs, and goals. By building a positive relationship with the client, the case manager can create a safe and supportive environment that promotes the client's well-being and empowerment.

Effective communication is essential in building rapport with clients. The case manager should use clear, concise language and active listening skills to ensure that they understand the client's needs and goals. It is also important to establish boundaries and expectations for the client and the case manager to ensure a professional and respectful relationship. These efforts can help to establish trust and respect, which can facilitate the development of a successful case management plan.

PROBLEM ASSESSMENT

Problem assessment is an important step in the case management process. It involves identifying the client's needs and challenges, determining the root causes of the problems, and understanding the client's goals and priorities. The case manager should use a comprehensive assessment approach that considers the client's physical, emotional, social, and economic needs. The assessment process may involve gathering information from the client, family members, healthcare providers, and other relevant sources. The case manager should use standardized assessment tools when possible to ensure that the assessment is comprehensive and consistent. By conducting a thorough problem assessment, the case manager can develop a service plan that addresses the client's specific needs and goals.

A key aspect of problem assessment is the use of a *strengths-based approach* (Crawford et al., 2012; Rapp et al., 2010). This approach focuses on the client's strengths, resources, and abilities rather than solely on their deficits and limitations. By identifying the client's strengths and resources, the case manager can create a service plan that builds on these assets to promote the client's success. The strengths-based approach also fosters a positive relationship between the client and case manager and promotes the client's empowerment and self-determination.

GOAL SETTING

Goal setting is an essential component of the case management process. Once the problem assessment has been completed, the case manager and client work together to identify the client's goals and priorities. The goals should be specific, measurable, achievable, relevant, and time-bound. The case manager should use a collaborative approach that takes into account the client's preferences, cultural background, and individual strengths and needs. By setting clear goals, the case manager and client can work together to develop a service plan that is focused on achieving those goals.

According to Kapp and Roesch (2005), goal setting is an essential component of effective case management. They suggest that case managers encourage clients to identify goals that are meaningful and relevant to them. The authors emphasize the importance of using a *client-centered approach* that takes into account the client's preferences and values. Further, it is suggested that goal setting should be an ongoing process, with goals being reviewed and revised as needed to ensure that they remain relevant and achievable (Cassell & Mulkey, 1985; Grubbs et al., 2006).

DEVELOPMENT AND IMPLEMENTATION OF SERVICES

The *development and implementation of a service plan* is a critical component of the case management process. After the problem assessment and goal-setting process, the case manager and client work together to develop a plan of action. The *service plan* outlines the specific interventions, services, and resources needed to achieve the client's goals. The case manager should work collaboratively with the client to identify the most appropriate services and resources to meet their needs. The service plan should be reviewed and revised as needed to ensure that it remains relevant and effective.

According to Wong and Law (2002), effective service planning requires a comprehensive and collaborative approach. They suggest that the case manager consider the client's strengths, needs, and preferences when developing the service plan. The authors also emphasize the importance of involving the client in the development and implementation of the service plan to ensure that it is client-centered and relevant. They suggest that the service plan be based on a thorough assessment of the client's situation and needs and should identify the specific interventions and services needed to achieve the client's goals.

EVALUATION

Evaluation is a critical component of the case management process, as it provides a means of assessing the effectiveness of the service plan and making necessary adjustments. The case manager should regularly monitor and evaluate the client's progress toward achieving their goals, using both quantitative and qualitative measures. The evaluation process should involve the case manager and client and should be ongoing throughout the course of the service plan. By regularly reviewing and evaluating the service plan, the case manager can make necessary adjustments to ensure that the client is receiving the most appropriate and effective services.

According to the CMSA (2017), the evaluation process should be an ongoing and collaborative effort between the case manager and the client. The CMSA recommends using a range of evaluation methods, including surveys, formal and informal interviewing processes, and observation, to assess the effectiveness of the service plan. The evaluation process should focus on the client's progress toward achieving their goals, as well as any barriers or challenges that may be hindering their progress. Further, emphasis is placed on the importance of regularly reviewing and updating the service plan to ensure that it remains relevant and effective.

TERMINATION

Termination is the final phase of the case management process and involves the closure of the service plan. It is an essential component of the process, as it provides an opportunity to reflect on the progress that has been made and to celebrate achievements. Termination should be planned and deliberate and should involve the case manager, the client, and any other relevant stakeholders. The case manager should work with the client to identify the most appropriate time to terminate the service plan and should ensure that the client has the necessary skills and resources to maintain their progress after the plan has been closed.

According to Frankel et al. (2019), termination is an important component of the case management process that should be planned and executed carefully. The authors recommend that the case manager work collaboratively with the client to develop a plan for the transition to post-case management services. The plan should include information about any ongoing services or resources that may be needed and should identify any potential barriers or challenges that may arise during the transition. Finally, it is recommended that the case manager and the client take time to reflect on the progress that has been made and to celebrate any achievements.

FOLLOW-UP AND REFERRAL

Follow-up and referral are critical components of the case management process, as they ensure that the client receives ongoing support and resources after the service plan has been closed. Follow-up involves the case manager checking in with the client after termination to ensure that they are maintaining their progress and to address any issues or concerns that may arise. Referral involves connecting the client with additional services or resources that may be needed to maintain their progress or address new issues. The case manager should work collaboratively with the client to identify the most appropriate follow-up and referral services and should ensure that the client has the necessary skills and resources to access and utilize these services.

According to Frankel et al. (2019) follow-up and referral are important components of the case management process that should be integrated into the service plan from the outset. The authors emphasize the importance of working collaboratively with the client to identify the most appropriate follow-up and referral services and recommend that the case manager provide ongoing support to the client as they access and utilize these services. Finally, the importance of maintaining accurate and up-to-date records of follow-up and referral services emerges, as this information can be useful in evaluating the effectiveness of the service plan and identifying areas for improvement.

SUMMARY

Case management is a complex and dynamic process that involves a range of functions, tasks, and responsibilities. The case manager plays a critical role in coordinating services and resources, advocating for the client, and working collaboratively with other stakeholders to achieve the client's goals. The case management process involves several phases, including building rapport, problem assessment, goal setting, development of service plan, evaluation, termination, and follow-up or referral. Each phase requires the case manager to engage in a range of tasks, such as developing a working relationship with the client, assessing the client's needs and strengths, setting achievable goals, developing and implementing a service plan, and evaluating the effectiveness of the plan.

The case management process is underpinned by a strengths-based approach that emphasizes the client's inherent strengths and resources and seeks to build on these to achieve positive outcomes. Effective case management requires the case manager to be skilled in a range of areas, including communication, problem-solving, advocacy, and cultural competence.

Rehabilitation case management is a vital component of helping individuals achieve their goals and improve their quality of life. Effective rehabilitation case management requires a collaborative and client-centered approach that focuses on the client's unique needs, strengths, and preferences. Case managers play an essential role in coordinating services and resources, advocating for clients, and working with a range of stakeholders to achieve positive outcomes. The rehabilitation case management process involves several phases, including assessment, planning, implementation, and evaluation. Each phase requires the case manager to engage in a range of tasks, such as developing a working relationship with the client, assessing the client's needs and strengths, setting achievable goals, developing and implementing a service plan, and evaluating the effectiveness of the plan.

A critical aspect of rehabilitation case management is the development of a comprehensive service plan that addresses the client's needs and goals. The service plan should be based on a collaborative and strengths-based approach that emphasizes the client's resources and preferences. The service plan should be regularly reviewed and updated to ensure that it remains relevant and effective in meeting the client's changing needs.

Effective rehabilitation case management also requires a high level of professionalism and ethical practice. Case managers should adhere to professional standards of conduct and practice, such as those developed by the Commission on Rehabilitation Counselor Certification (CRCC), while being committed to ongoing professional development to stay current with the latest research and best practices in the field of rehabilitation counseling.

QUESTIONS FOR DISCUSSION

1. What is the importance of the case management process in the field of rehabilitation?
2. Why is it important to develop effective case management skills when focusing on work with clients, services, and community resources?
3. What is the impact of case management when focusing on goal setting and client movement through the rehabilitation process?
4. Describe situations in an agency setting in which you might utilize the case management functions of outreach, assessment, treatment planning, and linking for appropriate services.
5. Why is it important to understand the tasks and responsibilities of the case manager?
6. When considering tasks and responsibilities of the case manager, which would be difficult for you as a case manager? Which would you feel would fit your skills, abilities, and personality?
7. Why is confidentiality important in the case management process?
8. Compare and contrast the tasks and responsibilities of the case manager.
9. Why do you feel so many stages are involved in the case management process?
10. Now that you have completed your chapter on case management, what can you conclude about the definition of case management and impact on provision of services in the field of rehabilitation?

PUTTING IT INTO PRACTICE

Ask yourself these questions to target issues or concerns with case management.

1. Are specialized strengths among counseling professionals crucial for effective case management in rehabilitation settings, particularly when working with individuals with disabilities in interprofessional environments? Is it necessary for case managers to excel in all aspects of case management to achieve success?

2. As a rehabilitation case manager, what are the key components of your daily work, such as counseling, paperwork, referrals, or other tasks? How do these core aspects influence your productivity and outcomes on a daily basis?

3. How can professionals integrate various aspects of case management while staying true to their unique personal styles of handling cases? Could it become necessary to evaluate your personal style to critically look at case management outcomes?

CASE STUDY

Mr. Ozaki, a 62-year-old individual, received a diagnosis of early-stage glaucoma more than a year ago, but unfortunately, his condition has rapidly progressed, resulting in extensive vision loss. Multiple vision specialists have informed him that his vision will continue to deteriorate as he ages. In light of this situation, Susie Lewis, the dedicated case manager assigned to Mr. Ozaki's case, is actively collaborating with him, his wife Louis, and the healthcare team to provide the necessary support for him to continue working in the field of computer science. As part of her efforts, Susie has initiated the process of obtaining Mr. Ozaki's medical records to verify his diagnosis and is working closely with his doctors to assess the potential speed of his future vision loss. This comprehensive approach aims to address the challenges posed by his vision impairment and enable him to maintain his career aspirations in the face of this difficult condition.

Case Study Question

1. In light of case management functions, what would be the subsequent course of action for Mr. Ozaki's case? What steps should be taken next, and how will this case progress?

A robust set of instructor resources designed to supplement this text is located at http://connect.springerpub.com/content/book/978-0-8261-5963-2. Qualifying instructors may request access by emailing **textbook@springerpub.com**.

REFERENCES

Allen, R. I., & Petr, C. G. (1996). Towards developing standards and measurements for family-centered practice in family support programs. In G. Singer, L. Powers, & A. Olson (Eds.), *Family support policy and America's caregiving families: Innovations in public–private partnerships* (pp. 57–86). Brookes.

American Case Management Association. (2017). *What is a case manager?* https://www.acmaweb.org/section.aspx?sID=4#:~:text=Professional%20case%20managers%20help%20navigate,right%20to%20self%2Ddetermination.%22

American Counseling Association. (2014, October). *New responsibilities when making referrals.* https://www.counseling.org/docs/default-source/ethics/ethics_ocober-2014.pdf?sfvrsn=2

American Public Human Services Association. (2013). *Case management: An overview*. https://www.aphsa.org/content/dam/aphsa/PDFs/Case-Management-An-Overview.pdf

Anastasi, A. A., & Zammit, S. (2022). Referrals for inpatient rehabilitation and the patient selection processes: Pre-pandemic challenges as a guide towards reforms moving forward. *Journal of Orthopaedics, Trauma and Rehabilitation, 29*(1). https://doi.org/10.1177/22104917221092162

Berger, G., Peikes, D., & Fouts, A. (2011). The effects of case management on the progression of chronic illness: A comparison of two models. *The American Journal of Managed Care, 17*(9), e362–e370.

Bickman, L., Lambert, E. W., Andrade, A. R., & Penaloza, R. V. (2010). The Fort Bragg continuum of care for children and adolescents: Mental health outcomes over 5 years. *Journal of Consulting and Clinical Psychology, 78*(4), 498–511.

Biegel, D. E., Sales, E., & Schulz, R. (1993). A longitudinal study of caregivers' burden and depressive symptoms. *The Gerontologist, 33*(2), 206–216. https://doi.org/10.1093/geront/33.2.206

Bond, G. R., Peterson, A. E., Becker, D. R., & Drake, R. E. (2012). Validation of the revised Individual Placement and Support Fidelity Scale (IPS-25). *Psychiatric Services, 63*(8), 758–763. https://doi.org/10.1176/appi.ps.201100476

Brown, M. A., & Jason, K. (2017). Disability, case management, and employment outcomes: A critical literature review. *Journal of Applied Rehabilitation Counseling, 48*(1), 20–30.

Brown, S. L., Nesse, R. M., Vinokur, A. D., & Smith, D. M. (2003). Providing social support may be more beneficial than receiving it: Results from a prospective study of mortality. *Psychological Science, 14*(4), 320–327. https://doi.org/10.1111/1467-9280.14461

Browning, M., Chappel, J. N., & Tamburri, L. M. (2013). Case management in rehabilitation. In J. L. Matkin & A. J. Steele (Eds.), *Rehabilitation case management* (4th ed., pp. 33–55). CRC Press.

Cesta, T. G., & Flanagan, M. E. (2019). Case management. In J. A. Menkhaus & M. E. Flanagan (Eds.), *Healthcare management: Theory, practice, and cases* (3rd ed., pp. 266–283). Routledge.

Case Management Society of America. (2017). *Standards of practice for case management*. https://www.cmsa.org/wp-content/uploads/2019/02/CMSA_Standards_of_Practice_for_Case_Management_2016_Revised.pdf

Case Management Society of America. (2021). *What is case management?* Centers for Medicare & Medicaid Services. https://cmsa.org/who-we-are/what-is-a-case-manager/

Cassell, J., & Mulkey, S. W. (1985). *Rehabilitation caseload management: Concepts and practice*. Pro-Ed.

Chan, F., & Leahy, M. J. (2013*). The essentials of rehabilitation counseling: A guide for practitioners*. Pearson.

Commission on Rehabilitation Counselor Certification. (2017, January 1). *Code of Professional Ethics for Certified Rehabilitation Counselors (CRC)*. https://www.crccertification.com/wp-content/uploads/2021/03/CRC_CodeEthics_Eff2017-FinaLnewdiesign.pdf

Connor, L., Dean, J., McNett, M., Tydings, D. M., Shrout, A., Gorsuch P. F., Hole, A., Moore, L., Brown, R., Melnyk, B. M., & Gallagher-Ford, L. (2023). Evidence-based practice improves patient outcomes and healthcare system return on investment: Findings from a scoping review. *Worldviews on Evidence-Based Nursing, 20*(1), 6–15. https://doi.org/10.1111/wvn.12621

Crawford, M. J., Kuforiji, J., & Ghosh, P. (2012). The use of the strengths-based approach in community mental health: A qualitative study. *Social Psychiatry and Psychiatric Epidemiology, 47*(1), 37–44. https://doi.org/10.1007/s00127-010-0343-3

Fadyl, J. K., & McPherson, K. M. (2009). Approaches to vocational rehabilitation after traumatic brain injury: A review of the evidence. *Journal of Head Trauma Rehabilitation, 24*(3), 195–212. https://doi.org/10.1097/HTR.0b013e3181a0d458

Frankel, A. J., Gelman, S. R., & Pastor, D. K. (2019). *Case management: An introduction to concepts and skills* (4th ed.). Oxford University Press.

Grubbs, L. A., Cassell, J., & Mulkey, S. W. (2006). *Rehabilitation caseload management: Concepts and practice* (2nd ed.). Springer Publishing Company.

Guo, Q., Li, X., Yang, S., Song, Y., Sun, C., & Ma, L. (2021). Effects of nurse-led care and case management on physical and psychological rehabilitation outcomes of patients with spinal cord injury. *Rehabilitation Nursing, 46*(3), 125–132.

Hager, E. (2013). Case management assessment: A framework for understanding, describing, and measuring process. *Journal of Case Management, 22*(3), 126–131.

Haggans, J. (2023). AOTA evaluation checklists: Enhancing quality reporting & interdisciplinary collaboration. *OT Practice, 28*(12), 33–34.

Herman, P. M., Fullerton, C. A., Mayer, A. R., Steward, W. T., & McKnight, B. N. (2016). The quality of information on rehabilitation services available to people with traumatic brain injury and their families. *Archives of Physical Medicine and Rehabilitation, 97*(2), 207–214.

Higginbotham, J. C., & Hundley, S. P. (2019). Vocational rehabilitation case management: An overview. In D. A. Harley, N. A. Ysasi, M. L. Bishop, & A. R. Fleming (Eds.), *Disability and vocational rehabilitation in rural settings* (pp. 103–115). Springer.

Iwanaga, K., & Chan, F. (2017). Job placement and job retention for people with disabilities: Impact of vocational rehabilitation and case management. *Journal of Vocational Rehabilitation, 47*(3), 263–270.

Kapp, S. A., & Roesch, R. (2005). Case management: An essential component of effective HIV care. *AIDS Reader, 15*(5), 241–248.

Lamper, C., Beckers, L., Kroese, M., Verbunt, J., & Huijnen, I. (2021). Interdisciplinary care networks in rehabilitation care for patients with chronic musculoskeletal pain: A systematic review. *Journal of Clinical Medicine, 10*(9), 2041. https://doi.org/ 10.3390/jcm10092041

Leahy, M. J., Chan, F., Iwanaga, K., Umucu, E., Sung, C., Bishop, M., & Strauser, D. (2019). Empirically derived test specifications for the certified rehabilitation counselor examination: Revisiting the essential competencies of rehabilitation counselors. *Rehabilitation Counseling Bulletin, 63*(1), 35–49. https://doi.org/10.1177/0034355218800842

Levit, K., Ryan, K., Elixhauser, A., Stranges, E., Kassed, C., Coffey, R., & Mark, T. (2017). *HCUP facts and figures: Statistics on hospital-based care in the United States, 2009-2014.* Agency for Healthcare Research and Quality. https://www.ncbi.nlm.nih.gov/books/NBK52994/

Maki, D. R., & Tarvydas, V. (2012). *The professional practice of rehabilitation counseling* (2nd ed.). Springer Publishing Company.

Mauk, K. L. (2018). Rehabilitation counseling and advocacy: A profession and a calling. In L. C. Koch & P. D. Rummrill, Jr. (Eds.), *Rehabilitation counseling and emerging disabilities* (pp. 3–26).

Miller, R. L. (2013). *Fundamentals of case management practice: Skills for the human services* (4th ed.). Brooks/Cole.

Minkoff, K., & Cline, C. A. (2004). Changing the world of mental health through a system of assertive community treatment. *Community Mental Health Journal, 40*(2), 113–118.

Morley, C. (2023). *The vital role of evidence-based practice in professional case management.* CMSA Today. https://cmsatoday.com/2023/11/29/the-vital-role-of-evidence-based-practice-in-professional-case-management/

Morrison, E. F., Lank, P. M., & Hsieh, P. (2017). *Case management in health care: Concepts and practices.* Routledge.

Mullahy, M. A. (2010). *The case manager's handbook.* Jones & Bartlett Publishers.

Nakamura, K., Maeda, K., Takase, S., Saito, K., & Yasunaga, H. (2020). Comprehensive geriatric assessment and individualized treatment plan for frail elderly patients: A single-center experience. *Journal of the American Medical Directors Association, 21*(5), 677–682.

National Association of Social Workers. (2017). *Code of ethics.* https://www.socialworkers.org/About/Ethics/Code-of-Ethics/Code-of-Ethics-English

National Association of Social Workers. (2018). *Case management.* https://www.socialworkers.org/Practice/Career-Center/Specialties/Case-Management

National Council on Aging. (2015). *Case management overview.* https://www.ncoa.org/article/case-management-overview/

National Council for Behavioral Health. (2018). *The role of case managers in mental health treatment.* https://www.thenationalcouncil.org/wp-content/uploads/2018/03/Role-of-Case-Managers-in-Mental-Health-Treatment.pdf

National Council for Behavioral Health. (2020). *A compelling argument for facilitating the equitable use of generally accepted standards of care: Strategies for mental health and substance use disorder providers.* https://www.thenationalcouncil.org/wp-content/uploads/2022/02/021020_NCBH_WitParityToolkit_v8.pdf

National Council on Disability. (2012). *The current state of health care for people with disabilities.* https://www.ncd.gov/sites/default/files/NCD_StateOfHealthCare_FullReport.pdf

National Rehabilitation Association. (2015). *Issue statements national rehabilitation association governmental affairs summit.* https://www.ohiorehab.org/pdf/NRA%202015%20Issue%20Statements%20-%2003-17-15.pdf

O'Connor, S. J., & Gardner, J. F. (2019). Rehabilitation case management: Roles and functions in the interdisciplinary team. In *Rehabilitation case management* (pp. 17–35). Springer.

O'Donnell, M., & Gordon, E. E. (2011). *Principles of program design and evaluation.* Sage.

Ozawa, M. N. (2015). Rehabilitation case management in the vocational rehabilitation process. *Journal of Applied Rehabilitation Counseling, 46*(2), 22–30.

Quanbeck, A., Gustafson, D. H., Brown, R. T., & Glass, J. E. (2013). The CareSpan collaborative: A case management program to reduce hospitalizations of frail elderly veterans. *The Gerontologist, 53*(5), 727–737.

Rapp, C. A., Goscha, R. J., & Carlson, L. S. (2010). *Strengths-based case management: Implementing a recovery approach to mental health practice.* Oxford University Press.

Rawlins-Alderman, L. A., & Dunn, P. L. (2015). A review of case and caseload management course availability in undergraduate rehabilitation and disability studies programs. *The Rehabilitation Professional*, 23(3), 163–168.

Roesseler, R. T., Rubin, S. E., & Rumrill, P. D. (2018). *Case management and rehabilitation counseling: Procedures and techniques* (5th ed.). Pro-Ed.

Scanlon, D. P., Christianson, J. B., & Hackbarth, G. (2016). Medicare payment and delivery system reform: Early lessons for the benetactarian movement. *The Milbank Quarterly*, 94(3), 368–392.

Schober, C. V., Schmitt, M. H., & Fogg, L. (2018). Comprehensive assessment: The foundation for effective case management. *Journal of Gerontological Nursing*, 44(4), 27–32.

Schuck, A., Gryglewicz, K., Bender, A., Nam, E., McNeil, M., Cosare, M., Rosler, M., & Karver, M. (2023). Examining the effectiveness of a family-focused training to prevent youth suicide. *Family Relations: Interdisciplinary Journal of Applied Family Science*, 72(1), 325–346.

Simon, M. A. (2014). *Rehabilitation counseling and case management* (8th ed.) Pearson.

Substance Abuse and Mental Health Services Administration. (2017). *Behavioral health screening and assessment tools for adults*. https://www.samhsa.gov/capt/tools-learning-resources/behavioral-health-screening-and-assessment-tools-adults

Tang, V. L., Sudore, R., Cenzer, I. S., Boscardin, W. J., Smith, A., Ritchie, C., Wallhagen, M., Finlayson, E., Petrillo, L., & Covinsky, K. (2017). Rates of recovery to pre-fracture function in older persons with hip fracture: An observational study. *Journal of General Internal Medicine, 32*, 153–158. https://doi.org/10.1007/s11606-016-3848-2

Tennant, L., Stellefson, M., & Dodd, V. (2015). Building rapport between nurse case managers and clients living with HIV/AIDS: A qualitative study. *Journal of the Association of Nurses in AIDS Care, 26*(6), 704–714. https://doi.org/10.1016/j.jana.2015.06.006

Tahan, H. M., & Treiger, T. M. (2017). *CMSA core curriculum for case* (3rd ed.). Wolters Kluwer Publishing.

Vos, A., Stolwijk-Swuste, J. M., Van Mierlo, M. L., & Post, M. W. (2019). Rehabilitation case management and employment outcomes for people with disabilities: A systematic review. *Journal of Occupational Rehabilitation, 29*(2), 197–212.

Wong, F. K. D., & Law, K. S. (2002). Developing and implementing a case management model for clients with chronic diseases in Hong Kong. *Journal of Advanced Nursing, 39*(6), 576–588. https://doi.org/10.1046/j.1365-2648.2002.02340.x

Wong, Y. G., Hang, J. A., Francis-Coad, J., & Hill, A. M. (2022). Using comprehensive geriatric assessment for older adults undertaking a facility-based transition care program to evaluate functional outcomes: A feasibility study. *BMC Geriatrics, 22*, 598. https://doi.org/10.1186/s12877-022-03255-5

CHAPTER 2

Rehabilitation Caseload Management: Quest for Competence

LEARNING OBJECTIVES

By the end of this chapter, learners will be able to:

- Discuss the historical context of rehabilitation caseload management, understanding its evolution and the factors that have shaped its current practices.

- Analyze the implications surrounding rehabilitation professional identity and competency as a caseload manager, recognizing the skills and knowledge required for effective caseload management.

- Define the key concepts and practices of rehabilitation caseload management, including its purpose, goals, and strategies.

- Describe the conceptual model of caseload management, identifying its core components and their interrelationships.

- Discuss the hierarchical arrangement of conceptual aspects within the caseload management process, recognizing the importance of each element in optimizing outcomes.

- Differentiate between case and caseload management in professional practice, understanding the distinctions and considerations associated with each approach.

- Identify the impact of improved caseload management on professional practice, evaluating the benefits in terms of client care, treatment continuity, and overall professional satisfaction.

INTRODUCTION

Some of the most ambiguous descriptions for guiding behavior ever confronted by developing professionals begin with the phrase "Caseload management is . . . ." In the field of rehabilitation these descriptions range from general to specific. However, a lack of comprehension of what constitutes caseload management has plagued professional practice. Because caseload management functions are so intricately entwined with all rehabilitation counselor functions, any quest for a competency base that uniquely characterizes this group of practitioners must take into account the role of caseload management in professional competence.

QUEST FOR COMPETENCE

The quest for a unique **competency base**, or what Roessler et al. (2018) term *"profession-alization,"* has led to the compilation of a vast array of abilities and skills. Historically, McGowan (1960) gives a list of counseling competencies, each of which could take extensive elaboration to enumerate the subparts. This list includes (a) an ability to establish and maintain a counseling relationship with individuals; (b) an ability to evaluate aptitudes, skills, interests, and educational background; (c) an ability to recognize manifestations of physical and mental disabilities and their relationships to vocational adjustment; (d) an ability to analyze occupations and workers in terms of job requirements, the skills required, and the physical demands of the job; and (e) an ability to make discriminating use of available community services and to maintain a cooperative working relationship with such sources.

In contrast, in the last 40 years the field of rehabilitation has seen an increase in specialization in multiple areas. Rubin and Roessler (2001, 2006, 2016) reflect on the increase in professionals and specialists as accompanied by greater societal influence. Generally, professionals act as **gatekeepers** of information and services, helping to define appropriate behaviors, goals, strategies, and supporting treatment for clients. Other areas important to the "professionalization" of counselors are medical-related knowledge, counseling skills, implementation of skills in management, ability to analyze occupational and industrial trends, and an understanding of legislative trends and federal laws relevant to rehabilitation programs (Mullahy, 1998, 2004; Shrey & Lacerte, 1995). Grubbs et al. (2006) point out that at the most basic level of career adjustment (i.e., mere survival) the counselor must have some management skills.

The field of rehabilitation counseling necessitates a thorough examination of **counselor competencies and skills** as these complexities continue to be explored and refined. Various authors, such as Dolce et al. (2022), Ervin (2008), Leahy (2004), Power (2012), Roessler and Rubin (1982, 2006), Rubin and Roessler (2006), Rubin et al. (2016), and Sink et al. (1979), have emphasized the importance of enhancing counselor skill development. While counselors possess a strong educational foundation, ongoing professional development should encompass job activities, knowledge acquisition, and skill enhancement. Rubin and coworkers (2006, 2016) specifically highlight the significance of specialized skills for different settings or areas of practice. These identify counseling as the foremost area of competence, complemented by expertise in assessment, case management, and job analysis/placement. Further, discussions underscore the importance of continuous skill development and the acquisition of specialized competencies to enhance the effectiveness of rehabilitation counselors in their direct service provision.

Similarly, rehabilitation counselors in the **private sector** have sought definitions of the skills and knowledge required for their professional roles (Beveridge et al., 2021; Kontosh, 2000; Lynch & Martin, 1982; Mullahy, 1998, 2004, 2017; Shrey, 1995). Although each professional brings a competency core of knowledge and skills from past educational encounters, to be effective, disability managers must recognize and understand the characteristics and trends of the rehabilitation system and how to integrate them into disability programs and professional practice. Hursch (1995) concludes that competencies required by independent and private rehabilitation practitioners will most often depend on the characteristics of the work environment and of the client population.

Patterson (1957), in his pivotal publication regarding the **counselor-versus-coordinator** controversy, offers what even today can be considered a summary statement to a process of compiling lists of performance competencies. He noted that these long lists of abilities, skills, and knowledge bases for rehabilitation counselors give one the impression of reading the curriculum for the complete content of the social and biological sciences. However, these lists cannot be summarized in any simple manner to produce a complete picture of a competent rehabilitation professional. This conclusion may have prompted Rubin and Roessler (2018) to call for the development of **multifaceted counselor roles**. This multifarious approach continues to perpetuate a dualism between counselor competencies and coordinator or manager competencies, that is, the Patterson (1957) "two hats" perspective. The field is long overdue in developing an integrative approach to rehabilitation counselor competency. Therefore, rather than continue in the current vein of broadening perspectives on counselor performance areas, a more productive approach would be the integration of the numerous functions of the rehabilitation professional into a core area toward which a majority of the competencies are directed. The core of counselor competency.

THE CORE OF COUNSELOR COMPETENCY

Counseling has long been recognized as the central component of competency within the rehabilitation profession (Bellini, 2002; Riggar & Maki, 1997; Thomason & Barrett, 1959). This emphasis on counseling places considerable pressure on rehabilitation counselors, both internally (self-generated) and externally (from organizational expectations), as they carry the responsibility for an entire caseload. Regardless of the source of accountability, be it organizational or personal, the ultimate goal remains the same: effectively managing individuals with disabilities through an informed and thoughtful process.

Contrary to the belief that direct client contact does not require management competency (Harrison & Lee, 1979), the core of rehabilitation counselors' work lies in their **management activities**. It is through these activities that counselors establish control over the demands of their caseloads. Successful rehabilitation counselors have embraced this understanding (Willey, 1978). In fact, counselors in the private sector have shifted their focus from traditional rehabilitation to a concept known as **disability management** (Kreider, 1983; Mullahy, 1998, 2004, 2017; Shrey, 1995). This shift highlights three distinct elements of disability management: healthcare delivery, cost-containment programs, and vocational placement. Clearly, caseload management in the private sector heavily relies on a management model to effectively navigate these elements.

Management is a function of counselor performance. Regardless of the setting, be it a public agency, private organization, or independent facility, the effectiveness of counseling activities relies on a well-structured management process. This process provides the necessary authority and accountability to the counseling function. It is important to note that effective caseload management does not seek to replace counseling as a critical responsibility; instead, its aim is to empower the counseling function by providing a solid power base. By implementing fully effective caseload management, counselors can enhance their ability to fulfill their responsibilities and deliver optimal client care.

THE COMMON THREAD

As we delve into the extensive lists of abilities, skills, and knowledge required of counselors, it becomes evident that there is a pressing need to unite them under a cohesive framework. This framework can be found in caseload management, which serves as the common thread tying these elements together. As early as 1965, a study group on caseload management recognized this connection, stating that caseload management should encompass the entirety of a counselor's work activities, including case work, caseload, case management, and other job responsibilities (Muthard, 1965, pp. 12–13). It is essential to acknowledge the holistic nature of caseload management and its role in integrating various aspects of a counselor's practice into a unified perspective.

The comprehensive integration of management concepts and principles is essential to unite the diverse functions and responsibilities of counselors, providing the necessary cohesion and consistency. Unfortunately, the management of caseloads has not historically received the recognition and emphasis needed to establish it as a distinct and valuable area for in-depth study and research. McLelland (1977), highlighting the significance of caseload management in the rehabilitation process, emphasized that the counselor's competence plays a critical role in the success of this process, surpassing the influence of any other variable. This underscores the importance of recognizing and developing the skills and expertise necessary for effective caseload management in achieving positive outcomes in rehabilitation practice.

DEFINING CASELOAD MANAGEMENT

The Definition Dilemma

The lack of consensus regarding a **common competency base** can be attributed to the ambiguity surrounding the definition of caseload management. Without a clear and agreed-upon understanding of what caseload management entails, it becomes challenging to establish a definitive competency framework. Currently, there is minimal consensus among practitioners, administrative personnel, researchers, and writers regarding the precise definition of caseload management. Interestingly, while the term "case management" is defined in dictionaries, "caseload management" lacks a universally accepted definition. This lack of consensus hinders the establishment of consistent competency levels among professionals, as the definitions vary significantly. To address this issue, this chapter explores a working definition of caseload management in detail. However, it is important to note that these initial concepts provided serve as a starting point. As the field evolves and new research and perspectives emerge, further elaborations and requirements for caseload management will need to be developed to ensure the continuous refinement and enhancement of professional practice.

Conceptual definitions give perspectives, or even quasi-boundaries, wherein individuals respond with appropriate duties and responsibilities. Therefore, if a definition of a concept is consistently vague, ambiguous, or incomplete, expected performance derived from this definitional base will be less than effective. If basic definitions are not developed through organized research, documented writings, and shared discussions among professionals, definitions will never evolve that have commonalities with potential for mutual acceptance. The end result will be individually derived definitional bases likely to be fragmented, unclear, incomplete, and disorganized.

The term **case management** has often been confused with **caseload management**. "In fact, these terms are sometimes used synonymously, without attempting to distinguish any difference" (Cassell & Mulkey, 2004, p. 254). This misuse adds to the confusion and frustration of establishing definitions. There are differences that have implications for the way counselors mentally rank germane activities as to their importance and value. Consequently, the motivational set that follows is affected also.

The *Commission for Case Manager Certification* (2022) reflects that case management is not considered a profession within itself, but a collaborative occurring in various settings and facilitated by diverse disciplines. Thus, with casework practices the counselor's perspective is naturally focused primarily on case-by-case specifics and not the more encompassing, interacting whole, which is the entire caseload. **Casework** is immersed in activities involving (a) moving clients from intake to closure, (b) performing proper case-by-case documentation, (c) acquiring necessary evaluations and examinations for justification purposes and satisfying established guidelines, (d) execution of master list activities and case findings, (e) individualized medical management programs, and (f) concern for case-by-case cost-containment practices. Roessler et al. (2018) offer procedures and techniques for developing case management skills. Their work delineates operational strategies and guidelines for the diagnosis, evaluation, treatment, and follow-up of the individual case.

In contrast, Grubbs et al. (2006) reflect on caseload management as performance encompassing, totally involving counselor attention, and integrating the coordination and control of many activities, one of which is case management. As the term *caseload management* implies, "it is a systematic process of organizing, planning, coordinating, directing, and controlling for effective and efficient counselor and manager decision-making, to enhance proactive practice" (Cassell & Mulkey, 1985, p. 11). In contrast to casework management, Henke et al. (1975) bring to prominence a description of caseload management. This description reads: "how to work with more than one case at a time, how to select which case to work with, how to move from one case to another, how to establish a system to insure (sic) movement of all cases, and how to meet the objective one has established in terms of numbers served" (p. 218). Additionally, Rawlins-Williams and Oswald (2021) enhance this definition with their focus on facilitating knowledge in caseload management and incorporating it into practice.

Other distinct characteristics are prominent when trying to define caseload management. These include (a) establishing a calendar of activities for a reasonably structured day or week for the most effective use of the counselor's time by filling the day with high-priority tasks, (b) orchestrating a group of other professionals to rehabilitate clients through this coordinated group effort, and (c) initiating actions through a consistent decision-making style that keeps activities moving toward targeted goals.

Whereas *control* is prominent in both caseload management and casework activities, caseload definitions are much broader and more encompassing in *caseload management* functions. Casework goals and objectives are typically microcosmic in scope, whereas caseload management goals and objectives are more macrocosmic. Implied, also, is the fact that counselors must effectively invoke salient counseling and managerial skills to be in control of a caseload management process.

This discussion has served to highlight a few of the identifying distinctions between the concepts of case management and caseload management. A more complete, more functional definition of caseload management will evolve in subsequent discussions. For **efficient action**, a counselor's extensive array of responsibilities must be met with case manager skills. Various bodies of work have stated that while professionals must be skilled counselors, rehabilitation counselors must also be competent case managers (Frankel & Beckman, 2020; Kanter, 2010; Roessler & Rubin, 1982; Snowden, 2003). However, without the perspective and skills founded in **effective** caseload management practices, overall competency will elude the counselor (Alderman & Oswald, 2016; Grubbs et al., 2006; Rawlins-Williams & Oswald, 2021).

Definitions in a Historical Context

The field has not yet accurately collected the components of caseload management into a basic definition that will serve as a major guidepost for describing the functions and actions required of the professional counselor. Thus, sustained efforts for upgrading knowledge and improving skill levels continue to be thwarted. Of those definitions existing in the literature, most are vague and general, some are scantly specific, and only a few are hauntingly accurate. Examples of past definitions for caseload management were noted by members of the Third Institute of Rehabilitation Services study group (Muthard, 1965).

The first is "the objective of CLM [caseload management] is to vocationally rehabilitate the greatest number of disabled persons at the least possible cost, consistent with the highest standards of quality" (p. 12). Although this definition is easily generalizable to a private or public rehabilitation setting, it is actually an outcome or result and does not describe the process of caseload management. As an objective or goal, the definition offers no real guidelines on which managerial behaviors can be founded. This is because one can never "do" a goal. That is, one can engage only in those activities that lead toward the goal. The study group provided an additional definition as the one they would collectively support: "the use of techniques (methods or details of procedure) to control the distribution, quality, quantity, and cost of all aspects of casework activities in order to accomplish the program goals of the agency" (p. 12). This definition admirably delineates process specifics (i.e., "techniques to . . . ") and outcomes (i.e., program goals). However, the definition is restricted in its perspective and does not deal with caseload management as a more encompassing, systematic, gestalt-like entity. It narrows to a case management definition and thus is circular: in other words, it makes an inference that caseload management is case management and case management is caseload management.

Muthard (1965) posits caseload management as techniques and procedures utilized to achieve the agencies' objectives. This definition is succinct to the point of complete vagueness. No functional base of operations could emerge from this beginning point. Also, the end result toward which the caseload management activities are to be directed is for the benefit of the fulfillment of agency objectives. Thus, the definition addresses only one of the four elements of caseload management to be described later in this chapter.

Henke et al. (1975) define caseload management with broad "how to" statements. They describe it as "how to work with more than one case at a time, how to select which case to work with, how to move from one case to another, how to establish a system to insure (sic) movement of all cases, how to meet objectives one has established" (p. 218). Greenwood (1982) characterized caseload management as a plan-manage-review conceptualization. He further states that "his approach to systematic caseload management is integrated into a case management model of rehabilitation counseling" (p. 159). Grubbs et al. (2006) provide an instructive definition as a systematic process merging counseling and managerial concepts and skills through application of techniques and research and other relevant related factors for anchoring a proactive practice.

Confusion over the nature of caseload management is not limited to academic groups, researchers, and writers. Counselors in the field also have a great deal of difficulty defining caseload management as it relates to them. To focus on recent definitions, the authors over time in training sessions have asked counselors employed by state rehabilitation agencies to write definitions of caseload management in their practices. They were told that definitions do indeed serve as descriptors for action or as guides to determine the direction of future activities. Therefore, serious consideration was to be given to writing definitions that accurately depicted what each counselor does as a caseload manager. The definitions presented here were written by the counselors. For purposes of description and analysis, the authors independently judged the definitions as falling into three categories: (a) functional definitions, (b) minimally functional definitions, and (c) nonfunctional definitions. The three categories were created to investigate the definitional formats that counselors most often utilize to guide their caseload management activities.

Functional Definition

A **functional definition** would be one on which the counselor could base an adequate program or management system. It would have enough elements to demonstrate that the counselor had a good grasp of what needs to go into a descriptive guide for behavior or an adequate perspective on the caseload as a more complete, systematized entity. Counselors were asked to complete the statement: "Caseload management is . . ." to form practical definitions. Three examples of those judged to be functional definitions are listed next:

1. *The process of analyzing, planning, supervising, and administering the smooth flow of rehabilitation services to the number of clients for which you have responsibility and the coordination of other professionals and resources utilized.*
2. *To effectively coordinate a system whereby individual clients are provided services toward eventual rehabilitation by predicting through evaluation, setting objectives, processing, co-ordinating, and maintaining an equitable and just flow of clients toward individual goals.*
3. *The ability to organize, coordinate, and effect the smooth flow of cases and services with maximum return from the services, to be utilized in returning clientele to the most independent status of which the counselor is capable.*

Definitions in this category are characterized by (a) the conceptualization of caseload management as a process or system; (b) the owning of managerial functions, such as planning, supervision, coordinating, and organizing, as a necessary part of a counselor's responsibility parallel to the therapeutic functions; (c) adequate length to "get into" the definition; (d) integration of work responsibilities and personal characteristics; (e) the proper differentiation between aspects of efficiency and effectiveness; and (f) the recognition of a dual role requirement, that is, counselor responsibilities and casework or caseflow responsibilities.

Minimally Functional Definition

A **minimally functional definition** would demonstrate that the counselor was giving thought to an adequate definition but could focus only marginally on the elements involved. That is, as a definition it would be a beginning, but it lacks completeness as an adequate behavioral guide. Examples of minimally functional definitions are given next. These follow the stem "Caseload management is . . ."

1. *The effective use and control of time, money, and people in such a way as to produce a desired result with a given case.*
2. *The effective administration and management of services to clients within a reasonable time period.*
3. *The process by which clients' cases are initiated and carried through the rehabilitation process in the most facilitative way possible by the vocational rehabilitation counselor.*

Minimally functional definitions are characterized by (a) vague generalities such as "*in the most facilitative way possible,*" (b) a focus on smaller units at the expense of a gestalt conceptualization of a caseload, (c) brevity but not succinctness, and (d) minimal concern for a sophisticated managerial approach.

Nonfunctional Definition

Nonfunctional definitions would be incomplete or inadequate attempts to describe the functions that make up the activities required in caseload management. Examples of nonfunctional definitions are given next. They also follow the stem "Caseload management is . . ."

1. *primarily "paper work." Your caseload is, however, those cases you choose to accept or ones you feel that you must accept based upon your interpretation of the regulations and what you can get by your supervisor.*

2. *your arrangement and coordination of client services.*
3. *the fine art of shuffling paper more effectively in order to facilitate a smooth transition from where the client is to a predetermined goal.*

Finally, nonfunctional definitions (a) have very little goal direction written in or are simply rambling collections of words, (b) are either vague to the extreme or attempt a universal explanation, (c) have a dearth of descriptive content, and (d) display some hostility or displeasure toward performing caseload management activities.

Of the 98 definitions gathered for analysis, the following percentages by categories were obtained: (a) 15% were judged to be functional definitions, (b) 45% were minimally functional definitions, and (c) 40% were nonfunctional definitions. Thus, 85% of the counselors in this study could not clearly demonstrate that they had an adequate base of knowledge or understanding of what constitutes caseload management and upon which they could base progressive caseload management activities.

The implications of this analysis are readily apparent, as is the awareness of the impact of attempting to function from some of these definitional bases. Again, if 85% of these counselors, the large majority of whom had more than 3 years of experience, have only a vague concept of themselves as in control of a process that necessitates managerial principles and concepts, then clearly a great deal of training or retraining lies ahead. Failure to arrive at more complete and comprehensive activity bases will perpetuate the tendency to manage by crises or, in many cases, not manage at all.

External forces and issues acting upon counselors and forces within their settings influence current definitions of caseload management. However, the basics are seldom altered or undergo any drastic revision over time. These basics stem from self-management issues, situation or setting management issues (i.e., private or public rehabilitation issues, state agency guidelines, or federal mandates), economic principles, and client management issues. These basics can be addressed with a knowledge base and practice format that will stabilize new counselors coming into the field, as well as continuing counselors who still grope for stability in an environment that often appears to have boundaries and limitations that will not stay constant for any extended period of time.

A Basic Definition

To this point, different definitions, all of which appear to be in various stages of incompleteness, have been given. All those we have encountered thus far have varying degrees of functionality, but none have a completeness that could be considered a standard. All counselors, of course, will arrive at some definition to guide their own behavior. However, for effective caseload management practices, an instructive definition is provided as follows:

Caseload management is a systematic process merging counseling and managerial concepts and skills through application of techniques from intuitive and researched methods, thereby advancing efficient and effective decision-making for functional control of self, client, setting, and other relevant related factors for anchoring a proactive and outcome-focused practice.

This definition contains components that provide greater depth than the majority of definitions found in the literature or in the field. A closer look at what this definition is communicating can be made by examining its individual components.

SYSTEMATIC PROCESS

Consistent patterns for performing caseload management responsibilities cannot exist without the counselor-manager being conceptually aware of the systematic process. These concepts establish two major points. First, counselors must operate from a model or system in order to achieve consistency. Whether practicing counselors realize it or not, their efforts to cope with or to control elements of caseload management activities fall into a system they have already devised for themselves. Assuredly, although consistency is the key element that signifies that a systematic approach is being taken, it does not ensure efficiency, nor does it address the extent of the effectiveness of counselors. Second, caseload management has beginning and ending phases that must be hierarchically and systematically arranged. The caseload management process consists of stages or a series of activities that must be sequenced properly in a logical, rational manner. The beginning and ending stages have separate requirements and considerations, but the idea of a flow or pipeline is paramount. The hierarchical arrangement (see **Figure 2.1**) of the process develops from a base of referral and interview biographical data. From this base develop interpersonal relationships, formalized and intuitive evaluations and insights, and, finally, professional judgments or decisions, all of which peak with an eventual successful rehabilitation. Each of the conceptual areas, of course, has its own skill and expertise requirements that must be well developed if the caseload manager is to be in effective control of this process.

MERGING COUNSELING AND MANAGERIAL CONCEPTS AND SKILLS

In the field of rehabilitation counseling, a professional must perform balanced, **dual roles** involving both typical counselor functions and managerial duties. Dualism must give way to interrelatedness with equal commitments for both roles in order for the process to be systematic (a discussion of these roles will be elaborated upon in Chapter 2).

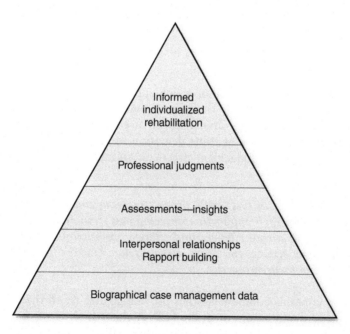

FIGURE 2.1 A hierarchical arrangement of conceptual aspects of the caseload management process.

APPLICATION OF TECHNIQUES FROM INTUITIVE AND RESEARCHED METHODS

This phrase draws from the systematic or model concept just discussed. However, here considerations are given to caseload management as a developing science that must be supported by techniques and methods derived by counselors through personal experiences and from intuitive approaches. These are "researched" and reported in the literature, used within practice, and then refined by counselor practice. This activity places much of the burden of the developing practice of caseload management with practitioners.

ADVANCING EFFICIENT AND EFFECTIVE DECISION-MAKING

This is a goal all rehabilitation professionals strive for, regardless of setting. It is especially the case in the field of rehabilitation, where there are rapport-building activities in human services endeavors, as well as management of financial resources to achieve the greatest benefit from constrained budgets in the public sector, and from cost-restrictive, insurance-applied rehabilitation programs in the private sector. The efficiency-effectiveness dimensions often are clouded unnecessarily by a continual dilemma that develops over the decision of which to sacrifice when discussing client concerns (i.e., the effectiveness dimension) and monetary, agency accounting-reporting demands (i.e., the efficiency dimension). This has been termed a dilemma (Cassell & Mulkey, 1985; Grubbs et al., 2006). The obvious, but very difficult-to-achieve, compromise is a balance between the two dimensions. **Efficiency** has a definite place in a management system and is necessary to achieve **effectiveness**. Hence, setting relatively strict schedule limits or conducting interviews in an efficient manner can be done without sacrificing the interpersonal or counseling relationship. It is by this efficient route that effectiveness is often achieved. However, it must be emphasized that efficiency will not always lead to effectiveness.

FUNCTIONAL CONTROL OF SELF, CLIENT, SETTING, AND OTHER RELEVANT RELATED FACTORS

The idea of control pervades the entire definition and is openly stated in its latter part for emphasis. Control is the key ingredient of a caseload management model and will be given extensive attention in later chapters. This component of our definition further extends the earlier discussion and reinforces the idea that boundaries are confronted consistently by professionals dealing with clients at the point of service delivery. The counselors' personal needs for performing work activities and deriving personal and professional satisfaction from these activities to meet the needs of clients are important considerations in defining caseload management as an entity consisting of a variety of factors. Also, clients' expectations generally exceed agency or company limitations. Control is the act of ensuring that this exceeding of limitations never reaches a critically high or abortive level. Or, if limits are exceeded, then alternatives (the control dimension) are enacted that diminish the critical nature of the events. It should be noted that "related factors" are considered in the generic sense. That is, legislative mandates (e.g., varying the disabilities allowable as eligible for services), employment outlook in varying economic conditions, counselors' drive and motivational strength, professional-ethical forces, need structures of counselors and clients, client personal strengths, drive and energy levels, and community resources are integral parts of this categorization. Culmination of the previously noted factors may result in strategies for empowering consumer involvement in maximizing the rehabilitation process.

ANCHORING A PROACTIVE AND OUTCOME-FOCUSED PRACTICE

The concepts brought together in this basic definition are given as boundary conditions or guidelines. Functional control, then, provides only a connection to link the concepts coherently.

The end result or action step, *a proactive, outcome-focused practice*, still rests with the execution of consistent daily practices and personal conduct that extends beyond self-defeating negative attitudes that can arise.

Conclusion

It should be noted that the authors' definition does not mention numbers of "successful outcomes" or "successful case closures" as part of caseload management. Because caseload management is considered a process to achieve these universally stated goals, success is an outcome dimension and generally will follow if the process is managed adequately from the outset.

There are two other issues that require attention when developing definitions. The first is the activity base from which counselors initiate caseload management functions (i.e., a proactive versus a reactive base). The second is the confusion of case management and caseload management as one and the same with identical theoretical underpinnings. These important issues are addressed in the following discussion.

A CONCEPTUAL MODEL OF CASELOAD MANAGEMENT

The practice of caseload management is not devoid of professionalism, nor is there an absence of consistent approaches. Rather, counselors often develop a personal methodology or approach but are unaware of the individual elements of their systems. Many of these counselors are unable to effect change or initiate improvement without this insight or perspective. For experienced counselors and for those who are being initiated to the demands of a caseload, this text attempts to systematize an approach to caseload management. The concepts offer a measure of organization and a professional base to help counselors develop a personal management style and personal management system.

The conceptualization of caseload management that follows stems from a model developed by Grubbs et al. (2006) and conclusions that this area is bounded by four essential elements. **Figure 2.2** depicts the four essential factors in this framework: (a) **personal elements,** (b) **data elements,** (c) **client elements,** and (d) **pehabilitation organization elements.**

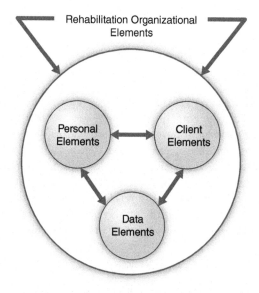

FIGURE 2.2 The essential elements of a caseload management model.

Each of these elements exerts a specific influence or force on the caseload management process. The methodology for coping with these factors is usually germane to the specific area of influence, and thus a separate knowledge base is required for each area. However, because these elements do not exist in isolation from one another, the interaction among them establishes the fact that knowledge about or experience gained from each element is usually synergistic with the others.

Clearly, it is this synergism that constitutes *caseload management*. These elements must be viewed and studied individually before they can be properly incorporated into a personalized management system. However, this text will concern itself with those two areas over which the counselor can exert the greatest control and can have the most immediate impact: personal elements and data elements. Client elements, of course, can be influenced greatly by a counselor's action (or inaction). The influence is more indirect, and sufficient literature has been developed to treat these elements. The subsequent discussion will present a brief overview of all four elements.

The management of a caseload is dependent first and foremost on the personal characteristics of the counselor. In order to manage a rehabilitation process, the counselor must first understand and be in control of aspects of managing themselves in the most effective manner possible. Hence, it is necessary for counselors to be as fully aware as possible of their internal dynamics: attitudes, beliefs, motivations, perceptions, decision-making skills, and general psychological makeup.

Personal elements have a wide range of components that require the caseload manager to exercise some measure of control. **Control** is defined very broadly and is not restricted to direct manipulation of overt actions. Basically, knowledge is control. To acquire an awareness or knowledge base in a particular area is to establish for oneself a measure of control. To lack information and knowledge in a specific personal area and to be forced to draw upon this area for interaction with external processes (persons and procedures) is to suffer the consequence of having these external processes control the caseload manager.

The authors believe that four content areas offer a framework for developing personal elements in a management process. These four areas are (a) learning the basics of management for counselors, (b) becoming aware of the specifics for establishing control, (c) developing an effective decision-making base, and (d) gaining effective management of time. These basics of management are an important area of consideration, as counselors do not often think of themselves as managers, or at least they most often prefer not to do so (Rawlins-Williams & Oswald, 2021; Rubin & Emener, 1979).

Personal Elements

One can never really *act* like a caseload manager unless one first begins to *think* like a caseload manager. When the basic information of a management framework is owned by the counselor, the "thinking process" has begun, and future constructive action is then dependent on the use to which the counselor puts the information gained.

Once the basics of a management model have been incorporated into a counselor's generic modus operandi, refinements of the basics are then possible. The caseload manager is then ready to focus directly upon the key management function: *control*. Without a firm level of control—at least personal control if not the difficult-to-achieve structural or organizational control—effective caseload management will always be elusive or achieved at very dramatic personal costs to counselors. Thus, "stress" (Brickham et al., 2021; Brill, 1995; Ling et al., 2014; Miller & Roberts, 1979; Selye, 1978), "role strain" (Duxbury & Halinski, 2014; Porter, 2010; Rubin & Emener, 1979; Vash, 2001; Woodside & McClam, 2003, 2019), and "counselor burn-out" (Emener, 1978; Faubion et al., 2001; Lee et al., 2007, 2010; Lizano 2015; Okun, 1999; Puig et al., 2014) all become relevant issues for practicing counselors.

Decision-making, of course, is the pivotal point upon which the caseload management process balances. Decision-making is a personal process and requires an individualized approach to make the process valid. However, if the basics for understanding this process and for objectifying it are learned well, decision-making becomes more than just an intuitive endeavor (see Chapter 6).

Effective decision-making, however, will depend on how well the counselor has developed the control function. When the counselor firmly believes a state of overall control is possible and consistently executes control, then the most formidable barrier to decision-making has been removed. Thus, we see how the acquisition of a true management style is highly dependent on a process arrangement or sequential building of one set of activities upon others.

Finally, the mortar for building any management program is the effective use of time. The counselor's consistency in managing a caseload will depend on whether they use a systematic approach to managing time. By relying on personalized principles and concepts for a complete understanding of time management, the counselor is in control of the flow of day-to-day management activities. Time management is conceptualized as a dual arrangement (i.e., a quantitative base and an intuitive base), with methodology and techniques specific to each leading to a comprehensive picture. Caseload managers must learn to manage their time by becoming aware of the specific manner in which they allot time to various activities (i.e., determining which activities are effective and which are time wasters). Also, caseload managers must often times manage time from an intuitive base that does not require the gathering of facts, figures, and other data. Instead, they must be spontaneous and ready to respond from internal processes that guide them through those time traps and time robbers that threaten effective time utilization.

These four areas are not all inclusive for establishing what rehabilitation counselors should understand about the personal elements of caseload management. They are the minimally necessary aspects. The information gained in this area should stimulate a thinking process that will allow the manager role to become cognitively and emotionally palatable. Although these are the minimally necessary aspects for control of personal elements, the incorporation of the principles learned in a counselor's total approach to the job is not minimal in terms of impact on performance and, thus, client services. These four areas also serve as the core for dealing effectively with the three remaining caseload management elements (i.e., data elements, client elements, and organization or agency elements) as they exert their influences on counselor practice.

Data Elements

Managers of caseloads most often perceive caseload data elements as the only area toward which to direct management efforts. Counselors come with the idea that they will be dealing only with data, including computerized lists, the basic classification system, case movement, and case recording. As one can see from what has already been stated, data elements are not the only area requiring the application of a managerial approach. Caseload data points do, however, constitute a significant portion of counselors' areas of responsibility in rehabilitation settings and must be managed, unless one would have them exert such an influence that the data begin to manage the counselor.

Part II of this text will be devoted primarily to aspects of getting this element of caseload management under counselor control. The areas emphasized focus on the applied aspects of this process and include (a) understanding the rehabilitation competency framework in various practical settings, (b) managing case flow, and (c) essentials of case recording and documentation.

The monitoring, assessment, and managing of client movement through any process require a systematic structure. In the rehabilitation field, individuals with disabilities who seek services in private and public rehabilitation organizations automatically become part of pre-established monitoring systems. Therefore, professional caseload managers who work within these organizations or those who work in association with them must have sufficient knowledge of the competency framework and how it is implemented into the private and public rehabilitation sectors. This system gives counselors the expertise required for moving clients through this monitoring system, and it gives counselors in the public sector and case managers in the private sector, who work with these agencies, an understanding of their terminology and nomenclature.

Caseloads in rehabilitation are systematized. The classification system itself is somewhat static. When the different zones accumulate numbers representing clients and when these clients move within the classification system, then a more dynamic case flow process is created. If effectiveness and efficiency are to be achieved within this caseload management framework, the counselor cannot move clients aimlessly through the system. Instead, priorities for action must be established and methods applied for assessment of actions that go beyond defined parameters. Next, the measure of control required to cope with changing pressure points must be initiated. This cannot be accomplished without structuring a management approach to caseload data.

With the establishment of a consistent, stable system for classifying cases and monitoring their movement comes an almost monumental amount of data, figures, and facts. If one is to manage in this area, one must exert control over the massive flow of data. The usual tendency would be merely to report the information according to the requirements of those asking for it and stop there. However, if caseload managers can establish a methodology for tracking the flow of cases from input to output stages, efforts to control the data elements will be successful.

Accountability has always been a professional issue, whatever the field in which an individual performs. It can be as nebulous as personally derived accountability or as formal as an official audit. In rehabilitation agencies, accountability stems from personal and external sources. External sources include those emanating from federal policy and regulations derived from congressional legislation and appropriate consumer groups. In the private sector, litigation factors and cost containment are among the taskmasters overseeing accountability issues. For these reasons, case recording and documentation are vital aspects of caseload management (see Chapter 8). A caseload manager should have the knowledge and skills required in these two areas to facilitate gaining of control over data elements.

Client Elements

The characteristics of empowered clients exert a definite influence on caseload management and thus constitute a significant element. These characteristics are not much different categorically from those involved in the personal elements. That is, clients' attitudes, affect, motivations, beliefs, perceptions, social factors, resilience, and general psychological makeup are integral parts of caseload management. Historically, DeLoach and Greer (1979) noted concern for accurate predictors to distinguish eventually successful clients from those who are not rehabilitated. This has been a research concern for decades and impacts the personality variables of self-esteem, self-acceptance, attitudes, and expectations correlated with client rehabilitation success.

Counselors in the private sector must deal directly with client elements from a management stance more than counselors in the public sector. The client characteristics of major concern emerge from five potential problem areas described by Kreider (1983): physical, emotional, financial, vocational, and motivational. The problems all concern balancing the injured or disabled client's welfare with cost-containment restrictions posed by the contracting organization.

Client elements are less directly affected by a managing practice than are the other three elements. That is, the execution of the action is incumbent on the client. This influence felt by the counselor on caseload management is controlled from a counseling or therapeutic approach. The techniques and methodologies relied on are complex and require extensive and appropriate integration into informed action plans. Rehabilitation counselors currently receive sufficient training and usually acquire the basic skills necessary to deal with client elements of a caseload at a relatively early stage in their professional education. This area is fortunate to have a plethora of information available from various sources with a variety of different models or approaches from which to choose. Hence, the significance of this element is duly noted and the rehabilitation counselor can go to these previously developed sources if a higher level of expertise is a personal or professional goal.

Rehabilitation Organization Elements

The final element of this conceptualization of caseload management has its roots in the organization or agency's structural and procedural processes. The influence is related to the guidelines, policies, federal government demands, changing emphases or priorities in serving different groups of disabled people, and changing priorities in general. The control the caseload manager has in this area is minimal. However, **Figure 2.2** depicts this element as providing the medium wherein the other three elements operate, interact, and gain their longevity.

Ideally, counselors will have input into the growth and development of the rehabilitation organization element through individual goal-setting exercises for output or production levels expected from a caseload, good record-keeping or reporting practices, and the cooperative, participatory teamwork philosophy they bring to the job. Although counselors have input into this element, higher-level administrative processes are in control wherein checks and corrective balances are achieved through a system over which the counselor has only minimal control. Thus, no specific approach or elaborations on techniques for managing in this area are included here. The counselor's intuitive skills and the knowledge gained throughout this text should be available, however, when the counselor encounters situations calling for these skills. The skills are generalized to all four of the basic elements of caseload management. Although counselors' conceptualizations of caseload management are bounded necessarily by these four areas, basic action (or inaction) orientation affects any form of practice. An action orientation for managing a caseload sets forth the preliminary condition for viewing any conceptualization of caseload management as falling into one of two summarizing classifications: reactive or proactive. Usually, one can predict the kinds of caseload management activities that counselors will engage in by their tendencies to place themselves into either part of this dichotomy.

Counselors who are aware of a tendency to consistently place themselves in one of these classifications will be in a position to lay one or more building blocks upon their efforts to construct a personalized style of managing. They will be aware of which actions to reinforce and which maladaptive behaviors to extinguish. The following discussion will concentrate on understanding what these orientations entail.

REACTIVE APPROACH

As the term implies, reactive orientations stem from a stimulus–observe–act model, which means the individual consistently fails to plan immediate coping strategies for most approaching events (see **Figure 2.3**). Instead, the counselor maintains a waiting posture, and problem areas predictably build up to a point where some corrective action is required.

FIGURE 2.3 The stimulus–observe–act model.

The counselor takes no real preventive actions. From this stance, only minimal management practices can occur. A struggle merely to stay even or not to get far behind is predominant; this struggle cannot be termed management, but rather a struggle for survival.

For discussion purposes, the following definition illustrates a **reactive orientation**: *Caseload management is a composite of duties and responsibilities directed toward relieving pressures from personal-professional domains, client domains, and agency reporting-case recording domains.*

The elements of a definition of the type presented earlier depict the counselor as a troubleshooter or a brushfire fighter. The counselor waits for pressures to occur before initiating action, thus taking a crisis orientation to caseload management. Procrastination is a characteristic aspect, as evidenced by the "relieving pressure" activities that come about from a wait-and-see posture, thereby permitting a problem to become a crisis.

No descriptions of action for preventative management are built into the definition. Counselors or case managers who adopt this position consistently view their approach as that of a problem-solver, deriving a great deal of reinforcement from this type of activity. The danger, of course, is that quite unknowingly counselors will at times create problems in order to demonstrate their skill at solving them because with the solution comes the traditional "atta-girl" or "atta-boy." Caseload management professionals consequently go about setting conditions to achieve as many "atta" awards from supervisors and agencies as possible. Other than this demonstration, no real personal control is built into a definition of this type.

The guiding objective in reactive practices is to stay even with the game. Thus, caseload management becomes something that happens to the counselor. To restate the old adage of whether the dog wags the tail or the tail wags the dog, the caseload wags the counselor.

PROACTIVE APPROACH

In contrast to the reactive approach, a proactive stance operates on an anticipate–act–assess–act–evaluate model (see **Figure 2.4**). Here an anticipate–act cycle replaces the stimulus variable of the reactive orientation. The "act" responses following the "assessment" mode represent the caseload manager's efforts to refine decisions and to act on those variables that could not be anticipated. This means that the counselor is now taking some action prior to a caseload management event reaching crisis or problem potential. It does not mean that problems will never occur and that no crises will ever be encountered. Rather, a proactive orientation lays the foundation for controlling situations by initiating some form of action that will continually lead one toward established goals instead of relying on urgency as a motivator that will incessantly shove one unceremoniously toward those goals. Consistency, of course, is the key concept because realistically one cannot always anticipate and plan for future actions. A reactive type of orientation might be the only response to certain situations. However, the proactive counselor will not rely on this orientation for any extended period of time.

The following statement is a definition of a proactive orientation: *Caseload management is an organized system of techniques or methods to effectively and efficiently control*

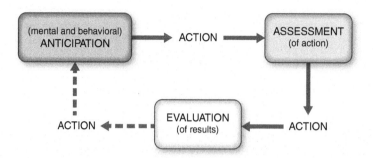

FIGURE 2.4 The proactive anticipation cycle.

anticipated personal, client, caseload, and setting demands on one's skills and resources and to react through immediate action steps to control unanticipated demands.

Inherent in this definition is the concept of a counselor as an individual who initiates or develops action steps to thwart agents that would disrupt a flow process in caseload management. Counselors or case managers operating from this orientation are not "holding tight." Involvement in higher risk-taking activities can be predicted, as opposed to the low-risk-taking approach characterizing the reactive stance. The proactive definition depicts the counselor as a *problem preventer*. The problem-prevention stance demands strong personal characteristics of counselors, as these activities most often do not come to the attention of the supervisor or others who could offer proper reward. Caseload managers operating from this base perceive reinforcement as derived from intrinsic personal sources, thus opting *not* to seek supervisory, agency, or other extrinsic rewards. Control occupies a central place in a proactive definition. Managers take the initiative in all phases of caseload management. These individuals make caseload management happen; therefore, they wag the caseload.

PROACTIVE VERSUS REACTIVE

Proactive and reactive stances abound among counselors in the field. Unfortunately, the latter variety is more abundant than the former. The definitions reported earlier were judged also on the basis of their *proactive* or *reactive* posture. The information shown in **Table 2.1** was used as a foundation for making comparisons. If a definition basically revealed a striving for control, avoiding possible pitfalls, or projecting an anticipatory approach to caseload management, the definition fell within the proactive area.

Reactive definitions reflect a procrastinating nature. A person may recognize that a problem arises and only then take some action. No preventative or anticipatory action is initiated. Another facet is the attempt of those guided by these definitions to equalize their efforts to all concerns without differentiating the degree and complexity of the demands of a situation or event.

Data not meeting the proactive or reactive protocols were defined as noncommittal. Noncommittal definitions are those responses following the stem, "Caseload management is . . ." taken by counselors who demonstrate a lack of a proactive or reactive position on the issue of control. The definitions used by these counselors lead them to avoid any real statement of anticipatory actions. The noncommittal category also includes those definitions that are too brief and so lacking in content as to suggest that these counselors either have no knowledge base upon which to conceptualize caseload management or prefer to remain in limbo and not commit themselves to a definite stance. As the average years of experience in this group were minimal, the lack of a knowledge base seems unlikely.

TABLE 2.1 APPROACHES TO CASELOAD MANAGEMENT

PROACTIVE	REACTIVE
1. Problem preventer.	1. Primarily a problem-solver.
2. Seeks intrinsic reinforcers.	2. Seeks extrinsic reinforcers.
3. Risk taker.	3. Low-risk taker.
4. Personal control.	4. No personal control built in.
5. "Wags" the caseload.	5. Caseload "wags" counselor.

However, owing to the past nature of caseload management as a less-than-fully conceptualized entity, the knowledge base quite possibly is fragmented and as such could contribute to this stagnating, noncommittal attitude.

In addition to the earlier definitions, which could be included in one of the categories just described, other examples of actual definitions falling within these groupings are given next.

Proactive Definitions

"Caseload management is . . ."

- a process whereby the caseload manager effectively controls and maintains the caseload at a maximum efficiency to obtain the maximum results.
- the prompt and adequate movement of all applicants for vocational rehabilitation services from an active status to case closure, without allowing delay of movement due to lack of decisions, paperwork, or other factors counselors can control.

Reactive Definitions

"Caseload management is . . ."

- the ability to keep the flow of work moving with as few snags as possible.
- the ability to be aware of casework flow and to spot any problem areas and be able to correct them.

Noncommittal Definitions

"Caseload management is . . ."

- the orderly and timely movement of the rehabilitation process.
- performing the duties involved in vocational rehabilitation programs in order to provide services necessary to rehabilitate individuals with disabilities.

The results from the analysis of the 98 definitions examined revealed that 26% were proactive, whereas 30% were reactive. The implication for the field is that presently the majority of rehabilitation counselors are laboring under a reactive stance. Seventy-four percent of counselors in this study find caseload management an area that must be tolerated but not identified with or, more than likely, an area that elicits their scorn. The cause–effect relationships are not clear. However, inappropriate organization reward systems for effective caseload management, confusing guidelines, unrealistic objectives, and other situational and individual elements are but a few symptoms that contribute to a reactive stance or merely a noncommittal one.

The implications for counselor and supervisory actions are clear. If a counselor is relying more heavily on one of these positions as a basic modus operandi, appropriate actions must be taken. That is, from a reactive position both supervisor and counselor must interact to move closer to resolving the negative aspects that arise. In contrast, mature counselors who operate from a proactive stance are usually already aware of their actions. Thus, the responsibility is primarily for supervisors to be aware of those proactive behaviors and to properly reward and reinforce these responses in their staff.

BENEFITS OF IMPROVED CASELOAD MANAGEMENT PRACTICES

The benefits for initiating a structured, ordered approach to caseload management come from a variety of sources. These outcomes assist in answering the question, "Why change or improve caseload management practices?" The five areas discussed next represent only a few of the many benefits that accrue from the enactment of a true management approach.

Increased Efficiency

A succinct definition for efficiency is, simply, doing things right. Consistently correct outcomes can come about only within a well-defined system of checks and balances, monitoring and evaluating stepwise actions. In their mention of realizable rewards, the study group of the Third Institute on Rehabilitation Services (Muthard, 1965) identified several products of improved caseload management, one of which is efficiency. Caseload management was seen as measurable in terms of increased efficiency: improving the ratio of output to input. To be efficient, rehabilitation professionals must recognize and understand the characteristics and trends of their operating system and how each of these must be integrated into service delivery (Havranek, 1995; Leahy et al., 2003, 2008; Riggar & Maki, 1997; Rubin & Rubin, 1988). To a large degree, these characteristics define the unique skills, competencies, and knowledge bases that counselors and case managers must utilize in order to be efficient throughout their practices (Hursch, 1995; Leahy et al., 2011; Rosenthal et al., 2007; Sculley et al., 1999; Spitznagel & Cody, 2003). Almost any professional is motivated to seek methods for satisfying the economy-of-effort principle. An improved caseload management system provides a means for achieving greater production with at least the same effort, if not with less effort. Woven properly into counselors' styles for action, increased efficiency will not mean a sacrifice in the therapeutic relationships with clientele. Rather, overall competence is more readily obtainable.

Increased Effectiveness

A succinct definition of effectiveness is doing the right thing. Thus, with ongoing correct and consistent actions (efficiency), the caseload manager must decide which prioritized action to take next. These actions evolve into management skills. The effective use of management skills when working with multiple rehabilitation services has several advantages. First, it allows the counselor to become aware of a vast array of rehabilitation services within the community. The effective manager can concentrate on providing those services for which they are trained while linking the client to the services of other professionals (Woodside & McClam, 2019). Second, not only do effective caseload management practices increase the efficiency of counselors, but they also increase the impact on the broader goal of assisting in the self-actualization and self-sustenance of individuals with disabilities. The study group mentioned earlier also spoke further to the point of improved caseload management as impacting counselor function. *"Another facet of this would be increasing the effectiveness of the counselor as counselor. That is, if the rehabilitation counselor is relieved of clerical and other routine tasks, whenever feasible, [the counselor] will have more time to engage in counseling"* (Muthard, 1965, p. 1).

Finally, caseload managers must become aware of the difference between tasks that fall within an operating category (i.e., tasks others should be performing or tasks that do not require the counselor's level of skill training) and those that fall within a managing category (i.e., tasks requiring the specialized skills and knowledge of the counselor). Then, understanding the necessity to delegate those operating tasks, where feasible, must follow.

It is not ironic that through a management approach the counseling role is enhanced and that this role establishes greater gains in authority and prominence for the counselor. The irony is the disbelieving attitudinal posture of many counselors, who find it difficult to mesh a seeming dichotomy (i.e., counselor versus manager roles) into a unity. This conflict of deferring commitment to one role while attempting to be effective at the other has robbed many counselors of effective performance.

Standards and Limitations

With a functioning caseload management system comes the opportunity to set standards and limits within which one will manage a process. Such standards offer goals to be attained and, at the same time, set boundaries for reality testing. The benefits should be a decrease in anxieties that, in the past, arose from the perception of a seemingly limitless set of variables to control. Further, a measure of reward is acquired when the individual performs within the standards established and begins to control those variables that can be controlled. The limits against which counselors will test themselves will emanate from personal and organization-established standards. The managing efforts directed toward operating within personally set limits, when these limits are maturely and wisely established, will provide a self-reinforcement program that is nonexistent in some agencies. Therefore, the overall effect will be a more relaxed approach to the job and a more enjoyable working environment.

Increased Professionalism

Logically, the next benefit for improved caseload management to follow from the previous discussion is that not only will it allow counselors to better utilize their professional skills, but improved practices will also add to their self-perception as competent professionals (Huber, 2017; Muthard, 1965; Patterson, 2009; Rubin & Roessler, 2001; Stebnicki, 2009). If indeed counselors are managing appropriately and meeting personal expectations by fulfilling the job functions for which they were trained, professionalism is a realizable goal. However, if counselors continue to flaunt the counselor role and show disdain for activities that are significantly managerial, then anxieties and frustrations will stunt any image counselors have of themselves as professionals.

Stress Reduction and Job Satisfaction

One of the most important roles for caseload managers is the coordination of services. Due to service limitation by agency mission, resources, and/or eligibility criteria, and due to employees' roles, functions, and expertise, arrangements must be made to match client needs with potential outside resources (Woodside & McClam, 2018). Therefore, a final benefit to be mentioned as a reason for improved caseload management is one that contributes not only to counselor well-being but also to the stability of the organization. With increased management skills, practitioners develop the ability to utilize important information regarding the availability of rehabilitation services (Bishop & Degeneffe, 2003). This benefit arises from the conclusion that improved counselors' caseload management practices will allow for more productive provision, coordination, and delivery of services in rehabilitation settings. Thus, practices build on the counselor's or case manager's knowledge about availability of services and the skills to put these services to use.

Counselors who practice effective management skills are more effective professionals and work to ensure client-informed choice and self-determination. However, improved counselors' caseload management practices, and thus more favorable perceptions of themselves as professionals, is often linked to the ongoing problem of retaining and recruiting trained professional staff (Grubbs et al., 2006). Although there are numerous reasons for counselors leaving their positions in both the public and private sectors, from the authors' perspective, many of those can be linked to disillusionment with the field of rehabilitation counseling as a panacea for fulfilling the professional aims of counseling persons with disabilities toward greater self-actualization (Cassell & Mulkey, 1985). Rapid staff turnover is another significant problem impacting all aspects of rehabilitation organizations and their services. Staff turnover is influenced by many factors, and the associated high and service-related costs are significant concerns for community-based rehabilitation programs (Mallik & Lemaire, 2003). Previous literature has noted four reasons for employee departure. They are (a) lack of opportunity for advancement, (b) little job satisfaction, (c) stress and burnout, and (d) personality differences with management/supervision (Brill, 1995; Luther et al., 2017; Mallik & Lemaire, 2003; Riggar et al., 1987; Woodside & McClam, 2003).

As consumers of rehabilitation services are responsible for directing the development of their plans and services, they are more involved than ever before in the decision-making processes regarding service delivery (Bishop & Degeneffe, 2003). Therefore, they must realize that rehabilitation professionals do not just help people through the rehabilitation process. Instead, counselors seek to empower individuals in the management of their rehabilitation processes, and they work to ensure client-informed choice and self-determination (Bishop & Degeneffe, 2003; Cassell & Mulkey, 1985; Grubbs et al., 2006).

The management base and philosophy support and augment the counseling function. Muthard (1965) has suggested that counselors discharged only approximately 25% of their time in what can be termed the counseling function, while the remaining 75% was allotted to other supporting functions. The "other supporting functions" fall within the purview of the role of the counselor as a manager. Thus, we can see evidence of the extent to which the counselor is involved in managerial efforts. From 1965 until today, it has become apparent that counselor functions have basically remained the same. Therefore, with full acceptance of manager orientation as a reality and the imbuing of it with a personal bias for constructive action, the profession will develop with greater solidarity, exhibit less contradiction, resolve many contrasting philosophical issues, and, in the end, establish firmer job stability and personal satisfaction for counselors.

CASELOAD MANAGEMENT: ART OR SCIENCE?

To conclude this chapter's attempt to define what does and what does not define caseload management, consideration should be given to whether caseload management is art or science. The field of rehabilitation continues to formalize practice tenets and guidelines. In the past, attempts at fully describing caseload management have defied definition to the point that one could conclude at times that it does not exist as a scientific entity. Very little research has contributed to a scientific base. The questions that arise are: (a) What gives this universally espoused term a basis for existence? and (b) If caseload management exists, who or what gives it continuity and definition?

A plausible explanation is that the acts and practices of professionals in the field culminate in a gestalt that is then labeled caseload management. With the individual parts and processes identified and isolated, they subsequently combine to produce "caseload management." However, these parts and processes cannot be totaled in any simple form. Thus, at the moment, one can only conclude with partial certainty that caseload management exists as an art emerging from cogent practices of many proficient professionals performing from individualized management styles.

This conclusion immediately provokes a critical inquiry. How does the field achieve transfer of knowledge and skills among all its practitioners? The answer lies with the identification and collection of the salient features of the art that are exhibited consistently by *successful* rehabilitation counselors or case managers. The next step is teaching these salient features to the motivated learner, who will then become a knowledgeable and skilled practitioner. The point to be developed in this text is that the art can be embellished or added to through an organized, structured information base. A more complete understanding of the parts and the processes of caseload management can be gained to give it order, consistency, and transference for increased learning by professionals and ongoing achievement of professional development as well as improved service delivery systems.

SUMMARY

This chapter has developed a rationale and overview that set the stage for content specifics to follow. It was noted that the competency upon which professionalism can evolve must come from the integration of a manager philosophy with a counselor philosophy. The benefits that can be gained from working toward improved caseload management were presented. These five areas were discussed: (a) increased efficiency, (b) effectiveness, (c) limits testing, (d) professionalism, and (e) job satisfaction. A conceptualization of caseload management was introduced. The chief components of this framework were organized around four essential elements of caseload management: (a) personal elements, (b) data elements, (c) client elements, and (d) rehabilitation organization elements. The purpose of the present text is to develop in detail the first two of these elements. Finally, the question of whether caseload management is art or science was posed. The conclusion is that the science of caseload management must be considered a functional developmental process to interface with the art. As such, the rehabilitation professional must continue to be an integral, contributing part of defining "Caseload management is . . . ."

QUESTIONS FOR DISCUSSION

1. What is the historical context of caseload management in the field of rehabilitation counseling? How has it evolved over time?

2. How does caseload management contribute to the professional identity and competency of rehabilitation counselors? What skills and knowledge are essential for effective caseload management?

3. Define and explain the conceptual model of caseload management. How does it provide a framework for organizing and structuring caseload management processes?

4. Discuss the hierarchical arrangement of conceptual aspects in the caseload management process. How do these components contribute to the overall effectiveness of caseload management?

5. Differentiate between case management and caseload management in professional practice. What are the key distinctions, and how do they impact the role of rehabilitation counselors?

6. Explore the potential impact of improved caseload management on professional practice. How can effective caseload management positively influence client outcomes and enhance overall service delivery?

7. Reflect on the challenges and complexities associated with defining caseload management. Why is there a lack of consensus in the field regarding its definition? How does this ambiguity affect the competency level of professionals?

8. Discuss the importance of collaboration and shared discussions among professionals in developing common definitions and understanding of caseload management. How can this contribute to more effective and unified practice?

9. Examine the role of caseload management in coordinating and controlling various activities within the rehabilitation counseling setting. How does it enhance decision-making processes and proactive practice?

10. Reflect on the characteristics of effective caseload management, such as establishing a structured schedule, coordinating efforts among professionals, and maintaining a consistent decision-making style. How can these characteristics be applied in real-world practice scenarios to optimize caseload management?

PUTTING IT INTO PRACTICE

Ask yourself these questions to target issues or concerns with caseload management quest for competence.

1. How do various factors influence the professional growth of rehabilitation counseling, and how do rehabilitation counselors adapt traditional roles and functions to meet the demands of a global society?

2. What lies at the heart of rehabilitation counselor competence? How do you define competency in this profession, whether it involves counseling, managerial responsibilities, or other supplementary roles related to professional practice?

3. How can professionals integrate the elements of a conceptual model of caseload management while maintaining their personal attributes and ethical values as practitioners?

 A robust set of instructor resources designed to supplement this text is located at http://connect.springerpub.com/content/book/978-0-8261-5963-2. Qualifying instructors may request access by emailing **textbook@springerpub.com**.

REFERENCES

Alderman, L. A., & Oswald, G. (2016). The current state of specialization and self-identity among certified rehabilitation counselors. *Rehabilitation Professional*, 24(2), 69–74. https://corescholar.libraries.wright.edu/human_services/27

Bellini, J. (2002). Correlates of multicultural counseling competencies of vocational rehabilitation counselors. *Rehabilitation Counseling Bulletin, 45*(2), 66–75. https://doi.org/10.1177/003435520204500201

Beveridge, S. F., McDaniel, R. S., & Glickman, C. P. (2021). Private practice in vocational rehabilitation. In D. R. Strauser (Ed.), *Career development, employment, and disability in rehabilitation: From theory to practice* (2nd ed., pp. 291–313). Springer Publishing Company.

Bishop, M. L., & Degeneffe, C. E. (2003). The implications for consumers of practices and policies in job development: Report of a pilot study. *Journal of Applied Rehabilitation Counseling, 34*(1), 31–37. https://doi.org/10.1891/0047-2220.34.1.31

Brickham, D., Yaghmaian, R., Morrison, B., Bowes, J., Rosenthal, D., & Tang, X. (2021). Mitigating rehabilitation counselor trainee stress and burnout through self-care initiatives in rehabilitation counseling programs. *Rehabilitation Research, Policy, and Education, 35*(4), 232–335. https://doi.org/10.1891/RE-20-03

Brill, N. I. (1995). *Working with people: The helping process* (5th ed.). Longman.

Cassell, J. L., & Mulkey, S. W. (1985). *Rehabilitation caseload management: Concepts & practice*. Pro-Ed.

Cassell, J. L., & Mulkey, S. W. (2004). Caseload management. In T. F. Riggar & D. R. Maki (Eds.), *Handbook of rehabilitation counseling* (pp. 252–270). Springer Publishing Company.

Commission for Case Manager Certification. (2022). *Certification Guide*. https://www.ccmcertification.org/sites/ccmc/files/docs/2022/CCMC-22-Certification-Guide-Update-web-%20NEW%20with%20Fees%20page%20updated%207.5.22_0.pdf

DeLoach, C., & Greer, B. (1979). Client factors affecting the practice of rehabilitation counseling. *Journal of Applied Rehabilitation Counseling, 10*(2), 53–59. https://doi.org/10.1891/0047-2220.10.2.53

Dolce, J. N., Goa, N., Bates, F. M., Banko, A. L., Stone, B. L., & Akhtar, I. (2022). A rapid response to training needs for rehabilitation practitioners: An exploratory study. *The Rehabilitation Professional, 30*(1), 37–48.

Duxbury, L., & Halinski, M. (2014). When more is less: An examination of the relationship between hours in telework and role overload. *Work, 48*(1), 91–103. https://doi.org/10.3233/WOR-141858

Emener, W. G. (1978). Professional burnout: Rehabilitation's hidden handicap. *Journal of Rehabilitation, 45*(1), 55–58.

Ervin, N. E. (2008). Caseload management skills for improved efficiency. *The Journal of Continuing Education in Nursing, 39*(3), 127–132. https://doi.org/10.3928/00220124-20080301-08

Faubion, C. W., Palmer, C. D., & Andrew, J. D. (2001). Rural/urban differences in counselor satisfaction and extrinsic job factors. *The Journal of Rehabilitation, 67*(4), 4–12. https://link.gale.com/apps/doc/A81759712/HRCA?u=anon~d3c4d1d5&sid=googleScholar&xid=b02d9183

Frankel, R. M., & Beckman, H. (2020). "Won't you be my doctor?": Four keys to a satisfying relationship in an increasingly virtual world. *Journal of Patient Experience, 7*(6), 851–855. https://doi.org/10.1177/2374373520957184

Greenwood, R. (1982). Systematic caseload management. In R. T. Roessler & S. E. Rubin (Eds.), *Case management and rehabilitation counseling: Procedures and techniques* (pp. 159–169). Pro-Ed.

Grubbs, L. A., Cassell, J., & Mulkey, W. (2006). *Rehabilitation caseload management: Concepts and practice* (2nd ed.). Springer Publishing Company.

Harrison, D. K., & Lee, C. C. (1979). Rehabilitation counseling competencies. *Journal of Applied Rehabilitation Counseling, 10*(3), 135–141.

Havranek, J. E. (1995). Historical perspectives on the rehabilitation counseling profession and disability management. In D. E. Shrey & M. Lacerte (Eds.), *Principles and practices of disability management in industry* (pp. 355–370). St. Lucie Press.

Henke, R. O., Connolly, S. G., & Cox, J. S. (1975). Caseload management: The key to effectiveness. *Journal of Applied Rehabilitation Counseling, 6*(4), 217–227.

Huber, M. J. (2017). Rehabilitation counseling: Current status and strategies for improving the professional's effectiveness and longevity (Special Issue). *Journal of Applied Rehabilitation Counseling, 48*(3), 4–5.

Hursch, N. C. (1995). Essential competencies in industrial rehabilitation and disability management: A skills-based training model. In D. E. Shrey & M. Lacerte (Eds.), *Principles and practices of disability management in industry* (pp. 303–352). St. Lucie Press.

Kanter, J. (2010). Clinical case management. In J. R. Brandell (Ed.), *Theory and practice of clinical social work* (2nd ed., Chapter 20). Columbia University Press.

Kontosh, L. G. (2000). Ethical rehabilitation counseling in a managed-care environment. *Journal of Rehabilitation, 66*, 9–13. link.gale.com/apps/doc/A62980224/AONE?u=anon~b045fd5f&sid=googleScholar&xid=4e037554

Kreider, J. (1983, January). *Rehabilitation in the private sector*. Paper presented at the midwinter conference of the National Council of Rehabilitation Educators, Atlanta, GA.

Leahy, M. J. (2004). Qualified Providers. In T. F. Riggar & D. R. Maki (Eds.), *Handbook of rehabilitation counseling* (pp. 142–158). Springer Publishing Company.

Leahy, M. J., Chan, F., & Saunders, J. L. (2003). Job functions and knowledge requirements of certified rehabilitation counselors in the 21st century. *Rehabilitation Counseling Bulletin, 46*(2), 66–81. https://doi.org/10.1177/00343552030460020101

Leahy, M. J., Chan, F., Sung, C., & Kim, M. (2011). *An analysis of job functions and knowledge requirements of certified rehabilitation counselors.* Commission on Rehabilitation Counselor Certification.

Leahy, M. J., Muenzen, P., Saunders, J., & Strauser, D. (2008). Essential knowledge domains underlying effective rehabilitation counseling process. *Journal of Applied Rehabilitation Counseling, 39*(4), 28–38.

Lee, S. M., Baker, C. R., Cho, S. H., Heckathorn, D. E., Holland, M. W., Newgent, R. A., Ogle, N. T., Powell, M. L., Quinn, J. J., Wallace, S. L., & Yu, K. (2007). Development and initial psychometrics of the counselor burnout inventory. *Measurement and Evaluation in Counseling and Development, 40*(3), 142–154. https://doi.org/10.1080/07481756.2007.11909811

Lee, S. M., Cho, S. H., Kissinger, D. B., & Ogle, N. (2010). A typology of professional counselors' burnout types. *Journal of Counseling & Development, 88,* 131–138. https://doi.org/10.1002/j.1556-6678.2010.tb00001.x

Ling, J., Hunter, S. V., & Maple, M. (2014). Navigating the challenges of trauma counselling: How counselors thrive and sustain their engagement. *Australian Social Work, 67*(2), 297–310. https://doi.org/10.1080/0312407X.2013.837188

Lizano, E. L. (2015). Examining the impact of job burnout on the health and well-being of human service workers: A systematic review and synthesis. *Human Service Organizations: Management, Leadership & Governance, 39*(1), 167–181. https://doi.org/10.1080/23303131.2015.1014122

Luther, L., Gearhart, T., Fukui, S., Morse, G., Rollins, A. L., & Salyers, M. P. (2017). Working overtime in community mental health: Associations with clinician burnout and perceived quality of care. *Psychiatric Rehabilitation Journal, 40*(2), 252–259. https://doi.org/10.1037/prj0000234

Lynch, R. K., & Martin, T. (1982). Rehabilitation counseling in the private sector: A training needs survey. *Journal of Rehabilitation, 48*(31), 51–53, 73.

Mallik, K., & Lemaire, G. S. (2003). Assessing departing employee's perceptions may lead to organizational change to reduce staff turnover. *Journal of Rehabilitation Administration, 27*(1), 23–32.

McGowan, J. F. (1960). *An introduction to the vocational rehabilitation process.* (U.S. Department of Health, Education, and Welfare, RSS No.555). U.S. Government Printing Office.

McLelland, S. (1977). Overview of caseload management in vocational rehabilitation. In S. Wayne Mulkey (Ed.), *Readings in caseload management in the vocational rehabilitation process* (pp. 1–31) [Unpublished manuscript]. University of Tennessee, Regional Rehabilitation Continuing Education Program, Knoxville.

Miller, L. A., & Roberts, R. R. (1979). Unmet counselor needs from ambiguity to the zeigarnik effect. *Journal of Applied Rehabilitation Counseling 10*(2), 60–65. https://doi.org/10.1891/0047-2220.10.2.60

Mullahy, C. M. (1998). *The case manager's handbook* (2nd ed.). Aspen Publishers.

Mullahy, C. M. (2004). *The case manager's handbook* (3rd ed.). Jones and Bartlett.

Mullahy, C. M. (2017). *The case manager's handbook* (6th ed.). Jones and Bartlett.

Muthard, J. E. (Ed.). (1965). *Training guides in caseload management for vocational rehabilitation staff* (Third Institute on Rehabilitation Services, RSS No.66-22). U.S. Government Printing Office.

Okun, B. F. (1999). *Effective helping: Interviewing and counseling techniques* (5th ed.). Brooks/Cole Publishing.

Patterson, C. H. (1957). Counselor or coordinator? *Journal of Rehabilitation, 23*(3), 13–15.

Patterson, J. B. (2009). Professional identity and the future of rehabilitation counseling. *Rehabilitation Counseling Bulletin, 52*(2), 129–132.

Porter, S. (2010). Counseling, suicide risk assessment, and retention in a community college (2004-2009). *College Quarterly, 13*(3), 1–6.

Power, P. (2012). *A guide to vocational assessment* (5th ed.). Pro-Ed.

Puig, A., Yoon, E., Callueng, C., An, S., & Lee, S. M. (2014). Burnout syndrome in psychotherapists: A comparative analysis of five nations. *Psychological Services, 11*(1), 87–96. https://doi.org/10.1037/a0035285

Rawlins-Williams, L. A., & Oswald, G. R. (2021). Facilitating knowledge in rehabilitation counseling professionals on caseload management: A pre-test/post-test evaluation. *The Rehabilitation Professional, 29*(1), 5–12.

Riggar, T. F., & Maki, D. R. (1997). Issues and perspectives: Profession and practice. In D. R. Maki & T. F. Riggar (Eds.), *Rehabilitation counseling: Profession and practice* (pp. 259–277). Springer Publishing Company.

Riggar, T. F., Hansen, G., & Crimando, W. (1987). Rehabilitation employee organizational withdrawal behavior. *Rehabilitation Psychology, 32,* 121–124. https://doi.org/10.1037/h0091562

Roessler, R. T., & Rubin, S. E. (1982). *Case management and rehabilitation counseling: Procedures and techniques.* Pro-Ed.

Roessler, R. T., & Rubin, S. E. (2006). *Case management and rehabilitation counseling: Procedures and techniques* (4th ed.). Pro-Ed.

Roessler, R. T., Stanford, E., & Rubin, S. E. (2018). *Case management and rehabilitation counseling: Procedures and techniques* (5th ed.). Pro-Ed.

Rosenthal, D. A., Hursch, N, Lui, J., Isom, R., & Sasson, J. (2007). A survey of current disability management practice: Emerging trends and implications for certification. *Rehabilitation Counseling Bulletin, 50*(2), 76–86. https://doi.org/10.1177/00343552070500020601

Rubin, S. E., & Emener, W. G. (1979). Recent rehabilitation counselor role changes and role strain-A pilot investigation. *Journal of Applied Rehabilitation Counseling, 10*(3), 142–147. https://doi.org/10.1891/0047-2220.10.3.142

Rubin, S. E., & Roessler, R. T. (2001). *Foundations of the vocational rehabilitation process* (5th ed.). Pro-Ed.

Rubin, S. E., & Roessler, R. T. (2006). *Foundations of the vocational rehabilitation process* (6th ed.). Pro-Ed.

Rubin, S. E., & Roessler, R. T. (2016). *Foundations of the vocational rehabilitation process* (7th ed.). Pro-Ed.

Rubin, S. E., Roessler, R. T., & Rumrill, P. D. (2016). *Foundations of the vocational rehabilitation process* (7th ed.). Pro-Ed.

Rubin, S. E., & Rubin, N. M. (1988). *Contemporary challenges to the rehabilitation counseling profession*. Paul H. Brookes Publishing.

Sculley, S. M., Habeck, R. V., & Leahy, M. J. (1999). Knowledge and skill areas associated with disability management practice for rehabilitation counselors. *Rehabilitation Counseling Bulletin, 43*(1), 20–29. https://doi.org/10.1177/003435529904300105

Selye, H. (1978). *The stress of life*. McGraw-Hill Publishing.

Shrey, D. E. (1995). Disability management practice at the worksite: Developing, implementing, and evaluating transitional work programs. In D. E. Shrey & M. Lacerte (Eds.), *Principles and practices of disability management in industry* (pp. 55–105). St. Lucie Press.

Shrey, D. E., & Lacerte, M. (1995). *Principles and practices of disability management in industry*. St. Lucie Press.

Sink, J. M., Porter, T. C., Rubin, S. E., & Painter, L. C. (1979). *Competencies related to the work of the rehabilitation counselor and vocational evaluator*. University of Georgia.

Snowden, F. (Ed.). (2003). *Case manager's desk reference*. Aspen.

Spitznagel, R. J., & Cody, L. S. (2003). The role and functions of vocational experts in workers' compensation in Florida. *Journal of Forensic Vocational Analysis, 6*(2), 127–134.

Stebnicki, M. A. (2009). A call for integral approaches in the professional identity of rehabilitation counseling: Three specialty areas, one profession. *Rehabilitation Counseling Bulletin, 52*(2), 133–137. https://doi.org/10.1177/0034355208324263

Thomason, B., & Barrett, A. M. (Eds.). (1959). *Casework performance in vocational rehabilitation* (U.S. Department of Health, Education, and Welfare). U.S. Government Printing Office.

Vash, C. L. (2001). Knowledge, models, and ideologies. *Contemporary Psychology, 46*(5), 481–483. https://doi.org/10.1037/002413

Willey, D. A. (1978). Caseload management for the vocational rehabilitation counselor in a state agency. *Journal of Applied Rehabilitation Counseling, 9*(4), 152–158. https://doi.org/10.1891/0047-2220.9.4.152

Woodside, M., & McClam, T. (2003). *Generalist case management: A method of human service delivery* (2nd ed.). Brooks/Cole Publishing.

Woodside, M., & McClam, T. (2018). *Generalist case management: A method of human service delivery* (5th ed.). Cengage.

Woodside, M., &McClam, T. (2019). *An introduction to human services* (9th ed.). Cengage.

CHAPTER **3**

Rehabilitation and the Management Model

LEARNING OBJECTIVES

By the end of this chapter, learners will be able to:

- Discuss the importance of implementing management processes at all levels of the organizational structure to achieve effective and efficient program success.
- Describe fundamental responsibilities of managers, regardless of their work environment, as identified in various rehabilitation settings.
- Discuss the impact of the five major skill clusters—*planning, organizing, coordinating, directing* and *controlling*—on the rehabilitation process.
- Describe each major skills cluster in relation to impact on individual counselor management skills.
- Discuss an overview of the fundamental groupings of skill patterns: interpersonal, technical and perceptual skills.
- Explore various styles of administering a caseload.
- Explore counselor clinical management styles as clients progress from low to high readiness.
- Discuss the impact of counselor clinical management and client readiness on rehabilitation caseload management progression.
- Discuss three basic strategies for caseload management to include process, marketing, and accounting strategies.

INTRODUCTION

Abraham Maslow, the renowned psychologist who developed the hierarchy of human needs, posited that a fundamental category of needs motivates behaviors that fulfill a desire for order, stability, and structure (Taormina & Gao, 2013). To operate at their optimal level and achieve maximum productivity, counselors must first meet the requirements of these fundamental needs before addressing relatedness, self-esteem, and self-actualization. Essentially, in order to function as an effective counselor with the necessary qualifications to maintain a professional standing, individuals must establish the requisite order, stability, and structure. However, this can only be accomplished through a comprehensive management philosophy or program that has the capacity and depth to navigate the complexities of both public and private rehabilitation organizations. Rehabilitation counselors often come to the field well prepared and well versed in several counseling models but ill-prepared to confront an entire process of multifarious variables and contingencies that must be managed, controlled, or otherwise kept within some realistic but preconceived boundaries.

Many counselors often overlook the fact that they are, in fact, managers. They may think to themselves, "I'm a counselor. Why do I need to understand management?" However, as Herr et al. (2006) highlight, there are individuals who function as managers even without the official title. Additionally, these authors suggest that if someone is working through others to accomplish a specific objective or goal, they are, in essence, managing. So, even if counselors don't consider what they do as "management," they are, in fact, carrying out managerial duties.

Ultimately, professionals involved in providing services to individuals with disabilities must acknowledge the importance of implementing management processes at all levels of the organizational structure to achieve effective and efficient program success. Administrative and supervisory personnel operate from a management foundation, and thus their role structures tend to follow recognizable patterns of duties and responsibilities, resulting in relatively conflict-free roles. However, the role of counselors in vocational rehabilitation agencies is often not well-defined, and there is a lack of commonly accepted and agreed-upon activities. The abundance of literature surrounding the coordinator versus counselor controversy and other works aimed at describing the counselor's role in the rehabilitation field supports this observation. When there is no systematic model to explain or describe the range of activities that counselors engage in, it can result in confused and frustrated performance, especially when there are no consistent and interdependent behavioral guideposts available.

This chapter presents a model that focuses on **managers** in a rehabilitation setting. This model will serve as a foundation for a personalized counselor management model. However, the effectiveness relies on the application phase, which cannot be easily taught and is more likely to emerge from an already established solid foundation. Therefore, while this chapter provides a broad cognitive base, other components such as personal motivation or drive must also be present in sufficient quantity to drive the knowledge gained. The model presented in this chapter is structured around three key conceptual areas: (a) base concepts, (b) process concepts, and (c) structure concepts (refer to **Figure 3.1**).

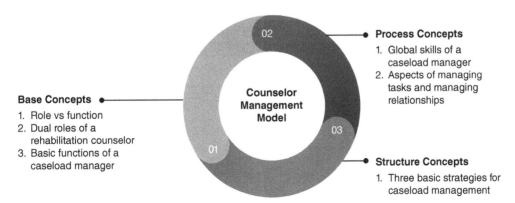

FIGURE 3.1 The major components of the Cassell-Mulkey rehabilitation counselor management model (1985).

THE MANAGEMENT MODEL

The **base concepts** represent the static aspects that serve as the foundation and basic support for the model, providing stability to the system. For instance, the model must include boundary definitions that distinguish between the role of a counselor in a rehabilitation setting and the functions or activities required of the counselor. This differentiation helps to clarify the counselor's job and ensures that proper affective and cognitive goal-directed behaviors are established. Therefore, resolving conflicting expectations from the role base is crucial to initiate performance from the proper skill area, which is the function base. Base concepts focusing on the roles of the professional in rehabilitation practice are explored extensively in Chapter 4.

Process concepts describe the dynamic aspects of a management program, specifically the outcomes that result from effectively combining technical skills, such as filling out forms and following procedures, with human-relations skills like counseling. These outcomes allow for a smooth progression of the process from beginning to end with minimal barriers. The main emphasis of this segment of the model is on the global skills of a caseload manager and how to facilitate the interface between the management of the mutually interacting task and relationship areas. These two crucial areas must be considered by any manager in a human-services organization.

The final component of the management model is **structure concepts**. While the first two components serve as the foundation for developing a management ideology, this collection of concepts and principles must be supported by a structure that can weave them into a unified whole. Therefore, structure concepts concentrate on the strategies that caseload management practices are typically based on. These practices can be traced back to one of three fundamental strategies or a combination of them.

BASIC CLUSTERS OF MANAGERS

The fundamental responsibilities of managers, regardless of their work environment, have been identified in different rehabilitation settings. Although the number of **functions** outlined by various authors may vary, most of them can be classified under the five essential skill categories outlined in **Table 3.1**. These five skill categories, in turn, serve as the basic functions of caseload managers. In the context of rehabilitation, counselor-managers rely

TABLE 3.1 BASIC MANAGER FUNCTIONS IN CASELOAD MANAGEMENT

TRADITIONAL MANAGERIAL FUNCTIONS	TYPICAL CORRESPONDING CASELOAD MANAGEMENT FUNCTIONS
Planning	Establishes method and setting for interpersonal communications to occur.
Organizing	Initiates and facilitates communication process with clients and others in the rehabilitation process.
Coordinating	Serves as a link to physical, social, and emotional rehabilitation services.
Directing	Executes an interpersonal-vocational problem identification process.
Controlling	Guides goal-setting activities and necessary corrective action phases within an individualized rehabilitation program structure.

on these functions to varying degrees, as discussed later. Nonetheless, individuals who effectively manage their caseloads at any given time intuitively utilize these five functions. By bringing these functions to a level of personal awareness, counselor-managers can significantly improve the caseload management process. The benefits of such an improvement are self-evident.

Skill Clusters

Skill clusters are patterns of actions that revolve around central themes or axes. A skill, in turn, is an acquired ability to perform an activity competently. Often, the execution of one skill relies on another prerequisite skill. Thus, skills often occur in clusters, each skill relating to another (Cassell & Mulkey, 2004; Grubbs et al., 2006). Each skill cluster comprises specific actions that caseload managers utilize to maintain consistency in their personal practices and meet organizational standards. For caseload managers, as reflected in **Table 3.1,** there are five major skill clusters: *planning*, *organizing*, *coordinating*, *directing* and *controlling*.

PLANNING

Planning is a key function in the management process, and it assists the counselor in guarding against the influences that interfere with the daily tasks that produce desired management outcomes (Cassell & Mulkey, 2004; Grubbs et al., 2006). Historically, Webber (1975) recalls the purpose of planning is not to demonstrate how accurately we can predict the future, but rather to identify the actions we need to take today to shape our future. Effective management of the future hinges on the development of strong planning skills today. The process of planning is intrasystemic, which implies that it generates its own internal system properties. Therefore, planning requires a systematic approach (Cassell & Mulkey, 2004; Grubbs et al., 2006). Planning long has been seen as a basic strategy for managers. More recently, the focus has begun to shift to **strategic planning** (Arend et al., 2017; Elbanna et al., 2016; George et al., 2019), which places an emphasis on planning as a critical, vital, crucial, and essential component to the management process. According to Webber (1975), dreams and visions are of noted importance in the planning process. Hence, having an understanding of the current developmental phase of the caseload, as well as where it should be, is an integral component of strategic planning (Cassell & Mulkey, 2004). Historically, Ackoff (1970) further extends this perspective by the contention that planning is anticipatory decision-making. Although planning is projected, the strategic planning process is applicable not only at the macro level but on the individual level as well. Grubbs et al. (2006) reflect on the steps projected for the individual level:

1. development of a personal vision,
2. writing down assumptions that shape a caseload,
3. from the assumptions listing, state the issues facing a caseload and state the desired objectives,
4. develop measures for each objective, and
5. choose strategies that will satisfy each objective.

Finally, **systematic planning** necessitates a shared purpose among all the managerial functions involved in caseload management. These functions are interconnected by factors that impact performance and outcomes. First and foremost, planning has an impact on the morale of both the counselor and the client in their professional interactions. This is why planning is closely associated with goal-setting activities. While it may not completely resolve the issue of unmotivated clients, it is a crucial first step in addressing the problem. Second, the statement given earlier suggests that planning has a direct impact on personal productivity. When planning is done properly, it can anticipate the degree to which the counselor, the client, and the agency as a whole can accomplish their respective tasks. Last, planning is essentially a problem-prevention activity and therefore is a crucial function for proactive rehabilitation professionals. Inadequate planning can result in professionals directing their attention solely toward planning instead of pursuing common objectives. Planning is seen as the conscious selection of successive plans, one building upon the other, and the creation of successful and informed outcomes.

ORGANIZING

The skill cluster of **organizing** involves a practical action-oriented approach, with a focus on identifying the next priority for the caseload manager. Unlike planning, which is primarily a mental exercise, organizing is an active process that involves bringing together various resources such as people, financial resources, placement sources, and equipment. The goal is to establish the most effective strategy for achieving the goals established during the planning process. In this sense, the rehabilitation professional functions as a "managerial architect," whose efforts are focused on integrating people variables with financial and budgetary demands, as well as other hardware elements. At the same time, the emphasis is on achieving a coordinated balance of people and supportive variables that will be sustainable over time.

Organizing is a priority setting and can be viewed as having two prime response–demand areas that elicit action from counselors: (a) structural demands and (b) humanistic demands.

STRUCTURAL DEMAND. **Structural demand** areas are an essential component of a rehabilitation professional's role. These areas require the professional to clarify responsibilities with their supervisor and other professionals within the rehabilitation unit. It is also necessary to clarify with clients who the responsible parties are for specific aspects of the rehabilitation program or plan. The rehabilitation professional must deal with centralization versus decentralization of authority within the unit and determine the span of control. This means establishing conditions or limits over which a counselor can effectively manage clients. Finally, setting standards, boundaries, or goals is crucial to structure action steps toward successful rehabilitation outcomes.

HUMANISTIC DEMANDS. **Humanistic factors** become significant when considering the organizing functions, particularly in regard to mental set or attitude, motivation, centralization versus decentralization, and commitment to action. Inadequate preparation can create chaos with a mental set or attitudinal factors, while the absence of motivation can lead to procrastination and ill-defined organizational attempts. Centralization versus decentralization is also important, as decentralizing control to clients when working jointly toward rehabilitation goals can be practical. Additionally, organization must be followed by sequenced steps toward program implementation, or else guilt and personal condemning behaviors may result.

Once the organizational cluster of skills has been identified, it is essential to consider the fundamental conceptual steps involved in organizing. According to Grubbs et al. (2006), these steps include:

1. *Sizing*. Comparable to preparing a wall before wallpapering, this conceptual step involves the rehabilitation professional creating the necessary conditions for organizing activities to take place. This includes gathering and integrating all pertinent data into a framework that, at this point, does not evaluate the collected information units.

2. *Patterning*. Patterning, or "chunking," involves the process of organizing related elements while disregarding other elements until they can be similarly patterned with their related elements.
3. *Selective ordering*. The process of organizing takes shape as the chunked elements are given values that mentally prioritize them for the upcoming action phase. Once there is a clear structure for ordering, the act of initiating actions becomes less intimidating and procrastination is avoided.
4. *Switching*. Ultimately, just like a railway mechanism has the ability to redirect movement along a set path, organizing also requires a mental mechanism. This mental mechanism involves switching and redirecting the ordered chunks toward the sizing phase to process them through the remaining steps in a continual process of organizing, thereby avoiding dead-end behaviors. It's important to note that one is always in the process of organizing and is never fully organized in actuality.

COORDINATING

The **coordination** function has been acknowledged as a significant responsibility of counselors, and there have been differing views on its relative importance. Some experts have advocated for coordination as the sole function of counselors, while others have advocated for a balance between coordination and counseling. However, our earlier discussions on roles and functions have resolved this debate. If any debate were to arise, it would be about whether counselors should focus more on planning or organizing. The literature and discussions in the field have placed such a strong emphasis on the coordination function that it may be challenging for readers to understand the importance of the other functions required for effectively managing a caseload.

The coordinating function of counselor-managers involves the critical task of linking together the requirements of multiple divergent systems. These professionals must act as intermediaries between the demands of the case management system and the service delivery system, which includes training facilities, placement sources, and others. Moreover, they must navigate client system variables like restoration needs, motivation, and skill levels, acting as a buffer to ensure that these factors align with the overall rehabilitation plan. In the public sector, counselor-managers must also negotiate between state and federal mandates and the limitations of available services. Similarly, in the private sector, practitioners must liaise between insurance companies, attorneys, and workers compensation boards, while ensuring that rehabilitation service strategies are tailored to meet individual client needs and restrictions.

Patterson (1957) first posed the question that rehabilitation professionals have long wondered: whether they are counselors or managers. Patterson reflected solely on the skill clusters in counseling. Hence, education and training that disregard management functions based on this premise are mistaken, as these functions are fundamental to the counselor-manager equation. Nevertheless, in the absence of either, the equation breaks down, and the rehabilitation professional is left struggling to manage the multitude of priorities associated with their caseload. To be an effective coordinator, one must possess the ability to identify and utilize community resources. This means that the professional should be well-informed and attentive to the rehabilitation entities that are most beneficial in achieving program goals for their caseload. Coordination requires the rehabilitation professional to serve as a bridge between the client's needs and the various services that can be accessed to meet those needs. As a result, the rehabilitation practitioner must acquire comprehensive skills that will boost their performance and personal functioning and enhance communication skills (Alderman & Oswald, 2016; Cassell & Mulkey, 2004; Grubbs et al., 2006).

DIRECTING

The **directing** function involves implementing the plans and preparations made during the previous functions. This highlights the interconnectedness of the skills clusters, as planning and organizing allow the rehabilitation professional to make and enforce decisions. Therefore, directing serves as the action step that puts the previous skills into operation. In a less overt manner, directing is closely linked with coordinating and serves as the culmination of a cycle of coordinating and directing. Grouping skill cluster activities under the directing function can offer a more concise and efficient conceptualization of the counselor-manager's responsibilities. These activities, including motivating, communicating, leading, guiding, and executing, are often listed separately, but they all fall under the umbrella of directing.

Rehabilitation counselors who aim to effectively manage their caseloads should familiarize themselves with the directing function, even if their initial involvement may seem minimal. Understanding the basic elements of directing is crucial, and the act of directing will naturally cause a counselor-manager style or a relatively consistent approach to develop (Grubbs et al., 2006). The skill cluster of directing is often considered the weakest. This is likely because directing involves behaviors such as pointing, steering, leading, instructing, regulating, and administering, which can be seen as opposing the helping, This statement is sometimes misconstrued as promoting a "hard-hearted" and nonempathetic approach to working with clients, which is not the case at all. The point being made is that clients often look to counselors for guidance and leadership in achieving their goals, as they may lack the necessary resources and support to do so themselves. However, some rehabilitation professionals who heavily prioritize counseling may overlook the subtle power of directing clients to become empowered. By demonstrating a command of situations and projecting an aura of solidarity in their approach to clients, counselors can influence clients to model these behaviors and achieve positive outcomes.

A second element that builds on the first is the **motivation** of clients and staff members under the counselor's responsibility. In this case, directing or leading involves providing clients with responses that foster personal motivation and enable them to meet expectations. Sakiz et al. (2020) have highlighted the significance of counseling managers on effectively guiding individuals toward taking initiatives while on a caseload. Within this study, the rehabilitation professional is encouraged to learn to transfer the initiative to clients, thereby allowing clients to make informed choices. There are five levels of **client initiative** (Carkuff, 1969; Carkuff & Pierce, 1975; Cassell & Mulkey, 2004; Felman et al., 2005; Grubbs et al., 2006; Oncken & Wass, 1974; Parker, 2002):

1. waiting to be told what to do,
2. asking, "What is the next thing to be done?,"
3. recommending a course of action and then taking some form of action,
4. actually taking action on one's own but reporting immediately to the caseload manager that the initiative has been taken, and
5. acting on one's own behalf and only reporting on a routine basis.

A final element of directing is maintaining a disciplined approach to managing oneself and others. To achieve this, the counselor-manager must appropriately reinforce desired behavior patterns and redirect unwanted ones in the desired direction. Over time, a stable pattern of responding to clients and others will emerge, reflecting the counselor-manager's personal attitude, structure, motivational base, and value system. This process of directing is crucial in effectively managing a caseload and achieving positive outcomes. Styles for directing are grouped into four categories (Cassell & Mulkey, 1985; Grubbs et al., 2006; Hersey & Blanchard, 1972). The counselor-manager should have a good understanding of the components that make up these four categories. By reflecting on their own behavior and approaches, counselors can identify which style they tend to exhibit.

According to Grubbs et al. (2006), these four styles of directing include **dictatorial directing, benevolent autocratic directing, democratic directing, and laissez-faire directing.**

1. *Dictatorial directing.* The counselor utilizing this approach seeks to achieve results through intimidation and fear, using criticism and negativity to interact with clients, colleagues, and subordinates. While this style can be displayed overtly, its effects are often more subtle, manifesting in inappropriate humor, sarcasm, and put-downs. This approach may yield quick, short-term improvements in performance, but it is ultimately ineffective in producing lasting change.
2. *Benevolent autocratic directing.* Here the counselor-manager presents a very forceful approach to guiding clients through the rehabilitation process, and clients are willing to allow themselves to be dictated to because of the benevolent, nurturing atmosphere. However, this can lead to a dependency on the counselor, and clients may not take initiative or make progress without their constant guidance. Although clients may initially comply with this type of directing, it can ultimately hinder their progress.
3. *Democratic directing.* This directing style is participatory and engaging for both clients and counselors. Clients are involved from the start in creating personalized rehabilitation plans, making decisions about their career and job selection, and organizing themselves to work toward their goals. With high motivation and morale, there are plenty of intrinsic rewards for all involved. Typically, this is the most well-received of the four styles mentioned.
4. *Laissez-faire directing.* This approach can hardly be considered as a form of directing, as it lacks guidance or leadership. Clients and others responsible to the counselor are left to generate their own goals, initiate movement, and sustain it. Unfortunately, this style is often adopted by default for a range of caseload responsibilities due to the counselor's personal career choices, overcommitments, and pressures from high caseloads.

These four styles provide a framework for comprehending the diverse aspects of the directing function. However, it's important to note that the counselor-manager may not have fixed approaches to caseload management, as the four styles suggest. Each style may be relevant in different circumstances, and it's not always a matter of choosing between them. Therefore, the intention is to expand our understanding of the directing function. To fully comprehend the approaches for managing caseload complexities, we will explore a more detailed treatment of styles later in this chapter.

Finally, directing involves multiple patterns, including effective communication, appropriate leadership, and motivating clients to seek services. It is considered a style that can be learned, but it often requires a paradigm shift for rehabilitation professionals, from a pure counseling orientation to guiding and directing clients toward constructive actions. This shift allows clients to experience the rewarding opportunity of establishing internal control over their own processes, leading to stable and long-lasting rehabilitation results (Cassell & Mulkey, 2004).

CONTROLLING

The skill cluster of **controlling** is the final component that governs the previous skills within operational boundaries. In this management model, the controlling function occupies a central position that significantly influences each of the other four functions. Although controlling is presented as a separate entity in the paradigm, it is an integral part of managing that interconnects the preceding skill clusters and integrates them into a system of interdependent decision-making, action initiation, and result evaluation and ensures the consistent repetition of the cycle (Grubbs et al., 2006). **Figure 3.2** depicts the relationship

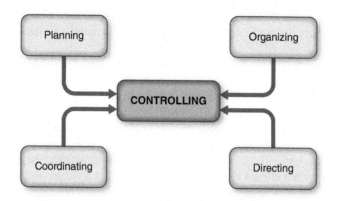

FIGURE 3.2 The five essential functions of management.

that each of the functions have to one another. Controlling appears as a separate but interlinked function. As an essential component of this management model for counselors, it is viewed readily as being involved in all the activities performed by counselors.

When examining the functions of organizing, coordinating, and directing, it becomes apparent that control is a crucial element. As such, control permeates every aspect of managing a caseload and warrants dedicated attention in this management model for counselors. Therefore, Chapter 5 will delve into the concepts and issues related to establishing control in caseload management, and most of the discussion on this crucial element will be postponed until then.

While these five functions of caseload management are described separately, in practice, they are all interconnected, and it is rare for any one function to exist independently of the others. Each activity within the management model is linked to the others, and at any given time, one activity may take precedence, but all five functions must be drawn upon in a coordinated and systematic manner to effectively manage a caseload.

It has been stated previously that caseload management is the key to **effectiveness** (Bellini & Rumrill, 2000; Cassell & Mulkey, 1985; Dunn et al., 2007; Grubbs et al., 2006; Henke et al., 1975; Oswald et al., 2016; Rawlins-Alderman & Dunn, 2015). To achieve effectiveness in caseload management, a rehabilitation professional must integrate all the elements of the process into a cohesive whole, which can be challenging. Many professionals may perceive control as outside their scope of practice. However, effectiveness can only be achieved when a mature professional has internalized these components and formed an operative gestalt. The key to effectiveness is the counselor's attitude, motivation, approach to caseload management, and willingness to accept and utilize both the self-actualizer and manager roles.

A counselor who is efficient at managing their caseload may not necessarily be effective. Simply focusing on short-term goals and achieving easily attainable outcomes with little value toward long-term objectives does not guarantee effective caseload management. Conversely, counselors who prioritize efficiency may be criticized by their colleagues for being ineffective, as they believe that both the self-actualizer and manager roles cannot coexist. The flawed assumption is that by prioritizing caseload management concerns, client welfare is compromised. This creates an imbalance in the hypothetical concern scale and tips it toward the self-actualizer role. However, it is important to note that rehabilitation professionals cannot be effective without first being efficient. This means that both programmatic goals and client concerns must be considered as equally important responsibilities.

SKILLS OF A CASELOAD MANAGER

It is evident that caseload management is a process that relies on principles encompassed within the complete roles, functions, and responsibilities of counselors. Before the process concepts can become viable alternatives, it is essential to firmly establish the base concepts as a counselor's personalized foundation. Therefore, the process concepts are necessary to bring this management model to a **state of maturity**.

The emergence of a process (through base concepts) creates a partially completed management model that needs to be shaped by skill patterns to attain the status of a system. The skills required for managing a process should not be excessively refined or specific to address a multitude of discrete actions. Enumerating every skill to match small units of action would not describe a model, but rather resemble a programmed learning situation. Instead, for a conceptual model, the skills should be global in nature to address the groups of actions required. Therefore, specialized skills should be developed within each group of actions to provide a basis for daily functioning on the job.

Clusters of skill patterns can be defined as collections of overt action sequences or organized passive response patterns that serve to bring process elements and expected outcomes together at the appropriate time. Skills act as intermediate links that bridge or close the gap between expectations and results. Mental activities such as perceptual awareness, foresight, and insight can only set the stage for what counselors hope or want to achieve, leaving them far from the goal of realistic outcomes (Cassell & Mulkey, 1985; Grubbs et al., 2006). To achieve consistent, positive results, counselors must acquire certain skill patterns that act on their immediate environment by keeping a multitude of variables within manageable limits. For instance, if the expected outcome is "career planning with clients," process variables may include agency or organizational requirements to help clients through a successful vocational program and gainful employment. Skill patterns, in this case, may include assessing functional limitations of clients; selecting, administering, and interpreting vocational testing-screening with clients; reconciling medical facts of client conditions with client motivation and job-market availability; conducting employer–employment negotiations; choosing and implementing the appropriate counseling approach required for a specific client; and organizing these various components into a conceptual, functional program in which all parts fit together in a coordinated manner (Grubbs et al., 2006). By focusing on separate skill patterns, counselors can effectively manage complex everyday demands and accurately match expectations with desired outcomes by acting on management-type responses.

Acquiring skill patterns involves a combination of gaining experience and undergoing task-relevant education and training programs. To have a better understanding of what one needs to acquire, it is essential to have a brief overview of the fundamental groupings of skill patterns. In general, a proficient caseload manager should possess adequate levels of four comprehensive skill patterns: technical skills, human skills, conceptual skills, and implementation skills. The following discussions elaborate on these skills.

Technical Skills

Technical skills refer to established, sequenced, and manipulative patterns that enable an individual to impact their immediate environment by utilizing past knowledge, methods, and techniques (Grubbs et al., 2006; Kluesner et al., 2005). These skills encompass various methods and techniques for counseling, processing cases through an organized system, using mandatory guidelines and policies of the organization, and finding and placing clients in appropriate vocational positions. The ultimate objective of these concrete skill patterns is achieving goals and production outcomes in the professional specialty of rehabilitation.

Moreover, technical skills serve as support mechanisms that extend the human and conceptual skills. The continuous application of these skills is influenced by several factors such as the discovery of new and more efficient ways of manipulating elements in the environment, the obsolescence of skills in the face of rapid change, legislative mandates, and rule or guideline modifications.

Interpersonal Skills

Interpersonal skills refer to established and sequenced patterns that enable individuals to effectively relate with others and work toward the fulfillment of personal, client, and organizational objectives. These skills prioritize the welfare of people over the larger processes or systems that clients are a part of. It is essential for counselors to possess adequate interpersonal skills to overcome potential barriers that can hinder them from understanding their clients. Good interpersonal skills enable counselors to navigate the complexities of emotions, such as the difference between empathy, sympathy, and unconditional positive regard, while motivating and encouraging clients (Coleman, 2022; Kim, 2018). Counselors with strong interpersonal skills create an environment that fosters genuine and two-way communication. They know when to give clients the freedom to express themselves and when to assert their leadership for therapeutic purposes.

While interpersonal skills are essential for a self-actualizer-manager in rehabilitation, they are not innate or automatic abilities. Unlike technical skills, which can attain a high degree of efficiency and reliability over time with minimal upkeep, interpersonal skills require constant practice, assessment, updates, and refinement. Interpersonal skills are continuously evolving, and they never truly reach a state of completion. The counselor's ability to maintain these skills at a high level is often hindered by personal frustrations, internal conflicts, and an unclear values system, which must be addressed before one can achieve higher skill levels.

Conceptual Skills

Conceptual skills refer to the established, sequenced mental patterns that enable caseload managers to understand the overall functioning of an organization or a process (Cassell & Mulkey, 1985; Grubbs et al., 2006; Katz, 1974). These skills allow caseload managers to visualize how individual goals and objectives fit into the larger whole, of which group goals and objectives are just a part. Additionally, conceptual skills allow managers to quickly identify the significant indicators for client success and anticipate potential problems or obstacles. In essence, it is the ability to grasp the big picture quickly and with precision.

Conceptual skills are essential for gathering and processing information about clients through various methods like case data, interviewing, and counseling. These skills allow caseload managers to maintain a balanced perspective of the client and choose a direction that leads to successful rehabilitation. They involve the ability to integrate different pieces of information, sense appropriate action paths even in the presence of conflicting objectives, and work within a broader perspective to operate effectively from an intuitive base. Conceptual skills enable caseload managers to have a comprehensive understanding of how all the components fit together to ensure client welfare, as they put together a complete picture of the client's needs and potential solutions. It is the total understanding of how all components fit together to ensure client welfare (McCarthy, 2014).

It can be challenging to acquire skill patterns falling into the conceptual skills area if the counselor does not possess pre-established generalization abilities. The ability to manage a multitude of factors while simultaneously fitting them into a coherent whole for each client in diverse settings is a difficult skill to train for if it has not been developed earlier in life. Nevertheless, to improve the skill levels of the individual practitioner, the counselor must learn to manage time pressures, overcome the fear of failure, and avoid trying to be everything to everyone. Excessive self-imposed pressure is likely to hinder the development of conceptual skills patterns (Grubbs et al., 2006).

The ability to maintain and improve these skills depends on various factors such as the extent to which the counselor gathers information, their ability to adopt a future-oriented perspective, and their capacity to establish and maintain a healthy and creative working relationship with information, individuals, and objects.

Implementation Skills

Muthard and Salomone (1969) and Katz (1974) suggests that all effective managers require a functional level of competence in multiple areas of skills (technical, conceptual, and interpersonal), but his model falls short in its completeness. We believe these basic skills lack extension into an **action mode**. That is, these skill patterns lack force, dynamism, or a base for movement. Thus, our conclusion is that due consideration must be given to Implementation skills.

As we have seen, conceptual, technical, and interpersonal skills are essential for effective management. However, to turn these skills into action, **implementation skills** are also crucial. Implementation skills include personal motivation, energy levels, commitments, priority systems, and attitude posture. These skills require a certain level of expertise in selecting appropriate reinforcers, maintaining high motivation levels, developing assertiveness, overcoming complacency and procrastination, and replacing inaction with necessary action. Without these skills, counselors may wait passively for external sources to initiate program implementation, which could negatively affect the success of their clients and the rehabilitation structure as a whole. Therefore, counselors must recognize the importance of implementation skills and practice them to ensure the success of their programs.

The significance of the previous statements and this discussion is often overlooked by many counselors. They fail to recognize that the act of implementation is a set of learned skill patterns. Instead, they tend to wait idly for some external energy source or providential intervention to achieve the goals of their clients and agencies. However, by acknowledging that implementation is a skill process that requires learning, practice, and rehearsal, counselors can increase the frequency and quality of program success for their clients, the rehabilitation structure, and the public and private sectors alike.

STYLES OF ADMINISTERING A CASELOAD

Counselors can acquire the skill patterns discussed earlier, but they often need a starting point to build a system of responses. Ambiguity can create anxiety and hinder skillful action, but structure can combat anxiety. The model concept provides a rubric for structure. By developing a model, counselors can gain technical and interpersonal skills and develop their conceptual skills by understanding how these areas interact. This approach can provide a significant boost to managing an entire caseload, as opposed to a trial-and-error approach. The model to be described later will suggest how to manage technical tasks and interpersonal relationships and how these areas interact with each other.

To provide rehabilitation counselors with a comprehensive understanding of the key components required for building and implementing an effective personal management model, we will now shift our attention to the second phase of our **process concepts: managing tasks, managing relationships** (refer to **Figure 3.1**). This area of focus encompasses two equally significant and opposing areas of responsibility that encompass all of the functions performed by counselors. Our aim is to explore the interplay between managing tasks and managing relationships and to identify the circumstances in which counselors can optimize their management capabilities by prioritizing these two areas.

A rehabilitation counselor, as the caseload administrator, is responsible for managing both task and relationship variables. Without a full awareness of these dichotomous areas and the ability to adopt an appropriate management style at the right time, a counselor cannot hope to be an effective and efficient caseload manager.

This brings up an important observation concerning the interrelationships among counselor variables, client variables, and the particular situations under which a counselor operates and situations under which clients operate. The observation is that the **effective administratorship** (EA) of a caseload is a **function of counselor** (CO), **client** (CL), and **situation variables** (S):

$$EA = f \ (CO, CL, S).$$

To be an effective caseload manager, counselors must consider all *three sets* of variables mentioned *at all times*. This requires responding to guiding questions such as: What are the client's needs? What are my biases and attitudes? And what external pressures or forces are at play in the situation (such as family involvement, available resources, or societal attitudes toward a particular disability group)? Ultimately, counselors must develop an administratorship style that can effectively manage the interaction between these three variables.

The following discussion will explore the process of choosing an appropriate response style for everyday situations that considers the interplay between task-related and relationship-related concerns. Historical and current viewpoints on the evolution of administratorship styles will be presented to provide context. This will be followed by an explanation of the four fundamental administrator styles that will equip the counselor with the knowledge to determine the most suitable style for the specific demands of the situation.

The idea of developing adaptable styles for caseload administration is not a novel concept. The development of adaptive styles for administering a caseload is a well-established concept. For further discussions on this topic, readers may refer to Fielder (1958, 1961, 1967); Stogdill (1956); Hersey and Blanchard (1972); Cassell and Mulkey (1985); Glass (1991); Grubbs et al. (2006); Zumitzavan and Michie (2015); Kunce & Angelone (1990); Okun (1999); Perls (1969, 1973); and Rogers (1951, 1961). Although these discussions may be framed in terms of styles of leadership functions, there are no significant conceptual or real deviations between leadership and administratorship. As a counselor, one must fulfill a leadership function in guiding clients toward rehabilitation goals, developing resources for restoration, placing clients in adequate community living environments, and navigating organizational structures. We highly recommend readers assess their style of leadership, and in particular, we recommend the Hersey and Blanchard (1972, 1974) inventory, which is readily available and easily comprehensible. Much of the following discussion is centered on their work.

Task Response Style

In terms of development, the earliest administrator styles were organization-focused, where the goal was to fulfill the needs and demands of the organization. This approach prioritized policy and guideline demands over humanistic elements. However, counselors who adopt a strictly task-oriented approach may be coercive toward their clients and fail to adjust the structure to meet their needs. In this orientation, interpersonal relationships are minimized, and the primary focus is on coordinating services. The rehabilitation field provides evidence of this evolving style, where service delivery personnel were called rehabilitation agents in the 1920s, rather than the current title of rehabilitation counselor or rehabilitationist. As agents, they were instruments of the organization, following policies and procedures. Thus, early management styles were predominantly focused on **task or structural elements**. Developmentally speaking, this approach was rooted in an organization base. Thus, many early management styles were essentially concerns for task or structure elements.

Human/Interpersonal Response Style

With the appearance of the work by Elton Mayo (1933), the trend in the management area was turned toward interpersonal relations concerns in industry and elsewhere. The concept that to make significant gains, rehabilitation organizations must deal with the power base that emanates from interpersonal relationships was slowly accepted. The human-relations style of administratorship prioritizes cooperative goal setting and coordinated efforts between clients and counselors for goal attainment. It also focuses on personal growth and development of clients by removing personally thwarting concerns. In the human- relations orientation, the primary concerns are the needs of the individuals being served, rather than the needs of the service organization.

Continuum Versus Separate Axes

With the advent of the human relations movement, a **continuum** was formed that placed administrator styles at one of two opposing poles depending on whether their behavior could be described as task-oriented or relationship-oriented (see **Figure 3.3**). Historically, research suggests leader behaviors can range from authoritarian styles at one extreme end of the continuum to democratic styles at the other (Blake & Mouton, 1985; Glass, 1991; Hannagan, 2002; Perls, 1969, 1973; Tannenbaum & Schmidt, 1958). Authoritarian behaviors call for the manager to make decisions and announce them to the appropriate person, while democratic behaviors allow for larger degrees of freedom of choice for individuals operating within the limits initially defined by the structure. There was controversy over which style was the most useful for achieving the greatest control and most productive outcomes (Cassell & Mulkey, 1985; Grubbs et al., 2006). Some writers favored a democratic style, while others supported an authoritarian role as the only approach to achieve adequate outcomes. Few supported a middle ground or compromise between these two opposing poles.

Hersey and Blanchard (1972) aimed to describe the fundamental dimensions of leader behavior, specifically in how administrators carry out their duties and responsibilities. They focused on two key aspects: **structure** and **consideration**. Cassell and Mulkey (1985) and Grubbs et al. (2006) build upon earlier work to argue that administrator styles cannot be reduced to a single continuum. Instead, they propose that these styles are situated

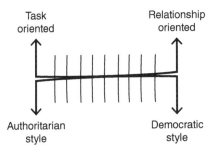

FIGURE 3.3 Continuum of contrasting administrator behaviors.

on two separate axes, as depicted in **Figure 3.4A**. By integrating these two axes, four quadrants are formed (**Figure 3.4B**), each representing a fundamental administrator style for managing task and relationship elements in caseload management. These quadrants indicate the various orientations that managers can adopt while administering a caseload.

The Best Style

All of the positions on styles described earlier consistently moved in the direction of the conclusion that there exists a one best style for an administrator. Earlier theories on administrator styles have consistently proposed a **"one best style"** approach, wherein certain styles are regarded as ideal and others as negative or to be avoided. However, research findings consistently showed that there were successful administrators who exhibited different styles, including some who were successful with low relationship, low task styles and others who were unsuccessful despite exhibiting high task–high relationship styles (Grubbs et al., 2006). While attempts were made to explain away these

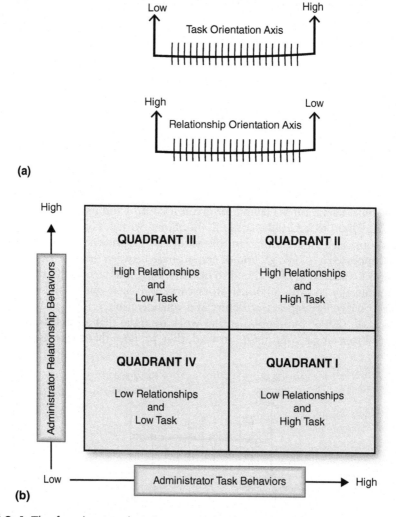

FIGURE 3.4 The four basic administrator styles for managing task and relationship elements of the caseload management process.

contradictions, it is clear that there cannot be a single ideal style of administration that suits all situations. As discussed earlier, the situational context is an important factor in determining effective administrator behavior. Therefore, an administrator of a caseload must be able to adopt different styles depending on the demands and needs of each individual situation.

ADAPTIVE ADMINISTRATOR BEHAVIOR

A caseload manager must be able to assess a situation correctly and to respond with the appropriate style required. In order that a counselor be equipped with the insight and background to enhance the ability to acquire expertise in diagnosing situations and responding adaptively to the demands that arise, the concept area of *clinical maturity level* in caseload management must be addressed. This concept, and interactions with counselor clinical maturity and client readiness later, have been adapted from the original work from Hersey and Blanchard (1982) focusing on the life cycle theory of leadership, and Grubbs et al.'s (2006) work on administrator response styles. This theory incorporates aspects of a maturity dimension or readiness level of a group to a basic concept. The new concept of *clinical maturity level* in relation to client readiness in the caseload management process will be discussed next.

Counselor Clinical Maturity Level and the Caseload Management Process

In an adapted cycle conceptualized for caseload management, the level of **client readiness** coming under the responsibility of a caseload manager plays a significant role in the *clinical maturity level* and behavior of that administrator. That is, as the readiness of clients increases, the clinical maturity level of the counselor decreases. For the rehabilitation counselor, less task or structure emphasis is needed, while the relationship dimension becomes increasingly necessary until a higher level of client readiness is reached in the rehabilitation process. However, it is important to keep in mind that only in relation to a specific task being performed can aspects of these variables be considered. A client or group of clients is not solely ready, but in relation to the tasks or functions in which the client is actively engaged. Therefore, a caseload manager must behave differently and distinctly with individuals than with the entirety of the caseload.

According to **Figure 3.5** (Part A), at lower levels of client readiness, client task variables are given greater emphasis, while the counselor/client relationship dimension is less emphasized. Conversely, as clients reach higher levels of readiness, the relative importance of the counselor's clinical maturity dimension decreases, while the emphasis on autonomy within the client increases. However, after reaching a midstage level of readiness, even the counselor/client relationship dimension loses its significance as a driving force in case interactions. This is because clients gain autonomy and the counseling relationship is no longer an urgent requirement. Clients emerge with autonomous skills such as preparedness, willingness, and ability to engage in the counseling process and make meaningful progress toward their goals. This term can also encompass the client's emotional and psychological stability, level of self-awareness, and their ability to take responsibility for their actions and choices. This suggests that client readiness develops along psychological dimensions instead of a chronological continuum.

When managing a caseload, it is important to strike a balance between task and relationship behaviors that align with the level of readiness of each client. Different counselor clinical management styles are necessary as clients progress from low to high

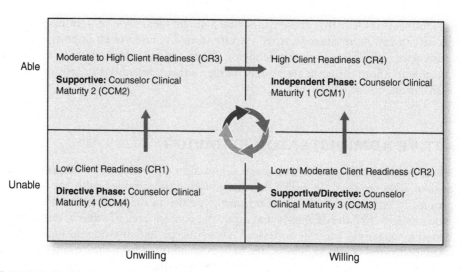

FIGURE 3.5 Client readiness and appropriate counselor clinical maturity.

readiness, moving from requiring direction to achieving independence. It is essential for caseload managers to understand that their clinical maturity, along with behavior and interactions, will vary with individual clients as opposed to the entire caseload as a group. **Figure 3.5** illustrates each clinical maturity level as it applies to the client readiness in rehabilitation caseload management practice. In the context of the rehabilitation process, *ability* pertains to the client's possession of the necessary skills or means to perform a task, while *willingness* relates to the state or quality of being prepared and ready to do something.

Let us look to see how the readiness of the client, the ability or willingness factors, and the counselor clinical concern for relationships all interact to provide an effective model for the caseload manager.

The **counselor clinical maturity cycle** suggests that as client behaviors move from a level of less readiness in the process to a mature client autonomy, the rehabilitation caseload manager's correct response style should move from:

1. High Clinical Maturity (Counselor Clinical Maturity 4)—Directive Phase
    TO
2. Moderate to High Clinical Maturity (Counselor Clinical Maturity 3)—Supportive/Directive Phase
    TO
3. Low to Moderate Clinical Maturity (Counselor Clinical Maturity 2)—Supportive Phase
    TO
4. Low Clinical Maturity (Counselor Clinical Maturity 1)—Independent Phase

To ensure a balanced and effective response to clients of different readiness levels, rehabilitation counselors must adopt an appropriate response style that aligns with their level of clinical maturity. It is crucial for counselors to understand the significance of response style in relation to their clinical maturity, as it helps them manage their caseload effectively.

Addressing the various levels of clinical maturity is necessary to fully appreciate the importance of response style for rehabilitation counselors. Each level requires a different response style that balances the client's ability and willingness to engage in the rehabilitation process. By taking into account the readiness level of the client and the counselor's own level of clinical maturity, rehabilitation counselors can provide personalized support that maximizes the client's potential for success.

COUNSELOR CLINICAL MATURITY 4 (HIGH CLINICAL MATURITY)–DIRECTIVE PHASE

The **directive phase** for low client readiness (CR1) refers to clients who may be characterized as both unable and unwilling to engage in the rehabilitation process. These clients may have limited understanding of the significance of rehabilitation for achieving their future goals, and they may feel insecure about the process. At this phase, the counselor utilizes their *clinical maturity at level 4* to guide the client toward engagement in the rehabilitation process.

When a new referral is being accepted, the counselor conducts an interview with the client to discuss policies, procedures, regulations, necessary diagnostic exams, and future goals and plans. The counselor prioritizes task-related behavior and provides structure to the client, who may not be fully aware of the process. During this interview, the rehabilitation counselor may identify deficiencies in the client's motivation, ability, and willingness to take on responsibilities, as well as their education in tasks that are relevant to the rehabilitation process.

As a result, the counselor responds with high structure and low concern for providing socioemotional (relationship) support at this stage, while still emphasizing the importance of establishing a supportive relationship. This approach aims to help the client understand and engage in the rehabilitation process, even if they initially lack motivation or confidence (**Figure 3.6A**).

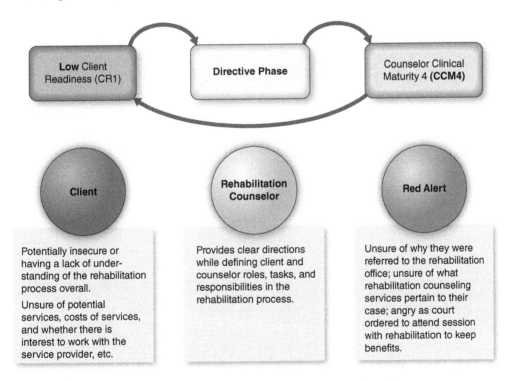

FIGURE 3.6A Client readiness and appropriate counselor clinical maturity: Directive phase.

COUNSELOR CLINICAL MATURITY 2 (MODERATE TO HIGH)– SUPPORTIVE/DIRECTIVE PHASE

Suppose the client is progressing and transitioning toward a higher readiness level (CR3), specifically moving into the **supportive phase**. At this stage, the client defines their readiness level and exhibits willingness in the rehabilitation process. As a result, the counselor must adjust their approach and utilize *counselor clinical maturity at level 3* to work with the client.

At this phase, the client's behavior is characterized as unable but willing, indicating that they are no longer considered completely unready but still lack the autonomy to be classified as fully autonomous. This results in a midstage readiness designation. To support the client's progress, the counselor should prioritize emphasizing task or structure elements, while also providing increased counseling (socioemotional) support. It is particularly important to attend to relationship factors that are of high concern to the client, even though they may display motivation toward rehabilitation.

To achieve client buy-in, the counselor must utilize effective communication techniques while explaining the services offered. If the counselor had provided too much emphasis on relationship factors before the client has progressed sufficiently, their behavior could be perceived as overly lenient, which could promote a permissive environment that fosters dependence on the counselor's willingness to forego structure or task elements for a friendly, feel-good, ego-boosting atmosphere.

However, it is also crucial to note that the counselor must be mindful of the client's potential for discouragement during this phase. Extensive two-way communication is critical to ensuring that the client remains motivated and engaged in the rehabilitation process (**Figure 3.6B**).

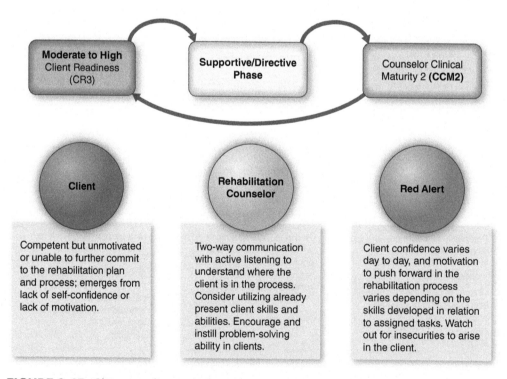

FIGURE 3.6B Client readiness and appropriate counselor clinical maturity: Supportive/Directive phase.

COUNSELOR CLINICAL MATURITY 3 (LOW TO MODERATE)– SUPPORTIVE PHASE

If the client continues to exhibit good midstage readiness level behaviors (CR2), progressing toward the **supportive/directive phase** may be appropriate. However, the counselor must first determine whether the client is ready to accept such counselor responses. If so, the counselor must consider moving into *counselor clinical maturity at level 2*.

At this stage, the client's style is characterized as able but unwilling. The counselor must continue to provide socioemotional support but places less emphasis on structure or task elements. The client is gradually taking on more self-control for the rehabilitation program but may still struggle with commitment at times. Despite this, the client is displaying growing self-direction and internal control, resulting in self-initiated goal setting and motivation to achieve these goals. However, the client's confidence levels may vary from day to day. The counselor must remain available to provide support and positive reinforcement as needed or desired. This is important in promoting the client's continued progress and maintaining their motivation toward rehabilitation (**Figure 3.6C**).

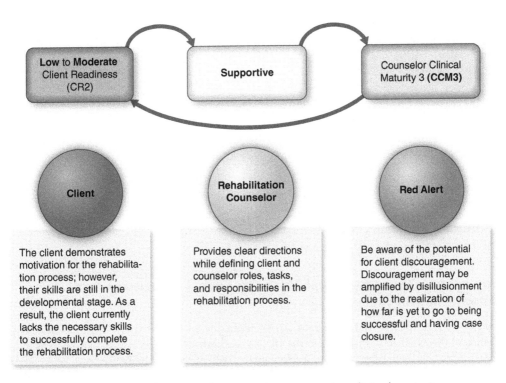

FIGURE 3.6C Client readiness and appropriate counselor clinical maturity: Supportive phase.

COUNSELOR CLINICAL MATURITY (LOW CLINICAL MATURITY 1)–INDEPENDENT PHASE

We have reached the *independent phase* for the client (CR4), which is the highest level of readiness. At this stage, the client is both willing and able to fulfill the requirements of the rehabilitation plan and process, and the counselor will achieve *clinical maturity at level 1*.

The client is functioning proficiently in the areas that define their maturity level, and they require minimal socioemotional support and task emphasis. This is because the client is largely rehabilitated, and the case is nearing closure. Typically, clients with adequate maturity require only oversight and minimal counselor responses, with an emphasis on promoting independence.

The counselor must ensure that the client has the necessary skills and knowledge to maintain their rehabilitation progress independently. They should also encourage the client to continue setting goals and developing plans for the future. Additionally, the counselor should establish a plan for follow-up and ensure that the client has access to appropriate resources for ongoing support (**Figure 3.6D**).

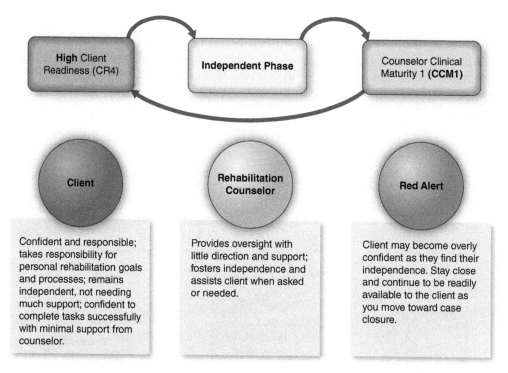

FIGURE 3.6D Client readiness and appropriate counselor clinical maturity: Independent phase.

Implementation of Clinical Maturity Levels in Caseload Management Practice

Let's explore how these **maturity levels** can be applied to caseload management practices with clients. In the event of a crisis, where the client's readiness level starts to decline, such as a decrease in achievement motivation or a reluctance to accept responsibility, the counselor clinical maturity process dictates that the counselor's response should regress to the moderate to high client readiness—supportive and directive phase (counselor clinical maturity 3). This involves providing increased socioemotional support while refraining from emphasizing additional tasks with the client, as doing so could hinder progress in the rehabilitation process.

However, if the crisis worsens and the client's ability to adapt deteriorates, the counselor may need to impose structure and emphasize the tasks that the client must accomplish. At this point, the client lacks the capability to affect structural or task variables, but the counselor must still maintain the same level of counseling support as before while guiding the client. The ultimate goal is to reverse the downward trend in the client's readiness level and provide a foundation for renewed progress toward greater independence and higher maturity.

The previous discussion highlights how the process is cyclical and adaptations may not always progress toward a desired goal in a linear fashion. Situations with negative or nonreinforcing aspects may necessitate a switch between phases. The pace at which counselors and clients adapt to different phases can vary, and some may require more time to develop the necessary knowledge base for awareness.

Counselors must tailor their response style to the demands of the situation rather than adhering to an ideal style. A successful caseload manager must be equipped with a range of adaptive styles to respond effectively to changing environments. Developing such flexibility requires personal and professional growth on the counselor's part and attentiveness to the situation's needs. Effective caseload management requires the counselor to consider the interplay between task and relationship elements and possess diagnostic skills to assess a client's readiness level and respond appropriately with the most adaptive style required by the situation. Ultimately, successful caseload management depends on the collaboration of the counselor, the client, and the situation working together for success (Cassell & Mulkey, 1985; Grubbs et al., 2006).

THREE BASIC STRATEGIES FOR CASELOAD MANAGEMENT

The caseload management process cannot operate within a **professional vacuum**. Numerous processes and structures will affect caseload management practices. This brings us to the final phase of the caseload management model described in this chapter, which is structure concepts (see **Figure 3.1**). Structure concepts have as their common beginning the insight that the caseload management process can be affected by current trends and higher-order socioeconomic philosophies of those individuals and elements invested with position and structure power (Grubbs et al., 2006). Just as the organization and management of a business must have basic orientations and responses to particular socioeconomic pressures, so must organizations and management within professional rehabilitation settings. Particular aspects of caseload management are affected by three basic strategies or models, which have emerged within industry. These models are (a) **process model**, (b) **marketing model**, and (c) **accounting model** (Grubbs et al., 2006). These distinct models from industry have implications for understanding outcomes in the field of rehabilitation. These models are professed to be the models for achieving optimal effectiveness in multiple organizations and business settings. The concern is not to select the best or worst of these models, but instead to explore the various elements of each of the models and allow situational dictates or management philosophies to select the structure to be applied. Table 3.2 depicts the three strategic approaches to caseload management and the selected essential components of each for comparison among them.

TABLE 3.2 THREE BASIC APPROACHES TO CASELOAD MANAGEMENT

	PROCESS MODEL	**MARKETING MODEL**	**ACCOUNTING MODEL**
Focus	Production	Consumption	Controllership
Product	Rehabilitation services	Client	Dollar savings
Customer	Consumer service	Others	Rehabilitation agency
Casefinding	Referral sources	Job capability	Financial cost
Organizational goals	Predicting input	Predicting market	Accounting techniques
Effectiveness	Quality of the process	Rehabilitation outcomes	Accountability cost-benefit money saved

Process Model

The **process model** used in industry is often compared to the well-known concept of the "rehabilitation process." This model has a long history, becoming popular in the early 1950s when production in all areas of the economy was thriving. During this time, the economic structure operated from a scarcity basis, with demand outweighing supply. The fundamental elements of this model are explained in further detail next.

FOCUS

Counselor-managers who primarily use the process model as their framework focus on production or rehabilitation outcomes. Their concern is the internal processes of the system, which they must monitor and improve to ensure that optimal quantities will be achieved at the appropriate end stages. They measure success in terms of quantities such as the number of successful rehabilitation closures, the number of people moved through the system in a specific amount of time (if they work in the public rehabilitation sector), or the number of clients who return to their preinjury level of functioning (if they work in the private rehabilitation sector).

PRODUCT

Given the production-oriented nature of the process model, it is essential for the model to have a product that can sustain its continued operation. This product is none other than rehabilitation services. As a result, efforts are directed toward providing or making available services that are in demand, or "sellable" to the target customer or client populations.

CUSTOMER

The individual with a disability or any condition that hinders their employment is the primary **customer** for the process model. This model is designed to cater to the client demand market by providing vocational rehabilitation services. Therefore, it can be said that the process model is "client-oriented" to the extent that it is geared toward meeting the needs of its customers. Despite its internal focus, the model does not compromise on the humanistic approach.

CASEFINDING

In the process model, casefinding plays a critical role in ensuring that the model's internal operations are sustained with an adequate supply of cases or clients. The counselor-manager's primary focus is to increase referral sources and modify existing strategies for referral acquisition to guarantee that the process is well-supplied from input to output stages. Counselor-managers use various strategies, including advocating for the expansion of eligibility criteria or passage of legislation to allow entrance of other disability groups into the process. These groups may include those from marginalized groups, those with varying health-related disorders. By implementing these casefinding activities, the process model ensures the continued demand for its product or services.

ORGANIZATIONAL GOALS

To operate effectively under the process model, it is necessary to adhere to the **organizational objectives** that are aimed at forecasting the input into the model. By maintaining a clear understanding of the flow of people through the process or the number of individuals entering the system, greater control can be exerted over the output. This is a critical aspect of the process model, as it places emphasis on production.

EFFECTIVENESS

The success of the process model is determined by the quality control measures put in place during service delivery. The counselor's effectiveness is judged by how well they establish criteria for success and select clients who meet or exceed these expectations. The main concern in this model is efficient delivery of rehabilitation services, rather than setting limitations on the final outcome.

Public-sector rehabilitation professionals prioritize service provision due to legislation, placing a high emphasis on success variables related to service quality throughout the rehabilitation process. Private-sector rehabilitation practitioners, on the other hand, focus on outcomes due to their business orientation. They prioritize cost-reduction programs, referral source requests, and expeditious rehabilitation regimens.

In summary, counselor-managers operating under the process model focus on producing services for clients with disabilities. They strive to maintain a steady supply of clients to justify the existence of their services. The effectiveness of the model is judged based on the process rather than the outcome, and vocational placement is not the primary concern. Nonetheless, placement into a vocational setting is still important, and it occurs naturally in an economy of scarcity with high demand for products and low unemployment.

CASELOAD DATA INDICATORS

Observing specific caseload data elements can provide evidence of the adoption of one of three models by counselors. Several indicators and combinations of data can help identify the model being used, provided the counselor lacks personal awareness of the model. Examples of elements that suggest a counselor is using the process model include:

1. large backlog of referrals,
2. consistently high acceptance rate,
3. concentration of cases in certain disability classification,
4. lack of clients in training,
5. rapid processing of cases through the caseflow system,
6. increasing numbers of unsuccessful cases, and
7. low levels of extended evaluation/trial work and waiting for employment.

However, the presence of one or two of these indicators in isolation should not be considered definitive evidence of the process model. It is necessary to observe several of these elements interacting with each other to determine the model being used.

Marketing Model

In contrast to the process model, the **marketing model** arose out of the needs and pressures of an economy and philosophy characterized by surplus. The supply and demand scale was tipped toward excess supply and unemployment was high.

FOCUS

The marketing model is focused on the employer or job market, and a counselor-manager operating under this model is primarily concerned with external factors such as job market trends, employer attitudes, and matching client skills to specific job demands.

PRODUCT

In contrast to the process model where the client was considered the customer, the marketing model considers the client as a product. In this model, clients are seen as possessing specific skills or traits. Marketing also includes many other areas such as advertising, designing and generating materials such as landing sites and social media content, enhancing customer service, and doing market research.

CUSTOMER

In the marketing model, the employer is considered the customer, and the focus is on tailoring the product to meet their demands. The product in this case is anything the rehabilitation professional provides to its customers in order to meet a demand.

CASEFINDING

To sustain the longevity of the marketing model, priority is given to feasibility of services, which relies on the prevailing trends of the job market or the identification of clients who possess the necessary skills for specific opportunities. Job analysis, development, modification, and reengineering have contributed to the identification of suitable candidates, resulting in a more comprehensive casefinding process. By removing structural and attitudinal barriers, individuals with disabilities can engage in higher-level competition with their nondisabled counterparts.

ORGANIZATIONAL GOALS

The behavior in this model is guided by the objective of predicting the extent to which the product will be absorbed into the rehabilitation market. Consequently, the process receives minimal attention, and more emphasis is placed on achieving goals related to predicting output. However, there is a danger that humanistic concerns may be neglected or compromised in the quest to meet the demands of external entities involved in the rehabilitation process.

EFFECTIVENESS

The marketing model's effectiveness is evaluated based on the number of successful placements, dollars saved, or outcomes focus. As a placement model, the main objective is to support clients in suitable rehabilitation outcomes. However, it is important to note that the process of achieving these outcomes is not disregarded. The marketing model does have controls, boundaries, and criteria that must be followed to ensure that the final product, the individual/candidate, is adequately prepared for the output stage.

Public rehabilitation counselors recently have begun to give the marketing model a prominent place in their caseload management philosophy and practice. For example, the federal government, in 1983, awarded a national grant to train counselors in the areas of applying marketing strategies to the public-sector job placement efforts. However, the private-sector professional has a primary concern of predicting a client's absorption into the job market. Several authors (Hursch, 1995; Matkin, 1985; Mullahy, 2004; Organist, 1979) have offered the following hierarchy suggesting the ranked predictors for successful rehabilitation:

1. Same job, same employer
2. Modified job, same employer

3. Different job—capitalizing on transferable skills, same employer
4. Same or modified job, different employer
5. Different job using transferable skills, different employer
6. Formal training leading to a change of occupation, same or different employer
7. Self-employment

In summary, those rehabilitation professionals operating from the marketing model attempt to produce a particular clientele for the market that is experiencing a surplus of individuals to fill most positions. Therefore, the counselor-manager must be equipped with an increased knowledge base and expertise in analyzing and predicting trends or feasibly modifying the rehabilitation environment to allow clients to "sell" themselves (Cassell & Mulkey, 1985; Fabian et al., 1994; Grubbs et al., 2006).

CASELOAD DATA INDICATORS

Clark and Wells (1980) suggest examples of caseload data elements that may assist in diagnosing a marketing model. These examples include:

1. acceptance rates that are lower than usual for the caseload,
2. large numbers in extended evaluation, work, and training,
3. tendency to do more vocational testing in the evaluation stage,
4. excessively high rates of successful rehabilitations,
5. tendency to have a smaller caseload, and
6. cases remaining in limbo for prolonged periods of time.

The same cautions mentioned for the process model also apply to the marketing model. It is a combination of the factors mentioned, and possibly other factors, that influence a counselor's decision to prioritize the marketing model over other models.

Accounting Model

This model with its proponents arose out of the need to establish control and establish efficient planning functions.

FOCUS

The primary focus is on controllership, which involves ensuring that the rehabilitation process functions in the most efficient and cost-effective manner possible.

PRODUCT

The primary focus of this model is financial gain, including material savings. Rehabilitation professionals, supervisors, and administrators who operate within this model prioritize the dollar savings that the vocational rehabilitation program generates in exchange for the resources invested.

CUSTOMER

If the product of the rehabilitation program is dollar savings, then the customers are the rehabilitation professionals themselves. They must focus on controlling and planning to eliminate waste and reduce excess expenses in order to benefit the rehabilitation agency.

CASEFINDING

Casefinding involves efforts to support the accounting structure with added resources. These resources stem from third-party funds, community resources, and economy of effort.

ORGANIZATIONAL GOALS

In this model, the primary objective is to achieve the most efficient accounting techniques possible. As a result, program efforts will focus on sacrificing convenience for the sake of worthwhile austerity.

EFFECTIVENESS

The effectiveness of this model is measured by accountability formulae, cost–benefit ratios, and the amount of money saved, which are tangible outcomes. The model considers itself successful if the financial books are balanced and the planning function has achieved its purpose.

CASELOAD DATA INDICATORS

The elements of a caseload that reveal an accounting model as the base from which particular counselors operate revolve around:

1. low-cost programs,
2. fast-moving client programs, and
3. descriptive language that speaks to monetary issues and subordinates people issues.

To summarize, the accounting model prioritizes the internal needs of the organization over the characteristics of the client. While this model may not prioritize a client-centered approach, it can still be useful for caseload managers in both private and public rehabilitation settings. In public rehabilitation, the priority selection process may require counselors to work with individuals who have significant disabilities, making the accounting model beneficial for cost containment. In private settings, this model is useful for companies looking to prioritize service delivery and achieve speedy closure through job placements or monetary settlements. The implementation of components of this model can help rehabilitation professionals eliminate waste and ensure lower-cost programs (Cassell & Mulkey, 1985; Diamond & Petkas, 1979; Grubbs et al., 2006; Lynch & Martin, 1982; Mullahy, 2004).

SUMMARY

Leadership in various settings and agencies must remain updated on key management models. Often, leaders, managers, and rehabilitation professionals work against each other. Counselors may operate differently than expected by the administration and may have different approaches from those followed by the model administration. This creates several problems and conflicting expectations for caseload managers. For instance, federal-level personnel and state-level administrative personnel within a state agency may start with an accounting model as their major approach. This model is emphasized because priorities focus on keeping rehabilitation programs solvent. As we move to the level of a district supervisor or regional director in a rehabilitation agency, the marketing model may gain greater emphasis with all its variables coming to prominence. This is a reasonable expectation since supervisors must respond to hierarchical pressures to focus on outcomes or output. Finally, at the service-delivery level, the process model becomes a primary emphasis. Counselors at this point are most often concerned with services and their customers or clients. Hence, the basis for internal conflicts exists, where the counselor plans to serve clients, while the administrator focuses on saving money and cutting costs. Thus, philosophical and administrative orientations seem to be in conflict. However, in the end, each is responding to the necessities required by their position, and everyone naturally defends their values system. The cost of differing perceptions could introduce conflict into the organization's structure. This could result in segmenting and cleaving into conflicting groups. Therefore, open and continuous communication within the organizational structure and within the rehabilitation field is vital.

Matkin (1983) raises the issue of potential conflict among practitioners in the private sector due to the "two masters" controversy, which centers around the question of who the client is: the person with the injury or the referring insurance carrier. This can result in conflicting demands placed on rehabilitation practitioners, as they attempt to balance the accounting model (costs to the funding source and billable time) with the process model (serving the needs of the individual with the injury) and the process model (maximizing vocational potential for legal purposes).

In public rehabilitation, serving individuals with significant disabilities has undergone a shift from the process model to the marketing model. Initially, the focus was on providing quality services to meet the needs of this population. However, there is an emphasis on job analysis, development, modification, and reengineering to better integrate individuals with significant disabilities into the job market (Crudden & Steverson, 2021; Riesen et al., 2021; Simonsen et al., 2015).

Rehabilitation professionals can make better predictions about the behavior and outcomes of counselors and other individuals if they are aware of the model from which they operate. Understanding the basic model that others use to orient themselves in rehabilitation helps to recognize the pressures and values that underlie their actions. This enables rehabilitation professionals to convince peers, supervisors, and others about their own positions based on their knowledge of others' orientations. Ultimately, knowledge of the orientation of significant others is a necessary component of any management endeavor, regardless of the level of operation, whether it involves caseload or organizational management.

QUESTIONS FOR DISCUSSION

1. Abraham Maslow has stated that one functional group of needs stimulates behaviors that satisfy a need for order, stability, and structure. Please explain this statement and how it directly relates to the field of rehabilitation.

2. Describe the similarities and differences between the traditional management role of supervisory personnel and the management requirements of a rehabilitation counselor.

3. Support or refute this statement, "Controlling is probably the least important of all the management functions."

4. Discuss the process model in relation to the various rehabilitation settings.

5. Discuss the marketing model in relation to various rehabilitation settings.

6. Discuss the impact of skill clusters on the roles and functions of rehabilitation professionals.

7. The term *counselor clinical maturity* is used extensively in this chapter. Discuss in depth the varied meanings of this term. In a group setting, explore other potential terminology as a more current descriptor of rehabilitation professionals.

8. Discuss the relationship between client readiness and counselor clinical maturity. Why or why not is this dicotomy important in professional practice?

9. Define the terms effectiveness and efficiency. Are these terms synonymous? Why or why not?

PUTTING IT INTO PRACTICE

Ask yourself these questions to target issues or concerns with rehabilitation and the management model.

1. Can the emotional responses of rehabilitation counseling professionals affect their level of clinical maturity in providing appropriate counseling? Could personal or professional situations influence their interactions and perceptions of clients' readiness?

2. How would you describe your individual approach to handling a caseload? What functions and principles characterize this style? What aspects do you feel might be missing or could be improved?

3. At the end of your workday, do you reach a point where you feel that all your tasks have been completed? If so, which aspects do you consider complete, and if not, what are the reasons for feeling otherwise?

 A robust set of instructor resources designed to supplement this text is located at http://connect.springerpub.com/content/book/978-0-8261-5963-2. Qualifying instructors may request access by emailing **textbook@springerpub.com**.

REFERENCES

Ackoff, R. L. (1970). *A concept of corporate planning.* Wiley Interscience.

Alderman, L. A., & Oswald, G. (2016). The current state of specialization and self-identity among Certified Rehabilitation Counselors. *The Rehabilitation Professional, 24*(2), 69–74. https://corescholar.libraries.wright.edu/human_services/27

Arend, R. J., Zhao, Y. L., Song, M., & Im, S. (2017). Strategic planning as a complex and enabling managerial tool. *Strategic Management Journal, 38*(8), 1741–1752. https://doi.org/10.1002/smj.2420

Blake, R. R., & Mouton, J. S. (1985). *The managerial grid III.* Gulf Publishing.

Carkuff, R. (1969). *Helping and human relations.* Holt, Rinehart & Winston.

Carkhuff, R. R., & Pierce, R. M. (1975). *Trainer's guide to the art of helping.* Human Resource Development Press.

Cassell, J. L., & Mulkey, S. W. (1985). *Rehabilitation caseload management: Concepts & practice.* Pro-Ed.

Cassell, J. L., & Mulkey, S. W. (2004). Caseload management. In T. F. Riggar & D. R. Maki (Eds.), *Handbook of rehabilitation counseling* (pp. 252–270). Springer Publishing Company.

Clark, B., & Wells, G. (1980). *Effective caseload management: Participant manual* [Unpublished manuscript]. Woodrow Wilson Rehabilitation Center, Rehabilitation Continuing Education Program, Fishersville, Virginia.

Coleman, M. L. (2022). The use of counseling skills within evaluative contexts. *Counseling Outcome Research and Evaluation, 13*(1), 22–29. https://doi.org/10.1080/21501378.2022.2025771

Crudden, A., & Steverson, A. C. (2021). Job retention and career advancement: A survey of persons who are blind or have low vision. *The Journal of Rehabilitation, 87*(2), 28–35.

Diamond, C. R., & Petkas, E. J. (1979). A state agency's view of private-for-profit rehabilitation. *Journal of Rehabilitation, 45*(3), 30–31.

Dunn, P., Grubbs, L. A., & Mulkey, S. W. (2007). Inclusion of case and caseload management in NCRE member rehabilitation curricula. *Rehabilitation Counselors & Educators Journal, 1*(1), 24–28.

Elbanna, S., Andrews, R., & Pollanen, R. (2016). Strategic planning and implementation success in public service organizations: Evidence from Canada. *Public Management Review, 18*(7), 1017–1042. https://doi.org/10.1080/14719037.2015.1051576

Fabian, E. S., Luecking, R. G., & Tilson, G. P. (1994). *A working relationship: The job development specialist's guide to successful partnerships with business.* Paul H. Brookes.

Fielder, F. E. (1958). *Leader attitude and group effectiveness.* University of Illinois Press.

Fielder, F. E. (1961). Leadership and leadership effectiveness traits: A reconceptualization of the leadership trait problem. In L. Petrullo & B. M. Bass (Eds.), *Leadership and interpersonal behavior* (pp. 179–186). Holt, Rinehart & Winston.

Fielder, F. E. (1967). *A theory of leadership effectiveness.* McGraw-Hill.

George, B., Walker, R., & Monster, J. (2019). Does strategic planning improve organizational performance? A meta-analysis. *Public Administration Review, 79*(6), 810–819. https://doi.org/10.1111/puar.13104

Glass, N. M. (1991). *ProActive management: How to improve your management performance.* Nichols Publishing.

Grubbs, L. A., Cassell, J. L., & Mulkey, S. W. (2006). *Rehabilitation caseload management: Concepts & practice* (2nd ed.). Springer Publishing Company.

Hannagan, T. (2002). *Management concepts and practice* (3rd ed.). Prentice Hall.

Henke, R. O., Connolly, S. G., & Cox, J. S. (1975). Caseload management: The key to effectiveness. *Journal of Applied Rehabilitation Counseling, 6*(4), 217–227.

Herr, E. L., Heitzmann, D. E., & Rayman, J. R. (2006). *The professional counselor as administrator: Perspectives on leadership and management of counseling services across settings.* Lawrence Erlbaum Associates.

Hersey, P., & Blanchard, K. H. (1972). *Management of organizational behavior.* Prentice-Hall.

Hersey, P., & Blanchard, K. H. (1974). So you want to know your leadership style? *Training and Development Journal, 28*(2), 22–37.

Hersey, P., & Blanchard, K. H. (1982). Leadership style: Attitudes and behaviors. *Training & Development Journal, 36*(5), 50–52.

Hursch, N. C. (1995). Essential competencies in industrial rehabilitation and disability management: A skills based training model. In D. E. Shrey & M. Lacerte (Eds.), *Principles and practices of disability management in industry* (pp. 303–352). St. Lucie Press.

Katz, R. L. (1974). Skills of an effective administrator. *Harvard Business Review, 52*(5), 90–102. https://www.hbr.org/1974/09/skills-of-an-effective-administrator

Kim, J. (2018). Consideration of the applicability of person-centered therapy to culturally varying clients, focusing on the actualizing tendency and self-actualization – from East Asian perspective. *Person-Centered & Experiential Psychotherapies, 17*(3), 201–223. https://doi.org/10.1080/14779757.2018.1506817

Kluesner, B., Taylor, D., & Bordieri, J. (2005). An investigation of the job tasks and functions of providers of job placement activities. *The Journal of Rehabilitation, 71*(3), 26–35.

Kunce, J., & Angelone, E. (1990). Personality characteristics of counselors: Implications for rehabilitation counselor roles and functions. *Rehabilitation Counseling Bulletin, 34*(1), 4–15.

Lynch, R. K., & Martin, T. (1982). Rehabilitation counseling in the private sector: A training needs survey. *Journal of Rehabilitation, 48*(31), 51–53, 73.

Mayo, E. (1933). *The human problems of an industrial civilization.* Macmillian

McCarthy, A. K. (2014). Relationship between rehabilitation counselor efficacy for counseling skills and client outcomes. *The Journal of Rehabilitation, 80*(2), 3–11.

Matkin, R. E. (1983). Insurance rehabilitation: Counseling the industrially injured worker. *Journal of Applied Rehabilitation Counseling, 14*(3), 54–58. https://doi.org/10.1891/0047-2220.14.3.54

Matkin, R. E. (1985). *Insurance rehabilitation: Service applications in disability compensation systems.* Pro-Ed.

Mullahy, C. M. (2004). *The case manager's handbook* (3rd ed.). Jones and Bartlett.

Muthard, J. E., & Salomone, P. R. (1969). The roles and functions of the rehabilitation counselor. *Rehabilitation Counseling Bulletin, 13*(Special Issue), 81–168.

Okun, B. F. (1999). *Effective helping: Interviewing and counseling techniques* (5th ed.). Brooks/Cole Publishing.

Oncken, W., Jr., & Wass, D. L. (1974). Management time: Who's got the monkey? *Harvard Business Review, 52*(60), 75–80.

Organist, J. (1979). Private sector rehabilitation practitioners-organize within NRA. *Journal of Rehabilitation, 45*(3), 52–55.

Oswald, G. R., Flexer, R., Alderman, L. A., & Huber, M. (2016). Predictive value of personal characteristics and the employment of transition-aged youth in vocational rehabilitation. *Journal of Rehabilitation, 82*(4), 60–66.

Parker, W. C. (2002). *Monkey management.* Retrieved October 2002 from http//workstar.net/library/monkey.htm.

Patterson, C. H. (1957). Counselor or coordinator? *Journal of Rehabilitation, 23*(3), 13–15.

Perls, F. (1969). *Gestalt therapy verbatim.* Real People Press.

Perls, F. (1973). *The gestalt approach & eye witness to therapy.* Science & Behavior Books.

Rawlins-Alderman, L. A., & Dunn, P. L. (2015). A review of case and caseload management course availability in undergraduate rehabilitation and disability studies programs. *The Rehabilitation Professional, 23*(3), 163–168.

Riesen, T., Keeton, B., Hall, S., & Snyder, A. (2021). Building consensus among experts regarding customized job development fidelity descriptors: A Delphi study. *The Journal of Rehabilitation, 87*(3), 22–30.

Rogers, C. R. (1951). *Client-centered therapy.* Houghton Mifflin.

Rogers, C. R. (1961). *On becoming a person.* Houghton Mifflin.

Sakiz, H., Saricali, M., & Turkum, A. S. (2020). Does disability matter in counselling? Views of counsellors with visual disabilities and their clients. *British Journal of Guidance & Counselling, 48*(2), 195–208. https://doi.org/10.1080/03069885.2017.1393496

Simonsen, M., Fabian, E., & Luecking, R. G. (2015). Employer preferences in hiring youth with disabilities. *The Journal of Rehabilitation, 81*(1), 9–18.

Stogdill, R. M. (1956). *Patterns of administrative performance.* Ohio State University, Bureau of Business Research.

Tannenbaum, R., & Schmidt, W. H. (1958). How to choose a leadership pattern. *Harvard Business Review, 36*(2), 95–102.

Taormina, R. J., & Gao, J. H. (2013). Maslow and the motivation hierarchy: Measuring satisfaction of the needs. *The American Journal of Psychology, 126*(2), 155–177. https://doi.org/10.5406/amerjpsyc.126.2.0155

Webber, R. A. (1975). *Management: Basic elements of managing organizations.* Richard D. Irwin.

CHAPTER 4

The Roles of the Professional in Rehabilitation Case and Caseload Management Practice

LEARNING OBJECTIVES

By the end of this chapter, learners will be able to:

- Define the multifaceted roles and functions of a rehabilitation counselor, including counseling, management, advocacy, crisis intervention, broker of services, and quality management.

- Discuss the impact of each role and function of a rehabilitation counselor on the quality of care provided to clients.

- Analyze the impact of current research and literature on the ongoing debate of the rehabilitation professional as counselor, manager, or some combination of the two.

- Identify challenges that rehabilitation counselors may face in fulfilling their multifaceted roles and functions, such as balancing competing demands and addressing the needs of diverse client populations.

- Explain the importance of interprofessional collaboration and communication with other service providers in the delivery of comprehensive care to clients.

- Evaluate the challenges that rehabilitation counselors face in fulfilling their roles and functions and identify strategies to address these challenges.

- Understand the importance of quality management in the rehabilitation counseling profession and the role of rehabilitation counselors in preventing potential problems and improving the quality of services provided.

INTRODUCTION

Rehabilitation case and caseload management practices play a crucial role in the healthcare industry, particularly in the field of rehabilitation. The success of rehabilitation programs heavily depends on the effective management of cases and caseloads, and this requires the expertise of professionals with specialized skills and knowledge. In this context, rehabilitation professionals assume important roles in managing cases and caseloads by ensuring that clients receive appropriate care and support throughout their rehabilitation journey. They work in an interprofessional team with other healthcare providers, including medical staff, mental health therapists, social workers, and community rehabilitation providers, to develop and implement comprehensive rehabilitation plans that address the unique needs and goals of each client.

This chapter provides a comprehensive overview of the **dual roles** and functions of caseload management in rehabilitation practice. Rehabilitation professionals are tasked with the complex and interdependent roles of counselor and manager, and this chapter examines the competencies and responsibilities necessary for effective performance in both capacities. Key areas of focus include communication, assessment, goal setting, problem-solving, crisis intervention, and service brokerage/facilitation.

In addition to these critical roles, the chapter highlights the significance of quality management in rehabilitation caseload management practice. It examines the various strategies and competencies used by rehabilitation professionals to monitor progress, evaluate service providers, develop quality improvement plans, and ensure compliance with industry standards. The chapter underscores the importance of various roles and functions of professional practice in this context, including quality management and service facilitation, in promoting and maintaining the highest standards of care for clients.

Overall, there emerges a comprehensive and nuanced exploration of the multifaceted roles and responsibilities of rehabilitation professionals in managing caseloads. It highlights the interconnectedness of their roles as counselors and managers, as well as the importance of quality management and service facilitation in ensuring the delivery of effective, client-centered care.

Base Concepts

Base concepts are the fundamental principles and building blocks that form the foundation of a particular field of study. In rehabilitation counseling, base concepts are essential for understanding the unique needs and challenges of individuals with disabilities and how to best support them in achieving their goals. These concepts provide the fundamental knowledge and skills that rehabilitation counselors need to work effectively with clients and help them overcome barriers to achieve greater independence and quality of life.

These components represent the static aspects that serve as the foundation and basic support for the model, providing stability to the system. For instance, the model must include boundary definitions that distinguish between the role of a counselor in a rehabilitation setting and the functions or activities required of the counselor. This differentiation helps to clarify the counselor's job and ensures that proper affective and cognitive goal-directed behaviors are established. Therefore, resolving conflicting expectations from the role base is crucial to initiate performance from the proper skill area, which is the function base.

ROLES VERSUS FUNCTIONS

A fundamental aspect of any management model is recognizing the differences between roles and functions. In practice, misunderstandings between the two can disrupt the entire performance framework, causing confusion and lack of direction. Therefore, clear definitions of roles and functions can help counselors make more significant personal commitments to their job activities and provide a solid foundation for taking on a management position.

Roles

The basic understanding of **roles** and **functions** is crucial for any caseload management model. To define a role, three fundamental concepts are used: (a) title descriptors, (b) implied expected behavior patterns, and (c) status within a group. Roles are outlined in agency documents that detail duties and responsibilities. However, they can also evolve through expected behavior patterns and status within groups. Implied expected behavior patterns develop over time as certain performance patterns are consistently reinforced. For example, some rehabilitation counselors are reinforced for their involvement in community development programs for individuals with disabilities. Status in a group can also determine roles, such as when an individual stands out as a leader among their peers. These three concepts can be used singly or in combination to understand an individual's role. However, in the field of rehabilitation, there is often a lack of clarity in the distinctions among these terms, which can lead to contradictions and role stress, ultimately hindering efforts toward appropriate management outcomes.

Job descriptions or conceptual activity listings are common ways to outline responsibilities for counselors. However, the key to establishing consistent and accepted role responsibilities is the authority to carry out these activities. In the rehabilitation field, if counselors who have the necessary maturity are not given a significant level of authority, their role responsibilities will be incomplete. Conversely, if appropriate authority is given but the counselor lacks initiative or leadership qualities, there will be a conflict between role demands and outcome expectations. Only when adequate responsibilities are outlined and significant authority is allowed can counselor-managers be justifiably held accountable for their expected roles. Furthermore, the authors suggest that counselors in rehabilitation must perform not one, but two roles, each with specific functions, duties, and responsibilities. These dual roles will be discussed later.

Functions

Functions, as defined in management terminology, refer to the tasks, acts, or operations expected of and performed by an individual (Das & Misra, 2016; Groene et al., 2014; Hannagan, 2002; Silvestri et al., 2022). They are a significant part of the description for a role, and they give definition to roles rather than the other way around. Each role an individual fulfills within an organization has corresponding functions that constitute it. However, a scattered list of functions lacks the completeness and boundary-setting qualities of a well-defined role. In the same way that a caseload manager has a role to fulfill through the performance of certain functions, a client or service recipient also has responsibilities inherent in fulfilling their role and functions within a rehabilitation process.

The traditional functions that managers are expected to perform in various settings can also be utilized to define the role of the counselor-manager in rehabilitation. In Chapter 3, management functions were explored along with several typical functions that counselors perform. However, it should be noted that the descriptions of counselor functions presented here are not meant to be comprehensive, but rather to provide the reader with an idea of the range of activities that stem from the counselor role. If additional information is needed, other historical research sources focusing primarily on this topic may be consulted (Kunce & Angelone, 1990; McGowan & Porter, 1967; Muthard & Salomone, 1969; Subich, 1984).

The tasks or functions expected of counselors in the rehabilitation field are complex and varied. Yet, a thorough analysis of these expectations and a systematic categorization of required functions lead to the conclusion that counselors in multiple rehabilitation settings must perform two distinct roles: that of a counselor and a manager. It is important to note that this dual role position does not create a contradiction or a paradox, but rather represents a practical solution to the demands and responsibilities currently expected of individuals in these rehabilitation settings.

DUAL ROLES OF THE REHABILITATION COUNSELOR

Rehabilitation literature has long debated the two primary roles required of counselors (Alderman & Oswald, 2016; Cassell & Mulkey, 1985; Dunn et al., 2007; Grubbs et al., 2006; Henke et al., 1975; Patterson, 1957; Riggar & Maki, 2004). The debate surrounding the roles of counselors in rehabilitation has been ongoing, with arguments revolving around whether they are counselors, coordinators, or a combination of both. However, this debate remains incomplete and has resulted in significant barriers to conceptual awareness and performance commitments, leading to deteriorating efficiency. The incompleteness of the argument is not solely due to semantic differences but also to basic conceptual flaws. The counselor framework is composed of several elements that come together as a larger whole. Nevertheless, it is crucial that this framework acknowledges the coordinator function as only one component of a more comprehensive management process that involves several other functions. While counselors in rehabilitation agencies rely on the coordination function for effective performance, an individual who solely fulfills the role of a coordinator is not necessarily a counselor.

Coordinating is just one of the five essential functions that managers need to perform, regardless of the setting. However, many arguments in rehabilitation literature suggest that counselors are only capable of performing one function (coordination) or one role (counselor), rather than the entire management process. This confusion arises from the elevation of a function to a role, which can lead to discrepancies and conflicts in the field. In rehabilitation, this usually results in practitioners being committed to the higher- status counselor role, but indifferent to the coordinator function. The critical issue is not whether counselors are capable of performing the manager role, but rather the lack of opportunity and properly established reward systems that hinder the merging of seemingly dichotomous roles into one unified role for efficient performance by counselors. Our position is that two primary roles are required of rehabilitation counselors (see **Figure 4.1**). One role is a restatement of the counselor's commonly accepted position as a **self-actualizer**. A self-actualizer is an individual who accepts responsibility for being part of a process that allows people's potential to reach the highest attainable level (i.e., potential within clients, peers, subordinates, and counselors themselves).

The remaining role required of rehabilitation counselors is that of a **manager** in the self-actualization process. Self-actualization does not solely come from the manager, but rather it is an evolving process that takes place within the manager over time. The administration of a specific process or sequence of events and activities through the manager

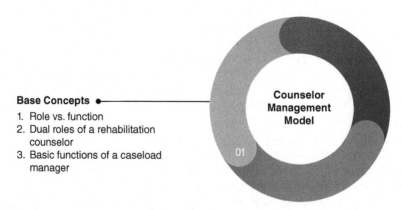

FIGURE 4.1 Base components of the Cassell-Mulkey rehabilitation counselor management model (1985).

role allows for access to the self-actualization level. In the following sections, both roles will be discussed, with a greater emphasis placed on the components of the manager role throughout this chapter.

Self-Actualizer (Counselor) Roles

According to Vaingankar et al. (2021) the rehabilitation system aims to assist disabled clients in achieving their maximum potential, while the private rehabilitation sector focuses on restoring individuals to a state of employability as close as possible to their preinjury level of employment. This difference in philosophy is reflected in the **self-actualization process**, with rehabilitation counselors striving to help clients achieve a level of functioning that is self-actualizing for them, or the highest level of functioning of which they are capable. In contrast, private rehabilitation counselors tend to follow a return-to-prior-functioning-level philosophy, which aims to restore individuals to their preinjury level of employment, or a state of employability that is as close as possible to their preinjury level. However, this does not necessarily contradict the self-actualization philosophy. It is important to recognize that self-actualization can be achieved through various means, including by helping individuals return to their preinjury level of functioning. Therefore, both public and private rehabilitation sectors can contribute to an individual's self-actualization by providing necessary support and resources to help them achieve their maximum potential. Overall, the goal of both sectors should be to provide the highest level of support to clients with disabilities, with a focus on achieving their self-actualization and helping them attain the highest level of functioning possible.

The term "*self*" refers to both the client and the provider or counselor. Therefore, the term "self-actualizer" is used to describe the role of the rehabilitation professional in the counseling process, as it better encapsulates the needs and goals of the role than the more commonly used term "counselor." As a self-actualizer, the rehabilitation professional can carry out various responsibilities, such as conducting interviews, establishing positive rapport with clients, identifying and addressing problems, providing occupational information, assisting with goal setting and guidance, and preparing clients for work adjustment and stabilization. These are just a few examples of the numerous characteristic responsibilities and duties performed by counselors, as outlined by several authors. Overall, the concept of self-actualization encompasses both the client and the rehabilitation professional, with the latter playing a crucial role in assisting clients in achieving their highest potential and functioning to the best of their abilities (Bellini & Rumrill, 2000; Blake & Mouton, 1985; Cassell & Mulkey, 1985; Grubbs et al., 2006; Kim, 2018; McGowan & Porter, 1967; Van Voorhis et al., 2000).

Historically, the literature extensively documents the self-actualizer role as a primary responsibility of counselors, and rehabilitation counselor education and training programs are designed to prepare individuals for this role. These programs typically incorporate counseling theory, counseling practicum, and counseling internships, as well as classic counseling models like Carkhuff, Perls, and Rogerian, or other models selected by continuing education training programs (Carkhuff, 1969; Carkhuff & Pierce, 1975; Cohen & Cohen, 1999; Okun, 1999; Perls, 1969, 1973; Rogers, 1951, 1961; Seligman, 2002; Thomas, 2000). After completing such training, rehabilitation counselors typically possess a solid foundation for assuming the self-actualizer role.

The self-actualizer role has historically been highly valued due to its potential for visible and immediate gratification, even more so than the role of manager. Through this role, counselors can create conditions that allow them to achieve personal rewards and experience a sense of fulfillment, regardless of any formal organizational reward system. Counselors who assume the self-actualizer role have control over their own personal reinforcers and draw from them to make further commitments to the role.

Manager Roles

In comparison to the self-actualizer role, the **manager role** has historically been undervalued and underrepresented in the public sector. There is a limited amount of literature on the managerial aspects of counseling in the rehabilitation field, and few academic courses teach principles of management for counselors or provide training for managing a caseload. As a result, the foundation for establishing the manager role has not been fully developed in public rehabilitation.

Furthermore, the manager role is often overlooked because its activities are not always visible or readily rewarded by agency systems. Unlike the self-actualizer role, the manager role does not offer immediate gratification or the same level of control over personal reinforcers. Intrinsic reinforcement processes require a mature counselor to maintain adequate motivation to continue performing managerial activities proficiently.

Historically, the private-sector rehabilitation has been viewed frequently as a business (Matkin, 1985), and the manager role takes on a relatively different emphasis. Research depicts the roles and functions of the private-sector rehabilitation professional (Dyck, 2016; Habeck & Munrowd, 1987; May, 2020; Millet & Vaittinen, 2011; Mullahy, 2004; Shrey, 1995; Zanskas & Strohmer, 2011). These bodies of work revealed five major task categories:

1. planning and coordinating client services,
2. business and office management,
3. job development and placement,
4. diagnostic assessment, and
5. other professional activities.

Role Integration

Although the self-actualizer and manager roles are typically perceived as distinct functions, they are, in fact, interrelated and interdependent. **Figure 4.2** depicts the presumed correlation between these two roles. In any professional environment, the optimal performance of a counselor necessitates the assimilation of both roles.

Although roles are discussed separately for ease of discussion, counselors must recognize the oneness of these roles and commit to fulfilling the requirements of both areas. The terms self-actualizer, manager, and counselor are used interchangeably throughout this text, but it should be noted that counselors should not limit themselves to solely performing counselor activities. The lack of knowledge and awareness of the functions involved in the manager role may hinder the acceptance of this role by counselors. However,

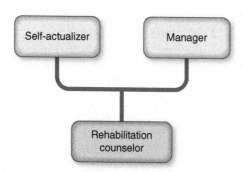

FIGURE 4.2 Dual roles of rehabilitation counselors in rehabilitation settings.

rehabilitation professionals are already fulfilling many managerial functions, and the only missing ingredient for effectiveness is a systematic and organized format from which to operate. Counselors should recognize this limitation and work toward fulfilling both roles for effective counselor performance.

ADDITIONAL ROLES OF THE REHABILITATION COUNSELOR

Role as Advocate

Advocacy is a crucial part of the rehabilitation counseling process and involves promoting policies that support the rights and welfare of people with disabilities. In fact, a case could be made that advocacy is the most critical case and caseload management role. Rehabilitation counselors serve as advocates for their clients to ensure that they receive the necessary resources, services, and opportunities that allow them to live fulfilling lives. Additionally, professionals advocate when clients may be unable or unwilling to act on their own behalf, or when a rehabilitation counselor could intervene to create a more effective provision of service in the process (Frankel et al., 2019). Clients may be unwilling or unskilled in advocacy, which does not support personal advocacy in the process. Examples of these types of situations are discussed when reflecting on client readiness and counselor maturity in Chapter 3.

Rehabilitation professionals frequently *advocate* for clients in several ways. Client advocacy may be helpful when it is apparent that a professional may have more well-known relationships, stronger professional understanding of a system, or more established connections than clients. For example, rehabilitation counselors may work with insurance companies and government agencies to secure funding for rehabilitation services. Additionally, they work with employers to identify job accommodations and other workplace modifications that can support clients with disabilities in performing their jobs effectively. Frequently, rehabilitation counselors must utilize advocacy skills to do what clients cannot, by utilizing formal or informal connections with various agencies or resources in order to access valued resources on behalf of the client.

Rehabilitation counselors also play a vital role in advocating for policies that support the rights and welfare of people with disabilities. The role of professionals presents itself most often in legislation, policies, and ethical standards of practice. For example, the Code of Professional Ethics for Certified Rehabilitation Counselors, adopted in September 2022, describes the advocate role as "fostering the self-advocacy skills of clients to achieve maximum independence, and advocating for clients who cannot self-advocate" (Commission on Rehabilitation Counselor Certification, 2022, p. 13). Rehabilitation counselors' participation in lobbying efforts or work with advocacy organizations to raise awareness of disability-related issues and promote legislative initiatives benefit clients at all levels. In addition, rehabilitation counselors may work with clients to understand their rights and develop self-advocacy skills, such as assertiveness, communication, and negotiation, which encourages clients to self-advocate and make informed autonomous decisions.

Overall, the role of the rehabilitation counselor as an advocate for clients is crucial in ensuring that people with disabilities have equal access to opportunities, services, and resources. Through their advocacy efforts, rehabilitation counselors empower clients to live independent, fulfilling lives and contribute to society in meaningful ways. Often the role as advocate emerges not by conscious choice, but by accident and through mentorship by other advocates in the field (Nichols & Carney, 2013). Additionally, this role is still often misunderstood across rehabilitation and other health professions, which complicates the ability to advocate effectively and provide the assistance necessary to individuals beyond care settings (Ng et al., 2015). To eliminate this ambiguity, advocacy in professional practice and training requires attention to approaches emphasizing the impact of social, cultural, and political contexts on both the client and the counselor. In order to enact change, roles as advocates must be explored and situated in a context that includes relations to power and structure. Finally, discussions must acknowledge the impact of awareness and content-specific knowledge as well as approaches to professional practice (Dobson et al., 2012).

Role in Crisis Intervention

The World Health Organization (WHO) reports that an increasing number of individuals are experiencing mental and emotional distress, resulting in a greater demand for **crisis intervention**. According to research conducted globally, there has been a 25% increase in serious psychological stress following the pandemic, with one in five adults reporting anxiety and depression that has had a significant impact on their overall mental health (Substance Abuse and Mental Health Services Administration, 2020). In addition to increases in the need for psychiatric care, percentages of disability-related injury and age-related fragility continue to rise as demographic projections indicate global populations are aging. The population aged 60 years and over will increase from 841 million in 2013 to more than 2 billion by 2050, exceeding the number of births by the year 2047 (Chatterji et al., 2015). Over the same period, global life expectancies are predicted to rise, with the gap between life expectancies expected to narrow. The rise of aging populations is happening concurrently with an increase in health disparities regarding access to healthcare and social support systems, as well as a widening of health gaps due to complex diseases. This, in turn, heightens the probability of various disabilities and other health risks emerging. Studies indicate that, while severe disability-free life expectancies may have declined, post–COVID-19 there has been an emergence in the co-occurrence of multiple diseases, where the prevention of one disease may lead to the emergence of disability due to another (National Academies of Sciences, Engineering, and Medicine et al., 2022).

Considering these impacts on changing demographics and the disability landscape, rehabilitation counselors play a crucial role in providing *crisis intervention* services to their clients. Their training equips them to offer short-term therapeutic assistance to individuals who are undergoing acute emotional distress, physical duress, or are in a state of crisis in diverse environments such as hospitals, schools, and community mental health centers (Lund et al., 2019; Macchiarulo et al., 2021; Tyuse, 2020). Additionally, rehabilitation professionals understand the impact of physical disabilities and are well versed in implications related to placement in employment. During the pandemic, 87% of jobs lost came in the services sector, primarily low-wage work offering little possibility of telecommuting, with women leaving the workforce at greater numbers than men (Kochhar, 2023).

Rehabilitation counseling professionals aim to assist individuals in attaining emotional stability and achieving positive outcomes through *crisis intervention services*. Their support includes emotional counseling, practical aid such as connecting clients to valued community resources, and referrals to additional services. Additionally, rehabilitation counselors strive to help prevent future crises by providing resources to clients to promote coping skills and strategies to manage stress and emotional challenges. Also, they may provide psychoeducation to clients and their families, increasing their awareness of warning signs and how to respond to varying disabilities in an effective manner. Overall, rehabilitation counselors' expertise is vital in providing crisis intervention services and helping clients achieve long-term physical and emotional stability (IBIS World, 2023).

Role as Service Coordinator

Effective coordination is a crucial aspect of case and caseload management. As Chapter 3 highlights, coordination has long been recognized as a significant responsibility of counselors. This responsibility is particularly important for rehabilitation counselors, as they must connect clients with valuable resources. Counselors navigate various systems to effectively implement rehabilitation strategies, often through **interprofessional collaborations**. Such collaborations clarify professional roles and responsibilities; foster teamwork; and enable interprofessional communication, conflict resolution, and shared decision-making processes, ultimately leading to positive outcomes (Mink et al., 2019).

In **interprofessional settings**, rehabilitation counselors often serve as service coordinators for their clients. As service coordinators, they are responsible for identifying and organizing a range of services and resources that meet their clients' diverse needs. This role involves collaborating with other professionals, such as physicians, social workers, and community-based organizations, to create a comprehensive plan of care for clients. Rehabilitation counselors assess their clients' needs and determine the necessary interprofessional services and resources to achieve their goals. Additionally, they provide support to clients to navigate complex healthcare and social services systems to access valuable resources and services. Rehabilitation counselors also monitor their clients' progress, adjust the rehabilitation plan when necessary, and facilitate independent client outcomes while ensuring clients' rights and needs are respected throughout the service coordination process (Tseng et al., 2011). Throughout this interactive process, various interprofessional service systems are integrated to develop a unified rehabilitation services approach (**Figure 4.3**).

Role as Broker/Facilitator of Services

Healthcare systems are increasingly relying on rehabilitation professionals to manage the complex process of **service brokering**. With the rise of specialized and standardized services, rehabilitation counselors often act as brokers or facilitators to ensure their clients receive the necessary resources and services to achieve their goals. Furthermore, changes in service provision and contemporary systems have led to fragmentation of an already complex system, making service brokering more important than ever. In-depth knowledge of available services and resources is crucial for connecting clients with the appropriate providers.

Brokering in rehabilitation includes basic case management functions connecting individuals with needed services. Intensive case management (ICM) and assertive community

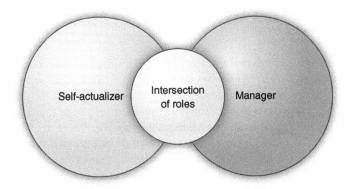

FIGURE 4.3 Interfaced self-actualizer and manager roles.

treatment (ACT) are additional forms of brokering that build on these basic services, including lower case sizes and outreach services provided by the case manager (Suzuki et al., 2019). Furthermore, brokering involves handling specific tasks, such as becoming brokers of coexisting objects of care, which include the body, the person, the organization, and the pathway (Wolf, 1956). Brokers of services must assist clients, through broker or self-direction, in identifying immediate and long-term needs, developing options to meet those needs, and accessing supports and services into the future (Mahoney et al., 2021).

However, this creates tension between service provision and self-direction, as clients seeking self-direction often do not desire traditional brokering or case management functions. Instead, there is a need for a supportive, proactively engaged, and culturally responsive coach (Mahoney et al., 2021). The **broker/coach role** involves providing guidance, support, and education to clients to ensure they are aware of available resources and services that can help them achieve their goals. Rehabilitation counselors serving in a broker/coaching role establish relationships with service providers and support clients to negotiate contracts for services on their own behalf. They ensure that the services provided meet the unique needs of their clients and are delivered in a timely and effective manner.

Rehabilitation counselors are instrumental in facilitating the delivery of services and resources to their clients. They collaborate with service providers to ensure that their clients receive the necessary resources and services to achieve their goals. Rehabilitation counselors monitor their clients' progress and adjust the plan of care as needed. As brokers, coaches, or facilitators of services, they ensure that their clients' rights are respected and that they are connected with the appropriate services and resources. In summary, rehabilitation counselors play a crucial role in supporting their clients to remain autonomous and achieve their goals.

Role of Quality Management

Total quality management *(TQM)* places an emphasis on improving processes, increasing overall customer satisfaction, and engaging in continuous improvement to achieve quality outcomes (Ozberk et al., 2019). According to Nakhai and Neves (2009), the essential components of TQM include customer satisfaction, continuous improvement, personnel relations, teamwork, and customer involvement. However, achieving overall quality is an ongoing process, as the needs of clients and society are constantly changing (Jayakumar et al., 2017). To reach this goal, processes must be constantly revised, refined, and adjusted (Freed et al., 1997). By utilizing quality tools, rehabilitation professionals and organizations can enhance their quality efforts, identify potential problems, and prevent defects from occurring.

Rehabilitation counselors also contribute significantly to *quality management* by ensuring that the services they provide to their clients are of the highest quality in terms of effectiveness, efficiency, and overall standard of care. As part of quality management, rehabilitation counselors may:

1. Monitor client progress: Rehabilitation counselors monitor the progress of their clients and evaluate the effectiveness of the services provided. They may use various assessment tools to measure client outcomes and identify areas for improvement.
2. Evaluate service providers: Rehabilitation counselors evaluate the effectiveness of service providers and make recommendations for improvement when necessary. They may conduct audits or site visits to assess the quality of services provided and ensure that service providers are meeting the needs of their clients.
3. Develop quality improvement plans: Rehabilitation counselors develop quality improvement plans that outline strategies for improving the quality of services provided. They may collaborate with service providers to develop these plans and identify areas for improvement.

4. Implement quality improvement strategies: Rehabilitation counselors implement quality improvement strategies and monitor their effectiveness. They may use data analysis to evaluate the impact of these strategies and make adjustments as necessary.
5. Ensure compliance with standards: Rehabilitation counselors ensure that service providers follow industry standards and regulations. They may review policies and procedures to ensure that they meet these standards and recommend changes when necessary.

Overall, the role of a rehabilitation counselor in quality management is critical in ensuring that clients receive high-quality services that meet their needs and promote their overall well-being. Rehabilitation counselors use their knowledge and skills to monitor progress, evaluate service providers, develop quality improvement plans, implement strategies, and ensure compliance with industry standards to improve the quality of services provided.

SUMMARY

In summary, the role of a rehabilitation counselor is complex and diverse. They serve as both counselors and managers, providing emotional support and overseeing the delivery of services to clients. Rehabilitation counselors also act as advocates, ensuring that their clients' needs and rights are respected. They may also offer crisis intervention services to assist clients in coping with unforeseen challenges. The diverse nature of their role allows rehabilitation counselors to provide comprehensive support and guidance to clients as they work toward their goals and strive for a fulfilling life.

The **multifaceted roles** and functions of rehabilitation counselors exemplify the intricate and dynamic nature of their profession. The diverse responsibilities assumed enable the opportunity to offer holistic and efficient support to clients, aiding in accomplishing their objectives and leading autonomous lives. Besides counseling, rehabilitation counselors act as brokers of services, liaising with other service providers to connect clients with the required resources and assistance. Additionally, quality management is another vital function of rehabilitation counselors, ensuring the consistent enhancement of services and anticipating potential issues. Overall, the comprehensive duties of rehabilitation counselors are pivotal in enabling clients to attain autonomy and success in their lives.

QUESTIONS FOR DISCUSSION

1. What are the impacts of the different roles and functions of rehabilitation professionals as counselors, managers, or a combination of the two, as discussed in current literature and research? What are some challenges they may face in fulfilling these multifaceted roles?

2. In what ways can rehabilitation counselors collaborate with other service providers to ensure their clients receive the best possible care?

3. How can rehabilitation counselors ensure that their clients' needs and rights are respected and upheld throughout the rehabilitation process?

4. What are some strategies that rehabilitation counselors can use to prevent potential problems and ensure the highest quality of services for their clients?

5. How can rehabilitation counselors provide effective crisis intervention services to clients in need?

6. In what ways can rehabilitation counselors support clients in achieving their goals and living fulfilling lives, beyond just managing their disabilities or illnesses?

7. How do rehabilitation counselors work collaboratively with other professionals and agencies to ensure that clients receive comprehensive and coordinated services?

8. In what ways can rehabilitation counselors advocate for policies and practices that promote the full inclusion and participation of individuals with disabilities in society?

9. How can rehabilitation counselors balance the need to provide emotional support and guidance to clients while also maintaining professional boundaries and avoiding burnout?

10. What are some strategies that rehabilitation counselors can use to effectively balance their roles as counselors, managers, advocates, crisis interveners, brokers of services, and quality managers?

PUTTING IT INTO PRACTICE

Ask yourself these questions to target issues or concerns with the roles of the professional in case and caseload management.

1. How do the specific roles and responsibilities you undertake influence the quality and value of services provided to your clients? Could these services be enhanced by reevaluating, clarifying, or adjusting your roles to better meet the evolving needs of professional practice?

2. As a rehabilitation counselor, how do you navigate effectively within a multidisciplinary team where colleagues may have conflicting priorities and demands during the rehabilitation process?

3. Do you feel content with your current role as a rehabilitation counselor in your present setting? Do you believe there are opportunities for you to enhance the provision of services for individuals with disabilities who are seeking rehabilitation support?

 SPRINGER PUBLISHING CONNECT™ A robust set of instructor resources designed to supplement this text is located at **http://connect.springerpub.com/content/book/978-0-8261-5963-2.** Qualifying instructors may request access by emailing **textbook@springerpub.com.**

REFERENCES

Alderman, L. A., & Oswald, G. (2016). The current state of specialization and self-identity among certified rehabilitation counselors. *Rehabilitation Professional, 24*(2), 69–74. https://corescholar.libraries.wright.edu/human_services/27

Bellini, J. L., & Rumrill, P. D. (2000). *Research rehabilitation counseling: A guide to design, methodology, and utilization.* Charles C Thomas Publisher.

Blake, R. R., & Mouton, J. S. (1985). *The managerial grid III.* Gulf Publishing.

Carkhuff, R. (1969). *Helping and human relations.* Holt, Rinehart & Winston.

Carkhuff, R. R., & Pierce, R. M. (1975). *Trainer's guide to the art of helping.* Human Resource Development Press.

Cassell, J. & Mulkey, S. W. (1985). *Rehabilitation caseload management: Concepts and practice.* Pro-Ed.

Chatterji, S., Bayles, J., Cutler, D., Seeman, T., & Verdes, E. (2015). Health, functioning, and disability in older adults—present status and future implications. *The Lancet, 385*(9967), 563–575.https://doi.org/10.1016/S0140-6736(14)61462-8

Cohen, E. D., & Cohen, G. S. (1999). *The virtuous therapist: Ethical practice of counseling and psychotherapy.* Brooks/Cole Publishing.

Commission on Rehabilitation Counselor Certification. (2022, September). *Code of professional ethics for certified rehabilitation counselors.* https://www.crccertification.com/wp-content/uploads/2023/04/2023-Code-of-Ethics.pdf

Das, J. P., & Misra, S. B. (2016). *Cognitive planning and executive functions: Applications in management and education.* Sage.

Dobson, S., Voyer, S., & Regehr, G. (2012). Agency and activism: Rethinking health advocacy in the medical profession. *Academic Medicine, 87*(9), 1161–1164. https://doi.org/10.1097/ACM.0b013e3182621c25

Dunn, P., Grubbs, L. A., & Mulkey, S. W. (2007). Inclusion of case and caseload management in NCRE member rehabilitation curricula. *Rehabilitation Counselors & Educators Journal, 1*(1), 24–28.

Dyck, D. E. (2016). Disability management education: Does the instructional delivery modality make a difference? *Workplace Health & Safety, 64*(2), 65–69. https://doi.org/10.1177/2165079915609951

Frankel, A. J., Gelman, S. R., & Pastor, D. K. (2019). *Case management: An introduction to concepts and skills* (4th ed.). Oxford University Press.

Freed, J. E., Klugman, M. R., & Fife, J. D. (1997). *A culture for academic excellence: Implementing the quality principles in higher education* (ASHE-ERIC Higher Education Report, Vol. 25, No. 1). George Washington University.

Groene, O., Sunol, R., Klazinga, N. S., Wang, A., Dersarkissian, M., Thompson, C. A., Thompson, A., & Arah, O. A. (2014). Involvement of patients or their representatives in quality management functions in EU hospitals: Implementation and impact on patient-centred care strategies. *International Journal for Quality in Health Care, 26*(1), 81–91. https://doi.org/10.1093/intqhc/mzu022

Grubbs, L. A., Cassell, J. L., & Mulkey, S. W. (2006). *Rehabilitation caseload management: Concepts & practice* (2nd ed.). Springer.

Habeck, R., & Munrowd, D. (1987). Employer-based rehabilitation practice: An educational perspective. *Rehabilitation Education, 1*(3), 1–13.

Hannagan, T. (2002). *Management concepts and practice* (3rd ed.). Prentice Hall.

Henke, R. O., Connolly, S. G., & Cox, J. S. (1975). Caseload management: The key to effectiveness. *Journal of Applied Rehabilitation Counseling, 6*(4), 217–227. https://doi.org/10.1891/0047-2220.6.4.217

IBIS World. (2023, March 1). *Family counseling & crisis intervention services in the US.* https://www.ibisworld.com/industry-statistics/market-size/family-counseling-crisis-intervention-services-united-states/

Jayakumar, V., Sheriff, F. M. A., Muniappan, A., Bharathiraja, G., & Ragul, G. (2017). Implementation of seven tools of quality in educational arena: A case study. *International Journal of Mechanical Engineering and Technology (IJMET), 8*(8), 882–891.

Kim, J. (2018). Consideration of the applicability of person-centered therapy to culturally varying clients, focusing on the actualizing tendency and self-actualization – from East Asian perspective. *Person-Centered & Experiential Psychotherapies, 17*(3), 201–223. https://doi.org/10.1080/14779757.2018.1506817

Kochhar, R. (2023). *The enduring grip of the gender pay gap.* Pew Research Center. https://www.pewresearch.org/social-trends/2023/03/01/the-enduring-grip-of-the-gender-pay-gap/

Kunce, J., & Angelone, E. (1990). Personality characteristics of counselors: Implications for rehabilitation counselor roles and functions. *Rehabilitation Counseling Bulletin, 34*(1), 4–15.

Lund, E. M., Schultz, J. C., McKnight-Lizotte, M., Nadorff, M. R., Galbraith, K., & Thomas, K. B. (2019). Suicide-related experience, knowledge, and perceived comfort and crisis competency among vocational rehabilitation support staff. *The Journal of Rehabilitation, 85*(4), 33–41.

Macchiarulo, E. E., Branca, F. F., Mallardi, A. A., Costanza, A. A., Amerio, A. A., Aguglia, A. A., Serafini, G. G., Amore, M. M., & Merli, R. R. (2021). Telephone counseling in coping with the COVID-19 lockdown consequences: Preliminary data. *Acta Bio-Medica de l'Ateneo Parmense, 92*(Suppl. 6). https://doi.org/10.23750/abm.v92iS6.12236

Mahoney, K. J., Mahoney, E. K., & Crisp, S. (2021). Care management and self-direction: Are they compatible? *Generations (San Francisco, Calif.), 45*(1), 1–11.

Matkin, R. E. (1985). *Insurance rehabilitation: Service applications in disability compensation systems.* Pro-Ed.

May, V. R. (2020). The international commission on health care certification life care planner role and function investigation. *Journal of Life Care Planning, 18*(2), 3–67.

McGowan, J. F., & Porter, T. L. (1967). An introduction to the vocational rehabilitation process (U.S. Department of Health, Education, and Welfare, RSS No. 68-32). U.S. Government Printing Office.

Millet, P., & Vaittinen, P. (2011). Job functions of Swedish public and private rehabilitation workers; their perceived level of importance and related knowledge. *Work (Reading, MA), 38*(2), 129–143. https://doi.org/10.3233/WOR-2011-1115

Mink, J., Mitzhat, A., Mihaljevic, A.L., Hauke, B.T., Gotsch, B., & Schmidt, J. (2019). The impact of interprofessional training ward on the development of interprofessional competencies: Study protocol of a longitudinal mixed-methods study. *BMC Medical Education, 19*(1), 48. https://doi.org/10.1186/s12909-019-1478-1

Mullahy, C. M. (2004). *The case manager's handbook* (3rd ed.). Jones and Bartlett.

Muthard, J. E., & Salomone, P. R. (1969). The roles and functions of the rehabilitation counselor. *Rehabilitation Counseling Bulletin, 13*(Special Issue), 81–168.

Nakhai, B., & Neves, J. S. (2009). The challenges of six sigma in improving service quality. *International Journal of Quality & Reliability Management, 26*(7), 663–684. https://doi.org/10.1108/02656710910975741

National Academies of Sciences, Engineering, and Medicine; Health and Medicine Division; Board on Health Care Services; Forstag, E. H., & Denning, L. A. (Eds.). (2022). Overview of long COVID and disability. In *Long COVID: Examining long-term health effects of COVID-19 and implications for the Social Security Administration: Proceedings of a workshop* (pp. 13–30). National Academies Press (US). https://doi.org/10.17226/26619

Ng, S. L., Lingard, L., Hibbert, K., Regan, S., Phelan, S., Stooke, R., Meston, C., Schryer, C., Manamperi, M., & Friesen, F. (2015). Supporting children with disabilities at school: Implications for the advocate role in professional practice and education. *Disability and Rehabilitation, 37*(24), 2282–2290. https://doi.org/10.3109/09638288.2015.1021021

Nichols, L. M., & Carney, J. V. (2013). Jane E. Myers: The evolution of an advocate. *Journal of Counseling and Development, 91*(2), 240–248. https://doi.org/10.1002/j.1556-6676.2013.00091.x

Okun, B. F. (1999). *Effective helping: Interviewing and counseling techniques* (5th ed.). Brooks/Cole Publishing.

Ozberk, O., Sharma, R. C., & Dagli, G. (2019). School teachers' and administrators' opinions about disability services, quality of schools, total quality management and quality tools. *International Journal of Disability, Development and Education, 66*(6), 598–609. https://doi.org/10.1080/1034912X.2019.1642455

Patterson, C. H. (1957). Counselor or coordinator? *Journal of Rehabilitation, 23*(3), 13–15.

Perls, F. (1969). *Gestalt therapy verbatim*. Real People Press.

Perls, F. (1973). *The gestalt approach & eye witness to therapy*. Science & Behavior Books.

Riggar, T. F., & Maki, D. R. (Eds.). (2004). *Handbook of rehabilitation counseling*. Springer Publishing Company.

Rogers, C. R. (1951). *Client-centered therapy*. Houghton Mifflin.

Rogers, C. R. (1961). *On becoming a person*. Houghton Mifflin.

Seligman, M. P. (2002). *Authentic happiness: Using the new positive psychology to realize your potential for lasting fulfillment*. Free Press.

Shrey, D. E. (1995). Disability management practice at the worksite: Developing, implementing, and evaluating transitional work programs. In D. E. Shrey & M. Lacerte (Eds.), *Principles and practices of disability management in industry* (pp. 55–105). St. Lucie Press.

Silvestri, E., Pellegrini, A., Di Sanzo, P., & Quaglia, F. (2022). Effective runtime management of tasks and priorities in GNU OpenMP applications. *IEEE Transactions on Computers, 71*(10), 1. https://doi.org/10.1109/TC.2021.3139463

Subich, L. (1984). Ratings of counselor expertness, attractiveness, and trustworthiness as a function of counselor sex-role and subject feminist orientation. *Sex Roles, 11*(11-1), 1033–1043. https://doi.org/10.1007/BF00288132

Substance Abuse and Mental Health Services Administration. (, 2020). *Key substance use and mental health indicators in the United States: Results from the 2020 National Survey on Drug Use and Health*. Author.

Suzuki, K., Yamaguchi, S., Kawasoe, Y., Nayuki, K., Aoki, T., Hasegawa, N., & Fujii, C. (2019). Core services of intensive case management for people with mental illness: A network analysis. *International Journal of Social Psychiatry, 65*(7-8), 621–630. https://doi.org/10.1177/0020764019867346

Thomas, R. M. (2000). *Comparing theories of child development* (5th ed.). Wadsworth Publishing.

Tseng, S. H., Liu, K., & Wang, W. L. (2011). Moving toward being analytical: A framework to evaluate the impact of influential factors on interagency collaboration. *Children and Youth Services Review, 33*(6), 798–803.

Tyuse, S. W. (2020). Crisis Intervention Team (CIT) programs and suicide. *Journal of Psychosocial Rehabilitation and Mental Health, 7*(3), 221–229. https://doi.org/10.1007/s40737-020-00186-5

Vaingankar, J. A., Teh, W. L., Roystonn, K., Goh, J., Zhang, Y. J., Satghare, P., Shahwan, S., Chong, S. A., Verma, S., Tan, Z. L., Tay, B., Maniam, Y., & Subramaniam, M. (2021). Roles, facilitators and challenges of employment support specialists assisting young people with mental health conditions. *Journal of Occupational Rehabilitation, 31*(2), 405–418. https://doi.org/10.1007/s10926-020-09930-x

Van Voohis, P., & Salisbury, E. J. (2016). *Correctional counseling and rehabilitation* (9th ed.). Routledge Publishing.

Wolf, E. R. (1956). Aspects of group relations in a complex society: Mexico. *American Anthropologist, 58*(6), 1065–1078. https://doi.org/10.1525/aa.1956.58.6.02a00070

Zanskas, S., & Strohmer, D. C. (2011). The work environment of the private-for-profit rehabilitation counselor. *The Journal of Rehabilitation, 77*(4), 13–22.

CHAPTER 5

Control: An Essential Element of the Case and Caseload Management Process

---

LEARNING OBJECTIVES

By the end of this chapter, learners will be able to:

- Discuss the concept of personal control and how it is related to rehabilitation practice.
- Discuss control as a prominent element and management function.
- Describe control as a central position in a management system.
- Examine the acronym PRIME as a method in establishing effective control of the caseload.
- Distinguish between internal and external control positions and influence on rehabilitation goals, process, and outcome.
- Explore deviation assessment in relation to deviation correction.

INTRODUCTION

The need for **personal control** is considered to be one of the basic innate psychological motives (Ryan & Deci, 2000; Whitson & Galinsky, 2008). Introna (1997) defines *control* intuitively as a systematic steering toward a defined final state or goal. Additionally, control can be defined as the ability to influence or direct the behavior of oneself or others toward a desired outcome (Baumeister et al., 2007). Control can manifest in various ways, such as exerting authority over others, regulating one's own thoughts and emotions, or manipulating the environment to achieve a desired outcome. Further, it emerges as a fundamental human need and plays a critical role in shaping our perceptions, behaviors, and well-being. In considering overall management functions, control is seen as implying insight into the current point or state; a defined ultimate point, state, or objective; and the ability to steer through systems throughout periods of transition (Cassell & Mulkey, 1985, 2004; Cassell et al., 1997). The essence of achieving a functional level of operations within any established system lies with the effective conceptualization and implementation of a *personal control concept*. This perspective is true regardless of whether the rehabilitation system involves managing an insurance case to a prompt resolution, managing case movement, or dealing with elements of the rehabilitation organizational structure.

CONTROL AS A KEY MANAGEMENT FUNCTION

As highlighted in Chapter 3, the interconnectedness of the five basic functions in a management approach is essential for maintaining continuity, with the control function playing a central role. In the context of rehabilitation counseling, where a professional orientation relies on a management foundation for all activities and responsibilities, control emerges as a critical element that contributes to overall effectiveness. For rehabilitation counselors to effectively manage caseloads and deliver high-quality services to clients, a solid grasp of control and its application is paramount. By harnessing the power of control, counselors can optimize their practice and facilitate positive outcomes for individuals receiving rehabilitation services.

Control plays a significant role in client counseling sessions. A counselor needs to consider and adapt to the client's existing control framework, whether it stems from internal dynamics, external influences, or powerful individuals. By comprehending the client's control base within the counseling relationship, counselors can enhance client satisfaction, foster better treatment outcomes, and ultimately, increase the likelihood of achieving rehabilitation goals. Applying reinforcements to the client's coping strategies becomes essential to facilitate continued progress and empower the client to further enhance their sense of personal control.

Control is a prominent element for every counselor, since the realistic appraisal of controllable and noncontrollable events is essential for personal discipline. Control is significant for a sense of power in the position; for developing self-confidence; and for thwarting frustrations, conflicts, and wasted efforts or just adjusting to burnout syndrome. Effective control of a system does not necessarily require an in-depth understanding of its internal processes. However, it is essential for the controller to have a clear understanding of the system's behavior, specifically how inputs relate to outputs. This knowledge allows the counselor to effectively manage their caseload and make informed decisions to achieve desired outcomes. Therefore, control is fundamental to the manner in which the counselor sets and meets case standards, achieves smooth movement of clients through the established rehabilitation process, and, in general, keeps within organizational demands that may impinge constantly on one's job. For example, self-discipline becomes a valued attribute for the caseload manager in private rehabilitation, since control is localized within the individual practitioner. Many of these practitioners operate on an independent basis in the field with only infrequent contact with central-office personnel (Golden & Veiga, 2005; Hertel et al., 2019; Lee et al., 2017). The necessity to set priorities, establish limits, and manage those various client and organizational related elements within acceptable limits therefore evoke control-related responses. Although many rehabilitation professionals in public rehabilitation agencies voice pessimism over their control position, control is exemplified through their professional decision-making activities (Crimando, 2004; Santana & Fouad, 2017; Savickas, 2011). Although certain parameters for practitioners are established by federal mandates and state policies—for example, eligibility determination—decisions such as case movement and placement activities operate through a control concept.

Therefore, as a powerful concept for performing, control pervades almost all actions of the counselor. It is crucial to understand control and establish techniques or methods that make effective control an essential aspect of the counselor's role, similar to counseling or placement techniques. This chapter aims to provide initial steps in supporting this premise and enhancing understanding of the impact of control as a management function in rehabilitation.

The authors conceptualize control into two essential areas: (a) elements of personal control and (b) elements of structural control. The first part of this chapter will concentrate on identifying the counselor's foundation for personal control and exploring significant factors in establishing a model of control for effective functioning. The second part will delve into the identification and understanding of elements that provide context to structural control, contributing to the overall development of the caseload manager's system.

ELEMENTS OF PERSONAL CONTROL

Personal control plays a vital role in the rehabilitation paradigm, serving as a driving force for effective professional practice. It involves recognizing and assessing the fundamental function in different areas of human behavior and taking corrective measures to address any deviations in performance that could lead to personal or caseload management challenges before they escalate into crises. This perspective aligns with the views of Cassell and Mulkey (1985) and Grubbs et al. (2006), highlighting the importance of maintaining control to attain positive outcomes in the field of rehabilitation.

While structural control refers to the external demands, requirements, and standards that influence control, there is also a personal aspect to control that involves internal processes within individuals. These **intrapersonal processes** enable practitioners to take charge of situations that could otherwise impede their ability to act in the best interest of their clients. Recognizing and assessing their own position in relation to control is crucial for practitioners, as it allows them to objectively evaluate their level of control. Without this self-awareness, practitioners may find themselves with limited control, making it difficult to effectively manage their caseloads. Personal control holds immense significance in the rehabilitation paradigm, as it serves as the driving force behind professional practice (Cassell et al., 1997; Ryan & Deci, 2000; Skinner, 2013).

INTERNAL AND EXTERNAL LOCUS OF CONTROL AND COMPARISON OF TRAITS

Personal control can be understood and approached from different perspectives. This section specifically examines the internal versus external control orientations as initially proposed by Rotter (1966, 1975). The framework known as locus of control has been extensively studied and offers a comprehensive set of concepts that rehabilitation practitioners can easily grasp and apply (Çelik & Naktiyok, 2018; Chen et al., 2016; Key, 2002; Livneh, 2000; Luszczynska & Schwarzer, 2005; Schwarzer & Jerusalem, 2010; Strauser et al., 2002). Rotter suggests that an individual's sense of control is influenced by their perception of the origin of reinforcers that shape their behavior. When counselors believe that their own actions are the primary determinants of the outcomes they experience, they exhibit an internal control expectancy (Cassell et al., 1997). In this perspective, rehabilitation counselors view events as controllable, as they attribute rewards following their actions or performance to their personal efforts. Conversely, if counselors perceive that outcomes and events are not influenced by their own actions but rather by luck, chance, or fate, they adopt an external locus of control and do not consider events to be within their control.

Suppose a counselor has successfully facilitated a client's employment placement and attributes the achievement predominantly to their own actions and the client's qualities, such as their interests and skills. The counselor acknowledges their accurate diagnosis of the client's challenges, their efforts to address skill gaps, their assessment of vocational potential and proficiency, their understanding of the job market, and their establishment of connections with employers and public relations. This counselor is inclined to repeat these activities and exhibit the necessary motivation to navigate through potential challenges in order to attain the desired outcome. This indicates that the counselor operates from an internal control base, believing that their actions and abilities significantly influence the outcomes they achieve.

In contrast, let's consider a counselor who has successfully facilitated a client's employment placement but attributes the achievement to factors beyond their control, such as luck or the client's independent efforts. This counselor may express statements like, "I was fortunate in finding this placement" or "The client's proactive job search made all the difference." Such a counselor operates from an external control base, perceiving that external circumstances or the client's actions primarily determine the outcome. As a result, they may not feel a strong sense of control over the process of placing clients and may be less motivated to actively influence future outcomes.

Individuals vary in their levels of personal control, with some exhibiting a greater sense of agency over their actions, while others allow external factors to exert more influence. For example, certain counselors may possess an internal orientation, enabling them to effectively manage their activities despite time constraints, heavy caseloads, or demanding clients. They maintain control over their work and make steady progress toward their goals. In contrast, counselors with an external orientation may feel overwhelmed by competing demands, perceiving limited control over their circumstances, which can hinder their ability to make significant strides in achieving their objectives.

If individuals rely on external sources to reinforce their goal-directed behavior, they exhibit an external orientation. Counselors with an external orientation generally believe that they have minimal influence over the outcomes achieved in caseload management. They attribute these outcomes to luck or chance factors. Consequently, they may face challenges in prioritizing tasks, procrastinate in decision-making, exhibit risk aversion, and be susceptible to manipulation by assertive or aggressive individuals. They may also struggle to establish a systematic approach to caseload management (Cassell & Mulkey, 2004; Cassell et al., 1997; Grubbs et al., 2006). These professionals allow external factors and others to control the reinforcements they receive, resulting in a tendency to wait for favorable conditions to replicate past successes, ultimately leading to decreased productivity. The findings from various research studies further describe this external orientation, as summarized in **Table 5.1**.

TABLE 5.1 COMPARISON OF INTERNAL AND EXTERNAL LOCUS OF CONTROL

INTERNAL CONTROLLERS	EXTERNAL CONTROLLERS
1. Can delay their need for reinforcement	1. Require immediate gratification.
2. Place great deal of value on time and manage accordingly	2. Tend to procrastinate, put things off. They thwart effective use of time.
3. Alertly read to take action to confront problems and difficulties. Dwell less on deficits and faults when doing problem-solving.	3. Tend toward inaction because they tend to be afraid of failure more than hope for success.
4. Are risk takers	4. Are not risk takers. Tend to play it safe and keep involvement down.
5. Cautious about data and general information accepted from others.	5. Accept information at face value.
6. Do preliminary steps for data gathering.	6. Engage less in preliminary data gathering.
7. Are resistant to pressures from external sources to direct their behavior.	7. Responsive to the influence of external sources.
8. Expend time and energy on decision-making and tasks demanding skill.	8. Expend minimal time in decision-making and tasks; take it as it makes its way down the path.

Typically, internally controlled individuals are highly **self-governing**. Those who possess an internal control position have a greater capacity to assume responsibility, take calculated risks, manage time efficiently, respond confidently, apply self-motivation and rewards for results, and direct the events that occur in caseload management. Intrinsic or internal rewards for performance are obtained by internally controlled persons, without relying on external recognition or other forms of reinforcement from outside sources to improve their performance. Such individuals perceive themselves and their own actions as the key factors that have the greatest impact on the outcomes achieved. **Table 5.1** summarizes additional research findings that characterize an internal control position.

In summary, individuals with an **internal control orientation** exhibit traits such as being knowledgeable about their priorities, actively seeking information to increase their chances of success, effectively managing their time, taking calculated risks based on informed decisions, and approaching skill tasks in a deliberate manner when they have control. On the other hand, externally controlled individuals are more inclined toward chance tasks, display impulsiveness and a preference for immediate gratification, are prone to procrastination, and may invest time and effort in decisions that seem less significant to internally controlled individuals. Regardless of one's control orientation, it is crucial for rehabilitation counselors to have a comprehensive understanding of control and its impact on caseload practices.

Locus of Control in Rehabilitation

To ensure that caseload managers have a comprehensive understanding of the internal versus external locus of control, it is crucial to examine its application in the field of rehabilitation. The following information provides a brief overview of the research conducted on individuals with disabilities or counselors working in the rehabilitation industry:

1. For individuals with disabilities, **internal or external locus of control** can determine attitudes and behaviors (Cuevas et al., 2019; Hall & Graff, 2011; Millet & Sandberg, 2003; Ordway et al., 2019; Selander et al., 2008; Siggeirsdottir et al., 2016).
2. Psychological adjustment to a spinal cord injury is largely devoted to correlates of adjustment, notably personality factors and locus of control (Peter et al., 2015; Russell et al., 2021; Sasse et al., 2014).
3. Rehabilitation counselors should consider the **locus of control** of their clients when formulating rehabilitation plans (Mertes & Harden, 2019; Sprong et al., 2018).
4. Locus of control orientation is useful in predicting the accurate perception of personal health status and the appropriate time for returning to work for individuals who have disabilities (Dionne et al., 2013; Vanovenberghe et al., 2021).
5. Individuals with learning disabilities develop adequate coping strategies which lead to the emergence of realistic self-awareness (Anuar et al., 2021; Chukwu et al., 2019; Kreider et al., 2019; Kurtek, 2018; Milligan et al., 2015; Taderera & Hall, 2017).
6. Research findings indicate that rehabilitation outcomes may be improved significantly if clients' control orientations could move from an external to a more internal locus of control (Berridge, 2018; De Tommaso & Turatto, 2022; Mizuno et al., 2022; Müller, 2021; Karsh et al., 2021).

Considering locus of control can be a crucial factor for counselors while managing their caseload. However, it should not be solely relied upon as a predictor of client behavior. When used in combination with other diagnostic tools available to the counselor, locus of control can be valuable in providing a more comprehensive understanding of the client's situation.

A Counseling Framework for Locus of Control

The basic concepts derived from the locus of control area offer a "mini-counseling" framework. According to Grubbs et al. (2006) and Cassell and Mulkey (1985), a counseling process that uses a **locus of control** approach would require four basic steps:

Step 1. Assess the Client's Locus of Control Orientation
The assessment of locus of control can be done with or without using the Rotter I-E Scale. A counselor can acquire the necessary knowledge and training to confidently determine the client's locus of control. Informal observations of the client's verbal and nonverbal behavior can provide important cues that indicate external locus of control, such as a tendency to attribute outcomes to luck or chance. Sufficient observation time is needed to ensure accuracy in assessing internal versus external orientation. Even when using the Rotter scale, the counselor should still collect observation data to validate the assessment conducted using the tool.

Step 2. Promote Behavior Recognition
The second step involves developing a process to help clients understand how they are relinquishing control if they have an external locus of control. Alternatively, for clients who already possess an internal locus of control, the focus is on reinforcing and building upon this positive orientation to further enhance their sense of control. The process is tailored to the individual's level of understanding.

Step 3. Accountability Counseling
The third step involves introducing the client to the concept of taking personal ownership of their behaviors identified in Step 2. This requires implementing strategies aimed at separating self-esteem elements from the negative outcomes of their actions. The client must recognize that negative outcomes do not diminish their self-worth, but rather are a result of their actions, and that new actions can lead to positive outcomes. By accepting responsibility for the negative results, clients can learn to reward themselves for producing positive outcomes, thereby shifting toward an internal locus of control. Once these foundational conditions have been established, the transition from an external to an internal locus of control can begin.

Step 4. Guide Preference Commitments
The final step involves weighing the available alternatives with the client and taking a proactive approach to empower them to drive the process. The client should be guided in a way that supports their autonomy in the decision-making process. The ultimate objective is to enable the internal locus of control to thrive such that the client's preferred actions and commitments stem primarily from their own personal perspective.

Organization Versus Personal Control

In the rehabilitation process, caseload managers have minimal control over various elements such as legislative and judicial actions, budgetary aspects, geographic region factors (such as a shortage of referral and placement sources), economic trends that result in higher costs for services to individuals with disabilities, decisions made by workers compensation boards, and the establishment of office and field standards for counselor practices (Cassell & Mulkey, 1985; Grubbs et al., 2006). These factors are beyond the control of counselors, and thus their ability to influence them is limited. However, these factors can potentially have a significant impact on the caseload manager. Integrating the demands from these areas with other management activities can help counselors adapt to their seemingly inevitable nature. While counselor behaviors directed toward these areas may not be perceived as under their control, it is possible to exercise control by learning to tolerate or adapt to these factors.

In contrast, some elements are more controllable for caseload managers, such as caseload size and projected numbers of individuals to be rehabilitated (although some counselors may question this), time structure, amount of paperwork (debated but ultimately controllable), referral acquisition and retention (when source scarcity is not a factor), and case flow and movement of clients through the rehabilitation process (Cassell & Mulkey, 1985; Grubbs et al., 2006). These factors are likely to be within the control of caseload managers, and individuals with an internal locus of control are more likely to have a greater impact than those with an external locus of control.

Counselors who are internally controlled are more likely to be aware of the extent and type of control they exert in managing the various aspects of caseload management. They have a greater opportunity to recognize the impact they have in these areas. On the other hand, counselors who argue that they have no control over the listed issues are likely to be externally controlled individuals who may miss the chance to realize the control they do have. By examining their activities more closely, it becomes evident that they do exert some control over these factors. However, by refusing to acknowledge any level of control, they deny themselves the valuable self-reinforcers they deserve.

ADMONITIONS: WARNINGS ON CONTROL POSITIONS

To fully grasp the utility and relevance of the locus of control concept, counselors must be aware of the limitations of the **Rotter I-E Scale**. The Rotter I-E Scale provides only a broad and generalized expectancy for prediction purposes. Moreover, it is essential to avoid conceptualizing I-E Scale results in a "good me–bad me" framework. Rotter (1975) emphasized that there is no evidence to suggest that all characteristics of internals are positive and those of externals are negative. Making value judgments such as concluding that internals are high achievers and externals are low achievers should be avoided. While there may be barriers and challenges associated with an external orientation, no value judgments should be attached to it. Differences in behavior have been observed between individuals with different internal and external locus of control orientations. However, caution should be exercised when attempting to categorize individuals as internal or external personality types. Evidence suggests that individuals can be placed on a continuum according to their degree of internality or externality. This representation acknowledges that individuals may possess varying degrees of internality or externality and can move toward one pole or the other (see **Figure 5.1**). A consistent orientation is established when behavior stemming from one of these expectation poles becomes dominant.

FIGURE 5.1 Depiction of locus of control as a continuum.

PRIME: PERCEPTION FACTORS FOR ESTABLISHING CONTROL

Historically, research has shown that one's orientation to control can be altered (Corey & Corey, 1997; Dua, 1970; Introna, 1997; Rubin & Rubin, 1988; Skinner & Edge, 2002; Van Voorhis et al., 2000). An individual counselor or client whose locus of control stems from an external orientation can move along the continuum toward the internal orientation through a process of self-awareness and constructive, practiced action. Additionally, it is possible that an individual who is localized on the internal control scale can maintain that present level of control, if desired, or can gain a higher level or firmer base for internal control.

Counselors can improve their ability to manage their caseload by consistently training themselves to establish greater control. This process begins with an awareness of the various factors that influence effective control. Grubbs et al. (2006) have identified five PRIME factors that play a key role in developing or establishing personal control. It is important to note that these factors are just a few of the many that can interfere with a professional's ability to maintain control. By receiving training and incorporating improved skills, counselors can establish a foundation for gaining and/or maintaining control. The five PRIME factors are depicted in **Figure 5.2**.

Perception

Perception ranks highest in importance among the five PRIME factors for establishing control. This factor can work to the counselor's disadvantage and exert great control on the individual's behaviors. Unwittingly or unknowingly, it can be a controller of much of the counselor's behavior, and therefore must be managed appropriately.

The process of perception involves gathering information about external events and using cumulative experiences to form a basis for interpreting future events. Personal factors like attitudes, emotions, and values heavily influence this interpretation. When counselors fail to actively manage the development of their perceptual sets, they risk losing control of the caseload management process. Compelling perceptions can then emerge and control the counselor's behavior, even if they are biased or inaccurate. To avoid this, counselors must critically evaluate their perceptions and consider alternative perspectives. However, perception tends to establish a prearranged or preorganized system for interpreting

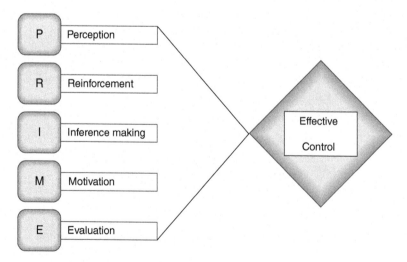

FIGURE 5.2 The PRIME factors for effective control.

information, so it can be challenging to gain control over it. Perception triggers automatic responses without necessarily going through a logical, rational, reasoning process, which makes it even harder to manage.

PERCEPTION AND PROBLEM-SOLVING

Counselors may face a barrier to effective problem-solving due to their own perceptions. They may become fixated on their perception of the situation and fail to accurately perceive current realities, which can lead to frustration and complicate the problem-solving process. An example of how neutral stimuli can be viewed through a perceptual framework that prevents a solution from being reached is shown in **Figure 5.3**. When counselors operate in this way, it can be said that the situation is controlling them. To address this issue, counselors should take a proactive approach to problem-solving and limit perception-based problems. To better understand this concept, individuals can refer to **Figure 5.3** and attempt to solve the problem several times before seeking input from others to arrive at a solution.

As illustrated in **Figure 5.3**, managing a caseload can sometimes make activities related to each case seem similar. However, this issue can be minimized if caseload managers have properly prepared themselves to manage through the five essential functions of management: planning, organizing, coordinating, directing, and controlling (as shown in Chapter 3, Table 3.2). By adopting a proactive approach and focusing on problem prevention, the issue of perception can also be addressed. This reduces the occurrence of loss of control in problem-solving and helps caseload managers avoid becoming fixated on their own perceptions.

Reinforcement

Reinforcement can serve as a powerful tool for behavior control, yet it is crucial for counselors to comprehend the origin of reinforcement. By embracing an internal frame of reference, counselors can exert greater influence over the reinforcement process. This approach

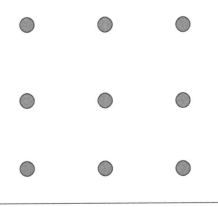

Rules:

Rule 1.   Connect all the dots with *four* straight, continuous lines. (When a line changes direction that constitutes a new line.)

Rule 2.   The lines may cross.

Rule 3.   DO NOT lift your pen from the paper.

FIGURE 5.3 A problem-solving example.

entails operating under the belief that rewards stem from their own actions, rather than depending on external factors beyond their control. By directing their attention toward internal sources of reinforcement, counselors can effectively manage and regulate behavior.

Recognizing the substantial influence of reinforcement on behavior, counselors must prioritize gaining control over this process. When counselors perceive that their own actions have directly contributed to a client's successful employment placement or the establishment of a favorable placement source, they hold the reins of their own reinforcement. By acknowledging their personal role in achieving positive outcomes, counselors can experience a sense of reward and fulfillment. However, some counselors may attribute success solely to external factors like the benevolence of an employer or mere chance, neglecting the significant impact of their own hard work, perseverance, and effective public relations. This approach undermines their contributions and leaves them feeling powerless. Hence, it is imperative for counselors to shift their focus to an internal frame of reference, enabling them to assert control over the reinforcement process.

Rehabilitation counselors who demonstrate a tendency toward externally controlled reinforcement often perceive their work as arduous, lacking in rewards, or monotonous. Their rewards may come sporadically and seemingly by chance, with the circumstances dictating the counselor's experience. On the other hand, individuals with internally controlled reinforcement tendencies can derive self-applied rewards from their efforts. This includes activities like maintaining thorough case records, fostering client self-improvement, preparing clients for employment, cultivating placement sources, and assessing client needs for community rehabilitation services. In this scenario, counselors become the primary source of their own reinforcement. To ensure that they maintain control over the reinforcement process and avoid relying on external factors beyond their control, counselors must ask themselves important questions such as "Who holds the reins—the client, the agency, or yourself?" and "Where do you typically seek reinforcement?" By addressing these crucial inquiries, counselors can assert control over the process and avoid becoming dependent on external factors.

Rehabilitation counselors need to recognize that seeking answers to certain questions from external sources may not yield fruitful results. While counselors may face challenges and frustrations, relying solely on their agency for validation or rewards is not a reliable approach. Instead, they should focus on self-applied reinforcement to enhance their personal sense of control over situations. It is crucial to understand that depending on external sources to manage personal reinforcers will ultimately transfer control to others or external processes. By prioritizing self-generated reinforcement, counselors can maintain autonomy and empower themselves in their professional practice.

Inference Making

To enhance control over caseload management, it is important for managers to recognize the role of a third control variable—the process of **making inferences**—and its potential impact on reactions. This distinction lies in drawing conclusions based on inferences versus actual observations. The process of making inferences involves gathering information and subjecting it to a decision-making or evaluation process before taking action. It differs from observations, which are based on firsthand experience through seeing, hearing, feeling, smelling, or touching the data directly. In contrast, inferences often rely on second-hand information derived from various sources, which themselves may be derived from secondary sources. Therefore, caseload managers must be aware of the potential influence of the inference-making process on their decision-making and take steps to minimize its impact. By prioritizing accurate and firsthand observations over inferences, managers can gain better control and make more informed decisions in caseload management.

Counselors must skillfully employ both inference and observation strategies to effectively manage caseloads. In many instances, counselors have to rely on inferences, as direct observations or factual data may not be readily accessible. However, a potential pitfall emerges when counselors treat inferences as equivalent to observations and solely base their actions on them, without considering the potential risks associated with incorrect or unreliable data. This approach leads to a loss of control for the counselor and can give rise to problems when acting on inferences as if they were verifiable observations or indisputable facts. Thus, maintaining a delicate balance between utilizing both inference and observation strategies is vital to prevent potential complications and ensure effective caseload management.

THE UNCRITICAL INFERENCE

The "uncritical inference test" originated from the work of Haney, who has utilized this test in his training and consulting endeavors. Haney (1971) established three essential criteria that must be fulfilled for an observation to be deemed valid. Failure to meet any of these criteria implies that the actions taken by an individual based on the data are merely assumptions. The three criteria for an observation, as outlined by Haney, are as follows:

1. The time element: Content statements can be made after or during the event, but not before the observation takes place. This criterion emphasizes the importance of basing statements on actual observations rather than making premature judgments.
2. The limitation element: Content statements must be confined to only those aspects that one has directly observed. This criterion emphasizes the necessity of limiting statements to what has been witnessed firsthand, avoiding speculation or assumptions about unobserved elements.
3. The source element: Content statements should be specific to an individual's own firsthand observations. This criterion underscores the significance of drawing conclusions based on personal experiences and observations, rather than relying on secondhand or indirect information.

By adhering to these criteria, individuals can ensure that their observations are grounded in valid and reliable data, enhancing the accuracy and credibility of their assessments and decisions. However, failure to evaluate the inference process can lead to errors, confusion, and undesirable outcomes. Here are examples of situations where reliance on inferences can result in negative consequences:

1. A counselor excludes a client from consideration for a specific job based on the assumption that the client's disability would hinder job performance. In this case, the time element is violated since the counselor has not directly observed the client working in that job.
2. A supervisor observes a counselor conducting a subpar counseling session with a client who has cerebral palsy and infers that the counselor is incapable of effectively counseling individuals with disabilities. This violates the limitations element as the supervisor has only witnessed the counselor's interaction with one client from a specific disability category.
3. A counselor assists a client in developing work objectives based solely on reports from a vocational evaluator, without any firsthand observation data. This counselor is in violation of the source element criterion as the conclusions drawn are solely based on inference rather than direct observation.

In each of these scenarios, the failure to adhere to the criteria for valid observations can lead to flawed judgments, impeding the counseling process and potentially compromising outcomes. Therefore, it is essential to evaluate and consider the limitations of the inference process to ensure accurate and informed decision-making.

Given the inherent nature of information processing, it is often not feasible to treat most information as observed facts. Consequently, counselors frequently rely on inference-based decision-making, as exemplified in the third example mentioned earlier. Making decisions inherently involves taking risks, which can result in a loss of control. To navigate this, Haney suggests the concept of "calculated risk" to minimize uncalculated risks. Counselors must acknowledge that a risk is being undertaken and that the chosen alternative may not align perfectly with the decision scheme. Furthermore, rehabilitation counselors must recognize that the decision may not lead to a successful outcome. This realization should prompt an evaluation of the trade-offs involved. Decisions that carry high costs and can significantly impact clients' lives require a higher probability of being correct. Thus, it becomes crucial to have access to as much observation data or near-to-the-event information as possible, minimizing risks in these cases. Conversely, low-cost decisions that do not disrupt a client's rehabilitation process can tolerate a margin of error. In such instances, it may be acceptable to utilize inference-based data with a 10% certainty level, freeing up the counselor's attention to focus on higher-priority tasks. By adopting a calculated risk approach and considering the appropriate level of certainty required for different decisions, counselors can effectively manage the inherent challenges of decision-making in their practice.

To distinguish between observations and inference-making, a checklist of questions is provided:

1. How closely connected or personally involved are you with the event? Are you making statements based on observations before actually making the observations?
2. Are your statements about the observation relevant to the event, or are you reverting to making excessive inferences?
3. Do you rely on your intuition to assess the probability of data certainty in high-risk situations when dealing with critical inferences?
4. Do you make a conscious effort to label your inferences as such when interacting with clients, and do you teach your clients to do the same? Additionally, do you establish appropriate risk levels with your clients?

By reflecting on these questions, one can better differentiate between observations and inferences, promoting greater awareness of the thought process involved and facilitating effective communication with clients.

Motivation

The fourth factor in our model will naturally expand on the previous three—perception, reinforcement, and inference-making. This motivational factor focuses on the events that trigger a person to act or the stimuli that drive individuals toward their goals. Thus, we should ask questions such as "How does motivation factor in as a control factor?" and "How does motivation control us, or how can counselors control motivation?"

Motivating individuals to perform can be approached through three general methods: force ("stick"), enticement ("carrot"), and identification. These methods can be categorized into two external control orientations and one internal orientation. In the upcoming sections, we will delve into each method to provide a more comprehensive understanding.

FORCE ("STICK")

This approach to **motivation** entails employing physical punishment, threats, or verbal reprimands as a means of controlling behavior. It relies on the external fear mechanism to exert control. While it is crucial to note that counselors would never resort to physical abuse with their clients, it is possible for some supervisory staff to adopt a berating approach when motivating personnel. Additionally, clients may perceive their counselors not as supportive helpers, but rather as authoritative figures, which can be seen as a manifestation of force. Consequently, it is important to establish a harmonious balance between the roles of counselor and manager to prevent the use of forceful tactics and ensure a more collaborative and supportive environment.

ENTICEMENT ("CARROT")

In this form of motivation, individuals are incentivized to perform their duties or achieve their goals through the promise of rewards. Examples of such rewards can include timely pay increases, promises of supervisory promotions, or involvement in special projects. However, relying solely on external sources of motivation can restrict behavior, as individuals become reliant on external processes to receive reinforcements, resulting in limited self-enhancement. To foster a more comprehensive and sustainable approach to motivation, counselors should avoid solely depending on external sources of motivation. Instead, professionals should encourage clients to cultivate internal motivations that drive them to achieve their goals. By maintaining commitment and motivation, individuals are more likely to experience personal growth, maintain long-term commitment, and experience a sense of fulfillment in their pursuits.

IDENTIFICATION

This form of motivation is rooted in an internal orientation. Counselors are driven to fulfill their duties because these responsibilities and obligations become deeply ingrained in their sense of self. Working with clients, understanding rehabilitation as a profession, being self-actualized, and serving as caseload managers become integral parts of their identity, rather than being perceived as external factors. When counselors possess this internal motivation, they feel a profound sense of accomplishment and take pride in their contributions to their role. Their job functions become intertwined with their self-esteem and sense of self-worth. They derive fulfillment from their work because it aligns with their personal values and aspirations. By cultivating this internal motivation, counselors can consistently deliver their best efforts and make a lasting impact in their profession. It becomes a natural extension of who they are and reinforces their dedication to providing quality care and support to their clients.

In a similar vein, clients who are encouraged to take ownership of their rehabilitation program will greatly benefit from an internal orientation approach. When clients perceive a structured service plan as their own program and take pride in the progress and achievements they make within it, they experience a sense of independence and empowerment. This proactive approach helps address the commonly observed issue known as "unmotivated client syndrome."

To effectively manage caseloads and promote personal control and motivation, it is essential for counselors to focus on attitude-based identification rather than relying solely on external motivators like rewards or punishments. Counselors need to recognize that caseload management encompasses more than just building relationships with clients. It involves various tasks such as maintaining case flow, developing referral sources, and completing case recordings, which are integral to the overall functioning required.

These activities should not be seen as additional burdens to counseling, but rather as essential aspects of effective caseload management.

Evaluation

The final factor of evaluation emphasizes the importance of maintaining control as an ongoing and continuous process. Given the constant change and dynamic nature of things and processes, counselors must consistently assess their current situation, define their desired goals, and identify the necessary steps to achieve them.

Evaluation is a critical component at every level of this control model. It is intricately connected with the other four factors and helps maintain a balanced perspective. Evaluation plays a vital role in understanding the limitations of perception and exploring new boundaries as insights expand. It is also instrumental in identifying the sources of reinforcement and selecting those that hold the greatest value. Evaluating the distinction between observations and inferences is another essential aspect. Ultimately, establishing a self-established evaluation system to determine the preferred course of action and the benefits that enhance personal self-worth is crucial. Only through this ongoing evaluation process can control be fully functional and sustainable.

In summary, the acronym PRIME represents the five key factors for establishing personal control: perception, reinforcement, inference-making, motivation, and evaluation. While these factors provide a foundation, it is important to recognize that they alone do not solve control problems. They serve as a starting point for counselors to establish effective personal control. Alongside personal control, counselors must also address the structural aspects of their functioning within the rehabilitation field, whether in agencies, facilities, or other settings. The following section will delve into strategies for gaining control over these structural aspects.

ELEMENTS FOR STRUCTURAL CONTROL

Efficient management of caseloads relies not only on personal control systems but also on strategies to manage and influence external factors, agency objectives, and other structural components. **Structural control** encompasses broader aspects beyond individual control. Scholars such as Cassell and Mulkey (1985), Freemantle (2002), Grubbs et al. (2006), Marshall and Oliver (1995), and Sartain and Baker (1978) have identified four crucial elements of a control system. These elements encompass (a) establishing standards for action or decision-making, (b) considering the implementation of performance criteria, (c) evaluating deviations from standards, and (d) implementing corrective measures for deviations.

The act of making decisions, whether in personal or business contexts, ultimately boils down to the act of choice (Freemantle, 2002). Freemantle (2002) suggests that being aware of available options and having a broader range of choices increases the likelihood of achieving desired outcomes. Alongside personal decision-making processes, standards function as tangible control mechanisms when they are set as limits or boundaries by individuals, organizations, or work units, allowing only specific deviations under exceptional circumstances. A standard can be defined as a predetermined, generally consistent minimum or maximum outcome necessary for successful performance (Cassell & Mulkey, 1985). Standards enable the comparison of ongoing behaviors with past or anticipated future performance, serving as a guiding framework for necessary actions. It is important to have standards at every level of the caseload management process.

As an example, the following standards may be included in a counselor's list:

1. Meet with rehabilitation assistant three times weekly to discuss case files and strategies in working with clients.
2. Do at least four rehabilitation plans in a month.
3. Ensure that timely flow is maintained in serving clients:
   i) Make decisions on referrals (i.e., accept or close from caseload) no later than 3 months after initial referral.
   ii) Move 80% of clients from plan formation to rehabilitation closure within 18 months, 24 months at the most.

Personal standards are crucial for guiding individuals in their day-to-day activities. As an example, counselors may adhere to the following standards in their daily work:

1. Use a daily to-do list for managing activities.
2. Establish a prioritizing system for selecting high- to lower-value activities, such as the A, B, C method.
3. Set aside one self-imposed hour daily for planning, organizing, and coordinating.
4. Make all call-backs within 24 hours of their reception.

When we consider the expectations of others, such as our peers or supervisors, regarding our performance, we are essentially focusing on standards. Standards are crucial because without them, caseload management would become a chaotic and indecisive battleground where rehabilitation professionals' actions would be hindered and uncoordinated.

Standards play a crucial role in guiding the structural aspects of caseload management, and these standards can be established either through legislative mandates or self-imposed regulations. In the public rehabilitation sector, for instance, there are nine standards mandated by legislation that provide guidelines and criteria for evaluating the effectiveness of counselors and the agency as a whole. These standards outline different performance levels against which counselors can gauge their progress toward achieving desired outcomes. Furthermore, rehabilitation organizations themselves impose standards to support their structure, which may include manuals of policies and procedures, service administration guidelines, regional or office rules, and occasional directives from agency directors. In the private rehabilitation sector, accountability is pursued through program evaluation. Shrey and Lacerte (1995) highlight two forms of accountability standards: minimal professional competencies and program evaluation of specialized service delivery systems. Program evaluation offers a systematic approach to regularly assess the outcomes achieved by clients and practitioners after receiving services, as well as the efficiency with which these outcomes are obtained on an ongoing basis (Matkin, 1981).

Effective standards possess common characteristics that make them valuable as behavioral guides. Authorities frequently emphasize that good standards are challenging yet attainable without excessive, prolonged effort. Furthermore, effective standards incorporate an element of competition among rehabilitation units and states, often reminding counselors that their state is the leader in certain aspects or possesses exceptional qualities. This competitive atmosphere motivates counselors to strive for excellence. Another essential characteristic of a sound standard is that it is perceived as fair by individuals responsible for achieving the desired outcomes. Fairness promotes a sense of ownership and commitment to meeting the standard. Additionally, standards must be clearly articulated and quantitatively expressed to ensure they are easily understood and measurable. This clarity enables accurate assessment and evaluation of progress toward meeting the standards.

In summary, good standards in the rehabilitation sector must possess several key characteristics to serve as effective guides for behavior. They should be challenging yet achievable, based on competition, perceived as fair, and clearly comprehensible and quantitatively stated. This balance ensures that standards push individuals and organizations to strive for improvement while remaining within reach. Incorporating an element of competition fosters motivation and innovation among rehabilitation units and states. When standards are perceived as fair, individuals feel a sense of ownership and commitment toward meeting them. Clear and quantifiable standards provide clarity and enable objective evaluation of progress. By embodying these characteristics, good standards play a vital role in guiding behavior and driving continuous improvement in the rehabilitation sector. They provide a framework for setting goals, monitoring progress, and promoting excellence in the delivery of services.

CONSIDERATIONS FOR APPLICATION OF A PERFORMANCE STANDARD

The applicability of a standard as a guiding framework for all counselors, both in public and private practice, depends on six essential elements. These elements encompass (a) the nature of the work task, (b) the shared physical and social environments, (c) the scope of work flow, (d) personal output control, (e) decision-making processes, and (f) a comprehensive understanding of the system's approach. These factors play a crucial role in determining the breadth of application for a standard.

Equated Work Task

In assessing the applicability of a specific standard to all counselors within a work setting, it is vital to consider the scope and complexity of tasks involved. For example, the caseload may consist of a high proportion of specialty cases or exclusively focus on significant disabilities such as blindness/low vision, deafness, traumatic brain injury, co-occurring conditions, various health-related issues, mental health, and so on. Consequently, it becomes crucial to carefully evaluate whether certain caseloads entail additional responsibilities and duties that could potentially burden the work task and necessitate operating under different standards.

Striving for efficiency while juggling multiple standards from various sources can lead to frustration and anxiety among professionals across different fields. Many of these standards prove counterproductive, consuming substantial energy and time on tasks that do not contribute to overall production goals. Hence, it becomes crucial to establish clear, concise, and relevant standards aligned with the objectives of the rehabilitation sector. These standards should be designed to minimize frustration and anxiety by enabling counselors to meet them efficiently and effectively, without compromising their own well-being or the quality of service provided to clients.

Common Physical and Social Environments

Creating a sense of commonality among counselors within an organization is essential when it comes to the physical and social environments in which they work. This commonality ensures that performance expectations remain realistic and prevent the risk of burnout. It would be unjust to hold one counselor's output to the same quantity standard as another counselor who operates under significantly different social and physical constraints. For instance, counselors working in regions facing economic downturn and limited placement possibilities should not be expected to achieve the same output as counselors in areas with greater resources. Similarly, counselors handling specialized caseloads should have different standards compared to those managing general caseloads. By recognizing and accounting for these variations, standards can be tailored to specific circumstances, promoting fairness and ensuring that counselors are not overwhelmed or disadvantaged in their work environments.

Extent of Workflow

The feasibility of a standard that prescribes the number or percentage of individuals to be rehabilitated from a specific caseload becomes evident when considering the availability of referral sources. If there are inadequate referral sources to consistently provide the required number of applicants, it becomes apparent that the standard is impractical. In such cases, it becomes essential to establish different standards that are applicable and attainable in these specific situations. By recognizing the limitations posed by insufficient referral sources, alternative standards can be developed to ensure a realistic and achievable framework for caseload management. These alternative standards may focus on factors such as the quality of services provided, the effectiveness of interventions, or the progress and outcomes of individual clients. Instead of solely measuring the quantity of individuals rehabilitated, these revised standards consider the unique circumstances and challenges faced by counselors in acquiring a sufficient number of applicants.

By adopting more nuanced standards, counselors can be evaluated and supported based on their ability to deliver high-quality services and achieve positive outcomes within the constraints of limited referral sources. This approach acknowledges the reality of the situation while still promoting excellence and accountability within the rehabilitation sector. Ultimately, different standards that adapt to specific situations ensure a fair and reasonable assessment of counselors' performance and enable effective caseload management in challenging circumstances.

Personal Output Control

Standards in rehabilitation units and among counselors are influenced by their control over their output. Factors like task scope, complexity, and personal responsibility for performance must be evaluated. For instance, counselors in different geographic areas with diverse conditions cannot be held to the same performance standards due to varying factors such as client populations, caseload sizes, and supervision structures.

When counselors lack effective control over these conditions, it can hinder their performance. Establishing effective control requires fulfilling all of these conditions. Nonetheless, counselors can proactively address this by utilizing their diagnostic skills to assess the situation and seeking active involvement from their supervisory structure. Taking these steps enables counselors to regain control over their output and meet performance criteria effectively.

Action Decision-Making Processes

Rehabilitation caseload managers must engage in action decisions, which involve setting objectives, being proactive, and maintaining an outcome focus. This process can be compared to planning a trip to a city: first, the destination is determined (objective); then, the necessary planning is done to ensure a smooth trip (proactive response); and finally, the focus remains on reaching the destination in a timely manner (outcome focus). Action decisions allow for the evaluation of competing demands and potential alternatives, such as taking side roads or changing cities, in order to achieve the desired results.

The importance of informed decision-making based on accurate information and agency standards is increasingly recognized within the field of rehabilitation (Cassell & Mulkey, 1985, 2004; Grubbs et al., 2006; Lauver & Harvey, 1997). In order to effectively navigate the selection of decision variables, it is crucial to consider the concept of compromise. Caseload managers must adopt a decision-making approach that integrates and distinguishes the various factors influencing the outcome or focus on a case-by-case basis. This necessitates the establishment of a guiding philosophy or viewpoint that shapes their decision-making process (Cassell & Mulkey, 2004). By incorporating these principles, rehabilitation professionals can make well-informed decisions that promote individual progress and overall success in caseload management.

Cassell and Mulkey (1985) and Grubbs et al. (2006) emphasize the importance of setting achievable objectives aligned with rehabilitation standards. These objectives should adhere to the SMART framework, meaning they should be Specific, Measurable, Attainable, Relevant, and Time-specific. The SMART acronym provides a structural framework for all stakeholders involved in the decision-making process. It is crucial to differentiate between objectives and intentions, and during the planning stage, feasible objectives should be established. Action decisions rely on personal and agency standards and pave the way for desired event outcomes. While uncertainties may persist, effective caseload managers must make informed decisions based on the best available information to maximize the potential for desired outcomes.

SYSTEMS THEORY AND APPROACH

Systems Theory

Systems theory is an important framework for understanding the complex nature of human behavior and how it relates to the broader social and cultural systems in which people live (Constantine et al., 2007). One important application of systems theory is in the field of rehabilitation counseling, where it has been used to understand the many factors that can influence an individual's ability to recover from a disability or injury. According to systems theory, rehabilitation counseling must take into account the many different systems that an individual is a part of, including their family, social networks, healthcare providers, and the broader cultural and economic systems in which they live (Goode et al., 2017). A key aspect of rehabilitation counseling is promoting personal control and self-efficacy in individuals with disabilities or injuries. In this context, personal control refers to an individual's belief in their ability to influence the outcomes of their lives, while self-efficacy refers to an individual's belief in their ability to achieve specific goals or outcomes (Bandura, 1977). Rehabilitation counselors support and promote personal control and self-efficacy in individuals by working with them to identify their strengths and abilities and by developing strategies for overcoming barriers and achieving their goals (Constantine et al., 2007).

According to the systems approach to personal control, an individual's sense of control is not only influenced by their own actions but also by external factors such as their social environment and cultural norms (Goode et al., 2017). For example, an individual's beliefs about disability and their ability to recover may be influenced by societal attitudes and beliefs about disability. Rehabilitation counselors must take these external factors into account when working with individuals with disabilities or injuries and must work to challenge negative attitudes and beliefs that may be hindering their clients' progress (Constantine et al., 2007).

In addition to promoting personal control and self-efficacy, rehabilitation counselors must also consider the many different systems that can either support or hinder an individual's recovery. For example, an individual's family and social networks can be a source of support and encouragement, while healthcare providers and insurance systems can present significant barriers to accessing needed services and support (Goode et al., 2017). Rehabilitation counselors must work with their clients to navigate these systems and to advocate for their clients' needs within larger systems that may be resistant to change (Constantine et al., 2007).

Systems theory provides an important framework for understanding the complex nature of human behavior and how it relates to the broader social and cultural systems in which people live. Rehabilitation counseling is a field that can greatly benefit from a systems approach, as it involves working with individuals who are navigating complex systems that can either support or hinder their recovery. By promoting personal control and self-efficacy in individuals with disabilities or injuries, and by working to navigate and challenge the many different systems that can influence their clients' lives, rehabilitation counselors can help promote positive outcomes and improve the quality of life for their clients.

Systems Approach

A **systems approach** signifies that without an adopted or self-constructed system of operations, effective practices will never evolve. All successful caseload managers employ a system or series of interconnected subsystems on which to base action and practice (Cassell & Mulkey, 2004; Grubbs et al., 2006). Regardless, having a systems lens is the only approach that will sustain a caseload manager in the face of multiple standards and demands in the profession of rehabilitation.

In a complex and diverse rehabilitation environment, professionals must adopt a systems perspective as their modus operandi to navigate the challenges they face. The "by the seat of the pants" approach is insufficient (Cassell & Mulkey, 2004). Caseload management operates independently from the politically mandated rehabilitation landscape, leading to a multitude of demands and competing priorities for rehabilitation managers. The organization itself has its own goals, objectives, and standards to uphold, while client populations have advocacy groups questioning professional decision-making (Cassell & Mulkey, 2004). Additionally, adjunctive groups and organizations that clients engage with further complicate the caseload manager's decision-making process. In such a complex landscape, setting priorities and taking action require a systematic evaluation and sometimes a delicate balancing act between competing standards and demands. Grubbs et al. (2006) emphasize that the most crucial guiding principle for an effective caseload manager is to develop a self-constructed system of operations aligned with the organization's standards, policies, and procedures.

Consistency and effectiveness in caseload and case management practices are essential, and to achieve this, there should be a level of commonality across counselors within an organization, particularly in the physical and social environments they operate in. This ensures that counselors are not subjected to undue burnout when their performance is compared to others operating under different constraints. For instance, counselors working in economically disadvantaged areas with limited placement opportunities cannot be expected to meet the same output standards as those in resource-rich areas. Similarly, counselors with specialized caseloads focusing on specific disability categories should have different standards than those managing general caseloads. In an environment where demands outweigh quality responses, survival necessitates differentiating standards. Ultimately, the convergence of consistency and effectiveness in caseload and case management practices aligns with the principles of system ideology.

DEVIATION ASSESSMENT

Once action and systems standards have been set, the subsequent crucial stage in establishing structural control is evaluating deviations from the established control. This assessment serves as the foundation for implementing corrective measures. There are two key strategies in deviation measurements that hold significance for counselors: strategic measurement points and sensitive limits testing. Counselors must strategically position measurement points at various stages of the caseload management process to monitor deviations before they escalate into crises. These measurement points assist in achieving the objectives of each standard and ensure they remain within manageable boundaries. By incorporating these proactive practices, counselors engage in problem prevention activities, enhancing their ability to address potential issues in advance.

To avoid unnecessary corrective measures for minor deviations, it is important to allow for a certain level of tolerance in counselor activities. By establishing well-defined standards and implementing a self-initiated measurement system, experienced counselors can accurately assess the magnitude of deviations and determine the appropriate course of action, if required. The decision-making process for addressing these deviations will be further discussed in Chapter 6.

DEVIATION CORRECTION

Once standards or guidelines for behavior have been established and a monitoring system is in place to provide feedback, the next crucial step in management is implementing corrective actions for deviations. These corrective actions are vital for stabilizing the management system and ensuring ongoing effectiveness. This aspect of structural control can be likened to a thermostatic system, where proactive measures are taken through built-in measurement controls to initiate automatic actions before crises or "compelled actions" arise. This approach reflects a proactive stance toward maintaining control and addressing deviations promptly.

To incorporate thermostatic controls into caseload management activities, it is crucial for an effective caseload manager to anticipate alternatives and establish a comprehensive counselor file system that indicates when a change is necessary for a client, triggering required, mandatory, or crisis-oriented actions. Moreover, corrective actions often involve reassessing actions that have already been taken or are needed in the remaining managerial functions of planning, organizing, directing, and coordinating. This iterative process ensures continuous evaluation and adjustment to maintain optimal performance in caseload management.

Structural control in caseload management requires the manager-counselor to go beyond administrative and tangible elements and consider the integration of personal control factors. This holistic approach, often referred to as the gestalt or "big picture," is achieved when the two control areas are interlinked and coordinated. By acknowledging the importance of both administrative structures and personal control, the manager-counselor can establish a comprehensive and effective system that addresses all aspects of caseload management.

SUMMARY

In this chapter, the focus is on the control aspects of caseload management. As discussed in this chapter, personal elements are crucial for effective outcomes in the rehabilitation process, and personal control elements within the process were discussed in detail. Rotter's locus of control conceptualization was introduced as a valuable concept for the rehabilitation field. The PRIME factors for establishing control were presented, and the elements of control were discussed to prepare the caseload manager for the personal and system approaches to action decisions encountered in field practices. The chapter concludes with a discussion on standards for action and deviation assessment.

It is important to note that control plays a central role in a management system, and the caseload manager must understand that without considering control, all efforts in the caseload management process may be futile.

QUESTIONS FOR DISCUSSION

1. Do you believe most individuals who become clients in the rehabilitation system have an internal or external control position? Why or why not?

2. Organizations exert many formal controls on rehabilitation professionals. What are some of the *informal controls,* and how does one's personal belief system affect the perception surrounding these *informal controls*?

3. Generate and discuss examples of perceptual limitations for personnel in public and private sectors of rehabilitation.

4. A rehabilitation professional has an *external* locus of control orientation. What are the likely responses toward clients with the same orientation? What would be the opposite orientation or perspectives?

5. A rehabilitation professional has an *internal* locus of control orientation. What are the likely responses toward clients with the same orientation? What would be the opposite orientation or perspectives?

6. Discuss and explore the proactive and reactive orientations in rehabilitation settings.

7. Regardless of the rehabilitation setting, organization controls, and type of caseload, a rehabilitation professional should always have control over a number of variables. Discuss what variables are controllable and why.

PUTTING IT INTO PRACTICE

Ask yourself these questions to target issues or concerns with the function of control in rehabilitation case and caseload management.

1. How does the concept of personal control manifest in your rehabilitation practice, and how does it influence clients' experiences and outcomes during their rehabilitation journey?

2. In what specific ways does your control as a prominent element in management impact the overall effectiveness or potential shortcomings of rehabilitation programs and services?

3. When critically evaluating your personal control position, do you find that it enhances or obstructs your role as a rehabilitation counselor? Are there any aspects that could be improved or adjusted to better support your work?

A robust set of instructor resources designed to supplement this text is located at http://connect.springerpub.com/content/book/978-0-8261-5963-2. Qualifying instructors may request access by emailing textbook@springerpub.com.

REFERENCES

Anuar, A., Anuar, A., Aden, E., Yahya, F., Ghazali, N. M., & Chunggat, N. A. (2021). Stress and coping styles of parents with children with learning disabilities. *Global Business and Management Research, 13*(2), 146.

Bandura, A. (1977). Self-efficacy: Toward a unifying theory of behavioral change. *Psychological Review, 84*(2), 191–215. https://doi.org/10.1037/0033-295x.84.2.191

Baumeister, R. F., Schmeichel, B. J., & Vohs, K. D. (2007). Self-regulation and the executive function: The self as controlling agent. In A. W. Kruglanski & E. T. Higgins (Eds.), *Social psychology: Handbook of basic principles* (pp. 516–539). The Guilford Press.

Berridge, K. C. (2018). Evolving concepts of emotion and motivation. *Frontiers in Psychology, 9*, 1–20. https://doi.org/fpsyg.2018.01647

Cassell, J. L., & Mulkey, S. W. (1985). *Rehabilitation caseload management: Concepts and practice.* Pro-Ed.

Cassell, J. L., & Mulkey, S. W. (2004). Caseload management. In T. F. Riggar & D. R. Maki (Eds.), *Handbook of rehabilitation counseling* (pp. 252–270). Springer Publishing Company.

Cassell, J. L., Mulkey, S. W., & Egen, C. (1997). Systematic practice: Case and caseload management. In D. R. Maki & T. F. Riggar (Eds.), *Rehabilitation counseling: Profession and practice* (pp. 214–233). Springer Publishing Company.

Çelik Ağırman, Ü. H., ve Naktiyok, A. (2018). Emotional intelligence traits and entrepreneurial intention in the context of perception of self-efficacy. *Journal of Social and Humanities Sciences Research, 5*(28), 3253–3262.

Chen, T., Li, F., & Leung, K. (2016). When does supervisor support encourage innovative behavior? Opposite moderating effects of general self-efficacy and internal locus of control. *Personnel Psychology, 69*(1), 123–158.

Chukwu, N. E., Okoye, U. O., Onyeneho, N. G., & Okeibunor, J. C. (2019). Coping strategies of families of persons with learning disability in Imo state of Nigeria. *Journal of Health, Population, and Nutrition, 38*(1), 9. https://doi.org/10.1186/s41043-019-0168-2

Constantine, M. G., Hage, S. M., Kindaichi, M. M., & Bryant, R. M. (2007). Social justice and multicultural issues: Implications for the practice and training of counselors and counseling psychologists. *Journal of Counseling & Development, 85*(1), 24–29. https://doi.org/10.1002/j.1556-6678.2007.tb00440.x

Corey, M. S., & Corey, G. (1997). *Groups: Process and practice* (5th ed.) Brooks/Cole Publishing.

Crimando, W. (2004). A model of cognitive-affective processing: Implications for career counseling and rehabilitation. *Journal of Rehabilitation, 70*(4), 12–19.

Cuevas, S., Vang, C., Chen, R. K., & Saladin, S. P. (2019). Determinants of self-efficacy among individuals who are hard-of-hearing. *Journal of Rehabilitation, 85*(2), 37–46.

De Tommaso, M., & Turatto, M. (2022). Control over reward gain unlocks the reward cue motivational salience. *Motivation and Emotion, 47*(4), 495–508. https://doi.org/10.1007/s11031-022-10001-2

Dionne, C. E., Bourbonnais, R., Frémont, P., Rossignol, M., Stock, S. R., & Laperrière, È. (2013). Obstacles to and facilitators of return to work after work-disabling back pain: The workers' perspective. *Journal of Occupational Rehabilitation, 23*(2), 280–289. https://doi.org/10.1007/s10926-012-9399-4

Dua, P. S. (1970). Comparison of the effects of behavioral oriented action and psychotherapy reeducation on introversion extraversion, emotionality, and internal external control. *Journal of Counseling Pscyhology, 17*, 567–572.

Freemantle, J. (2002). Case management in vocational rehabilitation: An exploratory study. *Journal of Vocational Rehabilitation, 17*(2), 115–122.

Golden, T. D., & Veiga, J. F. (2005). The impact of extent of telecommuting on job satisfaction: Resolving inconsistent findings. *Journal of Management, 31*(2), 301–318. https://doi.org/10.1177/0149206304271768

Goode, C., Keefer, L. A., Branscombe, N. R., & Molina, L. E. (2017). Group identity as a source of threat and means of compensation: Establishing personal control through group identification and ideology. *European Journal of Social Psychology, 47*(3), 259–272. https://doi.org/10.1002/ejsp.2259

Grubbs, L. A., Cassell, J. L., & Mulkey, S. W. (2006). *Rehabilitation caseload management: Concepts and practice* (2nd ed.). Springer Publishing Company.

Hall, H. R., & Graff, J. C. (2011). The relationships among adaptive behaviors of children with autism, family support, parenting stress, and coping. *Issues in Comprehensive Pediatric Nursing, 34,* 4–25. https://doi.org/10.3109/01460862.2011.555270

Haney, W. V. (1971). *The uncalculated risk (introductory manual for the film).* Roundtable Films.

Hertel, E., Cheadle, A., Matthys, J., Coleman, K., Gray, M., Robbins, M., Tufte, J., & Hsu C. (2019). Engaging patients in primary care design: An evaluation of a novel approach to codesigning care. *Health Expectations, 22*(4), 609–616 . https://doi.org/10.1111/hex.12909

Introna, I. D. (1997). *Management, information, and power.* MacMillan.

Karsh, N., Haklay, I., Raijman, N., Lampel, A., & Custers, R. (2021). Control alters risk-taking: The motivating impact of action-effectiveness in different risk contexts. *Motivation Science, 7*(4), 475–486. https://doi.org/10.1037/mot0000244

Key, S. (2002). Perceived managerial discretion: An analysis of individual ethical intentions. *Journal of Managerial Issues, 14*(2), 218–233. https://www.jstor.org/stable/40604385

Kreider, C. M., Medina, S., & Slamka, M. R. (2019). Strategies for coping with time-related and productivity challenges of young people with learning disabilities and attention-deficit/hyperactivity disorder. *Children, 6*(2), 28. https://doi.org/10.3390/children6020028

Kurtek, P. (2018). Prosocial vs antisocial coping and general life satisfaction of youth with mild intellectual disability. *Journal of Intellectual Disability Research, 62*(6), 581–592. https://doi.org/10.1111/jir.12497

Lauver, P., & Harvey, D. R. (1997). *The practical counselor: Elements of effective helping.* Brooks/Cole.

Lee, T. W., Hom, P., Eberly, M., & Li, J. (2017). Managing employee retention and turnover with 21st century ideas. *Organizational Dynamics, 47*(2), 88–98. https://doi.org/10.1016/j.orgdyn.2017.08.004

Livneh, H. (2000). Psychosocial adaptation to spinal cord injury: The role of coping strategies. *Journal of Applied Rehabilitation Counseling, 31*(2), 3–10.

Luszczynska, A., & Schwarzer, R. (2005). The role of self-efficacy in health self-regulation. In W. Greve, K. Rothermund, & D. Wentura (Eds.), *The adaptive self: Personal continuity and intentional self-development* (pp. 137–152). Hogrefe & Huber Publishers.

Marshall, K. T., & Oliver, R. M. (1995). *Decision making and forecasting.* Mc-Graw Hill.

Matkin, R. E. (1981). Program evaluation: Searching for accountability in private rehabilitation. *Journal of Rehabilitation, 47*(1), 65–68.

Mertes, A., & Harden, T. (2019). What life care planners need to know about the professional discipline of rehabilitation counselors. *Journal of Life Care Planning, 17*(1), 39–44.

Millet, P., & Sandberg, K. W. (2003). Locus of control and its relationship with vocational rehabilitation of unemployed sick leaves in Sweden. *Journal of Vocational Rehabilitation, 19*(1), 59–66.

Milligan, K., Badali, P., & Spiroiu, F. (2015). Using Integra mindfulness martial arts to address self-regulation challenges in youth with learning disabilities: A qualitative exploration. *Journal of Child and Family Studies, 24*(3), 562–575. https://doi.org/10.1007/s10826-013-9868-1

Mizuno, A., Karim, H. T., Newmark, J., Khan, F., Rosenblatt, M. J., Neppach, A. M., Lowe, M., Aizenstein, H. J., Mennin, D. S., & Andreescu, C. (2022). Thinking of me or thinking of you? Behavioral correlates of self vs. other centered worry and reappraisal in late-life. *Frontiers in Psychiatry, 13,* 780745. https://doi.org/10.3389/fpsyt.2022.780745

Müller, H. (2021). On the psychological importance of control and valorisation in psychiatric environments. *European Journal of Public Health, 31*(Suppl. 3). https://doi.org/10.1093/eurpub/ckab164.872

Ordway, A. R., Johnson, K. L., Amtmann, D., Bocell, F. D., Jensen, M. P., & Molton, I. R. (2019). The relationship between resilience, self-efficacy, and employment in people with physical disabilities. *Rehabilitation Counseling Bulletin, 63*(4), 195–205. https://doi.org/10.1177/0034355219886660

Peter, C., Müller, R., Post, M. W. M., van Leeuwen, C. M. C., Werner, C. S., Geyh, S., & Swiss Spinal Cord Injury Cohort Study Group. (2015). Depression in spinal cord injury: Assessing the role of psychological Resources. *Rehabilitation Psychology, 60*(1), 67–80. https://doi.org/10.1037/rep0000021

Rotter, J. B. (1966). Generalized expectancies for internal versus external control of reinforcement. *Psychological Monographs, 80*(1), 1–28. https://doi.org/10.1037/h0092976

Rotter, J. B. (1975). Some problems and misconceptions related to the construct of internal versus external control of reinforcement. *Journal of Consulting and Clinical Psychology, 43,* 56–67.

Rubin, S. E., & Rubin, N. M. (1988). *Contemporary challenges to the rehabilitation counseling profession.* Paul H. Brookes Publishing.

Russell, M., Ames, H., Dunn, C., Beckwith, S., & Holmes, S. A. (2021). Appraisals of disability and psychological adjustment in veterans with spinal cord injuries. *The Journal of Spinal Cord Medicine, 44*(6), 958–965. https://doi.org/10.1080/10790268.2020.1754650

Ryan, R. M., & Deci, E. L. (2000). Self-determination theory and the facilitation of intrinsic motivation, social development, and well-being. *The American Psychologist, 55,* 68–78. https://doi.org/10.1037//0003-066x.55.1.68

Santana, M. C., & Fouad, N. (2017). Development and validation of a self-care behavior inventory. *Training and Educaiton in Professional Psychology*, *11*(1), 140–145. https://doi.org/10.1037/tep0000142

Sartain, A., & Baker, A. (1978). *The supervisor and his job*. McGraw-Hill.

Sasse, N., Gibbons, H., Wilson, L., Martinez, R., Sehmisch, S., von Wild, K., & von Steinbüchel, N. (2014). Coping strategies in individuals after traumatic brain injury: Associations with health-related quality of life. *Disability and Rehabilitation*, *36*(25), 2152–2160. https://doi.org/10.3109/09638288.2014.893029

Savickas, M. L. (2011). Constructing careers: Actor, agent and author. *Journal of Employment Counseling*, *48*(4), 179–181. https://doi.org/10.1002/j.2161-1920.2011.tb01109.x

Schwarzer, R., & Jerusalem, M. (2010). The general self-efficacy scale (GSE). *Anxiety, Stress and Coping*, *12*(1), 329–345.

Selander, J., Marnetoft, S. U., Asell, M., Selander, U., & Millet, P. (2008). Internal locus of control and vocational rehabilitation. *Work (Reading, Mass.)*, *30*(2), 149–155. https://pubmed.ncbi.nlm.nih.gov/18413930/

Shrey, D. E., & Lacerte, M. (1995). *Principles and practices of disability management in industry*. St. Lucie Press.

Skinner, E. A. (2013). *Perceived control, motivation, and coping*. Sage.

Skinner, E. A., & Edge, K. (2002). Self-determination, coping, and development. In E. L. Deci & R. M. Ryan (Eds.), *Handbook of self-determination research* (pp. 297–337). University of Rochester Press.

Sprong, M. E., Soldner, J. L., & Dallas, B. K. (2018). Emergency preparedness knowledge and confidence in providing services for people with disabilities: An exploratory analysis among rehabilitation counseling students. *The Journal of Rehabilitation*, *84*(3), 57–65.

Strauser, D. R., Ketz, K., & Keim, J. (2002). The relationship between self-efficacy, locus of control and work personality. *Journal of Rehabilitation*, *68*(1), 20–26.

Taderera, C., & Hall, H. (2017). Challenges faced by parents of children with learning disabilities in Opuwo, Namibia. *African Journal of Disability*, *6*, 283. https://doi.org/10.4102/ajod.v6i0.283

Vanovenberghe, C., Du Bois, M., Lauwerier, E., & Van den Broeck, A. (2021). Does motivation predict return to work? A longitudinal analysis. *Journal of Occupational Health*, *63*, e12284. https://doi.org/10.1002/1348-9585.12284

Van Voorhis, P., Braswell, M., & Lester D. (2000). *Correctional counseling & rehabilitation* (4th ed.) Anderson Publishing Co.

Whitson, J. A., & Galinsky, A. D. (2008). Lacking control increases illusory pattern perception. *Science*, *322*(5898), 115–117. https://doi.org/10.1126/science.1159845

CHAPTER 6

Effective Decision-Making and Rationale for Professional Practice

LEARNING OBJECTIVES

By the end of this chapter, learners will be able to:

- Understand the relevance and importance of effective decision-making in the field of rehabilitation, recognizing its impact on client outcomes and overall professional practice.
- Identify and analyze decision patterns and structures commonly used in rehabilitation settings, such as the apex, base, and consequential decision patterns, to facilitate informed decision-making.
- Explore the rehabilitation decision model, examining its components and stages and how it can guide decision-making in rehabilitation counseling practice.
- Familiarize themselves with additional models of decision-making, including the behavioral, directive, analytical, conceptual, behavioral, and sequential models, and understand their applicability in rehabilitation contexts.
- Recognize the influence of cultural norms and biases in decision processes, and develop an awareness of conscious and unconscious biases that may impact decision-making in rehabilitation settings.
- Examine the concept of a decision variable schema, understanding how it influences the consideration and evaluation of different variables and factors in the decision-making process.

INTRODUCTION

Effective decision-making is a vital skill that permeates various aspects of our personal and professional lives. Whether in business, healthcare, or everyday situations, the ability to make informed and sound decisions can greatly impact outcomes and pave the way for success. This chapter explores the key elements that contribute to effective decision-making, particularly within the context of rehabilitation services.

Decisions made by rehabilitation professionals hold significant weight, as they directly influence the well-being and quality of life for individuals with disabilities. The complexities and unique challenges inherent in the rehabilitation field necessitate a thoughtful and systematic approach to decision-making (Athanasou, 2015). Therefore, understanding the fundamental elements that underpin effective decision-making is crucial for rehabilitation counselors and case managers to optimize service delivery and achieve desired outcomes.

This chapter will explore a range of concepts and models aimed at improving decision-making abilities within the field of rehabilitation. Emphasis will be placed on the significance of actively participating in decision-making processes and understanding the effects of both proactive and passive approaches. Furthermore, we will analyze decision-making frameworks and strategies designed to assist rehabilitation professionals in effectively managing intricate scenarios and finding the right balance amidst the various factors involved in delivering personalized services.

Through the incorporation of the key elements of effective decision-making, rehabilitation counselors can enhance their capacity to make informed choices, develop comprehensive plans, and take intentional actions. This, in turn, elevates their overall effectiveness in supporting individuals with disabilities as they progress toward their rehabilitation goals.

RELEVANCE OF DECISION-MAKING

Due to the specific responsibilities assigned to them in both public and private settings, rehabilitation professionals are inherently tasked with delivering timely and coordinated services to multiple individuals simultaneously. To effectively fulfill their roles, rehabilitation practitioners must address rehabilitation needs, identify appropriate services, provide those services, and carry out the necessary actions outlined in individualized plans. While recognizing individual needs and service availability form the foundation of rehabilitation counseling knowledge, the actual provision of services necessitates counselors to exhibit advanced decision-making abilities. Indeed, Moyer and Crews (2017) underscore the significance of **ethical decision-making** skills in effectively evaluating multiple pieces of information, enabling successful management of the diverse components within the overall caseload.

Rehabilitation counselors cannot perform their service-delivery duties unless they are capable of making decisions. While caseload managers should avoid making hasty and impulsive decisions based on incomplete or inadequate information, they must be willing and capable of making decisions even when faced with ambiguous or inconclusive data. In other words, rehabilitation counselors cannot postpone service provision until every inconsistency is resolved or until the data unequivocally support their decisions (Grubbs et al., 2006). Delays in decision-making often hinder the timely delivery of services and undermine responsible and cost-effective rehabilitation practice. It is important to recognize that by not making a decision, the counselor is effectively choosing not to deliver services at that particular time.

Rehabilitation counselors are not afforded the luxury of choice when it comes to decision-making. Due to their caseload management responsibilities and their crucial role in the rehabilitation process, counselors inherently act as decision-makers. The decisions they make, as well as those they fail to make, significantly impact their overall effectiveness in delivering services. Decision-making approaches can be categorized as either active (involving thinking, planning, and taking action) or inactive (resulting in minimal or no action). Consequently, the case manager's approach to decision-making directly influences whether progress is made or not within the case (Brunsson, 2007). Hence, the extent to which rehabilitation counselors can apply their knowledge in assisting individuals with disabilities depends on their ability to make active decisions and follow through with the necessary actions. Therefore, alongside acquiring a knowledge base, rehabilitation counselors must establish a framework for organizing and planning their management activities. This framework enables counselors to navigate the multitude of variables associated with delivering individualized services in complex situations. This section explores decision-making concepts, offers useful decision-making models, and presents a model specifically tailored for decision-making in the context of rehabilitation. These guidelines provide counselors with the initial tools to ensure the rehabilitation process advances toward well-defined goals.

A DECISION-MAKING STRUCTURE

ABC Decision Patterns

The pinnacle of rehabilitation decisions is built upon three fundamental components: **apex decisions, base decisions,** and **consequential decisions.** The initial exploration of these components was conducted by Cassell and Mulkey (1985) and later expanded upon by Grubbs et al. (2006), establishing the foundation of the **ABC decision patterns** for case-load managers (refer to **Figure 6.1**). The identified decision patterns provide a logical framework for understanding the decisions essential for effective performance as a reha-bilitation counselor-manager. Undoubtedly, decision-making plays a significant role in the counselor's daily responsibilities, whether it involves guiding clients through evaluation procedures, determining vocational goals, facilitating return to work, evaluating eligibility, or selecting appropriate rehabilitation services.

Decision-making is a learned skill that often relies on trial-and-error experiences to gen-eralize across various situations requiring choices among multiple alternatives. This process

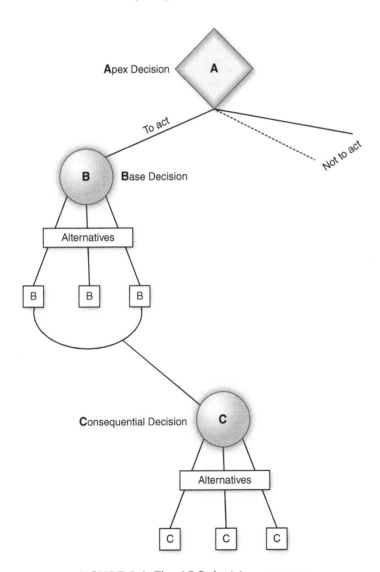

FIGURE 6.1 The ABC decision patterns.

often becomes ingrained as a "habit" when approaching decision situations (Vrchota & Švárová, 2015). However, a frequent lack of awareness or disregard for a systematic approach to alternative selection can lead to unfavorable programmatic outcomes. When such undesirable outcomes occur frequently, there is a risk of developing concurrent negative attitudes that can influence how a counselor-manager approaches future decision-making situations. The fear of making another poor decision may result in a reluctance to commit, which can be perceived as procrastination. Therefore, the first decision faced by the counselor-manager is whether to take action or not, known as the apex decision.

APEX DECISION

In any decision-making situation, the decision-maker is initially confronted with a choice between two alternative courses of action: to perform the action or not to perform it. This initial choice is referred to as the *apex decision*, as it serves as the foundation from which all other decisions stem. What makes it unique is that there are only two alternatives to consider (action or inaction), with the possibility of conveying a decision through inaction without noticeable effort. Apex decisions are often easily made (e.g., "I've been meaning to do that, but . . ."). However, in certain situations, the apex decision can be more challenging (e.g., "I'm not entirely sure what to do, but let's start with . . .").

Figure 6.1 depicts the extended duration of an inaction decision over several months. As the number of months (indicated by the broken line) increases, the likelihood of taking action decreases proportionally. In other words, the longer a decision to act is postponed, the more difficult it may become to implement any change at all (Arnold, 1976; Cassell & Mulkey, 1985). Situations evolve over time, exemplified by a scenario where an individual initially seeks rehabilitation services due to an urgent need for employment. However, 6 months later (counselor's decision of inaction) as the counselor-manager is ready to begin working toward rehabilitation goals (counselor's action decision), it is discovered that the potential client has been working for 2 months and is satisfactorily employed. Several variables have changed within this time frame, and the person no longer requires employment assistance.

Procrastination often hinders the decision to take action. However, rehabilitation counselors frequently encounter difficulties related to uncertainty. Caseloads consist of both symbolic and factual information about individuals, and as these symbols and facts intersect, decision situations arise. For instance, an individual completes an application (symbolic) expressing their interest in rehabilitation services to support their employment efforts. However, the merging of factual details (e.g., female, 53 years old, no work history, completed ninth grade, diabetic) creates opportunities for decisions that extend beyond the boundaries of rational certainty. Managing inherently involves confronting uncertainty by making "judgments" that go beyond mere facts and logic. The process of making action decisions is facilitated by a combination of human factors: intelligence and courage. Sometimes, internal pressures (e.g., guilt, feeling the need to address a situation) or external directives (e.g., a supervisor urging to move forward with a large number of applicant cases) are necessary to access the action alternative presented by the apex decision. As a result, some counselors feel comfortable making timely apex decisions that lead to base decisions. In contrast, other counselors may be influenced by internal or external forces that lead to inappropriate decision-making processes.

BASE DECISION

After choosing the "action" alternative as the apex decision, the caseload manager is then confronted with the task of selecting techniques and strategies that are likely to facilitate the progression of clients from their current circumstances to their desired rehabilitation goals. Whether the rehabilitation goal is specific, such as a return to prior employment, or more general, such as attaining remunerative employment, there is always an identifiable starting situation and a desired end result for each applicant in the caseload.

The *base decision*, in essence, is the alternative that is chosen as the most suitable means of assisting the client in transitioning from their present circumstances to the desired rehabilitation goal or negotiated settlement. Detailed procedures on how to make base decisions will be discussed later when examining decision models. At this point, it is crucial to emphasize that both the caseload manager and the client should identify the course of action that will contribute most effectively to achieving the rehabilitation goal. Base decisions, therefore, are decisions that represent the optimal choice leading to the negotiated settlement or the best possible outcome for the individual. It is important to acknowledge that assuming the existence of an "optimal" course of action implies that among the alternatives being considered, one stands out as the most favorable. The identification of the base decision can be relatively straightforward by eliminating less desirable alternatives. However, it should be noted that base decisions are not without risks, as caseload managers often have to make decisions based on ambiguous or inconclusive information.

CONSEQUENTIAL DECISION

The third type of decision that caseload managers are required to make pertains to the consequences of the base decision. In some cases, a rehabilitation program may not progress as initially planned. Various factors, such as the rejection of the proposed action plan by the workers compensation board or changes in conditions (e.g., client relocation), can divert the implementation of the base decision or hinder the achievement of rehabilitation objectives. In such instances, the caseload manager or the client is faced with the need to make a consequential decision. A consequence of the base decision "breaking down" is a change of plans. For instance, if new information necessitates additions to the existing program, such as modifying the vocational goal and implementing subsequent program initiatives, or even considering case closure, a consequential decision becomes necessary. Therefore, consequential decisions involve determining whether the program can proceed with modifications (such as supplemental or amended intermediate objectives) to ultimately achieve the original long-term goal, or if the prevailing circumstances hinder any further action toward the original vocational objective.

An examination of **Figure 6.1** reaffirms the conceptualization of apex, base, and consequential decision patterns utilized by rehabilitation caseload managers. However, it is important to recognize that not all decisions made by caseload managers can be solely derived from available data. There are instances when the appropriate decision is to temporarily postpone making a decision related to programmatic initiatives. Fulcher (1965) drew attention to the notion that while most decisions involve taking some form of action, a decision of "no action" can still be a very sound decision. This "no action" decision is distinct from a passive approach to decision-making and should not be confused with procrastination. To illustrate, an action decision could involve delaying the development of a rehabilitation program until the results of an admission examination or surgical procedure are known. The fundamental procedures for making responsible decisions remain the same, even when one of the considered alternatives is to refrain from taking any action.

REHABILITATION DECISION-MAKING MODEL

The important terms **theory** and **model** are used in a variety of ways through the literature on decision-making. However, each term commands universal respect for its contributions toward understanding the dynamics of decision structure. An exhaustive account of meaningful and aired theories and/or models would likely have limited influence on developing or shaping an appropriate, individualized approach to decision-making by rehabilitation professionals. Therefore, the next section will emphasize selected components of various theories and models to encourage the caseload manager to develop and use a preferred decision-making structure. A rehabilitation decision model is offered for consideration in **Figure 6.2** later in this chapter. Such a model may be helpful to the caseload manager as an organizational tool leading to effective personal and professional decision-making.

Need for a Process

In the role of a decision-maker, the rehabilitation counselor assumes the responsibilities of interpreting, classifying, describing, explaining, evaluating, prescribing, and predicting. Each of these activities involves making value judgments, and they often intersect within intricate problem contexts. Rehabilitation counseling places particular emphasis on evaluation and prescription, which entail identifying and resolving problems. These processes require the counselor to make thoughtful value judgments regarding various aspects, including the specific situations such as available resources and the job market; the institutions involved such as agencies, companies, and communities; and the people encompassing clients, families, lawyers, and vendors. Evaluating the vocational potential of each client and devising a program of services aimed at helping them realize their anticipated potential are vital obligations of the rehabilitation counselor.

Typically, the process of decision-making involves (a) identifying objectives, (b) exploring alternative options and their consequences, and (c) selecting the optimal alternative by eliminating choices with greater consequences (Anthony, 1988; Brill, 1995; Cohen & Cohen, 1999; O'Shaughnessy, 1972). This framework is widely utilized by professionals in the rehabilitation field and proves effective in many decision-making situations. However, there are instances where this model falls short in accommodating the available client-situation data. Particularly, complex decision models become necessary when dealing with issues that involve significant disability problems. For instance, models may tend to overlook the crucial steps of problem identification (despite its inherent presence) and evaluating its impact on the identified objectives.

Rehabilitation practitioners face a range of unique decisions that call for both simple and complex decision models, as illustrated in **Figure 6.2** reflecting the rehabilitation decision model (Grubbs et al., 2006). For straightforward decisions like choosing a physician for a medical examination or identifying a case zone, a simple decision model suffices. However, more intricate decisions such as determining vocational goals and evaluating functional limitations often require a complex decision model. These complex models may involve considering factors like time limits, estimating probabilities, or clarifying values. Irrespective of the decision's complexity, caseload managers must possess the ability to select appropriate decision-making models that align with the specific problem at hand. This function is facilitated by employing a systematic decision-making model, which involves following distinct sequential steps to address a precisely defined problem (Grubbs et al., 2006). In essence, caseload managers need to exhibit flexibility in selecting decision models since human-service problem situations are highly individualized with few commonalities. It is crucial to consider all possible alternatives and identify probable vocationally related goals before determining the "best alternative." Therefore, rehabilitation counselors should recognize the importance of systematic models that are relevant to specific decision situations, as mere repetition of decision-making does not necessarily enhance skill (Arnold, 1976).

Classifying Categories of Decisions

Rehabilitation counselors in the management of rehabilitation caseloads make decisions that can be classified in various ways, depending on the available information. Miller and Starr (1967) propose five classifications for problem decision-making situations: (a) *certainty,* (b) *risk,* (c) *uncertainty,* (d) *partial information,* and (e) *conflict.* These may be remembered using the acronym **CRUPIC.** Caseload managers often encounter decisions falling into each of these categories. Rehabilitation counselors face both routine decisions, involving familiar problem situations, and nonroutine decisions, involving unfamiliar problem situations, on a daily basis. To illustrate, let's explore how each of the five identified categories relates to a specific caseload management situation that requires a decision from the counselor-manager.

"*Decision-making under certainty*" can sometimes be problematic for the rehabilitation counselor. To provide an example, let's consider one of the initial decisions that a rehabilitation counselor faces: scheduling a client for a medical examination or additional medical evaluation. It is certain that an appointment can be arranged with any qualified physician. However, when it comes to the routine decision of selecting a physician who can promptly conduct the examination and deliver the required report within the shortest time frame, the counselor must rely on their judgment or past experiences, considering all relevant factors to make an informed choice.

"*Decision-making under risk*" is a familiar problem to most rehabilitation caseload managers since few (if any) caseload-related decisions are without risk. Counselors often encounter situations where clients fail to attend scheduled appointments with physicians or miss evaluation and training activities. Despite the apparent certainty of these situations, the risk of noncompliance or unforeseen circumstances may prevent the decisions from being executed as planned. Another scenario related to rehabilitation involves client employment. Caseload managers frequently face the challenge of placing individuals in employment situations with a high risk of job retention. Risk factors are inherent in every decision made in case management.

"*Decision-making under uncertainty*" can readily be related to rehabilitation of individuals with significant disabilities. Disabling conditions frequently introduce limitations or restrictions that give rise to significant uncertainties regarding rehabilitation or placement potential. In such cases, making program decisions of short duration becomes valuable, as it allows for the assessment of new information and the clarification of uncertain situations or conditions. In the public rehabilitation sector, extended evaluation procedures are employed to address this decision challenge, granting additional time for evaluation in order to gather information that reduces uncertainty concerning an individual's capacity to benefit from rehabilitation services. Conversely, in the private sector, rehabilitation planning developed by practitioners often carries inherent "uncertainty" until it undergoes scrutiny by the "compensation board" or is negotiated by appropriate representatives within the legal system. Given that rehabilitation revolves around the productive aspects of human beings, the intrinsic complexities of human nature contribute to uncertainties that must be taken into account in any rehabilitation endeavor.

"*Decision-making under partial information*" is a common aspect of almost all rehabilitation situations. It is neither practical nor necessary for the rehabilitation counselor-manager to possess comprehensive knowledge about an individual client or prospective client. Collecting all available information about a person would be cost-prohibitive and would considerably complicate the decision-making process. Therefore, decisions are made based on the best available information. This information should encompass the relevant data related to the established objectives. In other words, the accuracy and adequacy of information may vary for different clients, but all possible factors that could impact the outcome are taken into consideration. For instance, the rehabilitation practitioner may be unaware of the positive or negative influence exerted by family members or friends, which can significantly affect the success of an individual's rehabilitation journey. Consequently, the caseload manager must skillfully strike a balance between the quality and quantity of information, considering the unique circumstances of each individual, in order to make informed decisions.

"*Decision-making under conflict.*" Public Law 93-112, also known as the Rehabilitation Act of 1973, introduced the concept of client advocacy through community representatives. While this provision aimed to enhance the client's rights and representation, it also created potential situations of conflict of interest between the counselor and the client or the client's representative. In the private sector, counselors may face frequent decision-making under conflict due to the possibility of litigation. However, when all parties involved genuinely prioritize the client's best interests, maintaining a flexible approach can mitigate the nature of the conflict. Another scenario demonstrating decision-making under conflict arises when a client's vocational objective surpasses their demonstrated or evaluated performance levels. Even when negotiations help alleviate the conflict, the caseload manager must make decisions while navigating the existing conflicts.

The examples provided serve to illustrate the five decision problem situations and should not be considered exhaustive of all the categories of encounters experienced by rehabilitation counselors. There are numerous other situations that could be cited to demonstrate the diverse decisions made by rehabilitation caseload managers in public, private, and facility practice settings.

THE REHABILITATION DECISION MODEL

The rehabilitation counselor must make numerous decisions every day, and each one is made with varying amounts of information. It is likely that the decision-making process will include (a) apex decisions, (b) base decisions, and (c) consequential decisions at different stages in the rehabilitation process. The counselor should approach each decision as a challenge, requiring a systematic evaluation of the relevant factors involved. To accomplish this, a comprehensive assessment of the factors encompassed within state agency rehabilitation programs is necessary. Initially proposed by Cassell and Mulkey (1985) and further developed by Grubbs, Cassell, and Mulkey in 2006, the rehabilitation decision-making model presented in **Figure 6.2** has been adapted by Rawlins Williams to encompass professions in both public and private rehabilitation settings.

Upon examining **Figure 6.2**, it becomes evident that three significant dimensions (**problem diagnosis, service identification,** and **outcome evaluation**) form the decision structure for the sequential delivery of rehabilitation services. Each major dimension comprises various functions that contribute to the decision-making process. The relationship between these dimensions and functions in relation to decision-making is briefly discussed next.

Problem Diagnosis

The process of rehabilitation involves conducting a **diagnostic assessment** before determining eligibility and delivering services. However, the diagnostic evaluation is not a spontaneous occurrence, but rather a carefully determined segment of the rehabilitation process conducted by the rehabilitation counselor in accordance with agency policies and applicant requirements. The *initial intake/interview* serves as the counselor's first attempt to preliminarily evaluate the individual. Its purpose is to identify the applicant's functional capacities, limitations, their interest in rehabilitation services, and eventual employment prospects. The general *diagnostic assessment* encompasses various medical, psychiatric,

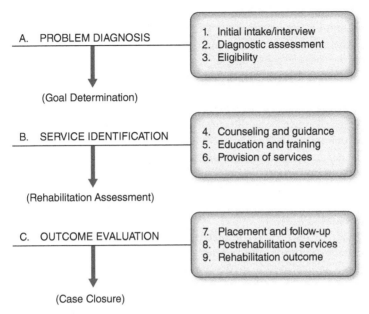

FIGURE 6.2 The Rawlins Williams rehabilitation decision-making model.

psychological, social, vocational, and other diagnostic procedures that are necessary to determine eligibility and explore suitable service options. Finally, *eligibility* is established when an individual is receiving Supplemental Security Income (SSI) or Social Security Disability Insurance (SSDI) based on their disability or when they have enduring medical and/or rehabilitation needs.

Service Identification

The services provided by public or private rehabilitation services can be categorized as effective solutions for challenging circumstances. *Counseling and guidance* play a crucial role in supporting clients and are often vital for the success of rehabilitation. Additionally, *education and training* may be necessary to equip clients with vocational or additional skills, facilitating their integration or reintegration into the job market. The *provision of services* involves the practical implementation of identified services, often through collaborative efforts with interprofessional rehabilitation providers. These collaborations aim to achieve the most suitable outcomes for clients throughout the rehabilitation process.

Outcome Evaluation

Every decision-making model must contain an evaluation dimension in order to determine whether the decision was an effective judgment. *Placement* (and *follow-up*) is certainly a valuable indicator as to whether the counselor has used good judgment. The provision of *post-rehabilitation services* can keep the counselor and client in contact with each other and provide an opportunity for additional evaluation of the rehabilitation outcomes. When the client does not achieve a *rehabilitation outcome,* the counselor should assess the situation to determine the reasons that the rehabilitation lacked a successful outcome.

Upon further examination of the model illustrated in **Figure 6.2**, it becomes evident that dimensions A (Problem Diagnosis) and B (Service Identification) are interconnected through Goal(s) Determination, while dimensions B (Service Identification) and C

(Outcome Evaluation) are connected through Rehabilitation Assessment. These two connections are essential for facilitating the seamless flow of the supra-decision-making structure known as the rehabilitation decision model. This decision model serves as a process for comprehensively understanding the current circumstances of clients and evaluating them in light of the established goals. The disparity between the client's present situation and the identified goals is then analyzed in conjunction with a thorough functional assessment of the individual.

It is crucial to establish rehabilitation goals at the earliest stage possible to ensure prompt service delivery and to effectively address identified functional limitations. Once the direction of rehabilitation is determined, decision-making becomes more straightforward, and the planning process is facilitated. Therefore, completing the diagnostic study and determining goals naturally pave the way for developing a service program (Berven, 2004; Cassell & Mulkey, 1985; Cox et al., 1981; Grubbs et al., 2006; Power, 2012; Rubin et al., 2016; Thomas, 1990).

Once a program of services is completed, the model offers an opportunity to assess the client's progress. The decision-maker must evaluate any new skills or improved functioning that enhance the likelihood of successful employment or rehabilitation outcomes. It is important to note that this assessment relies on clinical judgment since the actual measurement of outcomes will occur later when considering specific competitive work skills. In essence, the rehabilitation process can be viewed as a *supra-decision-making model*, providing a framework to guide the judgments made by the caseload manager. These professional judgments serve as the essential building blocks for creating an environment conducive to the successful rehabilitation of individuals with disabilities. The effectiveness of these decisions directly correlates with the skill of the decision-maker.

ADDITIONAL MODELS OF DECISION-MAKING PROCESSES

To effectively manage caseloads, rehabilitation professionals need an organizing concept that simplifies the complexities they encounter. Successful decision-makers understand the fundamental functions that drive the management process. Caseload managers are expected to possess decision-making skills, applying agency or company policies in certain cases, while also employing pragmatic approaches that consider the individual circumstances and progress of clients.

Various decision-making models offer an organized approach that can be applied to both public and private rehabilitation programs. However, due to theoretical differences among caseload managers and situational variables, some rehabilitation counselors may prefer an eclectic approach to decision-making. As a result, caseload managers are compelled to carefully consider the adoption or development of a functional model that can structure the decision process. The basic outline of these chosen models serves as a valuable resource for comprehending and cultivating an effective and efficient decision-making process.

The Directive Model

There is a strong historical literature in cross-cultural counseling that provides support for the **directive-style approach** (Berman, 1979; Draguns, 1981; Exum & Lau, 1988; Pedersen, 1991; Sue & Sue, 1990). The directive model refers to a decision-making model or approach that emphasizes efficiency, practicality, and a focus on getting results. It is often associated with autocratic or authoritative leadership styles, where the decision-making power is concentrated at the top of the hierarchy (Merta et al., 1992). In the directive model, decision-makers gather limited information, rely on their own expertise, and make decisions quickly without involving others extensively.

Key characteristics of the directive model include:

- Decisions are made by a few individuals or a single person in a position of authority.
- Decision-makers rely on their own knowledge and experience rather than seeking input from others.
- The decision-making process is typically quick and efficient.
- There is a clear chain of command and hierarchical structure.
- Communication tends to be one-way, with instructions flowing from the top down.
- The focus is on achieving outcomes and meeting targets.

This approach prioritizes efficiency and speed, often resulting in quick and efficient decision-making processes. The directive model is also associated with a clear chain of command and a hierarchical structure, where instructions flow from the top down (Islam et al., 2018). Communication in this model is typically one-way, with information and directives being conveyed from superiors to subordinates. This model is often employed in counseling settings where individuals may be facing challenges due to disabilities, injuries, or other factors that impact their ability to function effectively in daily life.

The directive model involves the counselor taking an active role in the decision-making process by offering specific advice and suggestions based on their expertise and knowledge (Duan et al., 2015). Instead of solely exploring options and facilitating the client's exploration of alternatives, the counselor provides a more authoritative stance to guide the decision-making process.

In the context of rehabilitation counseling, the directive model can be particularly useful when clients are struggling with decision-making due to their disabilities or limitations (Marini et al., 2018). By providing clear recommendations and direction, the counselor can help clients navigate complex choices and challenges more effectively. As reflected upon by Grubbs et al. (2006), the directive model for decision-making and rehabilitation counseling is characterized by several key aspects. First, the counselor provides expert guidance, drawing upon their knowledge and experience in rehabilitation and decision-making. They offer valuable information on various options, potential outcomes, and effective strategies for success. Additionally, the directive model adopts a goal-oriented approach. The counselor assists clients in identifying specific rehabilitation goals and offers guidance on the necessary actions and decisions to achieve them. This appropriate approach ensures that clients remain focused and motivated throughout their rehabilitation journey. Moreover, counseling sessions within the directive model are structured to provide a framework for decision-making. The counselor may utilize specific decision-making models or frameworks to help clients assess their options, carefully weigh the pros and cons, and ultimately make informed decisions aligned with their goals (Mackelprang & Salsgiver, 2015; Mackelprang et al., 2022).

Active involvement is a key aspect of the directive model. The counselor takes an active role in the decision-making process by offering recommendations, suggestions, and relevant resources. This active engagement helps clients benefit from the counselor's expertise and increases the likelihood of successful decision outcomes. While the counselor provides guidance, client collaboration is essential. The counselor recognizes and integrates the client's values, preferences, and unique circumstances into the decision-making process (Marini, 2012). The client's active participation ensures that decisions are tailored to their individual needs and promote their overall well-being.

Overall, the directive model for decision-making and rehabilitation counseling offers expert guidance, adopts a goal-oriented approach, employs structured sessions, emphasizes active involvement, and prioritizes client collaboration. This model proves beneficial for individuals seeking clear guidance and support in making decisions that facilitate their rehabilitation and enhance their overall quality of life. It's important to note that the directive model may not be suitable for every client or situation. Some individuals may prefer a more collaborative or exploratory approach to decision-making. The counselor should assess each client's needs and preferences and adapt their counseling style accordingly to provide the most effective support.

The Analytical Model

The **analytical decision-making model** is a systematic and logical approach to decision-making that involves gathering and evaluating relevant information, considering alternatives, and selecting the best course of action based on a rational analysis of the available data (Vroom & Jago, 1988). This model emphasizes a structured and evidence-based approach to decision-making.

An analytical model for rehabilitation decision-making refers to an approach that emphasizes gathering and analyzing information to make informed decisions regarding rehabilitation (Remley, 2012). This model utilizes a systematic and logical process to evaluate various options and their potential outcomes, enabling individuals to make decisions that align with their rehabilitation goals and overall well-being (Leahy, 2012). This model is characterized by several key steps incorporated into the rehabilitation counseling process (Commission on Rehabilitation Counselor Certification [CRCC], 2023). First, the counselor and client work together to identify and define the problem or decision at hand, considering the client's rehabilitation needs and desired outcomes. Then, relevant information and data are collected, such as medical records, assessments, and client preferences, to support the decision-making process effectively. The collected data are systematically analyzed and evaluated by the counselor. Together, client and counselor assess the strengths, weaknesses, risks, and benefits associated with each option, aiming to gain a comprehensive understanding of the available choices. Clear decision criteria are established, encompassing factors like effectiveness, feasibility, cost, and alignment with the client's goals and values. Next, each option is objectively evaluated against the established decision criteria. The counselor and client assess how well each option meets the identified criteria and consider the potential outcomes and implications of each choice (Grubbs et al., 2006). Through collaborative discussion, the counselor and client select the most appropriate decision or course of action based on the analysis, the evaluation, and the client's preferences and goals. Once a decision is made, the client is supported in implementing the chosen course of action (Shipp & Fried, 2014). Rehabilitation counselors provide guidance, resources, and ongoing monitoring to ensure effective execution and progress toward the client's rehabilitation goals. This implementation and monitoring phase ensures that the decision is put into practice and adjustments can be made as needed.

Overall, the analytical model for decision-making involves problem identification, data collection, information analysis, decision criteria establishment, option evaluation, decision selection, and implementation and monitoring. This approach emphasizes structure and logic, ensuring that decisions are based on objective analysis and the best available information, being deliberate and rational (Croskerry, 2013). This model helps individuals make informed choices that are aligned with their rehabilitation needs and desired outcomes. By utilizing data-driven analysis, the counselor can provide valuable support to clients throughout the decision-making process in the context of rehabilitation counseling.

The Conceptual Model

A **conceptual model** is an abstract or theoretical representation of a system, process, or phenomenon (Mayr & Thalheim, 2021). It is used to simplify complex ideas or relationships and provide a framework for understanding and analyzing a subject. Conceptual models are commonly used in various fields such as science, engineering, economics, and psychology to organize and communicate ideas (Engen et al., 2023).

Here are some key characteristics and uses of conceptual models:

- Abstraction and Simplification: Conceptual models involve simplifying complex real-world situations by focusing on the essential elements and relationships (Di Mitri et al., 2018). They strip away unnecessary details to provide a clear and concise representation of the subject matter.
- Visual Representation: Conceptual models are often presented graphically or visually to enhance understanding. They can be in the form of diagrams, charts, flowcharts, or other visual representations that depict the relationships and components of the system or process being modeled (Machin, 2014).
- Framework for Analysis: Conceptual models serve as a framework for analyzing and studying a subject. These models help identify key variables, interconnections, and patterns, allowing researchers or practitioners to explore and understand the subject in a structured manner (Nilsen, 2015).
- Communication and Collaboration: Conceptual models facilitate communication and collaboration by providing a shared language and understanding of the subject matter. They help individuals or teams communicate complex ideas, theories, or proposals effectively.
- Hypothesis Generation: Conceptual models can be used to generate hypotheses or test theories (Verhoeven, 2011). By defining the variables and relationships within a system, they provide a basis for formulating testable propositions or predictions.
- Tool for Decision-Making: Conceptual models can assist in decision-making by providing a framework to evaluate alternatives and understand the potential consequences of different choices. These models help decision-makers assess the potential impacts and trade-offs associated with different options.

It's important to note that conceptual models are simplifications and abstractions of reality and may not capture all the complexities and nuances of the subject being modeled (Verhoeven, 2011). These models are tools for understanding and analysis rather than exact replicas of the real-world system or phenomenon. Overall, conceptual models play a crucial role in organizing knowledge, facilitating understanding, and providing a foundation for analysis and decision-making in various fields (Wand et al., 1995).

A conceptual model for decision-making and rehabilitation counseling refers to an approach that focuses on understanding the underlying concepts, theories, and principles related to decision-making and rehabilitation. This model emphasizes several key aspects that contribute to effective client support and progress. In this model process, the counselor draws upon relevant theories and models from fields such as psychology, counseling, rehabilitation sciences, and decision science to establish a strong theoretical foundation (Hartley & Tarvydas, 2023). These theories provide a comprehensive framework for understanding the psychological, social, and cognitive processes involved in decision-making and the rehabilitation journey.

This model takes a holistic perspective by considering the multidimensional nature of decision-making and rehabilitation. It recognizes that various factors, including the client's physical abilities, cognitive functioning, emotional well-being, social support, and environmental context, contribute to their overall situation (Mpofu & Mpofu, 2023).

This holistic and individualized approach ensures that the counselor considers the entirety of the client's circumstances and tailors interventions accordingly, addressing both the immediate challenges and the underlying factors that impact the decision-making process and rehabilitation outcomes.

It acknowledges that each client is unique, with their own set of needs, preferences, and goals. The counselor collaborates closely with the client to gain a deep understanding of their values, aspirations, and personal circumstances. By doing so, the counselor can tailor the decision-making process and rehabilitation strategies to align with the client's individual needs, ensuring a personalized and meaningful approach that enhances engagement and progress (Smart & Smart, 2018).

The conceptual model integrates evidence-based practices and research findings to inform decision-making and rehabilitation interventions. The counselor utilizes current knowledge and empirical evidence to guide their recommendations and interventions, ensuring that they are based on the best available information and have a solid scientific foundation. By incorporating evidence-based practices, the counselor can provide interventions that are proven to be effective, increasing the likelihood of positive outcomes and client satisfaction.

Continuous assessment and adaptation are emphasized within the conceptual model. The counselor recognizes the dynamic nature of the rehabilitation process and the changing needs of the client. Ongoing assessment is conducted to monitor progress and evaluate the effectiveness of the interventions (Pebdani et al., 2022; Strauser & Greco, 2019). This enables the counselor to make informed decisions about potential adjustments or modifications to the approach, ensuring that it remains relevant and effective throughout the client's rehabilitation journey. Furthermore, the model places great importance on empowerment and self-determination. Recognizing the significance of client autonomy, the counselor fosters an environment that promotes client empowerment. The counselor supports clients in developing self-awareness, enhancing their problem-solving skills, and making choices that align with their values and preferences (Moore et al., 2021). By promoting client empowerment, the counselor fosters a sense of ownership and active participation in the decision-making and rehabilitation processes, increasing the likelihood of successful outcomes and long-term well-being.

In summary, by utilizing a conceptual model, rehabilitation counselors can go beyond surface-level decision-making and rehabilitation strategies. Underlying theories and concepts may be explored to gain a deeper understanding of the client's needs and apply evidence-based practices in a holistic and individualized manner. This approach enhances the counselor's ability to support clients effectively in their decision-making and rehabilitation journey.

The Behavioral Model

The **behavioral model** for decision-making is an approach that focuses on understanding how individuals actually make decisions, taking into account cognitive biases, heuristics, and psychological factors that influence their choices (Fontaine & Dodge, 2006). Unlike rational models that assume decision-makers are perfectly rational and objective, the behavioral model recognizes that human decision-making is often influenced by subjective perceptions and cognitive limitations.

Key principles and elements of the behavioral model for decision-making include:

- Bounded Rationality: The behavioral model acknowledges that individuals have limited cognitive capacity and information-processing abilities. Instead of considering all possible alternatives and evaluating them objectively, people tend to rely on simplified decision-making strategies, known as heuristics, to make choices efficiently (Selten, 2004).

- Cognitive Biases: Behavioral models recognize the presence of cognitive biases, which are systematic errors in thinking that can lead to deviations from rational decision-making (Croskerry, 2013). These biases include confirmation bias (favoring information that supports existing beliefs), availability bias (overemphasizing readily available information), and anchoring bias (being influenced by initial information).
- Emotions and Intuition: The behavioral model highlights the role of emotions and intuition in decision-making. Emotions can influence the evaluation of alternatives and the final decision. Intuitive judgments, based on previous experiences and patterns, can guide decision-making, sometimes leading to rapid and effective choices (Cheshin et al., 2011).
- Framing Effects: The way information is presented, or framed, can significantly impact decision-making. People may react differently to the same information depending on how it is framed, such as emphasizing gains or losses (Kapuściński & Richards, 2022). Framing effects can influence risk-taking behavior and preferences for different options.
- Social Influences: The behavioral model recognizes that decision-making is influenced by social factors. People may conform to group norms, be influenced by the opinions of others, or feel pressure to make decisions that align with social expectations (Goette & Tripodi, 2021). Social influence can affect both individual decision-making and group decision processes.
- Learning and Adaptation: The behavioral model acknowledges that decision-makers learn from feedback and adjust their decision-making strategies over time (Butz et al., 2007). Experience and feedback play a role in shaping future decisions and improving decision-making effectiveness.

Overall, the behavioral model provides insights into the actual decision-making processes of individuals, considering their cognitive limitations, biases, emotions, and social influences. By understanding these factors, organizations and individuals can make efforts to mitigate biases, improve decision-making processes, and enhance overall decision outcomes.

The Sequential Model

Drucker (1967) presents a comprehensive procedure for decision-making. This **sequential model** systematically defines the important aspects of a situation and considers the data in distinct sequential steps presented in **Figure 6.3**.

Six sequential steps of decision-making include:

1. Classification of the problem.
2. Definition of the problem.
3. Specifications that the answer to the problem must satisfy: What are the "boundary conditions"?
4. Decision as to what is "right" rather than what is acceptable, in order to meet the conditions.
5. Building in the decision the action to carry it out.
6. Feedback that tests the validity and effectiveness of the decision.

The first step, *classification*, aims to determine the nature of the problem. It involves identifying whether the problem is generic, which means it is a common situation with established procedures for resolution; unique, indicating an exceptional situation without recognized formal solutions; or the first manifestation of a new category, where rules are

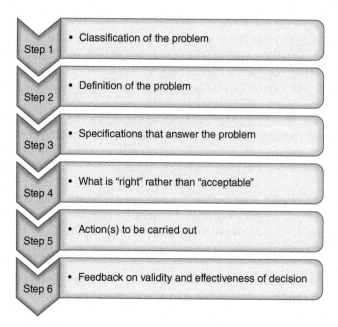

FIGURE 6.3 Sequential steps of the decision-making process.

yet to be developed. For example, this could include a federal policy stating eligibility for a new disability category when state or local procedures have not been established. Just as an athlete knows whether to run or dribble based on identifying the held object as a football or basketball, the caseload manager determines the appropriate action by correctly classifying the decision problem situation.

Defining (Step 2) the problem is often an easy task once it has been classified. Familiar questions that require answers include "What are the functional limitations?," "Is there a treatment regimen recommended for this disability?," and "What is the key to the situation solution?" Clearly, this is the beginning of the *rehabilitation diagnosis* activity.

At this stage of the decision-making process, effective decision-makers quickly recognize that the most significant risk is not making the wrong definition but rather an incomplete one. Just as half a dollar holds less value than a whole dollar, and an unfinished novel is unlikely to become a best-seller, an incomplete rehabilitation diagnosis can limit a client's vocational progress and even lead to incorrect identification of the underlying issue. Caseload managers must be vigilant in guarding against plausible but incomplete definitions of the problem.

To illustrate, let's consider a scenario where an academic training program is designed for a client with a diagnosed learning disability but there is no information available about the client's learning style. Shortly after starting the training program, it becomes evident that the client is performing below average and may face termination from the program. The client feels frustrated, and the counselor is perplexed about the reasons behind the difficulties experienced during the training activities. Despite the initial plausibility, such incidents can be avoided if caseload managers carefully observe all events associated with defining the problem.

Therefore, it is crucial for caseload managers to be thorough in considering all relevant factors when defining the problem. By doing so, they can mitigate the risk of an incomplete definition and its negative consequences. Therefore, the key safeguard against ending up with an incomplete definition is to meticulously review and verify all information to ensure its alignment with the defined problem. If the facts and evidence do not substantiate the derived definition, it is essential to initiate a process of immediate reconsideration. Addressing any shortcomings in the definition at this stage significantly reduces the overall costs in terms of time, resources, and frustration compared to making adjustments to an incomplete definition at a later point in time. The previous examples mainly highlight the elements of problem identification in relation to rehabilitation diagnosis. However, these illustrations were specifically utilized to exemplify this particular step in the decision-making process. It is important to bear in mind that defining the problem is relevant and essential in any decision situation.

Specifications (Step 3) should be viewed as both short- and long-term rehabilitation goals. This stage of the decision process requires a precise identification of the desired outcomes that the decision must achieve. In other words, it entails determining the objectives, such as attaining gainful employment or returning to a previous level of employment, that the decision needs to accomplish, as well as specifying the conditions, such as vocational training or job modification, that must be met to fulfill those objectives.

The rehabilitation process itself functions as a higher-level decision-making structure, as described in the section on the rehabilitation decision model earlier in the chapter. It prompts decisions based on the progression of cases through the classification system. Consequently, the rehabilitation process is composed of numerous foundational decisions, akin to building blocks. For instance, diagnostic decisions must precede service decisions. Attempting the reverse would be futile, as it would involve trying to fit the solution to the problem. In other words, an individualized plan for employment cannot be developed without a comprehensive understanding of the specific functional limitations. Thus, specifications are an integral part of both the higher-level decision-making structure, such as the individualized plan for employment, and the everyday building-block decisions, such as obtaining medical information. In both cases, specifications serve to clearly define the desired outcomes the decision must achieve.

During the *decision* (Step 4), the emphasis should be on identifying the "best alternative" rather than solely considering which alternative would be most acceptable to those involved. It is not productive to initially prioritize what will be most acceptable, as there will be opportunities for compromise later on. This principle is particularly relevant in distinguishing between original, supplemental, and amended service programs in public rehabilitation. The focus should be on determining the most effective and optimal alternative rather than solely catering to individual preferences.

Action (Step 5) involves translating the decision into tangible and measurable activities. This process requires careful consideration and responsiveness to the components essential for its implementation. The action commitments should be established from the outset to ensure the effectiveness of the decisions. It is crucial to allocate sufficient time and resources to the execution of these activities, as they form the backbone of turning decisions into tangible outcomes.

The progression toward a decision gains momentum when the responsibility for its execution is assigned to the client, caseload manager, vendor, or any other relevant party involved in the specific steps required for implementation. Clear timetables need to be established to ensure the completion of specific tasks. Therefore, service decisions outlined in the rehabilitation plan should consider the anticipated time needed for each task. Additionally, all individuals involved in carrying out the decision must be aware of their responsibilities and possess the necessary information and resources to fulfill them. It is of utmost importance that those who require information regarding a decision have access to it.

When the action commitment involves changing attitudes, habits, or behavior of individuals with a stake in the decision outcome, it is crucial to ensure that the planned action is feasible for those who bear the primary responsibility for its implementation.

It is not enough for them to simply be aware of their responsibility; they must also possess the capability to meet the established standards. For instance, consider an employer who reluctantly agrees to hire a worker with a disability but harbors doubts. In both cases, comprehending the responsibility for the action is only the first step; the capability to carry it out is equally important. In other words, failure comes at a high cost that can be mitigated if the decision-maker fully understands the standards that must be met. Such understanding helps ensure a proper alignment of capabilities with demands. However, this concern should not be misconstrued as an attempt to shield clients from failure; rather, it is a proactive approach to making effective decisions.

In the *Feedback* (Step 6), the process of information monitoring (validity) and reporting (effectiveness) plays a crucial role in any decision-making process. This activity is essential to assess whether the anticipated outcomes of a decision are actually being achieved. It involves documenting and obtaining periodic indications of the progress made in implementing previous decisions. These observations can pertain to individual case activities, such as tracking a client's progress in a specific training program, or to overall caseload actions, such as monitoring a reported 50% reduction in total cases. By consistently monitoring and documenting the results, rehabilitation caseload managers can ensure that decisions are on track and make any necessary adjustments to improve outcomes.

This step is crucial, as it provides valuable information about how specific decisions made by caseload managers are being implemented and whether adjustments are required to ensure their successful achievement. The dynamic nature of reality necessitates regular and accurate feedback on previous decisions, making it an essential management tool for effective decision-makers. In the field of rehabilitation, such feedback is vital for maximizing the benefits derived from service provision strategies. While progress reports and abstract communications like forms can provide some information, the most effective way to obtain valid feedback is through on-site inspections that incorporate appropriate interviews and discussions. Failing to "inspect" decision outcomes leaves room for incomplete observations, making it difficult to determine whether progress has actually been made. Caseload managers rely on both progress reports and on-site inspections to gather organized and comprehensive information for evaluating feedback. Based on this evaluation, strategies can be adjusted to align with the current reality.

In summary, it is important to note that this model advocates a systematic approach to decision-making, with the important elements clearly defined and considered in a distinct sequential order. Indeed, pervasive decision-making is mandated by virtue of the caseload manager position. However, it is a knowledgeable and alert manager who can make significant and positive impact on caseload movement and client performance. These results characterize the effective rehabilitation counselor-manager decision-maker.

Decision-making is, of course, a major task of rehabilitation caseload managers. The decision process requires an orderly approach to data consideration, and decision-makers need appropriate structures to assist them in reaching effective decisions. Thus, using a decision model ensures systematic and sequential treatment of the important issues related to the decision situation. The decision models presented are valuable tools for rehabilitation caseload managers, as they improve the consistency in handling decision input data. Systematic decision-making not only defines an effective decision-maker but, more importantly, reflects the adoption of efficient service delivery strategies for individuals with disabilities. These decision models contribute to the utility of rehabilitation caseload managers by ensuring consistent and effective decision-making processes that ultimately lead to efficient service delivery for persons with disabilities.

IMPACT OF CULTURAL NORMS AND BIAS IN DECISION-MAKING PROCESSES

Cultural norms and **biases** have a significant impact on decision-making processes. Our cultural background shapes our perception of the world and influences the decisions (Katz & Hoyt, 2014). Assumptions and expectations rooted in cultural norms can influence how information is interpreted, potentially leading to biased decision-making. These biases can contribute to stereotypes and generalizations about certain groups, affecting professional judgment and leading to unfair treatment or discrimination. In-group favoritism, where preferential treatment is given to individuals from one's own cultural, ethnic, or social group, can hinder objective decision-making and overlook the merits of those outside the group (Jami & Walker, 2022).

Confirmation bias, influenced by cultural biases, can prevent rehabilitation counselors from considering alternative viewpoints or information that challenges our existing beliefs or cultural norms. This bias can hinder objective decision-making by limiting our ability to see beyond our own perspectives. Cultural norms also influence decision-making processes at various levels. Organizational cultures shape decision-making practices within companies or institutions, while cultural norms regarding gender roles, hierarchy, or authority impact decision-making dynamics within teams or leadership structures (Sayre, 2021). Moreover, cultural norms play a significant role in shaping our ethical frameworks and moral judgments. Different cultures have varying perspectives on what is considered right or wrong, just or unjust, which can impact ethical decision-making. Individuals may prioritize values aligned with their cultural norms over universal ethical principles, affecting the fairness and inclusivity of their decisions.

Recognizing and addressing cultural biases in decision-making are crucial for promoting diversity and inclusion. Embracing diverse perspectives enhances decision-making by introducing alternative viewpoints, challenging assumptions, and promoting a comprehensive evaluation of information (National Education Association, 2016). To mitigate the impact of cultural norms and biases, it is important to foster awareness and cultural sensitivity. Encouraging open dialogue, providing diversity training, and creating inclusive decision-making processes can help minimize the influence of biases, leading to more objective and equitable decision-making outcomes.

Cultural Norms, Bias, and Rehabilitation Counseling

Rehabilitation counseling is a specialized field that focuses on assisting individuals with disabilities or health-related challenges in achieving their personal, social, educational, and vocational goals. Within this field, the impact of cultural norms and bias on decision-making processes is significant and should be given careful consideration.

Cultural competence plays a crucial role in rehabilitation counseling. Cultural norms and biases shape the experiences and needs of individuals from diverse cultural backgrounds (Larson & Bradshaw, 2017). Therefore, rehabilitation counselors must develop awareness, knowledge, and skills to effectively work with and support clients from varying cultures. Cultural competence enables counselors to understand and address the unique challenges and strengths of each individual.

In the assessment and treatment planning phase of rehabilitation counseling, cultural norms and biases can have a profound impact. Counselors need to recognize their own biases and be mindful of the influence of cultural norms when gathering information, conducting assessments, and developing treatment plans (CRCC, 2023). Failing to account for these factors can result in inaccurate assessments and inappropriate treatment recommendations, undermining the effectiveness of the counseling process (Bolton & Parker, 2008).

Communication and rapport-building are also influenced by cultural norms and biases in rehabilitation counseling (Henry et al., 2023; Matrone & Leahy, 2005; Middleton et al., 2010). Counselors must be attuned to cultural differences in communication styles, nonverbal cues, and interpersonal dynamics. Building rapport with clients from diverse cultural backgrounds requires sensitivity and the ability to create a safe and inclusive environment where individuals feel comfortable expressing themselves.

To ensure culturally responsive decision-making, rehabilitation counselors should continually engage in self-reflection, ongoing education, and training to address their own biases and enhance their cultural competence (CRCC, 2023). Embracing diversity and actively seeking to understand and respect cultural norms enable counselors to provide more effective and meaningful support to their clients, ultimately promoting positive rehabilitation outcomes.

IMPACT OF CONSCIOUS AND UNCONSCIOUS BIAS IN DECISION-MAKING PROCESSES

As we transition into adulthood, a significant portion of our cultural beliefs and norms becomes ingrained in our **subconscious** (Croskerry, 2013). Within this realm of consciousness, both conscious and unconscious biases play a crucial role in shaping our perceptions and judgments of others. These biases have the potential to impact how we interpret information, evaluate performance, and form impressions of individuals. Bias can manifest in the form of quick, impulsive judgments, unwarranted assumptions, and reliance on stereotypes, all of which can distort our decision-making processes and undermine the principles of fairness (Ridley, 2005). Consequently, influence emerges among various aspects of our lives, ranging from personal choices to professional decisions, such as those related to hiring, team assignments, resource allocation, and customer service.

Conscious bias encompasses biases that we are aware of and deliberately exhibit. These biases can arise from our cultural upbringing, personal beliefs, or explicit prejudices. When we make decisions under the influence of conscious bias, it can lead to favoritism, discrimination, or unfair treatment based on factors such as race, gender, age, or other characteristics. The presence of conscious bias can hinder our ability to make objective decisions and perpetuate inequities if left unrecognized and unaddressed. In contrast, unconscious bias, also known as implicit bias, refers to biases that operate outside of our awareness and conscious control. They are shaped by societal conditioning, learned associations, and automatic mental processes. Unconscious bias affects our decision-making even when we consciously strive to be fair and unbiased. It can manifest in subtle ways, such as subtle preferences, stereotyping, or microaggressions. Unconscious bias can have a significant impact on various decisions, including those related to hiring, promotions, evaluations, and interactions with others. Both conscious and unconscious bias can profoundly influence our judgments and decision-making processes, often resulting in inequitable outcomes (Hays & Erford, 2014). Recognizing and addressing these biases are essential steps toward fostering fairness, inclusivity, and equal opportunities in various domains of life.

The presence of bias in decision-making processes can pose significant challenges to diversity and inclusion efforts. Biases have the potential to exclude underrepresented groups, limit their opportunities for growth and advancement, and contribute to the perpetuation of systemic inequalities (Sue & Sue, 2013; Sue et al., 2022). Unchecked bias can result in the creation of homogeneous environments that lack diverse perspectives, stifling innovation and hindering creativity.

To promote fair decision-making, it is crucial to recognize and address bias. Implementing strategies to mitigate bias becomes imperative. This includes increasing awareness and understanding of unconscious biases that may influence our judgments and choices. Structured decision-making processes can help minimize the influence of subjective biases by introducing objectivity and consistency (Bonilla-Silva, 2018; Ritter & Graham, 2022). Providing diversity and bias training equips individuals with the knowledge and tools to identify and challenge biases. Using objective criteria and performance metrics can ensure that decisions are based on merit rather than subjective factors. Encouraging diverse perspectives and fostering an inclusive and respectful culture create an environment where different voices are valued and heard.

Actively recognizing and mitigating bias is a crucial step for organizations and individuals to promote fairness, diversity, and inclusion. By doing so, they contribute to the development of a more equitable society, enriched with diverse perspectives and increased innovation. However, the impact of bias in decision-making processes also raises important ethical concerns. To ensure fairness, equal opportunities, and respect for individuals' rights, it is necessary to examine our biases, acknowledge the potential harm caused by biased decisions, and actively work toward minimizing and eliminating bias to promote just outcomes (Saul, 2013). Creating inclusive and equitable decision-making processes requires fostering self-reflection, education, and cultural sensitivity. By raising awareness and taking deliberate actions to mitigate both conscious and unconscious bias, individuals and organizations can strive for fairer and more objective decision-making, leading to better outcomes for all involved.

Impact of Conscious and Unconscious Bias in Decision-Making Processes and Rehabilitation Counseling

The impact of conscious and unconscious bias in decision-making processes carries substantial implications within the field of rehabilitation counseling. Particularly in the assessment and treatment planning phase, biases can significantly influence the counselor's comprehension and evaluation of their clients (Lonner, 2016; Rose et al., 2013). Unintentionally, stereotypes or assumptions related to disabilities, cultures, or identities may shape the counselor's perceptions, resulting in inaccurate assessments and unsuitable treatment recommendations (Morrow & Deidan, 1992; Toporek & Williams, 2006). As a consequence, the counselor's capacity to tailor interventions according to the distinctive needs and experiences of their clients may be hindered, potentially impacting the overall effectiveness of the rehabilitation process.

Bias in rehabilitation counseling has multifaceted implications, affecting both the therapeutic relationship and access to equitable services. When clients perceive bias or feel judged based on their cultural background, disability, or personal characteristics, it erodes trust and impedes their willingness to engage fully. Establishing a trusting and nonjudgmental environment is vital in rehabilitation counseling, but biases can create barriers to achieving this goal (Appiah et al., 2022). Furthermore, bias can exacerbate disparities in access and equity within rehabilitation counseling services. Specific cultural, ethnic, or socioeconomic groups may encounter systemic barriers that hinder their access to appropriate and inclusive care (Bonilla-Silva, 2018; Nutter et al., 2020). Biases embedded in decision-making processes, such as resource allocation and referral systems, contribute to these disparities and perpetuate inequities. Recognizing and addressing biases is crucial to ensure that individuals from all backgrounds have equal opportunities to benefit from quality rehabilitation counseling.

To mitigate the impact of bias, rehabilitation counselors must engage in self-reflection, ongoing education, and cultural competence training. By cultivating awareness of their own biases and actively working to overcome them, counselors can embrace diversity, inclusivity, and cultural sensitivity. Fostering a nonjudgmental and inclusive environment becomes instrumental in better supporting clients and promoting positive outcomes throughout the rehabilitation process (Sue & Spanierman, 2020). By actively addressing bias, rehabilitation counselors can contribute to a more equitable and effective counseling experience for their clients.

SELF-REFLECTION AND TECHNIQUES FOR UNDERSTANDING PERSONAL BIAS IN WORKING WITH CLIENTS

Self-reflection is a valuable process where individuals examine their thoughts, emotions, and behaviors to gain a deeper self-understanding. It involves introspection and self-awareness to identify patterns, beliefs, and biases that influence our interactions with others. Biases are inherent tendencies shaped by personal experiences, cultural background, and societal influences. In professions involving client work, self-reflection is crucial, as it promotes awareness of personal biases and their impact in the workplace. Rehabilitation professionals benefit from self-reflection by utilizing **Table 6.1** to understand how it supports their practice.

Self-reflection is a potent tool for professionals who work with clients, as it enables them to gain a deeper understanding of their own biases and assumptions. By actively cultivating self-awareness and regularly examining their thoughts, emotions, and behaviors, professionals can provide more equitable and client-centered support. While self-reflection demands commitment and a willingness to engage in introspection, the personal and professional growth it offers is truly rewarding. Ultimately, through the practice of self-reflection, professionals can significantly enhance their capacity to deliver fair and client-focused assistance.

APPLICATION OF A DECISION-MAKING MODEL INTO PROFESSIONAL PRACTICE

Decision models are developed in many different ways in accordance with individualized need and purpose. Therefore, the structure of decision models differ, and occasionally a

TABLE 6.1 TECHNIQUES FOR UNDERSTANDING PERSONAL BIAS

PERSONAL BIAS AND TECHNIQUES FOR REHABILITATION PROFESSIONALS	
Cultivate Self-Awareness	Develop the habit of regularly examining your thoughts, feelings, and reactions during interactions with clients. Pay attention to any biases or assumptions and explore the reasons behind them.
Challenge Assumptions	Question your assumptions and preconceived notions about clients. Recognize unique experiences, perspectives, and backgrounds.
Seek Feedback	Actively seek feedback from colleagues, supervisors, or mentors who can provide constructive criticism and help identify blind spots or biases.
Engage in Continuous Learning	Stay informed about cultural, social, and systemic issues that may impact your clients. Read books, attend workshops or seminars, and participate in diversity and inclusion training.
Practice Empathy and Active Listening	Empathy is essential in understanding and appreciating your clients' experiences. Actively listen to their stories and concerns without judgment and try to put yourself in their shoes.
Regularly Examine Bias	Regularly reflect on your biases and their potential impact on your work. Consider how your biases may influence your assessment, treatment, or communication with clients.

specific model must be modified for use with a given organization or agency. Although decision-making models are usually presented in symbolic terms or structured frames, their purpose is to assist decision-makers in conceptualizing systematic procedures that yield effective judgments. It is therefore the purpose of this section to develop a decision-making framework that will be useful to rehabilitation caseload managers or others who work with persons with disabilities.

Many variables affect decision-making. Three significant ones are (a) the *situation*, (b) the *decision-maker*, and (c) the *process* of making decisions. The situation (problem, or state of nature) is, of course, the reason a decision is required if a desired goal is different from the given situation. Personality, *attitude,* aptitude, and related factors of the decision-maker are certainly dimensions that impair or facilitate the making of effective decisions. The process concept signifies that there is a mostly organized, sequential consideration of weighted characteristics in making decisions. Therefore, the process, or lack of, used by caseload managers to derive effective judgments has considerable effect upon the decisions rendered. Our concern is with this latter variable, the process of making decisions, which is a necessary management tool for appropriate case movement.

Decision Variable Schema

This design encompasses all relevant aspects that exert influence on the ultimate decision outcome. Consequently, these variables can exhibit both positive and negative attributes and possess varying degrees of impact on the identified alternatives. However, it is important to note that in the pursuit of determining decision alternatives, only a select few variables should be given consideration, while the remaining variables are discounted and assigned a lower level of significance within the parameters outlined in **Figure 6.4**. This approach allows for a focused analysis, enabling decision-makers to prioritize the most pertinent variables while minimizing the influence of less critical factors.

The significance of this concept becomes evident when considering the existence of decisions nested within larger decisions. The process of determining which variables hold importance and which do not becomes a crucial aspect of shaping the final decision. Early on, the focus lies in identifying the variables that will have the greatest impact on the desired outcome. Similar to a skilled poker player knowing which cards to keep and discard, the caseload manager must discern which variables to discount and which to prioritize in making the ultimate decision. Variables such as disability, education level, motivation, and familial support are typically key considerations in rehabilitation decisions. However,

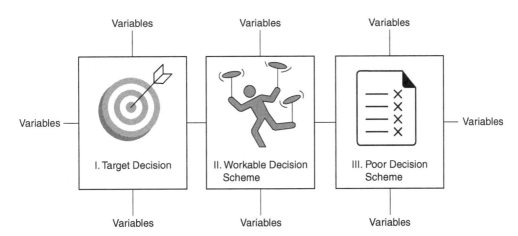

FIGURE 6.4 The decision variable schema.

their relative importance must be assessed on an individual basis. For instance, if a person's educational attainment surpasses the requirements of a particular job, the educational variable may hold less influence and be relegated to a secondary parameter (level III) with reduced effect. Conversely, if a person's motivation or family support appears questionable, these variables may require significant attention, as they are likely to impact the outcome. In such cases, the motivation and family-support variables would be considered within the primary scope of the target decision framework (level I). In other words, due to their perceived significance, these variables must remain within the purview of the target decision scheme, as they are expected to exert an influence on the final outcome.

It is crucial to recognize that decision-making should be based on a minimal number of variables. Due to inherent limitations in processing information, the selection of alternatives becomes significantly impaired as the number of decision variables increases. Studies conducted by Hayes (1962) revealed that decision speed and quality decline when more than four variables are taken into account. This finding is supported by Felsen (1976), who posited that decision-makers experience heightened confusion as the number of decision variables rises. Therefore, it is imperative to identify the key decision variables in order to arrive at effective decisions. However, even more important than determining these variables is ensuring that they are genuinely significant rather than arbitrarily assigned a value. Failing to adhere to this principle can lead to numerous subpar decisions due to errors in evaluating the importance of specific variables that influence decision-making. Additionally, since no decision-making model can encompass all variables relevant to a given decision situation, a systematic analysis of decision variables helps caseload managers prioritize those that are crucial and have a substantial impact on decision outcomes.

Upon further examination of **Figure 6.4**, it becomes evident that the *Target decision scheme* (level I) focuses on variables that have the strongest impact on the desired outcome. These variables exert a significant level of control over the rehabilitation process, influencing its success or failure. Variables such as disability, functional limitations, psychological factors, education, motivation, training, and family support are typically given high consideration in decision-making, making them essential target decision variables. Failing to accurately identify these variables can introduce additional risk factors and undermine the effectiveness of the resulting decision. It is crucial to avoid overlooking or disregarding critical decision variables to prevent program failures and ensure favorable outcomes for clients.

The *workable decision scheme* (level II) represents decisions based on variables that fall within "workable" parameters. These variables have a moderate level of control over the eventual outcome, and decisions made on these variables may yield mixed results. While some decisions within this scheme may fall within acceptable boundaries, many may require subsequent consequential decisions (refer to **Figure 6.1**) to achieve true success or the desired rehabilitation direction. Consequential decisions can be burdensome for all parties involved in the rehabilitation process, as they often involve unplanned adjustments to a client's program of services. These adjustments may indicate inadequate planning or the utilization of suboptimal decision variables. Caseload managers should invest sufficient effort in evaluating the impact of decision variables to accurately assess how each variable contributes to the resulting decisions made.

Limited attention is given to the variables linked to the poor decision scheme (level III). Decisions influenced by these variables tend to be random or founded on guesswork. Such variables hold little significance in attaining successful outcomes, and relying on them would lead to a haphazard or trial-and-error approach to problem-solving. Decision-makers striving to maintain their effectiveness should avoid basing their decisions on variables categorized as level III. The probability of achieving successful outcomes using *poor decision scheme* variables is exceedingly restricted. In practice, these variables (level III) rarely contribute to effective decision-making.

Therefore, decision-makers hold two essential responsibilities. First, they must establish guidelines by identifying the variables that hold the greatest influence on the ultimate outcome of the decision. Accurate determination of the significance of these decision variables can be accomplished by employing the ABC decision patterns, as depicted in **Figure 6.1**, once a comprehensive understanding of the decision context has been attained. Second, decision-makers must select from a range of available alternatives that offer potential solutions to the decision-requiring situation. In the realm of rehabilitation, the choice of alternatives is influenced by the strengths and limitations of the client, along with the resources provided by the community.

The importance of determining the appropriate variables to include in the ground rules can be demonstrated through a scenario involving reduced referrals in caseload management. Let's consider a counselor who has been receiving a low number of referrals. Initially, the counselor-manager believes that the main decision variable is the lack of awareness among community referral sources about the services offered by the rehabilitation agency. As a result, a decision is made to have the secretary send brochures describing agency services to all referral sources in the designated area. However, after several months, a review of caseload statistics reveals no increase in case referrals. It becomes evident that the decision to promote agency services through brochure distribution failed to address the underlying decision situation of having few referrals. In this case, it is possible that the counselor's performance or relationship with the referral agencies is the crucial target decision variable. If that is the case, a decision based on these specific decision variables is much more likely to yield the desired outcomes.

Recognizing the significance of variables that influence a decision situation is the responsibility of the decision-maker. These individuals are entrusted with implementing the concept of the decision variable schema and meticulously considering the utilization of decision variables in particular decision scenarios. The precision in identifying and determining crucial decision variables is directly connected to the capacity to make effective resulting decisions.

The Decision Checklist

Just as clients and community resources vary, each decision situation possesses its unique characteristics. However, the initial step in determining the rehabilitation direction is to identify probable service modes. Thus, the decision-maker's focus should be on organizing, integrating, and streamlining variables until the significant ones within a particular situation are identified. The rehabilitation counselor's main task is to determine which available alternatives offer a solution to the decision situation.

The decision-making process can be initiated using a simple method called the checklist assessment. This approach can be employed as early as the initial client interview, utilizing the counselor's direction-questions checklist (CDQ checklist) presented in **Table 6.2**. The 12 categorical service classifications in the table encompass a broad range of available rehabilitation alternatives for problem resolution. It is essential for the rehabilitation counselor and the potential client to collaboratively determine and agree upon the chosen alternative and promptly initiate the necessary steps to commence the program. Financial considerations related to the proposed service program should also be taken into account by the counselor and client.

Once a decision is made regarding the selection of an alternative, the counselor (and client) must become involved in the development of plans to reach the identified primary goal. While the rehabilitation cliché advises counselors to "plan your work, and work your plan," it lacks guidance on methodology and the underlying process. Given that planning is a significant aspect of the rehabilitation professional's role, it is beneficial to examine the planning activity in relation to rehabilitation decisions. According to Woodside and

TABLE 6.2 REHABILITATION COUNSELOR'S DIRECTION-QUESTIONS CHECKLIST (CDQ)

CHECK (✓)	CLIENT NEEDS
	A. General diagnostic evaluation?
	B. Extended evaluation/assessment?
	C. Vocational guidance?
	D. Psychological/psychiatric services?
	E. Disability management services?
	F. Medical/surgical services?
	G. Benefits counseling?
	H. Life care planning?
	I. Judicial services/expert witness testimony?
	J. Academic training?
	K. Vocational training?
	L. On-the-job training?
	M. Transition services?
	N. Other:
	O. Other:
ACTION NOTES:	

McClam (2018), planning in the context of rehabilitation involves several key characteristics: (a) planning is a process that encompasses setting goals, determining objectives, and selecting specific interventions; (b) planning becomes necessary when analysis is needed to identify desired outcomes; and (c) planning involves a thorough examination of information to gain a comprehensive understanding of the case. Therefore, readers are encouraged to refer to the planning section in Chapter 3.

The characteristics described previously directly pertain to the process of developing a program for rehabilitation services. When collaboratively creating a service plan, it is essential to engage in anticipatory decision-making and adopt a systematic approach to decision-making in order to attain the desired future state, which is the rehabilitation goal. The responsibility for effective planning, development, and documentation of the rehabilitation process lies with both the caseload manager and the client. Completing the necessary steps and meeting the appropriate requirements serve as prerequisites for initiating rehabilitation services.

SUMMARY

This chapter delved into the topic of decision-making within the context of rehabilitation. The concepts of apex, base, and consequential decisions were introduced, and their relevance to the role of rehabilitation counselors was discussed. A theoretical foundation for personalized decision-making models for caseload managers was provided by exploring appropriate decision theories. The decision-making process was examined and four models were identified that could inform the development of individual counselor models. The connection between risk factors and decision-making was explored, highlighting some of the challenges associated with professional judgments. Additionally, a rehabilitation decision model was presented as a framework for conceptualizing the decision-making process within rehabilitation agencies.

These concepts and tools are presented to support caseload managers in visualizing and developing a decision-making style that aligns with their personal and situational characteristics. However, if one is seeking a specific model or a step-by-step approach tailored to individual personality, the search may prove to be challenging and frustrating. Ultimately, the effectiveness of a caseload manager as a decision-maker hinges on their ability to learn and apply the decision variables and models. Application is the true test of any decision-making process, determining its impact and success.

QUESTIONS FOR DISCUSSION

1. How do the concepts of apex, base, and consequential decisions apply to the role of rehabilitation counselors? Provide examples to illustrate their relevance.

2. Discuss the importance of understanding and applying appropriate decision theories in the development of personalized decision models for caseload managers. How can a theoretical foundation enhance decision-making in the rehabilitation process?

3. Explore the four models of decision-making identified in the chapter. How can these models inform the development of individual counselor models? Discuss the strengths and limitations of each model.

4. Reflect on the relationship between risk factors and decision-making. What are some of the challenges associated with professional judgments in the context of rehabilitation? How can caseload managers navigate and mitigate these challenges?

5. Analyze the rehabilitation decision model presented in the chapter. How does this model conceptualize the decision-making process within rehabilitation agencies? Discuss its applicability and potential benefits in guiding decision-making.

6. Consider the statement that decision-making is an outcome and the test lies in the application of decision variables and models. What are your thoughts on this perspective? How can caseload managers ensure effective application of decision-making processes in their practice?

7. Reflect on your own decision-making style and preferences. How do your personal and situational characteristics influence your approach to decision-making in the rehabilitation context? How might you align your decision-making style with the concepts and tools presented in this chapter?

8. Discuss the challenges and considerations in balancing personalized decision-making with the need for standardized approaches in rehabilitation. How can caseload managers strike the right balance to ensure both individualized care and consistent outcomes?

9. Explore the role of collaboration between caseload managers and clients in the planning and development of rehabilitation services. How does shared responsibility for effective planning and documentation contribute to the success of the rehabilitation process? Share examples or experiences to support your discussion.

10. Reflect on your own experiences with decision-making in the rehabilitation field. What have been some of the most significant factors that influenced your decision-making processes? How have you learned and applied decision variables and models to improve your effectiveness as a caseload manager?

PUTTING IT INTO PRACTICE

Ask yourself these questions to target issues or concerns with effective decision-making and rationale for professional practice.

1. Do you possess a robust decision-making process that not only functions effectively but also allows you to flourish rather than just survive each day? Reflect on the steps involved in your decision-making process and consider if any crucial steps are missing.

2. Throughout your day, do you ever find yourself compelled to make quick decisions without sufficient time for reflection, especially concerning important and consequential matters? If so, what factors contribute to this rush, and how does this impact your ability to contemplate those decisions?

3. How do professionals handle situations in which the decisions made by rehabilitation counselors do not align with the preferences of their clients? What specific processes are employed to address and resolve such situations? What potential solutions are explored, and what happens if an impasse is reached? How can you continue to support client autonomy moving forward?

CASE STUDY

Sarah is a rehabilitation counselor working with a client who has recently experienced a spinal cord injury. The client is eager to return to work but faces significant mobility challenges. Sarah needs to make a decision about the most appropriate vocational training program for the client.

Case Study Questions

1. Using the rehabilitation decision model, what steps Sarah should take to gather relevant information in determining the problem and plan?

2. How should Sarah identify decision variables related to services identification?

3. What part of the process will most likely impact an informed decision that aligns with the client's goals?

4. How does the decision made by Sarah impact the outcome for the client?

5. What do you feel would strengthen this decision-making process?

A robust set of instructor resources designed to supplement this text is located at **http://connect.springerpub.com/content/book/978-0-8261-5963-2.** Qualifying instructors may request access by emailing **textbook@springerpub.com.**

REFERENCES

Anthony, R. N. (1988). *The management control function.* Harvard Business School Press.

Appiah, O., Eveland, W., Bullock, O., & Coduto, K. (2022). Why we can't talk openly about race: The impact of race and partisanship on respondents' perceptions of intergroup conversations. *Group Processes & Intergroup Relations, 25*(2), 434–452. https://doi.org/10.1177/1368430220967978

Arnold, J. D. (1976). 6 steps to effective decision-making. *Nation's Business, 64*(11), 71–74

Athanasou, J. (2015). Rehabilitation judgments with incomplete information: A case study. *The Australian Journal of Rehabilitation Counselling, 17*(2), 89–95. https://doi.org/10.1375/jrc.17.2.89

Berman, J. (1979). Counseling skills used by Black and White male and female counselors. *Journal of Counseling Psychology, 26,* 8 1–84. https://doi.org/10.1037/0022-0167.26.1.81

Berven, N. L. (2004). Assessment. In T. F. Riggar & D. R. Maki (Eds.), *Handbook of rehabilitation counseling* (pp. 199–217). Springer Publishing Company.

Bolton, B., & Parker, R. M. (2008). *Handbook of measurement and evaluation in rehabilitation* (4th ed.). Pro-Ed.

Bonilla-Silva, E. (2018). *Racism without racists: Colorblind racism and the persistence of racial inequality in America* (5th ed.). Rowman & Littlefield.

Brill, N. I. (1995). *Working with people: The helping process* (5th ed.). Longman.

Brunsson, N. (2007). *The consequences of decision-making.* Oxford University Press.

Butz, M. V., Sigaud, O., Pezzulo, G., & Baldassarree, G. (2007). Anticipations, brains, individual and social behavior: An introduction to anticipatory systems. In M. V. Butz, O. Sigaud, G. Pezzulo, & G. Baldassarre (Eds.), *Anticipatory behavior in adaptive learning systems: From brains to individual and social behavior* (pp. 1–18). Springer Publishing Company. https://doi.org/10.1007/978-3-540-74262-3

Cassell, J. L., & Mulkey, S. W. (1985). *Rehabilitation caseload management: Concepts & practice.* Pro-Ed.

Cheshin, A., Rafaeli, A., & Bos, N. (2011). Anger and happiness in virtual teams: Emotional influences of text and behavior on others' affect in the absence of non-verbal cues. *Organizational Behavior and Human Decision Processes, 116*(1), 2–16. https://doi.org/10.1016/j.obhdp.2011.06.002

Cohen, E. D., & Cohen, G. S. (1999). *The virtuous therapist: Ethical practice of counseling and psychotherapy.* Brooks/Cole Publishing.

Commission on Rehabilitation Counselor Certification. (2023). *Code of professional ethics for rehabilitation counselors.* Author.

Cox, C., McNair, W. C., DeFoor, J. N., Stephens, M., & Ladson, L. (1981). *Functional assessment: Limitations, capacities, and related factors*. Georgia Division of Vocational Rehabilitation.

Croskerry, P. (2013). From mindless to mindful practice—cognitive bias and clinical decision making. *The New England Journal of Medicine, 368*(26), 2445–2448. https://doi.org/10.1056/NEJMp1303712

Di Mitri, D., Schneider, J., Specht, M., & Drachsler, H. (2018). From signals to knowledge. A conceptual model for multimodal learning analytics. *Journal of Computer Assisted Learning, 34*(4), 338–349. https://doi.org/10.1111/jcal.12288

Draguns, J. G. (1981). Cross-cultural counseling and psychotherapy: History, issues, current status. In A. J. Marsella & P. B. Pedersen (Eds.), *Cross-cultural counseling and psychotherapy* (pp. 3–27). Pergamon Press.

Drucker, P. F. (1967). The effective decision. *Harvard Business Review, 45*(1), 92–98.

Duan, C., Hill, C. E., Jiang, G., Hu, B., Lei, Y., Chen, J., & Yu, L. (2015). The counselor perspective on the use of directives in counseling in China: Are directives different in China as in the United States? *Counseling Psychology Quarterly, 28*(1), 57–77. https://doi.org/10.1080/09515070.2014.965659

Engen, S., Muller, G., & Falk, K. (2023). Conceptual modeling to support system-level decision-making: An industrial case study from the Norwegian energy domain. *Systems Engineering, 26*(1), 177–198. https://doi.org/10.1002/sys.21649

Exum, H. A., & Lau, E. Y. (1988). Counseling style preference of Chinese college students. *Journal of Multicultural Counseling and Development, 16*, 84–92. https://doi.org/10.1002/j.2161-1912.1988.tb00644.x

Felsen, J. (1976). *Decision making under uncertainty: An artificial intelligence approach*. CDS Publishing.

Fontaine, R. G., & Dodge, K. A. (2006). Real-time decision making and aggressive behavior in youth: A heuristic model of response evaluation and decision (RED). *Aggressive Behavior, 32*(6), 604–624. https://doi.org/10.1002/ab.20150

Fulcher, G. S. (1965). *Common sense decision-making*. Northwestern University Press.

Goette, L., & Tripodi, E. (2021). Social influence in prosocial behavior: Evidence from a large-scale experiment. *Journal of the European Economic Association, 19*(4), 2373–2398. https://doi.org/10.1093/jeea/jvaa054

Grubbs, L. A., Cassell, J. L., & Mulkey, S. W. (2006). *Rehabilitation caseload management: Concepts and practice* (2nd ed.). Springer Publishing Company.

Hartley, M. T., & Tarvydas, V. M. (2023). Rehabilitation counseling: A specialty practice of the counseling profession. In M. T. Hartley & V. M. Tarvydas (Eds.), *The professional practice of rehabilitation counseling* (3rd ed., pp. 1–20). Springer Publishing Company.

Hayes, J. R. (1962). *Human data processing limits in decision making* (Report No. ESK-TDR-62-48). Air Force System Command, Electronics System Division.

Hays, D. G., & Erford, B. T. (2014). *Developing multicultural counseling competence: A systems approach* (2nd Ed.). Pearson.

Henry, J. S., Kulesza, E. T., Williams Awodeha, N. F., Hicks, S. B., Middleton, R. A., & Robinson, M. (2023). A way forward with multicultural considerations, advocacy, and accessibility across the 2023 Revised Code of Professional Ethics for Rehabilitation Counselor Educators and Practitioners. *Rehabilitation Counseling Bulletin*. https://doi.org/10.1177/00343552221146164

Islam, T., Tariq, J., & Usman, B. (2018). Transformational leadership and four-dimensional commitment: Mediating role of job characteristics and moderating role of participative and directive leadership styles. *The Journal of Management Development, 37*(9/10), 666–683. https://doi.org/10.1108/JMD-06-2017-0197

Jami, P. Y., & Walker, D. I. (2022). Exploring situational empathy and intergroup empathy bias among people with two opposing cultural norms: Collectivism and individualism. *International Journal of Intercultural Relations, 91*, 282–296. https://doi.org/10.1016/j.ijintrel.2022.11.002

Kapuściński, G., & Richards, B. (2022). Destination risk news framing effects—the power of audiences. *The Service Industries Journal, 42*(1–2), 107–130. https://doi.org/10.1080/02642069.2018.1441402

Katz, A. D., & Hoyt, W. T. (2014). The influence of multicultural counseling competence and anti-Black prejudice on therapists' outcome expectancies. *Journal of Counseling Psychology, 61*(2), 299–306. https://doi.org/10.1037/a0036134

Larson, K. E., & Bradshaw, C. P. (2017). Cultural competence and social desirability among practitioners: A systematic review of the literature. *Children and Youth Services Review, 76*, 100–111. https://doi.org/10.1016/j.childyouth.2017.02.034

Leahy, M. (2012). Qualified providers of rehabilitation counseling services. *In D. R. Maki & V. M. Tarvydas (Eds.), The professional practice of rehabilitation counseling* (2nd ed., pp. 193–211). Springer Publishing Company.

Lonner, W. J. (2016). Assessment of persons in cross-cultural counseling. In P. B. Pedersen, W. J. Lonner, J. G. Draguns, J. E. Trimble, & M. R. Scharron-del Rio (Eds.), *Counseling across cultures* (7th ed., pp. 51–74). Sage.

Machin, D. (2014). *Visual communication*. De Gruyter Mouton Publishing. https://doi.org/10.1515/9783110255492

Mackelprang, R. W., & Salsgiver, R. O. (2015). *Disability: A diversity model approach in human service practice* (3rd ed.). Oxford University Press.

Mackelprang, R. W., Salsgiver, R. O., & Parrey, R. C. (2022). *Disability: A diversity model approach in human service practice* (4th ed.). Oxford University Press.

Marini, I. (2012). *The psychological and social impact of illness and disability*. Springer Publishing Company.

Marini, I., Glover-Graf, N. M., & Millington, M. (2018). *Psychosocial aspects of disability: Insider perspectives and strategies for counselors* (2nd ed.). Springer Publishing Company.

Matrone, K. F., & Leahy, M. J. (2005). The relationship between vocational rehabilitation client outcomes and rehabilitation counselor multicultural counseling competencies. *Rehabilitation Counseling Bulletin, 48*(4), 233–244. https://doi.org/10.1177/00343552050480040401

Mayr, H. C., & Thalheim, B. (2021). The triptych of conceptual modeling: A framework for a better understanding of conceptual modeling. *Software and Systems Modeling, 20*(1), 7–24. https://doi.org/10.1007/s10270-020-00836-z

Merta, R. J., Ponterotto, J. G., & Brown, R. D. (1992). Comparing the effectiveness of two directive styles in the academic counseling of foreign students. *Journal of Counseling Psychology, 39*(2), 214–218. https://doi.org/10.1037/0022-0167.39.2.214

Middleton, R. A., Robinson, M., & Mu'min, A. (2010). Rehabilitation counseling: A continuing professional imperative for multiculturalism and advocacy competence. In M. J. Ratts, R. L. Toporek, & J. A. Lewis (Eds.), *ACA advocacy competencies: A social justice framework for counselors* (pp. 173–183). American Counseling Association.

Miller, D. W., & Starr, M. K. (1967). *The structure of human decisions*. Prentice-Hall.

Moore, E., Holding, A. C., Moore, A., Levine, S. L., Powers, T. A., Zuroff, D. C., & Koestner, R. (2021). The role of goal-related autonomy: A self-determination theory analysis of perfectionism, poor goal progress, and depressive symptoms. *Journal of Counseling Psychology, 68*(1), 88–97. https://doi.org/10.1037/cou0000438

Morrow, K. A., & Deidan, C. T. (1992). Bias in the counseling process: How to recognize and avoid it. *Journal of Counseling & Development, 70*(5), 571. https://doi.org/10.1002/j.1556-6676.1992.tb01663.x

Moyer, M., & Crews, C. (2017). *Applied ethics and decision making in mental health*. Sage.

Mpofu, N., & Mpofu, E. (2023). Assessment. In M. Hartley & V. M. Tarvydas (Eds.), *The professional practice of rehabilitation counseling* (3rd ed.). Springer Publishing Company.

National Education Association. (2016). *Why cultural competence?* http://www.nea.org/home/39783.htm

Nilsen, P. (2015). Making sense of implementation theories, models and frameworks. *Implementation Science, 10*(53), 1–13. https://doi.org/10.1186/s13012-015-0242-0

Nutter, S., Russell-Mayhew, S., Ellard, J. H., & Arthur, N. (2020). Reducing unintended harm: Addressing weight bias as a social justice issue in counseling through justice motive theory. *Professional Psychology, Research and Practice, 51*(2), 106–114. https://doi.org/10.1037/pro0000279

O'Shaughnessy, J. (1972). *Inquiry and decision*. Allen and Unwin.

Pebdani, R. N., Zeidan, A. M., Fearn-Smith, E. M., & Matthews, L. R. (2022). Telehealth assessment in rehabilitation counseling during the COVID-19 pandemic. *Rehabilitation Counseling Bulletin*. https://doi.org/10.1177/00343552221115866

Pedersen, P. B. (1991). Counseling international students. *The Counseling Psychologist, 19*(1), 10–58.

Power, P. (2012). *A guide to vocational assessment* (5th ed.). Pro-Ed.

Remley, T. P. (2012). Evolution of counseling and its specializations. *In D. R. Maki & V. M. Tarvydas (Eds.), The professional practice of rehabilitation counseling* (2nd ed., pp. 17–38). Springer Publishing Company.

Ridley, C. R. (2005). *Overcoming unintentional racism in counseling and therapy a practitioner's guide to intentional intervention* (2nd ed.). Sage.

Ritter, L. A., & Graham, D. H. (2022*). Multicultural health* (3rd ed.). Cognella Academic Publishing

Rose, A. K., Brown, K., Field, M., & Hogarth, L. (2013). The contributions of value-based decision-making and attentional bias to alcohol-seeking following devaluation. *Addiction, 108*(7), 1241–1249. https://doi.org/10.1111/add.12152

Rubin, S. E., Roessler, R. T., & Rumrill, P. D. (2016). *Foundations of the vocational rehabilitation process* (7th ed.). Pro-Ed.

Saul, J. (2013). Implicit bias, stereotype threat and women in philosophy. In K. Hutchison & F. Jenkins (Eds.), *Women in philosophy* (pp. 39–60). Oxford University Press.

Sayre, N. K. (2021). Addressing health disparities: Cultural proficiency. *In* S. B. Buchbinder, N. H. Shanks, & B. J. Kite *(Eds.), Introduction to health care management* (4th ed., pp. 351–370. Jones & Bartlett Publishing.

Selten, R. (2004). Boundedly rational qualitative reasoning on comparative statistics. *In* S. Huck (Ed.), *Advances in understanding strategic behaviour* (pp. 1–8). Palgrave Macmillan. https://doi.org/10.1057/9780230523371_1

Shipp, A. J., & Fried, Y. (2014). *Time and work: How time impacts groups, organizations and methodological choices (Vol. 2)*. Psychology Press.

Smart, J. F., & Smart, D. W. (2018). Models of disability: Implications for the counseling profession. In I. Marini & M. A. Stebnicki (Eds.), *The psychological and social impact of disability* (7th ed., pp. 49–68). Springer Publishing Company.

Strauser, D. R., & Greco, C. E. (2019). Introduction to assessment in rehabilitation. In D. R. Strauser, T. N. Tansey, & F. Chan (Eds.), *Assessment in rehabilitation and mental health counseling* (pp. 1–11). Springer Publishing Company.

Sue, D. W., & Spanierman, L. (2020). *Microaggressions in everyday life*. Wiley.

Sue, D. W., & Sue, D. (1990). *Counseling the culturally different* (2nd ed.). Wiley.

Sue, D. W., & Sue, D. (2013). *Counseling the culturally diverse: Theory and practice* (6th ed.). Wiley.

Sue, D. W., Sue, D., Neville, H. A., & Smith, A. (2022). *Counseling the culturally diverse: Theory and practice* (9th ed.). Wiley.

Thomas, S. W. (1990). Vocational assessment of multiple and severe physical impairments. *In* S. J. Scheer *(Ed.), Multidisciplinary perspectives in vocational assessment of impaired workers* (pp. 31–46). Aspen Publishers.

Toporek, R., & Williams, R. (2006). *Ethics and professional issues related to the practice of social justice in counseling psychology*. Sage. https://doi.org/10.4135/9781412976220

Verhoeven, N. (2011). *Doing research: The hows and whys of applied research*. Lyceum.

Vrchota, J., & Švárová, M. (2015). Comparison of decision-making skills of students and managers. *Acta Universitatis Agriculturae et Silviculturae Mendelianae Brunensis, 63*(3), 1073–1077. https://doi.org/10.11118/actaun201563031073

Vroom, V. H., & Jago, A. G. (1988), Managing participation: A critical dimension of leadership. *Journal of Management Development, 7*(5), 32–42. https://doi.org/10.1108/eb051689

Wand, Y., Monarchi, D. E., Parsons, J., & Woo, C. C. (1995). Theoretical foundations for conceptual modeling in information systems development. *Decision Support Systems, 15*(4), 285–304. https://doi.org/10.1016/0167-9236(94)00043-6

Woodside, M., & McClam, T. (2018). *Generalist case management: A method of human service delivery* (5th ed.). Cengage.

CHAPTER 7

The Operational Management of Time

LEARNING OBJECTIVES

By the end of this chapter, learners will be able to:

- Understand the dimensions and properties of time, including the finite nature of time and the importance of prioritizing tasks.
- Describe the principles of effective time management, including techniques for organizing schedules and optimizing productivity.
- Identify interfaced systems and the importance of communication, collaboration, and coordination with others for efficient time management.
- Recognize fundamental time laws, such as Parkinson's law and the Pareto principle, and leverage these principles to enhance productivity.
- Identify common time traps that hinder effective time management, such as interruptions, procrastination, overcommitment, and poor communication.
- Describe strategies to overcome time traps and maintain focus on important tasks.
- Understand the importance of self-care for maintaining high energy levels, focus, and productivity.
- Identify self-care activities that promote a healthy work–life balance.
- Describe technology as a valuable tool for time management and identify examples of technological solutions that can streamline processes and enhance organization.
- Develop effective time management skills and strategies for maximizing productivity and achieving greater balance in personal and professional life.

INTRODUCTION

Time is one of the most precious and finite resources available to individuals, organizations, and societies. Effective **time management** is essential for achieving success in any endeavor, as it allows us to prioritize tasks, set goals, and meet deadlines. In today's fast-paced world, where competition is fierce and demands are high, efficient management of time has become a crucial factor in determining the success or failure of the professional (Grissom et al., 2015). This chapter explores the operational management of time, which involves optimizing the use of time in all aspects of a rehabilitation counselor's operations. Various strategies and techniques for managing time will be discussed, such as goal-setting, **prioritization**, delegation, and time-tracking. Additionally, the role of technology in time management will be examined, including the use of productivity apps, time-tracking tools, and project management software. By the end of this chapter, a deeper understanding of the importance of effective time management will emerge, along with the strategies and tools available to optimize it in personal and professional practice and setting.

According to Brian Tracy (2014), time is an essential feature of life and serves as the prime organizing tool. People use time to create, shape, and order their worlds. While time management in rehabilitation settings has its unique components, problems related to overall time management are common across all rehabilitation settings, vocations, and practitioners. Based on observations by Cassell and Mulkey (1985, 2004), and Grubbs et al. (2006), rehabilitation counselors usually report time as the most formidable element to be managed. The necessity for multiple categories of activities, such as client interviews, case recording and documentation, gathering medical data, counseling for personal adjustment problems, testing, vocational counseling, consulting with other professionals, industrial surveys, client placement, and other follow-up activities, place considerable demands on a counselor's time allotment for a day or week. The frequent interactions with other professional groups, who face similar problems, are also a typical example of why this perception is a reality. Counselors who strive for consistency and reliable patterns of action in their work quickly discover that the job is characterized by a constant state of flux and rapid change, leaving little room for stability in time management. Thus, there is little constancy in managing time in rehabilitation settings (Cassell & Mulkey, 1985).

The counselor's understanding and awareness of time as a crucial management concern is essential. It is important to know what counselors understand about time and the principles and theoretical bases for managing it successfully. Counselors who cannot answer the following four basic questions should seriously consider gaining a knowledge and understanding of time: (a) What personal characteristics do you possess that affect your control of time? (b) How aware are you of how you spend your time? (c) What methods have you initiated to control your time? (d) Could you describe your system for managing time and the principles and concepts that guide your activities? The answers to these questions cannot always be found in a text, and experience on the job is necessary to solve time management problems. However, understanding time as an entity with definable limits and a conceptual framework is crucial. This chapter provides an initial base for understanding and managing time, upon which a counselor's personal commitment to control this aspect of caseload management can evolve.

While it's true that the answers to these questions may not always be found in a text or a single chapter of a text, rehabilitation counselors can gain a deeper understanding of time management through real-world experience and problem-solving. However, this understanding is built upon a foundation of awareness and conceptual understanding of time as a structured entity with clear limits. Therefore, this chapter serves as an initial starting point for rehabilitation counselors to develop their understanding and skills in managing time. By committing to this process, counselors can evolve their own honest and effective time management system to better manage their caseloads.

DIMENSIONS AND PROPERTIES OF TIME

In order to develop an effective time management program, a rehabilitation counselor must first have a solid understanding of the various dimensions, elements, and properties that impact their efforts. This means gaining an awareness of the **nature of time** and **time use**, which can initially appear ambiguous and omnipresent. By approaching time management from a rational perspective, counselors can ensure that their efforts are organized and effective. Ultimately, awareness and understanding are essential initial steps toward achieving control in any undertaking, as emphasized by Cassell and Mulkey (1985).

The following are the fundamental properties or dimensions that give time its conceptual reality, which one experiences in everyday life, whether at work dealing with clients, supervisors, and paperwork or at home dealing with the variables that make up post-work living. These dimensions must be described as distinct entities, but ultimately, it is their combining or coalescing properties that provide the theoretical basis for understanding time or what constitutes time use.

Time Has Structure and Perception

Time is a fundamental aspect of daily living that affects everyone, and it is crucial for rehabilitation professionals to understand the **structure of time** to support their clients. Time has structure in the sense that it can be divided into distinct units such as seconds, minutes, and hours. Additionally, time can be organized into different categories such as work time, leisure time, and sleep time (Kwapinska et al., 2018). Understanding the structure of time can help rehabilitation professionals assess how their clients are spending their time, identify any potential issues with time management, and develop effective interventions to improve their clients' overall functioning.

In addition to understanding the structure of time, rehabilitation professionals should also be aware of the concept of **time perception**. Time perception refers to the subjective experience of time, which can vary from person to person and can be influenced by factors such as age, culture, and psychological state (Avnet & Sellier, 2011). By considering their clients' individual experiences of time, rehabilitation professionals can develop interventions that are tailored to their clients' specific needs and goals. This can help their clients achieve a more balanced and fulfilling life, both in terms of their time use and their overall well-being.

Time on a Continuum

In the context of rehabilitation counseling, time being on a **continuum** implies that the rehabilitation process is a continuous and ongoing journey. It is not a fixed point in time that can be achieved and then forgotten. Rather, it is a process that evolves and changes over time. The rehabilitation process is dependent on various factors such as the individual's physical, emotional, and psychological condition; the severity of the disability; and the resources available for rehabilitation. The continuum of time is a reminder that rehabilitation professionals must be flexible in their approach and willing to adapt to changing circumstances. They must be prepared to work with individuals for an extended period and continue to support them through the ups and downs of the rehabilitation process.

Moreover, the **continuum of time** in rehabilitation counseling highlights the importance of setting realistic goals and expectations for clients. Rehabilitation professionals must work with clients to set achievable goals based on their current condition and pace of progress. They must also be willing to adjust these goals as the rehabilitation process progresses. This requires constant communication and collaboration between the rehabilitation professional and the client. By understanding time as a continuum, rehabilitation professionals can help clients maintain motivation and momentum throughout the rehabilitation process, leading to better outcomes in the long run. Ultimately, time being on a continuum emphasizes the need for rehabilitation professionals to take a patient-centered approach, working with clients to tailor their rehabilitation program to their unique needs and circumstances.

Time Involves "Humanization"

One way that time can be **humanized** is through our perception and experience of it. While time itself may be a constant stream that moves forward at a predictable pace, our subjective experience of time can vary depending on our emotional state, level of engagement, and other contextual factors. For example, when we are having fun or engaged in a meaningful activity, time may seem to fly by, whereas when we are bored or waiting for something, time may seem to drag on endlessly. These experiences can make time feel more human and relatable, rather than just an abstract concept.

Another way that time can be humanized is through cultural and social practices that give it meaning and value. Different cultures and societies may place different emphasis on the importance of time and have different rituals and practices surrounding it, such as religious observances, seasonal celebrations, or work schedules. These practices can give time a human context and imbue it with significance beyond just a measurement of seconds and minutes. By recognizing and participating in these practices, we can connect with others and create a shared sense of time that is meaningful and relevant to our lives.

PRINCIPLES FOR TIME MANAGEMENT

Effective time management is essential for success in both personal and professional life. It involves the ability to prioritize tasks, set goals, and make efficient use of time to achieve those goals. Time management also includes the ability to handle distractions and interruptions, maintain focus, and adjust as necessary. To master the principles of time management, one must learn self-motivation, planning, concentration, and how to deal with the tyranny of the urgent. By implementing these principles, individuals can increase their productivity, reduce stress, and achieve their goals in a timely manner while ensuring they utilize "ICE" while functioning in the various roles in the field of rehabilitation.

Principle of Self-Motivation

Time management programs are no different from any structured behavior change program one attempts, because at the outset one must have a real need or voiced desire to make changes. There must be a willingness to initiate actions and accept the consequences, to make sacrifices and be willing to tolerate concomitant change anxieties. Without this strong desire to make some change, the counselor should abandon the idea of making any change in current practices and merely accept one's present level of performing (Cook, 2011). Without this desire, counselors must accept themselves as ineffective time managers or time wasters and cease perseverating emotionally over poor performance, that is, if they are willing to accept the costly consequences. With continual feelings of distress come anxieties and further deterioration in performance. Thus, one's high levels of **motivation** to make real constructive changes are a prerequisite that cannot be waived or compromised if one's goal is an adequate time management program (Cassell & Mulkey, 1985).

Principle of Planning

As reflected upon in Chapter 3, **planning** is a key function in the management process.

The principle of time management as planning is essential for effectively utilizing one's time and achieving desired goals. Planning involves setting clear objectives, breaking them down into smaller tasks, and creating a roadmap to accomplish them within specific time frames. It helps individuals prioritize their activities, allocate resources appropriately, and avoid unnecessary distractions.

When practicing time management through planning, individuals can create schedules or **to-do lists** that outline their tasks and deadlines. This allows them to visualize their workload and allocate time slots accordingly. By identifying priorities and establishing realistic timelines, individuals can ensure that important tasks are completed on time while minimizing procrastination and last-minute rushes. Planning also provides a sense of direction and clarity, enabling individuals to make better decisions about how to allocate their time and resources (Wolters & Brady, 2021). Additionally, planning allows for better coordination and collaboration with others, as everyone involved can be aware of the tasks at hand and their respective timelines. Ultimately, effective planning helps individuals stay organized, focused, and in control of their time, leading to increased productivity and a greater sense of accomplishment.

LISTING FOR GOAL PLANNING

As described in Chapter 3, this tool falls under the purview of a manager's planning and organizing functions. According to Alan Lakein (1973), the first step for a manager is to clarify their goals and what they aim to achieve. Lakein suggests a practical approach where one takes a blank page of paper and spontaneously lists their lifetime goals, professional or work goals, and short-term goals. The emphasis should be on quantity rather than quality during this brainstorming exercise. It is crucial for the goals to be specific and attainable. For instance, a reasonable goal could be "to successfully close X number of 'rehabilitated' cases within the next year, 6 months, or month," rather than a vague statement like "I will be a better counselor."

After listing the goals, it becomes essential to assign different levels of importance to them, considering that the counselor might have a greater number of goals than can be realistically achieved within the given time frame. Alan Lakein proposes a priority system known as the A, B, C technique. This technique involves ranking the goals based on their significance to oneself at the present moment, where A represents the most important goals and C represents the least important ones (Lakein, 1973). By prioritizing goals, the counselor can focus their efforts on the most crucial objectives and ensure that they receive the necessary attention and resources, while minimizing time spent on less critical tasks.

To maximize the effectiveness of this **listing approach,** the counselor should proceed by identifying specific activities that will contribute to the attainment of their desired end results. This step is crucial because goals themselves cannot be directly accomplished. Once again, the A, B, C technique is employed to distinguish high-value activities from those of lesser value to the counselor. The primary focus should be on tackling the A activities first, rather than the B or C activities. However, it is important to remain attentive to any B activities that may need to be elevated to A priority. To determine the most valuable A activity to begin with, the counselor can further categorize the A activities as A1, A2, A3, and so forth.

Once these lists are created and the items are rated as A, B, or C, they only require periodic or as-needed updates. The time invested in this process yields significant returns in terms of saved time and increased productivity. By strategically investing time up-front in prioritizing and planning, the counselor can optimize their efforts and achieve their goals more efficiently.

TO-DO LISTS

The daily **to-do list** is a widely recognized and extensively utilized tool in the realm of time management, particularly among successful managers (Buck, 2003; Cassell & Mulkey, 1985). It serves as a daily roadmap, guiding counselors to their intended destinations by the end of the day. For optimal effectiveness, the daily to-do list should be created and reviewed on a daily basis. Interestingly, when asked about their use of daily to-do lists, some counselors in training sessions amusingly responded with "sometimes." To ensure efficiency, it is advisable to have only one comprehensive to-do list instead of scattering tasks across multiple scraps of paper.

Establishing a **priority system** is crucial in determining the relative importance of activities on the to-do list. One popular method is the A, B, C approach already mentioned. Alternatively, some counselors use columns marked with asterisks (*, * *, * * *), with three asterisks indicating the highest-value activity. To maximize its impact, the to-do list should ideally be created in the evening or early morning. However, if the counselor maintains a running list of tasks and assigns asterisks to indicate their value, the assigned level of importance can dictate the prioritization order of items on the list, rather than setting priorities in the evening or morning.

When executed correctly, the time manager's to-do list should consist of a few A-level tasks, slightly more B-level tasks than A-level ones, and a larger group of C-level or low-priority activities. These low-priority items can be problematic because they are often quick and easy to accomplish, providing a sense of gratification upon completion. However, counselors often find themselves prioritizing these low-priority tasks at the expense of giving adequate attention to the high-priority A-level items. It is crucial to resist the temptation of pursuing psychological closure by simply crossing off activities from the list. Instead, the primary focus should be on taking action or making progress on the A-level items. The ultimate goal should not solely revolve around checking off tasks, but rather on actively advancing the A-level objectives. Guarding against the inclination to seek completion as the ultimate measure of success is essential. By prioritizing movement and progress on the A-level tasks, one can ensure that the most crucial and significant goals receive the necessary attention and effort, leading to meaningful accomplishments rather than mere task completion.

To-do lists of counselors often become notorious for having unfinished tasks at the end of the day. It is not uncommon to find numerous items left undone when reviewing the list. It is acceptable to transfer these unfinished tasks to the agenda for the next day without any penalty. However, it is crucial for the diligent time manager to question whether the items carried over for more than a day or so are truly authentic A-level tasks. Otherwise, there is a risk that procrastination may be seeping into what initially appears to be a well-intentioned and disciplined management program. By carefully evaluating the nature and importance of the carried-over items, one can identify any potential tendencies to delay or defer critical tasks, ensuring a more effective and proactive approach to time management.

Principle of Concentration

Concentration is a fundamental principle of time management that plays a crucial role in maximizing productivity and efficiency in rehabilitation professional practice. It involves the ability to focus one's attention and mental energy on a specific task or objective, while minimizing distractions and interruptions. By cultivating the skill of concentration, individuals can make the most of their available time and accomplish tasks more effectively.

Maintaining concentration requires creating an environment conducive to deep work. This involves minimizing external distractions such as noise, interruptions, or unnecessary notifications. Finding a quiet and dedicated space, utilizing time-blocking techniques, and setting boundaries with colleagues or family members can help create a focused work environment. Additionally, managing internal distractions, such as limiting multitasking or controlling the urge to check emails and social media frequently, is essential for maintaining concentration.

Implementing strategies such as the **Pomodoro technique** can be valuable in enhancing concentration and combating mental fatigue. This technique involves breaking work into focused intervals, typically around 25 minutes, followed by short breaks. This structured approach not only helps manage time effectively but also promotes sustained attention and concentration (Content Engine, 2023; Mandal, 2020). By working in concentrated bursts and allowing brief periods of rest, rehabilitation counselors can maintain their focus, prevent burnout, and optimize productivity.

In addition to time management techniques, incorporating **mindfulness** exercises or **meditation** into daily routines can have a profound impact on concentration. These practices cultivate self-awareness and the ability to direct attention to the present moment. By training the mind to stay focused and avoid distractions, rehabilitation counselors can enhance their concentration skills, improve their ability to engage deeply in tasks, and achieve higher levels of productivity (Droit-Volet et al., 2019). Prioritizing concentration as a fundamental principle of time management empowers individuals to harness their cognitive resources effectively. By consciously managing external and internal distractions, rehabilitation counselors can unlock their full potential, accomplish more meaningful work, and experience greater success in both their professional and personal lives.

Principle of Tyranny of the Urgent

The **"tyranny of the urgent"** is a time management principle coined by Charles E. Hummel (1967), which refers to the tendency for urgent tasks or issues to dominate our attention and drive our actions, often at the expense of important but nonurgent tasks. It describes the phenomenon where the immediate demands and pressures of the moment take precedence over activities that contribute to long-term goals and overall effectiveness.

When faced with numerous urgent tasks, it is common for individuals to become reactive and constantly firefight, jumping from one urgent matter to another without considering the bigger picture. This can lead to a cycle of perpetual urgency, where important tasks and strategic planning are neglected, causing stress, inefficiency, and hindered progress.

To overcome the tyranny of the urgent, it is important to prioritize and differentiate between tasks that are truly important and those that are merely urgent (Cannon, 2004). This involves distinguishing between what is necessary for long-term success and what is simply demanding immediate attention. By consciously allocating time and resources to important tasks, individuals can regain control over their time and focus on activities that align with their goals and values.

Implementing strategies such as proactive planning, goal setting, and time blocking can help mitigate the impact of the tyranny of the urgent. By setting aside dedicated time for important tasks, individuals can ensure that they receive the necessary attention and avoid being overwhelmed by the constant influx of urgent matters. This approach allows for better decision-making, increased productivity, and a sense of progress toward meaningful objectives. By recognizing and addressing the tyranny of the urgent, individuals can regain control of their time and work more intentionally, making room for strategic thinking, personal growth, and achieving long-term success. It involves breaking free from reactive patterns and embracing a proactive mindset that focuses on important tasks while effectively managing urgent demands.

Principle of "ICE"–Insulate, Concentrate, and Eliminate

The principle of **"ICE"** stands for **Insulate, Concentrate, and Eliminate,** and it serves as an effective time management principle to enhance productivity and focus (Grubbs et al., 2006). It provides a structured approach to optimize time utilization and minimize distractions. Let's explore each element of the **ICE principle:**

1. Insulate: Insulating refers to creating a conducive work environment that shields you from unnecessary interruptions and distractions. This involves finding a physical space that minimizes noise, interruptions, and other external disturbances. Additionally, it entails setting boundaries and managing interruptions from colleagues, email notifications, and phone calls. By insulating yourself from external distractions, you can create a focused work environment that promotes concentration and efficiency.

2. Concentrate: Concentrating involves directing your full attention and mental energy toward the task at hand. This means eliminating multitasking and resisting the temptation to switch between various activities simultaneously. Instead, focus on a single task and give it your complete attention until completion or until a designated break time. By concentrating on one task at a time, you can achieve a higher level of productivity, produce better-quality work, and reduce errors.

3. Eliminate: Eliminating refers to removing or reducing distractions, including nonessential tasks and activities that do not contribute to your goals or priorities. It involves identifying time-wasting activities, low-value tasks, or unnecessary commitments and finding ways to eliminate or delegate them. By consciously eliminating or reducing nonessential elements, you create more time and mental space for important and meaningful activities. This allows you to focus on high-priority tasks and allocate your resources effectively.

By following the ICE principle, individuals can improve their time management skills and enhance productivity. Insulating oneself from distractions, concentrating on one task at a time, and eliminating nonessential activities can lead to increased focus, better time allocation, and improved overall efficiency. It helps rehabilitation counselors to make the most of their time, accomplish meaningful work, and achieve their goals effectively.

MANAGING INTERFACED SYSTEMS

Figure 7.1 showcases the remarkable consistency with which counselors relinquish control over aspects of their daily activities that are initiated by others (with a combined percentage of 88% across all categories, excluding self-imposed activities). This realization brings to light the fact that we are not operating in isolation. **Figure 7.1** visualizes the interconnection and interdependence of others' time systems with our own. Consequently,

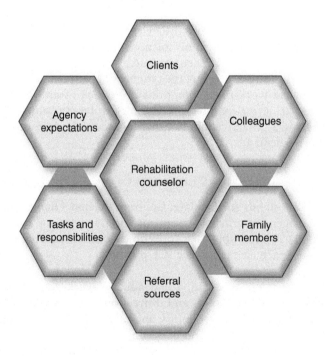

FIGURE 7.1 The influence of interfaced time systems.

it becomes evident that if inefficiencies exist in how others manage their time, these inefficiencies will also impact the counselor through their interactions with them. Therefore, it becomes necessary to allocate efforts toward effectively managing these **interconnected systems.**

The **team approach** has gained significant popularity as a viable solution for improving overall time management. Counselors are encouraged to engage in a collaborative effort with individuals who impose substantial demands on their time. This entails the counselor taking the following steps: (a) identifying the individuals with whom the most significant challenges arise, (b) pinpointing the specific areas in which these challenges manifest (employing conceptual categories as necessary), and (c) assessing the extent or priority level of these problems to determine the order in which they should be addressed (Grubbs et al., 2006). By adopting this team-oriented approach, counselors can effectively manage their time and enhance productivity in collaboration with those who have a direct impact on their schedule and workload.

Once the counselor has harnessed all the available resources, techniques, and tools, it becomes feasible to harness their collective power to address the potential obstacles that arise when different professional systems intersect. This marks a significant milestone in achieving more effective time management. The initial step in this process involves engaging with significant individuals in the counselor's time management sphere. By engaging in discussions about common time management challenges and identifying specific areas of conflict, a supportive and facilitative framework gradually takes shape. It is at this point that the management of interconnected time systems starts to come under the counselor's control, allowing for more efficient coordination and utilization of time resources.

The principle of **self-reinforcement** for action requires careful monitoring to avoid misapplication, which can hinder progress. It is essential to remember that self-reinforcement should primarily focus on action structuring, which refers to the purposeful and goal-directed initiation of the first forward step by counselors. While acknowledging the completion of individual tasks is important, it is crucial to avoid providing deep, gratifying rewards.

Historically, reinforcements have often been strongly tied to specific outcomes, task completion, or maze solving. However, this approach can be highly detrimental to human motivation (Dezfouli et al., 2020). The reliance on gratification during the process can temporarily immobilize individuals due to the closure effect. As a result, elaborate reward systems are not suitable for initial action-setting endeavors. Instead, by circumventing this effect and experiencing only minimal yet satisfying positive feelings when taking the first movement toward structuring a new action step, common obstacles to effective time management, such as procrastination and nonmotivational inactivity, become less menacing and less likely to impede progress.

Lastly, it is crucial to initiate action structuring based on a solid management foundation. Without proper planning, organizing, directing, coordinating, and controlling, effective action is unlikely to occur. It is important to remember that in the pursuit of end goals, without a clear plan for action, any path can lead to an outcome. This implies that inefficient routes will arise as frequently as efficient ones, and the costs associated with taking such paths will become evident. Therefore, prioritizing strategic planning and implementing efficient management practices become imperative for achieving optimal results.

Reevaluation and Interfaced Systems

In reality, it is the system that connects all other elements together to formalize them. The principle of **reevaluation** emphasizes that an effective time management system can only be as successful as the extent to which its interactions are regularly reassessed. If a counselor's activities are based on outdated data, perceptions, and information, achieving effectiveness will remain a challenging endeavor. To maintain a proactive approach, the effective time manager must continuously evaluate current conditions, forces, and issues, as well as stay updated on others' perspectives. By engaging in reevaluation activities, the counselor enhances problem-prevention efforts and reduces the frequency of time-consuming crises or "firefighting" situations (Grubbs et al., 2006).

The **practice of reevaluation** involves developing self-awareness cues and making vigilance an integral part of everyday activities. It entails assessing questions such as "Where have I been?," "Where am I now?," and "What am I progressing toward?" These self-reflective guideposts may initially seem time-consuming and draining, but with consistent commitment to these principles, they soon become timesaving and energy-conserving practices. The act of reevaluation empowers the counselor to stay on track, adapt to changing circumstances, and make informed decisions that align with their goals.

In conclusion, recognizing the impact of interfaced time systems is crucial for establishing effective strategies to manage time more efficiently. Ultimately, without a clear understanding of how time is being utilized, it is impossible to gain control over time management issues. By acquiring the necessary skills to manage oneself efficiently and effectively, counselors will find that they have more time available to accomplish tasks that previously required significant sacrifice and were often left unfinished. Taking proactive steps toward better time management will lead to increased productivity and a sense of accomplishment in both personal and professional endeavors.

CATEGORIZED TIME USE

In order to foster an intuitive understanding of time management, counselors often need to recognize the patterns of **time motivation** that shape their behaviors. This entails classifying time into different motivational elements to establish a coherent framework for addressing the challenges at hand.

Historically, Bliss (1976) conceptualized five basic categories of which four necessitate the time manager to effectively navigate the demands associated with each category.

1. *Important and urgent.* The category of "important and urgent" tasks is easily identifiable and clearly requires immediate attention. Counselors readily recognize these time-related challenges as genuine crisis situations. Caseload managers typically face minimal obstacles when it comes to taking prompt action on such time problems. These situations demand and receive immediate attention.
2. *Important but low in urgency.* This particular category of time usage can indeed pose challenges for counselors. The majority of activities or demands on counselors' time, although highly important, lack urgency. As a result, there is a tendency to postpone taking action. Unfortunately, what we postpone often ends up being abandoned altogether. In cases where action is not abandoned, counselors often resort to a "crisis style" of functioning, relying on adrenaline rushes to propel themselves into action when the appropriate time arrives. However, this approach does not constitute effective management.

    Ultimately, it becomes crucial for counselors to cultivate their own sense of urgency. According to Bliss's observation, if our activities are driven solely by other people's priorities or externally imposed deadlines that create a sense of urgency, we will never find the time to address our own priorities (Bliss, 1976).
3. *High urgency–low importance.* This category of time usage encompasses those activities that initially appear to be urgent but upon closer examination or clarification are actually of much lower priority. These situations are characterized by what Mackenzie (1972) referred to as a "tyranny of urgency." The urgent-but-not-important scenario

can frequently mask low-value tasks as high-priority projects that demand immediate attention. Counselors often encounter a large number of these demands, which usually belong to someone else's A-list, or come from individuals in positions of authority, or from someone to whom the counselors feel an elevated degree of responsibility.

4. *Diversionary work.* This category encompasses the busywork activities that counselors often find themselves engaged in. It involves dedicating time to the numerous Cs that tend to dominate daily to-do lists. Bliss (1976) points out that working in this area provides an excuse to postpone tackling tasks from category II, which are the tasks that offer a significantly higher payoff for the counselor.

5. *Wasted time.* This category poses fewer challenges compared to the more disguised categories III and IV mentioned earlier. Wasted time in this category is usually apparent to most individuals without much effort. There is often an immediate awareness of wasted time when a negative feeling arises after completing an activity, indicating that the time could have been utilized for something far more productive.

Time-Use Laws

A caseload manager's approach to time utilization can be influenced positively or negatively based on their understanding and wise application of two daily operating laws or principles that impact their efforts. Two examples of such **time-use laws** that are often discussed are (a) **Parkinson's law** and (b) **Pareto's law.**

PARKINSON'S LAW

Parkinson's law, a critical principle of time management, states that tasks will naturally expand or take longer to complete if more time is made available for their completion. This can be a fallacy because the counselor might continue to add finishing touches or improve the task under the guise of achieving perfection. This can result in the counselor spinning their wheels and wasting time. Although they might argue that they are serving the best interests of their clients and the agency, this argument is usually weak. To overcome Parkinson's law, counselors must set deadlines, establish a daily plan without mental margins of error, and limit the time available for specific tasks. Once these deadlines are set, they must be strictly adhered to, and tasks must be completed within the established time frame. Darnell et al. (2022) posits not allowing perfection to be the enemy of what is good or correct, but to focus on supporting this change in mindset to strive for excellence rather than perfection.

PARETO'S "LAW"

Vilfredo Pareto, an Italian sociologist from the 19th century, introduced a significant principle that is often regarded as a law. **Pareto's principle** asserts that a small portion of items within a group holds the greatest significance and value, while the majority of items are relatively insignificant (Cassell & Mulkey, 1985; Grubbs et al., 2006). This principle is also referred to as the "trivial many" versus the "vital few" (Mackenzie, 1970) or the 80/20 rule (Lakein, 1973). It provides insight into many aspects of our daily and professional activities. For instance:

1. Around 80% of phone calls received by counselors originate from just 20% of the callers.
2. Approximately 80% of a counselor's time is dedicated to working on 20% of the cases in their caseload.
3. Roughly 80% of grocery expenses are allocated to 20% of the meat and grocery items purchased.

4. The majority of eating out, about 80%, occurs at only 20% of the favorite restaurants available.
5. When reading a newspaper, roughly 80% of one's time is spent on 20% of the pages.
6. About 80% of employee absenteeism can be attributed to just 20% of the employees.
7. During a training session, approximately 80% of the discussion originates from 20% of the participants.

This principle can be applied to time management, where it becomes evident that a counselor's extensive investment of time, energy, and effort is often consumed by numerous trivial problems or situations, which make up around 80% of their time. Surprisingly, these efforts yield only about 20% of the overall results achieved. On the other hand, the critical situations or problems that require the counselor's attention typically account for only 20% of their time. However, this focused 20% of time generates around 80% of the total results achieved. Similarly, when a counselor has a long list of, let's say, 20 tasks to accomplish, by prioritizing and working on 4 of these tasks, they can achieve the highest value, utilizing approximately 80% of their time effectively, provided their priorities are well-defined and valid.

To effectively apply Pareto's principle, several steps can be taken. First, it is important to establish clear boundaries and define the scope of work, such as by creating a list of tasks. Second, prioritize the tasks using a method like the A, B, C system. Finally, identify the two or three most crucial items (the "vital few") that will yield the highest results. Dedicate a significant block of time to these tasks and remain focused until completion. By concentrating efforts on this concentrated period of time and effort, even small improvements (e.g., from 20% to 23% or 25%) can lead to tremendous overall output increase in the long run. If counselors are facing frustrations and anxieties regarding meeting new and heightened production goals set for a specific period, they can find the solution by harnessing the positive power of Pareto's principle and implementing it effectively.

TIME TRAPS

No matter how diligently counselors strive to measure time, analyze activities, and establish action plans, there are various processes and situations that can undermine their efforts and diminish their efficiency. These obstacles form a group characterized by their tendency to cause significant time loss for counselors. However, it is possible to gain control over these **time traps** by adopting an intuitive and personalized approach (Grubbs et al., 2006).

Having conducted training sessions with counselors for several years, the authors have identified a collection of time traps that are consistently voiced by participants. The following list outlines eight of these common time traps:

1. Interruptions
2. Procrastination
3. Drop-ins
4. Incomplete information
5. Overcommitment
6. Poor communication
7. Meetings
8. Personal disorganization

In order to provide caseload managers with a starting point for understanding and addressing these time robbers, each of the eight traps will be discussed briefly. It is important to note that this initial understanding serves as a foundation and should be followed by a well-thought-out and implemented time management program.

Interruptions

There are two primary types of **interruptions**: self-initiated interruptions and interruptions initiated by others. It is crucial for rehabilitation caseload managers to understand the significant impact these interruptions can have on a time management program. It is common to experience multiple interruptions throughout the day (Cassell & Mulkey, 1985; Riley et al., 1976; Smith, 1994; Woodside & McClam, 2003), emphasizing the high time cost associated with them.

One reason interruptions are so time-consuming is because of the nature of most interruptions. **Figure 7.2** illustrates the anatomy of an interruption, revealing that the overhead portions of an interruption (technical and social overhead) consume a significantly larger proportion of time compared to the actual purpose or content for which the interruption was initiated (Riley et al., 1976). Typically, the technical overhead (e.g., preparing papers and gathering notes) and the social overhead (e.g., lengthy greetings and warm-up conversations) exist in ratios of 2:1, 3:1, or even 10:1 in relation to the core of the interruption. Furthermore, interruptions often arise from issues within the communication process. If clients, parents, vendors, employers, and other professionals do not fully grasp the required actions or procedures after communicating with the counselor, it leads to frequent renewed contacts, some of which occur as interruptions.

To control interruptions, several strategies can be employed: (a) practicing self-discipline, (b) blocking specific time periods for dedicated activities and allowing only genuine crises to interrupt (remember, 1 uninterrupted hour can be worth 2 to 3 uncontrolled hours), (c) permitting interruptions or interrupting others only when vital and urgent matters are at stake, (d) arranging desks and office furniture in a way that discourages interruptions, (e) using body language and attitudes that convey a polite busyness, and (f) giving due respect and attention to the communication process.

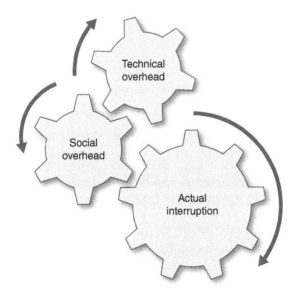

FIGURE 7.2 The component parts of an interruption.

Procrastination

Interruptions are a common form of time robbery inflicted by others, while **procrastination** is the most prevalent self-inflicted time robber (Van Eerde, 2015). Procrastination can stem from various causes, such as a lack of confidence, the pursuit of perfection, resentment toward task requirements, fear of failure, or a generally passive and low-keyed approach (a characteristic of true procrastinators). Fear tends to greatly exaggerate the problems and barriers a counselor experiences. "Putting it off" has probably caused more failure than all other management problems combined (Smith, 1994; Southerton, 2003). Consequently, procrastination often results in feelings of guilt due to perceived inaction.

If counselors were to ask others the straightforward question, "Do you see me as a procrastinator?" the answer would likely confirm that the real adversity lies in the guilt rather than the act of procrastination itself. To confront procrastination, it is important to (a) embrace the notion that errors are valuable learning experiences and not to fear them, (b) establish a prioritizing system and have faith in it, (c) begin each day by tackling the most unpleasant task (not necessarily the most important) first, and (d) avoid ending the day feeling insufficiently accomplished to prevent falling into the guilt syndrome. Remember, if your management system is effectively working for you, it means you have filled your day with all the high-priority activities it could accommodate, and other important tasks will have to wait for another day.

Drop-Ins

Drop-ins can be categorized into two main groups: (a) clients, including new, current, or former clients, and (b) others, such as fellow counselors. During the day, it may be necessary to tolerate some drop-ins from new clients. Occasional drop-ins from former or current clients may also need to be accommodated, but steps can be taken to train them to respect time management and prioritize their interactions. The "others" mentioned earlier can be tactfully trained to recognize and respect a counselor's efforts in establishing an effective time management program.

There are several effective strategies for dealing with drop-ins: (a) maintain tactful honesty when communicating with drop-ins, as their recognition of your honesty can influence their own time management practices; (b) suggest scheduling meetings with them later in their offices; (c) occasionally close your door to convey your focus and availability; (d) if possible, remain standing during the interaction to signal a brief and time-limited encounter; (e) train support staff to assist drop-ins by scheduling appointments and providing requested information; and (f) designate intake counselors in a rehabilitation unit to handle drop-ins on a rotating basis, particularly for new clients.

Incomplete Information

This time trap can have the counselor chasing around expending time at an enormous rate. However, as was learned earlier, one characteristic of internally controlled counselors is the drive to attain more information in order to be more cognizant and in greater command of their situation. This gathering of complete information will improve the decision-making process, ensure more valid planning, and lower risk-taking and inference-based action. The time used for seeking out further and more complete information is a trade-off for a larger portion of time saved later on.

Overcommitment

The experience of **overcommitment** is perhaps the most significant time trap faced by vocational rehabilitation counselors. These counselors are responsible for managing caseloads that bring them into contact with a wide range of systems, each with its own unique requirements and demands on the counselor's time. In addition to addressing a client's personal values, attitudes, and psychological conditions, counselors must also navigate interactions and responses to various systems, including social services, parental and familial systems, community and organizational systems, medical/psychological examinations and treatments, industry and placement systems, vocational evaluation training, tracking and follow-up systems, and attorney and judicial demands for clients (Rothbard & Ollier-Malaterre, 2016). Each of these systems necessitates acquiring knowledge and establishing ongoing relationships. It is no surprise, then, that overcommitment can become a challenge.

Effectively managing overcommitment requires the development of comprehensive management skills that complement the counselor's existing expertise. The alternative approach of superficially dealing with some systems while giving greater attention to others is only a temporary solution and ultimately leads to reduced quality and quantity of outcomes. Therefore, counselors must strive to establish viable and complete management skills to effectively navigate and balance their commitments to these various systems.

Poor Communication

The consequences of this time trap manifest in a consistent pattern of client interruptions, duplicated efforts by counselors (when communication breakdown occurs downward in the organization), duplicated efforts by clients, and the burden of shouldering others' responsibilities. A vigilant caseload manager should be able to recognize these patterns as indicators of a flawed communication process.

Poor communication networks with others arise from various problem areas that have reached critical levels. These problem areas include conflicting value systems, which lead individuals to only perceive what aligns with their own beliefs, overcommitment that weakens connections with communication targets, inattention to detail (often resulting from basing actions on assumptions rather than observations), and anxieties arising from the struggle to prioritize effectively.

Historically, Treon (1979) illustrates the cost of poor communication for caseload managers, particularly in the context of private rehabilitation for injured individuals. He points out that rehabilitation professionals and lawyers representing injured individuals often fail to understand each other and lack a shared perspective. Treon states that better understanding and communication would greatly improve client service.

Addressing poor communication issues begins by incorporating positive forms of redundancy into the communication process. This includes actively seeking clarity from communicators during interactions and confirming understanding through mental or verbal assessments of the transaction. By striving for clarity and reinforcing understanding, caseload managers can rectify communication problems and foster more effective interactions.

Meetings

Meetings are often met with disdain by almost everyone involved. However, conscientious managers understand the importance of being prepared for specific meetings and actively contribute to keeping the meeting focused and progressing at a reasonable pace. They provide progress summaries when the meeting seems to be unproductive and opt for standing meetings to maintain engagement. Additionally, effective caseload managers set clear objectives for meetings and acquire knowledge about the psychology of group processes. In certain situations, it may be more productive for a counselor to receive meeting minutes later rather than attend in person. A counselor with a mature mindset will regularly ask themselves, "What is the most valuable use of my time at this moment?" and make appropriate decisions based on that assessment.

Personal Disorganization

Personal disorganization is a comprehensive concept that encompasses many of the time traps discussed earlier, emphasizing the importance of implementing coping strategies to deal with time-related issues. Although time problems often originate from external sources, it is crucial to first look inward and focus on areas that can be easily controlled to achieve immediate results. To become a time manager rather than a "time subordinate," counselors must make a strong personal commitment to consistently applying a management system. The cost of time lost to these time traps is so high that it is surprising any significant work can be accomplished. However, even minimal management efforts can result in immediate payoffs in terms of productivity and personal job satisfaction.

PRIORITIZATION

In today's fast-paced world, time has become an increasingly valuable commodity. As a result, it is essential to manage time effectively in order to maximize productivity and achieve one's goals. **Prioritization** is a key component of time management and involves identifying tasks and activities that are most important and need to be completed first (Forsyth, 2013). By prioritizing effectively, individuals can make the most of their time, increase efficiency, reduce stress, and achieve their desired outcomes.

Tickler System as a Prioritization Approach

Tickler systems are excellent examples of prioritization in time management. A tickler system is a method used to organize and prioritize tasks, reminders, and deadlines. It involves setting up a system that prompts individuals to act on specific dates or at predetermined intervals. With a tickler system, tasks and deadlines are categorized and scheduled in a way that ensures important items are addressed in a timely manner. This method allows individuals to prioritize their workload, ensuring that critical tasks are completed on time while also providing a structure for managing future obligations (Cassell & Mulkey, 1985; Cook, 2011; Grubbs et al., 2006; Pollar et al., 1998). Here's how a tickler system typically works:

1. *Centralized system.* The tickler system consists of a centralized location, such as a physical folder or a digital calendar or task management app, where all time-sensitive items are stored.
2. *Date-based organization.* The system is organized based on dates. It typically includes 31 folders for each day of the month and 12 folders for each month of the year. Some tickler systems may also have additional folders for long-term planning, such as a "Next Year" folder.
3. *File and retrieve.* Items are filed in the corresponding date or month folders based on when they need to be addressed or revisited. For example, if you have a meeting scheduled for July 10, you would file any relevant documents or notes in the "July" folder or specifically in the "10" folder if needed.
4. *Daily review.* At the beginning of each day, you review the contents of the current day's folder to see what tasks or appointments are scheduled for that day. This helps you stay focused on what needs to be done and ensures that important items are not overlooked.
5. *Future planning.* As you come across items or commitments that need attention in the future, you file them in the corresponding date or month folder so that they can be retrieved when the time comes. This allows you to offload future tasks from your immediate to-do list while ensuring they won't be forgotten.

A tickler system offers individuals a range of options for prioritizing their tasks and obligations. By incorporating a tickler system into their time management approach, individuals can effectively organize their workload and stay on top of critical deadlines and appointments. This systematic approach minimizes the chances of overlooking important events or tasks, ensuring that all necessary actions are completed in a timely manner. With a tickler system in place, individuals can confidently prioritize their responsibilities and maintain a proactive and organized approach to managing their time.

SELF-CARE: AN ESSENTIAL TIME MANAGEMENT TOOL

Incorporating **self-care** is not only essential for our overall well-being, but it also plays a crucial role in effective time management. Research suggests that understanding several key elements of time management and its correlation with health is essential for cultivating a comprehensive work–life balance (Aeon et al., 2021). Taking care of ourselves physically, mentally, and emotionally allows us to maintain a high level of energy, focus, and productivity. By integrating self-care activities into our daily routines, we can recharge, reduce stress, and improve our overall time management skills. This may include activities such as exercise, proper nutrition, adequate sleep, mindfulness practices, relaxation techniques, hobbies, socializing, and setting boundaries to protect our personal time. Prioritizing self-care means investing in our own well-being, which in turn enhances our ability to manage time effectively and achieve greater balance in all areas of life.

Self-Care and Rehabilitation Counseling

Self-care is of utmost importance in the field of rehabilitation counseling. As rehabilitation counselors, we often work with individuals facing various challenges, and it is essential for us to prioritize our own well-being to effectively support others. Engaging in self-care practices allows us to maintain our physical, mental, and emotional well-being, which directly impacts our ability to provide quality care to our clients. By taking time for ourselves, practicing self-reflection, seeking support when needed, and engaging in activities that recharge us, we can ensure that we are in a better position to help others navigate their rehabilitation journeys. Self-care not only benefits us as individuals but also strengthens our ability to make a positive impact on the lives of those we serve.

TECHNOLOGY AS A TIME MANAGEMENT TOOL

Technology has revolutionized the way we manage our time, offering numerous tools and resources to enhance productivity and efficiency. One of the challenges of living in a network-connected society is using available time effectively. Time is regarded as something that must be carefully planned in the context of a day full of tasks to complete, roles to be played, and information to be processed (Stoilov, 2012). Utilizing **technology** as a time management tool can significantly improve our ability to organize tasks, streamline processes, and stay on track. Here are some examples of how technology can be utilized for effective time management:

1. *Calendar and scheduling apps.* Applications like Google Calendar, Microsoft Outlook, or Apple Calendar allow us to schedule and manage our appointments, meetings, and deadlines in one centralized place. They offer reminders and notifications to keep us on track and ensure we don't miss important events.

2. *Task management software.* Tools such as Trello, Asana, or Todoist help us create task lists, set priorities, and track progress. These platforms often provide features like due dates, reminders, and the ability to collaborate with others, making it easier to manage and prioritize our work.

3. *Time tracking apps.* Applications like Rescue Time, timeBro, or Toggl can help us monitor how we spend our time by tracking activities and providing detailed reports. This insight allows us to identify time-wasting habits, optimize productivity, and allocate our time more effectively.

4. *Project management tools.* Platforms such as Basecamp, Jira, or Monday.com assist in planning and managing complex projects. They enable us to assign tasks, track progress, set deadlines, and facilitate collaboration among team members, ensuring that projects stay on schedule.

5. *Communication and collaboration tools.* Technologies like Slack, Microsoft Teams, or Zoom provide efficient communication channels for team collaboration, reducing the need for lengthy email threads. Real-time messaging, video conferencing, and file sharing features enable effective communication and quick decision-making.

6. *Note-taking apps.* Applications like Evernote, OneNote, or Notion help us capture and organize our ideas, meeting notes, and important information in a digital format. These apps allow us to easily search and retrieve information, eliminating the need for paper-based notes and ensuring everything is accessible at our fingertips.

Remember, while technology can be a powerful time management tool, it is important to choose the tools that align with your needs and preferences. Embrace technology that enhances your productivity, but also be mindful of not getting overwhelmed by excessive digital distractions.

SUMMARY

In summary, this chapter highlighted the importance of developing techniques and practices for effective time management in order to achieve desired outcomes. It provided a comprehensive overview of time management, covering dimensions and properties of time, principles for effectiveness, interfaced systems, time laws, time traps, self-care, and technology. By understanding the finite nature of time and implementing strategies to optimize productivity, individuals can make the most of their time and achieve a healthy work–life balance. The concept of interfaced systems emphasized the significance of communication and collaboration in efficient time management. Additionally, recognizing common time traps and employing strategies to overcome them can help individuals stay focused on important tasks. The chapter also emphasized the importance of self-care for maintaining high energy levels and productivity. Lastly, technology was identified as a valuable tool, providing examples of how it can streamline processes and improve time management efficiency. By applying the principles and strategies discussed in this chapter, individuals can develop effective time management skills, increase productivity, and attain greater balance in both their personal and professional lives.

QUESTIONS FOR DISCUSSION

1. What are some common time management challenges faced by rehabilitation counselors? How do these challenges affect their overall productivity and effectiveness?

2. How does the principle of concentration contribute to effective time management? What strategies can counselors employ to enhance their ability to concentrate on tasks?

3. The chapter discusses the "tyranny of the urgent" as a time management principle. How can counselors avoid falling into the trap of constantly prioritizing urgent tasks over important ones? What strategies can be employed to strike a balance between urgent and important responsibilities?

4. The **ICE** principle (Insulate, Concentrate, Eliminate) is introduced as a time management strategy. How can counselors apply this principle to their daily routines? Can you think of specific examples where each component of the ICE principle can be utilized?

5. The concept of self-reinforcement for action is discussed. How can counselors effectively use self-reinforcement to stay motivated and maintain momentum in their time management efforts? Are there any potential pitfalls or challenges associated with self-reinforcement?

6. The chapter emphasizes the importance of reevaluation in time management. Why is ongoing reevaluation necessary? How can rehabilitation counselors incorporate reevaluation into their routines to ensure continuous improvement in their time management practices?

7. Reflecting on the chapter, what are some practical steps rehabilitation counselors can take to formalize their time management systems and bring their time use within manageable limits? How can they gain an objective understanding of their current use of time?

8. How can counselors balance the demands of their professional responsibilities with their personal lives? What strategies can be employed to prevent work–life imbalance and ensure a healthy integration of both aspects?

9. What are some potential barriers or obstacles that counselors may face when implementing effective time management strategies? How can these barriers be overcome?

10. How might the principles and strategies discussed in this chapter be applicable to individuals in other professions or fields beyond rehabilitation counseling? Are there any specific adaptations or modifications that would be necessary?

PUTTING IT INTO PRACTICE

Ask yourself these questions to target issues or concerns with the operational management of time.

1. How do you personally manage interruptions throughout your day while working on rehabilitation tasks and responsibilities? Interruptions can be quite disruptive, so what strategies do you employ to handle them effectively at all levels?

2. Technology plays a significant role in our daily lives, both inside and outside of the workplace. Considering the technology utilized regularly, is it viewed as a helpful ally or a hindrance when it comes to accomplishing your case and caseload tasks and responsibilities?

3. Self-care is often overlooked but crucial in the field of rehabilitation counseling. What steps are you taking to practice self-care on a daily basis? Additionally, what aspects of your self-care routine do you believe need improvement to enhance your overall effectiveness in the workplace?

CASE STUDY

Laura is a counselor who works in a busy community mental health center. She finds herself constantly overwhelmed with a high caseload and numerous administrative tasks. Her time management skills are lacking, and she struggles to prioritize her tasks effectively. As a result, she often feels stressed and unable to meet deadlines.

Case Study Questions

1. What specific challenges or tasks contribute to Laura's feeling of being overwhelmed?

2. How does Laura currently prioritize her workload? Are there any patterns or strategies she uses?

3. What are the consequences of Laura's poor time management skills on her work and overall well-being?

4. Are there any external factors or organizational issues that may be contributing to Laura's workload and time management challenges?

5. What strategies or techniques has Laura tried in the past to improve her time management? What were the results?

6. How does Laura's lack of effective time management impact her ability to provide quality care to her clients?

 A robust set of instructor resources designed to supplement this text is located at **http://connect.springerpub.com/content/book/978-0-8261-5963-2.** Qualifying instructors may request access by emailing **textbook@springerpub.com.**

REFERENCES

Aeon, B., Faber, A., & Panaccio, A. (2021). Does time management work? A meta-analysis. *PLoS One,* *16*(1), e0245066. https://doi.org/10.1371/journal.pone.0245066

Avnet, T., & Sellier, A.-L. (2011). Clock time vs. event time: Temporal culture or self-regulation? *Journal of Experimental Social Psychology, 47*(3), 665–667. https://doi.org/10.1016/j.jesp.2011.01.006

Bliss, E. C. (1976). *Getting things done: The ABC's of time management.* Bantam Books.

Buck, G. (2003). *Assessing listening.* Cambridge University Press. https://www.assets.cambridge.org/97805216/61621/sample/9780521661621ws.pdf

Cannon, B. (2004). Tyranny of the urgent. *Motor Age, 123*(3), 4.

Cassell, J. L., & Mulkey, S. W. (1985). *Rehabilitation caseload management: Concepts & practice.* Pro-Ed.

Cassell, J. L., & Mulkey, S. W. (2004). Caseload management. In T. F. Riggar & D. R. Maki (Eds.), *Handbook of rehabilitation counseling* (pp. 252–270). Springer Publishing Company.

Content Engine. (2023). *Pomodoro technique: How does the methodology improve time management?* (English ed.). ContentEngine. https://www.proquest.com/docview/2779232232/fulltext/708637AECFB54BE9PQ/1?accountid=9255

Cook, S. (2011). How successful are you as a time manager? In *Essential time management and organization: A pocket guide* (pp. 10–15). IT Governance Publishing. http://www.jstor.org/stable/j.ctt5hh72n.6

Darnell, J. S., Perry, M., Lamoureux, N., & Lee E. (2022). Don't let perfect be the enemy of good: A proof of concept for a custom national data repository of quality measures for free and charitable clinics. *Health Equity, 6*(1), 708–716. https://doi.org/10.1089/heq.2022.0078

Dezfouli, A., Nock, R., & Dayan, P. (2020). Adversarial vulnerabilities of human decision-making. *Proceedings of the National Academy of Sciences, 117*(46), 29221–29228. https://doi.org/10.1073/pnas.2016921117

Droit-Volet, S., Chaulet, M., Dutheil, F., & Dambrun, M. (2019). Mindfulness meditation, time judgment and time experience: Importance of the time scale considered (seconds or minutes). *PLoS One, 14*(10), 1–22. https://doi.org/10.1371/journal.pone.0223567

Forsyth, P. (2013). *Successful time management*. (3rd ed.). Kogan Page.

Grissom, J. A., Loeb, S., & Mitani, H. (2015). Principal time management skills: Explaining patterns in principals' time use, job stress, and perceived effectiveness. *Journal of Educational Administration, 53*(6), 773–793. https://doi.org/10.1108/JEA-09-2014-0117

Grubbs, L. A., Cassell, J., & Mulkey, S. W. (2006). *Rehabilitation caseload management: Concepts & practice* (2nd ed.). Springer Publishing Company.

Hummel, C. E. (1967). *Tyranny of the urgent*. InterVarsity Press.

Kwapinska, M. S., Jankowski, T., Przepiorka, A., Oinyshi, I., Sorokowski, P., & Zimbardo, P. (2018). What is the structure of time? A study on time perspective in the United States, Poland, and Nigeria. *Frontiers in Psychology, 9*(Article 2078), 1–10. https://doi.org/10.3389/fpsyg.2018.02078

Lakein, A. (1973). *How to get control of your time and your life*. Signet.

Mackenzie, R. A. (1970). *Managing time at the top*. The President's Association.

Mackenzie, R. A. (1972). *The time trap*. McGraw-Hill.

Mandal, A. (2020). The Pomodoro technique: An effective time management tool. *The NICHD Connection, 11*(120), 1–17. Retrieved May 16, 2023, from https://science.nichd.nih.gov/confluence/display/newsletter/2020/05/07/The+Pomodoro+Technique%3A+An+Effective+Time+Management+Tool

Pollar, O., Woodbury, D., & Mapson, R. (1998). *Organizing your workspace: A guide to personal productivity*. Course Technology Crisp.

Riley, R. T., McKinney, J. M., & Mantel, S. J., Jr. (1976). *Time management: Concepts and techniques for doing more in less time (a workbook)*. Penton Publishing.

Rothbard, N. P., & Ollier-Malaterre, A. (2016). Boundary management. In T. D. Allen & L. T. Eby (Eds.), *The Oxford handbook of work and family* (pp. 109–122). Oxford University Press.

Smith, H. W. (1994). *The 10 natural laws of successful time and life management: Proven strategies for increased productivity and inner peace*. Warner Books.

Southerton, D. (2003). "Squeezing time": Allocating practices, coordinating networks and scheduling society. *Time & Society, 12*, 5–25. https://doi.org/10.1177/0961463X03012001001

Stoilov, T. (2012). *Time management*. IntechOpen. https://doi.org/10.5772/2280

Tracy, B. (2014). *Time management*. AMACOM.

Treon, R. T. (1979). Private rehabilitation of injured persons: A plaintiff lawyer's perspective. *Journal of Rehabilitation, 45*(3), 34–36.

Van Eerde, W. (2015). Time management and procrastination. In M. D. Mumford & M. Frese (Eds.), *The psychology of planning in organizations: Research and applications* (pp. 312–333). Routledge.

Wolters, C. A., & Brady, A. C. (2021). College students' time management: A self-regulated learning perspective. *Educational Psychology Review, 33*(4), 1319–1351. https://doi.org/10.1007/s10648-020-09519-z

Woodside, M., & McClam, T. (2003). *Generalist case management: A method of human service delivery* (2nd ed.). Brooks/Cole Publishing.

Applied Aspects of Caseload Management

CHAPTER 8

Case Recording and Documentation in Rehabilitation

LEARNING OBJECTIVES

By the end of this chapter, learners will be able to:

- Appreciate the function of case recording in the vocational rehabilitation system.
- Differentiate between various types of case documentation.
- Explore basic elements of the case recording process.
- Understand client-centered approaches to documentation management.
- Recognize pitfalls and legal considerations in documentation practices.

INTRODUCTION

Collecting artifacts, developing case notes, and organizing documents are all fundamental responsibilities and tasks of a case manager. Considering what is to be collected from outsides sources, how to effectively convey what has transpired throughout an open case, and everything that must occur and be documented based on external and internal policies and procedures are all essential components to efficient case management. A productive practitioner understands that the case file serves dual purposes: compliance verification and service facilitation. Properly recording the time spent with their clients fosters accountability and supports both expediting and evaluating forward momentum. It is a bedrock of the process, influencing how counselors structure their time and effort. This chapter will explore the various components of case recording and case documentation, models for counselor-developed artifacts, best practices, and cautions. How to balance a client-centered approach with client expectations, communication styles and conflict resolution, and the potential for litigation will also be explored.

Case Recording Versus Case Documentation

Although **case recording** and **case documentation** are frequently used interchangeably by rehabilitation practitioners, each term encompasses a distinct artifact even when they merge at the practitioners' operative level in the process of case file/folder development (Cassell & Mulkey, 1985). Case recording is the individual rehabilitation professional's contributions to case file development. Such contributions may reflect factual information (i.e., the client's work history) or subjective information (i.e., observations from the intake appointment) regarding the client–counselor interaction. More broadly, case documentation includes all case file contributions from the totality of various resources that affect the client's rehabilitation efforts (Austin & McClelland, 1996; Woodside & McClam, 2003). Records from the workers compensation board, medical or psychological reports, academic records, and other pertinent information acquired during the course of the case represent *documentation* efforts. In addition, completed case recording by the rehabilitation practitioner becomes documentation material once it is admitted to the case file and made a part of the official record of the client.

There are enormous responsibilities inherent in the roles and functions of a rehabilitation practitioner. Therefore, an essential case management skill is the ability to balance the facilitation and documentation requirements of the **rehabilitation process**. Otherwise, high-quality work remains hidden from both the profession and the legislative community that assesses the accountability factor inherent in the field of **vocational rehabilitation** (VR). One unfortunate outcome of opaque documentation is the criticism of practitioners, supervisors, and agencies for an apparent lack of rehabilitation engagement between clients and staff. Such feedback is based on an inaccurate reflection of service delivery due to poorly developed case records or lack of the documentation provided by the caseload manager.

A common strategy of supervisory personnel to determine the quality of a practitioner's work is to read the case file/folder. This type of review generally provides a comprehensive snapshot of service delivery to clients. As service delivery is often completed privately through the one-to-one relationship with the client, case record development is the best method of illustrating the rehabilitation process. Therefore, satisfactory case file development requires the practitioner to function with skill in both case recording and case documentation aspects throughout the process.

This chapter considers methods and procedures designed to develop or enhance skills in case recording and documentation that can mean the difference between mediocrity and excellence as a caseload manager. There is no attempt to standardize case recording practices, only to offer access to a structural framework with which the caseload manager can objectify the practice of effective case development. Individuality of practices among the various state agencies or companies in case file requirements precludes standardization.

RATIONALE FOR CASE RECORDING FOR EFFECTIVE CASELOAD PRACTICE

Adequate and accurate case recording is one of the most significant aspects contributing to the role and function of a rehabilitation practitioner (Cassell & Mulkey, 1985). Case recording offers a dynamic aid to effective service delivery through a visible description of case progression and direction. Consider private-sector rehabilitation where documented case folders are scrutinized by many parties with varied interests in the rehabilitation outcome or negotiated settlement. For example, typical parties participating in medical or postmedical rehabilitation include the injured claimant, an insurance carrier representative, the rehabilitation company representative, attorney(s) representing the client, attorney(s) representing the insurance carrier, an individual from a state or federal agency, and the rehabilitation specialist (Conte & Parker, 1983; Matkin, 1983; Mullahy, 2004; Shrey & Lacerte, 1995). In reality, rehabilitation perspectives can differ regarding effective rehabilitation and planning within a given client situation. Both case recording *and* documentation assist with communication and case movement justification among the involved participants.

The primary purpose of case recording and documentation, in both public and private rehabilitation programs, is to collate *all* pertinent data that facilitates the relationship of *all* persons associated with efforts toward rehabilitation (Young, 2001). Complete and factual information is essential to the provision of quality rehabilitation services. Thus, case recording serves to aid all parties directly involved in the rehabilitation process: (a) the client, (b) the rehabilitation counselor/practitioner, and (c) the agency or company.

The Client

A prime rationale for case recording is to facilitate the client–practitioner relationship by accumulating pertinent data about the client at strategic points to affect the rehabilitation process. Historically, there has been a general agreement (Cassell & Mulkey, 1985; Cassell et al., 1997; McGowan & Porter, 1967; Thomason & Barrett, 1959) that the most important objective of case recording in **public rehabilitation** is to serve as an aid in providing better services to the client. In 1992, Public Law 102-56, commonly referred to as the Rehabilitation Act of 1973 as Amended, continued legal emphasis upon greater client involvement in the rehabilitation process, especially in the development of the individualized plan for employment, and underscored the centrality of informed choice within rehabilitation outcomes. It is during this participative, rehabilitation case recording process that a client's interests, attitudes, and aptitudes become evident. The resulting formal documentation on which decisions can be made regarding rehabilitation direction provides the information necessary for establishing a professional relationship with the client. Services should be noted and justified in accordance with the client's plan and progress toward the rehabilitation goal.

The Rehabilitation Counselor/Practitioner

The continuity afforded by appropriate case recording enables the practitioner to better engage with the client, cultivate a holistic understanding of the client's needs and goals, and assume sound reasoning practices in the management of a rehabilitation case. The case record, particularly the last practitioner contact entry, provides a reference point for making decisions about initial programs or additional services necessary to predict rehabilitation direction and/or outcomes. Case recording can offer information regarding the client's interests and motivations toward the ultimate rehabilitation goal, as well as participation in rehabilitation efforts. Reviewing past interactions with the client can support evaluating case progression, anticipating future or understanding current barriers and challenges that may arise, and initiating solution-focused thinking. Sufficient case recording should reflect the problem-solving abilities of the practitioner by detailing activities related to any proposed solution (Frankel et al., 2019).

All written materials should be relevant and foster a comprehensive understanding of the case situation. Integral to this effort are any meanings drawn from the experiences of the client and their relationship to their rehabilitative services. Then, as other data outlining the needs of the client are compiled through information gathering, assessment, and service delivery activities, the practitioner is able to assemble the key components resulting in a dynamic understanding of the individual and case for planning purposes. Thus, documentation of the logical sequences of decisions pertinent to the informed choice of the individual client is preserved. Evidence of a practitioner's decisions and activities affords a record in the event such actions are later challenged.

In addition, appropriate case recording and periodic case review provides the practitioner a means of evaluating personal effectiveness and enhancing professionalism. The record is indispensable as a tool for assessing the quality of individual skills associated with the provision of rehabilitation services. A meaningful review of progress made toward the cultivation of skills is contingent upon the study of past performance through quality assurance, case records, and documents.

The Agency or Service Provider

Beyond benefits to the individuals involved, case recording and folder documentation are essential to effective supervision and administration. They provide a means for the agency or company to maintain and improve the quality of operations while testing the effectiveness of the services being provided. Case records contain an inordinate amount of information that can be used in an individual supervisory context, when developing and revising group training programs, and for research purposes. Administratively, case recording and documentation serve to establish whether services are being provided in accordance with legislation, regulations, or policies specific to the program, thus forming the basis of a monitoring tool. In other words, the expenditure of public or private funds is justified through case documentation that establishes the need for client services, identifies the cost and kind of services provided, substantiates any circumstances resulting in a need for further client services, and reflects a measurement of the outcome related to client benefits. Ultimately, adequate and accurate case records are essential to effective agency administration.

REHABILITATION PROFESSIONALS AND CASE RECORDINGS FOR EFFECTIVE CASE AND CASELOAD PRACTICE

Every state rehabilitation agency has the primary responsibility for developing basic standards for case recording within the rehabilitation program. The resulting requirements and guidelines become policy and will dictate the style of case recording used by individual VR counselors and supporting professionals. The agency's standards are usually contained in a casework manual issued to each caseload manager or are maintained at an office location to ensure conformity in case development. Often, agencies foster consistency in case recording by use of basic forms or templates that can be tailored individually for each client. Perhaps these forms are related to a general need to assist practitioners in the identification of significant and insignificant information surrounding the specific case study. More likely, the forms contribute to principles of good management. The agency's standards and guidelines for case recording should be under constant review and revision to preclude continued use of antiquated forms or templates that no longer serve to facilitate service delivery. Any repetition or duplication should be eliminated from the current standards. The process used for case development should be functional and streamlined, supporting the process instead of an encumbrance to the service delivery system.

Effective case recording should, in essence, tell the story of the client's case. Anything left out of the case file does not exist or did not occur for all intents and purposes. Case recordings afford the practitioner the opportunity to demonstrate the relationship developed between the counselor and client, the journey they undertook together, and how and when the client made informed choices along the way. How individualized VR services led to a successful employment outcome can also be illustrated. With well-crafted tools, practitioners will be well positioned to demonstrate compliance with policies, regulations, and procedures. In totality, the case file provides the evidence of the professionalism and skill mastery of a VR counselor and all required justifications for actions taken and services provided.

Practically, some entries will require the precise detailing of components of the process (i.e., diagnostic interpretations or service program justification), while others may suffice with nothing more than simple demographic entries (i.e., gender or age) for identification. Five common styles of recording were reported by the First Institute on Rehabilitation Services Committee on Case Recording (Macdonald, 1963) as appropriate for use in rehabilitation programs. The four styles currently utilized include (a) recording on established forms, (b) process or verbatim recording, (c) summary recording, and (d) narrative recording. As research is generally completed post hoc through records review measures, the research recording style is beyond the scope of this text.

Recording on Established Forms

Typical forms used in the VR system often correspond with steps in the process. Although tailored by each agency, it is customary to utilize **established forms** at referral, application, initial intake (including a health or disability questionnaire), eligibility, individualized plan for employment (which may outline the comprehensive assessment), plan amendments as needed, and case closure. Forms are useful when minimal amounts and types of information must be gathered uniformly in all cases. For uniform reporting to other entities and data processing, established or prescribed forms are essential.

Process and Verbatim Recording

Process recording refers to a highly detailed record that covers the series of actions, emotions, and events that transpire in the interview situation. Verbatim recording actually refers to the complete record or word-by-word transcription of the interview. These types of records are primarily useful for such purposes as psychological evaluation, content or thematic analysis, and training purposes to demonstrate methods and techniques in interviewing and counseling. Within the rehabilitation realm, legal transcripts become part of case development activities for specialists in the private sector.

Summary Recording

More common are **summary recordings** which are a condensed account of transactions between the client, rehabilitation practitioner, and agency or company. This may be a summary of what occurred in a given interview or over several interviews, with particular notations as to the important characteristics of the client or of the events that transpired during the interview(s). This form of recording may also be a periodic review of progress toward an objective agreed upon by the client, rehabilitation professional, and agency or company. Summary recording works best when a clear-cut objective is spelled out early in the case record. Summary accounts, then, describe any progression or lack thereof regarding the vocational or rehabilitation objective during the time interval the summary covers.

Narrative Recording

The **narrative recording** form is considered the standard format. Usually, this technique *tells a story* about the client, the counselor, and the agency. Therefore, the content should include client-reported background information related to past and current employment experiences, strategies and interventions attempted previously and the results of such efforts, and the motivations of the client in seeking help at this time. The narrative should describe the client's total situation as it pertains to and may impact planning and services. Any information shared or observations of relationships between the client and significant people, such as family, community or work associates, friends, and authority figures, as well as the counselor and agency, should be detailed. This format may lend itself to brief shorthand descriptions or to a more lengthy and reflective recording. Also, recording may be either descriptive or analytic, or both. The culmination of the narratives should be a dynamic picture of what has happened, is happening, and will be happening through the rehabilitation process.

CASE RECORDING BASICS

Basic Elements of Case Recording

As mentioned, case recording is the information created by the rehabilitation professional during the course of a case. Case recordings document the *what, when, where, who, why,* and *how* of all activities. The record tells the story of the process including events, milestones, successes and challenges, client progress, course corrections, emerging information, lessons learned, changing goals, and evolving interventions. It provides an opportunity to explain and justify all actions, delays, goals, decisions, services provided, directions taken, and informed choice. In addition, the working alliance between practitioner and client is illustrated. In fact, case recordings and documentation provide the primary evidence of the practitioner's professionalism, ethical practice, and compliance with policy, procedures, and federal regulations.

Case Recording and Documentation Authors

Beyond the lead rehabilitation counselor or case manager, other individuals may have responsibilities and roles that require them to add case recordings or artifacts to the overall case document. When situations arise in which the lead practitioner is unavailable, a backup professional may be assigned to the case to maintain continuity of care. There may also be a need for an administrator, supervisor, and director to be involved in the process. With VR staffing shortages, agencies may employ paraprofessionals, specialists, and technicians to assume some case responsibilities. A benefits specialist may be required to review and explain specifics related to a person's disability benefits. Employment specialists, job developers, and job coaches spend a considerable amount of time with clients. Reports and case notes outlining their activities, staff/client interactions, and progress are generally received at regular intervals (often monthly) for review and inclusion in the case file. Finally, receptionists, administrative assistants, and financial (authorization) processors may be in a position to add meaningful information and documentation. Ultimately, anyone who interacts with the client on behalf of the agency may be an author of a case note (**Figure 8.1**).

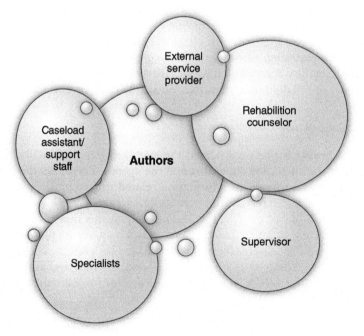

FIGURE 8.1 Case recording and documentation authors.

Potential Audiences

With so many possible content creators, let's not forget the potential audience of all of this information as well. Who might be reviewing the file and why? What is their level of knowledge, expertise, and understanding? What information or evidence might they be looking for? What key elements are necessary for different audiences? Conversely, what parts of the story are interesting but not essential? When developing case recordings and inserting documentation, effective rehabilitation professionals recognize the importance of understanding how each item may be interpreted by clients, client representatives, parents, significant others, advocates and the Client Assistance Program (CAP) representatives, lawyers, judges, supervisors, agency administration, state and federal auditors, the professional's replacement, service providers, so forth (see **Figure 8.2**). Knowing who can obtain what information and how that information may be used is essential in crafting documentation to meet the needs of all constituents in a fair and accurate way.

In discussing case document "crafting," some cautions or clarifications might be in order. First, just like service delivery, case recordings and documentation should always be done in an ethical and professional manner. Although we all want to be effective and efficient, it is not appropriate to cut corners, fabricate events or details, or misrepresent information to present more timely, reasonable, compliant, efficacious, or progressive services. As a basis for a (hopefully never needed) legal defense, the same accuracy and clarity are required to demonstrate compliance with federal regulations, agency policy and procedures, and the practitioner's scope of practice and competency. Records should also be able to stand up to any scrutiny by fiscal managers and financial auditors from various government entities who will, on occasion, assess cases to determine return on investment; effectiveness and efficiency; accountability; and any instances of fraud, waste, or abuse.

Others will review these cases from a **quality assurance** perspective. For instance, a client might request access to their case to attest to its accuracy, equity, and fairness. They may also seek evidence of cultural competency, professionalism, progress, informed decision-making, confidentiality, and outcomes. A coworker may inherit a case due to short-term reassignment, turnover, or retirement. The new case manager will not appreciate a confusing, inaccurate, or incomplete case document file. Finally, administrators often review cases as part of their supervisory responsibilities. This may occur on a predetermined regular basis for counselor professional development and performance management, or it may be due to complaints, compliance issues, or a pattern of undesired outcomes.

Common Errors and Pitfalls

There are several common potential errors case managers make. The first is the mistake of omission. When actions are not documented, justified, or explained, there is no evidence that they occurred. "If it's not documented, it didn't happen." Therefore, it is essential to document, document, and document some more. Specifically, explain all decisions,

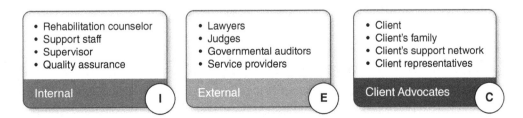

FIGURE 8.2 Case file audiences.

especially if other case documentation is contradictory of such decisions or actions, and any delays. Things happen, services get delayed; yet if those delays aren't explained, the assumption will be that the practitioner was failing to manage the progress.

The need for documentation also applies to counselor engagement and efforts. The work done during and in between appointments is an essential task of the job and should be part of the story. Focus on what is provided by way of vocational counseling and guidance, rather than the employment targeted. Career exploration, career pathway planning, labor market information, measurable skill gains, industry-recognized credentials, work readiness skills, and career preparation are typical concepts we investigate with our clients and should be illustrated in the record. Don't forget disability information or the reasons a person was deemed eligible for services. What has been done to address functional limitations? What accommodations, modifications, assistive technologies, and services have been explored? What has been determined to be appropriate and why?

A final caution is stating an opinion that has no supporting facts or evidence. Effective practitioners stay objective and professional, avoiding personal judgments, value impositions, and assumptions. Considering again the broad potential audience, ensure all notes are clear and unambiguous to reduce the potential for individual interpretations. As well, be organized and systematic. Not only because chaotic or disordered files invoke a negative impression of the creator, but a methodical approach to documentation saves time, maintains focus, ensures consistency and compliance, and demonstrates competence and professionalism.

In conclusion, the recorded information about an applicant or client should be accurate and reliable. The case should be concise and consistent with the counselor's professional understanding of the client's behavior, as well as any conditions or circumstances associated with the client's current situation. Any significant information about precedent experience or behavior of the client should be considered by the caseload manager for appropriate admission into the case record (Holt, 2000). Observations or generalizations about a client should be explained adequately and labeled as such when included in case recording. Likewise, conflicting or contradictory reports should be reconciled or explained to reduce or remove any confusion about the information or its accuracy to the client situation. Thus, one might assume that counselors are successful at case recording because of hard work, a professional attitude, and decision-making ability. Case recording is not an easy process since it demands that the counselor be personally and professionally secure and willing to risk documentation of judgments.

However difficult case recording may be for practitioners, it is crucial to the rehabilitation process since a counselor's focus is on the client. The objectives of the client, counselor, and agency must be appropriately defined, pursued, and evaluated for inclusion as case recording entries to the client file. This process is logical and dynamic in presentation of the basis for service eligibility and program development. However, when the counselor has integrated a style or technique for case recording that includes a logical organization of germane data, what formerly seemed difficult becomes much easier. Beyond expected improvement in the quality of recorded information, less time will be spent since the counselor will not linger over insignificant aspects of the client situation.

ACTIVE LISTENING AND INTERVIEWING

In order to capture the appropriate information during interactions for case recording, effective **active listening and interviewing skills** are essential. Observing and noting the essential details of pertinent information shared verbally and nonverbally in the moment is a skill worth developing. Understanding not only the standard information that must be collected

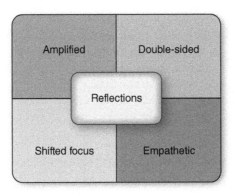

FIGURE 8.3 Reflections.

but also when and how to probe deeper is key to really developing a complete picture of each multidimensional and unique client. Strategies to reinforce active listening include:

1. Be on alert for discrepancies between what the client says and their body language or how they are presenting today and what past records would suggest.
2. Listen to understand what the person is trying to convey, not to formulate a response.
3. Don't prepare a reply while the person is still sharing.
4. Be comfortable with silence, as it provides an opportunity for the person to think and reflect on what they have said.
5. Repeat back what is heard, allowing the person to hear what they have said, evaluate if it is accurate to what they are thinking and feeling, and revise or clarify.

Reflections are a key component of ensuring an understanding of what the client is trying to say and that they are conveying their thoughts accurately (see **Figure 8.3**). Reflections can be very simple, such as merely repeating the client verbatim, or more complex. An **amplified reflection** can exaggerate words or tone of voice. **Double-sided reflections** share two conflicting thoughts, illustrating the client's ambivalence about a subject. **Shifted focus reflections** move a spiraling conversation in a new (hopefully more productive) direction. An **empathetic reflection** takes a guess at how someone is feeling to allow them to consider what was said and correct the assumption if it isn't quite on target. There might also be value in a **metaphor** or **reframing** what the client has said to shed a new light on the topic.

CASE NOTE FRAMEWORKS FOR EFFECTIVE RECORDING

Traditional Case Note Structures

A common structure of case notes within the mental health, counseling, social work, and medical fields is the SOAP note. The format for a **SOAP note** includes Subjective, Objective, Assessment, and Plan information. Subjective statements highlight pertinent information relayed by the client or observations that are open to interpretation. Observable and measurable data collected by the professional fall under objective statements. The assessment portion of the note involves the professional's evaluation of both subjective and objective information obtained. Finally, the plan for anticipated next steps is then detailed. An example of a SOAP note for VR might look like this:

I met with client X today to follow up on the progress of her job search. The client reported feeling frustrated by the lack of communication with her job developer (S). During the session, the client raised her voice and hands multiple times to add emphasis to her statements of unmet needs and unfulfilled expectations (O). Based on the client's statements and my in-session observations, the client would like more contact from her job developer and more consistent job search activities (A). I will contact the job developer to schedule a meeting between the three of us to explore current activities between the job developer and client, negotiate expectations for each party, and outline a revised plan for weekly responsibilities and actions of each party (P).

Similar case note templates include BAR, BIRP, DAP, APSO, and STIPS:

- **BAR:** Behavior, Action, Response
- **BIRP:** Behavior, Intervention, Response, Plan
- **DAP:** Data, Assessment, Plan
- **APSO:** Assessment, Plan, Subjective, Objective
- **STIPS:** Symptoms, Topics discussed, Interventions, Progress/Plan, Special issues

DRIVE Notes

A new model within the field of rehabilitation is the **DRIVE note** (see **Figure 8.4**). Developed by Kyle Walker at the University of Wisconsin-Stout, DRIVE notes are a model of client record progress notes designed specifically for VR by VR counselors. DRIVE notes tell the story of the case in a manner that covers all the important facts in a way that will be understood by all possible audiences in a quick and efficient manner. They offer a conceptual tool that can be applied directly to practice and adjusted to

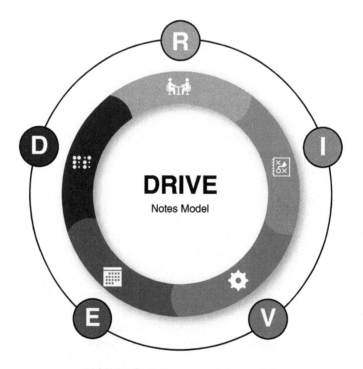

FIGURE 8.4 DRIVE notes model.

personal style and preference. They can be particularly helpful for new rehabilitation practitioners learning how to document case progress relating to counseling and guidance interventions and services. DRIVE notes help keep the direction of the case focused on disability rehabilitation, employment and employment-related interventions, activities, and services. In addition, they help set the tone for each session and guide the counselor's thinking in a way that retains the connection between eligibility and service provision.

DRIVE notes can be conceptualized through the image of a steering wheel and broken down into five components: Disability, Rehabilitation, Intervention, Vocational, and Evaluation:

- **Disability Notes:** What is being done to address the disability and related functional limitations that made the individual eligible for VR services in the first place? Disability notes should be brief yet complete, objective and nonjudgmental, and connect back to the disability or functional limitations. They should take all potential audiences into account and only share what needs to be shared in an easily understandable narrative. Types of information typical in a disability note include:
  - The client's personal adjustment to disability, disability acceptance, adaptations, and level of restoration
  - Any medical/psychological services justification and/or progress notes
  - Assistive technology assessment, justifications, and follow-up notes
  - Other restoration notes
- **Rehabilitation Notes:** What contribution is VR counseling and guidance making toward this person's employability? Rehabilitation notes explore the following:
  - The story of the counselor–customer relationship.
  - How did the counseling and guidance ensure informed decisions and customer rights, due process, and advocacy (CAP)?
  - What counseling and guidance were provided; what issues were addressed?
  - How did the customer benefit from the rehabilitation practitioner's expertise?
  - Counselor observations; client comments; additional or emerging barrier identification; and emerging client concerns, fears, and worries.
  - Guidance provided to ensure utilization of comparable benefits, workforce development system, and community resources.
- **Intervention Notes:** What interventions, services, activities, and so forth are being provided to the client for the purpose of preparing for, obtaining, or maintaining their vocational goal? Intervention notes typically address:
  - Identification and justification for paid/unpaid interventions/services based on functional limitations.
  - Informed choice notes (both about provider selection and service delivery settings).
  - Comparable benefit notes.
  - Progress notes.
  - Vocational or other training progress notes.
  - Measurable skill gain progress notes.
  - Supported employment, customized employment, individualized placement and support, and work-based training progress notes.
  - Life skills, work readiness skills, job seeking skills, and interview skills development.
  - Industry-recognized credential progress notes.
- **Vocational Notes:** How are vocational counseling, guidance, and services helping prepare the client for employment? This is an important concept to keep front of mind, as

having a vocational discussion during every contact keeps the focus of services on the employment outcome. Vocational notes illustrate:

- Discussions about volunteer, temporary, part-time, and work-based learning experiences.
- Career exploration, labor market information, and career pathways.
- Job search, resume development, interviewing, and employment skill development notes.
- Work readiness, soft skills, and employability skills notes.
- Vocational informational interviewing notes.
- Reviewing online job boards together for career exploration or job search purposes.

- **Evaluation Notes:** How did this meeting go, and what are our next steps? Evaluation notes evaluate what was accomplished during the current meeting and what needs to happen next. They also document who is responsible for doing what and by when. As a blueprint for where the case is heading, these notes also offer an excellent refresher when reviewed before the next appointment with the individual. Evaluation notes consider the following:
  - When is the next appointment?
  - What homework/follow-through needs to happen and by whom?
  - What emerging concerns or issues need to be monitored?
  - What is the plan for the next appointment?
  - What progress is being made toward employment?

In conclusion, use the DRIVE note model as a conceptual mental tool to create an agenda for each counseling session or touchpoint. The notes will help maintain a focus on the reason the person was made eligible (i.e., disability, impediments, functional limitations, and the goal of employment). DRIVE notes can highlight the professional practice of VR counseling and guidance, as well as make a clear connection between the person's functional limitations and any interventions or services provided. Overall, this framework will support the client and counselor in remaining laser focused on the end goal of employment, while assisting with case load management, audits, case reviews, and so forth. When reviewed prior to the next appointment, DRIVE notes help prepare the practitioner and demonstrate that they are professional and organized. Consider the following case illustration examples of DRIVE notes.

DRIVE CASE NOTE ILLUSTRATION 1

- D: Met Karen. She is engaged w/ doctor (private health insurance) treating back injury. Reports pain controlled, lifting restrictions remain, limited twisting, bending, standing for at least next 12 months.
- R: Voc. goal is accountant. Provided counseling and guidance to prepare for upcoming job search. Refined resume, identified job search strategy, discussed social network contacts. Explained value of internship/volunteer, get foot in door. Explored her anxiety, fear of failure, introduced positive self-talk.
- I: Job training graduation next month, 3.0 GPA. Needs job interview appropriate clothes, added to individualized plan for employment (IPE), no comp. benefit available. Need for interview/job seeking skills training, added to IPE, provided by American Job Center. Arranged several mock interviews with some partner employers.
- V: Training near complete, progressing to job search preparation. Seeking internship/volunteer opportunity through college career services. Registered w/AJC, created profile on LinkedIn and Talent Acquisition Portal.
- E: Next appointment 7/9/2021. She will provide final transcripts, receipts for interview clothing, and report her follow-up on job search.

DRIVE CASE NOTE ILLUSTRATION 2

- D: Met George. His doctor (private health insurance) released from prior work restrictions. Reports continued limitations standing/sitting over 30 minutes (stiffness), ADLs difficult b/c of range of motion issues (Arms).
- R: Prior limitations prevented return/former job as Warehouse Manager. Discussed ADA/reasonable accommodations, wants to return to former job. Spoke w/former employer by phone, reviewed essential job functions, identified reasonable accommodations, employer agreed, will provide adjusted schedule & stand/ sit adjustable desk.
- I: Added several assistive technology devices to IPE, support completion of ADLs to support employability. (No Comp Benefits). Added pair steel toe work boots to IPE, required by employer. (Documentation in File)
- V: Amended IPE to change vocational goal to Warehouse Manager. Start date 8/2/2021. (Employment Letter in file)
- E: Scheduled check-in call on 9/9/2021. Assess developing needs, job satisfaction, and postemployment services. Prepare case for successful closure in 90 days.

Pro Tips for Documentation

Certain basic case recording rules or techniques must permeate the counselor's awareness in order to accommodate documentation of the individualized needs of clients. Otherwise, the recording process becomes a mere mechanical activity rather than selection of data that have meaning for both the counselor and the client. The particular circumstances of each case will be different; thus, there can be no specific rules regarding the amount of information that should be included in the case record. The information recorded by the counselor in each case file should, at a minimum, be adequate to support a clear understanding of the client's total situation. However, there are some best practices to follow when creating case records.

Pro Tip 1: Record the information while the experience is fresh. Any delay can result in forgotten or uncaptured information and the buildup of work tasks.

Pro Tip 2: Use a pre-established format to organize thoughts and ensure all essential components are addressed.

Pro Tip 3: Accept the role and responsibility of case decision-making and capture those decisions accurately and adequately in the record. Commit to a continuity of action, instead of deferring difficult decisions or delaying case activities due to discomfort or a lack of self-efficacy.

Pro Tip 4: Separate and properly distinguish between objective and subjective data, using reasonable caution when making inferences and using subjective data for decision-making purposes.

Pro Tip 5: Record only pertinent data necessary to provide a complete understanding of the client and the situations relevant to the efforts at rehabilitation. Counselors must be able to conceptualize the major variables involved in the system they manage, as well as categorize and summarize information into a concise and easily consumable artifact.

Pro Tip 6: Consult with coworkers and supervisors to establish self-efficacy and diminish procrastination habits. Consultations with other counselors who have superior case recording skills or supervisors, as well as case review personnel who judge the adequacy of case recording, are a means of establishing one's own professional practices. Find a good role model or mentor to provide guidance and opinions on decisions and techniques to facilitate case development.

CLIENT-CENTERED APPROACH TO DOCUMENTATION MANAGEMENT

Client-Centered Planning

Engaging the client in the process has much broader implications than checking the *informed choice* box or remaining in compliance. Authentic engagement requires that the individual understands what is going on, what options are available and the implications of each choice, how to make the decision (self-determination), and self-efficacy in their own autonomy and self-advocacy skills (see **Figure 8.5**). To support meaningful inclusion of the client, one essential ingredient is to remain **client-centered** throughout the process.

Client-centered services focus on completing tasks and making decisions as a team. In other words, client-centered practitioners move through the entire process (information gathering, assessment, planning, and service provision) with their clients. They do not do VR to or for the client. They help their clients gain the knowledge and skills necessary to make informed choices and feel empowered to make those decisions.

This does not mean that a client-centered practitioner agrees with every decision that a client makes or supports every vocational goal and service selected. Counselors are still bound by agency policies and procedures, legislative regulations, and their ethical responsibilities to do no harm. What it does mean is that the client is involved, informed, and included every step of the way. It is inappropriate to assume someone understands or honestly agrees with a counselor-driven plan because it is well-defined, realistic, or logical and the client does not verbally or nonverbally disagree. Remember, many factors may play a role in a person's silence or compliance (i.e., cultural norms around respect of authority figures, power differentials, age differences). A client-centered counselor actively seeks the input of the person, assessing for comprehension and alignment between the person's preferences and the topic being discussed. The practitioner will *make* the time to confirm the client is in agreement with decisions and activities, recognizing and addressing any signs of ambivalence, passive aggressive behaviors, and inauthentic compliance.

Communication and Conflict Resolution

The working alliance between practitioner and client is built on the rapport and trust developed early on in the relationship. Putting in the time and effort at the beginning of a case to establish respectful, balanced, and open communication between both parties will support the continuation of such communication during times of disagreement. It is much easier to remain empathetic, receptive, and approachable when that is the standard practice within a relationship.

However, there are occasions that inevitably will result in conflict. Maybe a client's behavior has drastically changed, and the counselor must address the lack of progress or

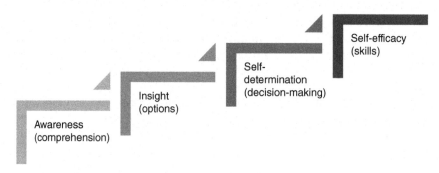

Self-efficacy (skills)

Self-determination (decision-making)

Insight (options)

Awareness (comprehension)

FIGURE 8.5 Authentic engagement components.

FIGURE 8.6 Conflict resolution strategies.

inappropriate behaviors. Or maybe a client is requesting a service that the counselor cannot approve based on policy or professional judgment. One would be naive to ignore the reality that conversations can quickly overheat and emotions boil to the surface. Preparing for and practicing strategies for stress management and conflict resolution will support the ability to remain calm and professional when faced with a displeased client or other stakeholder in the process (see **Figure 8.6**). Strategies may include:

1. Don't ignore discord. Address any concerns before they become open conflicts.
2. Focus on active listening skills, attempting to demonstrate empathy and understand the true root issue.
3. Use the nonviolent communication framework to observe, identify feelings and unmet needs, and make requests (Rosenberg, 2015).
4. Take three deep breaths before responding.
5. If no progress is being made or the situation reaches a hostile level, suggest taking a short break or adjourning the meeting to allow both sides to regain their composure and regroup.

Managing Client Expectations in the Rehabilitation Process

Many factors may contribute to resistance or disagreements. However, establishing mutually agreed upon expectations for both practitioner and client from the start of the relationship can greatly reduce future discord. Clearly outlining what types of communication can and should be expected from each, an appropriate response time for communications, and level of involvement will ensure everyone is on the same page. It provides guidelines to determine when someone is not meeting their responsibilities. It also can help establish when one side is making unreasonable requests or holding too high of expectations of the other side.

LITIGATION AND THE IMPACT ON REHABILITATION CASE AND CASELOAD MANAGEMENT

Appropriate Documentation for Litigation

The intent of this section is not to dwell on all the ramifications of the legal actions possible in this area, but simply to develop *awareness* of the counselor's vulnerability to legal action regarding the contents of the case record. Therefore, it offers neither discussion of precedent litigation nor strategies for the counselor concerned with possible litigation. The basic premise is that, aside from ethical responsibility, the counselor *may* also have a legal responsibility to maintain accuracy and authenticity in the contents of the case file.

Riscalla (1974) notes that the case file "contains a legal record" and that the possibility of litigation could encourage "defensive recordkeeping" by the practitioner. However, the *possibility* of legal action should not preclude the acquisition of adequate and accurate information necessary for the provision of services to rehabilitate the individual. The entire area of record maintenance is still in a considerably ambiguous state.

The report from the Third Institute on Rehabilitation Issues (1976) on Legal Concerns of the Rehabilitation Counselor indicates that although the counselor's responsibilities, liabilities, and protections vary from state to state, the legal liability is personal and may result in personal judgment against the counselor. However, the Prime Study Group of the Third Institute found that most state agencies have formal or informal procedures for obtaining legal counsel if such is necessary. The authors recommend that rehabilitation practitioners have access to, and study, the previously cited document for its application to the legal concerns associated with the system of rehabilitation service delivery. The counselor's awareness of the current legal issues facilitates effective and reasonable approaches to the legal concerns of the rehabilitation counseling position. However, counselors should not forget that *adequate* case recording can be a positive reinforcer to caseload managers who have concerns about the legal implications of their jobs.

Reporting of Unusual Occurrences

Every now and again something completely unexpected happens in a case. When there is no clear policy/protocol or prior precedent for how to handle a situation in the agency, the best course of action is to contact a supervisor for guidance. In addition to being the ethical route to take (per many ethical decision-making models), consultation can uncover new information on policies, procedures, best practices, prior precedent, and legal requirements. Seeking guidance and then documenting everything is the safest bet to responding appropriately and ensuring the agency will support the decision. Make sure to document what occurred, what guidance was sought and from whom, what decision was made, and any outcome of that decision. A supervisor and organization cannot provide the most comprehensive assistance to a professional if they are left uninformed or brought in after the fact.

SUMMARY

This chapter has considered case recording and case documentation and briefly called attention to pitfalls and legal concerns for the rehabilitation counselor. Case recording, as a tool for the client, the counselor, and the agency, was explored and distinguished from case documentation. Common styles of case recording procedures were presented for consideration in total case file development activities. A systematic approach to case recording was discussed in relation to the basic elements that constitute a responsive procedure for relating significant referral–applicant–client aspects to the specified rehabilitation process goals. Formats were presented with brief discussion to structure efforts in the area of the development of effective case recording skills. Case file documentation was viewed with appropriate discussion to establish conceptual understanding of the value of such information. Illustrations and examples were presented to provide insight to procedures for acquisition of such data. Finally, attention was called to the ambiguous state of the legal issues involving case record maintenance and the caseload manager's responsibility for accountability. It was further noted that the counselor has a personal, legal liability for actions or inactions pursuant to rehabilitation service delivery.

QUESTIONS FOR DISCUSSION

1. What are some concerns you have related to case recording development, and how might you alleviate some of those concerns?

2. What organizational skills and strengths do you possess that will support you as a case manager?

3. What are some time management strategies for balancing time spent with clients and the time required to manage case files and document activities that might work for you?

4. What skills and abilities could you strengthen to support the wide range of activities and responsibilities required of a case manager?

5. Who do you feel could support you as a mentor or in a consultative capacity when the need arises?

6. In what ways can you continue to professionally develop as it relates to case recording and documentation?

7. How will you engage your client in the process, and in what ways can you promote a client-centered approach?

8. How will you reduce and mitigate counselor–client discord and support conflict resolution?

9. What concerns, if any, do you have related to litigation, and how might that impact your provision of services?

10. How can you best protect yourself against litigation?

PUTTING IT INTO PRACTICE

Ask yourself these questions to target issues or concerns with case recording and documentation.

1. Is the recording of cases effective in conveying the client's story? Do you find your cases well-organized, with comprehensive documentation that outlines the client's history and future trajectory?

2. Do you tend to delay case recording and documentation due to the time and effort it takes, or a combination of both? Be mindful of potential pitfalls, such as procrastination, and strive to maintain a consistent practice of documentation.

3. What case framework do you currently employ in your professional practice? Are you following an established framework or using a self-taught format? Always remember that case documentation should be professional, ethical, and easily accessible for client review, so it's essential to write in a manner that shows respect.

SPRINGER PUBLISHING CONNECT™ A robust set of instructor resources designed to supplement this text is located at **http://connect.springerpub.com/content/book/978-0-8261-5963-2.** Qualifying instructors may request access by emailing **textbook@springerpub.com.**

REFERENCES

Austin, C. D., & McClelland, R. W. (1996). Introduction: Case management-everybody's doing it. In C. D. Austin & R. W. McClelland (Eds.), *Perspectives on case management practice* (pp. 1–16). Families International.

Cassell, J. L., & Mulkey, S. W. (1985). *Rehabilitation caseload management: Concepts & practice*. Pro-Ed.

Cassell, J. L., Mulkey, S. W., & C. Engen. (1997). Systematic practice: Case and caseload management. In D. R. Maki & T. F. Riggar (Eds.), *Rehabilitation counseling: Profession and practice* (pp. 214–233). Springer Publishing Company.

Conte, L., & Parker, D. (1983). Private rehabilitation and the rural client: Four perspectives of a case study. *Journal of Rehabilitation, 49*(4), 25–29.

Frankel, A. J., Gelman, S. R., & Pastor, D. K. (2019). *Case management: An introduction to concepts and skills* (4th ed.). Oxford University Press.

Holt, B. J. (2000). *The practice of generalist case management*. Allyn and Bacon.

Macdonald, R. W. (Ed.). (1963). *Case recording in rehabilitation* (First Institute on Rehabilitation Services, RSS No.65-12). U. S. Government Printing Office.

Matkin, R. E. (1983). Insurance rehabilitation: Counseling the industrially injured worker. *Journal of Applied Rehabilitation Counseling, 14*(3), 54–58.

McGowan, J. F., & Porter, T. L. (1967). *An introduction to the vocational rehabilitation process* (U.S. Department of Health, Education, and Welfare, RSS No. 68-32). U.S. Government Printing Office.

Mullahy, C. M. (2004). *The case manager's handbook* (3rd ed.). Jones and Bartlett.

Riscalla, L. M. (1974). Records: A legal responsibility: Uses and abuses of case records. *Journal of Rehabilitation, 40*(1), 12–14.

Rosenberg, M. B. (2015). *Nonviolent communication: A language of life*. PuddleDancer Press.

Shrey, D. E., & Lacerte, M. (1995). *Principles and practices of disability management in industry*. St. Lucie Press.

Third Institute on Rehabilitation Issues. (1976). *Legal concerns of the rehabilitation counselor*. Research and Training Center, University of Wisconsin-Stout.

Thomason, B., & Barrett, A. M. (Eds.). (1959). *Casework performance in vocational rehabilitation* (U.S. Department of Health, Education, and Welfare). U.S. Government Printing Office.

Woodside, M., & McClam, T. (2003). *Generalist case management: A method of human service delivery* (2nd ed.). Brooks/Cole Publishing.

Young, M. E. (2001). *Learning the arts of helping* (2nd ed.). Merrill Prentice Hall.

CHAPTER 9

Specialized Skills in Public Vocational Rehabilitation Caseload Management

---

LEARNING OBJECTIVES

By the end of this chapter, learners will be able to:

- Understand the vocational rehabilitation process.
- Explain the basic elements within vocational rehabilitation process stages.
- Differentiate between public and private rehabilitation roles.

INTRODUCTION

Rehabilitation practitioners have many employment pathways available to them (Oswald & Taylor, 2020) based on their level of education and professional credentials. Every career path shares some features (such as basic case recording and case documentation requirements), while other aspects of each occupation may be vastly different. Two areas of divergence in rehabilitation work center on the system in which the work takes place and the nature of the work. **Vocational rehabilitation** (VR) can occur in public (governmental) or private (nongovernmental) entities. **Public rehabilitation services** may be provided at the federal (i.e., Veterans Administration), state (state-specific VR agencies that serve all people with disabilities or specialize in assisting persons with visual impairments or total blindness through a combination of state and federal funding), or local level (i.e., county agencies that serve individuals with specific disabilities such as intellectual and development disabilities or severe mental health impairments). **Private VR services** may be available through nonprofit (community rehabilitation providers, often working under a fee-for-service contract with a public agency) or for-profit entities.

Depending on the setting and position, a rehabilitation professional may not only be responsible for vocational planning and case management tasks but also direct job placement service provision. Although the fundamental tasks may be delegated to multiple practitioners within the same agency or coordinated between agencies, the overarching VR process remains the same. The core components of the VR process include referral and case finding, initial interview, routine contacts, records review, eligibility determination, vocational evaluation and assessment, and goal setting and plan formation (see **Figure 9.1**). Through this process, a plan for services through successful closure is crafted and, eventually, executed. In this chapter, we will explore the traditional VR process and corresponding documentation recommendations.

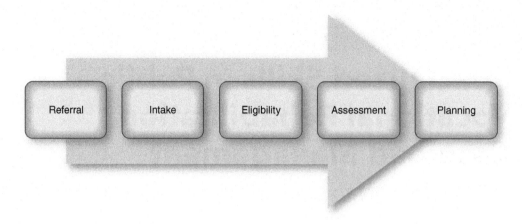

FIGURE 9.1 Vocational rehabilitation process.

Procedural Forms

To effectively move through each stage of the VR process, a rehabilitation professional will need specialized skills. Not only will the practitioner be responsible for completing the task at hand, but they will also need to develop appropriate documentation. Corresponding to each stage, many agencies utilize a standardized **procedural form** to ensure consistency between staff and compliance-driven artifacts. Although forms are very agency-specific, most follow a universal format (a conceptual entity that provides a general design for arranging or organizing case recording activities along definite dimensions) for each stage. Therefore, universal formats offer a framework to *guide* the counselor's case recording endeavors and provides continuity to the recorded entries that contribute to the flow of case development. In comparison to established forms, a universal format offers a greater latitude for counselor freedom and creativity.

The specialized skills and formats presented here relate to the content areas of case development; they in no way attempt to standardize case recording in rehabilitation programs, nor are they forms to be filled out mechanically. The format can provide scaffolding to help the practitioner select the kinds of case data that are significant to the development of a particular case. Consequently, it is essential to identify and consider seven critical components of the rehabilitation process: (a) referral and case finding, (b) initial interview, (c) routine contacts, (d) records review, (e) eligibility determination, (f) vocational evaluation and assessment, and (g) goal setting and plan formation. Each process component is clarified through a brief introduction, outline of specialized skills, and universal format. The formats themselves are designed to highlight the significant elements within a rehabilitation case.

Specialized Case Management Skills

Beyond personal entries, the caseload manager must obtain and document significant information from other sources to lay the foundation for the entire process. Information that provides insight into the client and the direction of the rehabilitation efforts should be obtained in support of *any significant case action*. For example, prior to implementation of a training program with a client, the caseload manager must collect supportive data to document the particular client's interests, needs, and abilities prior to implementing a training program, thus supplying the rationale for a logical expectation of success. In addition, the practitioner must also demonstrate managerial skills to direct, expedite, and oversee the case development process. Therefore, it is the caseload manager functions of

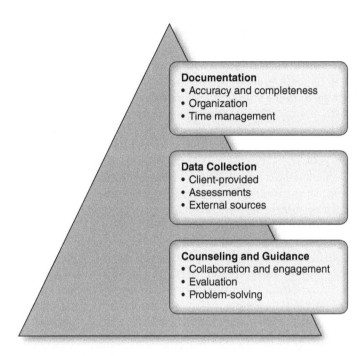

FIGURE 9.2 Case manager functions that require specialized skills.

the professional counselor that come into guiding focus as file documentation is explored and accepted. A blending of external and internally developed documentation supplies the materials for the case file and provides a roadmap of the client's progress. Moreover, balancing the demands of vocational counseling and guidance, critical evaluation, day-to-day problem-solving, documentation, case file organization, and time management is an essential skill for effective case management (see **Figure 9.2**).

REFERRAL AND CASE FINDING

Generally, **case finding** in VR refers to the identification of persons with disabilities for the purpose of considering services in accordance with their needs and interests. Within many organizations, active case finding activities are not necessary, as many agencies are inundated with referrals. A **referral** is the submission of a potential client by another source (either through self-identification by the person with a disability or through another individual such as a medical provider, knowledgeable community member, or family member). Although many state and federal VR agencies as well as nonprofit community rehabilitation providers are consistently overwhelmed with referrals, there are both public and private agencies that have times in which they operate under capacity and will benefit from case finding activities.

No general rule can be stated for establishing a "standard" case finding program since situational and personal variables contribute to the development of any adequate referral source. However, when the counselor approaches case finding and referral development functions professionally, a systematic program can evolve that produces a continuous flow of possible clients for consideration of their eligibility and potential for entering services. Recognizing the broad diversity in practitioner interests, agency needs, and regional dynamics, three core strategies for referral development include (a) client targeting, (b) agency targeting, and (c) system targeting.

Client Targeting

It is critical that the counselor begins to target specific populations, particularly those at risk for high-cost institutional care or those in need of multiple services provided by the public VR system. As various agencies move into "order of selection" restrictions, service provision is contingent on the level of disability or need. Under these restrictions, eligibility determinations are more readily justified and service provision authorizations prioritized for individuals with the most significant disabilities. Take the time to establish any professional expertise and preferences. Does the practitioner have a specialized skill in American Sign Language or assistive technology? Will the professional offer a wide range of services or focus on a particular area of need (i.e., career counseling for youth seeking to go to college, facility-based vocational evaluations, benefits advisement, or community-based work experiences and direct job placement services)? Should the provider narrow down the populations to be served based on client age, disability type, geographic location, vocational goal sector, or funding stream? It is crucial that counselors seeking future clients (a) understand the function of all possible sources of referral within the given geographic region, (b) identify current and consistent service delivery areas of need and opportunities for case finding, (c) cross-reference their expertise and professional interests with populations in need of services (i.e., veterans, justice-involved youth, individuals with specific types of disabilities), and then (d) develop a working relationship with potential referral sources to ensure the delivery of appropriate referrals that align client needs with the provider's expertise and available services. Improving the chances of a referral match (or appropriate linkage between applicant and service provider) will not only support constructive case progression but also more referrals in the future.

Agency Targeting

The rehabilitation caseload manager should be aggressive and comprehensive in reviewing all potential referral sources within the viable geographic territory. Any analysis of service delivery region feasibility should recognize that, although virtual service delivery options have gained traction, some services are better suited for remote work. For example, providing career counseling and guidance to a young adult via a video meeting platform may be perfectly reasonable and even increase the client's engagement, whereas attempting to provide job placement services in another state will likely be futile for a job developer due to a lack of knowledge of the local labor market, direct business connections, and opportunities for employer interactions. Referrals may be received from secondary and postsecondary educational settings, training facilities, residential and long-term care facilities, independent living centers, medical and rehabilitation providers, psychological and substance use treatment centers, and governmental agencies such as the Social Security Administration and various federal and state VR agencies.

A consistent referral pipeline is contingent on developing community relationships and resourcing. Professional outreach fulfills the counselor's responsibility for assuring that referral sources realistically understand the general and/or overall objectives of the agency. One aim in coordinating agencies' activities is to create seamless services and maximize resources available to individuals with disabilities. This notion of synchronized delivery of services has challenged the organizational ownership of certain client populations. In addition, emphasis has been placed on cooperation across agencies and sectors. In fact, many agencies are explicitly focused on this goal based on the expectations outlined in the Workforce Innovation and Opportunity Act of 2014 (WIOA). Rather than providing only those services that can be offered through a single agency, rehabilitation professionals have the opportunity to resource and work in collaboration (in partnership) with a variety of service providers and agencies within the community (Davis et al., 2009;

Honeycutt et al., 2014), thus creating an environment conducive to stronger interagency ties, which leads to a greater cost-effective use of informal, contracted, and interagency resources (Gursansky et al., 2003).

System Targeting

The impact of current and past service delivery on case finding and referral development can be an easily overlooked task. Practitioners can be so focused on actually doing the work that they sometimes miss the interconnection of certain components and how one can influence another. Acknowledging the cyclical nature of referrals and how volume can ebb and flow, rehabilitation professionals will be better positioned long-term through the use of a client feedback monitoring, tracking, and maintenance system (e.g., annual satisfaction surveys).

Of particular importance is tracking clients once they have been placed in employment. Along with system tracking and monitoring of clients, rehabilitation professionals conduct assessments, collect information, and form hypotheses regarding how clients may remain successful while in their places of employment. This is a crucial part of the system targeting process for rehabilitation professionals due to the rates of recidivism in the rehabilitation services delivery system. "Recidivism involves the general breakdown in a community support system that is unable to help clients make significant and lasting lifestyle changes" (Frankel & Gelman, 1998, p. 136). Tracking allows rehabilitation professionals to identify and address potential concerns before they have the opportunity to become an issue.

Moreover, monitoring the delivery of services and supports assists rehabilitation professionals in determining how well the service plan is being implemented. Thus, it is during this monitoring phase that the rehabilitation professional begins to foster credibility. Reliability is established when the counselor can provide services (a) that significantly benefit the referred individual, (b) as requested, (c) in the time frame agreed upon, and (d) to the satisfaction of the funder and client. To facilitate a professional reputation for quality services, the caseload manager should maintain preplanned periodic contacts with all potential sources within the system.

A final option for referral development is through community outreach and raising public awareness. Speaking before community groups (i.e., civic organizations, churches, and schools) is an outreach effort that not only locates potential clients but is also a valuable asset to the counselor in the establishment of community public relations. Although such efforts in case finding are time-consuming and may not result in an immediate return on the time invested, they are a critical dimension of effective caseload management. Whether starting a new rehabilitation business venture and in need of referrals in the present or just laying the foundation for future lean times, a combination of these strategies will serve any practitioner well for case finding and referral development.

INITIAL INTERVIEW

Once a client has been referred, a practitioner will often open a case through an application and/or **intake process**. The **initial interview** between the counselor and the referral has immense importance, as it facilitates the information gathering stage and dictates the path forward. Basic demographic information (i.e., gender, race/ethnicity, age) is often collected during this phase for federal reporting and compliance measures; however, such information is also crucial for research activities and quality assurance measures, as personal characteristics have consistently been linked to case closure outcomes (Oswald et al., 2016; Wang & Ethridge, 2022; Yin et al., 2022). Beyond the information required by standardized or established agency forms, the interview will offer other data that should be reported through the recording process. Both what the client reports and what the interviewer observes during the interaction should be captured. Furthermore, an effective interviewer will also acknowledge areas of discrepancy between what is submitted via referral documentation, verbally reported by the client, and behaviorally observed during the meeting. All of this information will lay the foundation for the case, ultimately playing a key role in case direction. In addition, the caseload manager must continually be aware of emerging content that supports a preliminary understanding of the potential client's condition and situation.

To record appropriate information during the interview, the counselor should:

1. Give identification of the potential client, counselor, and date.
2. Explain the stated reason for the referral.
3. Describe any preliminary perceptions or observations of the individual (including disposition, demeanor, and physical presentation).
4. Discuss the individual's abilities, current accommodations/supports/assistive technologies, functional limitations, and areas of concern or need.
5. Identify the individual's verbalized vocational interest.
6. Explore any work experience.
7. Clarify the individual's understanding of the rehabilitation program.
8. Discuss the individual's current circumstances, including family involvement and available supports, residential arrangements, and availability of transportation.
9. Consider the individual's personality characteristics.
10. Explore highest level of completed education or vocational training.
11. Discuss any significant social or leisure activities that may impact or provide motivation during the case.
12. Identify the source and amount of any financial assistance.
13. Justify opening a case (if appropriate).
14. List the records to be obtained and types of evaluations necessary to determine the individual's functional capabilities and limitations for eligibility and planning purposes.
15. State the next steps of action.

There may be other information with particular significance to the specific situation of the potential client. If so, it should be appropriately recorded, identifying the proper meaning to the counselor or the individual. While the previous format outlines significant information elements that should be obtained during any intake meeting, the initial interview also offers the first opportunity to collect in-depth data on the complex social and vocational dimensions of the individual.

Social Data

The applicant or potential client is the primary source of social data. Nevertheless, such data can sometimes be acquired from staff at other organizations or significant individuals in the person's life. Information may be obtained through workers at social services agencies, educational entities, and treatment and medical facilities, or the individual's family members, friends, and employers/coworkers. Regardless, the caseload manager should remain focused on the necessity of acquiring the desired information, ensuring confidentiality and privacy practices are respected, and being objective in the interpretation of all obtained data. Forms or formats are used consistently to guide the counselor in acquisition of the pertinent social data necessary for documentation. Also, it is important to remember that social data become part of the permanent record as a result of counselor-entry documents.

Disability and Functional Limitations

During that first meeting, it will be important to explore any disabilities that may impact work. While appropriate documentation will likely need to be secured to support and expound upon information gathered, the client is the expert on their lived experience with their disability, **functional limitations**, and current accommodations and assistive technologies. Often, conversations on this topic are supported through a health questionnaire or disability checklist that requests information on diagnoses, limitations, hospitalizations, and medications. Functional limitations result in loss of employment through job termination or the inability to obtain a job or perform a specific function at work based on a disability or disabilities. Functional limitations may also be framed through a checklist or general conversation around common categories such as:

- *Communication*: the inability to exchange thoughts, messages, or information with other people.
- *Interpersonal skills*: the inability to interact in a socially acceptable and mature manner with coworkers, supervisors, and others to facilitate normal flow of work or activities.
- *Mobility*: the inability to move from one place to another and/or physically manipulate the environment.
- *Self-care*: the inability to perform tasks that involve caring for self and living environment, or the inability to manage physical, emotional, and safety needs.
- *Self-direction*: the inability to plan, initiate, problem-solve, organize, or independently carry out goal-directed activities related to independent living and work.
- *Work skills*: the inability to perform specific tasks required to carry out job functions, benefit from training in the necessary skills, or practice the work habits needed to stay employed.
- *Work tolerance*: the inability to effectively and efficiently perform jobs that require various levels of physical, emotional, and psychological demands of work over a sustained period of time.

As mentioned, disability and functional limitations information can be obtained through a variety of sources including observation of and discussions with the client and significant others. In addition to this information, the rehabilitation professional should explore strengths, current accommodations and assistive technologies, and solutions or strategies that have been effectively used in the past. Documenting what is ascertained through various avenues will not only support compliance standards for eligibility determination but also the VR process. Understanding a person's abilities, as well as areas requiring support or accommodations, will be advantageous to the vocational goal setting and service planning phases. Case managers seeking further guidance in this area should consult resources such as the Job Accommodation Network (askjan.org), which offers a cornucopia of searchable information on disabilities, limitations, work-related functioning, and common accommodations.

Vocational Data

Although the initial source of vocational information is again the applicant or client, there may be times when it would be appropriate for the counselor to further explore a situation with a current employer. As an example, an individual may already have a job that is in jeopardy due to functional limitations that are impacting work performance. A job modification, insertion of assistive technology, or additional services such as the support of a short-term job coach may render an employment situation more sustainable for the individual. If the applicant is currently unemployed, it will be important to ascertain whether the individual has work experience and, if so, to understand the client's employment record including any consistent or sporadic patterns of unemployment or problems on the job. If a particular vocational interest is stated by the applicant or client, it should be explored through the lens of the totality of data obtained and developed through the assessment process. The significance of the vocational situation is usually interpreted and recorded as counselor-entry documentation to the individual case record. Certainly, since the goal of rehabilitation services has vocational ramifications, it is advisable for public and private practitioners to document clearly the vocational base the individual has already established.

ROUTINE CONTACTS

It is appropriate to discuss routine case recording at this time, as the counselor will need to periodically document relevant data after each appointment or interaction. Numerous **progress reports** may be generated during the life of a case file to demonstrate movement toward the rehabilitation goal. Generally, the purpose of routine contact reports is to facilitate the working relationship through a concentration on germane data about the individual. Moreover, routine recordings assist the practitioner to systematically monitor service provision, prepare for future meetings, and exhibit compliance with required policies and procedures.

To capture meaningful information during a routine contact, the case manager should:

1. Identify the client, counselor, and date.
2. Identify persons, agency, company, or institution contacted, as well as the method for contact.
3. Explain reasons for the contact.
4. Discuss what transpired and was accomplished or learned during the contact.
5. State or explore the next action steps.

The caseload manager should consider carefully *all* situational circumstances of the applicant or client for possible significant documentation to the case record. As with all recorded entries, the professional should avoid procrastination or undue delay in recording the acquired information. Otherwise, the full impact and meaning of the data will likely escape documentation. It is important to recognize that documentation of situational elements are generally counselor-entry descriptions of factors that may have a *positive, neutral,* or *negative* influence upon the individual, the individual's potential for rehabilitation, or flow of the rehabilitation process. Therefore, all information should be presented in objective terms, devoid of potentially biased judgments and interpretations. The source and context of information gathered should also be considered when determining how and what to represent in the record.

RECORDS REVIEW

Since case development may be referred to as an individualized, client-oriented process, it is appropriate to envision a systematic managerial approach to the acquisition of necessary data while protecting the individuality of the applicant or client. In addition to social and vocational information, pertinent information may be ascertained from medical, psychological, and educational records as well. The amount of information available in each area will likely vary in accordance with the individuality of the applicant or client.

Although evaluative activities should occur throughout the life of a case, the initial assessment component of the rehabilitation process is generally concerned with the determination of eligibility for rehabilitation services and then used to inform plan development. As the eligibility process is for the benefit of the agency and can result in a delay of service provision, it is imperative that the caseload manager act as expeditiously as possible to secure any necessary evaluative data pertinent to understanding and documenting a disability diagnosis from a qualified professional and the functional limitations of the applicant. Research shows that time spent in a holding pattern or inactive stage of services will increase attrition and decrease successful employment outcomes (Honeycutt & Stapleton, 2013). Hence, eligibility for services should be determined as quickly as possible, allowing an individual to move into the active phase of plan development. Although more information may be beneficial for planning purposes, eligibility should be completed as soon as the minimal amount of information is obtained, with additional records requests and assessment activities shifted to the planning phase.

Depending on the agency, information required for eligibility determination and planning services may vary. For state VR services, the acquired data are used to determine whether the applicant meets the established criteria for services or whether further evaluation will be needed. The three criteria for eligibility require the individual to (a) have a physical or mental impairment that results in a substantial impediment to employment, (b) require VR services to obtain or maintain employment, and (c) benefit from VR services to achieve employment and maximize career goals. If the applicant would not be deemed eligible, the case would be closed. Other public and private entities typically have specific eligibility criteria based on type and severity of disability, funding available, and service needs.

The practitioner must secure specific diagnostic information relative to each applicant. Case recording should reflect information relative to:

1. Applicant, counselor, and date identification.
2. Evaluations or consultations scheduled.
3. Records requested (when and from whom).
4. A comprehensive summarization of records obtained and functional limitations established through self-report, observation, and records review.

Once the necessary data are acquired, the counselor must consider carefully the information to gain an understanding of the applicant's total disability, impediments to employment, and any problems preventing satisfactory work adjustment. The result of such an analysis must be recorded appropriately in the case file, showing the counselor's reasoning for the decisions relevant to the situation. As additional information is obtained, further analyses may be necessary and updates to the record completed.

Medical Data

The rehabilitation professional will need to coordinate the acquisition of appropriate medical data on *every* applicant prior to eligibility consideration. Even if someone is presumed eligible, based on an obvious disability or eligibility status from another recognized governmental system (i.e., Social Security Administration disability determination), medical information can illustrate the capabilities and limitations of an individual for documentation purposes and ensure the physical appropriateness of a future vocational goal. Whether the necessary data include a comprehensive evaluation with multiple examinations, records from across multiple medical providers, or simply a required general examination, the caseload manager must be effective and efficient in collecting adequate medical data to establish the existence and boundaries of a defined disability.

Generally, medical documentation is only requested during the initial phase of the process, but occasionally, as some clients' conditions change or progress, it is necessary to update the medical data. Depending on the medical data received at referral and through records requests or the lack thereof, the rehabilitation practitioner may wish to acquire additional medical *or* psychological evaluations or consultations. This is considered more common in private practice scenarios and is used sparingly, on a case-by-case basis, in public VR agencies.

Psychological Data

Psychological data from a psychologist, psychiatrist, or other treatment professional can be very helpful in establishing an emotional or psychological disorder and any potential functional limitations to employment. Just as with medical data related to physical disabilities, hospitalization and treatment records can support eligibility, establish areas of concern or need, and suggest strategies and accommodations that may be appropriate. The counselor may also wish to secure a psychological evaluation when no current treatment provider is identified and available records are unable to supply information on the individual's past, present, and potential future behavior. These psychological data usually are acquired directly from a psychologist following an interview and evaluation of the applicant or client.

Educational Data

Educational documentation may come from the applicant or client as well as any academic institution or other training site with which the individual has prior association. The caseload manager should obtain academic, performance, and disability support (i.e., individual education program, 504 Plan) records whenever possible because of their value in reflecting the present proficiency of the individual. Other beneficial information that may be gleaned from records include cognitive (standardized aptitude and achievement testing) and psychological assessment results that may support eligibility, observed learning and behavioral difficulties that may translate into functional limitations on a job site, and the implementation and success of past intervention strategies. This information will be much more meaningful in the vocational planning and goal development stage than simply asking for, and denoting, the highest grade completed or level attained. It is important, however, to be reminded that numerous factors (i.e., geographical location; mental, emotional, and physical health; and cultural influence) have contributed to an individual's educational achievements. Therefore, interpretations of the individual's educational and training performance should be developed within the context of the previous situational circumstances and not automatically assumed to be an absolute indicator of any future potential or challenges of the client.

VOCATIONAL EVALUATION AND ASSESSMENT

Eligibility Determination

The first piece of the assessment process is generally the determination of service eligibility. Although it may feel most appropriate to wait to determine eligibility until all requested documentation is obtained and reviewed, counselors are not encouraged to delay eligibility once enough information has been procured. By expediting eligibility, the rehabilitation practitioner can engage the client more quickly. On the other hand, leaving a potential client in a holding pattern, waiting for documentation that may arrive in a timely fashion or may take upwards of 60 to 90 days, will more likely foster frustration, disengagement, and attrition from services. Unless there is a compelling reason otherwise, counselors should place themselves in their client's shoes. What good could come from being left waiting for much-needed services for months on end? Additional information-gathering measures and assessments can continue within the planning phase, after eligibility is determined and the counselor and client can actively begin to meet and work together.

One compelling reason to defer **eligibility determination** when there is sufficient documentation to establish the existence of disability and impediments to employment would be if there are concerns around the person's ability to benefit from services. In this instance, additional evaluative services may be necessary. The primary purpose of providing extended evaluation/trial work services is to assess the effect of specific services on the applicant to determine whether the individual can and/or will benefit from rehabilitation services in terms of employability. For states operating under the employment first philosophy, the right to competitive, integrated employment is extended to all individuals with disabilities, regardless of severity of disability (Office of Disability Employment Policy, n.d.); therefore, an evaluation to determine a person's ability to work or benefit from services would not be involved in eligibility determination.

Since the goals of extended evaluation/trial work and VR services differ, the recorded information will also be different. When the case data yield a decision for the necessity of a program for extended evaluation, the case recording should clearly justify the reasons for further evaluation of the applicant, what will be evaluated, how and when the evaluation will be completed, and the ways the proposed evaluation will assist in eligibility determination.

In most cases, the records review process should provide the practitioner with sufficient information to determine that the applicant is eligible for some services of the agency. As well, at the conclusion of extended evaluation/trial work programs, the applicant *may* be determined eligible for rehabilitation services. For this eligibility narrative, the professional should:

1. Identify the client, counselor, and date.
2. Identify the client's primary, and any secondary, disability.
3. Explain the functional limitations imposed by each disability.
4. Describe how the client has impediments to employment.
5. Explore the client's motivation toward employment.
6. Tell how the client can benefit from agency services.
7. State whether the client has a significant or most significant disability.
8. Discuss tentative problem solution strategies.
9. Indicate the next appropriate step toward rehabilitation efforts.

The counselor must document the client's disability and impediments to employment at eligibility. As additional information is compiled through new medical/psychological records, formal and informal assessment strategies, and observations, the eligibility record can be amended to continually expand or enhance understanding of the client and their specific situation. Case recording should begin to focus on the client's progress toward vocational goal selection and prognosis for a successful employment closure.

General Assessments

Either in conjunction with eligibility determination or afterward, **vocational evaluation and assessment** is crucial to developing a comprehensive overview of the client and case that will inform the planning process. Several types of assessments can provide insight into the individual's abilities, limitations, interests, and preferences. Understanding these unique data points will help support, refine, or reject potential vocational goals and even highlight areas of strengths or concern to be addressed in the job placement phase and any services and accommodations planning activities.

Assessments may be formal (standardized to all test takers) or informal (adaptable to meet the individual's needs or circumstances) in nature. Some **formal assessments** that are typically received through the records request process include medical/functional evaluations, psychological evaluations, and standardized aptitude and achievement testing. When assessment results are not available yet necessary to complete a **comprehensive vocational evaluation,** the rehabilitation professional may refer the client to another professional who is qualified to administer the specific evaluation and can then submit a report with their findings.

In VR, **informal assessments** are more commonly completed directly by the rehabilitation practitioner during the career exploration phase. A few examples of nontraditional or informal assessment methods include completing a discovery profile or client profile checklist, having a conversation with the individual to evaluate communication and interaction skills, obtaining the perspectives of others through an interview, observing the individual in a variety of settings to understand typical behaviors and interaction patterns, career interest inventories, strengths and values assessments, and learning style inventories. These activities may be done during regularly scheduled appointments, between meetings as "homework" as in the case of interest inventories, or as a component of a larger career exploration service.

The combination of formal and informal assessments lays the foundation for a preliminary vocational goal that can then be further assessed through more specialized and community-based assessments. No matter the origin or type of assessment employed, caution should be exercised when interpreting and using data. Recognizing the impact of potentially confounding factors will be helpful to ensuring appropriate utilization of assessment results. Considerations may include the impact of disability and anxiety levels on assessment measures, assessor bias, cultural factors, the norms used and generalizability of standardized testing interpretations, low expectations of the client, past experiences, availability of disability accommodations, diversity in knowledge or skill demonstration opportunities, and potential impact of learned helplessness.

Specialized and Community-Based Assessments

Once the counselor and client have narrowed down potential vocational goals, it may be helpful to complete some targeted assessment activities that focus on comparing the abilities and limitations of the individual to specific work tasks and positions. Specialized **work samples** (i.e., the Purdue Peg Board) are helpful in determining an individual's distinct skills, fine and gross motor dexterity, and tolerance for work tasks. Work samples, typically completed in a facility by an individual specifically trained to administer the test, have become far less common. Conversely, **community-based assessments** can assess similar information in a natural work setting, while also offering insight into how an individual will react and perform in a typical employment environment. These situation-specific evaluation opportunities, sometimes called **situational assessments,** also allow the client to more authentically and realistically explore the vocational goal, which can lead to a more informed choice.

Generally, a combination of formal and informal assessments will be necessary to develop the data required to complete a comprehensive vocational evaluation of the client and move forward with planning. However, assessment for the sake of assessment is unwarranted. An effective rehabilitation practitioner will first determine what information is necessary and then the most appropriate and expeditious way to obtain such data. In addition, all assessment activities (completed by the rehabilitation professional or an external entity) should be used mindfully, exploring the impact of cultural differences, personal biases or lowered expectations, the influence of disability and the availability of accommodations, and other factors that may have impacted completion or interpretation. No matter what assessments are to be completed, it will be important to engage the client in the process. Taking the time to help the client understand the purpose and value of the assessment activities will cultivate a good-faith effort on the part of the client and, ultimately, more accurate results.

GOAL SETTING AND PLAN FORMATION

The **counseling and guidance** activity in VR mandates involvement with a client's personal world (counselor role) as well as involvement with various systems or service delivery components (the manager role). These roles fluctuate according to client need and counselor competence to meet those needs. For instance, research shows that those receiving disability benefits are more likely to be closed successfully if they receive work incentives benefits counseling (Kaya et al., 2023); however, this form of counseling is generally outside the scope of a rehabilitation counselor's purview. The skill and efficiency with which a rehabilitation professional can guide a client through the process are a critical dimension affecting case movement. The counselor's orientation (e.g., directive versus nondirective) and ability to apply theory is undoubtedly influenced by the strength of the managerial procedure developed.

Motivational Interviewing

Beyond basic counseling and guidance skills, **motivational interviewing** is an evidence-based practice that rehabilitation professionals can use to support case movement (Chan et al., 2018; Leahy et al., 2018). A counselor will initially want to meet the client wherever they are at in the process; however, practitioners also need skills to help clients gain insight and increase motivation to inspire forward momentum. Motivational interviewing was originally developed as a goal-directed substance use disorder intervention that has been adapted to support a broad range of individuals in motivation development and behavioral change (Substance Abuse and Mental Health Services Administration, 2021). The emphasis throughout the process is on the collaboration between counselor and client, an offshoot from person-centered therapy. Key techniques are designed to increase awareness of the individual's internal discrepancies related to the pertinent topic or behavior, resolve ambivalence, and promote a motivation to change.

At the core, motivational interviewing is grounded in the **transtheoretical model** and its **stages of change** proposed by Prochaska and DiClemente (1984). The stages of change framework involves six potential stages in which a client might present (see **Figure 9.3**). It is important to note that although the arrows and flow move in one direction, a person can go back to an earlier stage at any time.

1. *Precontemplation*: in this stage, an individual has shown no insight or motivation. They have not acknowledged that there is a problem behavior or need for change. Common strategies employed during this time are empathy, inquiry, listening and reflections, acceptance, and affirmation.
2. *Contemplation*: when a client has moved into contemplation, they are actively acknowledging that there is a problem. However, the client is not ready to make any changes, which may be due to a lack of desire to change or confidence in the ability to make a change. Common strategies exercised with clients in contemplation focus

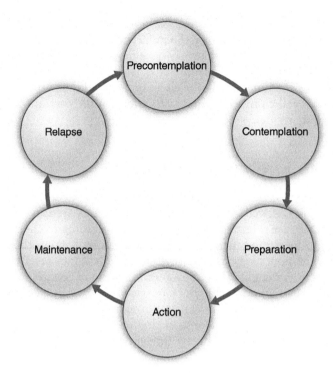

FIGURE 9.3 Stages of change model.

on (a) exploring their motivation, barriers/challenges, and strategies for change; (b) creating an employment vision (or self-revisioning); and (c) helping them clarify for themselves:

a. Why do they want to change the behavior? (pros)
b. Why shouldn't they try to change the behavior? (cons)
c. What would it take for them to change the behavior? (What's my strategy to overcome my cons?)

3. *Preparation/determination:* the preparation or determination stage is initiated when a person commits to the change and begins to make plans. Common strategies that support a person in preparation include (a) making sure the vision, motivators, barriers, strategies, and conditions to support success are clear to the individual; (b) supporting the client in designing Specific, Measurable, Attainable, Relevant, and Time-bound (or **SMART**) goals connected to their employment vision (Grubbs et al., 2006); and (c) encouraging small steps or wins as they try out or experiment with strategies and changing the behavior.

4. *Action/willpower:* in this stage, the person is actively making the change or decision. The person is putting their strategies or plan into action. Common strategies involve building the client's confidence, brainstorming strategies and solutions to issues that may arise, exploring conditions that will support success, preparing for lapses or setbacks, and the use of rewards.

5. *Maintenance:* during the maintenance stage, the client is consistent in their action plan and sustaining the behavioral change. A person would transition from action to maintenance after approximately 6 months. Many professionals assume all is well once a person has reached maintenance and that no further intervention or support is needed. However, many individuals benefit from longer-term encouragement and reinforcement of their efforts. Common strategies for those in this stage incorporate the creation of new goals to reach for and celebrating successes.

6. *Relapse*: the final stage, relapse, should not be overlooked. In relapse, a person has moved to an earlier stage in the model, reverting back to past behaviors and ambivalence. Relapse can occur at any time and may occur multiple times over the case or the individual's life. If a relapse does occur, it will be important for the rehabilitation professional to assess at which stage the person has regressed to (precontemplation, contemplation, or preparation) and provide assistance congruent with that stage.

In the VR context, counselors determine which stage of change or the planning process the individual is in and respond accordingly. In addition, the rehabilitation professional will work to incorporate the "spirit" of four interwoven motivational interviewing processes: partnership, acceptance, compassion, and evocation (Miller & Rollnick, 2013; see **Figure 9.4**).

1. *Partnership*: the active collaboration between counselor and client. A client will be more willing to express concerns when the counselor is empathetic and shows genuine curiosity about their perspective. In this partnership, the counselor gently influences the client as an expert in the employment field, while the client drives the conversation as the expert in their lived experience (Miller & Rollnick, 2013).
2. *Acceptance*: the act of demonstrating respect for and approval of the client. Acceptance shows the counselor's intent to understand the individual's point of view and concerns. Counselors can use the four components of acceptance within the context of motivational interviewing—absolute worth, accurate empathy, autonomy support, and affirmation—to help them appreciate the client's situation and decisions.
3. *Compassion*: the counselor's active promotion of the client's welfare. In this process, the counselor prioritizes the client's needs.
4. *Evocation*: the process of eliciting and exploring a client's existing motivations, values, strengths, and resources.

In practice, motivational interviewing relies on two overarching techniques. First, the professional can establish and validate the partnership through *asking permission* throughout the process. This practice allows the client to be involved in the process and how the conversation will move forward. Second, the professional will use the OARS set of techniques. **OARS** involves **O**pen-ended questions, **A**ffirmations, **R**eflective listening, and **S**ummaries (Buckley & Powers, 2022). Combined, these simple yet effective techniques and active listening skills foster collaboration and promote successful outcomes.

FIGURE 9.4 Motivational interviewing processes.

Ultimately, the interplay of the stages of change model with motivational interviewing provides a mindset and concrete framework from which to work with individuals with disabilities within the goal setting and plan formation process. More specifically, the associated techniques have the potential to inspire and activate clients who may be struggling with ambivalence related to their desire or motivation to work, resistance to the process, or realistically evaluating their abilities and interests as matched to the local labor market and employment conditions. Recently, motivational interviewing has been posited as a useful tool for verbal de-escalation in VR settings when paired with the best practices of the English Modified De-Escalating Aggressive Behavior Scale (Buckley & Powers, 2022). Therefore, rehabilitation professionals can benefit from developing these specialized skills for client engagement and case movement.

Plan Formation

Throughout the eligibility determination and vocational evaluation phases of a case, the rehabilitation counselor should be gathering information that will inform the planning process. This will allow for plan development to proceed expeditiously in order to maximize the client's potential for successful rehabilitation. In this stage, the rehabilitation professional has several roles that include (a) assisting the client to select appropriate services through informed choice, (b) documenting the collaborative efforts of every person associated with the client's rehabilitation program, (c) determining required services to prepare the client and secure successful employment outcomes, and (d) managing service delivery and coordination through case closure.

Three primary dimensions of the service component require counselor attention for effective case recording. These relate to the activities surrounding the (a) *planning,* (b) *provision,* and (c) *completion* of the required rehabilitation services. Specific information is admitted to the case file showing any exploration or analysis relevant to the dimension being considered. In some agencies, the specified data are recorded in conjunction with a particular classification change, while in other agencies, it may simply be allowed to merge within routine case recording. Either way, certain information must be systematically stored in the case file for counselor use in the supervision of the client's rehabilitation program. The following three formats provide assistance in selecting specific data associated with each dimension that merits recording consideration.

In the first dimension, the counselor and client must cooperatively share responsibility (informed choice) for the planning and development of the program of rehabilitation services. Nevertheless, it is the counselor who is responsible for accurate *documentation* of the *planning* process. For recording purposes, the case record should:

1. Identify client, counselor, and date.
2. Review the client's vocational interests.
3. Discuss available employment in the area of stated interests.
4. Describe the client's abilities or potential abilities in interest areas.
5. Address any contraindicators of the vocational goal and appropriate accommodations, modifications, assistive technologies, and other services that will be used for mitigation.
6. Explain why the vocational objective was selected.
7. Show the client's participation in the planning process.
8. State specific action plans for job placement and employment.
9. Identify necessary services.
10. Identify and justify selection of providers or *vendors* of services. Justifications may be strengthened through the use and documentation of evidence-based and promising practices as outlined in recent research (Leahy et al., 2018; Mazzotti et al., 2020).
11. Justify expenditures to be authorized.
12. Make a statement relative to program prognosis.

Through case recording, the caseload manager shows the development of decisions that culminate in a specific program of rehabilitation services and client involvement. This documentation becomes the support system to the efforts in monitoring the provision of the defined services. The caseload manager must not allow the continuity of case flow to stall at this point. The client is ready to go to work (or is already employed), and appropriate efforts must be applied to the service provision function of the process.

Service Provision

Moving into the second dimension, any case recording related to the *provision* of rehabilitation services may be identified as a *routine* recording. However, the following format offers more specificity in documentation of service delivery. Records related to service delivery should:

1. Identify client, professional, and date.
2. Indicate counselor activities in establishing (i.e., warm hand-off measures; Peterson, 2023) and coordinating services.
3. Verify vendor performance in provision of authorized services.
4. Describe client progress in the program of services.
5. Identify any areas of concern in either vendor performance or client progress.
6. Indicate counselor activities in facilitating the program.
7. Recommend any modification of the service program.

The principle of the periodic review of service programs provides a continuity of energy directed to the potential success of the rehabilitation program. This systematic approach keeps the counselor continuously in touch with case flow. It further provides a base of information for use in resolution of many problems that threaten a successful outcome of the program.

The Job Placement/Employment Process

One crucial service delivery element, **job placement**, warrants special attention, as it directly relates to the whole purpose of VR services and the securing of an employment outcome. The placement/employment process is not a single event in the life of the client–professional relationship, but rather a series of events leading to the acquisition of employment (or related activity). In fact, one could argue that the placement process can or should begin as early as the initial meeting between practitioner and prospective client through the exploration of past vocational experiences and current interests and preferences. It is important to note that although the public VR counselor is delegated the legal responsibility for vocational placement of individuals with disabilities through the administration of a state and federally funded program, how this responsibility is executed will vary. To illustrate, the caseload manager may:

1. Actively engage in employer contacts seeking placement opportunities.
2. Simply *urge* the client to explore placement possibilities.
3. Cooperatively work with the client in locating potential employment situations.
4. Refer the client out to a community rehabilitation provider for job placement services.

It is imperative that the counselor embrace a systematic approach to the job placement/employment responsibility in order to effectuate the flow of cases through the process. A plan that includes continual or periodic review of the progress of placement activities is essential, even more so when this service is contracted out to another entity. Establishing clear expectations for the types, frequency, and timeliness of activities for all responsible parties, as well as any reporting requirements, will be integral to proper oversight and evaluation.

Case Closure

Finally, once the program has reached *completion,* the rehabilitation practitioner should evaluate the effect of the individualized program of services on the client and the employment outcome. The case recording entry used by the counselor to substantiate closure of the successful rehabilitation case should focus on the contribution of the various rehabilitation services directed toward the total adjustment of the rehabilitated client. Job and wage considerations are important, of course, but so is a comprehensive analysis of the way the client differs from the previously documented problem situation. This assessment should:

1. Identify the client, counselor, and date.
2. Summarize the services provided.
3. Outline the outcome of services (i.e., successful competitive integrated employment).
4. Specifically describe the employment situation.
5. Discuss appropriateness of the client's job.
6. Explore impressions of the client's total adjustment.
7. Indicate how services contributed to the client's vocational objective.
8. Describe client's feelings about rehabilitation efforts.

In order to accomplish this, the rehabilitation practitioner must complete follow-up inquiries to acquire feedback relative to the appropriateness of the client's placement and the value of services prior to official closure of the case. Follow-up may be viewed as research efforts with a specific focus on evaluating the overall satisfaction with the placement situation and for assisting the agency in its information gathering for the accountability reports to the federal agency. It is important to the success of the placement process that the client is content with the job situation and the employer be satisfied with the performance of the client. It is the responsibility of the rehabilitation counselor to intervene and attempt problem resolution with any difficulties that occur during the designated follow-up period. As such, follow-up does not assure long-term client employment, but it does reinforce to the employer that the counselor is invested in a sustainable outcome, not just the placement itself.

The number of follow-up contacts with the client or employer is difficult to recommend, as the characteristics of each situation will mandate the appropriate quantity of follow-up interaction. When a placement situation is stable and free of crises, monthly contacts or *check-ins* may be sufficient. Other situations will require professional judgment as to the required number of contacts. Follow-up, as a correlative dimension to caseload management, should be viewed in terms of both *immediate* and *long-term* aspects. The immediate aspects will dictate the necessity of interventions within the client–employer relationship regarding the specific placement situation. Long-term aspects, on the other hand, are more concerned with developing employment opportunities for future job seekers. Keeping the doors open to further engagement with the employer may lead to a whole host of benefits (i.e., community-based assessments and work experiences, informational interviews and job shadowing activities, and direct placements).

Unfortunately, not all cases will end in a successful employment outcome. In these instances, the case closure entry to the case file provides an excellent opportunity for practitioner self-evaluation and service evaluation. The willingness to review and critique one's performance is an important early step toward improvement of the skills necessary for effective rehabilitation counseling. In addition, the counselor's case recordings provide a snapshot of quality of services provided, red flags or contraindicators that may have been missed, and opportunities for intervention that could have been initiated. Strategies to be employed in future cases can then be developed and inserted into the case management process. The significance of this step alone in the success of future cases should cause any rehabilitation professional to seek improvement of case recording techniques.

SUMMARY

In this chapter, we have explored VR as it generally unfolds through public agencies. We reviewed the various steps in the process from case finding and information gathering to plan formation and case closure. Skills and features central to each stage were outlined. Key considerations and recording recommendations were also offered. An effective rehabilitation practitioner understands the necessity to cultivate within the case file both what is helpful to caseload management and what is required within their agency. By following best practices at each level and implementing a continual process of evaluation, rehabilitation practitioners are better prepared to offer impactful services and professional development.

QUESTIONS FOR DISCUSSION

1. In preparation of future case finding and referral development activities, how would you narrow down the populations to be targeted based on your individual expertise and preferences when considering factors such as service type, client age, disability type, geographic location, vocational goal sector, and funding stream?

2. What are determining factors in either the completion or delay of eligibility determination?

3. What types of information should a rehabilitation professional look for in a records review?

4. What are some examples of situations in which further assessment or consultation might be required in the eligibility determination and planning process?

5. What are some cautions or considerations related to determining the need for, implementing, and interpreting assessment activities?

6. How might a rehabilitation professional document the client's involvement in the planning process?

7. What ambivalence or resistance might a case manager encounter and how can motivational interviewing support client engagement and case movement?

8. How might a rehabilitation professional document their contributions and the impact of those contributions to the VR process?

9. In what ways should service provision be documented and evaluated?

10. What are some strategies a rehabilitation practitioner can employ to evaluate their effectiveness throughout the VR process and after case closure?

PUTTING IT INTO PRACTICE

Ask yourself these questions to target issues or concerns with specialized skills in public VR.

1. What sets public VR apart from other professional rehabilitation fields?

2. Have you examined how the public VR process influences client outcomes? In terms of case and caseload management, it is crucial to assess individual cases and their impact on overall caseload management. How does the public VR process contribute to or impede caseload management practices?

3. Imagine a scenario where client referrals unexpectedly decline, and you need to find clients to maintain your caseload. How would you approach this situation? Whom would you reach out to, and what steps would you take to seek assistance in the process?

SPRINGER PUBLISHING
CONNECT™

A robust set of instructor resources designed to supplement this text is located at http://connect.springerpub.com/content/book/978-0-8261-5963-2. Qualifying instructors may request access by emailing **textbook@springerpub.com**.

REFERENCES

Buckley, C. P., & Powers, B. F. (2022). Targeted motivational interviewing techniques assist the process of verbal de-escalation in vocational rehabilitation. *Journal of Vocational Rehabilitation, 56,* 217–222. https://doi.org/10.3233/JVR-221185

Chan, F., Iwanaga, K., Umucu, E., Yaghmaian, R., Wu, J., Bengston, K., & Chen, X. (2018). Evidence-based practice and research utilization. In V. M. Tarvydas & M. T. Hartley (Eds.), *The professional practice of rehabilitation counseling* (2nd ed., pp. 359–380). Springer Publishing Company.

Davis, M., Green, M., & Hoffman, C. (2009). The service system obstacle course for transition-age youth and young adults. In H. B. Clark & D. K. Unruh (Eds.), *Transition of youth and young adults with emotional or behavioral difficulties: An evidence-supported handbook* (pp. 25–46). Paul H Brookes Publishing.

Frankel, A. J., & Gelman, S. R. (1998). *Case management: An introduction to concepts and skills.* Lyceum Books.

Grubbs, L. A., Cassell, J., & Mulkey, S. W. (2006). *Rehabilitation caseload management: Concepts and practice* (2nd ed.). Springer Publishing Company.

Gursansky, D., Harvey, J., & Kennedy, R. (2003). *Case management: Policy, practice and professional business.* Columbia University Press.

Honeycutt, T., Bardos, M., & McLeod, S. (2014). *Bridging the gap: A comparative assessment of vocational rehabilitation agency practices with transition-age youth.* Mathematica Policy Research.

Honeycutt, T., & Stapleton, D. (2013). Striking while the iron is hot: The effect of vocational rehabilitation service wait times on employment outcomes for applicants receiving social security disability benefits. *Journal of Vocational Rehabilitation, 39*(2), 137–152. https://doi.org/10.3233/JVR-130645

Kaya, C., Bishop, M., & Torres, A. (2023). The impact of work incentives benefits counseling on employment outcomes: A national vocational rehabilitation study. *Journal of Occupational Rehabilitation, 33*(3), 538–549. https://doi.org/10.1007/s10926-022-10092-1

Leahy, M. J., Del Valle, R. J., Landon, T. J., Iwanaga, K., Sherman, S. G., Reyes, A., & Chan, F. (2018). Promising and evidence-based practices in vocational rehabilitation: Results of a national Delphi study. *Journal of Vocational Rehabilitation, 48*(1), 37–48. https://doi.org/10.3233/JVR-170914

Mazzotti, V. L., Rowe, D. A., Kwiatek, S., Voggt, A., Chang, W., Fowler, C. H., Poppen, M., Sinclair, J., & Test, D. W. (2020). Secondary transition predictors of postschool success: An update to the research base. *Career Development and Transition for Exceptional Individuals, 44*(1), 47–64. https://doi.org/10.1177/2165143420959793.

Miller, W. R., & Rollnick, S. (2013). *Motivational interviewing: Helping people change* (3rd ed.). The Guilford Press.

Office of Disability Employment Policy. (n.d.). *Employment first.* https://www.dol.gov/agencies/odep/initiatives/employment-first

Oswald, G. R., Flexer, R., Alderman, L. A., & Huber, M. (2016). Predictive value of personal characteristics and the employment of transition-aged youth in vocational rehabilitation. *Journal of Rehabilitation, 82*(4), 60–66.

Oswald, G. R., & Taylor, R. (2020). Careers and credentials: Employment settings for rehabilitation practitioners. In J. D. Andrew & C. W. Faubion (Eds.), *Rehabilitation services: An introduction for the human services professional* (pp. 282–307). Aspen Professional Services.

Peterson, S. (2023). Facilitating a warm handoff in state vocational rehabilitation service delivery. *Journal of Applied Rehabilitation Counseling, 54*(1), 33–47. https://doi.org/10.1891/JARC-2021-0019

Prochaska, J. O., & DiClemente, C. C. (1984). *The transtheoretical approach: Crossing traditional boundaries of therapy.* Dow Jones/Irwin.

Substance Abuse and Mental Health Services Administration. (2021). *Using motivational interviewing in substance use disorder treatment. Advisory.* https://store.samhsa.gov/sites/default/files/SAMHSA_Digital_Download/PEP20-02-02-014.pdf

Wang, Y. C., & Ethridge, G. (2022). Identifying factors that promote successful vocational rehabilitation case closure: Comparison of individual characteristics, VR experiences and state economic conditions. *Journal of Vocational Rehabilitation, 56,* 139–147. https://doi.org/10.3233/JVR-221178

Yin, M., Pathak, A., Lin, D., & Dizdari, N. (2022). Identifying racial differences in vocational rehabilitation services. *Rehabilitation Counseling Bulletin, 66*(1), 13–24. https://doi.org/10.1177/00343552211048218

CHAPTER 10

Specialized Skills in Private Rehabilitation Caseload Management

LEARNING OBJECTIVES

By the end of this chapter, learners will be able to:

- Understand the role of specialized skills in private rehabilitation caseload management.
- Identify the key components of rehabilitation disability management and its importance in facilitating client recovery and functional improvement.
- Explore the complexities of workers compensation in the context of private rehabilitation, including navigating legal processes and coordinating vocational rehabilitation services.
- Gain insights into forensic rehabilitation and its role in providing expert opinions within the legal system, such as evaluating employability and offering guidance on vocational options.
- Comprehend the principles and techniques involved in life care planning, including assessing long-term needs, estimating associated costs, and developing comprehensive care plans.
- Develop a working knowledge of Social Security expertise, including eligibility criteria, documentation requirements, and effective advocacy for disability benefits.
- Understand the significance of community rehabilitation partnerships and the benefits of collaborating with external rehabilitation contractors and community organizations.
- Analyze case studies and real-world scenarios to apply the specialized skills discussed in the chapter to practical situations.
- Explore ethical considerations and professional standards relevant to private rehabilitation caseload management.
- Reflect on the importance of ongoing professional development and staying updated with evolving best practices in private rehabilitation.

INTRODUCTION

The profession of private sector rehabilitation counseling is experiencing rapid growth and constant change, making it one of the most dynamic fields. Since its inception with the passage of the Smith-Fess Act in 1920, rehabilitation has continuously been in a state of transition. According to Grubbs et al. (2006), the field of rehabilitation undergoes a perpetual process of moving from one state to another. Change is an integral and recognized part of the rehabilitation profession, with the understanding that the only consistent element within the field is the presence of change itself. The dynamic nature of rehabilitation is particularly evident in the expansion of private sector rehabilitation.

In 1970, the majority of rehabilitation professionals worked for state-federal vocational rehabilitation agencies. Although the Social Security Administration collaborated with these agencies to provide rehabilitation services to Social Security Disability recipients, the impact of such services remained limited in scope. However, during the 1970s, there was a significant increase in benefit levels and costs associated with workers compensation and other disability policies, which brought attention to the financial implications of disabilities. This led to the establishment of private rehabilitation services (Havranek, 1995). The rapid growth of the private-for-profit sector in the rehabilitation field can be attributed to the perceived personal and economic advantages it offered. Furthermore, organizations dedicated to reducing disability benefit costs played a role in the expansion of these services. Throughout the 1990s, efforts persisted to improve the cost-effectiveness and efficiency of rehabilitation services, aiming to provide more impactful and effective rehabilitation outcomes.

The field of rehabilitation has undergone significant transformation and evolution, particularly with the emergence of private sector rehabilitation. The recognition of the financial implications of disabilities and the perceived benefits, both personal and economic, have played a pivotal role in driving the expansion of private-for-profit rehabilitation. Additionally, organizations focused on minimizing disability-related expenses have contributed to the growth of these services. In the 1990s, continuous efforts were made to enhance the cost-effectiveness and efficiency of rehabilitation services, with the goal of delivering more impactful outcomes.

Rehabilitation in the private sector includes a wide range of services provided by practitioners and other professionals who are employed in private businesses rather than in public service agencies. As described by Shaw and Betters (2004), the term private sector rehabilitation encompasses a wide array of rehabilitation personnel within both for-profit and not-for-profit businesses who support individuals with disabilities at varying levels. The services provided in the private sector are similar in many ways to those provided by practitioners regardless of their work settings. These services may include vocational planning and assessment, disability case management, case documentation and reporting, and job placement and development (Beveridge et al., 2016; Lynch & Martin, 1982; Zanskas & Strohmer, 2011).

The **nature of work** in private sector rehabilitation significantly impacts caseload management, requiring professionals to adapt to unique challenges and dynamics (Chan et al., 2003; Leahy et al., 2009). Understanding the characteristics of private sector work is vital for effectively managing caseloads. One crucial aspect is the emphasis on efficiency and productivity. According to Shaw and Betters (2004), what makes the work of private sector professionals unique is the business environment in which they function, regardless of the mission or services that may characterize profit as the nature of the business. Private sector rehabilitation operates within a **profit-driven framework**, where time and resources are highly valued (Mann, 2016; Shaw & Betters, 2004). This emphasis on efficiency often leads to more intense and focused caseloads compared to the public sector, necessitating strong organizational and prioritization skills to meet the demands of a highly focused workload (Gardner, 2017).

Furthermore, effective caseload management in the private sector necessitates a business-oriented approach. Practitioners are required to actively engage in marketing and networking in order to attract clients and establish referral networks, thus fostering a consistent caseload. Additionally, they must possess proficient skills in managing the financial aspects of their practice, including budgeting, billing, and client invoicing (American

Association of Managed Care Nurses, 2016; Prentice et al., 2011). A comprehensive understanding of the business aspects of private sector rehabilitation is crucial for maintaining a sustainable practice and ensuring effective caseload management. By incorporating business strategies and honing financial management skills, professionals can optimize their caseloads and cultivate long-term success in the private sector (Mullahy, 2017).

Changing Target Populations

The field of rehabilitation has often experienced a shift in its focus, moving from one disability group to another, driven by an unspoken desire to cater to the needs of all individuals. There was a time when a comprehensive range of rehabilitation services was envisioned, aiming to serve individuals across the entire spectrum of life. However, this constant fluctuation and change in caseload management practices resulted in confusion and stress, making it more challenging for individuals to become competent professionals in the field.

The emergence of private sector rehabilitation can be attributed to several factors, including changes in the client demographics within the public rehabilitation system, caseload sizes, and the extent of service provision. In the 1920s, vocational rehabilitation services became available to civilians, while workers compensation statutes already existed to provide medical services to federal and private workers, as noted by Matkin (1997). These vocational rehabilitation services were initially intended to be provided through state agencies. Consequently, the primary client population served by the state agencies until the mid-1970s consisted of working-age individuals who were expected to return to gainful employment. The characteristics and services in the public sector also changed drastically with the definition and inclusion of developmental disabilities.

The passage of the 1973 Rehabilitation Act and subsequent amendments expanded the priority of clients to be served by the public agency system to include individuals with significant disabilities acquired at birth or later in life (Matkin, 1997). This broadened the scope of services to cover a wider range of citizens with disabilities. However, the public rehabilitation professionals faced challenges of managing increasing caseloads and longer average case durations. Consequently, the expansion of the disability population and government funding for rehabilitation services led to the emergence of private rehabilitation facilities.

During this time, rehabilitation units and centers were exempted from the prospective payment system, which was the prevailing method of healthcare reimbursement. As a result, many tertiary care centers opted to establish their own rehabilitation units (Shaw & Betters, 2004). Community rehabilitation programs also began focusing on service integration and vocational rehabilitation. At the same time, a report on cost-containment strategies caught the attention of state workers compensation boards, who were grappling with cost-containment issues. The report suggested that introducing vocational rehabilitation services could expedite the return to work for individuals with disabilities, thus reducing costs. This concept gained traction, leading to an increased utilization of rehabilitation services within the workers compensation field.

However, workers compensation companies often became dissatisfied with the services provided by the public sector. Services were perceived as slow to implement, focused on training rather than placement, and lacking in cost-containment measures (Shaw & Betters, 2004; Weed & Hill, 2001). Consequently, private practitioners began shifting their focus from public services to the private sector, which catered to various disabling conditions commonly resulting from diseases, accidents, or work injuries covered by workers compensation insurance.

Private sector rehabilitation professionals strive to restore their clients to their previous level of functioning to the best extent possible (Matkin, 1995). In the pursuit of cost-efficiency, the private sector offers a comprehensive package of services that are more easily accessible and adaptable. This area of rehabilitation is characterized by a diverse range of clients and conditions, necessitating flexible approaches to caseload management. Practitioners encounter individuals with varying types and degrees of disabilities, injuries, or impairments, requiring them to tailor interventions and treatment plans according to each client's unique needs and goals (Grubbs et al., 2006; International Association of Rehabilitation Professionals, n.d.).

Furthermore, the private sector introduces considerations related to insurance coverage and reimbursement, which significantly influence caseload management. Rehabilitation services often rely on insurance reimbursement, such as workers compensation or private health insurance. Effective caseload management in the private sector involves navigating insurance policies, ensuring accurate documentation and billing, and advocating for appropriate coverage to meet clients' rehabilitation needs. Professionals must possess knowledge of insurance regulations and procedures to optimize reimbursement and ensure the financial sustainability of their practice (Grubbs et al., 2006).

PROCEDURES IN THE PRIVATE SECTOR

Caseload management is the nucleus of the private sector and/or disability management system. Caseload managers may be selected from the internal ranks of **human resource management personnel**, may be recruited and hired to complement an already existing disability management team, or may be accessed through a consultant from a private rehabilitation vendor in the community. Several professional roles have evolved to meet the challenges faced by practitioners in the private sector. Private sector professionals have become caseload managers, disability management specialists, consultants to business and industry, specialists in the area of workers compensation vocational rehabilitation, and vocational experts in the legal arena (Brodwin, 2001).

Caseload management in the private sector requires coordination and monitoring of medical and rehabilitation services. Private sector professionals need to coordinate multidisciplinary prevention, rehabilitation, and treatment activities for workers. These professionals collaborate with medical and healthcare providers, public and private rehabilitation providers, and members of disability management teams (Grubbs et al., 2006; Mullahy, 2017; Shrey, 1995a, 1995b). These counselors emphasize early intervention, minimize functional limitations associated with disability, control cost-effective services, prevent industrial accidents, are associated with wellness in the workplace, and develop disability management and/or return-to-work programs.

Private rehabilitation professionals formalize disability management programs, which require the development of transitional work plans and a systematic effort to coordinate information in implementation of return-to-work or worker-retention plans. These managers also coordinate an employer's response to an injury and issues directly related to disability through evaluations to determine transferable skills, rehabilitation plans, and transitional programs. According to Shrey (1995a, 1995b), along with these duties, private sector practitioners have important functions in recommending corporate policy and procedure. The roles and functions of disability managers must be clearly delineated and exhaustively communicated to others actively participating in the overall process (Grubbs et al., 2006).

Communication

In the private sector, case management has become an integral component of mainstream medical practices. As a result, it is crucial to establish new dialogues and enhance communication channels. **Disability management** is a profession that heavily relies on face-to-face interactions, underscoring the importance of maintaining open pathways for effective communication. The Case Management Society of America (2022) emphasizes the need for improved and intentional communication among caseload managers, physicians, patients, families, payer sources, and relevant legal entities. This necessitates a focused and proactive approach to foster efficient collaboration and information sharing. To communicate more effectively with these specific groups, disability managers must acknowledge communication barriers and actively work to eliminate or overcome them.

Communicating With Supervision

In the field of disability management, effective communication between the disability manager and the employee's supervisor is of utmost importance. Historically noted by Shrey (1995a), a majority of injuries, subsequent disabilities, and work disruptions originate within the work environment. The employee's supervisor possesses valuable insights regarding the employee, specific job requirements, and circumstances surrounding the onset of disability. Thus, the disability manager plays a crucial role in facilitating communication with the supervisor and implementing appropriate work-return options for employees with restrictions. It is essential to develop and implement a comprehensive return-to-work plan that establishes clear goals, objectives, and responsibilities. These plans not only improve communication but also ensure the effective coordination of services by the disability manager.

Communicating With Clients

The introduction and explanation of the case management role to a client hold significant importance. Early involvement of the caseload manager can effectively benefit all parties involved. As Mullahy (2017) emphasizes, a continual objective for caseload managers is to educate clients about the optimal timing for case management intervention. However, since caseload managers often have limited control over referral timing, it becomes crucial to develop effective communication skills with clients. To facilitate the best possible exchange, the caseload manager should be well-informed about the client and the reason for referral. Similarly, the rehabilitation professional should possess a comprehensive understanding of the disability or injury, including any financial hardships or other challenges faced by the client. By maintaining an open communication style, the client remains informed about their medical circumstances, and the counselor can provide valuable assistance in the rehabilitation process while demonstrating empathy.

Communication and Private Sector Burnout

Case managers will often have tragic and difficult cases. Many of these cases result in life-altering changes for clients and their families. There seems to be little balance between success and tragedy in more traditional healthcare delivery systems. Often, caseload managers deal with individuals who are angry at the system and who tend to voice their opinions to their caseload manager rather than to their physician. Caseload managers who try to totally distance themselves emotionally from the pain of handling tough situations may lose their ability to be effective because the interaction with the client may be impacted over time. Therefore, private sector professionals must develop a balance by finding the appropriate level of involvement between clients and themselves. Caseload managers must understand where the function of case management begins and where it ends. They must be able to develop a strategic plan that addresses all issues related to the problem, while simultaneously understanding and acknowledging their own limitations. Despite the day-to-day issues that arise, counselors must maintain a state of equilibrium. Otherwise, they will become overwhelmed and burned out (Mullahy, 2017).

In order to prevent counselor burnout, it is crucial for professionals in the private sector to examine their attitudes toward their roles and the boundaries that come with them. Research has shown that counselors' attitudes toward their clients significantly impact their effectiveness in combating burnout (Brodwin, 2001). To be effective in their work, rehabilitation professionals must have a thorough understanding of their own attitudinal biases toward clients and the issues they encounter in their job. It is also important for private rehabilitation practitioners to have a realistic understanding of the parameters of their positions and avoid idealizing them. When counselors take on a case management role, they should be prepared for the requirements of the role and have a clear understanding of the expectations involved. Many professions have hidden expectations, but by recognizing and comprehending these expectations, counselors can proactively address burnout and find effective solutions to manage workplace stress.

PRIVATE SECTOR SKILLS AND SKILL CLUSTERS

Private Sector Skills

Working in private rehabilitation and effectively managing caseloads require a specific set of professional **skills** to meet the diverse needs of clients and ensure successful outcomes. **Figure 10.1** demonstrates key skills necessary for professionals in private rehabilitation and caseload management:

1. *Clinical expertise.* Professionals in private rehabilitation need strong clinical knowledge and skills essential for accurately assessing clients' conditions, developing appropriate rehabilitation plans, and delivering evidence-based interventions. This includes proficiency in rehabilitation practice, functional assessments, and understanding the latest advancements in the field.
2. *Communication and interpersonal skills.* Effective communication is crucial when working with clients, their families, and other healthcare professionals. Professionals in private rehabilitation must possess active listening skills, empathy, and the ability to convey complex information in a clear and understandable manner. Building strong relationships and establishing rapport with clients are vital for successful caseload management.
3. *Organization and time management.* Private rehabilitation settings often involve managing multiple clients with varying needs. Professionals must excel in organizational skills to prioritize tasks, set realistic goals, and manage time effectively. This includes maintaining detailed documentation, scheduling appointments efficiently, and ensuring timely follow-ups.
4. *Problem-solving and critical thinking.* The ability to analyze complex situations, think critically, and develop innovative solutions is essential in private rehabilitation. Professionals must be skilled in identifying barriers to progress, adjusting treatment plans as needed, and addressing unexpected challenges that may arise during caseload management.
5. *Legal and ethical understanding.* Private rehabilitation practitioners must have a solid understanding of legal and ethical frameworks relevant to their practice. This includes adhering to privacy regulations, understanding consent and confidentiality guidelines, and complying with professional codes of conduct. Awareness of legal considerations related to insurance reimbursement and workers compensation is also crucial.
6. *Business and financial acuity.* Professionals working in private rehabilitation must possess a basic understanding of business principles and financial management. This includes knowledge of billing and coding practices, budgeting, and managing insurance claims and reimbursements. Competency in marketing and networking can also contribute to building a sustainable caseload.

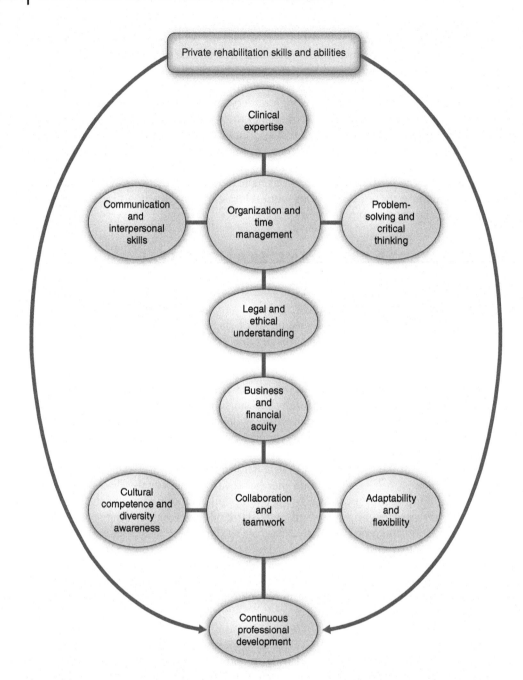

FIGURE 10.1 Private sector rehabilitation caseload management skills.

7. *Cultural competence and diversity awareness.* Clients in private rehabilitation come from diverse backgrounds, cultures, and communities. Professionals must demonstrate cultural competence, sensitivity, and the ability to provide inclusive care. Understanding and respecting diverse perspectives and tailoring interventions accordingly are essential for effective caseload management.

8. *Collaboration and teamwork.* Private rehabilitation often involves working in multidisciplinary teams. Professionals must excel in collaborating with other healthcare providers, including physicians, therapists, and specialists. Effective teamwork and communication contribute to comprehensive care coordination and enhance client outcomes.

9. *Adaptability and flexibility.* Private rehabilitation settings can present dynamic and evolving challenges. Professionals must be adaptable and open to change, able to adjust their approaches based on individual client needs, emerging research, and shifting healthcare policies.
10. *Continuous professional development.* Staying updated with current research, best practices, and advancements in the field is crucial for professionals in private rehabilitation. Engaging in ongoing professional development activities, attending conferences, and participating in relevant training programs ensure the delivery of high-quality care and effective caseload management.

By honing these skills, professionals can navigate the complexities of private rehabilitation, manage caseloads effectively, and provide comprehensive care to clients, ultimately promoting positive outcomes and improved quality of life.

Private Sector Skill Clusters

As described in Chapter 3 (Table 3.1), **skill clusters** are patterns of actions that concern central themes or axes. A skill is a learned ability for doing an activity in a competent manner. Often, the execution of one skill relies on another prerequisite skill. Thus, skills are often interrelated and occur in clusters (Cassell & Mulkey, 2004; Grubbs et al., 2006). Each cluster gathers sets of specific actions that the caseload manager uses for consistency of personal practice and for fulfilling organization standards. Whether in the private or public sector, there are skill clusters that may be applied to any rehabilitation setting. Illustrated in **Table 10.1** are five major skill clusters that reflect management application in the private sector.

Planning

Caseload management is a process that allows private sector practitioners to identify and solve problems. For private sector rehabilitation professionals, the key issue in any case is to focus on the best and/or most appropriate treatment, as well as the most appropriate setting for the treatment. Caseload managers must use their skills in various situations to appropriately plan effective rehabilitation outcomes. Some information in case files may be beyond the expertise of some practitioners. It is then that the caseload manager has a responsibility to become familiar with the area in question, and it is always appropriate to ask or to acknowledge that there is a need for further information.

TABLE 10.1 BASIC MANAGERIAL CLUSTERS IN THE PRIVATE SECTOR

MANAGERIAL FUNCTIONS	TYPICAL CORRESPONDING CASELOAD MANAGEMENT FUNCTIONS
Planning	Establishes a process of identifying and solving problems.
Reporting	Initiates and facilitates an effective communication process with clients.
Obtaining approval	Serves as adjunctive link to proceeding with the recommendations in the rehabilitation report.
Coordination	Executes the recommended services and puts these services into place.
Follow-up	Evaluates recommended activities and takes the necessary corrective action within a rehabilitation structure to maintain cost-effectiveness and quality services.

At this phase of the rehabilitation process case managers need to begin evaluating the funds available for services. With the impact of costs of medical equipment, supplies, physician bills, and therapies, case managers must pay close attention to price, quality, and delivery sites. Therefore, it is crucial that the case manager consider the services already in place, look at the overall costs, and reevaluate where and how time may be well spent. Overall, it is the case manager's job to plan an effective rehabilitation program and then, in measurable steps, follow the procedures necessary to ensure that the ultimate goals are attainable and realistic for the client.

Reporting

The nature of the referral source will impact on communication from the initial evaluation through the reporting stage (Mullahy, 2017). The focus needs to remain on the client, and the information needs to be balanced to present an accurate picture of the client's overall situation. A report in a disability case should be specific and the medical information complete. The frequency and length of the report should be established by the referral source, and the nature of the report should be pertinent to the specific medical situation. Reports should be written a minimum of once per month and should contain all pertinent case activity recorded in a specific, standard, or recommended form and clarify the client's current medical situation. This type of recording (i.e., specific) should continue for the duration of the case and be modified according to the referral source.

Case managers must focus on the situation, the line of insurance, the payer, and the needs of the client. Therefore, case management records need to address medical costs; medical, physician, client, and family issues; the individuals consulted; rehabilitation actions agreed upon and actions taken; and outcomes (Mullahy, 2017). Regardless of the client's situation or need, the report should adequately present the information that captures the general and specific aspects of the case.

Obtaining Approval

After the case management plan has been created and the report has been sent to the client and the referral source, the caseload manager must obtain approval to proceed with the rehabilitation plan as outlined. At this point in the process the caseload manager will communicate directly with the payer regarding the list of recommendations that define the rehabilitation plan. This bidirectional communication process allows the counselor and payer to address cost issues and alternative forms of care.

There will be times when caseload managers will have to use personal judgment and consideration for those they are representing. They may receive direct communication from an employer, referral source, or payer that prohibits the payment of some aspect of the plan due to cost containment or expense. If the rehabilitation professional's opinion is that the client is located in the most appropriate setting and is receiving the most cost-effective treatment, then the caseload manager should not allow the employer, referral source, or payer to override their professional judgment.

Coordination

The caseload manager's roles and responsibilities are to coordinate case resolution services, prevention services, medical treatment, rehabilitation services, and evaluation services through direct links with internal and external resources (Grubbs et al., 2006; Shrey, 1995a, 1995b). The caseload manager will often work in collaboration with employer-based human resources departments to coordinate third-party insurance payments for services.

For those caseload managers with medical management skills, provision of services to injured clients and important utilization reviews ensure quality rehabilitation and treatment outcomes.

For clients with prolonged work disruptions or for those hospitalized more than 2 weeks, rehabilitation services and medical management activities should be closely monitored. Case managers may be assigned to coordinate visits to rehabilitation and treatment programs, functioning as the liaison between the client and the community treatment team provider. The case manager may coordinate office visits with physicians and make visits to homebound clients to monitor recovery processes and facility rehabilitation planning activities (Cromwell & King, 2010; Harris & Popejoy, 2019; Shrey, 1995a, 1995b).

The focus of case management is on a more comprehensive coordination of services across the continuum of care, focusing on client perspective and need (Knox et al., 2022; Uittenbroek et al., 2018). The nature of case and medical management activities vary according to the acuity, chronicity, and other mediating circumstances surrounding the injury and/or disability (Shrey, 1995a). Therefore, it is imperative for caseload managers to expand their coordination beyond basic monitoring skills to include utilization review, evaluation of treatment plans, and promotion of medical opinions. It is the goal of the coordination process to reduce lost time by providing effective healthcare services and coordinating realistic and attainable return-to-work options (Fabbri et al., 2017; Shrey, 1995a, 1995b; Uittenbroek et al., 2018).

Follow-Up

Attention must be given to each detail of the rehabilitation process. Any time a caseload manager becomes responsible for a case, recommendations for services, or implementation of services, the counselor must ensure that what has been put into place is working effectively. Approval to monitor or follow up a case may be difficult to obtain from the payer or source; yet managing a case without follow-up can lead to disaster.

The monitoring process varies from case to case. Joo and Huber (2019) highlight the significance of a persistent and extensive monitoring process in reducing healthcare costs associated with chronic illness care and improving the quality of care. This is particularly important, as many practitioners depend on case management to achieve these goals. In situations where multiple services are involved, it becomes necessary for the case manager to conduct on-site or home visits to ensure a comprehensive understanding of the actual circumstances. Additionally, continuous follow-up reports play a crucial role in helping the case manager establish and maintain a connection with the client during the assessment process. These reports also support the case manager in fulfilling their role throughout the entire case.

Follow-up services are necessary to facilitate the continued implementation of rehabilitation strategies and return-to-work plans for workers with disabilities. These strategies blend the management of information with supportive policies. Mullahy (2017) reflects on the continuity of the case manager's position during the management process and throughout follow-up by reflecting on the case manager as someone who contributes to the entire treatment plan. Thus, rehabilitation professionals are part of this process from the beginning and follow it through with the client until the end.

REHABILITATION AND DISABILITY MANAGEMENT

Private rehabilitation and **disability management** entails addressing the needs of individuals with disabilities, empowering them to regain independence and maximize their quality of life (White, 2011). The nature of work in private rehabilitation and the area of disability management involves comprehensive assessments, developing personalized rehabilitation plans, coordinating services, and advocating for clients within legal and insurance frameworks (Currier et al., 2001).

Professionals working in the field of private rehabilitation and disability management must possess a diverse range of skills to effectively manage caseloads and support their clients (Grubbs et al., 2006). Clinical expertise is essential for accurately assessing disabilities, understanding their impact on functional abilities, and implementing evidence-based interventions. Knowledge of legal and insurance systems is also crucial for navigating complex regulations, facilitating disability claims, and coordinating services accordingly (Hoynes et al., 2021).

In addition to skills, various tools and technologies play a significant role in supporting private rehabilitation and disability management. Electronic health records and case management software help organize client information, track progress, and facilitate efficient communication among team members (Kisekka & Giboney, 2018). Assessment tools, such as functional evaluations and standardized measures, aid in identifying client needs and setting appropriate goals. Assistive technologies and adaptive equipment are instrumental in enhancing clients' functional independence and promoting their active participation, and integration of artificial intelligence (AI) continues to foster the potential for disability management practice (Skerritt & Wolstein, 2023).

Effective communication skills are fundamental in private rehabilitation and disability management. Professionals must establish rapport with clients, effectively communicate treatment plans, and collaborate with multidisciplinary teams. Active listening, empathy, and cultural competence are essential in building strong relationships and understanding clients' unique circumstances (Weger et al., 2014). Problem-solving, critical thinking, and creativity are also vital for developing tailored solutions to address clients' specific challenges. Furthermore, time management skills ensure the timely delivery of services and meeting clients' needs within specified timelines. Knowledge of community resources, social support systems, and available funding options facilitates comprehensive care and ensures access to necessary services (Hains et al., 2020).

Overall, private rehabilitation and disability management require professionals to possess a multidimensional skill set and effectively utilize tools and technologies. By leveraging these resources and skills, professionals can provide personalized and holistic care, empowering individuals with disabilities to achieve their goals and lead fulfilling lives.

WORKERS COMPENSATION

In the realm of private rehabilitation **workers compensation**, professionals are dedicated to meeting the specific needs of individuals who have suffered work-related injuries or illnesses. The nature of work in this field revolves around facilitating their recovery and ensuring a safe return to work. To achieve this, rehabilitation practitioners engage in a range of activities, including conducting comprehensive assessments to evaluate the impact of injuries or illnesses, developing customized rehabilitation plans, coordinating services with healthcare providers and employers, and advocating for clients within the workers compensation system (Roberts-Yates, 2003).

In private rehabilitation workers compensation, professionals require a specific skill set to effectively manage caseloads and provide support to injured workers. Clinical expertise is crucial for evaluating the functional limitations resulting from work-related injuries and designing appropriate treatment interventions (Bean et al., 2020). A deep understanding of workers compensation laws and regulations is also necessary to navigate the complex claims process and ensure compliance with legal requirements.

Various tools and resources support private rehabilitation workers compensation. Electronic health records and case management software assist in documenting and tracking clients' progress, managing appointments, and coordinating care among different stakeholders (Campanella et al., 2015). Vocational assessment tools are utilized to evaluate an injured worker's skills, abilities, and work capacity, enabling professionals to facilitate appropriate job placement or modification. Additionally, knowledge of ergonomic principles and workplace accommodations is essential to help injured workers transition back to their job duties safely (Herzog & Buchmeister, 2020).

Effective communication and documentation skills play a vital role in private rehabilitation workers compensation. Professionals must establish clear and productive communication with injured workers, employers, insurers, and healthcare providers to ensure collaboration and successful return-to-work outcomes. Professionals need to convey and document complex medical information in a clear and understandable manner, while advocating for their clients' needs, and facilitate effective coordination of care (Upton et al., 2021). Additional skills include problem-solving, negotiation, and conflict resolution. Professionals may need to address potential barriers to return to work, mediate disputes, and negotiate suitable accommodations for injured workers. Time management skills are crucial to prioritize tasks, meet deadlines, and ensure the timely delivery of services (Rawlins-Williams & Oswald, 2021).

In summary, private rehabilitation workers compensation requires professionals with a diverse skill set, including clinical expertise, knowledge of workers compensation regulations, effective communication, and problem-solving abilities. The use of electronic health records, case management software, vocational assessment tools, and communication platforms aids in efficient caseload management and the successful rehabilitation and return-to-work of injured employees.

FORENSIC REHABILITATION-CIVIL LITIGATION

Forensic rehabilitation refers to the comprehensive evaluation of vocational, medical, and economic harm within the framework of legal proceedings (Sprong et al., 2023). Forensic rehabilitation plays a crucial role by offering expert insights and assessments concerning disabilities, injuries, and vocational capabilities. The primary objective is to aid legal professionals, courts, and insurance companies in comprehending how disabilities affect employability and vocational opportunities. This field encompasses various areas, such as assisting private attorneys specializing in medical malpractice or catastrophic injury law, supporting the state worker compensation system, and aiding the Social Security Administration's Office of Disability Adjudication and Review (Herlihy et al., 2015). Key responsibilities within forensic rehabilitation in civil litigation include conducting comprehensive assessments, delivering expert testimony, and providing guidance on rehabilitation strategies that align with the legal framework (Barros-Bailey, 2014).

Professionals in forensic rehabilitation-civil litigation require a specialized skill set to effectively manage caseloads and contribute to the legal decision-making process. Clinical expertise is essential for evaluating the functional limitations resulting from disabilities or injuries and assessing an individual's vocational capabilities. Professionals need to be proficient in conducting comprehensive vocational assessments, analyzing medical records, and interpreting complex diagnostic information (Sprong et al., 2023).

Expert knowledge of legal principles, regulations, and case law relevant to civil litigation is critical. Professionals must understand the legal standards for determining vocational capacity, assessing earning potential, and calculating damages. Private rehabilitation professionals must also possess strong research and analytical skills to stay updated on legal precedents and effectively apply them to their evaluations and testimony (Shahnasarian, 2015). Effective communication skills are paramount in forensic rehabilitation-civil litigation. Professionals must have the ability to convey complex medical and vocational information in a clear and concise manner to legal professionals, judges, and juries. Further, there is a need to be adept at producing detailed reports and delivering credible expert testimony that can withstand cross-examination (Dunn, 2014). Collaboration and teamwork are essential in this field, as professionals often work closely with attorneys, insurance companies, and other experts involved in the litigation process. Effective collaboration ensures that the vocational and rehabilitation aspects of the case align with legal strategies and goals. To support their work, professionals have access to various tools and resources in forensic rehabilitation–civil litigation. These include medical databases, vocational assessment tools, assistive technology, and research materials (Robinson, 2014). Case management software and electronic document management systems further facilitate the efficient organization and retrieval of case-related information.

Forensic rehabilitation–civil litigation requires professionals with a unique combination of clinical expertise, legal knowledge, strong communication skills, and collaboration abilities. Professionals rely on specialized tools, access to pertinent databases, and efficient documentation systems to efficiently manage their caseloads and provide expert opinions within the legal context. This multidimensional approach ensures the seamless integration of clinical knowledge and legal principles, enabling professionals to navigate the complexities of civil litigation while providing valuable insights and guidance.

LIFE CARE PLANNING

Life care planning, established since 1998, is an internationally recognized interdisciplinary specialty practice that encompasses various aspects such as rehabilitation planning, service implementation, healthcare resource management, discharge planning, educational and vocational planning, and long-term managed care (McCollom, 1998). It plays a crucial role in private rehabilitation by serving as a long-standing case management tool to coordinate present and future medical and rehabilitation requirements for individuals who have experienced significant injuries or illnesses (Cary et al., 2021). The work of life care planning entails the development of comprehensive and detailed plans that encompass medical treatments, therapies, assistive devices, home modifications, and essential services. These plans aim to enhance the quality of life and independence of individuals with disabilities (Barros-Bailey, 2020; Weed, 2018). Life care planners collaborate closely with healthcare providers, therapists, and other professionals to create customized plans tailored to the unique needs of each client.

Professionals in life care planning require specific skills to effectively manage caseloads and provide comprehensive care. Clinical expertise is essential for evaluating the functional limitations resulting from disabilities or injuries and determining the appropriate medical interventions and therapies required for optimal recovery and ongoing support. Life care planners need to be knowledgeable about medical procedures, treatment options, and the latest advancements in the field of rehabilitation (Berens & Weed, 2018). Additionally, effective assessment skills are crucial in life care planning. Professionals must be able to thoroughly evaluate the physical, cognitive, and functional abilities of individuals and accurately estimate their long-term needs. This includes conducting functional assessments, analyzing medical records, and considering the individual's goals and aspirations for the future. Additionally, strong financial insight is necessary to estimate the costs associated with the recommended medical treatments, therapies, assistive devices, and services. Life care planners must have a comprehensive understanding of healthcare billing and reimbursement practices, insurance coverage, and the financial resources available to support the recommended care plan and have the ability to present this information in a way that supports clients in various rehabilitation settings (Preston, 2022).

Communication and interpersonal skills are essential for working with clients, their families, and a multidisciplinary team of healthcare professionals. Professionals must effectively convey complex medical information, discuss options, and address the concerns and expectations of clients and their families. Collaboration with other professionals involved in the individual's care is vital to ensure coordinated and holistic support. Various tools and resources support life care planning and caseload management. These include standardized assessment tools, cost estimation software, and electronic health records to document and track client information and progress (Barros-Bailey, 2020). Collaboration platforms and communication tools facilitate effective communication among team members and stakeholders.

To summarize, the provision of life care planning within private rehabilitation necessitates the presence of proficient experts possessing clinical knowledge, assessment proficiency, financial acumen, and strong communication skills. Leveraging specialized tools, assessment instruments, and electronic records facilitates streamlined caseload management and the creation of thorough life care plans that cater to the distinctive requirements of individuals with disabilities or injuries.

SOCIAL SECURITY VOCATIONAL EXPERT

Professionals in the field of **Social Security vocational expert** work play a vital role in assisting individuals who are seeking disability benefits from the Social Security Administration (SSA). Vocational experts provide expertise and guidance throughout the application process. In a recent publication by Thomas (2023), a comprehensive toolkit specifically tailored for vocational experts is discussed. This toolkit serves as an invaluable resource, offering support in defining key concepts and providing expert witness testimony. It covers a wide range of important aspects, including detailed definitions of the nature of work, assessing how disabilities impact an individual's ability to work, and effectively advocating during functional and environmental evaluations. By equipping vocational experts with comprehensive definitions and insights, this toolkit enables them to deliver accurate and compelling testimony to support disability benefit claims.

Professionals engaged in Social Security vocational expert work must possess specialized knowledge and skills to successfully handle caseloads and navigate the intricate Social Security system. One crucial skill is the ability to evaluate an individual's functional limitations arising from disabilities and comprehend how these limitations affect their capacity to perform work-related activities (Thomas, 2023). This entails conducting thorough vocational assessments and carefully analyzing medical records to determine the individual's vocational capabilities and limitations.

Professionals engaged in expert testimony must dedicate their efforts to collecting and organizing relevant medical and vocational evidence, which necessitates strong research and analytical skills. This involves thoroughly examining medical records, evaluating diagnostic information, and interpreting medical and vocational reports to construct a persuasive argument in favor of an individual's claim for disability benefits (Lutz, 2010). Moreover, vocational experts must possess a comprehensive understanding of the guidelines and regulations set forth by the SSA regarding vocational assessments and disability determinations. This knowledge is essential in ensuring that their assessments align with the established criteria and contribute effectively to the disability determination process.

Effective communication skills are crucial in Social Security vocational expert work, just as in other areas of professional practice within the private sector of rehabilitation. Professionals in this field must possess the ability to clearly and persuasively articulate complex medical and vocational information to various stakeholders, including the SSA, administrative law judges, and other involved parties in the claims process. Professionals must skillfully prepare detailed reports and deliver expert testimony that effectively communicates the individual's vocational limitations and their impact on their ability to work (Cary et al., 2023). By employing strong communication skills, professionals in Social Security vocational expert work can enhance the understanding and recognition of an individual's vocational challenges, contributing to a more accurate and fair evaluation of disability claims.

Strong advocacy skills are crucial in Social Security vocational expert work. Professionals must be able to advocate persuasively for their clients' rights and entitlement to disability benefits. This entails presenting persuasive arguments supported by medical and vocational evidence, addressing objections or challenges, and ensuring that the individual's vocational limitations are accurately considered during the decision-making process (Chamberlin, 2017).

Various tools and resources support Social Security vocational expert work and assist in managing caseloads. These include access to medical databases, vocational assessment tools, industry-specific resources, and research materials. Additionally, case management software and electronic document management systems aid in organizing and tracking case-related information, correspondence, and deadlines. These tools enable professionals to efficiently gather and manage the necessary information and documentation, enhancing their ability to provide comprehensive and well-supported expert opinions.

In summary, Social Security vocational expert work within the realm of private rehabilitation necessitates professionals who possess assessment skills, research and analytical abilities, effective communication, and strong advocacy skills. The availability of specialized tools, access to relevant resources, and efficient documentation systems greatly contributes to effective caseload management and the successful navigation of the Social Security system. These resources support professionals in providing comprehensive support to individuals seeking disability benefits and enable them to effectively advocate for their clients' rights and entitlements.

COMMUNITY REHABILITATION PROVIDERS (OUTSIDE CONTRACTS)

Collaborating with **community rehabilitation partners** is a vital component of private sector rehabilitation and effective caseload management. This collaborative effort involves establishing partnerships with external rehabilitation contractors, healthcare providers, vocational training programs, and job placement agencies. The aim is to provide holistic, interdisciplinary, and coordinated care for clients. In this field, professionals focus on building relationships with community partners to leverage their expertise and resources in supporting clients' rehabilitation goals (Cernich, 2020). Regular communication and collaboration with these partners are essential. Professionals work closely with community rehabilitation partners to coordinate services, exchange client information, and ensure smooth transitions between different phases of the rehabilitation process. By fostering these collaborative relationships, professionals can enhance the quality and effectiveness of rehabilitation services, creating a seamless and comprehensive support system for clients.

To effectively work with community rehabilitation partners and manage caseloads, professionals require specific skills. Strong interpersonal and communication skills are essential for building and maintaining collaborative relationships with external partners. Effective collaboration involves active listening, clear and concise communication, and the ability to navigate diverse professional cultures and perspectives (World Health Organization, 2010).

Organizational and coordination skills are crucial to manage the logistics of working with multiple community partners. Professionals must be able to prioritize tasks, schedule appointments and services, and ensure timely follow-ups. Attention to detail is necessary to track and document client progress, monitor service delivery, and manage contractual agreements. Negotiation and advocacy skills are important when working with community partners to ensure that clients receive appropriate services and support. Professionals may need to advocate for clients' needs, negotiate service contracts, and resolve any conflicts or challenges that may arise during the collaboration (Almost et al., 2016).

Professionals also benefit from an understanding of business principles and contract management. This includes knowledge of legal and ethical considerations, financial agreements, renegotiation of contracts, and performance monitoring to ensure that contractual obligations are met and services are delivered effectively (Shonk, 2020). In addition, various tools and resources are available to support professionals in their work with community rehabilitation partners and caseload management. Communication platforms and collaboration tools can facilitate effective communication and information sharing among all parties involved. Project management software can be used to track and monitor progress, deadlines, and deliverables associated with contractual agreements (Zulch, 2014). Moreover, electronic document management systems can aid in the organization and accessibility of relevant contractual documents and client information (Kittanah et al., 2016). These tools enhance efficiency, streamline processes, and contribute to effective caseload management and collaboration with community partners.

To summarize, successful collaboration with community rehabilitation partners in the private sector of rehabilitation relies on professionals who possess strong interpersonal skills, organizational abilities, negotiation and advocacy skills, and an understanding of business principles. These skills enable professionals to establish and maintain productive relationships with community partners, ensuring comprehensive and coordinated care for clients. Furthermore, the utilization of communication tools, project management software, and document management systems greatly supports effective caseload management and enhances collaboration with community partners. These tools streamline communication, track progress, manage deadlines, and facilitate efficient access to relevant information and documentation. By leveraging these skills and utilizing appropriate resources, professionals can effectively work with community rehabilitation partners, resulting in enhanced client outcomes and the delivery of high-quality rehabilitation services.

SUMMARY

This chapter explores the specific skills essential for effectively managing caseloads in private rehabilitation settings. It sheds light on critical areas including rehabilitation disability management, workers compensation, forensic rehabilitation, life care planning, Social Security vocational expertise, and community rehabilitation partnerships.

Private rehabilitation professionals must be adept at navigating legal frameworks, utilizing assessment techniques, and engaging in collaboration with external stakeholders. Successful caseload management in private rehabilitation necessitates a combination of essential skills, including clinical expertise, effective communication and interpersonal skills, strong organization and time management abilities, problem-solving and critical thinking proficiencies, a solid understanding of legal and ethical considerations, business acumen and financial knowledge, cultural competence and diversity awareness, and collaboration and teamwork aptitude, as well as adaptability and flexibility. Moreover, a commitment to continuous professional development is vital to stay updated and enhance one's capabilities in this field.

Additionally, the chapter explores the range of tools and technologies employed in private sector rehabilitation caseload management. These tools include electronic health records, case management software, assessment tools, outcome measures, treatment planning templates, communication and collaboration platforms, appointment scheduling systems, reporting and analytics tools, billing and reimbursement software, and mobile applications.

By honing these specialized skills and leveraging the right tools, professionals in private rehabilitation can maximize client outcomes, cultivate collaboration among stakeholders, and deliver comprehensive care. This chapter serves as a valuable resource, offering insights into the nature of the work, the necessary skills, and the tools employed in private rehabilitation caseload management. Professionals must continue to gain a comprehensive understanding of this vital aspect within the field, enabling individuals in professional practice to navigate the complexities of private rehabilitation more effectively as this area continues to grow into the future.

QUESTIONS FOR DISCUSSION

1. How does the nature of work in private rehabilitation settings differ from that of public or government-funded rehabilitation? What are the implications for caseload management?

2. What are some challenges that rehabilitation professionals may encounter when managing larger caseloads in the private sector? How can these challenges be addressed effectively?

3. How do specialized skills in areas such as rehabilitation disability management, workers compensation, forensic rehabilitation, life care planning, Social Security expertise, and community rehabilitation partnerships contribute to successful caseload management in the private sector?

4. How can professionals in private rehabilitation balance the need for efficiency and productivity while providing high-quality personalized care to their clients?

5. What are some key considerations and strategies for effectively navigating insurance policies and reimbursement processes in private sector rehabilitation caseload management?

6. How does the business aspect of private sector rehabilitation impact caseload management? What business skills and strategies are essential for maintaining a viable practice in this context?

7. How can professionals in private rehabilitation effectively collaborate with external stakeholders, such as healthcare providers, vocational training programs, and job placement agencies, to ensure comprehensive care and successful client outcomes?

8. What are some ethical considerations that professionals in private rehabilitation should keep in mind when managing caseloads and advocating for their clients' needs?

9. How can the use of specialized tools and technologies, such as electronic health records, case management software, and assessment instruments, enhance caseload management in private rehabilitation settings?

10. How do ongoing professional development and staying up-to-date with advancements in the field contribute to effective caseload management in private rehabilitation?

These discussion questions can help facilitate a deeper exploration of the topic, promote critical thinking, and encourage the sharing of insights and experiences among professionals in the field of private rehabilitation caseload management.

PUTTING IT INTO PRACTICE

Ask yourself these questions to target issues or concerns with specialized skills in private rehabilitation caseload management.

1. Are the disability populations being served in the private sector leading to a shift in the required specialized skills for private rehabilitation practitioners? Is this shift necessitating additional credentialing or education to meet the evolving demands for specialized services?

2. How do individuals in the private sector ensure a continuous "pipeline" of services for their clients? How do they incorporate managerial functions to maintain both cost-containment and high-quality services across all service levels?

3. Does the business aspect of private case and caseload management impact the overall quality of services provided? If so, how do rehabilitation providers strike a balance between delivering quality services and respecting client autonomy and choice?

CASE STUDY

Idris, a private rehabilitation counselor, has been called upon to provide expert witness testimony in a personal injury lawsuit involving Sonia, a 55-year-old woman who suffered a traumatic brain injury in a car accident. As Idris assumes this critical role, he faces the responsibility of making decisions regarding the selection of appropriate interventions and services to support Sonia's recovery and potential return to work. To accomplish this task effectively, Idris must utilize specialized skills, taking into consideration Sonia's demographic information, including her age, cognitive abilities, pre-accident occupation, and social support network.

Case Study Questions

1. How can Idris assess Sonia's cognitive and functional abilities to identify areas of impairment and potential strengths?

2. What role does a neuropsychological evaluation play in understanding Sonia's brain injury and potential for recovery?

3. How will Idris ensure a comprehensive understanding of Sonia's demographic information, including her age, cognitive abilities, pre-accident occupation, and social support network?

4. What strategies will be employed to effectively communicate complex rehabilitation concepts and assessments to the court and to the jury?

5. What measures will be taken to maintain objectivity and avoid any conflicts of interest in your role as an expert witness?

REFERENCES

Almost, J., Wolff, A. C., Stewart-Pyne, A., McCormick, L. G., Strachan, D., & D'Souza, C. (2016). Managing and mitigating conflict in healthcare teams: An integrative review. *Journal of Advanced Nursing, 72*(7), 1490–1505. https://doi.org/10.1111/jan.12903

American Association of Managed Care Nurses. (2016). *Care Management Institute guidelines.* http://www.aamcn.org/Guidelines_Final%20Draft.pdf

Barros-Bailey, M. (2014). History of forensic vocational rehabilitation consulting. In R. H. Robin (Ed.), *Foundations of forensic vocational rehabilitation* (pp. 13–31). Springer Publishing Company.

Barros-Bailey, M. (2020). Life care planning report writing foundations, standards, methods, and ethics: Development of a checklist. *Journal of Life Care Planning, 18*(2), 69–79. https://rehabpro.org/global_engine/download.aspx?fileid=C8583859-033C-491F-BA3F-1A0E31E02635&ext=pdf

Bean, M., Erdil, M., Blink, R., McKinney, D., Seidner, A., & ACOEM Utilization Review Task Force. (2020). Utilization review in workers' compensation: Review of current status and recommendations for future improvement. *Journal of Occupational and Environmental Medicine, 62*(6), 273–286. https://doi.org/10.1097/JOM.0000000000001893

Berens, O. E., & Weed, R. O. (2018). The role of the vocational rehabilitation counselor in life care planning. In R. O. Weed and D. E. Berens (Eds.), *Life care planning and case management handbook* (4th ed.). Routledge Publishing.

Beveridge, S., Karpen, S., Chan, C., & Penrod, J. (2016). Application of the KVI-R to assess current training needs of private rehabilitation counselors. *Rehabilitation Counseling Bulletin, 59*(4), 213–223. https://doi.org/10.1177/0034355215590770

Brodwin, M. G. (2001). Rehabilitation in the private-for-profit sector: Opportunities and challenges. In S. E. Rubin & R. T. Roessler (Eds.), *Foundations of the vocational rehabilitation process* (5th ed., pp. 475–495). Pro-Ed.

Campanella, P., Lovato, E., Marone, C., Fallacara, L., Mancuso, A., Ricciardi, W., & Specchia, M. L. (2015). The impact of electronic health records on healthcare quality: A systematic review and meta-analysis. *European Journal of Public Health, 26*(1), 60–64. https://doi.org/10.1093/eurpub/ckv122

Cary, J. R., Choppa, N., Johnson, C. B., Fountaine, J., & Choppa, T. (2023). A walk-through from referral to testimony: Methodology & admissibility. *Journal of Life Care Planning, 21*(1), 69–84.

Cary, J. R., Choppa, N., & Layton, K. (2021). Vocational, economic and life care planning in the era of COVID-19. *Journal of Life Care Planning, 19*(1), 3–17.

Case Management Society of America. (2022). *Standards of practice for case management.* https://cmsa.org/about/standards-of-case-management-practice/

Cassell, J. L., & Mulkey, S. W. (2004). Caseload management. In T. F. Riggar & D. R. Maki (Eds.), *Handbook of rehabilitation counseling* (pp. 252–270). Springer Publishing Company.

Cernich, A. N. (2020). Leadership of the ultimate interdisciplinary team: Rehabilitation science at NIH. *Journal of Neuroengineering and Rehabilitation, 17*(1), 67. https://doi.org/10.1186/s12984-020-00696-0

Chamberlin, J. (2017). Take the stand: Strategies for effective testimony. *Monitor on Psychology, 48*(1), 1–56. https://www.apa.org/monitor/2017/01/effective-testimony

Chan, F., Leahy, M. J., Saunders, J. L., Tarvydas, V. M., Ferrin, J. M., & Lee, G. (2003). Training needs of certified rehabilitation counselors for contemporary practice. *Rehabilitation Counseling Bulletin, 46*(2), 82–91. https://doi.org/10.1177/00343552030460020201

Cromwell, D. L., & King, C. L. (2010). A coordinated approach to disability management. *HR Magazine, 55*(4), 55–60.

Currier, K. F., Chan, F., Leahy, M. J., Taylor, D. W., & Lui, J. (2001). Functions and knowledge domains for disability management practice: A Delphi study. *Rehabilitation Counseling Bulletin, 44*(3), 134–144. https://doi.org/10.1177/003435520104400303

Dunn, P. (2014). Introduction to the American legal system and rules of civil procedure: A primer for vocational experts. In R. H. Robin (Ed.). *Foundations of forensic vocational rehabilitation.* Springer Publishing Company.

Fabbri, E., De Maria, M., & Bertolaccini, L. (2017). Case management: An up-to-date review of literature and a proposal of a county utilization. *Annals of Translational Medicine, 5*(20), 396. https://doi.org/10.21037/atm.2017.07.26

Gardner, M. (2017, May 23). *Private case management vs. public case management services.* Case management basics. https://www.casemanagementbasics.com/2017/05/private-case-management-vs-public-case.html

Grubbs, L. A., Cassell, J. L., & Mulkey, S. W. (2006). *Rehabilitation caseload management: Concepts and practice* (2nd ed.). Springer Publishing Company.

Hains, K. D., Hains, B., White, S., Standard, V., & Rios, M. (2020). Knowledge, values and skills essential for effective community development practice: A Delphi study. *Journal of Community Practice, 28*(4), 416–429. https://doi.org/10.1080/10705422.2020.1838021

Harris, R. C., & Popejoy, L. L. (2019). Case management: An evolving role. *Western Journal of Nursing Research, 41*(1), 3–5. https://doi.org/10.1177/0193945918797601

Havranek, J. E. (1995). Historical perspectives on the rehabilitation counseling profession and disability management. In D. E. Shrey & M. Lacerte (Eds.), *Principles and practices of disability management in industry* (pp. 355–370). St. Lucie Press.

Herlihy, B., Corey, G., Herlihy, B., & Corey, G. (2015). Focus on specialty areas: Disaster mental health, private practice, addictions counseling, and rehabilitation counseling. In B. Herlihy and G. Corey (Eds.), *Boundary issues in counseling* (pp. 221–240). Wiley.

Herzog, V., & Buchmeister, B. (2020). Workplace design and ergonomic analysis for workers with disabilities. In W. Karwowski, R. Goonetilleke, S. Xiong, R. Goossens, A. Murata (Eds.), *Advances in physical, social & occupational ergonomics.* AHFE 2020. *Advances in intelligent systems and computing* (*Vol. 1215*) (pp. 127–134). Springer Publishing Company.

Hoynes, H. W., Maestas, N., & Strand A. (2021). *Legal representation in disability claims.* National Bureau of Economic Research, Center Paper: NB19-29, Summer Institute 2023. https://www.nber.org/programs-projects/projects-and-centers/retirement-and-disability-research-center/center-papers/nb19-29

International Association of Rehabilitation Professionals. (n.d.). *What is private rehabilitation?* Retrieved June 18, 2023, from https://rehabpro.org/general/custom.asp?page=private_rehab

Joo, J. Y., & Huber, D. L. (2019). Case management effectiveness on health care utilization outcomes: A systematic review of reviews. *Western Journal of Nursing Research, 41*(1), 6–28. https://doi.org/10.1177/0193945918762135

Kisekka, V., & Giboney, J. S. (2018). The effectiveness of health care information technologies: Evaluation of trust, security beliefs, and privacy as determinants of health care outcomes. *Journal of Medical Internet Research, 20*(4), 1–11. https://doi.org/10.2196/jmir.9014

Kittanah, K. S., Bujarour, S. A., & Jordan, A. (2016). The impact of electronic documents management on performance. *Global Journal of Management and Business Research, 16*(1), 1–9. https://globaljournals.org/GJMBR_Volume16/1-The-Impact-of-Electronic-Documents.pdf

Knox, M., Esteban, E. E., Hernandez, E. A., Fleming, M. D., Safaeinilli, N., & Brewster, A. L. (2022). Defining case management success: A qualitative study of case manager perspectives from a large-scale health and social needs support program. *BMJ Open Quality, 11*(2), e001807. https://doi.org/10.1136/bmjoq-2021-001807

Leahy, M., Muenzen, P., Saunders, J., & Stauser, D. (2009). Essential knowledge requirements of certified rehabilitation counselors in the 21st century. *Rehabilitation Counseling Bulletin, 46*(2), 66–81.

Lutz, D. (2010). Vocational rehabilitation assessments. In S. Walfish (Ed.), *Earning a living outside of managed mental health care: 50 ways to expand your practice* (pp. 103–105). American Psychological Association.

Lynch, R. K., & Martin, T. (1982). Rehabilitation counseling in the private sector: A training needs survey. *Journal of Rehabilitation, 48*, 51–73.

Mann, B. (2016, December 22). *As addiction deaths surge, profit-driven rehab industry faces "severe ethical crisis."* NPR. https://www.wgbh.org/news/national-news/2021/02/15/as-addiction-deaths-surge-profit-driven-rehab-industry-faces-severe-ethical-crisis

Matkin, R. E. (1995). Private sector rehabilitation. In S. E. Rubin & R. T. Roessler (Eds.), *Foundations of the vocational rehabilitation process* (4th ed., pp. 375–398). Pro-Ed.

Matkin, R. E. (1997). Public and private rehabilitation counseling practices. In D. R. Maki & T. F. Riggar (Eds.), *Rehabilitation counseling: Profession and practice* (pp. 139–150). Springer Publishing Company.

McCollom, P. (1998). Dialog for tomorrow. *International Academy of Life Care Planners Academy Letter, 1*(1), 6–13.

Mullahy, C. M. (2017). *The case manager's handbook* (6th ed.). Jones & Bartlett Learning.

Prentice, D., Ritchie, L., Reynolds, M., Kitson, M., Smith, J., & Schenck, T. (2011). A case management experience: Implementing best practice guidelines in the community. *Care Management Journals: Journal of Case Management, 12*(4), 150–153. https://doi.org/10.1891/1521-0987.12.4.150

Preston, K. (2022). Standards of practice for life care planners, 4th edition. *Journal of Life Care Planning, 20*(3), 5–24. https://cdn.ymaws.com/rehabpro.org/resource/collection/9D348803-F86B-4F1B-B5D1-2CDFC57ED3C7/JLCP-Vol-20-No-3.pdf

Rawlins-Williams, L. A., & Oswald, G. R. (2021). Facilitating knowledge in rehabilitation counseling professionals on caseload management: A pre-test/post-test evaluation. *The Rehabilitation Professional, 29*(1), 5–12.

Roberts-Yates, D. (2003). Examining the role of rehabilitation in the South Australian workers' compensation system. *The Australian Journal of Rehabilitation Counselling, 9*(2), 82–101. https://doi.org/10.1017/S1323892200000399

Robinson, R. H. (2014). *Foundations of forensic vocational rehabilitation.* Springer Publishing Company.

Shahnasarian, M. (2015). Consultation in litigation. In P. J. Hartung, M. L. Savickas, & W. B. Walsh (Eds.), *APA handbook of career intervention, Vol. 2. Applications* (pp. 521–534). *American Psychological Association.*

Shaw, L. R., & Betters, C. (2004). Private sector practice. In T. F. Riggar & D. R. Maki (Eds.), *Handbook of rehabilitation counseling* (pp. 235–251). Springer Publishing Company.

Shonk, K. (2020). *Contract renegotiation in a time of crisis. Harvard Law School program on Negotiation Blog.* https://www.pon.harvard.edu/daily/business-negotiations/contract-renegotiation-in-a-time-of-crisis/

Shrey, D. E. (1995a). Disability management practice at the worksite: Developing, implementing, and evaluating transitional work programs. In D. E. Shrey & M. Lacerte (Eds.), *Principles and practices of disability management in industry* (pp. 55–105). St. Lucie Press.

Shrey, D. E. (1995b). Worksite disability management and industrial rehabilitation: An overview. In D. E. Shrey & M. Lacerte (Eds.), *Principles and practices of disability management in industry* (pp. 303–352). St. Lucie Press.

Skerritt, C., & Wolstein, D. (2023). Use of artificial intelligence to enhance case management and job development practices in rehabilitation counseling. *The Rehabilitation Professional, 31*(2), 19–26.

Sprong, M. E., Thomas, L., Fuscaldo, N., Purinton, J., & Oakes, T. (2023). Examination of forensic vocational rehabilitation models: Prior graduate-level training and current use per forensic setting. *The Rehabilitation Professional, 31*(1), 13–26.

Thomas, L. B. (2023). Practitioner tool-kit: Social security definitions for vocational experts. *The Rehabilitation Professional, 30*(3), pp. 7–12.

Uittenbroek, R. J., van der Mei, S. F., Slotman, K., Reijneveld, S. A., & Wynia, K. (2018). Experiences of case managers in providing person-centered and integrated care based on the Chronic Care Model: A qualitative study on embrace. *PLoS ONE, 13*(11), e0207109. https://doi.org/10.1371/journal.pone.0207109

Upton, T. D., Sanchez, J., & Sprong, M. (2021). Forensic rehabilitation services in the United States. In M. A. Joseph & M. Robinson (Eds.), *Fundamentals of clinical rehabilitation counseling* (pp. 41–51). Cognella Publishers.

Weed, R. O. (2018). Life care planning: Past, present and future. In R. O. Weed & D. E. Berens (Eds.), *Life care planning and case management handbook* (4th ed., pp. 3–20). Routledge Publishing.

Weed, R. O., & Hill, J. A. (2001). *Rehabilitation consultant's handbook.* Elliott & Fitzpatrick.

Weger, H., Bell, G. C., Minei, E. M., & Robinson, M. C. (2014). The relative effectiveness of active listening in initial interactions. *International Journal of Listening, 28*(1), 13–31. https://doi.org/10.1080/10904018.2013.813234

White, A. (2011). Disability management services in unionised environments: A Delphi study. *International Journal of Disability Management, 6*(1), 22–36. https://doi.org/10.1375/jdmr.6.1.22

World Health Organization. (2010). *Rehabilitation—community-based rehabilitation: CBR guidelines.* https://www.ncbi.nlm.nih.gov/books/NBK310933/

Zanskas, S., & Strohmer, D. C. (2011). The work environment of the private-for-profit rehabilitation counselor. *Journal of Rehabilitation, 77*, 13–22.

Zulch, B. G. (2014). Communication: The foundation of project management. *Procedia Technology, 16*(1), 1000–1009. https://doi.org/10.1016/j.protcy.2014.10.054

CHAPTER 11

Ethical Practice in Case and Caseload Management

LEARNING OBJECTIVES

By the end of this chapter, learners will be able to:

- Identify academic standards related to ethical practice.
- Recognize the impact of professional ethics on case and caseload management.
- Differentiate between various professional codes of ethics related to rehabilitation professionals.
- Utilize an ethical decision-making model for difficult situations.

INTRODUCTION

Considered broadly, ethics can be defined as (a) a discipline dealing with what is good and bad and with moral duty and obligation; (b) a set of moral principles and/or a theory or system of moral values; (c) the principles of conduct governing an individual or a group; or (d) a guiding philosophy. Ethics may be mandatory or aspirational in nature. **Mandatory ethics** are related to minimal standards required for compliance purposes, whereas **aspirational ethics** refer to the highest standard of thinking and conduct.

Professional ethics are established by a recognized organization based on shared values and agreed-upon behavioral expectations. Work within the rehabilitation field can present many ethical and moral dilemmas. Common interactions and situations within vocational rehabilitation require professionals to assess and determine the most appropriate response on a consistent basis. Such responses are typically either dictated or guided by past experience, knowledge, best practices, consultation with colleagues, and professional ethics. Professional ethics provide a key element or cornerstone to any professional practice, offering broad principles and specific standards of conduct. It is important to note that rehabilitation professionals may also be bound to one or more codes of professional ethics, depending on their credentials and employment setting.

Ethics are often developed through education and classroom instruction, professional development trainings, modeling by and observation of others, and on-the-job experience. An ethical practice is generally fostered through reviewing the code regularly, consultation, case reviews, and specific tools and resources. Tools and resources may include **ethical decision-making models**, guidance from a professional association, and consultation opportunities. In this chapter, academic standards, common credentials that enforce codes of ethics, relevant codes of professional ethics, and tools beneficial to the cultivation of an ethical practice will be discussed and illustrated through case examples.

ACADEMIC AND PROGRAMMATIC STANDARDS

The first true exposure to professional ethics for individuals entering skilled occupations often occurs through some type of training program. Training may be provided on the job to some extent; however, many career pathways require formalized instruction, whether through an apprenticeship/trades-related program or higher education. In addition to application-based learning objectives, academic programs convey theories, philosophies, and expectations established for the profession. The accreditation process for academic programs standardizes curricular and programmatic requirements between programs. Within rehabilitation, there are two distinct entities that oversee the voluntary process of accreditation for undergraduate and graduate-level programs in the United States.

Undergraduate Curricular Standards

For undergraduate programs, the Committee on Rehabilitation Accreditation (CoRA) provides curricular standards for programs that fall under the broad category of inclusive rehabilitation sciences (IRS). Under the sponsorship of the Commission on Accreditation of Allied Health Education Programs (CAAHEP) since 2018, CoRA seeks to (a) develop, maintain, and revise IRS standards; (b) support the development and improvement of programs; and (c) gather and use stakeholders' data to guide and improve the accreditation process and related standards (n.d.). Moreover, IRS programs train rehabilitation generalists who "focus on the nature, meaning, consequences, and impact of impairment and disability, while exploring the environmental, personal, vocational, historical, culture, economic, physiological, socio-political, and geo-political dynamics that affect individuals" (n.d.). Rehabilitation generalists often work as part of an interdisciplinary team to assist their clients in attaining and maintaining individualized goals and optimal quality of life through person-centered services.

When determining curricular standards, CoRA drew from over six decades of undergraduate rehabilitation educational history and recent research studies that explored employment outcomes of IRS graduates (Perry et al., 2018). In 2007, Evenson and Holloway established knowledge and skill competencies based on the perspectives of graduates from four IRS programs. Top knowledge competencies included problem-solving, liaison with other agencies, case recording, interfacing with other professionals, and case presentation. Important skills related to caseload management, individualized rehabilitation plan development, intake interviewing, and decision-making. The role of case and caseload management is further illustrated through a role of function study of IRS graduates whereby the most important and frequent work tasks reported were emotional support of clients, writing client progress and summary notes, advocating for clients, conducting interviews, and identifying community resources (Herbert et al., 2010). Oswald and colleagues (2018, 2020) also established that the majority of IRS students (pre- and post-graduation) were interested in and entering rehabilitation-related occupations and/or pursuing further education related to rehabilitation.

Although further educational research continues to be warranted (Huck et al., 2023), CoRA curricular standards offer broad content requirements to support rehabilitation generalists across the gambit of occupational pathways. In addition to a plethora of supportive content areas, case management activities are addressed under the pre-experiential learning requirements (CAAHEP, 2019). Specifically, students must demonstrate knowledge of elements and principles of case management, ethical issues that may occur in case management settings (such as boundary issues, confidentiality, privacy, and allocation of resources), and the advantages and disadvantages of models of case management. Related skill areas required within the standards include interviewing techniques, person-centered planning, the working alliance, and the utilization of evidence-based practices. Furthermore, the section on professionalism and ethical practices outlines ethical principles, concepts, and decision-making models that must be addressed by programs (CAAHEP, 2019).

In spite of the fact that accreditation through CoRA is a relatively new opportunity for IRS programs, the majority of programs appear to already be broadly aligned with the curricular standards. Oswald and Jenkins (2022) demonstrated the most frequently required courses within rehabilitation-related undergraduate programs covered the topics of employment, case management, interviewing skills, assessment, and community resources. In addition, 74% of programs required content on professionalism, which included professional attitudes and ethics (Oswald & Jenkins, 2022). Moving forward, the comprehensive and all-purpose nature of IRS curriculum will remain extremely important as programs require the flexibility in their requirements to meet local labor market needs, student preferences, and faculty interests (Oswald & Jenkins, 2022). As the field continues to evolve and respond to legislative mandated and employment conditions, IRS programs and accreditation standards will need to remain vigilant in keeping a pulse on needs from the field and adjust accordingly.

Graduate Curricular Standards

For graduate-level programs, the Council for Accreditation of Counseling and Related Educational Programs (CACREP) offers the opportunity for accreditation to both traditional and specialized counseling programs. Acknowledging the two primary guiding principles of the revised standards (quality first and unified counselor identity; CACREP, 2023), rehabilitation counseling educational programs must meet all general CACREP curricular standards plus those specifically related to rehabilitation counseling or clinical rehabilitation counseling. Through this universal lens, all counseling students should graduate with a strong counselor identity and functional professional dispositions and skills. Beyond that baseline, graduates of specialized counseling programs can build additional knowledge and skills in a focused practice area.

Similar to undergraduate requirements, professional ethics and tasks related to case management are essential elements within CACREP standards. Within the first section (Professional Counseling Orientation and Ethical Practice), professional ethics are addressed through (a) ethical standards of professional counseling organizations and credentialing bodies and applications of ethical and legal considerations in professional counseling across service delivery modalities and specialized practice areas and (b) self-care, self-awareness, and self-evaluation strategies for ethical and effective practice (CACREP, 2023). In support of this emphasis on ethics is the recognition that over 80% of licensed professional counselors sanctioned for ethical violations were graduates from non–CACREP-accredited educational programs (Even & Robinson, 2013).

As well, case management and aspects of the vocational rehabilitation process are outlined through standards within foundational content areas such as:

- Career development (i.e., strategies for assessing abilities, interests, values, personality, and other factors that contribute to career development; career development program planning, organization, implementation, administration, and evaluation; developmentally responsive strategies for empowering individuals to engage in culturally sustaining career and educational development and employment opportunities)
- Counseling practice and relationships (i.e., case conceptualization skills using a variety of models and approaches; consultation models and strategies; application of technology related to counseling; ethical and legal issues relevant to establishing and maintaining counseling relationships across service delivery modalities; interviewing, attending, and listening skills in the counseling process; goal consensus and

collaborative decision-making in the counseling process; record-keeping and documentation skills; principles and strategies of caseload management and the referral process to promote independence, optimal wellness, empowerment, and engagement with community resources)

- Assessment and diagnostic processes (i.e., culturally sustaining and developmental considerations for selecting, administering, and interpreting assessments, including individual accommodations and environmental modifications; use of assessments in academic/educational, career, personal, and social development; use of environmental assessments and systematic behavioral observations; use of structured interviewing, symptom checklists, and personality and psychological testing; procedures to identify substance use, addictions, and co-occurring conditions; procedures for using assessment results for referral and consultation)

Although some content on professional ethics and case management functions is present in general CACREP-accredited counseling program curriculum, further detail is offered for specializations. Depending on the specialized practice area (rehabilitation counseling or clinical rehabilitation counseling), additional standards include (a) rehabilitation counseling services and organizational settings, including independent living, community rehabilitation, and public/proprietary vocational rehabilitation programs; (b) intake interview, mental status evaluation, biopsychosocial history, mental health history, and psychological assessment for treatment planning and caseload management for people with disabilities; and (c) case management strategies that facilitate rehabilitation and independent living planning (CACREP, 2023). These supplementary standards highlight some of the unique knowledge and skills rehabilitation counselors bring to their work with clients with disabilities. In this way, individuals with disabilities are not only served through traditional mental health–focused counseling theories and techniques but also benefit from professionals who understand and address disability-related dimensions through specialized services.

In addition to the two specific sets of accredited rehabilitation-related academic standards, there are curricular standards and guidelines for educational programs that fall under related fields through various accrediting bodies and professional associations. Examples of related fields include human services, social work, applied behavioral analysis, public health, human resources, and special or inclusive education. To level-set for the diversity in educational pathways and lived experiences an individual might bring to their rehabilitation work, all case managers and their supervisors should ensure the appropriate knowledge, skills, and abilities are cultivated through further education, professional development, or mentoring opportunities. Taking active measures to assess, monitor, and enhance practitioner effectiveness will support the ultimate goal of rehabilitation services: successful and ethical service provision of and in partnership with clients with disabilities.

REHABILITATION CREDENTIALS

To establish uniformity and durability of agreed-upon professional knowledge and skills across any field, professional credentialing that requires a baseline examination and continuing education units is often maintained through a reputable professional organization. According to Remley and Herlihy (2020), "Credentialed individuals possess some type of indicator that they are legitimate professionals. Credentialing comes in many forms, which is the basic reason people are so confused by it" (p. 33). In addition, the availability of diverse credentialing opportunities has resulted in split perceptions between individuals and agencies ranging from a credential being viewed as essential to the profession, desired but not necessary for practice, or questionable in its value or worthiness. One of the persistent challenges faced by new rehabilitation professionals is the exploration and selection of relevant national and state credentials applicable to various career pathways (Remley & Herlihy, 2020).

In the field of rehabilitation, there are many opportunities for credentialing. However, the following section will address the most common nationally available credentials recognized in vocational rehabilitation and case management employment opportunities. These credentials include (a) **Certified Rehabilitation Counselor (CRC)**, (b) **National Certified Counselor** (NCC), and (c) **Certified Case Manager** (CCM). A brief discussion of other national and state-specific credentials will follow.

Certified Rehabilitation Counselor

In the field of rehabilitation, the CRC credentialing process is the oldest and most established (Leahy et al., 2019). Offered by the Commission on Rehabilitation Counselor Certification (CRCC), this credential is designed for professionals practicing rehabilitation counseling, a specialty for those assisting individuals with disabilities. There are several rehabilitation disciplines and service provision processes represented within the CRC, including vocational evaluation, job development and placement, work adjustment, and case management (Mullahy, 2016). The scope of practice for a CRC (and Canadian counterpart, the Canadian Certified Rehabilitation Counselor or CCRC) as outlined by CRCC, n.d.-a) states that "Rehabilitation counseling is a systematic process that assists persons with physical, mental, developmental, cognitive, and emotional disabilities to achieve their personal, career, and independent living goals in the most integrated setting possible through the application of the counseling process. The counseling process involves communication, goal setting, and beneficial growth or change through self-advocacy, psychological, vocational, social, and behavioral interventions. The specific techniques and modalities utilized within this rehabilitation counseling process may include, but are not limited to:

- assessment and appraisal
- diagnosis and treatment planning
- career (vocational) counseling
- individual and group counseling treatment interventions focused on facilitating adjustments to the medical and psychosocial impact of disability
- case management, referral, and service coordination
- program evaluation and research
- interventions to remove environmental, employment, and attitudinal barriers
- consultation services among multiple parties and regulatory systems
- job analysis, job development, and placement services, including assistance with employment and job accommodations
- provision of consultation about and access to rehabilitation technology"

Since inception in 1974, over 40,000 professionals have participated in the CRC certification process (CRCC, n.d.-b). Currently, there are over 15,000 practicing CRCs in the United States and throughout the world. In support of aspiring rehabilitation professionals, CRCC provides a number of eligibility levels to sit for the exam (related to educational and experiential requirements), as well as certification knowledge standards, a Code of Professional Ethics, and several tools and resources to assist CRCs in ethical decision-making and professional development based on continuing education requirements. The certification standards and content for the examination have been validated empirically and represent the education, experience, and knowledge competencies required of qualified rehabilitation professionals (Leahy et al., 2019; Remley & Herlihy, 2020). Moreover, many state vocational rehabilitation agencies either require or prefer the CRC credential in vocational rehabilitation counselor employment job descriptions or tie attainment of various counselor position levels to CRC eligibility.

National Certified Counselor

The National Board for Certified Counselors, Inc. (NBCC, n.d.) has offered a nationally recognized general practice counseling credential, the NCC, since 1982. In order to obtain this credential, a professional must have a graduate-level degree or advanced certificate in counseling through a CACREP-accredited program and other program from a regionally accredited institution, meet the experiential requirements with appropriately documented supervision, submit a professional endorsement, pass the National Counselor Examination or National Clinical Mental Health Counselor Examination, and adhere to the NBCC Code of Ethics (NBCC, n.d.). The examination content areas and questions are based on CACREP curricular standards and a national job analysis of more than 16,000 credentialed counselors. NBCC supports the professional practice of counselors and their employers through resources such as their Code of Ethics (NBCC, 2023a) and Ethics Case Procedures (NBCC, 2023b). Currently, more than 67,000 counselors throughout the United States and in over 40 other countries hold this voluntary professional credential (Surpass Assessment, 2021). Although the NCC credential seldom is required for independent practice and is not a substitute for the legislated state credentials, those who hold the credential appreciate the opportunity to demonstrate that they have met national standards developed by counselors, not legislators.

A notable specialty certification offered by the NBCC is the Certified Clinical Mental Health Counselor (CCMHC) credential. This credential holds significant recognition within the field of mental health counseling, particularly for professionals working in diverse capacities and roles, including private practice. The CCMHC certification requires candidates to fulfill certain prerequisites, such as holding the NCC credential. Additionally, candidates must have completed a specified number of graduate-level academic credits in counseling from an institutionally accredited program to be eligible for the examination. Furthermore, specific content areas must be covered, along with completing nine semester or 15 quarter hours of supervised field experience in clinical training. Candidates are also required to document at least 100 hours of postgraduate clinical supervision and obtain endorsement from a professional colleague who holds a master's degree or higher in a mental health field. Lastly, candidates must provide documentation of at least 3,000 hours of postgraduate clinical client work experience. These rigorous requirements ensure that individuals holding the CCMHC credential have demonstrated a high level of competence and expertise in clinical mental health counseling (NBCC, n.d.).

Certified Case Manager

Established in 1992, the Commission for Case Manager Certification (CCMC, n.d.-a) currently credentials over 50,000 case managers and disability management specialists throughout the nation. The CCM examination is intended to be the tool for the evaluation of the skills necessary for the practice of case management in private and public sectors. To be eligible to sit for the exam, a professional must qualify based on education (which may be established through an acquired degree, licensure, or certification) and experience (12–24 months of full-time work related specifically to the provision or supervision of case management services). Employment experience must also include providing at least five of the following six core components (psychosocial aspects, healthcare reimbursement, rehabilitation, healthcare management and delivery, principles of practice, and case management concepts; Oswald & Taylor, 2020). Under each component, applicants must:

- include all eight essential activities in service delivery: assessment, planning, implementation, coordination, monitoring, evaluation, outcomes, and general activities,
- provide a continuum of care beyond a single episode of care that addresses the ongoing needs of the individual being served,
- be responsible for communicating with pertinent parties within the client's healthcare system, and
- be primarily responsible for dealing with the client's broad spectrum of needs.

On face value, the CCM may be construed as the most appropriate credential for any professional holding the title of case manager or main responsibility of case management. This can be further supported when considering the eight essential activities of case management as outlined by CCMC (Oswald & Taylor, 2020). However, with approximately 82% of all CCMC-certified professionals originating from the nursing field and less than 4% comprising the disability and counseling fields, the CCM credential is most often utilized and recognized in traditional healthcare settings (CCMC, n.d.-b). Based on the diversity of professional opportunities within the field of rehabilitation, the credential may demonstrate a standard qualification and level of knowledge and abilities across many private employment settings. Yet, ultimately, the applicability and value of the CCM will likely be largely employer and employment setting determined.

Other Credentials

As explained in this section, credentials vary significantly among rehabilitation practitioners. The previous section addressed in detail three common credentials noted in the rehabilitation services profession (i.e., CRC, NCC, and CCM). In addition, many states offer licensure opportunities to those planning to deliver counseling and rehabilitative services. Most commonly, states require licensure for professionals providing counseling, marriage and family therapy, social work, and substance use treatment services through state-specific educational and experiential qualifications. Although the professional title and licensure designation may seem parallel (i.e., licensed professional counselor), there is no national parity standard that would support portability for counselors wishing to move or practice between states, and the majority of states have not established universal parity agreements.

Furthermore, a number of credentials have emerged due to changes in private sector rehabilitation and case management services. Examples of these certifications include (a) Certified Disability Management Specialist (CDMS), (b) Qualified Intellectual Disabilities Professional (QIPD), (c) Case Management Administrator, Certified (CMAC), (d) National Certified Addiction Counselor (NCAC), (e) Certified Life Care Planner (CLCP), (f) American Board of Vocational Experts (ABVE) Fellow or Diplomate, and (g) Certified Professional in Health Care Quality (CPHQ; Oswald & Taylor, 2020). To date, there is no current unifying undergraduate-level rehabilitation credential. However, recent research of IRS program coordinator perspectives illustrated concerns related to a lack of awareness and visibility of programs, relationships with graduate-level programs, and professional identity, resulting in over half of the respondents reporting an interest in the development of both a credential and specific code of ethics (Oswald et al., 2018). These concerns are further amplified when paired with recent research that outlined a lack of clarity within IRS students around professional identity, credentialing opportunities, and codes of ethics (Oswald et al., 2020).

Due to the nature of case management and cross-disciplinary practice, there will continue to be variances in the credentials of case managers. As more public agencies and private companies specify a credential to their employees, the perceived value of certain credentials will evolve and potentially diminish the permanence of some. Certain credentials will gain prominence as highly sought-after and recognized indicators of established professionals (Mullahy, 2016). Therefore, it is crucial that private sector practitioners become aware of which credential will meet their needs and the needs of their clients.

Ultimately, attaining a credential that encompasses and actively promotes evidence-based and best practices in case management should be the goal of professional rehabilitation practitioners. Thereafter, a professional should maintain both competency and credential through continued education and training. Doing so demonstrates a commitment to the case management process and quality outcomes (Mullahy, 2016). By maintaining a qualified workforce through credentialing mechanisms, the profession of rehabilitation is strengthened through unity and standardization of practice. For case managers, the credentialing process can underscore and further complement professional contributions to the field of rehabilitation.

ETHICAL STANDARDS OF PROFESSIONAL PRACTICE

Based on common credentials and field standards, four main codes of ethics are recognized for rehabilitation practitioners. For the purposes of this discussion, we will focus on:

1. CRCC's Code of Professional Ethics (2023)
2. NBCC's Code of Ethics (2023)
3. American Counseling Association's Code of Ethics (2014)
4. CCMC's Code of Professional Conduct (2023)

In addition to these codes, professionals may be bound to or voluntarily choose to adhere to other professional codes of ethics. Examples of related codes include the Association of Persons Supporting Employment First (APSE) Ethical Guidelines for Professionals in Supported Employment (1998), the National Association of Social Workers (NASW) Code of Ethics (2021), and the National Organization of Human Services (NOHS) Ethical Standards for Human Services Professionals (2015). Whether mandated by credential, employer, or personal belief system and commitment to quality services, every rehabilitation practitioner should feel compelled to understand and follow an established professional ethical code of conduct.

CRCC Code of Professional Ethics (2023)

PURPOSE OF THE CODE OF PROFESSIONAL ETHICS

As reported by CRCC, the purpose of the Code of Professional Ethics is "to provide standards of practice for practitioners, trainees, recipients of services, and society on the ethical practice of certified rehabilitation counselors, henceforth referred to as CRCs/CCRCs" (2023, p. 4). In addition, the basic objectives are to promote public welfare, establish principles that guide behavior, offer guidance on a professional course of action, and create a process for allegations of code violations (CRCC, 2023). There are many benefits to the establishment and active use of ethical standards in everyday practice. Overall, ethical behavior improves service provision and the client experience, as their engagement is encouraged and various rights are protected and respected. The working alliance or relationship between counselor and client will be enhanced as roles are established, boundaries maintained, and any power differentials managed appropriately. The professional may be supported in the process through a preservation of their focus, increasing efficiencies and effectiveness. Such measures may result in better alignment of case activities and the provision of services with the employment goal and improved outcomes. Furthermore, the professional can also exhibit increased professionalism and demonstrate accountability through ethical practice.

VALUES AND PRINCIPLES

Professional ethics are based on values, principles, and best practices. For example, the primary values that serve as a foundation for the CRCC Code of Professional Ethics (2023) include a commitment to:

- respecting human rights and dignity of all people;
- ensuring the integrity of all professional relationships;
- acting to alleviate personal distress and suffering;
- enhancing the quality of professional knowledge and its application to increase professional and personal effectiveness;
- promoting empowerment through self-advocacy and self-determination;
- respecting and understanding the diversity of human experience and appreciating culture;
- emphasizing client strengths versus deficits;
- serving individuals holistically; and
- advocating for equitable and appropriate provision of services.

In conjunction, the six principles (see **Figure 11.1**) that guide ethical behavior for CRCs are:

1. **Autonomy:** To respect the rights of clients to be self-governing within their social and cultural framework.
2. **Beneficence:** To do good to others; to promote the well-being of clients.

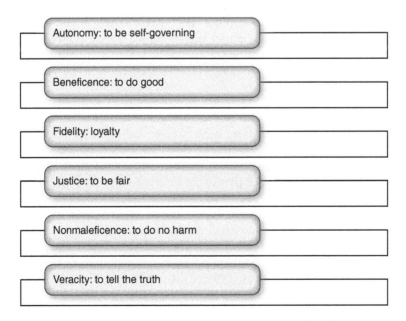

FIGURE 11.1 The six principles of the CRCC's Code of Professional Ethics.

3. **Fidelity:** To be faithful; to keep promises and honor the trust placed in rehabilitation counselors.
4. **Justice:** To be fair in the treatment of all clients; to provide appropriate services to all.
5. **Nonmaleficence:** To do no harm to others.
6. **Veracity:** To be honest.

SPECIFIC ETHICAL STANDARDS IN RELATION TO CASE AND CASELOAD MANAGEMENT

Grounded through agreed-upon values and principles of the profession, ethical standards of practice have been outlined for CRCC. Not only an awareness of but also a true understanding of the purpose and spirit of the standards are essential to any case management practice. Although a thorough review of each specific standard and Section J (Research and Publications) is beyond the scope of this chapter, an overview of major sections will be offered as they relate to case and caseload management.

Section A: The Counseling Relationship of the Code of Professional Ethics (CRCC, 2023) focuses on several areas deeply intertwined with any discussion related to case and caseload management. For each element, not only is a rehabilitation counselor charged with upholding the standard but also documenting such actions by the counselor and agreement from the client. For example, CRCC states "CRCs/CCRCs understand that trust is the cornerstone of the counseling relationship, and they have the responsibility to respect and safeguard the client's right to privacy and confidentiality" (2023, p. 4). Rehabilitation professionals work to build rapport and gather sensitive information from clients for eligibility and planning purposes. Clients must feel comfortable with the practitioner and have faith that the information shared will be treated appropriately. Boundaries must be maintained, power dynamics considered, appropriate relationship expectations determined and outlined, and the impact of group work and dynamics addressed. Case recordings should illustrate all pertinent conversations between counselor and client, as well as any verbal or written consent provided by the client to the counselor especially as it relates to transmitting information to external entities or within internal groups. Signed documents should be included in the case file.

Section A also established the need to ensure the autonomy and engagement of the client throughout the rehabilitation process. The development of goals and plans should be a collaborative effort between practitioner and client. All activities should be client-centered and individualized, emphasizing integrated and mutually agreed-upon outcomes. Professionals use their specialized skills to assist clients in building insight into their unique abilities, assets, characteristics, preferences, potential barriers to employment, and service and accommodations needs. Case recordings should highlight how and when the client made informed decisions and the rehabilitation practitioner's contributions to the process via expertise and knowledge transfer. In addition, other activities completed by the client should be reported through artifacts such as case recordings of meetings, assessment results, counselor observations, and follow-up notes on tasks completed by the client between meetings. It is not enough to build an effective working alliance between counselor and client. Intentional actions on the part of the rehabilitation professional and resulting outcomes of such interactions must be clearly documented.

Section B: Confidentiality, Privileged Communication & Privacy (CRCC, 2023) has many case and caseload management implications. A careful review of this section as it relates to the rehabilitation professional's current practices, as well as internal agency policies and procedures, is warranted for all practitioners. Differentiating necessary and beneficial informational sharing practices between various stakeholders (such as with service providers, physical and mental healthcare providers, employers, and external support network members like family, friends, and community members) can foster productive conversations with the client and lay the foundation for informed consent where appropriate.

Helping someone understand the why in addition to the how is a critical step in respecting and supporting a client's autonomy regarding communication parameters, observation, and disclosure. With a new and clear emphasis on duty to warn and mandated reporting within the latest code revisions (CRCC, 2023), practitioners must first understand their legal and ethical obligations and then work with their agency to ensure protocols and policies align with professional ethical expectations and standards.

As would be expected, case recording and documentation are key tools in implementing, ensuring, and demonstrating ethical confidentiality, privileged communication, and privacy measures. A careful examination of agency and individual professional practices can highlight established forms, policies, and written protocols for information requesting and sharing; rules on client access to records; procedures for working with individuals who cannot provide consent; promoted best practices of service delivery and client engagement; personal consultation activities; and unwritten internal *understandings* that either support, hinder, or directly violate ethical principles and standards. Equipped with such knowledge, the rehabilitation practitioner can rest assured in measures that enhance or facilitate their abilities to maintain an ethical practice and address areas of concern, implementing appropriate adjustments to ensure compliance with the spirit and expectations of the code.

Section C: Advocacy & Accessibility (CRCC, 2023) highlight two key aspects or characteristics of rehabilitation professionals. As case managers, rehabilitation practitioners not only provide services but also coordinate services between other entities. To that end, it is extremely important to have the knowledge, skills, and abilities to understand the need for opportunities and access, identify internal and external barriers (stemming from agency policies and procedures, environmental features, societal attitudes and stigma, and greater systemic impediments), and participate in advocacy measures to eliminate obstacles to client empowerment and outcomes. Advocacy may be in the form of professional advocacy actions within an agency or at the local, state, or national level (Henry et al., 2023). Another avenue is through infusing client skill development and encouragement within the vocational rehabilitation process. Arranging structured and progressive opportunities, building confidence through modeling and role-playing interactions, and exploring the importance and impact of self-advocacy with clients can be accomplished in routine meetings with some forethought. Recognizing the wide range of advocacy opportunities/needs and potential strategies allows for both professionals and clients to use their time wisely and establish their personal level of comfort and effectiveness in undertaking impactful, strength-based actions.

Section D: Multicultural Considerations (CRCC, 2023) addresses the greatest evolution in the CRCC Code of Professional Ethics. Although the topic was previously present within earlier versions of the code, the emphasis permeating throughout the document and completely new concentrated section illustrates CRCC's recognition of the overarching nature and impact of identity, worldview, and lived experience of both the counselor and client on the working alliance and case progression. Rehabilitation research has consistently demonstrated the predictive nature of personal characteristics of the client (such as race, ethnicity, and gender) on the vocational rehabilitation process and associated negative impact on employment outcomes (Ji et al., 2015; Johnson et al., 2017; Oswald et al., 2016; Salimi et al., 2023; Yin et al., 2022). Although difficult to investigate, experts also make a compelling argument regarding needs related to members of the LGBTQ community and those with disabilities whose identities intersect with at least one other marginalized community (Stevens et al., 2020). There is a clear call to professionals to seek awareness and understanding into their own personal biases and potential microaggressions, knowledge of the client, and how factors such as power, intersectionality, and systemic racism influence and potentially impede service delivery. CRCC provides clear directives to rehabilitation counselors on recommended professional development activities and cultural competences (CRCC, 2023). One introspective expectation for CRCs is cultural humility or a personal lifelong commitment to self-evaluation and self-critique whereby the individual not only learns about another's culture, but one starts with an examination of their own beliefs and cultural identities (Tervalon & Murray-Garcia, 1998). While the practice of cultural humility can be difficult to capture within case documentation, actions such as using affirming language, ensuring services are devoid of racism and discriminatory practices, and engaging in social justice can not only promote equality in case management services but also strengthen the working alliance and improve client outcomes. In support of practitioners, further guidance and recommendations continue to be developed and disseminated (Ahonle et al., 2023; Henry et al., 2023; Jorgensen-Smith, 2021).

Section E: Professional Responsibility (CRCC, 2023) focuses on both outward and inward actions that rehabilitation professionals must take to foster quality in services, professionalism, and ethical behavior. As a baseline, CRCC restricts practitioners to completing jobs and tasks within their abilities based on education and training, experience, and applicable credentials. Due to community connectedness requirements of various case manager functions, the expectation on public presentations, professional statements, exploitation of others, truthfulness, and conflicts of interest are outlined. As case management and teams-based processes may create confusion in role and responsibility expectations, the code acknowledges the need for team members to be clear on their individual expertise, competencies, and position within the group. CRCs can only delegate work (such as through the case management and referral for service processes) to other qualified professionals. There is also a strong emphasis on functional competence and the recognition that professions must continually assess and monitor their own effectiveness in service delivery. In fact, the code specifically requires that "CRCs/CCRCs engage in self-care activities to maintain and promote their own emotional, physical, mental, and spiritual well-being to best meet their professional responsibilities" (CRCC, 2023, p. 16). As there are many evidence-based and helper-specific self-care recommendations available (Brickham et al., 2021; Centers for Disease Control and Prevention, 2022; National Institute on Health, 2022; National Institute on Mental Health, n.d.; Plath & Fickling, 2022), case managers should identify and prioritize activities based on personal preference that decrease levels of burnout, compassion fatigue, and vicarious traumatization. Finally, CRCC addresses criterion for selecting and using appropriate practices and interventions, with particular attention to the targeted utilization of culturally appropriate and evidence-based practices and cautions related to the exploration and implementation of novel or potentially harmful techniques. Overall, ensuring professional competence and personal wellness should be paramount to any rehabilitation professional, as the consequences of ignoring these factors could be disastrous for the individuals, their organization, the profession, the individuals they serve, and the public at large.

Section F: Relationships With Other Professionals & Employers (CRCC, 2023), although sometimes overlooked or minimized, has immense implications for case managers due to the collaborative and interactive nature of case management. In order to navigate and streamline services between internal colleagues and external treatment and service providers, case managers must facilitate and foster productive professional relationships on a regular basis. Within the vocational rehabilitation settings, this may extend to members of personal support networks, employers, and coworkers of the client. The value and intricacies of team-based services are outlined, as well as the expectations for meaningful client engagement and group consensus. Consultation and the attainment of evaluations and reports are limited to information deemed essential, reducing the practice of sharing or acquiring confidential information that is unnecessary to the process. Adherence to the standards within this section will actively promote effective responsibility sharing between stakeholders and case progress through productive and seamless collaborative efforts across various service providers.

Section G: Forensic Services (CRCC, 2023) generally refers to the expert review, evaluation, and analysis by rehabilitation professionals for the purposes of case consultation and testimony. Although typical case manager duties do not include forensic services, some caseload management activities are required within a forensic practice setting. Recognizing the high incidence of ethical complaints and violations related to this section (Saunders et al., 2007), a brief overview is warranted. Individuals working within this arena should remain vigilant in maintaining the rights of the person under evaluation, their own professional competence and conduct, and forensic practices. As in other settings, forensic experts are cautious to only accept cases that fall within their knowledge and skills and adhere to ethical business practices related to payments/fees and outcomes. In addition, the realities of service delivery are evolving, and rural areas disproportionately require the expansion of individual professional responsibilities to meet current needs. The part played by role changes in the process and how to make such adjustments are provided (Lloyd et al., 2023). Although specifically outlined within this section, these considerations should not be viewed as confined to forensic settings alone and are applicable to any individual tasked with caseload management.

Section H: Assessment & Evaluation (CRCC, 2023) is crucial to the vocational rehabilitation process as outlined in the previous chapter discussing specialized skills. Whether completed internally, externally, or through historical records, care must be ensured when completing assessment activities and interpreting and using assessment results. Assessments should be selected and completed with a justified and specific purpose in mind by a qualified professional. Recognition and mitigation of influencing factors on the completion of assessment activities and interpretation of results (as described in detail in Chapter 9) are fundamental to an ethical practice. In addition, the appropriateness and impact of the dissemination of results to the client and other interested parties must be considered and addressed accordingly.

Section I: Supervision, Training and Teaching (CRCC, 2023) can be crucial in case management, as it is quite common practice to promote and train from within an organization. Although logical when viewed through a career ladder lens, many managers are promoted in human services organizations based on their skills and abilities in service provision as opposed to those related to supervision and leadership. This may be due to the assumption that knowledge and skills will translate to the supportive, instructive, and corrective responsibilities within supervision in lieu of formal training, guidance, and oversight during the transition to the new role and duties. However, it is not enough to *hire or promote good people* and *hope for the best*. Supervisors hold an elevated ethical responsibility to further "the mission, goals, values, and knowledge of the rehabilitation counseling profession by fostering supervisee growth and welfare and supporting them in development and progression toward professional goals" (CRCC, 2023, p. 25). Moreover, supervisors understand their role and influence in supervisee maturation and ethical fluency (i.e., knowledge acculturation, fluid reasoning, and accuracy and speed of recognition and processing of ethical dilemmas; Landon & Schultz, 2018). Based on interventions and activities grounded in the working alliance (Landon & Schultz, 2018), supervision in an ever more technology-based work environment can present additional ethical considerations (Bernacchio et al., 2022; Lund & Schultz, 2015). Although outside the scope of case and caseload management, supervisors play a critical supportive role to case managers and are encouraged to understand their responsibilities in this realm, persist in remaining current on pertinent information, and infuse ethical knowledge and skills development best practices in supervisory interactions (Bernacchio et al., 2022; Landon & Schultz, 2018; Landon et al., 2023).

Section K: Technology, Social Media, Virtual Counseling (CRCC, 2023) is no longer a fringe section, relevant to the few who ascribed to the viability and appropriateness of remote services over the past few decades. Due to the COVID-19 pandemic, rehabilitation professionals were faced with unprecedented circumstances and forced to either close indefinitely or convert their practices to a virtual platform expeditiously (Hartley et al., 2023). Practitioners were left to acquire new technological and professional skills with little to no previous experience or transitional period (Hartley & Bourgeois, 2020). Although many practices and policies were adapted to address acute healthcare risks and stay-in-place orders, the expansion of electronic information sharing and communication modalities such as videoconferencing and electronic signatures and the reconsideration of the benefits and acceptable utility of technology-based services have spurred what might become a sustained evolution in vocational rehabilitation service delivery in many regions.

Therefore, a review of Section K standards is timely and necessary for professionals across the field. Having the ability to complete assessments through online inventories, communicate with a client in real time from anywhere on the globe, and explore virtual repositories of occupational information and social media–driven job opportunities all with a few clicks on a smartphone or laptop can open up a world of opportunities for many clients and providers. Yet with greater convenience and availability come many cautions and ethical considerations (Hartley et al., 2023). Focusing on the security of communication and the maintenance of confidentiality and privacy is essential when considering the potential for data breaches, overuse and misuse of social media platforms, and exposed nature of some virtual meeting venues (i.e., a service provider or client joining a meeting from a shared space such as a family living room or a public location; Froehlich, Henry, et al., 2023). With this in mind, it is essential for professionals to develop an understanding of ethical principles related to technology use and virtual counseling, clinical competence in technology-assisted services, and safety planning for distance clients (Bernacchio & Wilson, 2018; Bourgeois et al., 2022; Lin et al., 2021; Maier et al., 2021). To this end, CRCC posted an additional resource on technology, social media, and virtual counseling considerations that can also be used for professional development and discussion (CRCC, n.d.-c).

Section L: Business Practices (CRCC, 2023) encompasses advertising to and soliciting new clients, client records, and fees bartering and billing. Case and caseload management practices play a key role in promoting efficiency and ethical responsibility within specific tasks. CRCC is clear on the protection of privacy and maintenance of records. In addition, CRCC instructs "regardless of format, CRCs/CCRCs create, protect, and maintain documentation necessary for rendering professional services. CRCs/CCRCs include sufficient and timely documentation to facilitate the delivery and continuity of services. CRCs/CCRCs ensure that documentation accurately reflects client progress and the services provided, including who provided the services. If records or documentation need to be altered, it is done so according to organizational policy and in a manner that preserves the original information. Alterations are accompanied by the date of change, the identity of who made the change, and the rationale for the change" (CRCC, 2023, p. 38). One area that should not be overlooked relates to succession planning and the need for continuity of services in the event that the rehabilitation professional is unable to complete duties based on incapacitation, death, retirement, closure, or termination of practice (CRCC, 2023; Lloyd et al., 2023). With consistent concerns over staffing shortages and turnover (Herbert et al., 2023), contingency planning is integral to any ethical case management practice.

Section M: Resolving Ethical Issues (CRCC, 2023) offers guidance on how to respond to ethical dilemmas. First and foremost, professionals need to be aware of the code of ethics and outlined standards. Second, a process for addressing ethical violations should be consistent and fair. With so many benefits to establishing an ethical practice, "the new CRCC Code of Ethics should be used as a resource and a source of training for counselors and trainees to engage in ethical practices" (Ahonle et al., 2023, p. 7). This is even more important when considering the realities facing rehabilitation counselors around ethical concerns related to core roles and functions of case managers, the working alliance and confidentiality, privileged communication, and privacy (Hill et al., 2023).

However, bringing lofty ethical standards to everyday practice can be daunting in fast-paced, task-oriented work settings. Agency policies and unwritten organizational rules are no substitute, and therefore, should not be the basis for the justification of lapses or personal ignorance when it comes to everyday actions with ethical implications. Simple suggestions to intentionally infuse ethical thinking and discussions into a professional practice include making time at each staff meeting to review an ethical dilemma or case study (either real or hypothetical in nature), highlighting ethical dimensions and standards during case reviews, posting an image of ethical principles in office spaces to normalize and encourage discussion of the topic, and providing data to staff on global or local ethical violation trends and consequences. Creating a safe environment and reminder prompts for regular ethical dilemma exploration can cultivate a work culture built on openness and trust, supporting the further development of knowledge and skills for professional ethical practice within rehabilitation practitioners.

In addition to worksite strategies, practitioners have several tools and resources to facilitate everyday ethical behaviors. Resources available through CRCC include sample forms and templates of professional disclosure forms for various employment settings (CRCC, n.d.-c), the ability to request an advisory opinion for a current situation and explore past opinions, and a formal grievance process (Froehlich, Hicks, et al., 2023). As noted, "the CRCC Ethics Committee provides advisory opinions on select situations having ethical implications. These advisory opinions are provided as a general educational service and are rendered in response to limited and unverified information provided to the Committee. Therefore, it should not be construed as direct advice regarding the unique or specific ethical or legal action recommendations that should be followed regarding the issues raised" (CRCC, n.d.-d). Prior to submitting a request for an opinion, CRCs are expected to engage in consultation with their colleagues and review past advisory opinions. There are already nearly 150 opinions resulting from past field-initiated reviews available through Ethics Committee meeting minutes established between 1996 and 2022 (CRCC, n.d.-e). In addition, guidance is provided on the key components and utilization of contemporary ethical decision-making models (Froehlich, Hicks, et al., 2023), an essential tool in any professional's toolkit that will be discussed in greater detail later in this chapter.

OTHER ETHICAL STANDARDS OF PROFESSIONAL PRACTICE

NBCC Code of Ethics (2023)

NBCC also published a revised code of ethics in 2023, specifically for those with the NCC credential. This allows NBCC to hold all credentialed professionals to a minimum standard of conduct. "Central to the purpose of the NBCC Code of Ethics is the commitment to maintain behavioral standards that will be used to enforce required disclosure procedures and compliance concerns brought forward through complaints. The Code serves as the foundation of an effective and fair method for submitting complaints and disclosures for the protection of both the public and counselors" (NBCC, 2023a). The values and beliefs upheld by the code include:

- Counselors will be civil in their actions and words, avoiding arrogance, assumptions, and hubris. Counselors seek to listen to others with intention and respond with respect. When engaged in challenging dialogues, counselors do so to seek answers—not confrontations or harm. Counselors strive to be sensitive to differences in attitudes and culture. Counselors always seek to minimize undue harm and take particular care of those who are vulnerable or in anguish. With respect to all clients and work, counselors seek to be mindful of their humanity as they fulfill their counseling duties.

- Counselors strive to enhance the social and mental well-being of their clients while supporting the overall physical health of each client. Counselors must engage in self-care and self-reflection.
- Access and equity are essential to the profession of counseling and fundamentally important for the success of any society. Counseling services should be provided to achieve the best mental health outcomes. Counselors provide services to all of those in need, utilizing available resources, and advocating for the expansion of resources in underserved communities.
- Certified counselors and candidates demonstrate their commitment to ethical behaviors by demonstrating, and representing to their clients, sensitivity to multicultural issues, avoiding discrimination, oppression, and/or any form of social injustice.

As the NBCC Code of Ethics is tied to a national credential, there is a formal grievance process for filing a complaint. NBCC also offers an FAQ and Ethics Case Procedures document to support counselors seeking guidance for the resolution of ethical issues (NBCC, 2023b). Although "NBCC recognizes that ethical decision-making by counselors exists within the context of the legal parameters and licensure requirements enacted by States, territories, and other jurisdictions" (NBCC, 2023a, p. 1), no further recommendations of specific models are provided.

American Counseling Association Code of Ethics (2014)

Similar to NBCC, the American Counseling Association (ACA) also has an established Code of Ethics for those in the larger counseling profession (2014) and guidance on ethical decision-making (Forester-Miller & Davis, 2016). However, this code is not tied to a specific credential and therefore only provides a formal complaint process for professional members within the organization and penalties related to membership status (ACA, 2020). The code is built on the following core professional values of the counseling profession:

- enhancing human development throughout the life span;
- honoring diversity and embracing a multicultural approach in support of the worth, dignity, potential, and uniqueness of people within their social and cultural contexts;
- promoting social justice;
- safeguarding the integrity of the counselor–client relationship; and
- practicing in a competent and ethical manner.

The fundamental principles of professional ethical behavior for counselors parallel CRCC principles in spirit if not exact definition:

1. autonomy, or fostering the right to control the direction of one's life;
2. nonmaleficence, or avoiding actions that cause harm;
3. beneficence, or working for the good of the individual and society by promoting mental health and well-being;
4. justice, or treating individuals equitably and fostering fairness and equality;
5. fidelity, or honoring commitments and keeping promises, including fulfilling one's responsibilities of trust in professional relationships; and
6. veracity, or dealing truthfully with individuals with whom counselors come into professional contact.

Overall, there are many similarities and parallels between the CRCC Code of Professional Ethics and codes available to other counseling professionals through NBCC and ACA, such as a firm commitment to the working alliance, appropriate documentation, and culturally responsive services. However, CRCC provides a clear focus on client empowerment and self-advocacy, emphasizing a strength-based approach and viewing individuals through a holistic lens. In addition, not all standards sync up seamlessly or offer as much detail as others. Finally, guidance on how to use the code, espoused ethical decision-making models, and available resources differ between organizations.

CCMC Code of Professional Conduct for Case Managers (2023)

Although the CCM is a less traditional credential within the rehabilitation field, the code of professional conduct established through CCMC warrants an overview, as it offers somewhat distinct values and principles that expand consideration to a less counselor- and more healthcare-focused practice. With deference to a strong commitment to their clients and protecting the public interest, supporting the profession, and creating positive outcomes for all stakeholders (including the healthcare system and payers), the underlying philosophy is calibrated through a slightly different professional lens. According to the 2023 code, the values that drive the principles and ethical standards for CCMs are:

- CCMs believe that case management is a means for improving client health, wellness and autonomy through advocacy, communication, education, identification of service resources, and service facilitation.
- CCMs recognize the dignity, worth, and rights of all people.
- CCMs understand and commit to quality outcomes for clients, appropriate use of resources, and the empowerment of clients in a manner that is supportive and objective.
- CCMs embrace the underlying premise that when the individual(s) reach(es) the optimum level of wellness and functional capability, everyone benefits: the individual(s) served, their support system, the healthcare delivery system, and the various reimbursement systems.
- CCMs understand that case management is guided by the ethical principles of *autonomy, beneficence, nonmaleficence, justice,* and *fidelity.*

In addition, guiding principles outlined by CCMC are that CCMs will:

1. place the public interest above their own at all times,
2. uphold the rights and inherent dignity of all of their clients,
3. always maintain objectivity in their relationships with clients,
4. act with integrity and fidelity with clients and others,
5. maintain their competency at a level that ensures their clients will receive the highest quality of service,
6. honor the integrity of the CCM designation and adhere to the requirements for its use,
7. obey all laws and regulations, and
8. help maintain the integrity of the Code by responding to requests for public comments to review and revise the code, thus helping ensure its consistency with current practice.

As with the other codes reviewed in this chapter, the CCMC code covers similar areas and dimensions of professional practice. Specifically, major sections include the client advocate; professional responsibility; case manager/client relationships; confidentiality, privacy, security, and record-keeping; and professional relationships.

ETHICAL DECISION-MAKING MODELS

Finally, there are several ethical decision-making models endorsed by CRCC. The key components of an ethical decision-making model as relayed by CRCC and originally outlined by Corey et al. (2014) are illustrated in **Figure 11.2**. An important feature that should not be overlooked is the active participation of the client in the various steps. Ethical decision-making is not intended to be an insulated action undertaken by the practitioner, but a collaborative process between case manager and client as they seek to understand the situation and cocreate the solution.

Beyond the previously mentioned framework, CRCC refers to several contemporary ethical decision-making models that may assist counselors experiencing a dilemma, noting that no one model is proven more effective or universally effective (CRCC, n.d.-f). These models are resources for professional development and everyday ethical practice delivery, offering tangible steps for theoretical exploration and real-life scenario action plans (Corey et al., 2014; Cottone, 2001; Cottone et al., 2021; Garcia et al., 2003; Herlihy & Watson, 2007). As highlighted through a comparison by CRCC, salient themes between models include information gathering, exploration of influencing factors (such as laws, relationships, individual worldviews, and ethical codes), consultation with stakeholders and knowledgeable support networks (i.e., the client, a supervisor, legal counsel, and colleagues), selection and planning of a course of action, and implementation with some type

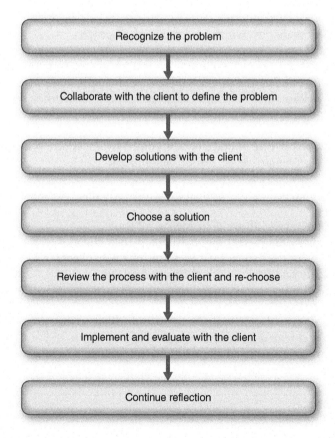

FIGURE 11.2 Key components of an ethical decision-making model.

of evaluation or follow-up to any action. Ultimately, it is generally accepted that consultation and thorough case recordings are two of the best strategies for ethical decision-making and documentation of professional practice in the event disagreement or discord persists in the professional–client relationship. As unpleasant an unexpected or particularly negative consequence may be, careful documentation can provide supervisors and agencies the information, confidence, and ability to support a practitioner who may be served with a formal grievance or some other action requiring arbitration.

Similarly, ACA provides a practitioner's guide to ethical decision-making (Forester-Miller & Davis, 2016). In addition to expounding on the guiding principles of autonomy, justice, beneficence, nonmaleficence, and fidelity, the guide offers a list of steps to take when encountering an ethical dilemma. The model recommends:

1. Identify the problem.
2. Apply the ACA Code of Ethics.
3. Determine the nature and dimensions of the dilemma.
4. Generate potential courses of action.
5. Consider the potential consequences of all options and determine a course of action.
6. Evaluate the selected course of action.
7. Implement the course of action.

Forester-Miller and Davis (2016) are careful to remind counselors that ethical dilemmas are complex in nature. They do not offer one easily determined and correct solution. There will likely be many options for how to proceed, each with its own benefits and pitfalls. The outcome is never completely foreseeable. However, Van Hoose and Paradise (1979) suggest that a counselor "is probably acting in an ethically responsible way concerning a client if (1) he or she has maintained personal and professional honesty, coupled with (2) the best interests of the client, (3) without malice or personal gain, and (4) can justify his or her actions as the best judgment of what should be done based upon the current state of the profession" (p. 58). In conjunction, intentionally using an ethical decision-making model and documenting the process are recommended as a supportive measure in future justifications of professional actions (Brennan, 2013; Forester-Miller & Davis, 2016).

With the foundational knowledge, tools, and resources available, exploring potential real-life scenarios can be beneficial to cultivating a deeper understanding of the values, principles, and standards that offer the foundation of an ethical practice. Use the following situations to contemplate the various ethical implications, competing interests, and potential consequences of actions available to a case manager. What is clearly required by the standards outlined in the code(s) of ethics? What is open to interpretation? Is there additional guidance provided through professional organizations and other available resources (such as peer-reviewed research and best practices)? How might a case manager use an ethical decision-making model or other process to work through complicated and unprecedented situations?

As the working alliance is essential yet sometimes fragile, consider the following scenario. Jasmine, a 35-year-old with an intellectual disability, is seeking vocational rehabilitation at her local state agency. She has an engaged and committed support network that includes her parents, residential services provider, and church community. Jasmine has a pleasant and quiet disposition, relying on her support network to vocalize her abilities and other pertinent information during all meetings. When discussing vocational goals, her support network was very supportive of her working at a local thrift shop connected to her church community. However, observations of Jasmine in meetings and through community-based assessments raise concerns. Jasmine's demeanor at job sites is detached, while her attention to task appears minimal and frustration levels elevated. What are some ethical concerns in this situation? How should the assessment results be addressed with the client and/or support network? What might be some strategies the counselor can employ moving forward? Does *the code* provide any guidance pertinent to Jasmine's case? What are major case recording and documentation considerations for the case file?

Recognizing and respecting privileged communication and privacy can require a delicate balance of competing guideline principles, ethical standards, professional judgment, and unique dimensions of the working relationship and situation. Consider the complexities and ramifications of the following scenario. Petey is a 16-year-old receiving pre-employment services while in high school. Petey has cerebral palsy that affects their mobility. Petey, a typically verbose and engaged participant, conveys the message that they don't want to pursue employment services anymore or attend any further meetings to their teacher. The counselor relays an altercation that occurred during Pride Week at school the week before, convincing Petey to keep their appointment with the employment specialist. Petey does eventually show up to the appointment, albeit visibly downcast and withdrawn. Petey is reluctant to participate in the conversation and leaves abruptly when, in the course of pulling up a shirt sleeve, accidentally reveals several parallel incisions on their forearm (possible signs of cutting or self-injurious behavior). What are some practical and ethical concerns in this scenario? How does Petey's age affect possible courses of action? What might be some important information, resources, and strategies to consider? Does *the code* or corresponding ethical resources provide any guidance pertinent to Petey's case? What are major case recording and documentation considerations for the case file?

Finally, explore the wide-reaching ethical implications of this practitioner. The practitioner is just filling in for a coworker who is on vacation. One of the coworker's previously stable clients goes into crisis. Because the case was running on *autopilot*, the coworker didn't brief the person covering the caseload on this specific client, and the case notes do not provide sufficient information. The coworker graciously agrees to a quick virtual meeting to offer some insight and ensure continuity of care. The practitioner is hoping for some context and guidance. As the practitioner logs onto the virtual meeting platform, they realize that the coworker is using a live background, exposing the location to be somewhere on the Las Vegas strip. The coworker also appears to be in an uncharacteristically good mood and/or mildly intoxicated. What are the possible ethical considerations in this scenario? What standards should be reviewed, and does *the code* provide guidance on how to handle this situation in the moment and afterward? What are possible responses or actions that the practitioner might undertake? What potential consequences exist for the client, practitioner, coworker, and agency? What, if any, expectations for case recording and documentation might be pertinent to this scenario?

Unfortunately, ethical dilemmas are difficult by nature. Understanding the values, principles, and standards outlined in a professional code of ethics is the first step to determining the availability of specific guidance. When the circumstances are not clearly covered by directives within the code, practitioners should seek consultation, explore resources, and follow an ethical decision-making model. Ultimately, using professional recommendations for resolving ethical issues and accurately documenting what occurred and how a response was determined will support the external evaluation of the counselor's actions and, in turn, increase the likelihood that the results of any review will conclude that ethical behavior was exhibited.

SUMMARY

National organizations support their respective professions through various efforts that legitimize and solidify standards of practice. Professional ethics, a key component in the process, are established based on shared values and agreed-upon behavioral expectations. Which professional ethical standards are appropriate to follow may be dictated by a person's credentials or employment setting. As the rehabilitation field presents many situations rife with ethical implications, professionals should possess or work to cultivate personal skills through knowledge attainment and professional development of ethical standards, best practices, and tools and resources accessible to them. Professionals should also feel empowered and supported through the availability of consultation with colleagues and supervisors, as well as other constructive mechanisms. In this chapter, academic standards, relevant codes of professional ethics, and tools beneficial to the development of an ethical professional practice and opportunities for exploration through case examples were provided. Remember, professional ethical standards, caseload characteristics, needs of clients, and the realities of *the work* evolve over time. Whether a seasoned counselor or recent graduate, knowledge of and skills that support a professional ethical practice should be continually revisited and reinforced.

QUESTIONS FOR DISCUSSION

1. In what ways can professional ethics be both mandatory and aspirational? Provide examples.

2. Beyond mandatory or compliance-driven ethics, when and how might a counselor demonstrate aspirational ethics and the highest level of ethical practice in vocational rehabilitation?

3. Based on the available employment opportunities and your specific interests, what credentials might make sense to obtain, and what will be required to acquire those credentials?

4. How do CRCC values and principles align or misalign with your personal values and beliefs?

5. Is there any parity between educational and experiential requirements between credentials in which you have an interest in obtaining? Will any state-specific credentials offer portability if you move geographically?

6. In what ways can a rehabilitation professional's working alliance with a client improve or impede case management?

7. What might be some ways in which a counselor can assess their level of cultural humility and any potential impact of their personal biases on their work with clients?

8. What are some of the challenges to maintaining an ethical practice? How are ethical challenges different based on practice setting?

9. How might technology benefit rehabilitation services? What cautions and considerations should go into technology selection and service provision decisions?

10. Can case managers realistically delineate personal and professional social media presences? Considering the benefits and pitfalls of various social media platforms, what personally defined guidelines might you employ if you so choose to leverage this tool to support your service provision and clients?

PUTTING IT INTO PRACTICE

Ask yourself these questions to target issues or concerns with ethical practice in case and caseload management.

1. Mandatory ethics are related to minimal standards required for compliance purposes, whereas aspirational ethics refer to the highest standard of thinking and conduct. How do you strive each day to achieve aspirational ethics in case and caseload management professional practice? Is it something that comes naturally or do you have to work at it?

2. Do you feel that there is importance to having and maintaining ethical practices through professional credentialing? If so, what are your credentials and how did you select them specifically? Are there other credentials that you feel would benefit you in the field of rehabilitation practice?

3. As you reflect on the credentials in this chapter, do you feel that one would suit the field of rehabilitation counseling better than another? Reflect on your feelings regarding where the field is going in the future and what credentials would be best to help it thrive.

CASE STUDY

The rehabilitation agency where William Scoggins, CRC, CVE, LPC, CCM, is employed recently made significant reductions in the number of qualified rehabilitation counselors, leaving a shortage of staff. As a result, the agency has mandated that the remaining professionals, including William, work overtime and take on the additional caseloads left open due to the vacancies. Unfortunately, this has led to William's caseload ballooning to over 400 clients, causing several negative consequences in his work.

Case Study Questions

1. What potential consequences could William experience in his work due to the significantly increased caseload?

2. Are there any potential ethical concerns or implications arising from the agency's decision to mandate overtime and increased caseloads for its rehabilitation counselors?

3. What support systems or coping mechanisms are available to assist rehabilitation counselors in managing stress and burnout during challenging times like these?

4. Could the increase in workload affect William's work–life balance and overall well-being?

 A robust set of instructor resources designed to supplement this text is located at **http://connect.springerpub.com/content/book/978-0-8261-5963-2.** Qualifying instructors may request access by emailing **textbook@springerpub.com.**

REFERENCES

Ahonle, Z. J., Hill, J. C., Rumrill, P., Degeneffe, C. E., & Dillahunt-Aspillaga, C. (2023). The 2023 revision to the CRCC code of ethics: Implications for defining and protecting the counselor-client relationship. *Rehabilitation Counseling Bulletin, 66*(4), 257–264. https://doi.org/10.1177/00343552221147220

American Counseling Association. (2014). *2014 ACA code of ethics.* http://www.counseling.org/docs/ethics/2014-aca-code-of-ethics.pdf?sfvrsn=4

American Counseling Association. (2020). *ACA policies and procedures for processing complaints of ethical violations.* https://www.counseling.org/docs/default-source/center-resources/p_and_p_complaints_of_ethical_violations.pdf?sfvrsn=fe0c292c_2

Association of Persons Supporting Employment First. (1998). *APSE ethical guidelines for professionals in supported employment.* https://apse.org/wp-content/uploads/2021/04/APSE-Ethical-Guidelines.pdf

Bernacchio, C. P., Kuo, H. J., Schultz, J. C., Brink, E. A., & Soldner, J. L. (2022). A technology-assisted supervision option in rehabilitation counseling: Ethical considerations and best practices. *Journal of Rehabilitation, 88*(4), 4–12.

Bernacchio, C., & Wilson, J. (2018). VR online in rehabilitation counseling preparation: An integrative pilot initiative. *Journal of Applied Rehabilitation Counseling, 49*(2), 24–33. https://doi.org/10.1891/0047-2220.49.2.24

Bourgeois, P., Shaw, L., Hartley, M. T., & Clarke, B. (2022). Technology and distance counseling. In J. Stano (Ed.), *Ethics in rehabilitation counseling* (2nd ed., pp. 321–330). Aspen Professional Services.

Brennan, C. (2013). Ensuring ethical practice: Guidelines for mental health counselors in private practice. *Journal of Mental Health Counseling, 35,* 245–261. https://doi.org/10.17744/mehc.35.3.9706313j4t313397

Brickham, D., Yaghmaian, R., Morrison, B., Bowes, J., Rosenthal, D., & Tang, X. (2021). Mitigating rehabilitation counselor trainee stress and burnout through self-care initiatives in rehabilitation counseling programs. *Rehabilitation Research, Policy, and Education, 35*(4), 323–335. https://doi.org/10.1891/RE-20-03

Centers for Disease Control and Prevention. (2022, June 16). *Benefits of physical activity.* https://www.cdc.gov/physicalactivity/basics/pa-health/index.htm

Commission for Case Manager Certification. (n.d.-a). *CCMC at a glance.* https://ccmcertification.org/ccmc-at-a-glance

Commission for Case Manager Certification. (n.d.-b). *2019 role & function study key findings.* https://ccmcertification.org/about-ccmc/2019-role-function-study/2019-role-function-study-key-findings

Commission for Case Manager Certification. (2023). *Code of professional conduct for case managers.* https://ccmcertification.org/sites/ccmc/files/docs/2023/Code%20of%20Professional%20Conduct%20for%20Case%20Managers%20FINAL%202023.pdf

Commission on Accreditation of Allied Health Education Programs. (2019). *Standards and guidelines for the accreditation of educational programs in inclusive rehabilitation sciences.* https://assets.website-files.com/5f466098572bfe97f28d59df/603da59d98b90a0d4b630fcc_InclusiveRehabilitationServices-Nov2019.pdf

Commission on Rehabilitation Counselor Certification. (n.d.-a). *Rehabilitation counselor scope of practice.* https://crccertification.com/scope-of-practice/

Commission on Rehabilitation Counselor Certification. (n.d.-b). *About us.* https://crccertification.com/about-crcc/

Commission on Rehabilitation Counselor Certification. (n.d.-c). *Sample forms and templates.* https://crccertification.com/code-of-ethics-4/sample-forms-and-templates/

Commission on Rehabilitation Counselor Certification. (n.d.-d). *Guidelines for requesting advisory opinions from CRCC's Ethics Committee.* http://crccertification.com/wp-content/uploads/2020/10/Guidelines-for-Requesting-Advisory-Opinions.pdf

Commission on Rehabilitation Counselor Certification. (n.d.-e). *Advisory opinions from Ethics Committee minutes 1996–2022.* https://crccertification.com/wp-content/uploads/2022/12/AdvisoryOpinions-2023-01.pdf

Commission on Rehabilitation Counselor Certification. (n.d.-f). *Contemporary decision-making models.* https://crccertification.com/code-of-ethics-4/decision-making-models/

Commission on Rehabilitation Counselor Certification. (2023). *Code of professional ethics for rehabilitation counselors.* https://crccertification.com/wp-content/uploads/2023/04/2023-Code-of-Ethics.pdf

Committee on Rehabilitation Accreditation. (n.d.). *About us.* https://www.caahep.org/committees-on-accreditation/inclusive-rehabilitation-sciences

Corey, G., Corey, M. S., Corey, C., & Callanan, P. (2014). *Issues and ethics in the helping professions* (9th ed.). Brooks/Cole.

Cottone, R. R. (2001). A social constructivism model of ethical decision-making in counseling. *Journal of Counseling Development, 79,* 39–45. https://doi.org/10.1002/j.1556-6676.2001.tb01941.x

Cottone, R. R., Tarvydas, V. M., & Hartley, M. T. (2021). Ethical decision-making processes. In R. R. Cottone, V. M. Tarvydas, & M. T. Hartley (Eds.), *Ethics and decision making in counseling and psychotherapy* (pp. 53–84). Springer Publishing.

Council for Accreditation of Counseling and Related Educational Programs. (2023). *2024 CACREP standards.* https://www.cacrep.org/wp-content/uploads/2023/10/2024-Standards-Combined-Version-10.09.23.pdf

Even, T. A., & Robinson, C. R. (2013). The impact of CACREP accreditation: A multiway frequency analysis of ethics violations and sanctions. *Journal of Counseling & Development, 91*(1), 26–34. https://doi.org/10.1002/j.1556-6676.2013.00067.x

Evenson, T., & Holloway, L. (2007). Undergraduate education: An essential rung on the rehabilitation career ladder. *Rehabilitation Education, 21*(2), 73–86. https://doi.org/10.1891/088970107805059760

Forester-Miller, H., & Davis, T. E. (2016). *Practitioner's guide to ethical decision making.* https://www.counseling.org/docs/default-source/ethics/practioner-39-s-guide-to-ethical-decision-making.pdf

Froehlich, R. J., Henry, J. S., Tichy, N., Hill, J. C., & Thompson, K. (2023). Rehabilitation counselors and technology, social media, and distance counseling: Contemporary considerations. *Rehabilitation Counseling Bulletin, 66*(4), 265–273. https://doi.org/10.1177/00343552221147219

Froehlich, R. J., Hicks, S., Hill, J. C., Tichy, N., & Riedy-Rush, C. (2023). Using the revised CRCC code of professional ethics for rehabilitation counselors as a tool in resolving ethical issues. *Rehabilitation Counseling Bulletin, 66*(4), 301–309. https://doi.org/10.1177/00343552221148200

Garcia, J., Cartwright, B., Winston, S., & Borchukowska, B. (2003). A transcultural integrative ethical decision-making model in counseling. *Journal of Counseling and Development, 81*, 268–276. https://doi.org/10.1002/j.1556-6678.2003.tb00253.x

Hartley, M. T., & Bourgeois, P. (2020). The Commission on Rehabilitation Counselor Certification Code of Ethics: An emerging approach to digital technology. *Rehabilitation Research, Policy and Education, 34*(2), 73–85. https://doi.org/10.1891/RE-19-04

Hartley, M. T., Bourgeois, P., & Clarke, B. J. (2023). Ethics of technology practice: Beliefs and behaviors of certified rehabilitation counselors during the COVID-19 pandemic. *Rehabilitation Counseling Bulletin, 66*(4), 244–256. https://doi.org/10.1177/00343552221147216

Henry, J. S., Kulesza, E. T., Williams Awodeha, N. F., Hicks, S. B., & Robinson, M. (2023). A way forward with multicultural considerations, advocacy, and accessibility across the 2023 revised code of professional ethics for rehabilitation counselor educators and practitioners. *Rehabilitation Counseling Bulletin, 66*(4), 274–282. https://doi.org/10.1177/00343552221146164

Herbert, J. T., Barrett, K., Evenson, T., & Jacob, C. J. (2010). Work roles and functions of undergraduate rehabilitation services alumni: A pilot study. *Rehabilitation Education, 24*(3), 149–166.

Herbert J. T., Yoon, H. J., O'Shea, A., & Balushi, I. A. (2023). Recruitment and retention of state vocational rehabilitation counselors: A mixed methods analysis. *Journal of Rehabilitation, 89*(1), 61–71.

Herlihy, B., & Watson, Z. E. (2007). *Social justice and counseling ethics.* In C. C. Lee (Ed.), Counseling for social justice (2nd ed., pp. 181–199). American Counseling Association.

Hill, J. C., Stokes, L. E., Froelich, R. J., Emmanuel, D., Landon, T., & Hicks, S. (2023). Ethical dilemmas: Current and projected concerns reported by certified rehabilitation counselors. *Rehabilitation Counseling Bulletin, 66*(4), 231–243. https://doi.org/10.1177/00343552221146159

Huck, G., Horton, C., Oswald, G. R., Fredricey, D., & Scarfella, E. (2023). Undergraduate rehabilitation education and clinical practice: Stakeholder perspectives on areas of research need. *Journal of Applied Rehabilitation Counseling, 54*(2), 105–118. https://doi.org/10.1891/JARC-2022-0011

Ji, E., Schaller, J., Pazey, B., & Glynn, K. (2015). Education and employment outcomes from the RSA data file for transition-age African American, White, and Hispanic youth with learning disabilities. *Journal of Applied Rehabilitation Counseling, 46*(3), 15–24. https://doi.org/10.1891/0047-2220.46.3.15

Johnson, E. T., Kaya, C., Chan, F., Dutta, A., Yaghmaian, R., Kundu, M., & Devebakan, N. (2017). Vocational rehabilitation services for African-American women with HIV/AIDS: An examination of acceptance rates and employment outcomes. *Journal of Vocational Rehabilitation, 47*, 235–245. https://doi.org/10.3233/JVR-170898

Jorgensen-Smith, T. (2021). Multicultural ethics in rehabilitation services. *Journal of Vocational Rehabilitation, 54*, 295–304. https://doi.org/10.3233/JVR-211140

Landon, T. J., Levine, A., Sabella, S. A., Hill, J. C., Khan, U., & Kulesza, E. T. (2023). Supervision and ethics: Updates to the CRCC Code of Professional Ethics. *Rehabilitation Counseling Bulletin, 66*(4), 283–293. https://doi.org/10.1177/00343552221146163

Landon, T. J., & Schultz, J. C. (2018). Exploring rehabilitation counselor supervisors' role in promoting counselor development of ethical fluency. *Rehabilitation Counseling Bulletin, 61*(1), 18–29. https://doi.org/10.1177/0034355217728912

Leahy, M. J., Chan, F., Sung, C., Kim, J., Strauser, D., & Steadman, C. (2019). Empirically derived test specifications for the certified rehabilitation counselor examination: Revisiting the essential competencies of rehabilitation counselors. *Rehabilitation Counseling Bulletin, 63*(1), 3–12. https://doi.org/10.1177/0034355218800842

Lin, T., Heckman, T. G., & Anderson, T. (2021). The efficacy of synchronous teletherapy versus in-person therapy. *Clinical Psychology: Science and Practice, 29*(2), 167–179. https://doi.org/10.1037/cps0000056

Lloyd, L., Barros-Bailey, M., Vercillo, A., & Landon, T. (2023). Forensic and business ethics. *Rehabilitation Counseling Bulletin, 66*(4), 294–300. https://doi.org/10.1177/00343552221147222

Lund, E. M., & Schultz, J. C. (2015). Distance supervision in rehabilitation counseling: Ethical and clinical considerations. *Rehabilitation Research, Policy, and Education, 29*, 88–95. https://doi.org/10.1891/2168-6653.29.1.88

Maier, C. A., Riger, D., & Morgan-Sowada, H. (2021). "It's splendid once you grow into it": Client experiences of relational teletherapy in the era of COVID-19. *Journal of Marital and Family Therapy,* 47(2), 304–319. https://doi.org/10.1111/jmft.12508

Mullahy, C. M. (2016). *The case manager's handbook* (3rd ed.). Jones and Bartlett.

National Association of Social Workers. (2021). *NASW code of ethics.* https://www.socialworkers.org/About/Ethics/Code-of-Ethics/Code-of-Ethics-English

National Board for Certified Counselors, Inc. (n.d.). *Candidate handbook for National Certified Counselor Certification.* https://www.nbcc.org/assets/exam/handbooks/nce_applicant_handbook_for_national_certification.pdf

National Board for Certified Counselors, Inc. (2023a). *NBCC code of ethics.* https://www.nbcc.org/assets/ethics/nbcccodeofethics.pdf

National Board for Certified Counselors, Inc. (2023b). *NBCC code of ethics case procedures.* https://www.nbcc.org/assets/Ethics/ethics_case_procedures.pdf

National Institute on Health. (2022, August 8). *Emotional wellness toolkit.* https://www.nih.gov/health-information/emotional-wellness-toolkit

National Institute on Mental Health. (n.d.) *Caring for your mental health.* https://www.nimh.nih.gov/health/topics/caring-for-your-mental-health

National Organization of Human Services. (2015). *Ethical standards for human services professionals.* https://www.nationalhumanservices.org/ethical-standards-for-hs-professionals

Oswald, G. R., Flexer, R., Alderman, L. A., & Huber, M. (2016). Predictive value of personal characteristics and the employment of transition-aged youth in vocational rehabilitation. *Journal of Rehabilitation,* 82(4), 60–66.

Oswald, G. R., Huck, G., & Duncan, J. C. (2018). The state of undergraduate rehabilitation education: Current program coordinator perspectives. *Rehabilitation Research, Policy, and Education,* 32(4), 253–261. https://doi.org/10.1891/2168-6653.32.4.253

Oswald, G. R., Huck, G., & Rawlins Williams, L. A. (2020). Undergraduate rehabilitation student perceptions of post-graduation outcomes and professional identity. *Journal of Applied Rehabilitation Counseling,* 51(3), 249–263. https://doi.org/10.1891/JARC-D-19-00018

Oswald, G. R., & Jenkins, B. (2022). Current trends and characteristics of required undergraduate rehabilitation curriculum. *Journal of Applied Rehabilitation Counseling,* 53(4). https://doi.org/10.1891/JARC-2021-0007

Oswald, G. R., & Taylor, R. (2020). Careers and credentials: Employment settings for rehabilitation practitioners. In J. D. Andrew & C. W. Faubion (Eds.), *Rehabilitation services: An introduction for the human services professional* (pp. 282–307). Aspen Professional Services.

Perry, D. C., Schiro-Geist, C., Marm., M., Duncan, J. C., Robertson, R., & Willmering, P. (2018). Undergraduate rehabilitation education and accreditation: The importance of being persistent. *Journal of Applied Rehabilitation Counseling,* 49(4), 34–41. https://doi.org/10.1891/0047-2220.49.4.34

Plath, A. M., & Fickling, M. J. (2022). Tase-oriented self-care: An innovative approach to wellness for counselors. *Journal of Creativity in Mental Health,* 17(1), 55–66. https://doi.org/10.1080/15401383.2020.1842274

Remley, T. P., & Herlihy, B. (2020). *Ethical, legal and professional issues in counseling.* Pearson Merrill Prentice Hall.

Salimi, N., Gere, B., Dallas, B., & Shahab, A. (2023). State vocational rehabilitation service patterns and employment outcomes predictors among Native American VR clients. *Journal of Rehabilitation,* 89(1), 4–16.

Saunders, J., Barros-Bailey, M., Rudman, R., Dew, D. W., & Garcia, J. (2007). Ethical complaints and violations in rehabilitation counseling: An analysis of Commission on Rehabilitation Counselor Certification Data. *Rehabilitation Counseling Bulletin,* 51(1), 7–13. https://doi.org/10.1177/00343552070510010301

Stevens, R. L., Wondolowski, E. L., & Wilson, G. A. (2020). Navigating the unique landscape of clients who identify as LGBTQ+ in vocational rehabilitation: A social justice primer. *Journal of Applied Rehabilitation Counseling,* 51(4), 304–322. https://doi.org/10.1891/JARC-D-20-00022

Surpass Assessment. (2021, March 4). *The National Board for Certified Counselors (NBCC) joins the Surpass community.* https://surpass.com/news/2021/the-national-board-for-certified-counselors-nbcc-joins-the-surpass-community/

Tervalon, M., & Murray-Garcia, J. (1998). Cultural humility versus cultural competence: A critical distinction in defining physician training outcomes in multicultural education. *Journal of Health Care for the Poor and Underserved,* 9(2), 117–125. https://doi.org/10.1353/hpu.2010.0233

Van Hoose, W. H., & Paradise, L. V. (1979). *Ethics in counseling and psychotherapy: Perspectives in issues and decision making.* Carroll.

Yin, M., Pathak, A., Lin, D., & Dizdari, N. (2022). Identifying racial differences in vocational rehabilitation services. *Rehabilitation Counseling Bulletin,* 66(1), 13–24. https://doi.org/10.1177/00343552211048218

CHAPTER **12**

Technology in the Virtual World: Influence on Rehabilitation Practice

---

LEARNING OBJECTIVES

By the end of this chapter, learners will be able to:

- Understand the benefits of integrating technology in rehabilitation caseload management, including improved accessibility, enhanced communication, and effective data management.

- Recognize the importance of maintaining confidentiality and data privacy when utilizing technology platforms in rehabilitation caseload management.

- Identify the challenges and strategies for bridging the digital divide to promote equitable technology access among individuals with disabilities.

- Explore specific applications of technology in rehabilitation caseload management, such as telehealth services, mobile applications, and artificial intelligence (AI) and their potential impact on assessments, interventions, and progress monitoring.

- Understand the concept of digital interconnectivity among rehabilitation agencies and its role in promoting collaboration and information sharing among service providers.

- Recognize the integration of technology in emergency preparedness and its significance in disaster response and recovery for individuals with disabilities.

- Gain insight into the use of technology platforms for emergency communication, virtual assessments, and remote support during crises.

- Reflect on the future implications and possibilities of technology in rehabilitation caseload management, considering emerging technologies and their potential to enhance care quality and inclusivity in the field.

INTRODUCTION

In today's rapidly evolving digital landscape, the integration of **technology** has become essential across various professional domains (Kisekka & Giboney, 2018). One such area where technological advancements have significantly impacted efficiency and effectiveness is case and caseload management practice. Technology has revolutionized the way cases are handled, tracked, and managed, enabling professionals to streamline processes, improve data accuracy, enhance collaboration, and ultimately provide better outcomes for clients (Stoumpos et al., 2023).

Traditionally, case and caseload management relied heavily on manual paperwork, cumbersome filing systems, and time-consuming administrative tasks. However, with the advent of **innovative technologies**, professionals in the legal, social work, rehabilitation, and healthcare sectors, among others, are now empowered with sophisticated tools and software solutions that optimize their workflow.

One of the key advantages of technological utilization in case and caseload management practice is the ability to centralize and organize information. Gone are the days of sifting through stacks of physical files; now, professionals can store and access case-related data in secure **digital platforms**. These platforms often offer robust search functionalities, allowing practitioners to retrieve information quickly, analyze trends, and make informed decisions based on comprehensive and up-to-date data (Kraus et al., 2022; Yadav & Pavlou, 2014).

Moreover, technology has introduced automation and customization capabilities to case and caseload management, saving professionals valuable time and effort. Tasks such as scheduling appointments, generating reports, and sending notifications can now be automated, freeing practitioners to focus on higher-value activities (Larco et al., 2018). Furthermore, software solutions tailored to specific domains allow professionals to customize workflows and processes according to their unique requirements, thereby increasing efficiency and adaptability.

Collaboration and communication among team members have also been greatly facilitated through technology. **Cloud-based platforms** enable real-time collaboration on case files, enabling multiple professionals to work simultaneously and seamlessly exchange information (Lilly et al., 2020). Additionally, integrated messaging systems and shared calendars enhance communication, ensuring that all stakeholders are updated on case progress, deadlines, and important events.

The utilization of technology in case and caseload management practice also contributes to improved client experiences. Digital platforms provide secure portals where clients can access relevant information, communicate with their assigned professionals, and participate actively in their own cases (Baum et al., 2020; Benjamin & Potts, 2018; der Schaft et al., 2020). This enhanced transparency and accessibility foster a sense of trust and engagement, leading to better outcomes and client satisfaction. However, it is crucial to recognize that as technology advances, it brings forth new challenges and considerations. Data security, privacy, and ethical implications must be carefully addressed to protect sensitive client information and ensure compliance with legal and professional standards.

The integration of technology in case and caseload management practice has revolutionized the way professionals handle their responsibilities. By centralizing information, automating tasks, facilitating collaboration, and enhancing client experiences, technology has significantly improved efficiency and effectiveness in this field. As technology continues to evolve, practitioners must embrace the opportunities it offers while navigating the associated ethical and security considerations to harness its full potential in serving their clients and achieving positive outcomes.

TECHNOLOGICAL UTILIZATION IN CASE AND CASELOAD MANAGEMENT

Technological advancements have brought about significant changes in various professional fields, and case and caseload management are no exception. The integration of technology in this practice has revolutionized the way cases are handled, tracked, and managed, offering numerous benefits for professionals and their clients (Hudson et al., 2016; Lustgarten & Elhai, 2017; McLaughlin-Davis, 2018). By leveraging innovative tools and software solutions, practitioners can streamline processes, improve data accuracy, and enhance collaboration.

One of the primary advantages of technological utilization in case and caseload management is the ability to centralize and organize information. Traditional methods relied on manual paperwork and physical filing systems, which were not only time-consuming but also prone to human error. However, with the advent of digital platforms, professionals can now store and access case-related data in a secure and centralized manner. As a result, practitioners can swiftly retrieve information, monitor case progress, and analyze trends using these platforms' robust search functionalities, leading to more informed and efficient decision-making and ultimately improved outcomes for clients.

Automation is another significant benefit of technological utilization in case and caseload management. Repetitive administrative tasks that once consumed valuable time can now be automated, freeing up practitioners to focus on more critical activities. Scheduling appointments, generating reports, sending notifications, and tracking deadlines can be seamlessly handled by software solutions (Harvard Business Review, 2023). This automation not only increases efficiency but also reduces the risk of errors, ensuring that essential tasks are completed in a timely and accurate manner, and ultimately provides better outcomes.

Moreover, technological utilization in case and caseload management practice contributes to enhanced client experiences. Digital platforms often provide secure portals where clients can access relevant information, communicate with their assigned professionals, and actively participate in their own cases (Kisekka & Giboney, 2018; Mtemeri et al., 2022). This increased transparency and accessibility empower clients, allowing them to stay informed, provide input, and make informed decisions about their legal, social work, or healthcare matters. As a result, client engagement and satisfaction are improved, fostering a stronger practitioner–client relationship.

Utilization for Caseload Management Evaluation

Technological utilization for caseload management evaluation offers significant benefits and opportunities for professionals in various areas of rehabilitation. By leveraging technology, practitioners can enhance the evaluation process, improve data analysis, and gain valuable insights to inform their decision-making and resource allocation. Technology enables practitioners to collect and record caseload data efficiently, eliminating the need for manual data entry and reducing the chances of errors or data inconsistencies. Digital platforms and **software solutions** streamline the data collection process, allowing practitioners to capture relevant information in a structured and standardized format (Mohanty et al., 2021). This comprehensive and systematic approach to data analysis empowers rehabilitation counseling professionals to identify patterns, trends, and correlations within their caseloads. With the help of **data analytics** tools and software, practitioners can gain valuable insights into client demographics, case outcomes, resource utilization, and other key metrics (Cozzoli et al., 2022; Galetsi et al., 2019). These insights inform decision-making, allowing rehabilitation counselors the ability to allocate resources effectively, identify areas for improvement, and ultimately enhance client outcomes. Technological utilization in caseload management evaluation revolutionizes the evaluation process, making it more efficient, data-driven, and impactful.

INTEGRATION OF TECHNOLOGY INTO THE CASE AND CASELOAD MANAGEMENT PROCESS

The integration of technology has revolutionized the field of case and caseload management, offering numerous advantages in terms of efficiency, collaboration, and client outcomes. However, as technology becomes more prevalent in this domain, it is crucial to explore its impact on important aspects such as **confidentiality, data privacy,** access to re-cords and documentation, and access to **interdisciplinary resources** (Bani-Issa et al., 2016, 2020; Klein, 2011; Kruse et al., 2017).

The integration of technology in case and caseload management has brought about remarkable improvements in managing sensitive information while ensuring confiden-tiality and data privacy. Digital platforms and secure software solutions have replaced traditional paper-based systems, providing enhanced protection against unauthorized access and physical vulnerabilities (Akhu-Zaheya et al., 2018). Robust **encryption measures, access controls,** and **two-factor authentication** protocols help safeguard sensitive client data, ensuring confidentiality and complying with legal and ethical obligations (Lustgarten, 2015; Lustgarten & Colbow, 2017; Munn et al., 2019). Additionally, technology has made accessing records and documentation more efficient and convenient. **Digital storage** and archiving systems allow practitioners to store and retrieve case-related information quickly and securely. This digital access to records enables professionals to locate and review documents promptly, enhancing their ability to make informed decisions and pro-vide effective services to clients. The streamlined accessibility of records also facilitates seamless collaboration among **interdisciplinary teams,** enabling professionals from dif-ferent fields to share and access information more efficiently (McLaney et al., 2022; Vos et al., 2020). Furthermore, the integration of technology has significantly improved access to interdisciplinary resources. Digital platforms and online databases provide profession-als with a wealth of resources, research articles, legal precedents, and support development of interprofessional competencies from various disciplines (Croker et al., 2012; McLaney et al., 2022). This easy access to interdisciplinary resources empowers practitioners to stay updated on the latest developments in their respective fields, enhancing their knowledge base and enabling them to provide comprehensive and informed support to their clients.

While the integration of technology offers numerous benefits, it also presents chal-lenges related to confidentiality, data privacy, and ethical considerations. Professionals must be mindful of maintaining the privacy and security of client data, ensuring com-pliance with applicable regulations and ethical guidelines (Rahnama & Pentland, 2022; Tariq & Hackert, 2023). Robust data protection measures, secure storage, and controlled access to information are essential to safeguard client confidentiality and protect against unauthorized disclosure or breaches.

The shift to digital platforms and secure software solutions has enhanced confidenti-ality and data privacy and facilitated access to records and interdisciplinary resources. However, it is vital for professionals to navigate the challenges and ethical considerations associated with technology, ensuring that client data remain confidential and secure while harnessing the benefits it offers to improve client outcomes and provide effective interdis-ciplinary support.

Impact on Confidentiality

Confidentiality plays a crucial role in caseload management, and the integration of technology has both positive and negative implications for maintaining confidentiality. Technology offers opportunities for more secure and controlled storage of client infor-mation. Digital platforms and secure software systems provide options for encryption, access controls, and authentication, thereby reducing the risk of unauthorized access to sensitive data (Devereaux & Gottlieb, 2012; Lustgarten, 2015). However, technology also introduces new challenges to confidentiality. The ease of digital communication and data sharing increases the potential for unintended disclosures or breaches (Elhai & Frueh, 2016; Elhai & Hall, 2016; Elhai et al., 2017; Penney, 2016). Rehabilitation pro-fessionals must be vigilant in ensuring that client information is appropriately protected throughout the entire technological ecosystem, including data transmission, storage, and access points. It is essential for practitioners to stay informed about the latest security measures and best practices to safeguard client confidentiality in the digital age. Regular training and education on privacy laws, data protection regulations, and ethical guidelines are crucial to maintaining the trust and privacy of clients (Elhai & Frueh, 2016). Additionally, rehabilitation counseling professionals must be vigilant in understanding professional codes of ethics and overall impact of ethical guidelines surrounding confidentiality in the field.

Moreover, practitioners must be aware of the limitations of technology and exercise caution in sharing information electronically. Understanding the risks associated with email communication, **cloud storage**, and **electronic record systems** allows professionals to make informed decisions about the appropriate methods and platforms for sharing sensitive information (Devereaux & Gottlieb, 2012; Elhai & Frueh, 2016; Grisold et al., 2023). Ultimately, the integration of technology in caseload management requires a thoughtful and proactive approach to ensure the confidentiality of client data. By implementing robust security measures, staying informed about privacy regulations, and exercising discretion in electronic communication, professionals can navigate the challenges posed by technology while maintaining the privacy and trust of their clients.

Data Privacy

Data privacy is a critical consideration in the context of technology integration in caseload management. The utilization of technology introduces both benefits and challenges to maintaining the privacy of client data (McKinsey & Company, 2020). With the integration of technology, professionals can implement robust data privacy measures to protect sensitive client information. Encryption, secure access controls, and authentication protocols provide safeguards against unauthorized access and breaches. These technological tools enhance data privacy by ensuring that client information remains confidential and protected from external threats. However, technology also brings forth potential risks to data privacy. The digital nature of information exchange and storage increases the vulnerability to data breaches and unauthorized disclosures (Cheng et al., 2017; Kisekka & Giboney, 2018; Seh et al., 2020). Professionals must remain vigilant and proactive in implementing comprehensive data protection strategies to mitigate these risks.

Compliance with data protection regulations, such as general data protection regulation (GDPR) or Health Insurance Portability and Accountability Act (HIPAA), is essential in ensuring data privacy in caseload management. Professionals must understand and adhere to the legal requirements and ethical guidelines specific to their respective fields (Klein, 2011; Lustgarten & Elhai, 2017). This includes obtaining informed consent, securely transmitting and storing data, and implementing measures to prevent data breaches. As stated in other sections, ongoing education and training on data privacy best practices are crucial for professionals to stay informed about emerging threats, technological advancements, and evolving privacy regulations. By continuously updating their knowledge, practitioners can adapt their practices to ensure the highest standards of data privacy. While technology enables secure storage and controlled access to client information, it also requires proactive efforts to mitigate the risks associated with data breaches. Compliance with regulations, implementing robust security measures, and staying informed about data privacy best practices are essential steps to protect the privacy of client data in the digital age (Panelists, 2020).

Access to Records and Documentation

The integration of technology in caseload management has significantly transformed the way rehabilitation counseling professionals access, manage, and utilize records and documentation. Digital platforms and software solutions have revolutionized the accessibility of medical records and documentation in caseload management (Tsai et al., 2020; Upadhayay & Hu, 2022). Digital storage and archiving systems allow professionals to store, retrieve, and share case-related information quickly and efficiently. This streamlined access to records eliminates the need for manual searches through physical files, saving valuable time and improving overall efficiency (Tsai et al., 2020). Additionally, digital platforms offer robust search functionalities, allowing practitioners to easily locate specific records and extract relevant information. Advanced search **algorithms** and filters enable professionals to quickly retrieve specific case details, track case progress, and analyze trends (Bramer et al., 2018). This enhanced search capability contributes to more informed decision-making and efficient case management.

The digital nature of record-keeping also facilitates seamless collaboration among interdisciplinary teams. Professionals from different disciplines can securely share and access records, fostering effective communication and coordination. This interdisciplinary collaboration promotes a holistic approach to caseload management, allowing for comprehensive assessment, planning, and delivery of services. Furthermore, technology enables professionals to utilize various tools for documentation, such as electronic forms, templates, and digital notetaking (Croker et al., 2012; McLaney et al., 2022; Vos et al., 2020). These tools enhance accuracy, organization, and legibility of documentation, reducing the risk of errors and ensuring consistency in record-keeping practices. However, with the increased accessibility of records and documentation through technology, it is essential to maintain strict security measures to protect sensitive information. Rehabilitation professionals must ensure that appropriate data protection protocols, access controls, and encryption are in place to safeguard client confidentiality and comply with privacy regulations (Commission on Rehabilitation Counselor Certification, 2023).

The integration of technology has revolutionized access to records and documentation in caseload management. It has streamlined the storage, retrieval, and sharing of information, promoting efficiency, collaboration, and informed decision-making. While technology offers numerous benefits, practitioners must prioritize data security to maintain confidentiality and protect sensitive client information.

Access to Interdisciplinary and Interprofessional Resources

The integration of technology in caseload management has opened up vast opportunities for accessing and utilizing interdisciplinary and **interprofessional resources**, fostering collaboration and enhancing the quality of client care. Technology serves as a gateway to a wealth of interprofessional resources in the caseload management process. Online databases, research repositories, and digital libraries provide rehabilitation counseling professionals with a vast array of information from diverse fields. This includes research articles, case studies, legal precedents, and best practices from various disciplines relevant to caseload management (Grubbs et al., 2006). Access to these interdisciplinary resources allows professionals to stay informed about the latest developments, evidence-based interventions, and emerging trends in their varying areas in the field of rehabilitation. Professionals emerge with the ability to leverage this knowledge to enhance their understanding, expand their skill set, and deliver comprehensive services to their clients. The ability to tap into interprofessional resources enables practitioners to approach caseload management from a holistic perspective, integrating insights from different disciplines within the field of rehabilitation for more effective and client-centered interventions (McLaney et al., 2022). Furthermore, technology facilitates collaboration among professionals from different disciplines. Online platforms, forums, and **virtual spaces** provide avenues for interdisciplinary communication, knowledge sharing, and joint problem-solving. Professionals can engage in discussions, seek advice, and collaborate on complex cases, benefiting from the diverse expertise and perspectives of their peers (Keshmiri & Ghelmani, 2023).

Also, the integration of technology enables seamless interdisciplinary coordination in caseload management. Shared digital platforms and collaborative **software solutions** allow professionals to access and update shared documents, exchange information, and coordinate services. This streamlined communication and coordination enhance efficiency, reduce duplication of efforts, and promote a multidisciplinary approach to client care (Campanella et al., 2015). However, while technology offers unprecedented access to interdisciplinary resources, professionals must critically evaluate and apply the information they encounter. In this context discernment must be exercised, considering the context of the specific caseload and applying interdisciplinary as well as interprofessional insights in an appropriate and ethical manner.

Technology continues to transform the landscape of interdisciplinary resources. The digital era provides professionals with access to diverse knowledge, research, and expertise, enhancing their understanding and enabling collaborative approaches to client care. Leveraging these interdisciplinary resources can lead to improved client outcomes and a more comprehensive and holistic approach to caseload management (Grubbs et al., 2006).

COORDINATED APPROACHES TO REHABILITATION PRACTICE

Coordinated technology approaches in rehabilitation practice involve the intentional integration and use of various technologies to enhance the delivery of rehabilitation services, improve outcomes, and support the overall rehabilitation process. Technology plays a significant role in rehabilitation practice by providing tools and resources that aid in assessment, intervention, and ongoing support for individuals with disabilities or impairments. Coordinated technology approaches involve leveraging multiple technologies in a cohesive and integrated manner to address the unique needs of each individual and optimize their rehabilitation journey. One example of a coordinated technology approach is the use of assistive technologies. These technologies, such as mobility aids, communication devices, and adaptive equipment, are designed to assist individuals with disabilities in performing daily activities, increasing independence, and improving their quality of life (Smith, 2021). Coordinating the selection, customization, and training for the appropriate assistive technologies ensures a tailored approach that meets the specific needs of the individual.

Another aspect of coordinated technology approaches in rehabilitation practice involves the use of **electronic health records (EHRs)** and telehealth solutions. EHRs enable seamless sharing of patient information among different rehabilitation professionals, fostering interprofessional collaboration and coordinated care (Pyron & Carter-Templeton, 2019). Telehealth technologies, including videoconferencing and remote monitoring tools, allow for virtual consultations, therapy sessions, and remote monitoring of progress, enabling access to rehabilitation services from a distance and increasing the reach of care. Furthermore, wearable technologies and sensor-based devices are increasingly being integrated into rehabilitation practice. These technologies can track and monitor various aspects of movement, performance, and physiological data, providing valuable insights to rehabilitation professionals (Seshadri et al., 2019). By collecting objective data, these technologies support evidence-based decision-making, enable personalized treatment plans, and facilitate progress tracking. Coordinated technology approaches also include the use of **virtual reality (VR)** and **augmented reality (AR)** technologies in rehabilitation, addressed in detail later in this chapter. VR and AR can create immersive and interactive environments that simulate real-life situations, allowing individuals to practice and develop skills in a controlled and safe setting (Cheng et al., 2020). These technologies have been utilized in areas such as physical therapy, cognitive rehabilitation, and pain management, offering engaging and effective rehabilitation experiences.

Coordinated technology approaches in rehabilitation practice involve the intentional integration and use of various technologies to optimize the rehabilitation process. By leveraging a combination of assistive technologies, EHRs, telehealth solutions, wearable devices, and immersive technologies, rehabilitation professionals can enhance assessment, intervention, and support, ultimately improving outcomes and promoting the well-being of individuals with disabilities or functional limitations.

IMPACT OF THE DIGITAL DIVIDE ON TECHNOLOGICAL UTILIZATION AND PRACTICE

The **digital divide**, characterized by disparities in access to and use of technology, has far-reaching implications for technology utilization in rehabilitation counseling practice. This divide creates barriers that limit access to healthcare, exacerbate inequities, and hinder the effectiveness of rehabilitation interventions. One significant consequence of the digital divide is limited access to technology, including internet connectivity and devices, particularly in underserved or remote areas (Rawlins-Williams & Williams, 2021; Thomas, 2014). This lack of necessary infrastructure and resources restricts individuals from benefiting from technological advancements that could enhance rehabilitation outcomes. Further, the digital divide continues to lead to unequal access to information and resources (Alkureishi et al., 2021; Ayanso et al., 2010; Helsper & Reisdorf, 2017; Mihelj et al., 2019). Individuals without internet access or digital literacy skills face challenges in accessing online databases, research articles, and educational materials related to rehabilitation (Rawlins-Williams & Williams, 2021). This disparity in knowledge impedes the ability of both individuals and rehabilitation professionals to stay updated on the latest evidence-based practices. Also, the digital divide significantly impacts telehealth and remote rehabilitation services. These services rely on technology for virtual consultations, remote monitoring, and teletherapy. However, it is well noted that individuals who lack the necessary technology or internet connectivity face difficulties in accessing these services, resulting in unequal access to vital care and exacerbating healthcare disparities (Alkureishi et al., 2021; Van Dijk, 2020; Weiss et al., 2018). The digital divide impedes engagement and full participation in rehabilitation. Mobile applications, wearable devices, and online platforms play a crucial role in engaging individuals, promoting self-management, and providing real-time feedback. However, clients without access to these technologies due to the digital divide may miss out on the benefits of these interactive tools, affecting their motivation and overall progress in rehabilitation.

The digital divide poses significant challenges to technology utilization in rehabilitation practice. Limited access to computers and smartphones, unequal access to information and resources, low technological literacy, barriers to telehealth services, and reduced engagement in rehabilitation all hinder the ability to deliver equitable and effective case and caseload management services in the rehabilitation process (Rawlins-Williams & Williams, 2021). Addressing the digital divide is crucial to ensuring that technology can be harnessed to its fullest potential in improving rehabilitation outcomes and promoting equal access to quality services for all individuals.

INTEGRATION OF TECHNOLOGY INTO CASE AND CASELOAD MANAGEMENT

Telehealth

Telehealth has emerged as a valuable and convenient tool, enabling remote delivery of services and expanding access to care (Jury & Kornberg, 2016). Telehealth refers to the use of telecommunications technology, such as videoconferencing and remote monitoring, to provide healthcare services at a distance (Mayo Clinic, 2015). In the context of rehabilitation counseling, telehealth allows individuals to receive counseling services remotely, eliminating barriers related to distance, mobility, and transportation. This is particularly beneficial for individuals with disabilities or limited mobility who may face challenges in accessing traditional in-person counseling services (Cary et al., 2016; Pebdani et al., 2022). Through telehealth, individuals can engage in counseling sessions from the comfort of their own homes, reducing the need for travel and ensuring continuity of care. Telehealth in rehabilitation counseling offers several advantages. First, it enhances access to services, especially for those in rural or underserved areas with limited availability of rehabilitation counselors. Telehealth eliminates geographical barriers, enabling individuals to connect with qualified counselors regardless of their physical location. Next, telehealth promotes convenience and flexibility. By eliminating the need for physical appointments, individuals can schedule counseling sessions at times that are most convenient for them, reducing disruptions to their daily routines. This flexibility also extends to individuals who may have limited availability due to work or caregiving responsibilities. Finally, telehealth can foster a sense of privacy and comfort for individuals receiving counseling services (Dinesen et al., 2016). Counseling sessions conducted through secure video platforms allow individuals to engage in therapy from a familiar and safe environment, potentially increasing their willingness to open up and participate actively in the counseling process. This can lead to more effective outcomes and improved engagement in the rehabilitation process. However, it is important to acknowledge that telehealth in rehabilitation counseling also presents challenges. Limited access to reliable internet connections, technological barriers, and concerns regarding privacy and security are among the factors that need to be addressed to ensure equitable and effective implementation of telehealth services in rehabilitation counseling (United Nations, 2021; Weiss et al., 2018).

Telehealth has emerged as an effective approach in rehabilitation counseling, providing individuals with increased access to counseling services, convenience, and flexibility. It has the potential to bridge geographical gaps, improve engagement, and promote continuity of care. As technology continues to advance, and as the field of rehabilitation counseling evolves, telehealth is likely to play an increasingly important role in enhancing the accessibility and effectiveness of rehabilitation counseling services.

Telecommuting

Telecommuting, also known as remote work or telework, refers to the practice of working from a location other than a traditional office setting, usually from one's home or a remote location (Allen et al., 2015). In the context of rehabilitation counseling, telecommuting can have both advantages and challenges. Telecommuting in rehabilitation counseling offers several benefits. First, it provides flexibility for both rehabilitation counselors and clients. Counselors can schedule appointments with clients without the constraints of physical office spaces, allowing for more convenient meeting times and accommodating individuals with busy schedules or limited availability. This flexibility can enhance engagement and participation in counseling sessions, as clients can choose a time and place where they feel most comfortable and receptive to the counseling process (Meek, 2023). Additionally, telecommuting can improve accessibility to rehabilitation counseling services. Clients who face barriers to attending in-person sessions, such as transportation challenges, mobility limitations, or residing in remote areas, can still access counseling support through telecommuting (Kysely et al., 2020). This enables individuals to receive necessary rehabilitation services, regardless of their location, contributing to more equitable access to rehabilitation counseling services (Lewis et al., 2017; Peretti et al., 2017). Furthermore, telecommuting can enhance privacy and confidentiality for clients. By engaging in counseling sessions from their own homes or private environments, clients may feel more at ease and secure in discussing sensitive topics. This can foster a deeper sense of trust and openness in the counseling relationship, ultimately facilitating the effectiveness of rehabilitation counseling interventions.

Telecommuting in rehabilitation counseling also presents challenges that need to be addressed. Technology-related issues, such as internet connectivity problems or disruptions in communication platforms, can impact the quality and continuity of counseling sessions. It is essential for rehabilitation counselors to ensure that they have access to reliable and secure communication tools to maintain the integrity and confidentiality of client information (Omboni et al., 2022). Telecommuting may require rehabilitation counselors to adapt their counseling approaches to the virtual setting. Professionals need to consider how to establish rapport, effectively engage clients, and address nonverbal cues in an online environment. Adequate training and ongoing professional development can equip rehabilitation counselors with the necessary skills and competencies to navigate these challenges and deliver high-quality counseling services through telecommuting (Mahmoud et al., 2022).

Telecommuting in rehabilitation counseling opens up new avenues to improve flexibility, accessibility, and privacy. Utilizing technology to connect with clients remotely, it allows counseling services to reach individuals who face barriers to in-person sessions, promoting greater inclusivity. However, rehabilitation counselors must be mindful of the unique challenges that come with virtual environments and equip themselves with the requisite resources and skills to deliver effective counseling in these settings (Elhadi et al., 2021). By proactively addressing these considerations, telecommuting can truly enhance the quality and availability of rehabilitation counseling services.

Electronic Submission of Documentation

Based on a report on comprehensive error rate testing in 2019, it was found that 59% of incorrect payments were attributed to inadequate documentation. This deficiency was mainly caused by cumbersome workflows and the sluggish, error-prone nature of paper or fax-based communication methods (U.S. Department of Health and Human Services, 2019). With the changing landscape of medical and health information and previous technology moving toward obscurity, rehabilitation providers are being encouraged to explore the use of cases involving electronic submission. This practice involving the use of digital platforms and technologies to submit, store, and manage client-related documents and information has become increasingly prevalent in the field of rehabilitation counseling, offering numerous benefits and streamlining administrative processes (Stanhope & Matthews, 2019). One significant advantage of electronic submission is the increased efficiency and convenience it brings to the documentation process. Instead of relying on physical paperwork, rehabilitation counselors can electronically transmit and receive important documents, such as intake forms, treatment plans, progress notes, and assessment reports. This eliminates the need for manual handling, printing, and mailing, saving time and reducing the risk of document loss or misplacement. Furthermore, electronic submission enhances data accuracy and organization (Wroten et al., 2020). With digital systems, rehabilitation counselors can input and store client information in structured formats, making it easier to retrieve and update as needed. This promotes consistency in record-keeping and ensures that vital information is readily accessible during counseling sessions or when collaborating with other professionals. Additionally, electronic submission enables secure data sharing and collaboration among multidisciplinary teams (Holden et al., 2018). Rehabilitation counselors can securely share client documentation with other healthcare providers, such as physicians, occupational therapists, or vocational specialists, facilitating coordinated care and a holistic approach to rehabilitation. The smooth sharing of information fosters a well-informed team and promotes collaboration toward shared objectives, ultimately elevating the standard of client care. Additionally, electronic submission facilitates adherence to privacy and confidentiality regulations, exemplified by **HIPAA** in the United States (HIPAA Journal, 2023). To safeguard sensitive client data from unauthorized access, digital platforms must continue employing robust security measures, such as **biometric security** (e.g., fingerprint and optical scan, facial recognition) and a **system audit trail** (International Biometric Group, n.d.). Rehabilitation counselors can further establish stringent data management protocols to ensure ongoing client confidentiality and privacy during the electronic submission process.

It is crucial for rehabilitation counselors to remain mindful of potential challenges and concerns related to electronic submission. These may include technological barriers, such as limited access to reliable internet connectivity or difficulties in adapting to new software systems. Additionally, counselors must ensure they have appropriate policies and procedures in place to safeguard client information and adhere to ethical guidelines regarding data privacy and security. Electronic submission may bring efficiency, accuracy, and enhanced collaboration to the documentation process, but privacy and confidentiality must remain at the forefront of rehabilitation caseload management practice (Grubbs et al., 2006). By embracing electronic submission practices, rehabilitation counselors can streamline administrative tasks, improve communication with interdisciplinary teams, and ultimately deliver more effective and client-centered rehabilitation counseling services, but professionals must continue to be focused on securing and protecting client data at all levels.

Mobile Applications

Mobile applications (mobile apps) have transformed the field of rehabilitation, offering a wide range of tools and resources to support clients in their journey. These apps, designed specifically for smartphones and tablets, provide convenient access to various interventions and support systems. One significant advantage of mobile apps in rehabilitation counseling is their ability to promote engagement and self-management. Apps such as *MyFitnessPal* allow clients to track their nutrition and exercise, set goals, and receive reminders, empowering them to take an active role in their care. Similarly, *Headspace* provides guided meditation and mindfulness exercises to help individuals manage stress and enhance emotional well-being.

Mobile apps also offer a wealth of educational materials and resources that complement rehabilitation sessions. They provide information on specific conditions, offer exercise demonstrations, coping strategies, mindfulness techniques, and psychoeducation materials. Clients can access these resources at any time, fostering continuous learning and skill development in all areas of life. Furthermore, mobile apps facilitate communication and remote support between rehabilitation counselors and clients. Apps like *BetterHelp* and *Talkspace* offer secure messaging and videoconferencing capabilities, enabling counselors to provide guidance, answer questions, and maintain regular contact outside of scheduled sessions. This real-time communication helps establish a sense of connectedness and support, particularly for individuals facing geographical or logistical barriers (Nelson et al., 2021). Additionally, mobile apps enhance data collection and tracking, enabling clients to input information on symptoms, activities, and progress. Apps like *PainScale* and *CareClinic* allow individuals to monitor their pain levels, log activities, and track medication usage. Rehabilitation counselors can access these data to assess progress, identify trends, and make informed treatment decisions, facilitating personalized care.

Examples of mobile apps commonly used in rehabilitation counseling and mentioned already here include MyFitnessPal for nutrition and exercise tracking, Headspace for mindfulness and stress reduction, BetterHelp and Talkspace for remote counseling, and PainScale and CareClinic for pain management and symptom tracking. However, it is crucial to assess the reliability, effectiveness, and privacy features of mobile apps before recommending these to clients. Rehabilitation counselors should ensure that the apps align with evidence-based practices, prioritize client confidentiality, and provide enhanced data security.

Mobile apps have revolutionized rehabilitation counseling by promoting engagement, providing educational resources, facilitating communication, and supporting data collection. By incorporating well-designed and evidence-based apps into their practice, rehabilitation counselors can harness the power of technology to enhance client outcomes and empower individuals in their rehabilitation journey. This section has merely skimmed the surface of the numerous mobile apps accessible to individuals undergoing rehabilitation. The aim is to initiate a conversation with clients about the potential for improving rehabilitation services through the wide range of available apps online. Clients should be motivated to choose apps that align with their specific needs and contribute to their success in the rehabilitation journey. By offering opportunities for autonomy, clients can progress toward self-sufficiency, while rehabilitation professionals prioritize client choice.

Text Messaging Alerts

Text messaging alerts have become a valuable tool in rehabilitation counseling, providing convenient and timely communication between counselors and clients. These alerts can serve various purposes, offering reminders, motivational messages, educational content, and support throughout the rehabilitation process. For example, a rehabilitation counseling program may utilize text messaging alerts to send regular reminders to clients about their scheduled therapy sessions, exercise routines, or medication schedules. These reminders can help individuals stay on track with their rehabilitation goals and ensure they do not miss important appointments or activities.

Text messaging alerts can also be used to send motivational messages and positive affirmations to clients. These messages can serve as encouraging reminders of their progress, boost motivation during challenging times, and reinforce the importance of sticking to their rehabilitation plan (Nesmith, 2019). In addition to reminders and motivational messages, text messaging alerts can be used to deliver educational content related to rehabilitation. Counselors can send information about specific conditions, treatment options, coping strategies, or self-care tips directly to clients' phones. This allows for ongoing education and empowers individuals to actively participate in their recovery process.

Text messaging alerts can provide an avenue for ongoing support and check-ins between counseling sessions. Counselors can send messages to inquire about clients' well-being, ask about their progress, or offer additional resources or guidance. This real-time communication helps maintain a connection and ensures that clients feel supported throughout their rehabilitation journey (Baker & Bickel, 2019; Hudenko et al., 2020). Examples of text messaging alert platforms commonly used in rehabilitation counseling include platforms like *Twilio, EZ Texting*, or *SimpleTexting*. These platforms allow counselors to schedule and send automated text messages to clients, ensuring that important information and support reach them in a timely manner. It is important to note that when using text messaging alerts in rehabilitation counseling, client consent and privacy considerations should be carefully addressed. Counselors should obtain informed consent from clients regarding the use of text messaging and ensure that their personal information is protected and handled securely (Barnett et al., 2013). Text messaging alerts have become a valuable communication tool in rehabilitation counseling, providing reminders, motivation, educational content, and ongoing support to clients. By leveraging this technology, counselors can enhance client engagement, adherence to treatment plans, and overall outcomes in the rehabilitation process.

Digital Interconnectivity of Agencies (Cloud-Based or Data Platforms)

The **digital interconnectivity** of agencies through cloud-based or data platforms has the potential to significantly impact rehabilitation counseling. These technological advancements offer numerous benefits and opportunities for collaboration, communication, and data sharing among different entities involved in the rehabilitation process. One key impact of digital interconnectivity is the seamless exchange of information and records between different agencies involved in rehabilitation (McLaney et al., 2022). Cloud-based platforms and data-sharing systems enable secure and efficient sharing of client information, treatment plans, progress reports, and other relevant documentation. This facilitates effective coordination and collaboration among professionals, including rehabilitation counselors, healthcare providers, therapists, and case managers. The availability of shared data platforms also promotes a holistic approach to rehabilitation (Tedersoo et al., 2021). It is well documented that the impact of different professionals working with a client can access and contribute to a centralized database, ensuring that everyone involved has access to the most up-to-date and comprehensive information (Baker & Bufka, 2011; Barnett et al., 2013; Goss et al., 2015). This shared knowledge enhances the coordination of care, improves communication, and reduces the risk of duplicated efforts or conflicting recommendations.

Digital interconnectivity enables real-time monitoring and tracking of client progress. Rehabilitation counselors can access data and analytics from various sources to assess the effectiveness of interventions, track outcomes, and make informed decisions about treatment adjustments. This data-driven approach enhances the ability to tailor counseling strategies to individual needs, identify trends, and evaluate the impact of interventions on clients' rehabilitation journeys. Additionally, digital interconnectivity supports interdisciplinary collaboration and access to a broader range of resources (Tedersoo et al., 2021). Through shared platforms, rehabilitation counselors can easily connect with professionals from other disciplines, such as medical practitioners, psychologists, social workers, and vocational specialists. This interdisciplinary collaboration fosters a comprehensive and integrated approach to rehabilitation, ensuring that clients receive holistic care addressing their physical, psychological, social, and vocational needs. However, it is crucial to address potential challenges and considerations when implementing digital interconnectivity in rehabilitation counseling. Privacy and data security are of paramount importance to protect client confidentiality and comply with relevant regulations. Adequate safeguards must be in place to ensure the secure storage and transmission of sensitive client information. Furthermore, as stated in previous sections in the chapter, training and education on the use of digital platforms and data-sharing systems are essential for rehabilitation professionals. Rehabilitation professionals need to be equipped with the necessary skills to effectively navigate and utilize these technologies to maximize their benefits in counseling practice.

The digital interconnectivity of agencies through cloud-based or data platforms holds great potential to positively impact rehabilitation counseling. It facilitates seamless information exchange, enhances collaboration, enables real-time monitoring of progress, and promotes interdisciplinary teamwork. By harnessing these technological advancements, rehabilitation counselors can provide more effective and coordinated care, leading to improved outcomes for their clients.

Artificial Intelligence and Machine Learning

The ongoing integration of **artificial intelligence (AI)** and **machine learning** technologies has the power to bring about profound changes in the world today. AI has become an integral part of doing work globally and is becoming more integrated into healthcare and monitoring (Gursoy et al., 2019; Steyvers & Kumar, 2023). These cutting-edge advancements present rehabilitation counselors with a range of innovative tools and capabilities that can greatly enhance the effectiveness, efficiency, and personalization of their interventions. By harnessing the potential of AI and machine learning, rehabilitation counselors can revolutionize their practice and deliver more impactful and tailored support to their clients.

AI and machine learning technologies have transformative impacts on rehabilitation counseling, particularly in the areas of data analysis, personalized treatment planning, and virtual support. With the ability to process extensive volumes of client diagnostic information, treatment records, and research data, these technologies excel at identifying patterns, trends, and correlations (National Center for Biotechnology Information, 2023). This data analysis empowers rehabilitation counselors with deeper insights into client needs, treatment outcomes, and the effectiveness of various interventions. Additionally, AI and machine learning contribute to the development of personalized treatment plans by leveraging algorithms and predictive modeling. By analyzing individual client characteristics, preferences, and responses to interventions, these technologies recommend tailored counseling approaches (Schwartz et al., 2021). This personalization enhances the precision and relevance of counseling strategies, resulting in improved outcomes for clients. Furthermore, AI-powered virtual assistants and chatbots play a vital role in providing continuous support and guidance to individuals during their rehabilitation journey (de Cock et al., 2020). These virtual agents offer a wealth of information, address common questions, deliver coping strategies, and provide motivational messages. By offering 24/7 accessibility, they enhance client engagement and self-management, while providing support to circumvent professional burnout (Anmella et al., 2023; Liu et al., 2022). Moreover, these virtual assistants serve as valuable resources between counseling sessions, delivering ongoing support and reinforcement to clients (Graham et al., 2019). Together, the data analysis capabilities, personalized treatment planning, and virtual support offered by AI and machine learning technologies advance the field of rehabilitation counseling, empowering counselors to deliver more effective and tailored interventions to their clients.

AI and machine learning technologies can also contribute to the development of innovative assessment tools. Through natural language processing and sentiment analysis, these technologies can analyze verbal and written client responses to identify emotions, cognitive patterns, and changes in mental health (Petersen et al., 2020). This information can aid in the evaluation of progress, treatment effectiveness, and the identification of potential areas requiring additional support. However, it is important to note that while AI and machine learning offer promising possibilities, they should not replace human interaction and counseling expertise. These technologies should be used as supportive tools, augmenting the role of rehabilitation counselors rather than replacing them. The human element of empathy, understanding, and therapeutic alliance remains crucial in the counseling process (Grodniewicz & Hohol, 2023; Lee et al., 2021). Ethical considerations also need to be addressed when utilizing AI and machine learning in rehabilitation counseling. Privacy, confidentiality, and data security must be prioritized to protect client information and maintain trust (Sedlakova & Trachsel, 2023). Transparent communication with clients about the use of these technologies and obtaining informed consent is essential.

Rehabilitation counseling stands on the brink of a transformative era, thanks to the remarkable potential of AI and machine learning. These cutting-edge technologies have the power to revolutionize the field by offering sophisticated data analysis, tailor-made interventions, virtual assistance, and groundbreaking assessment tools. Through careful and ethical integration, these advancements hold the promise of amplifying the impact and efficiency of counseling interventions. As a result, we can expect to witness improved outcomes for individual cases and caseloads, as well as the delivery of superior services within the rehabilitation community.

EMERGENCY PREPAREDNESS AND TECHNOLOGY UTILIZATION IN CASELOAD MANAGEMENT PRACTICE

The aftermath of a disaster can bring about severe and lasting consequences, both economically and environmentally. The level of assistance provided by federal and private sources may or may not align with the magnitude of damage caused by natural or human-made events. Communities, tribes, and states often face years of arduous rebuilding and recovery efforts following such disasters. The initiation of federal recovery aid hinges on the declaration process, a crucial step that sets these resources in motion (Congressional Research Service, 2019).

In 1979, the establishment of the **Federal Emergency Management Agency (FEMA)** marked a significant milestone in the institutionalization of emergency management. This federal entity emerged from the consolidation of five previously separate agencies, each responsible for different aspects of emergency response. Subsequently, numerous state and local organizations followed suit by incorporating the term "emergency management" into their names. This change in nomenclature reflects a shift in focus from preparing for specific or limited hazards to embracing a comprehensive all-hazards approach focusing on prevention, protection, mitigation, response, and recovery (Stienstra, 2021). This comprehensive approach recognizes and addresses potential threats to life and property stemming from environmental and technological hazards, as well as domestic and foreign attacks. Importantly, this shift in terminology does not imply a reduction in security measures; instead, it underscores the significance of maintaining responsive and adaptable emergency management capabilities to effectively handle any major emergency situation (Feng & Cui, 2021).

In the realm of case and caseload management practice, it is crucial to be prepared for emergency situations that may arise. Emergencies can range from natural disasters to unexpected events that disrupt normal operations. The integration of technology plays a vital role in enhancing emergency preparedness and response in caseload management practice. By leveraging a human–computer interactive approach, practitioners can effectively manage caseloads, ensure continuity of services, and respond promptly and efficiently in times of crisis (Carver & Turoff, 2007). In this section, we will explore the intersection of emergency preparedness and technology utilization in caseload management, highlighting the benefits, challenges, and best practices for utilizing technology to enhance emergency response capabilities.

Emergency Initiatives (Pandemic, Natural Disaster)

In the aftermath of World War II, emergency management primarily focused on preparedness, mainly in anticipation of enemy attacks. Over time, this approach expanded to include community preparedness for all types of disasters, requiring the identification of resources and expertise in advance and meticulous planning for their effective utilization during emergencies (Wagner, 2022). However, it is essential to recognize that preparedness is just one facet of comprehensive emergency management. In recent years, emergency management has undergone significant updates to address evolving challenges, including the emergence of pandemics and the increasing frequency and severity of natural disasters (Government Accountability Office, 2020). These updated initiatives acknowledge the ever-present threats posed by infectious diseases and the potential devastation caused by natural calamities. For instance, in response to the COVID-19 pandemic, emergency management strategies emerged that were geared towards mitigating the spread of the virus. This included implementing measures such as testing, contact tracing, and vaccination programs, while also ensuring sufficient healthcare resources and promoting public awareness and education (Li et al., 2022; O'Connell & O'Keffee, 2021) Furthermore, the management of natural disasters, such as hurricanes, wildfires, and floods, has become a critical aspect of emergency management. Initiatives now focus on proactive measures to mitigate the impact of these events, including effective early warning systems, evacuation plans, and the allocation of resources for rapid response and recovery.

In addition to the updated emergency initiatives of pandemic and natural disaster management, another crucial aspect that has gained prominence is how to manage electronic information in areas of case and caseload management. Caseload management refers to the effective coordination and allocation of resources to handle the increasing volume of cases and individuals affected during emergencies (Grubbs et al., 2006). During a pandemic such as the COVID-19 outbreak, case and caseload management became essential in ensuring that varying rehabilitation systems could adequately cope with the surge in clients. This involved strategies to optimize the allocation of rehabilitation personnel, equipment, and facilities, as well as implementing triage protocols to prioritize cases based on severity and urgency. In the realm of natural disasters, effective caseload management is crucial to efficiently meet the needs of those affected. When it comes to evacuation planning, it is essential to consider the unique requirements of individuals with diverse disabilities. This entails ensuring accessibility in evacuation shelters, providing mobility assistance, and guaranteeing reliable power sources to operate vital equipment like power wheelchairs and communication devices (Quaill et al., 2018). Furthermore, rehabilitation professionals play a pivotal role in collaborating with external support systems to facilitate the location, coordination, rescue, and evacuation efforts (Stough & Kelman, 2018). They work hand in hand with these supports to establish temporary shelters, coordinate medical assistance, and address the logistical challenges that arise from the large-scale displacement of individuals with disabilities.

Effective caseload management requires careful planning, collaboration between various stakeholders, and the utilization of technology and data analysis to streamline processes and optimize resource allocation (Grubbs et al., 2006; Rawlins-Williams & Oswald, 2021). Experienced case managers establish strong relationships with applicants from the beginning by listening, showing empathy, providing excellent customer service and support, and communicating program requirements. Consistency in all these areas is important, especially in times of disaster (Anderson, 2021; Bartsch et al., 2021). By proactively managing cases within rehabilitation caseloads, professionals can enhance their response capabilities, minimize bottlenecks, and ensure that those affected receive timely and appropriate assistance. Integrating caseload management into emergency management frameworks further strengthens the overall preparedness and response efforts, enabling a more efficient and coordinated approach to address the challenges posed by emergencies, pandemics, natural disasters, and other crises.

DESIGNING AND INCORPORATING THE EMERGENCY PLAN (MITIGATION, PREPAREDNESS, RESPONSE, RECOVERY)

As **emergency management** has evolved, a comprehensive approach has emerged, encompassing four distinct phases: *mitigation, preparedness, response,* and *recovery*. These phases are widely recognized and form the basis of dedicated courses and emergency preparedness training programs. **Figure 12.1** illustrates this framework, highlighting the interconnected nature of these phases in effective emergency management.

Rehabilitation counseling is a specialized field that focuses on helping individuals with disabilities overcome barriers and achieve their personal, social, and vocational goals. In the context of emergency management, rehabilitation counseling plays a crucial role in providing support and assistance to individuals with disabilities during and after disasters. It aims to provide support to individuals with physical, emotional, and psychological disabilities that they may facilitate their recovery and integration back into the community.

Phases of **emergency preparedness** must be explored in the context of rehabilitation caseload management for rehabilitation professionals to be successful in times of crisis. **Table 12.1** incorporates aspects of the phases of the emergency management process, with basic information surrounding each step of the phase related to the rehabilitation professional.

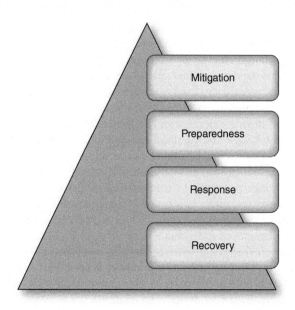

FIGURE 12.1 Phases of the emergency management process.

TABLE 12.1 EMERGENCY PREPAREDNESS AND THE
REHABILITATION COUNSELOR

Mitigation *Preventing future emergencies or minimizing their effects*	• This phase includes discussing with clients activities that prevent an emergency, reduce the likelihood of occurrence, or reduce the damaging effects of unavoidable hazards. • These preventative activities should be considered long before an emergency, and discussions should begin at initial application.
Preparedness *Preparing to handle an emergency*	• This phase includes developing plans along with clients for what to do, where to go, or who to call for help before an event occurs. • Discussion of the preparation of a disaster kit to include essential supplies, emergency telephone numbers, and other needs is essential.
Response *Responding safely to an emergency*	• A client's safety and well-being in an emergency depend on preparation and individual response to crisis. • Clients should be contacted individually to determine resources and services. • Ongoing conversations must occur to upgrade or downgrade provision and delivery of services.
Recovery *Recovering from an emergency*	• During the recovery period, rehabilitation counselors must first take care of themselves and then provide case management support to clients. • After an emergency (pandemic, natural disaster, etc.) and once the immediate danger is over, continued safety and well-being will depend on the rehabilitation counselor's ability to cope with rearranging their work environment to meet the needs of clients. • During recovery, the rehabilitation counselor should evaluate what has occurred in working with clients and how to adjust in the future.

Designing and Incorporating the Emergency Plan Related to Case and Caseload Management

When developing and integrating an emergency plan for caseload management in rehabilitation, several crucial factors need to be considered:

1. *Inclusive Needs Assessment*: Conducting a thorough assessment of the specific needs, abilities, and limitations of individuals with disabilities within the caseload. This assessment should consider factors such as communication requirements, mobility aids, assistive technology, and any other accommodations needed during emergencies.
2. *Personalized Emergency Plans*: Developing individualized emergency plans for each client, considering their unique circumstances, disabilities, and support requirements. These plans should outline specific actions to be taken during different types of emergencies and address factors such as evacuation routes, communication methods, and access to necessary support services.
3. *Collaboration With Stakeholders*: Collaborating with various stakeholders, including the clients themselves, their families, healthcare professionals, disability organizations, and relevant community agencies. This collaboration ensures that the emergency plan reflects the specific needs and preferences of the clients and that necessary resources and support systems are in place.
4. *Training and Education*: Providing training and education to clients, their families, and relevant caregivers on emergency preparedness, including specific instructions outlined in the emergency plan. This helps to enhance understanding of potential risks, response strategies, and available resources.
5. *Ongoing Support and Communication*: Establishing clear lines of communication with clients and their support networks to provide ongoing support and updates regarding emergency preparedness. This ensures that the emergency plan remains up-to-date, relevant, and effective in meeting the evolving needs of individuals with disabilities.
6. *Continuity of Care*: Incorporating mechanisms to ensure the continuity of rehabilitation services and support during and after emergencies. This may involve coordination with healthcare providers, therapists, and other professionals to maintain critical interventions and therapies even in challenging circumstances.

By designing and incorporating an emergency plan for case and caseload management in rehabilitation counseling, individuals with disabilities receive the necessary support and accommodations during emergencies, promoting their safety, well-being, and successful recovery.

SUMMARY

This chapter provides a forward-thinking perspective on the integration of technology in rehabilitation caseload management. It emphasizes numerous advantages, including improved accessibility, enhanced communication, and effective data management. The chapter highlights the significance of maintaining confidentiality and data privacy while utilizing technology platforms. Furthermore, the chapter explores strategies to bridge the digital divide, aiming to ensure equitable technology access for all individuals, considering socioeconomic factors and geographical disparities. It discusses the potential of emerging technologies, such as telehealth services, mobile applications, and AI, in revolutionizing caseload management practices. Moreover, the chapter delves into the possibilities of digital interconnectivity among rehabilitation agencies, promoting seamless information sharing and collaboration among different service providers. It envisions a future where technology plays a central role in streamlining processes and enhancing the quality of care for individuals with disabilities. Additionally, the chapter highlights the integration of technology in emergency preparedness, recognizing its vital role in disaster response and recovery. It explores the use of technology platforms for emergency communication, virtual assessments, and remote support, envisioning a future where technology enables efficient and effective assistance during crises.

Overall, this forward-thinking chapter encourages the exploration and adoption of innovative technologies in rehabilitation caseload management, paving the way for a future where technology empowers individuals, promotes inclusivity, and enhances the overall quality of care in the field.

QUESTIONS FOR DISCUSSION

1. In what ways can the integration of technology in rehabilitation caseload management improve accessibility for individuals with disabilities? How does technology enhance communication between rehabilitation professionals and their clients?

2. Discuss the importance of maintaining confidentiality and data privacy when utilizing technology platforms in rehabilitation caseload management. What strategies and safeguards can be implemented to ensure the security of client information?

3. What are some of the challenges faced in bridging the digital divide to promote equitable technology access among individuals with disabilities? How can these challenges be addressed, and what strategies can be employed to ensure equal opportunities for all?

4. Explore specific applications of technology, such as telehealth services, mobile applications, and AI, in rehabilitation caseload management. How can these technologies impact assessments, interventions, and progress monitoring? What are the potential benefits and limitations?

5. Discuss the concept of digital interconnectivity among rehabilitation agencies and its role in promoting collaboration and information sharing among service providers. How can technology facilitate effective communication and coordination among different stakeholders in the rehabilitation field?

6. Reflect on the integration of technology in emergency preparedness and its significance for individuals with disabilities. How can technology platforms be utilized to support disaster response and recovery efforts, ensuring the safety and well-being of individuals with disabilities during crises?

7. Gain insight into the use of technology platforms for emergency communication, virtual assessments, and remote support during crises. What are the potential advantages and challenges associated with these technologies in emergency situations?

8. Reflect on the future implications and possibilities of technology in rehabilitation caseload management, considering emerging technologies. How do you envision these technologies enhancing care quality and promoting inclusivity in the field? What are the potential ethical and practical considerations that need to be addressed?

PUTTING IT INTO PRACTICE

Ask yourself these questions to target issues or concerns with technology in the virtual world.

1. When it comes to issues of confidentiality, do you struggle to place complete trust in technology? What specific strategies and safeguards would you like to see implemented in your workplace or home office to address these concerns? Additionally, are there any existing practices that have proven effective or ineffective and should be either retained or eliminated?

2. How at ease are you with utilizing technology? This aspect can significantly influence your perspective on the world and your ability to promptly resume working with clients after a crisis or emergency. What resources do you require to enhance your proficiency in technology usage and to ensure your comfort in handling potential emergencies?

3. Regarding the impact on the specific clients served on your caseload, what does your professional emergency preparedness plan entail? Is there a combination of personal and organizational plans considered, or is the organizational plan the sole focus when dealing with clients during crisis or emergency preparedness?

CASE STUDY

John is a 35-year-old individual with a mobility impairment due to a spinal cord injury. He relies on a wheelchair for mobility and requires assistance with activities of daily living. John lives independently in an apartment building located in a coastal area prone to hurricanes. As a rehabilitation counselor, your role is to assist John in developing an emergency preparedness plan that addresses his specific needs and ensures his safety and well-being during hurricanes or other emergencies.

Case Study Questions

1. What are the key considerations in assessing John's needs and limitations as an individual with a mobility impairment in the context of emergency preparedness?

2. How can you collaborate with John to develop a personalized emergency plan that addresses his unique circumstances and ensures his safety during hurricanes or other emergencies?

3. What resources and support systems should be incorporated into John's emergency plan to assist him in evacuating the apartment building safely during a hurricane?

4. How can you involve John's support network, such as family members or friends, in the development and implementation of his emergency plan?

5. What strategies can you employ to ensure effective communication with John during emergencies, considering his mobility impairment and potential disruptions in traditional communication methods?

REFERENCES

Akhu-Zaheya, L., Al-Maaitah, R., & Bany Hani, S. (2018). Quality of nursing documentation: Paper-based health records versus electronic-based health records. *Journal of Clinical Nursing, 27*(3–4), 578–589. https://doi.org/10.1111/jocn.14097

Alkureishi, M. A., Choo, Z. Y., Rahman, A., Ho, K., Benning-Shorb, J., Lenti, G., Velázquez Sánchez, I., Zhu, M., Shah, S. D., & Lee, W. W. (2021). Digitally disconnected: Qualitative study of patient perspectives on the digital divide and potential solutions. *JMIR Human Factors, 8*(4), p. 1–20. https://doi.org/10.2196/33364

Allen, T. D., Golden, T. D., & Shockley, K. M. (2015). How effective is telecommuting? Assessing the status of our scientific findings. *Psychological Science in the Public Interest, 16*(2), 40–68. https://doi.org/10.1177/1529100615593273

Anderson, C. (2021). *5 best practices for case management after a disaster.* ICF. https://www.icf.com/insights/disaster-management/5-best-practices-case-management

Anmella, G., Sanabra, M., Primé-Tous, M., Segú, X., Cavero, M., Morilla, I., Grande, I., Ruiz, V., Mas, A., Martín-Villalba, I., Caballo, A., Esteva, J. P., Rodríguez-Rey, A., Piazza, F., Valdesoiro, F. J., Rodriguez-Torrella, C., Espinosa, M., Virgili, G., Sorroche, C., . . . Hidalgo-Mazzei, D. (2023). Vickybot, a chatbot for anxiety-depressive symptoms and work-related burnout in primary care and health care professionals: Development, feasibility, and potential effectiveness studies. *Journal of Medical Internet Research, 25*, e43293. https://doi.org/10.2196/43293

Ayanso, A., Cho, D. I., & Lertwachara, K. (2010). The digital divide: Global and regional ICT leaders and followers. *Information Technology for Development, 16*(4), 304–319. https://doi.org/10.1080/02681102.2010.504698

Baker, C., & Bickel, R. (2019). Reaching young people through texting-based crisis counseling. *Advances in Social Work, 20*(1), 1–14. https://doi.org/10.18060/21590

Baker, D. C., & Bufka, L. F. (2011). Preparing for the telehealth world: Navigating legal, regulatory, reimbursement, and ethical issues in an electronic age. *Professional Psychology: Research and Practice, 42*(6), 405–411. https://doi.org/10.1037/a0025037

Bani-Issa, W., Al Akour, I., Ibrahim, A., Al Marzouqi, A., Abbas, S., Hisham, F., & Griffiths, J. (2020). Privacy, confidentiality, security, and patient safety concerns about electronic health records. *International Nursing Review, 67*, 218–230. https://doi.org/10.1111/inr.12585

Bani-Issa, W., Al Yateem, N., Al Makhzoomy, I. K., & Ibrahim, A. (2016). Satisfaction of healthcare providers with electronic health records and perceived barriers to its implementation in the United Arab Emirates. *International Journal of Nursing Practice, 22*, 408–416. https://doi.org/10.1111/ijn.12450

Barnett, J. E., Wise, E. H., Johnson-Greene, D., & Bucky, S. F. (2013). Informed consent: Too much of a good thing or not enough? *Professional Psychology: Research and Practice, 44*(5), 309–316. http://dx.doi.org/10.1037/0735-7028.38.2.179

Bartsch, S., Weber, E., Buettgen, M., & Huber, A. (2021). Leadership matters in crisis induced digital transformation: How to lead service employees effectively during the COVID-19 pandemic. *Journal of Service Management, 32*(1), 71–85. https://doi.org/10.1108/JOSM-05-2020-0160

Baum, M., Danner-Schroeder, A., Mueller-Seitz, G., & Rabl, T. (2020). Organizational emergence – interdisciplinary perspectives against the backdrop of the digital transformation. *Management Revue, 31*(1), 31–54. https://doi.org/10.5771/0935-9915-2020-1-31

Benjamin, K., & Potts, H. W. W. (2018). Digital transformation in government: Lessons for digital health? *Digital Health, 4*(1). https://doi.org/10.1177/2055207618759168

Bramer, W. M., de Jonge, G. B., Rethlefsen, M. L., Mast, F., & Kleijnen, J. (2018). A systematic approach to searching: An efficient and complete method to develop literature searches. *Journal of the Medical Library Association, 106*(4), 531–541. https://doi.org/10.5195/jmla.2018.283

Campanella, P., Lovato, E., Marone, C., Fallacara, L., Mancuso, A., Ricciardi, W., & Specchia, M. L. (2015). The impact of electronic health records on healthcare quality: A systematic review and meta-analysis. *European Journal of Public Health, 26*(1), 60–64. https://doi.org/10.1093/eurpub/ckv122

Carver, L., & Turoff, M. (2007). Human-computer interaction: The human and computer as a team in emergency management information systems. *Communication of the ACM, 50*(3), 33–38. https://doi.org/10.1145/1226736.1226761

Cary, M. P., Jr., Spencer, M., Carroll, A., Hand, D. H., Amis, K., Karan, E., Cannon, R. F., Morgan, M. S., & Hoenig, H. M. (2016). Benefits and challenges of delivering tele-rehabilitation services to rural veterans. *Home Healthcare Now, 34*(8), 440–446. https://doi.org/10.1097/NHH.0000000000000441

Cheng, A. S. K., Ng, P. H. F., Sin, A. P. T., Lai, S. H. S., & Law, S. W. (2020). Smart work injury management (SWIM) system: Artificial intelligence in work disability management. *Journal of Occupational Rehabilitation, 30*(1), 354–361. https://doi.org/10.1007/s10926-020-09886-y

Cheng, L., Liu, F., & Yao, D. (2017). Enterprise data breach: Causes, challenges, prevention, and future directions. *WIREs Data Mining and Knowledge Discovery, 7*(5), 1–14. https://doi.org/10.1002/widm.1211

Commission on Rehabilitation Counselor Certification. (2023). *Code of Professional Ethics for Rehabilitation Counselors*. https://crccertification.com/wp-content/uploads/2023/04/2023-Code-of-Ethics.pdf

Congressional Research Service. (2019). *The Federal Emergency Management Agency (FEMA): Its history and selected legal issues* (Report No. R43784). https://crsreports.congress.gov/product/pdf/R/R43784

Cozzoli, N., Salvatore, F. P., Faccilongo, N., & Milone, M. (2022) How can big data analytics be used for healthcare organization management? Literary framework and future research from a systematic review. *BMC Health Services Research, 22*, 809. https://doi.org/10.1186/s12913-022-08167-z

Croker, A., Trede, F., & Higgs, J. (2012). Collaboration: What is it like? Phenomenological interpretation of the experience of collaborating within rehabilitation teams. *Journal of Interprofessional Care, 26*(1), 13–20. https://doi.org/10.3109/13561820.2011.623802

de Cock, C., Milne-Ives, M., van Velthoven, M. H., Alturkistani, A., Lam, C., & Meinert, E. (2020). Effectiveness of conversational agents (virtual Assistants) in health care: Protocol for a systematic review. *JMIR Research Protocols, 9*(3), e16934. https://doi.org/10.2196/16934

der Schaft, A., Lub, X., der Heijden, B., & Solinger, O. N. (2020). The influence of social interaction on the dynamics of employees' psychological contracting in digitally transforming organizations. *European Journal of Work and Organizational Psychology, 29*(2), 164–182. https://doi.org/10.1080/1359432X.2019.1656284

Devereaux, R. L., & Gottlieb, M. C. (2012). Record keeping in the cloud: Ethical considerations. *Professional Psychology: Research and Practice, 43*(6), 627–632. https://doi.org/10.1037/a0028268

Dinesen, B., Nonnecke, B., Lindeman, D., Toft, E., Kidholm, K., Jethwani, K., Young, H. M., Spindler, H., Oestergaard, C. U., Southard, J. A., Gutierrez, M., Anderson, N., Albert, N. M., Han, J. J., & Nesbitt, T. (2016). Personalized telehealth in the future: A global research agenda. *Journal of Medical Internet Research, 18*(3), e53. https://doi.org/10.2196/jmir.5257

Elhadi, M., Elhadi, A., Bouhuwaish, A., Bin Alshiteewi, F., Elmabrouk, A., Alsuyihili, A., Alhashimi, A., Khel, S., Elgherwi, A., Alsoufi, A., Albakoush, A., & Abdulmalik, A. (2021). Telemedicine awareness, knowledge, attitude, and skills of health care workers in a low-resource country during the COVID-19 pandemic: Cross-sectional study. *Journal of Medical Internet Research, 23*(2), e20812. https://doi.org/10.2196/20812

Elhai, J. D., Chai, S., Amialchuk, A., & Hall, B. J. (2017). Cross-cultural and gender associations with anxiety about electronic data hacking. *Computers in Human Behavior, 70*, 161–167. https://doi.org/10.1016/j.chb.2017.01.002

Elhai, J. D., & Frueh, B. C. (2016). Security of electronic mental health communication and record-keeping in the digital age. *Journal of Clinical Psychiatry, 77*(2), 262–268. https://doi.org/10.4088/JCP.14r09506

Elhai, J. D., & Hall, B. J. (2016). Anxiety about internet hacking: Results form a community sample. *Computers in Human Behavior, 54*, 180–185. https://doi.org/10.1016/j.chb.2015.07.057

Feng, Y., & Cui, S. (2021) A review of emergency response in disasters: Present and future perspectives. *Natural Hazards, 105*, 1109–1138. https://doi.org/10.1007/s11069-020-04297-x

Galetsi, P., Katsaliaki, K., & Kumar, S. (2019). Values, challenges, and future directions of big data analytics in healthcare: A systematic review. *Social Science & Medicine, 241*(5), 112533. https://doi.org/10.1016/j.socscimed.2019.112533

Goss, S., Anthony, K. K., & O'Hara, M. W. (2015). Technology-based mental health treatment and the impact on the therapeutic alliance. *Clinical Psychology: Science and Practice, 22*(1), 72–86. https://doi.org/10.1007/s11920-019-1055-7

Government Accountability Office. (2020). *National preparedness: Additional actions needed to address gaps in the nation's emergency management capabilities* (Publication No. GAO-20-297). https://www.gao.gov/products/gao-20-297

Graham, S., Depp, C., Lee, E. E., Nebeker, C., Tu, X., Kim, H. C., & Jeste, D. V. (2019). Artificial intelligence for mental health and mental illnesses: An overview. *Current Psychiatry Reports, 21*(11), 116. https://doi.org/10.1007/s11920-019-1094-0

Grisold, T., Kremser, W., Mendling, J., Recker, J., Brocke, J. V., & Wurm, B. (2023). Keeping pace with the digital age: Envisioning information systems research as a platform. *Journal of Information Technology, 38*(1), 60–66. https://doi.org/10.1177/02683962221130429

Grodniewicz, J. P., & Hohol, M. (2023). Therapeutic conversational artificial intelligence and the acquisition of self-understanding. *The American Journal of Bioethics, 23*(5), 59–61. https://doi.org/10.1080/15265161.2023.2191021

Grubbs, L. A., Cassell, J. L., & Mulkey, S. W. (2006). *Rehabilitation caseload management: Concepts and practice* (2nd ed.). Springer Publishing Company.

Gursoy, D., Chi, O. H., Lu, L., & Nunkoo, R. (2019). Consumers acceptance of artificially intelligent (AI) device use in service delivery. *International Journal of Information Management, 49*(1), 157–169. https://doi.org/10.1016/j.ijinfomgt.2019.03.008

Harvard Business Review. (2023). *Intelligent process automation can give your company a powerful competitive advantage.* https://hbr.org/sponsored/2022/01/intelligent-process-automation-can-give-your-company-a-powerful-competitive-advantage

Helsper, E. J., & Reisdorf, B. C. (2017). The emergence of a 'digital underclass' in Great Britain and Sweden: Changing reasons for digital exclusion. *New Media & Society, 19*(8), 1253–1270.

HIPAA Journal. (2023, May 1). *HIPAA explained – updated for 2023.* https://www.hipaajournal.com/hipaa-explained/

Holden, R. J., Binkheder, S., Patel, J., & Viernes, S. H. P. (2018). Best practices for health informatician involvement in interprofessional health care teams. *Applied Clinical Informatics, 9*(1), 141–148. https://doi.org/10.1055/s-0038-1626724

Hudenko, W. J., Dollard, N., & Levine, D. S. (2020). Text messaging: The next gen of therapy in mental health. *Psychiatric Services, 71*(8), 836–839. https://doi.org/10.1176/appi.ps.202000155

Hudson, C., Chouinard, M., Lambert, M., Dufour, I., & Krieg, C. (2016). Effectiveness of case management interventions for frequent users of healthcare services: A scoping review. *BMJ Open, 6*, 012353. https://doi.org/10.1136/bmjopen-2016-012353

International Biometric Group. (n.d.). *Biometric data safeguarding technologies analysis and best practices [PDF].* https://apps.dtic.mil/sti/pdfs/ADA555403.pdf

Jury, S. C., & Kornberg, A. J., (2016). Integrating telehealth in to 'business as usual': Is it really possible? *Journal of Telemedicine and Telecare, 22*(8), 499–503. https://doi.org/10.1177/1357633X16675802

Keshmiri, F., & Ghelmani, Y. (2023). The effect of continuing interprofessional education on improving learners' self-efficacy and attitude toward interprofessional learning and collaboration. *Journal of Interprofessional Care, 37*(3), 448–456. https://doi.org/10.1080/13561820.2022.2084053

Kisekka, V., & Giboney, J. S. (2018). The effectiveness of health care information technologies: Evaluation of trust, security beliefs, and privacy as determinants of health care outcomes. *Journal of Medical Internet Research, 20*(4), 1–11. https://doi.org/10.2196/jmir.96014.

Kraus, S., Durst, S., Ferreira, J. J., Veiga, P., Kailer, N., & Weinmann, A. (2022). Digital transformation in business and management research: An overview of the current status quo. *International Journal of Information Management, 63*(102446), 1–18. https://doi.org/10.1016/j.ijinfomgt.2021.102466

Kruse, C. S., Smith, B., Vanderlinden, H., & Nealand, A. (2017). Security techniques for the electronic health records. *Journal of Medical Systems, 41*, 127. https://doi.org/10.1007/s10916-017-0778-4

Kysely, A., Bishop, B., Kane, R., Cheng, M., De Palma, M., & Rooney, R. (2020). Expectations and experiences of couples receiving therapy through videoconferencing: A qualitative study. *Frontiers in Psychology, 10*, 2992. https://doi.org/10.3389/fpsyg.2019.02992

Larco, J. A., Fransoo, J. C., & Wiers, V. C. S. (2018). Scheduling the scheduling task: A time-management perspective on scheduling. *Cognition, Technology and Work, 20*(1), 1–10. https://doi.org/10.1007/s10111-017-0443-1

Lee, E. E., Torous, J., De Choudhury, M., Depp, C. A., Graham, S. A., Kim, H. C., Paulus, M. P., Krystal, J. H., & Jeste, D. V. (2021). Artificial intelligence for mental health care: Clinical applications, barriers, facilitators, and artificial wisdom. *Biological Psychiatry: Cognitive Neuroscience and Neuroimaging, 6*(9), 856–864. https://doi.org/10.1016/j.bpsc.2021.02.001

Lewis, A. N., Quamar, A. H., McKeon, A. B., Schein, M. L., Schein, R. M., & Hartman, L. M. (2017). Improving the evidence base of telerehabilitation: A future modality for delivering clinical services to people with disabilities. *Journal of Applied Rehabilitation Counseling, 48*(3), 31–36. https://doi.org/10.1891/0047-2220.48.3.29

Li, Y., Zhang, T., & Wang, Y. (2022). The effectiveness of COVID-19 testing and contact tracing in a metropolitan area of the United States. *Proceedings of the National Academy of Sciences of the United States of America, 119*(1), e2200652119. https://doi.org/10.1073/pnas.2200652119

Lilly, J. F., Verma, N., Jordan, S. G., Oldan, J. D., Fordham, L. A., Noone, P. G., & Beck Dallaghan, G. L. (2020). Medical student imaging case files in the cloud. *The Clinical Teacher, 17*(3), 275–279. https://doi.org/10.1111/tct.13059

Liu, H., Peng, H., Song, X., Xu, C., & Zhang, M. (2022). Using AI chatbots to provide self-help depression interventions for university students: A randomized trial of effectiveness. *Internet Interventions, 27*, 100495. https://doi.org/10.1016/j.invent.2022.100495

Lustgarten, S. D. (2015). Emerging ethical threats to client privacy in cloud communication and data storage. *Professional Psychology: Research and Practice, 46*(3), 154–160. https://doi.org/10.1037/pro0000018

Lustgarten, S. D., & Colbow, A. J. (2017). Ethical concerns for tele-mental health therapy amidst governmental surveillance. *American Psychologist, 72*(2), 159–170. https://doi.org/10.1037/a0040321

Lustgarten, S. D., & Elhai, J. D. (2017). Technology use in mental health practice and research: Legal and ethical risks. *Clinical Psychological Science and Practice, 25*(2), e12234. https://doi.org/10.1111/cpsp.12234

Mahmoud, K., Jaramillo, C., & Barteit, S. (2022). Telemedicine in low- and middle-income countries during the COVID-19 pandemic: A scoping review. *Frontiers in Public Health, 10*, 914423. https://doi.org/10.3389/fpubh.2022.914423

Mayo Clinic. (2015). *Telehealth: Technology meets health care.* https://www.mayoclinic.org/healthy-lifestyle/consumer-health/in-depth/telehealth/art-20044878

McKinsey & Company. (2020, April 27). *The consumer data opportunity and the privacy imperative.* https://www.mckinsey.com/capabilities/risk-and-resilience/our-insights/the-consumer-data-opportunity-and-the-privacy-imperative

McLaney, E., Morassaei, S., Hughes, L., Davies, R., Campbell, M., & Di Prospero, L. (2022). A framework for interprofessional team collaboration in a hospital setting: Advancing team competencies and behaviours. *Healthcare Management Forum, 35*(2), 112–117. https://doi.org/10.1177/08404704211063584

McLaughlin-Davis, M. (2018). The integrated case management program: Essential for today's case manager. *Professional Case Management, 23*(3), 147–149. https://doi.org/10.1097/NCM.0000000000000288

Meek, W. D. (2023). The flexible care model: Transformative practices for university counseling centers. *Journal of College Student Psychotherapy, 37*(1), 1–10, https://doi.org/10.1080/87568225.2021.1888365

Mihelj, S., Leguina, A., & Downey, J. (2019). Culture is digital: Cultural participation, diversity and the digital divide. *New Media & Society, 21*(7), 1465–1485. https://doi.org/10.1177/1461444818822816

Mtemeri, J., Madhovi, Y., Mutambara, J., & Maziti, E. (2022). Technology and counselling in Africa: Reflections from MSc counselling students at a selected university in Zimbabwe. *Counselling and Psychotherapy Research, 22*, 377–384. https://doi.org/10.1002/capr.12443

Munn, L., Hristova, T., & Magee, L. (2019). Clouded data: Privacy and the promise of encryption. *Big Data & Society, 6*(1). https://doi.org/10.1177/2053951719848781

National Center for Biotechnology Information. (2023). *Artificial intelligence for medical diagnostics—existing and future AI trends.* https://www.ncbi.nlm.nih.gov/pmc/articles/PMC9955430/

Nelson, E. L., Barnard, M., & Cain, S. (2021). Couples therapy delivered through videoconferencing in rural areas: A systematic review. *Frontiers in Psychology, 12.* https://doi.org/10.3389/fpsyg.2021.773030

Nesmith, A. (2019). Reaching young people through texting-based crisis counseling. *Advances in Social Work, 19*(1), 1–15. https://doi.org/10.18060/21590

O'Connell, J., & O'Keffee, D. T. (2021). Contact tracing for Covid-19—a digital inoculation against future pandemics? *New England Journal of Medicine, 385*(1), 484–487. https://doi.org/10.1056/NEJMp2102256

Omboni, S., Padwal, R. S., Alessa, T., Benczúr, B., Green, B. B., Hubbard, I., Kario, K., Khan, N. A., Konradi, A., Logan, A. G., Lu, Y., Mars, M., McManus, R. J., Melville, S., Neumann, C. L., Parati, G., Renna, N. F., Ryvlin, P., Saner, H., . . . Wang, J. (2022). The worldwide impact of telemedicine during COVID-19: Current evidence and recommendations for the future. *Connected Health, 1*, 7–35. https://doi.org/10.20517/ch.2021.03

Panelists. (2020). *Best practices for managing data privacy & responding to privacy breaches.* Security Intelligence. https://securityintelligence.com/posts/manage-data-privacy-breaches-response/

Pebdani, R. N., Zeidan, A. M., Fearn-Smith, E. M., & Matthews, L. R. (2022). Telehealth assessment in rehabilitation counseling during the COVID-19 pandemic. *Rehabilitation Counseling Bulletin.* https://doi.org/10.1177/00343552221115866

Penney, J. W. (2016). Chilling effects: Online surveillance and Wikipedia use. *Berkeley Technology Law Journal, 31*(1), 117. https://doi.org/10.15779/Z38SS13

Peretti, A., Amenta, F., Tayebati, S. K., Nittari, G., & Mahdi, S. S. (2017). Telerehabilitation: Review of the state-of-the-art and areas of application. *JMIR Rehabilitation and Assistive Technologies, 4.* https://doi.org/10.2196/rehab.7511

Petersen, C. L., Halter, R., Kotz, D., Loeb, L., Cook, S., Pidgeon, D., Christensen, B. C., & Batsis, J. A. (2020). Using natural language processing and sentiment analysis to augment traditional user-centered design: Development and usability study. *JMIR mHealth and uHealth, 8*(8), e16862. https://doi.org/10.2196/16862

Pyron, L., & Carter-Templeton, H. (2019). Improved patient flow and provider efficiency after the implementation of an electronic health record. *CIN: Computers, Informatics, Nursing, 37*(10), 513–521. https://doi.org/10.1097/CIN.0000000000000553

Quaill, J., Baker, R. N., & West, C. (2018). Experiences of individuals with physical disabilities in natural disasters: An integrative review. *Australian Journal of Emergency Management, 33*(3), 28–34. https://knowledge.aidr.org.au/resources/ajem-jul-2018-experiences-of-individuals-with-physical-disabilities-in-natural-disasters-an-integrative-review/

Rahnama, H., & Pentland, A. (2022). *Data management: The new rules of data privacy.* Harvard Business Review. https://hbr.org/2022/02/the-new-rules-of-data-privacy

Rawlins-Williams, L. A., & Oswald, G. R. (2021). Facilitating knowledge in rehabilitation counseling professionals on caseload management: A pre-test/post-test evaluation. *The Rehabilitation Professional, 29*(1), 5–12.

Rawlins-Williams, L. A., & Williams, T. (2021). The experiences of community college students impacted by COVID-19: Transitions from traditional didactic learning to online formats. *The Rehabilitation Professional, 29*(3), 185–198.

Schwartz, B., Cohen, Z. D., Rubel, J. A., Zimmermann, D., Wittmann, W. W., & Lutz, W. (2021). Personalized treatment selection in routine care: Integrating machine learning and statistical algorithms to recommend cognitive behavioral or psychodynamic therapy. *Psychotherapy Research, 31*(1), 33–51. https://doi.org/10.1080/10503307.2020.1769219

Sedlakova, J., & Trachsel, M. (2023) Conversational artificial intelligence in psychotherapy: A new therapeutic tool or agent? *The American Journal of Bioethics, 23*(5), 4–13, https://doi.org/10.1080/15265161.2022.2048739

Seh, A. H., Zarour, M., Alenezi, M., Sarkar, A. K., Agrawal, A., Kumar, R., & Khan, R. A. (2020). Healthcare data breaches: Insights and implications. *Healthcare (Basel, Switzerland), 8*(2), 133. https://doi.org/10.3390/healthcare8020133

Seshadri, D. R., Li, R. T., Voos, J. E., Rowbottom, J. R., Alfes, C. M., Zorman, C. A., & Drummond, C. K. (2019). Wearable sensors for monitoring the internal and external workload of the athlete. *NPJ Digital Medicine, 2*, 71. https://doi.org/10.1038/s41746-019-0149-2

Smith, E. M. (2021). Assistive technology research: Evidence for a complex and growing field. *Assistive Technology, 33*(4), 177. https://doi.org/10.1080/10400435.2021.1958650

Stanhope, V., & Matthews, E. B. (2019). Delivering person-centered care with an electronic health record. *BMC Medical Informatics and Decision Making, 19*, 168. https://doi.org/10.1186/s12911-019-0897-6

Steyvers, M., & Kumar, A. (2023). Three challenges for AI-assisted decision-making. *Perspectives on Psychological Science.* https://doi.org/10.1177/17456916231181102

Stiensra, L. R. (2021). *Strengthening National Preparedness* (Report No. IG10027). Congressional Research Service. https://crsreports.congress.gov/product/pdf/IG/IG10027

Stough, L. M., & Kelman, I. (2018). People with disabilities and disasters. In H. Rodríguez, W. Donner, & J. Trainor (Eds.), *Handbook of disaster research: Handbooks of sociology and social research.* Springer Publishing Company. https://doi.org/10.1007/978-3-319-63254-4_12

Stoumpos, A. I., Kitsios, F., & Talias, M. A. (2023). Digital transformation in healthcare: Technology acceptance and its applications. *International Journal of Environmental Research and Public Health, 20*(4), 3407. https://doi.org/10.3390/ijerph20043407

Tariq, R. A., & Hackert, P. B. (2023). Patient confidentiality. *In StatPearls.* StatPearls Publishing.

Tedersoo, L., Küngas, R., Oras, E., Köster, K., Eenmaa, H., Leijen, Ä., Pedaste, M., Raju, M., Astapova, A., Lukner, H., Kogermann, K., & Sepp, T. (2021). Data sharing practices and data availability upon request differ across scientific disciplines. *Scientific Data, 8*, 192. https://doi.org/10.1038/s41597-021-00981-0

Thomas, D. (2014). Factors that influence college completion intention of undergraduate students. *The Asia-Pacific Education Researcher, 23*(2), 225–235. https://doi.org/10.1007/s40299-013-0099-4

Tsai, C. H., Eghdam, A., Davoody, N., Wright, G., Flowerday, S., & Koch, S. (2020). Effects of electronic health record implementation and barriers to adoption and use: A scoping review and qualitative analysis of the content. *Life, 10*(12), 327. https://doi.org/10.3390/life10120327

United Nations. (2021, February 18). *Leveraging digital technologies for social inclusion.* Department of Economic and Social Affairs Social Inclusion. https://www.un.org/development/desa/dspd/2021/02/digital-technologies-for-social-inclusion/

Upadhyay, S., & Hu, H. (2022). A qualitative analysis of the impact of electronic health records (EHR) on healthcare quality and safety: Clinicians' lived experiences. *Health Services Insights*, 15. https://doi.org/10.1177/11786329211070722

U.S. Department of Health and Human Services. (2019). *2019 medicare fee-for-service supplemental improper payment data*. https://www.cms.gov/files/document/2019-medicare-fee-service-supplemental-improper-payment-data.pdf

Van Dijk, G. (2020). *The digital divide*. Wiley and Sons Publishers.

Vos, J. F. J., Boonstra, A., Kooistra, A., Seelen, M., & van Offenbeek, M. (2020). The influence of electronic health record use on collaboration among medical specialties. *BMC Health Services Research, 20*, 676. https://doi.org/10.1186/s12913-020-05542-6

Wagner, S. L. (2022). Information technology and operational issues for emergency preparedness and response. In J. M. Kiel, G. R. Kim, & M. J. Ball (Eds.), *Healthcare information management systems: Case, strategies and solutions*. Springer Publishing Company. https://doi.org/10.1007/978-3-031-07912-2_11

Weiss, D., Rydland, H. T., Øversveen, E., Jensen, M. R., Solhaug, S., & Krokstad, S. (2018). Innovative technologies and social inequalities in health: A scoping review of the literature. *PLoS One, 13*(4), e0195447. https://doi.org/10.1371/journal.pone.0195447

Wroten, C., Zapf, S., & Hudgins, E. (2020). Effectiveness of electronic documentation: A case report. *The Open Journal of Occupational Therapy, 8*(3), 1–10. https://doi.org/10.15453/2168-6408.1722

Yadav, M. S., & Pavlou, P. A. (2014). Marketing in computer-mediated environments: Research synthesis and new directions. *Journal of Marketing, 78*(1), 20–40. https://doi.org/10.1509/jm.12.0020

CHAPTER 13

Rehabilitation Caseload Management Competency Framework

LEARNING OBJECTIVES

By the end of this chapter, learners will be able to:

- Understand the core competencies outlined in the WHO Competency Framework for effective rehabilitation practice.
- Identify the unique challenges associated with caseload management in rehabilitation and the need for a focused approach.
- Explore the integration of the WHO Competency Framework with Rehabilitation Caseload Management to establish an effective practice model.
- Examine the application of the assessment domain in prioritizing clients and allocating resources within a rehabilitation caseload.
- Discuss how the planning and implementation domain can guide the development of individualized care plans within the constraints of caseload management.
- Investigate the role of the evaluation and outcome measurement domain in monitoring progress and adjusting interventions in the context of caseload management.
- Explore the significance of teamwork and collaboration in efficient resource allocation and interdisciplinary care delivery within a rehabilitation caseload.
- Understand the importance of professionalism in caseload management, including ethical conduct, confidentiality, and continuous professional development.
- Highlight the role of advocacy and leadership in promoting inclusive services and advocating for the rights and needs of individuals with disabilities within a rehabilitation caseload.
- Gain practical strategies and insights for integrating the WHO Competency Framework with Rehabilitation Caseload Management to enhance resource allocation, individualized rehabilitation services, and quality improvement in rehabilitation practice.

INTRODUCTION

Rehabilitation plays a vital role in optimizing functioning and reducing disability in individuals with health conditions (Mills et al., 2017). To ensure the delivery of high-quality rehabilitation services, the **World Health Organization (WHO)** developed the **Rehabilitation Competency Framework (RCF)** (WHO, 2020, 2021a, 2021b). This comprehensive framework outlines the core competencies necessary for effective rehabilitation practice and serves as a guideline for the development of rehabilitation professionals, education programs, and policies. However, the management of caseloads poses unique challenges in the field of rehabilitation, requiring a focused approach to ensure efficient resource allocation and individualized planning. Therefore, this chapter aims to explore the integration of the WHO Competency Framework with rehabilitation caseload management, establishing a new model that optimizes the allocation and management of clients within a rehabilitation professional's workload (WHO, 2016).

The WHO Competency Framework encompasses six core competency domains: *assessment, planning and implementation, evaluation and outcome measurement, teamwork and collaboration, professionalism, and advocacy and leadership*. These domains provide a comprehensive guide for effective rehabilitation practice (WHO, 2022). However, the framework does not specifically address the intricacies of caseload management, which require professionals to balance the needs of multiple clients within limited resources and time constraints (Cassell & Mulkey 1985; Grubbs et al., 2006). By overlaying the WHO Competency Framework with rehabilitation caseload management, professionals can establish a new model that bridges the gap between competency-based practice and efficient caseload management. This integration allows rehabilitation professionals to align their workload management practices with the core competencies required for effective rehabilitation care.

Throughout this chapter, we will delve into each competency domain of the WHO Competency Framework and explore how it can be applied to caseload management. We will examine how the assessment domain can inform the prioritization of clients, the planning and implementation domain can guide the development of individualized care plans, and the evaluation and outcome measurement domain can support monitoring and adjustment of interventions (WHO, 2020). Additionally, we will explore the significance of teamwork and collaboration, professionalism, advocacy, and leadership in the context of caseload management, highlighting the promotion of efficient resource allocation, ethical conduct, and inclusive rehabilitation services.

By developing a new model that integrates the WHO Competency Framework with rehabilitation caseload management, professionals can ensure that their workload management practices align with evidence-based, person-centered practice. This integration promotes effective resource allocation, individualized rehabilitation plans, and continuous quality improvement within the context of a rehabilitation caseload. Ultimately, the aim is to enhance the well-being and functional independence of individuals with disabilities receiving rehabilitation services while maintaining a sustainable and efficient practice environment.

In the forthcoming sections, this chapter will thoroughly examine each competency domain outlined in the WHO Competency Framework and its direct relevance to rehabilitation caseload management. It will offer valuable insights and practical strategies aimed at assisting rehabilitation professionals in optimizing their caseload management practices within the presented integrated framework. By merging these two components, professionals can enhance their efficiency and effectiveness in providing comprehensive rehabilitation services while efficiently managing their workload (Cassell & Mulkey, 2004; Grubbs et al., 2006; Rawlins-Williams & Oswald, 2021).

WORLD HEALTH ORGANIZATION AND GENERAL COMPETENCY FRAMEWORK

The WHO is a specialized agency of the United Nations responsible for international public health. It plays a crucial role in addressing global health issues, setting health standards, providing guidance and support to member countries, and promoting health and well-being worldwide (WHO, n.d.). The WHO recognizes the importance of developing competent and skilled health professionals to deliver quality healthcare services.

In line with this objective, the WHO has developed the **General Competency Framework (GCF) for Health Workers** to guide the education, training, and development of health professionals across various disciplines. The GCF encompasses a set of core competencies that are essential for health workers to effectively meet the needs of individuals, families, and communities. These competencies reflect the knowledge, skills, attitudes, and behaviors required for delivering patient-centered care, promoting health, preventing diseases, and addressing health inequalities. The GCF is designed to be flexible and adaptable to different health systems, contexts, and professional roles. It can be customized to specific healthcare settings, professions, and levels of practice (WHO, 2022). The framework provides a foundation for curriculum development, competency-based education, workforce planning, and continuing professional development.

The core competencies included in the GCF cover a wide range of areas and are noted in **Figure 13.1**. These areas include:

1. *Person-Centered Care*: Focusing on meeting the unique needs and preferences of individuals, respecting their autonomy and rights, and fostering a collaborative and trusting relationship between the health worker and the patient.

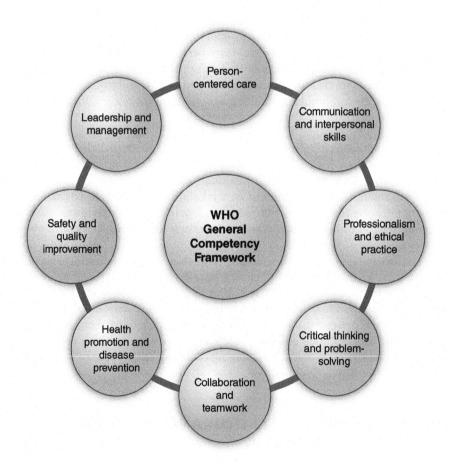

FIGURE 13.1 The World Health Organization General Competency Framework.

2. *Communication and Interpersonal Skills*: Emphasizing effective communication, active listening, empathy, cultural sensitivity, and the ability to convey information clearly and appropriately.
3. *Professionalism and Ethical Practice*: Highlighting the importance of ethical conduct, integrity, confidentiality, respect for diversity, commitment to continuous learning, and adherence to professional standards and codes of conduct.
4. *Critical Thinking and Problem-Solving*: Developing the ability to think critically, analyze complex situations, make evidence-based decisions, and solve problems creatively and effectively.
5. *Collaboration and Teamwork*: Promoting effective teamwork, interdisciplinary collaboration, coordination, and communication among healthcare professionals to ensure comprehensive and coordinated care.
6. *Health Promotion and Disease Prevention*: Focusing on promoting health, preventing diseases, and encouraging healthy lifestyles through education, counseling, and the implementation of evidence-based strategies.
7. *Safety and Quality Improvement*: Emphasizing the provision of safe and high-quality care, understanding and implementing patient safety practices, and engaging in continuous quality improvement.
8. *Leadership and Management*: Developing leadership skills, the ability to work effectively in teams, manage resources, and contribute to the planning, organization, and evaluation of healthcare services.

The GCF provides a valuable guide for the education, training, and development of health professionals worldwide. By ensuring that health workers possess the necessary competencies, the framework aims to improve the quality, effectiveness, and equity of healthcare services and ultimately contribute to better health outcomes for individuals and populations (Connor et al., 2023; Jagals & Ebi, 2021).

THE WHO REHABILITATION COMPETENCY FRAMEWORK

The WHO is a global organization dedicated to addressing health challenges worldwide and providing leadership in areas such as public health, health policy, and healthcare system development. Recognizing the crucial role of rehabilitation in promoting health, function, and well-being for individuals with disabilities and other health conditions, the WHO has developed the **RCF**. The creation of this framework was a direct response to the imperative of establishing a universally applicable approach in addressing various needs.

On a global scale, the rehabilitation workforce faces a shortage of resources and lacks the necessary competence, knowledge, skills, and abilities to effectively meet the diverse needs of individuals with disabilities (Jesus et al., 2017). As the demand for rehabilitation services continues to soar, the RCF assumes a prominent role, serving as a critical tool in equipping rehabilitation professionals with the indispensable competencies required to provide exceptional services that encompass the entire range of rehabilitation needs.

The WHO RCF is an essential tool designed to communicate the expected performance standards for rehabilitation professionals across different disciplines, specializations, and healthcare settings. It serves as a guide for ensuring the delivery of high-quality rehabilitation services by establishing clear expectations and benchmarks for the workforce. Developed as a response to workforce challenges, the RCF is a valuable resource for stakeholders worldwide. It supports professionals, organizations, and policy makers in effectively addressing the unique demands and complexities of the rehabilitation field (Fernandes et al., 2022; Jesus et al., 2017). The framework's applicability extends to all rehabilitation disciplines, specializations, and settings, ensuring its relevance and usefulness across the spectrum of rehabilitation practice. By utilizing the WHO RCF, stakeholders can enhance the capacity and capability of the rehabilitation workforce, promoting consistent and standardized performance, ultimately, fostering the provision of quality rehabilitation services that contribute to improved health outcomes and enhanced quality of life for individuals with disabilities and other health conditions.

The WHO RCF comprises various interconnected components that focus on core values and beliefs, competencies and behaviors, activities and tasks, and knowledge and skills. Apart from core values and beliefs, these components are categorized into five thematic domains: Practice (P), Professionalism (PM), Learning and Development (LD), Management and Leadership (ML), and Research (R). Each domain encompasses core values and beliefs, competencies and behaviors, activities and tasks, and knowledge and skills (WHO, 2020).

The WHO (2020, 2021a, 2021b) RCF functions as an organizational framework, offering a conceptual structure and shared terminology (**Figure 13.2**). It can be customized and applied to specific situations and objectives. Additionally, the RCF provides a comprehensive framework that enables organizations, institutions, and services to create competency frameworks that cater to their unique requirements while aligning with the broader rehabilitation community. By leveraging this framework, stakeholders can establish a unified and standardized approach to evaluating and enhancing competencies in the field of rehabilitation. Further, it promotes consistency, collaboration, and a mutual comprehension of the knowledge, skills, and values essential for effective rehabilitation practice across various settings and professional roles.

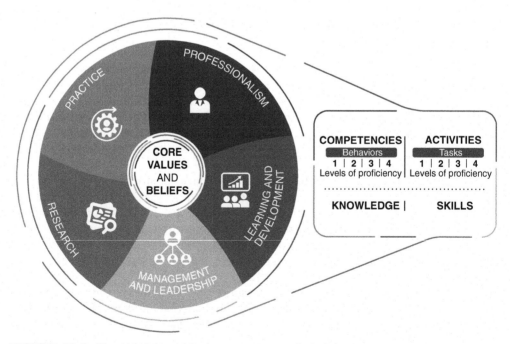

FIGURE 13.2 The World Health Organization Rehabilitation Competency Framework.

THE REHABILITATION CASELOAD MANAGEMENT COMPETENCY FRAMEWORK: CONCEPTS AND PRACTICE

Core Values and Beliefs

This section reflects on the **core values** and **beliefs** within the Rehabilitation Caseload Management Competency Framework (CLM-CF). The Rehabilitation CLM-CF serves as a guiding compass for professionals in the field of rehabilitation. It is a comprehensive framework that has been adapted from the WHO GCF and RCF, incorporating the Rehabilitation Counseling Competency Framework (RC-CF) developed by Rawlins-Williams (2023). This integration ensures that the CLM-CF encompasses the essential competencies required for effective caseload management within the rehabilitation counseling context. By drawing from these established frameworks, the CLM-CF provides a solid foundation for professionals to deliver person-centered and high-quality caseload management services. This adapted framework aligns with the specific focus of caseload management in professional practice. These core values and beliefs represent the fundamental principles and convictions that form the bedrock of rehabilitation professionals' work and shape their interactions with clients (Peterson, 2020). By embracing these values and beliefs, rehabilitation professionals can establish a robust foundation for delivering person-centered, ethical, and effective caseload management services.

The **core values and beliefs** presented in this section epitomize the foundational principles that form the basis of rehabilitation professionals' practice. These values encompass a historically steadfast dedication to respect, empowerment, advocacy, collaboration, and ethical conduct (Leahy et al., 2009; Matthews et al., 2015: Scully et al., 1999; Thielsen & Leahy, 2001). Each of these serve as a testament to rehabilitation professionals' unwavering commitment to upholding the well-being and dignity of their clients, as well as their determination to champion equal access, foster independence, and elevate the overall quality of life for individuals with disabilities or other health conditions. By internalizing these core values and beliefs, rehabilitation professionals create a supportive and inclusive environment where clients feel valued, heard, and empowered. These values guide professionals in developing collaborative partnerships, advocating for clients' rights, and delivering services that are responsive to their unique needs and aspirations.

The inclusion of these core values and beliefs within the CLM-CF underscores the significance of their role in caseload management within the field of rehabilitation. By adhering to these principles, professionals establish a solid framework for their practice, fostering meaningful connections with clients and inspiring confidence in their ability to effectively manage caseloads. Embracing the core values and beliefs outlined in the CLM-CF enables rehabilitation professionals to move beyond mere technical competence, infusing their work with purpose and meaning. This commitment to ethical, person-centered care ensures that caseload management services are delivered with integrity, professionalism, and compassion, ultimately making a positive and lasting impact on the lives of individuals with disabilities or other health conditions (Grubbs et al., 2006).

CORE VALUES

The **core values** of a rehabilitation counselor encompass a set of guiding principles that inform their professional practice and interactions with clients. These core values are reflected in the fundamental beliefs and ideals that underpin the Rehabilitation CLM-CF. The core values of rehabilitation counseling reflective in this framework include:

1. *Respect:* Rehabilitation counselors value and respect the dignity, autonomy, and worth of every individual they serve. They recognize the uniqueness of each client and approach their work with a nonjudgmental and accepting attitude.

2. *Empowerment:* Rehabilitation counselors believe in the inherent strengths and abilities of individuals with disabilities or other health conditions. They strive to empower their clients by providing support, resources, and opportunities that promote self-determination and personal growth.

3. *Client-Centered Approach:* Rehabilitation counselors prioritize the needs, preferences, and goals of their clients. They actively involve clients in the decision-making process and tailor their interventions to align with each client's unique circumstances and aspirations.

4. *Advocacy:* Rehabilitation counselors are advocates for their clients, working to promote their rights, access to services, and equal opportunities. They strive to eliminate barriers and create a more inclusive society that recognizes and values the potential of individuals with disabilities.

5. *Collaboration:* Rehabilitation counselors believe in the power of collaboration and teamwork. They actively engage with clients, families, and other professionals to foster interdisciplinary cooperation and holistic support for clients' well-being.

6. *Ethical Practice:* Rehabilitation counselors adhere to a professional code of ethics, maintaining the highest standards of integrity, confidentiality, and ethical conduct. They prioritize the well-being and best interests of their clients and engage in ongoing professional development to enhance their competence and effectiveness.

These core values guide the actions, decisions, and relationships of rehabilitation counselors, ensuring that their practice is grounded in principles of respect, empowerment, client-centeredness, advocacy, collaboration, and ethical behavior. By upholding these values, rehabilitation counselors strive to make a positive difference in the lives of individuals with disabilities, supporting their journey toward independence, fulfillment, and improved quality of life.

CORE BELIEFS

The **core beliefs** of a rehabilitation counselor are the foundational principles and convictions that shape their professional identity and guide their work with clients. These beliefs reflect the counselor's understanding and perspective on the rehabilitation process and the potential for growth and change in individuals with disabilities or other health conditions. The core beliefs of a rehabilitation counselor reflected in the Rehabilitation CLM-CF include:

1. *Growth and Potential:* Rehabilitation counselors believe that individuals with disabilities have the capacity for growth, development, and achieving their full potential. They view disability as a part of a person's identity but not a limitation to their abilities or aspirations.

2. *Self-Determination:* Rehabilitation counselors believe in the importance of self-determination, autonomy, and personal choice for individuals with disabilities. They respect and support their clients' right to make decisions about their own lives and encourage their active involvement in the rehabilitation process.

3. *Hope and Resilience:* Rehabilitation counselors maintain a belief in the power of hope and resilience. They recognize the ability of individuals to overcome challenges, adapt to change, and find meaning and purpose in their lives despite the impact of disability.

4. *Equality and Social Justice:* Rehabilitation counselors advocate for equality, social justice, and equal access to opportunities for individuals with disabilities. They work toward eliminating discrimination, prejudice, and barriers that hinder full participation and inclusion in society.

5. *Strengths-Based Approach*: Rehabilitation counselors focus on identifying and leveraging their clients' strengths, resources, and abilities rather than solely focusing on limitations or deficits. They promote a positive and empowering perspective that emphasizes what clients can do rather than what they cannot.

6. *Lifelong Learning and Growth*: Rehabilitation counselors value continuous professional development, ongoing learning, and staying current with research and best practices. They believe in the importance of evolving and adapting their skills and knowledge to better serve their clients.

These core beliefs provide a guiding framework for rehabilitation counselors, shaping their approach to client interactions, rehabilitation planning, advocacy efforts, and professional development. By embracing these beliefs, rehabilitation counselors work toward facilitating positive change, promoting independence, and enhancing the overall well-being and quality of life for individuals with disabilities or other health conditions.

The Rehabilitation Caseload Management Competency Framework

The **Rehabilitation CLM-CF** is specifically tailored to meet the distinctive competencies required for effective rehabilitation caseload management (see **Figure 13.3**). It draws upon the core competencies outlined in both the WHO GCF and the RCF to create a comprehensive framework that enhances caseload management practice. By integrating these models, the CLM-CF establishes the essential requirements for successful caseload management in rehabilitation across various settings and professional roles. This cohesive approach empowers professionals to deliver impactful caseload management practices while addressing the unique challenges and needs of individuals with disabilities throughout the rehabilitation process.

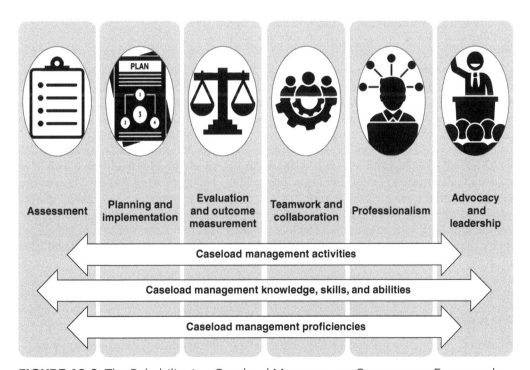

FIGURE 13.3 The Rehabilitation Caseload Management Competency Framework.

The CLM-CF comprises six distinct competency domains that emphasize specific competencies and activities:

1. *Assessment*: This domain focuses on the ability to conduct comprehensive assessments of individuals' functional abilities, needs, and goals. It includes skills related to gathering and analyzing relevant information, using appropriate assessment tools, and interpreting assessment results.
2. *Planning and Implementation*: This domain emphasizes the development and implementation of individualized rehabilitation plans based on assessment findings and in collaboration with the individual and their support network. It includes skills related to goal-setting, intervention planning, and selecting and applying evidence-based interventions.
3. *Evaluation and Outcome Measurement*: This domain involves the ongoing evaluation of individuals' progress and the measurement of outcomes related to rehabilitation interventions. It includes skills related to the selection and use of outcome measures, data collection and analysis, and using evaluation results to inform decision-making and adjust interventions.
4. *Teamwork and Collaboration*: This domain highlights the importance of effective teamwork and collaboration among rehabilitation professionals, individuals receiving rehabilitation services, and their families or caregivers. It includes skills related to communication, interdisciplinary collaboration, shared decision-making, and coordination of services.
5. *Professionalism*: This domain focuses on professional values, ethics, and behaviors that are integral to rehabilitation practice. It includes skills related to ethical decision-making, maintaining confidentiality, engaging in reflective practice, and continuous professional development.
6. *Advocacy and Leadership*: This domain emphasizes the role of rehabilitation professionals in advocating for the rights and needs of individuals receiving rehabilitation services and in providing leadership within their professional practice. It includes skills related to advocating for inclusive services, influencing policy development, and assuming leadership roles within interdisciplinary teams.

The Rehabilitation CLM-CF serves as a cornerstone for the education, training, and growth of rehabilitation professionals in the area of caseload management. It provides guidance for the development of curricula, assessment methods, and competency-based education approaches within rehabilitation programs. Furthermore, the CLM-CF acts as a valuable resource for professional associations, policy makers, and healthcare organizations in promoting exceptional rehabilitation services and supporting the ongoing professional development of rehabilitation professionals. By adopting and implementing the CLM-CF, rehabilitation educational systems, organizations, and agencies can ensure that professionals possess the requisite knowledge, skills, and attitudes to deliver effective and person-centered services. This, in turn, leads to improved outcomes and enhanced quality of life for individuals with disabilities and other health conditions. Further, by incorporating the CLM-CF, rehabilitation professionals can ensure that their workload is managed in a manner that aligns with the core competencies required for effective rehabilitation practice. This integration promotes efficient resource allocation, individualized planning, and continuous quality improvement within the context of a rehabilitation caseload.

Activities

Activities are fundamental in the Rehabilitation CLM-CF, acting as the cornerstone of effective caseload management in the field of rehabilitation. Within the CLM-CF, a comprehensive range of activities is incorporated to provide guidance for rehabilitation professionals in their daily practice, ensuring the provision of high-quality and person-centered services. These activities cover a broad spectrum of responsibilities that address diverse aspects of caseload management across various settings and professional roles within the CLM-CF. They serve as crucial tasks that rehabilitation professionals undertake, providing them with a framework for effective caseload management practice.

By integrating the activities outlined in the CLM-CF into their practice, rehabilitation professionals can establish a standardized and comprehensive approach to caseload management. This framework fosters consistency, collaboration, and a shared understanding of the activities necessary for effective rehabilitation practice. Furthermore, the CLM-CF emphasizes the acquisition of specific skills related to these activities, such as risk management, quality improvement, and navigating caseload management transitions. Developing these skills enables professionals to manage their caseloads effectively and efficiently, ensuring the optimal allocation of time and resources for providing client-centered services.

Next, you will find further illustrations of activities linked to each category within the framework:

Category 1: Assessment
- Conducting comprehensive assessments of clients' functional abilities, impairments, and rehabilitation needs.
- Evaluating the effectiveness of interventions and adjusting treatment plans accordingly.

Category 2: Planning and Implementation
- Managing and organizing a caseload of clients, including prioritizing client needs, scheduling appointments, and allocating resources effectively.
- Coordinating and integrating care plans to ensure holistic and seamless rehabilitation services.

Category 3: Evaluation and Outcome Measurements
- Monitoring and evaluating outcomes to measure the impact of interventions and identify areas for improvement.
- Participating in quality improvement initiatives to enhance the effectiveness and efficiency of rehabilitation services.

Category 4: Teamwork and Collaboration
- Facilitating effective communication and coordination among interdisciplinary team members, clients, and their families.
- Collaborating with outside providers to develop and implement comprehensive rehabilitation plans for clients.

Category 5: Professionalism
- Engaging in continuous professional development to enhance knowledge and skills in rehabilitation counseling and caseload management.
- Adhering to ethical standards, promoting client autonomy, and advocating for the rights and well-being of clients.

Category 6: Advocacy and Leadership
- Advocating for the needs and rights of clients within the rehabilitation system.
- Taking on leadership roles in promoting high-quality rehabilitation services and advocating for policy changes to improve outcomes for individuals with disabilities.

Ultimately, by embracing the activities outlined in the CLM-CF, professionals can enhance their ability to provide effective and person-centered care, leading to improved outcomes and quality of life for individuals with disabilities and other health conditions.

Knowledge, Skills, and Abilities

The Rehabilitation CLM-CF recognizes the critical importance of **knowledge, skills, and abilities** in ensuring effective caseload management. Within the CLM-CF, these competencies are organized into distinct categories, each representing crucial areas of expertise that rehabilitation professionals must possess. This framework emphasizes the significance of acquiring and applying knowledge relevant to caseload management, cultivating essential skills to execute tasks effectively, and developing the necessary abilities to navigate various challenges in rehabilitation practice. By focusing on these foundational components within each category, the CLM-CF provides a comprehensive framework for enhancing the competence and proficiency of rehabilitation professionals in managing caseloads efficiently and delivering high-quality services to individuals with disabilities:

Category 1: Assessment
- *Knowledge*: Understanding of assessment tools, diagnostic processes, and relevant evaluation methods.
- *Skills*: Proficiency in conducting comprehensive assessments and interpreting assessment results.
- *Abilities*: Capability to gather and analyze client information, synthesize assessment findings, and formulate appropriate treatment plans.

Category 2: Planning and Implementation
- *Knowledge*: Familiarity with evidence-based practices, treatment modalities, and individualized rehabilitation planning.
- *Skills:* Competence in developing client-centered rehabilitation plans, setting realistic goals, and implementing effective interventions.
- *Abilities*: Proficiency in adapting rehabilitation plans, managing resources efficiently, and ensuring successful implementation of interventions.

Category 3: Evaluation and Outcome Measurements
- *Knowledge*: Knowledge of outcome measurement tools, data analysis, and interpretation.
- *Skills*: Proficiency in measuring and documenting client progress, evaluating rehabilitation outcomes, and identifying areas for improvement.
- *Abilities*: Ability to analyze and interpret outcome data, modify treatment plans accordingly, and contribute to continuous quality improvement.

Category 4: Teamwork and Collaboration
- *Knowledge*: Understanding of interdisciplinary collaboration, effective communication strategies, and teamwork principles.
- *Skills:* Competence in collaborative communication, respectful interactions, and active participation in team decision-making.
- *Abilities*: Proficiency in fostering a collaborative team environment, resolving conflicts, and promoting effective teamwork to enhance client care.

Category 5: Professionalism
- *Knowledge*: Familiarity with ethical guidelines, legal standards, and professional boundaries.
- *Skills*: Competence in maintaining confidentiality, demonstrating ethical behavior, and upholding professional standards.
- *Abilities:* Ability to engage in reflective practice, seek professional development opportunities, and exhibit professionalism in all interactions.

Category 6: Advocacy and Leadership
- *Knowledge:* Understanding of advocacy principles, relevant policies, and leadership strategies.

- *Skills:* Proficiency in advocating for clients' rights, engaging in professional leadership roles, and influencing positive change.
- *Abilities:* Ability to advocate for system-level improvements, lead interdisciplinary teams, and effectively communicate and collaborate with stakeholders.

By prioritizing these core knowledge areas, honing relevant skills, and cultivating the necessary abilities, rehabilitation professionals can elevate their caseload management practices and deliver exceptional care to individuals with disabilities and other health conditions. The Rehabilitation CLM-CF acts as a valuable roadmap for professionals, guiding them in acquiring and advancing their knowledge, skills, and abilities throughout their career. By continuously developing and refining these competencies, rehabilitation professionals can ensure they are equipped to provide the highest standard of care and support to their clients, promoting positive outcomes and improving the overall quality of life for those they serve in the rehabilitation process.

Levels of Proficiency and Rehabilitation Professional Practice

Proficiency levels are a crucial component of the Rehabilitation CLM-CF, providing a valuable framework for evaluating and enhancing the knowledge, skills, and abilities of rehabilitation professionals. These proficiency levels serve as essential benchmarks for assessing expertise and performance in key categories, such as assessment, planning and implementation, evaluation and outcome measurements, teamwork and collaboration, professionalism, and advocacy and leadership.

The Rehabilitation CLM-CF incorporates proficiency levels that serve as valuable indicators of competence for professionals in the field. These levels provide a structured pathway for professionals to assess their current capabilities and identify areas for growth and development. The proficiency levels within the CLM-CF range from basic proficiency, where professionals demonstrate foundational knowledge and skills under supervision, to intermediate proficiency, which reflects independent competence and proficiency in daily caseload management practice. Advancing further, advanced proficiency represents mastery and exceptional performance in caseload management. It is important to note that similar to the WHO RCF, the CLM-CF proficiency levels are not determined by educational attainment, professional credentials, or training duration. Rather, professionals may vary in their alignment with the basic, intermediate, and advanced levels based on personal experiences, role expectations, cultural norms, or individual areas of interest. This recognition allows for a flexible and individualized approach to assessing and advancing proficiency levels within the framework.

Proficiency levels within each category serve as invaluable guides for professionals as they strive to improve their caseload management practice. These levels enable professionals to set clear goals, develop personalized learning plans, and actively seek out opportunities for growth. By assessing their proficiency level, professionals can identify areas for improvement and focus their efforts on acquiring the necessary knowledge and skills. Additionally, these proficiency levels provide a framework for supervisors, educators, and organizations to offer targeted support and guidance, ensuring that professionals receive the resources and mentorship needed to enhance their practice. Together, these proficiency levels foster a culture of continuous learning and professional development, benefiting both the individual professionals and the quality of caseload management services provided.

Next is an overview of proficiency levels for each category provided in the Rehabilitation CLM-CF:

Category 1: Assessment
- Basic Proficiency: Demonstrates a foundational understanding of assessment tools and methods, conducts assessments with guidance, and interprets assessment results under supervision.
- Intermediate Proficiency: Conducts comprehensive assessments independently, selects appropriate assessment tools, and accurately interprets and synthesizes assessment findings.
- Advanced Proficiency: Exhibits expertise in a wide range of assessment techniques, demonstrates critical thinking skills in analyzing complex assessment data, and integrates assessment results into comprehensive treatment plans effectively.

Category 2: Planning and Implementation
- Basic Proficiency: Participates in the development of client-centered treatment plans, follows established protocols and guidelines, and implements interventions with supervision and guidance.
- Intermediate Proficiency: Develops client-centered treatment plans independently, sets realistic goals, and implements interventions with proficiency, adapting as needed based on client progress.
- Advanced Proficiency: Demonstrates mastery in developing individualized treatment plans, utilizes evidence-based practices, and implements interventions with flexibility and creativity, achieving optimal outcomes.

Category 3: Evaluation and Outcome Measurements
- Basic Proficiency: Participates in outcome measurement activities, collects data accurately, and contributes to outcome evaluation with supervision.
- Intermediate Proficiency: Independently collects and analyzes outcome data, documents and interprets results effectively, and makes informed recommendations for treatment modifications.
- Advanced Proficiency: Conducts comprehensive outcome measurements, employs advanced statistical analysis techniques, and utilizes data-driven insights to refine treatment plans and improve outcomes.

Category 4: Teamwork and Collaboration
- Basic Proficiency: Participates actively in team discussions, communicates effectively within the team, and contributes to collaborative decision-making.
- Intermediate Proficiency: Engages in interdisciplinary collaboration, communicates clearly and respectfully, and effectively contributes to team goals and decision-making processes.
- Advanced Proficiency: Demonstrates exceptional teamwork and collaboration skills, fosters a positive and inclusive team environment, resolves conflicts, and promotes effective interdisciplinary collaboration to optimize client care.

Category 5: Professionalism
- Basic Proficiency: Demonstrates basic understanding of professional ethics, maintains confidentiality, and adheres to professional standards under guidance.
- Intermediate Proficiency: Displays professionalism in all interactions, upholds ethical guidelines and legal standards, and consistently demonstrates integrity and ethical behavior.
- Advanced Proficiency: Exhibits exemplary professionalism, engages in reflective practice, seeks ongoing professional development, and serves as a role model for ethical and professional conduct.

Category 6: Advocacy and Leadership
- Basic Proficiency: Recognizes the importance of client advocacy and leadership, participates in advocacy initiatives, and demonstrates leadership potential under supervision.

- Intermediate Proficiency: Engages in client advocacy, takes on leadership roles within the team, and influences positive change within the organization or community.
- Advanced Proficiency: Demonstrates exceptional advocacy skills, leads interdisciplinary teams effectively, and advocates for systemic improvements in rehabilitation services at the local, regional, or national level.

These proficiency levels provide a framework for assessing and developing competencies within each category of the Rehabilitation CLM-CF. Professionals can progress through these levels by gaining experience, continuing education, and actively practicing and refining their skills in case and caseload management. By incorporating proficiency levels into practice, rehabilitation professionals can effectively track their progress, tailor their learning experiences, and continuously improve their case and caseload management skills.

SUGGESTIONS FOR IMPLEMENTATION AND SUCCESS OF THE REHABILITATION CASELOAD MANAGEMENT COMPETENCY FRAMEWORK

The Rehabilitation CLM-CF provides valuable suggestions for the implementation and success of competency-based practices in the field of rehabilitation. These suggestions are designed to enhance the effectiveness and impact of the framework, ensuring its successful integration into professional development, education, and practice settings. By following the suggestions provided in the following figure, rehabilitation professionals and organizations can maximize the benefits of the framework and promote positive outcomes for individuals with disabilities or other health conditions.

Suggestions for implication and success: The Rehabilitation Caseload Management Competency Framework.

1. *Awareness and Understanding*: To ensure successful implementation, it is crucial for stakeholders to have a comprehensive awareness and understanding of the Rehabilitation CLM-CF. This includes familiarizing themselves with its core concepts, domains, and proficiency levels. Building a shared understanding among professionals, educators, and policymakers sets the stage for effective utilization and alignment of competencies across various contexts.

2. *Integration Into Education and Training*: The successful implementation of the framework requires its integration into education and training programs for rehabilitation professionals. This involves aligning curriculum content, learning objectives, and assessment methods with the competencies outlined in the framework. By incorporating the framework into educational curricula, future professionals can acquire the necessary knowledge, skills, and attitudes to provide high-quality rehabilitation services.

3. *Continuous Professional Development*: Rehabilitation professionals should embrace a lifelong learning mindset and engage in continuous professional development aligned with the competencies outlined in the framework. This includes participating in training programs, workshops, conferences, and other learning opportunities that focus on enhancing competency-based skills. By continuously updating their knowledge and skills, professionals can stay abreast of advancements in the field and deliver evidence-based and client-centered care.

4. *Collaboration and Interdisciplinary Approach*: The framework encourages collaboration and an interdisciplinary approach to rehabilitation practice. Professionals should actively seek opportunities to work collaboratively with colleagues from different disciplines, fostering a holistic and integrated approach to client care. By leveraging diverse perspectives and expertise, professionals can provide comprehensive and coordinated services that address the complex needs of individuals undergoing rehabilitation.

5. *Quality Assurance and Evaluation*: Regular evaluation and quality assurance processes should be established to assess the effectiveness of the framework's implementation. This involves monitoring the application of competencies, measuring outcomes, and collecting feedback from professionals, clients, and stakeholders. By regularly reviewing and refining the implementation strategies, organizations can ensure the framework's ongoing relevance and impact.

6. *Stakeholder Engagement*: Successful implementation of the framework requires the active involvement and engagement of stakeholders, including rehabilitation professionals, educators, policy makers, and clients. Collaborative efforts in developing, implementing, and evaluating the framework promote a sense of ownership and shared responsibility, increasing the likelihood of success and sustainability.

By considering these suggestions and adapting them within unique contexts, rehabilitation professionals and organizations can successfully implement the caseload management framework and capitalize on its advantages. Embracing competency-based practices empowers professionals to provide exceptional, person-centered rehabilitation services that significantly improve the well-being and quality of life for individuals with disabilities. The framework fosters consistency, collaboration, and a shared comprehension of the competencies essential for effective rehabilitation practice.

Furthermore, the CLM-CF serves as an invaluable resource for the development of curricula, the design of assessment methods, and the implementation of competency-based education approaches in rehabilitation programs. It offers a comprehensive framework that guides educators in shaping the knowledge, skills, and attitudes of future rehabilitation professionals, ensuring their readiness to meet the demands of the field. By utilizing the CLM-CF, educational institutions can cultivate a workforce that is well-equipped and proficient in delivering high-quality rehabilitation services.

Overall, the incorporation of these suggestions and the integration of competency-based practices into rehabilitation settings have far-reaching benefits. They enhance service provision, promote collaboration, and ultimately contribute to the betterment of the lives of individuals with disabilities. Through the CLM-CF, rehabilitation professionals and organizations can embark on a transformative journey that elevates the standard of practice and empowers individuals on their path to full autonomy and improved well-being.

SUMMARY

This chapter explored the WHO GCF and RCF and influence of these on the development of the Rehabilitation CLM-CF. The implications for effective caseload management in the field of rehabilitation were explored. We began by discussing the core values and beliefs that underpin the work of rehabilitation professionals, emphasizing their commitment to respect, empowerment, advocacy, collaboration, and ethical conduct. These values provide a strong foundation for person-centered and ethical caseload management services. Next, the activities outlined in the CLM-CF explored encompassing a wide range of responsibilities across assessment, planning and implementation, evaluation and outcome measurements, teamwork and collaboration, professionalism, and advocacy and leadership. These activities serve as a comprehensive guide for rehabilitation professionals, ensuring the delivery of high-quality and client-centered services.

Throughout this chapter, we thoroughly examined the knowledge, skills, and abilities required for each category within the Rehabilitation CLM-CF. We explored various aspects, ranging from conducting assessments and developing comprehensive plans to measuring outcomes and fostering collaboration. By highlighting these essential competencies, we emphasized the key attributes necessary for excelling in caseload management. Furthermore, the chapter provided valuable proficiency-level information for each category, offering a clear understanding of the expected levels of expertise and proficiency in caseload management activities. This information serves as a valuable tool for professionals to assess their own skills and competencies, enabling them to identify areas for growth and improvement. In addition to examining the knowledge, skills, and abilities, the chapter also addressed suggestions for implementing and achieving success with the CLM-CF. These suggestions encompassed crucial aspects such as raising awareness and promoting understanding of the framework, integrating it into education and training programs, fostering continuous professional development, encouraging collaboration among stakeholders, ensuring quality assurance, and engaging relevant parties. By adhering to these suggestions, rehabilitation professionals and organizations can effectively implement the caseload management framework and maximize its benefits, ultimately achieving a high level of competence in this vital area of the field.

Overall, this chapter provided a comprehensive exploration of the knowledge, skills, and abilities within the CLM-CF and offered guidance on implementing the framework for success. By embracing the competencies, assessing proficiency levels, and following the suggested strategies, rehabilitation professionals and organizations can enhance their caseload management practices, resulting in improved outcomes and enhanced services for individuals in need of rehabilitation support.

QUESTIONS FOR DISCUSSION

1. How does the nature of work in private rehabilitation settings differ from that of public or government-funded rehabilitation? What are the implications for caseload management?

2. What are some challenges that rehabilitation professionals may encounter when managing larger caseloads in the private sector? How can these challenges be addressed effectively?

3. How do specialized skills in areas such as rehabilitation disability management, workers compensation, forensic rehabilitation, life care planning, Social Security expertise, and community rehabilitation partnerships contribute to successful caseload management in the private sector?

4. How can professionals in private rehabilitation balance the need for efficiency and productivity while providing high-quality personalized care to their clients?

5. What are some key considerations and strategies for effectively navigating insurance policies and reimbursement processes in private sector rehabilitation caseload management?

6. How does the business aspect of private sector rehabilitation impact caseload management? What business skills and strategies are essential for maintaining a viable practice in this context?

7. How can professionals in private rehabilitation effectively collaborate with external stakeholders, such as healthcare providers, vocational training programs, and job placement agencies, to ensure comprehensive care and successful client outcomes?

8. What are some ethical considerations that professionals in private rehabilitation should keep in mind when managing caseloads and advocating for their clients' needs?

9. How can the use of specialized tools and technologies, such as electronic health records, case management software, and assessment instruments, enhance caseload management in private rehabilitation settings?

10. How does ongoing professional development and staying up-to-date with advancements in the field contribute to effective caseload management in private rehabilitation?

11. These discussion questions can help facilitate a deeper exploration of the topic, promote critical thinking, and encourage the sharing of insights and experiences among professionals in the field of private rehabilitation caseload management.

PUTTING IT INTO PRACTICE

Ask yourself these questions to target issues or concerns with the RCF.

1. How do you perceive the impact of the Rehabilitation CLM-CF presented in this chapter on your professional practice as a rehabilitation counselor? Which core values from the framework resonate most strongly with you and influence your interactions with clients?

2. Regardless of your education or experience, how do you assess your proficiency level as a rehabilitation counselor? Do you believe that the training, knowledge, and skills provided are sufficient for success in working with clients and within the rehabilitation field? What improvements, developments, or new initiatives would you propose to foster ongoing growth in proficiency?

3. What qualities define a competent rehabilitation case or caseload manager in your opinion? Having explored the Rehabilitation CLM-CF, how do you incorporate the presented concepts to support your continuous development and future growth in the field?

A robust set of instructor resources designed to supplement this text is located at http://connect.springerpub.com/content/book/978-0-8261-5963-2. Qualifying instructors may request access by emailing **textbook@springerpub.com**.

REFERENCES

Cassell, J. L., & Mulkey, S. W. (1985). *Rehabilitation caseload management: Concepts & practice*. Pro-Ed.

Cassell, J. L., & Mulkey, S. W. (2004). Caseload management. In T. F. Riggar & D. R. Maki (Eds.), *Handbook of rehabilitation counseling* (pp. 252–270). Springer Publishing Company.

Connor, L., Dean, J., McNett, M., Tydings, D. M., Shrout, A., Gorsuch, P. F., Hole, A., Moore, L., Brown, R., Melnyk, B. M., & Gallagher-Ford, L. (2023). Evidence-based practice improves patient outcomes and healthcare system return on investment: Findings from a scoping review. *Worldviews on Evidence-Based Nursing, 20*(1), 6–15. https://doi.org/10.1111/wvn.12621

Fernandes, J. B., Vareta, D., Fernandes, S., Almeida, A. S., Peças, D., Ferreira, N., & Roldão, L. (2022). Rehabilitation workforce challenges to implement person-centered care. *International Journal of Environmental Research and Public Health, 19*(6), 3199. https://doi.org/10.3390/ijerph19063199

Grubbs, L. A., Cassell, J. L., & Mulkey, S. W. (2006). *Rehabilitation caseload management: Concepts and practice* (2nd ed.). Springer Publishing Company.

Jagals, P., & Ebi, K. (2021). Core competencies for health workers to deal with climate and environmental change. *International Journal of Environmental Research and Public Health, 18*(8), 3849. https://doi.org/10.3390/ijerph18083849

Jesus, T. S., Landry, M. D., Dussault, G., & Fronteira, I. (2017). Human resources for health (and rehabilitation): Six rehab-workforce challenges for the century. *Human Resources for Health, 15*(1), 8. https://doi.org/10.1186/s12960-017-0182-7

Leahy, M. J., Muenzen, P., Saunders, J. L., & Strauser, D. (2009). Essential knowledge domains underlying effective rehabilitation counseling practice. *Rehabilitation Counseling Bulletin, 52*(2), 95–106. https://doi.org/10.1177/0034355208323646

Matthews, L. R., Buys, N., Randall, C., Marfels, B., Niehaus, M., & Bauer, J. F. (2015). A comparative study of the job tasks, functions, and knowledge domains of rehabilitation professionals providing vocational rehabilitation services in Australia and Germany. *Rehabilitation Counseling Bulletin, 58*(2), 80–90. https://doi.org/10.1177/0034355213504304

Mills, T., Marks, E., Reynolds, T., & Cieza, A. (2017). Rehabilitation: Essential along the continuum of care. In D. T. Jamison, H. Gelband, S. Horton, P. Jha, R. Laxminarayan, C. N. Mock, & R. Nugent (Eds.), *Disease control priorities: Improving health and reducing poverty* (3rd ed.). The International Bank for Reconstruction and Development/The World Bank.

Peterson, S. (2020, February 6). Celebrating the role of rehabilitation counseling. *Counseling Today*. https://ct.counseling.org/2020/02/celebrating-the-role-of-rehabilitation-counseling/

Rawlins-Williams, L. A. (2023). *Rehabilitation counseling competency framework (RC-CF)* [Unpublished manuscript].

Rawlins-Williams, L. A., & Oswald, G. R. (2021). Facilitating knowledge in rehabilitation counseling professionals on caseload management: A pre-test/post-test evaluation. *The Rehabilitation Professional, 29*(1), 5–12.

Scully, S. M., Habeck, R. V., & Leahy, M. J. (1999). Knowledge and skill areas associated with disability management practice for rehabilitation counselors. *Rehabilitation Counseling Bulletin, 43*(1), 20–29. https://doi.org/10.1177/003435529904300105

Thielsen, V. A., & Leahy, M. J. (2001). Essential knowledge and skills for effective clinical supervision in rehabilitation counseling. *Rehabilitation Counseling Bulletin, 44*(4), 196–208. https://doi.org/10.1177/003435520104400402

World Health Organization. (n.d.). *Definition of health*. https://www.who.int/about/

World Health Organization. (2016). *Enhanced WHO global competency model*. Author. https://www.who.int/publications/m/item/enhanced-who-global-competency-model

World Health Organization. (2020). *Rehabilitation competency framework*. https://www.who.int/teams/noncommunicable-diseases/sensory-functions-disability-and-rehabilitation/rehabilitation-competency-framework

World Health Organization. (2021a). *Adapting the WHO Rehabilitation Competency Framework to a specific context: A stepwise guide for competency framework developers*. https://www.who.int/publications/i/item/9789240015333

World Health Organization. (2021b). *WHO competency framework: Building a response workforce to manage infodemics*. https://apps.who.int/iris/handle/10665/345207

World Health Organization. (2022). *Global competency framework for universal health coverage*. https://www.who.int/news/item/19-07-2022-global-competency-framework

PART III

Caseload Management Emerging Trends From the Field of Rehabilitation

CHAPTER **14**

Rehabilitation Management Issues and Special Populations

LEARNING OBJECTIVES

By the end of this chapter, learners will be able to:

- Appreciate the impact of co-occurring disorders on functional limitations and vocational planning.
- Explore unique features of special populations common in vocational rehabilitation services.
- Address functional limitations of special populations.
- Identify case management and employment considerations and evidence-based practices related to special populations.

INTRODUCTION

Within **vocational rehabilitation** (VR), there are several disabilities that may benefit from heightened attention to case management responsibilities and efficiencies. A high prevalence rate and/or complicated nature can present unique considerations for rehabilitation counselors. This chapter will set the stage through a discussion of the impact of functional limitations and dual diagnoses on case management tasks. Next, various disability categories will be dissected to understand their current prevalence, characteristics, common functional limitations, and potential impacts on case management and employment activities. A review of two common specialized caseloads will conclude the chapter.

Functional Limitations

As outlined in Chapter 9, uncovering and understanding a person's functional limitations are specialized skills of rehabilitation professionals. In fact, functional limitations are often more informative than a specific diagnosis when working with individuals with disabilities on employment goals, so being able to identify and address what may be a barrier to entering the job market is essential. This is more so important as rehabilitation practitioners recognize the unique impact disability can have on a person and the process. Two people may have identical diagnoses yet very different levels of ability and need. The magnitude of the functional limitations of an individual will be based on their personal experience of the disability, environmental features and barriers, and their access to and skill with self-advocacy, common accommodations, strategies for independence and task completion, assistive technologies, and problem-solving. Therefore, it is essential to take the time to explore the broad categories of functional limitations with each client and ascertain what has been problematic in the past, as well as possible solutions, accommodations, and strategies that can mitigate those limitations.

Beyond eligibility determination reviews, case managers should also consider the impact of functional limitations on a client's ability to engage in the working alliance between client and counselor and contribute to the process. See **Table 14.1** for a review of major categories of functional limitations with tasks or features associated with each. As particularly relevant and complex conditions are discussed later, consider the functional limitations that may impact the person communicating effectively in meetings, engaging in self-advocacy, participating in services, and completing tasks independently between appointments. What are unique case management strategies and implications that may be pertinent when working within the population? What skills might be addressed and fostered through the case management process? What issues and resources (both inclusive and specialized) are available to support needs tangential to employment (i.e., transportation, housing, socialization, interventions, or treatment providers)?

TABLE 14.1 FUNCTIONAL LIMITATIONS

CATEGORIES	EXAMPLES
Communication: the inability to exchange thoughts, messages, or information with other people.	• Unable to communicate verbally • Unable to use formal language of any type (spoken or sign) • Cannot readily understand or be understood by others • Unable to converse via telephone • Unable to initiate or sustain conversation • Limited to single words or short phrases in conversation • Has speech that is rambling or illogical • Talks/interrupts excessively • Unable to follow written instructions or interpret written materials
Interpersonal skills: the inability to interact in a socially acceptable and mature manner with coworkers, supervisors, and others to facilitate normal flow of work or activities.	• Unable to understand/demonstrate interaction or behavior appropriate to worksite • Unable to determine appropriate social response to others • Isolated/withdrawn from coworkers • Unable to effectively resolve conflict with coworkers • Has a spotty, intermittent work history • Has had problems accepting supervisory monitoring and criticism
Mobility: the inability to move from one place to another and/or physically manipulate the environment.	• Unable to safely move about within common training or work settings without the help of others or use of assistive devices • Significantly restricted or limited in the distance they can safely move within common training or work settings • Takes significantly longer than the average person to move about within common training or work environments • Cannot safely change body positions without help of others or use of assistive devices • Cannot drive • Requires specialized transportation services for travel within community

(continued)

TABLE 14.1 FUNCTIONAL LIMITATIONS *(CONTINUED)*

CATEGORIES	EXAMPLES
Self-care: the inability to perform tasks that involve caring for self and the living environment, or the inability to manage physical, emotional, and safety needs.	• Needs monitoring to prevent injury • History of poor decision-making or is unaware of consequences of behavior • Requires a personal care attendant • Unable to manage money or finances • Requires assistive technology, modifications, adaptations, or accommodations not typically needed by others (i.e., button fastener, utensil gripper, modified work schedule, split work schedule, modified workstation, etc.) to perform most self-care or independent living activities necessary to obtain or maintain employment
Self-direction: the inability to plan, initiate, problem-solve, organize, or independently carry out goal-directed activities related to independent living and work.	• Unable to organize information in a logical manner • Unable to recognize and acknowledge problems, seek remedies, take corrective action, and arrive at solutions • Unable to effectively seek employment independently • Unable to regulate maladaptive behavior • Serious difficulty working independently • Serious difficulty shifting focus between activities or tasks • Serious difficulty adjusting to new situations or changes • Easily distracted/has a short attention span leading to repeatedly poor task completion
Work skills: the inability to perform specific tasks required to carry out job functions, benefit from training in the necessary skills, or practice the work habits needed to stay employed.	• Reading, spelling, or math skills at/below fifth-grade level • Difficulty learning new tasks • Limited task sequence recall ability • Performs at significantly reduced speed • Unable to plan/initiate/sequence/recall/process complex information needed on the job • Requires continual monitoring, skill training, behavior management, support, assistive technology, or accommodations and adaptations not typically made for other employees to maintain work skills and stable job performance • Inconsistent and unreliable in their work habits
Work tolerance: the inability to effectively and efficiently perform jobs that require various levels of physical, emotional, and psychological demands of work over a sustained period of time.	• Unable to lift and carry more than 10 pounds • Unable to sustain continual or prolonged paced movement of the arms, hands, or fingers over an 8-hour day • Unable to sustain continual or prolonged standing or sitting required to perform the job over an 8-hour day • Requires work in a controlled or specific working environment • Unable to tolerate common psychological stresses of work • Requires assistive technology, modifications, or accommodations to the work schedule • Unable to tolerate changes in routine and/or job tasks • Unable to work at an acceptable pace

Co-occurring Conditions

In addition to considering the functional limitations of each individual, it will be critical to determine if there are co-occurring conditions that may also impact the client. Although there may be one primary disability that forms the basis of eligibility and VR service need, there may be secondary disorders that will also have the power to impact a person's ability to make appropriate and meaningful decisions about their case, engage in services, or secure and retain employment. **Co-occurring disorders**, sometimes interchanged with comorbid or dual diagnosis, can compound limitations as well as present unique intersectionality within an individual. For instance, an individual with a **substance use disorder** (SUD) may cause a motor vehicle accident that results in a spinal cord injury (Beaulieu-Bonneau et al., 2017). Although the SUD may not be the primary disability when considering functional vocational limitations of a new spinal cord injury and eligibility, the new disability will not automatically resolve the SUD, which may actually be complicated or amplified through symptom management strategies for physical pain and emotional trauma from the accident.

In spite of the infinite combinations of disabilities a person can experience, consider the following information on comorbidity. In general, common comorbidities include anxiety disorders, arthritis, cancer, depression, diabetes, heart disease, lung disease, obesity, and sleep apnea (Yetman, 2022). Individuals with traumatic brain injuries (TBIs) are more likely to experience TBI-related conditions such as hypertension, diabetes, obesity, and stroke (Dreer et al., 2018; Yi et al., 2018). Individuals with chronic conditions (such as autoimmune diseases, cancer, heart disease, diabetes, hypothyroidism, and multiple sclerosis) are more likely to experience depression, while individuals with depression are at higher risk of conditions such as cardiovascular disease, stroke, pain, and diabetes (National Institute of Mental Health [NIMH], 2021a). As alluded to in the scenario earlier, SUDs may also contribute to the worsening of symptoms or development of certain physical disabilities (Reif et al., 2022). Reciprocally, adults with disabilities have a heightened risk of SUDs than those without disabilities (Reif et al., 2022). Individuals with intellectual and/or developmental disabilities "frequently abuse alcohol, tobacco, and cannabis, but are largely underdiagnosed and undertreated for SUDs. Treatment for SUDs in these patients is critical because substance abuse among patients with ID [intellectual disabilities] is associated with developing mood disorders, long-term health consequences, incarceration, and interpersonal instability" (Bhatt & Gentile, 2021, p. 480). In 2021, 842,000 adolescents aged 12 to 17 were dual diagnosed with a major depressive episode and an SUD and almost 18 million adults experienced both a mental illness and SUD (Substance Abuse and Mental Health Services Administration [SAMHSA], 2022).

No one disability precludes a client from another disability. A person with a visual disability may also have an SUD, just as a person with an intellectual disability may have a mental health condition. Even if a client seems straightforward and the case uncomplicated, take the time to review a comprehensive health checklist and ask follow-up questions when answers suggest there is more to the story. Having a secondary or tertiary disability pop up after the fact can create a lot of frustration, lost time and effort, and friction with service providers and employers. In order to holistically and effectively serve individuals, rehabilitation professionals should seek to understand all pertinent conditions in order to determine best practices, such as collaboration of services between providers (i.e., Davis et al., 2022; Johnson et al., 2020; Zhang et al., 2023), to pursue. As various conditions are explored next, consider how the intersection of functional limitations may amplify the complexity of individual cases and need for strategic case management practices.

MENTAL HEALTH AND CHRONIC MENTAL ILLNESS

Prevalence, Characteristics, and Functional Limitations

Whether a standalone or dually diagnosed condition, a discussion of **severe mental illness** (SMI) is highly prevalent, as approximately 1 in 20 U.S. adults live with substantial limitations to major life activities and over 2 million receive Social Security disability benefits based on an SMI (NIMH, 2021b; SAMHSA, 2020; Social Security Administration, 2020). SMI is often a result of a mental health disability such as anxiety disorders, major depression, mood disorders, SUD, schizophrenia spectrum disorders, or personality disorders (American Psychiatric Association [APA], 2013). The prevalence of SMI is even more relevant for those with VR case management responsibilities, as research continues to demonstrate a disparity in employment outcomes for those with SMI when compared to clients with other conditions in the VR system (Kaya & Chan, 2017; Peterson & Olney, 2021; Sevak & Khan, 2017). Postulated contributing factors include a lack of coordination in services, inherent bias in VR counselors and other service providers, and a lack of training on how to best support individuals living with SMI (Amsalem et al., 2018; Hoy & Miner Holden, 2014; Olney & Gill, 2016; Peterson, Alkhadim, et al., 2021; Peterson & Olney, 2020, 2021). Common functional limitations that can impede the VR process and case management activities include limitations in interpersonal skills, dependability, logical thinking and decision-making, motivation or initiative, follow-through, self-confidence, concentration and memory, stress management, and adaptability to change.

Case Management and Employment Planning Considerations

Current research recommends improved counselor knowledge and utilization of psychiatric rehabilitation and evidence-based practices (EBPs) for working with individuals with SMI (Cimera, 2009; Kaya & Chan, 2017; Peterson, 2023; Peterson & Olney, 2021). Professional development activities should address symptoms of SMI and their potential impact on engaging in the process and employment, systemic bias of VR clients with SMI, and effective service strategies (Kaya & Chan, 2017; Leahy et al., 2018; Peterson & Olney, 2021; Salzer et al., 2011; Sevak & Khan, 2017; White, 2011). Particular focus should be given to understanding and delivering research-based, recovery-oriented, and integrated strategies that include the Assertive Community Treatment (ACT) model of case management, the Individual Placement and Support (IPS) model of supported employment, the Wellness Recovery Action Plan (WRAP), peer supports, benefits counseling, mental health and SUD screening, and integrating mental health and VR services (Drake, 2020; Heinemann et al., 2014; Lusk et al., 2016; Olney & Emery-Flores, 2017; Olney et al., 2014; Peterson & Olney, 2021; Peterson, Saia, et al., 2021; Topitzes et al., 2019; Waynor et al., 2018).

Often serving as coordinators of services and bridges between service providers, case managers can be the essential ingredient to success through the warm handoff approach. A warm handoff is an intentional introduction of the client to another member of the service delivery team. This simple act can facilitate improved and rapid rapport building and information sharing between the client and the internal or external service provider (Cabán-Alemán et al., 2020; Peterson, 2023; Taylor & Minkovitz, 2021; Young et al., 2020). Implementation of a warm handoff should be considered in all phases of the VR process (assessment, vocational planning, job development services, and case closure/post-VR service supports; Peterson, 2023).

SUBSTANCE USE

Prevalence, Characteristics, and Functional Limitations

Individuals with SUD are often viewed within the VR system as a distinctive population under the SMI umbrella, presenting unique policy and procedural considerations. Prevalence is difficult to specify, as many individuals with SUD are underdiagnosed, as well as underserved or underreported (wherein another disability is the primary or documented disability for eligibility) in VR services (Heinemann et al., 2008; Sprong et al., 2014). Estimates of the incidence of SUD range from 22% to 50% in VR clients (Heinemann et al., 2014; Moore et al., 2008). As mentioned earlier, individuals with chronic physical, sensory, mental health, TBI, or spinal cord injuries are more likely to be living with a comorbid SUD when compared to the general population (Anderson et al., 2014; Beaulieu-Bonneau et al., 2017; Ebener & Smedema, 2011; Niemeier et al., 2016; Walker & Druss, 2017), complicating case management responsibilities such as eligibility determination, assessment of functional limitations, and the need for SUD treatment prior to or in conjunction with VR services. Counselor attitude and self-efficacy also remain a relevant consideration for effective service provision (Chan et al., 2017; Lusk & Paul, 2017; Nash et al., 2017; Yang et al., 2017). Furthermore, research demonstrates inconsistent or insufficient agency policies related to the provision of services to clients with SUD, a disconnect between everyday practice and policy, and discord between written policies and counselor perceptions of such policies (Xiao & Zhou, 2020).

The essential feature of SUD is a maladaptive pattern of substance use manifested, resulting in significant, recurring adverse consequences (APA, 2013). Diagnosis is based on 11 criteria related to four basic categories (impaired control, physical dependence, social problems, and risky use) and severity (mild, moderate, or severe). Functional limitations may be explored based on psychological, personal behavior, and learning/communication dimensions (see **Figure 14.1** for common functional limitations; Glenn et al., n.d.).

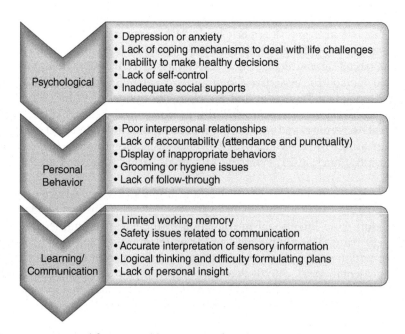

FIGURE 14.1 Potential functional limitations for clients with substance use disorder.

Case Management and Employment Planning Considerations

A rehabilitation professional's knowledge of and skills in serving clients with SUD can support or hinder progress when factoring in the complicated puzzle involving individual functional limitations, treatment and service coordination, agency policies, and practitioner attitudes. Clients with SUD may present more intense challenges to the case management process than individuals with other SMI diagnoses via difficulties in developing the working alliance (due to a lack of trust and/or motivation), current or past involvement in the criminal justice system, temporary or permanent driving restrictions, and health issues related to long-term substance use (Glenn et al., n.d.). In addition to previously mentioned recommendations and EBPs for working with individuals with SMI, counselors should consider routine screenings for SUD in the intake process, as well as any phase of the VR process when indicators are observed (Glenn & Keferl, 2008; Heinemann et al., 2008, 2014). Research-supported recommendations focus on individualized services, service integration among multiple providers, and long-term supports (Magura & Marshall, 2020). Practitioners should be clear on current agency policies, procedures, and services for supporting clients with SUD (Lusk & Stipp, 2018; Wang et al., 2018; Xiao & Zhou, 2020), as there can be significant differences across state/federal agencies' policies and disagreement between agency policy and counselor interpretations or practices (Xiao & O'Sullivan, 2019). One example is the discrepancy between agencies on recommended sobriety waiting periods that range from 3 days to 6 to 9 months or may even be completely prohibited (Xiao & O'Sullivan, 2019). Finally, rehabilitation practices operating in states with legalized cannabis usage (either medical or recreational) should be familiar with their state's laws on usage and how their agency's services are still restricted by federal regulations (ADA National Network, 2021a, 2021b). Current personal usage may be deemed legal and reasonable in a state and not impact eligibility determination, while employment goals related to the cannabis industry may still be prohibited.

TRAUMATIC BRAIN INJURY

Prevalence, Characteristics, and Functional Limitations

Traumatic brain injury (TBI) "can be caused by a forceful bump, blow, or jolt to the head or body, or from an object that pierces the skull and enters the brain. Not all blows or jolts to the head result in a TBI," and not all TBIs result in severe and/or permanent disability (National Institute of Neurological Disorders and Stroke, n.d.). The Centers for Disease Control and Prevention (CDC, 2023a) estimates that about 1.5 million Americans develop a TBI every year, with 5.3 million Americans living with long-term effects. As approximately 75% of all TBIs are classified as mild and receive little to no medical treatment, these estimates may be vastly lower than reality (Taylor & Seebeck, 2020). Depending on the location and severity of the disability, functional limitations may be explored as they relate to physical, cognitive, and psychological dimensions of ability. Physical limitations may include chronic pain, diminished strength and stamina, fatigue, fine and gross motor disturbances, hearing loss, spasticity, speech dysfluencies, tremors, and visual and perceptual impairments (Falvo & Holland, 2018). Cognitive limitations relate to analytic abilities, attention control and task adherence, executive function, information retrieval and memory (short-, intermediate-, and long-term), self-management, and social cognition (Frain et al., 2012). Individuals with TBIs are also at an elevated risk for anxiety disorders, depression, disinhibited speed and behavior, feelings of persecution and isolation, low frustration tolerance, irritability and impatience, posttraumatic stress disorder, suicidal ideation, and SUD (Dillahunt-Aspillaga et al., 2017; Frain et al., 2012; Taylor & Seebeck, 2020).

Combined, the resulting residual abilities and support needs may offer a dynamic challenge for rehabilitation practitioners, who will best see each case from a solution-focused, problem-solving paradigm.

Case Management and Employment Planning Considerations

As with other populations, rehabilitation practitioners should be trained or independently develop knowledge and skills specific to supporting individuals with TBI. Severe interventions and programs have been implemented to address the complex nature of the diagnosis, coordination of multiple providers, and employer expectations (Rumrill & Koch, 2020). Although no two cases are identical and clients should be served based on the unique characteristics of their disability, service needs, personal and regional resources, and available services, research can now offer evidence to what practices may be most appropriate and effective (Degeneffe et al., 2023a, 2023b). For instance, on-the-job supports, job placement, and on-the-job training have all proven associated with competitive employment outcomes (Ahonle et al., 2020; Tucker & Degeneffe, 2017). Understanding the importance of such case management functions and services as outreach and eligibility, assessment (including transferable skills analyses, assistive cognitive technologies, and neuropsychological evaluations), diagnosis and treatment (especially physical restoration, standard and complementary therapies, and psychological support), counseling and guidance, job placement and skills development services, transportation, and benefits counseling for a person with a TBI will be instrumental in ensuring steps within the VR process aren't overlooked or rushed (Rumrill & Koch, 2020). In addition, the impact of a sudden TBI on the family unit is significant and should be considered within the context of assessment, planning, and service delivery. Persistent strains on the client's support network through familial role adjustments, financial concerns, and in home care and support services provided by family members may present significant limitations to the support network's capacity to encourage and facilitate service and employment activities (Degeneffe & Lee, 2015; Degeneffe et al., 2023a, 2023b). The ability to view the individual's life context holistically will foster a more accurate appreciation for the day-to-day experience of the individual, the appropriateness and availability of natural supports, and other contributing factors that may enhance or hinder the process.

DEVELOPMENTAL DISABILITIES

Prevalence, Characteristics, and Functional Limitations

As established in the Developmental Disabilities Assistance and Bill of Rights Act of 2000 (Public Law 106-402), **developmental disabilities (DDs)** are a cluster of conditions that develop prior to the age of 22 and result in physical, learning, language, or behavioral impairments (CDC, 2022a). Approximately one in six children have one or more DDs (CDC, 2022a); therefore, looking toward future caseloads with an understanding of the prevalence of co-occurring disorders, it is appropriate for every rehabilitation professional to have a working knowledge of this population. Common DDs include specific learning disabilities and generalized intellectual disabilities (IDs), cerebral palsy (CP), Down syndrome, fetal alcohol syndrome (FAS), and autism spectrum disorder (ASD).

Specific learning disabilities present targeted mental limitations. The three types of learning disabilities include dyslexia (difficulty acquiring and processing language through activities such as reading, spelling, and writing), dysgraphia (difficulty putting thoughts onto paper), and dyscalculia (difficulty in number-related concepts and calculations; APA, 2013).

Unlike specific learning disabilities, **intellectual disabilities** result in general cognitive limitations related to a wide range of daily activities (APA, 2013). Contrary to past diagnostic criteria, IDs are no longer established through a person's intellectual quotient (IQ), but their functional abilities in thoughts, social situations, and self-management. Functional limitations may impact the ability to organize work, manage time and conceptualize information, make decisions and problem-solve, concentrate, communicate clearly, and follow instructions.

Some DD conditions manifest with both cognitive and physical components. **Cerebral palsy** is a broad term applied to individuals with nonprogressive motor disorders caused by abnormal brain development or injury to the developing brain (CDC, 2022b). CP, characterized by spasticity, uncontrollable movements, or poor balance and coordination, can also affect a client's other physical, cognitive, psychosocial, and sensory abilities depending on the location and extent of the injury. An extra chromosome in individuals with **Down syndrome** causes differences in brain and body to develop, often resulting in a lowered IQ, language impediment, and related health and sensory conditions (CDC, 2023b). Similarly, individuals with prenatal substance exposure (leading to diagnoses such as **fetal alcohol syndrome**) experience both brain and physical growth problems (Mayo Clinic, 2018). The combination of brain and body development changes expands considerations of functional limitations from cognition alone to include possible deficits in mobility, stamina, sensory abilities, bowel and bladder control or function, and behavior management.

Specific to **autism spectrum disorder**, counselors should become familiar with the diagnostic criteria established in the *Diagnostic and Statistical Manual of Mental Disorders,* fifth edition (*DSM-5*) and severity rating scale of required supports (APA, 2013). Currently, the previous diagnoses of Autistic Disorder, Asperger Syndrome, and Pervasive Development Disorder Not Otherwise Specified are combined under the unifying diagnosis of ASD. In addition to having two or more restrictive or repetitive behaviors, an individual should only be diagnosed if they demonstrate difficulties in (a) social emotional reciprocity, (b) nonverbal communication used for social interactions, and (c) developing and maintaining relationships with others (APA, 2013). Unlike other DDs, common ASD functional limitations include difficulty in learning language, impaired social interactions and inappropriate response to others, extreme resistance to change, difficulty choosing a topic of conversation or engaging in one-sided conversations, inability to recognize that other people think and feel differently than they do, displaying unusual nonverbal communication or inability to understand nonverbal cues (e.g., facial expressions, body language) or humor, using a voice that is monotonous or rigid, abnormal responses to sensory stimulation (i.e., light, sound, touch, smell, taste, and movement), and showing an intense obsession with one or two targeted subjects (Andrew & Andrew, 2017).

Case Management and Employment Planning Considerations

DDs can impact individuals in any of the major areas of functional limitations, leading to support needs related to housing, transportation, community integration, employment, recreation and leisure activities, and socialization. As with many individuals with complex and significant disabilities, holistic and long-term services are often required. Rehabilitation practitioners often serve as the coordinator and facilitator of an interagency team that includes the client, VR staff, employment service providers, DD-specific agencies, school personnel, healthcare providers, and the client's personal support network members.

As services have evolved, there has been much work done recently on how employment is viewed for people with DD. Through the Employment First initiative, policies, research findings, and advocacy efforts (Kim et al., 2023; Office of Disability Employment Policy [ODEP], n.d.-a; Workforce Innovation and Opportunity Act, 2014), the

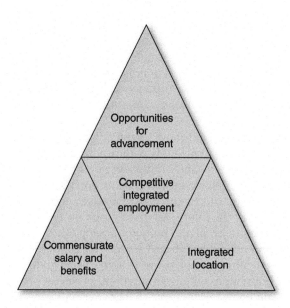

FIGURE 14.2 Competitive integrated employment framework.

foundation for employment outcomes is now set at **competitive integrated employment** (CIE; see **Figure 14.2**). The definition of CIE requires (a) competitive and commensurate earnings and benefits eligibility at or above minimum wage for full- or part-time work, (b) an integrated setting in the community with individuals without disabilities, and (c) commensurate opportunities for advancement (ODEP, n.d.-b).

CIE placements for individuals with developmental and/or intellectual disorders are often developed through **supported employment** strategies or **customized employment** (Almalky, 2020; Friedman & Rizzolo, 2017; Kim et al., 2023). Broadly, supported employment can be viewed as the overarching process whereby an employment specialist assists an individual with a significant disability obtain and maintain employment. Various general supported employment strategies can be designed and implemented to identify the job seeker's abilities, determine vocational interests and preferences, develop a job offer through preexisting positions or the creation of a new job description, and provide individualized on-the-job training through a job coach (Wehman, 2012).

Customized employment is specified by the Workforce Innovation and Opportunity Act of 2014 (WIOA) as "competitive integrated employment, for an individual with a significant disability that is based on an individualized determination of the strengths, needs, and interests of the individual with a significant disability, and is designed to meet the specific abilities of the individual with a significant disability and the business needs of the employer" (29 U.S.C §705(7), p. 1634). Specific strategies supporting customized employment include (a) exploring jobs with the individual; (b) working with employers to facilitate placement, including customizing a job description based on current employer needs or on previously unidentified and unmet employer needs; (c) developing a set of job duties, a work schedule, and job arrangement, along with specifics of supervision (including a performance evaluation review) and determining a job location; (d) representing a professional chosen by the individual, or self-representation of the individual in working with an employer to facilitate placement; and (e) providing services and supports at the job placement (29 U.S.C §705 et seq.). As a model for individuals unable to obtain CIE through more traditional VR processes and employment service models, the customized employment process can be implemented congruently with the various phases of a case from intake and assessment through job development and follow-along (Kim et al., 2023; Smith et al., 2015; see **Figure 14.3**).

FIGURE 14.3 The customized employment process aligned to the vocational rehabilitation process.

For individuals with ASD, it will be important to recognize the anxiety that might result from social situations, as well as the client's potential to learn unwritten social and communication rules. In addition, how might their unique talents and characteristics be used as an asset through a strength-based approach? Specific learning disabilities should be addressed based on considering all of the various ways the affected mental areas may impact securing and retaining work. Clients with FAS may present maladaptive behavior that is difficult to understand and address at a worksite. Therefore, focus should be placed on exploring and addressing concerns through the assessment and planning phases. Understanding the behavior's antecedent (triggering event) or what the client is trying to communicate or accomplish through the behavior can support the development of behavior management strategies.

If given the opportunity to work with **transition-aged youth** with DD, focus on **evidence or research-based and promising practices** that predict employment and postschool education success as outlined in Mazzotti et al. (2020; see **Table 14.2**).

Recognize the impact a disability may have had on the foundational experiences and milestones children often go through on their pathway to adulthood. Understand that an individual with a disability may have been excluded from opportunities to build self-efficacy, self-esteem, self-determination, and self-advocacy. Acknowledge the potential that a client may have experienced reduced independence and a lack of autonomy up until that point. Appreciate the differences in eligibility, responsibility, and availability between school-based services and those offered to adults and how this can create confusion,

TABLE 14.2 EVIDENCE-BASED TRANSITION SERVICES PREDICTORS

EVIDENCE- OR RESEARCH-BASED PRACTICES	EMPLOYMENT	POSTSCHOOL EDUCATION	PRACTICE
	X	X	Career technical education
	X	X	Goal setting
	X	X	Inclusion in general education
	X	X	Paid employment or work experience
	X		Parent expectations
	X	X	Program of study
	X	X	Self-advocacy/ self-determination
	X		Student support
		X	Transition program
	X		Work study
	X	X	Youth autonomy/ decision-making
PROMISING PRACTICES	**EMPLOYMENT**	**POSTSCHOOL EDUCATION**	**PRACTICE**
	X	X	Career awareness
	X		Community experiences
	X	X	Interagency collaboration
	X	X	Occupational courses
		X	Parent expectations
	X		Parent involvement
	X	X	Psychological empowerment
	X	X	Self-care/independent living
	X		Self-realization
	X	X	Social skills
		X	Student support
	X		Technology skills
	X		Transition program
	X		Travel skills

FIGURE 14.4 The five required pre-employment transition services.

unrealistic expectations, and frustration for the client and their support network. Explore the compendium of research outlining services, predictor variables, and outcomes of transition-aged youth in the VR system (i.e., Currier Kipping et al., 2021; Honeycutt et al., 2014; Mazzotti et al., 2020; Oswald et al., 2016; Pickens & Dymond, 2022; Roux et al., 2021). When appropriate, collaborate with school personnel and connect youth with DD with pre-employment transition services (pre-ETS), as 15% of all federal VR funding must be allocated to the provision of this service to students with disabilities who are eligible or potentially eligible for VR services (National Technical Assistance Center on Transition [NTACT], n.d.). Pre-ETS are designed to "improve the transition of students with disabilities from school to postsecondary education or to an employment outcome, increase opportunities for students with disabilities to practice and improve workplace readiness skills, through work-based learning experiences in a competitive, integrated work setting and increase opportunities for students with disabilities to explore post-secondary training options, leading to more industry recognized credentials, and meaningful post-secondary employment" (NTACT, n.d.). See **Figure 14.4** for the five required pre-ETSs. Whether working with a specialized caseload of individuals with disabilities or not, rehabilitation professionals who support youth or adults with disabilities will be well served with the knowledge and skills to serve clients with DD.

CHRONIC ILLNESS

Prevalence, Characteristics, and Functional Limitations

Chronic conditions are considered disorders that can be treated yet never cured (Center for Managing Chronic Illness, 2011). Approximately 60% of all adult Americans are currently living with one chronic illness (CDC, 2023c), while one in three adult Americans have two or more chronic conditions (Multiple Chronic Conditions Resource Center, n.d.).

Common chronic illnesses represented within the VR system include **arthritis, asthma and other respiratory disorders, cardiovascular disease, chronic fatigue syndrome, chronic pain, diabetes, fibromyalgia, long COVID, muscular sclerosis, obesity, seizure disorders, and sleep disorders** (see **Table 14.3** for brief descriptions).

Chronic illnesses result in lifelong limitations to clients with one or more conditions. Moreover, chronic disorders can present complicated symptomatology, making it difficult to receive a proper diagnosis and coordinated care, which often prolongs the assessment period, increases personal frustrations and fear, and impedes the ability of healthcare professionals to effectively treat the condition (Koch & Rumrill, 2017; Multiple Chronic Conditions Resource Center, n.d.). Although each chronic condition has specific symptoms related to the body part or region impacted and level of severity, common limitations or barriers across disorders include physical and cognitive impairment, loss in stamina, reduced self-efficacy and coping resources, environmental factors, and employer bias (de Dios Pérez et al., 2022; Hill et al., 2017; Linge et al., 2021). In addition, it is critical that rehabilitation professionals recognize any progressive nature of the chronic conditions. Individuals may experience ever-increasing symptoms with decreased efficacy in reversing or managing limitations. In addition, flare-ups, or acute spikes in symptoms are common with many chronic conditions, resulting in alternating periods of high and low needs (Arthritis Foundation, n.d.; Cleveland Clinic, 2022; Pradeep et al., 2013). Flare-ups can be a significant form of stress for clients, as they may be a result of a triggering event or present without warning. As well, sleep disruptions (whether caused by a sleep disorder or other chronic conditions) have an overarching impact on cognitive, emotional, and physical functioning (National Institute of Health, 2013).

TABLE 14.3 CHRONIC CONDITIONS WITH BASIC DESCRIPTIONS

CHRONIC CONDITION	DESCRIPTION
Arthritis	Inflammation or swelling in one or more joints
Asthma	Narrowing and swelling of the airway
Cardiovascular disease	Disease of the heart or blood vessels
Chronic fatigue syndrome	Extreme fatigue, worsened by physical or mental activity
Chronic pain	Persistent pain despite medication or treatment
Diabetes	A group of diseases resulting in too high of blood glucose (sugar) levels
Fibromyalgia	Pain and fatigue felt throughout the body
Long COVID	Symptoms and conditions that continue or develop after COVID-19 infection
Muscular sclerosis	Disease of the brain, spinal cord, and optic nerves
Obesity	Abnormal or excessive fat accumulation that presents a health risk
Seizure disorders	Sudden, uncontrolled burst of electrical activity in the brain
Sleep disorders	A group of disorders that disturb normal sleep patterns

Case Management and Employment Planning Considerations

Individuals with one or more chronic conditions have complex needs that may result in feelings of ambivalence toward employment and engaging in VR services (Iwanaga et al., 2021). Cases of clients with chronic illnesses are more likely to be longer in duration and more expensive (Fleming et al., 2014). However, research shows that VR can have far-reaching benefits beyond the employment outcome (Hall et al., 2013; Muller et al., 2017). For example, one study demonstrated how participation in VR improved health-related quality of life, decreased body mass index, and increased work self-efficacy (Linge et al., 2021). Therefore, individuals with chronic conditions may benefit from motivational interviewing, self-determination and self-efficacy supports, and work incentives benefits counseling (Buckley & Powers, 2022; Delin et al., 2012; Iwanaga et al., 2021; Nazarov, 2013) to fully engage in services. In addition, specific insight into the benefits of employment, the impact disability can have on employment, the legal rights of job seekers and employees with disabilities under the Americans with Disabilities Act, and effective accommodations and assistive technologies to mitigate and support symptom management through valuable resources (such as the Job Accommodation Network) will be helpful in securing client participation and confidence in the process and their potential. With accurate knowledge on chronic conditions and tools to assist persons with chronic illness, VR counselors will be better prepared to coordinate and provide ethical services to an often-misunderstood population (Hill et al., 2017; Larsson et al., 2021).

SPECIALTY CASELOADS

Blindness and Low Vision

PREVALENCE, CHARACTERISTICS, AND FUNCTIONAL LIMITATIONS

The CDC estimates that approximately 6 million Americans are living with vision loss and 1 million are blind (2021). "Vision loss is defined as permanent or uncorrectable vision loss based on the best-corrected visual acuity (BCVA) in the better-seeing eye, as measured using the methodology of the National Health and Nutrition Examination Survey (NHANES). These estimates measure the best visual function obtainable with proper glasses or contact lenses. These estimates do not include vision loss due to inadequate corrective glasses or contacts (uncorrected refractive error). They also do not capture impairment caused only by visual field or contrast sensitivity problems. Vision Loss: best-corrected visual acuity 20/40 or worse. Blindness: best-corrected visual acuity 20/200 or worse" (CDC, 2022c). Vision loss and blindness may be caused by infection, injury, tumors, diabetic retinopathy, macular degeneration, cataracts, glaucoma, and genetic conditions. Many factors such as current age, age at onset, accommodations and services available and utilized, social supports, and personal characteristics can influence an individual's experience of or adjustment to a vision loss or blindness. In addition to the loss of sight, a person may experience a decrease in quality of life and physical and mental health based on falls, isolation, depression, and anxiety (CDC, 2021). Functional limitations to explore include reading, writing, walking, driving, night vision, and perception deficits related to space, form, depth, and color.

CASE MANAGEMENT AND EMPLOYMENT PLANNING CONSIDERATIONS

Dating back to the Congressional Act of 1879, individuals who are blind or have low vision (B/LV) received differentiated services and additional protections in the United States when compared to other disability categories. Legislation and governmental programs were initiated to specifically improve the education and employment of persons with B/LV. With the passing of the Randolph-Sheppard Act of 1936 (PL 74-732) and Wagner-O'Day Act of 1938 (PL 75-739), the federal government granted the exclusive right to operate vending machine businesses in federal buildings and agreed to purchase designated products from facilities that trained and employed individuals from this population. To date, 22 states maintain a distinct VR agency to serve B/LV clients (Rehabilitation Services Administration [RSA], n.d.). In addition, RSA offers federal funding to states to provide independent living services to this population. With the availability of targeted nonprofit and public agencies and services, rehabilitation practitioners should become familiar with any additional resources, funding, and opportunities accessible to clients with B/LV.

When supporting this population, case managers need to be particularly aware of the impact technology has on case work, as some individuals with B/LV may not have assistive technologies set up to independently complete tasks such as review emails and documents, execute e-signatures, and participate in internet-based activities. Conversely, individuals may have assistive technologies at home to facilitate most independent living and internet-based actions yet are not equipped for the same out in the community. Clients with B/LV may or may not have mobility and safety concerns related to navigating to and from work, within work sites, and in novel environments such as may be required to participate in the job search process. For planning purposes, current research demonstrates the positive correlation between the provision of rehabilitation technology, on-the-job supports, job placement assistance, and job search assistance and successful employment outcomes (Cimera et al., 2015; Giesen & Hierholzer, 2016; Giesen & Lang, 2018). Understanding the characteristics, challenges, and resources unique to the individual with B/LV, their environment (personal residence, community and geographic region), and aspirations and preferences will guide how case workflow tasks can be completed and services planned in support of goal achievement and client independence.

Deaf and Hard of Hearing

PREVALENCE, CHARACTERISTICS, AND FUNCTIONAL LIMITATIONS

Approximately 13 million Americans (aged 12 and over) have a moderate to profound hearing loss (Wirth et al., 2023). An estimated 13% of adults experience difficulty hearing even with a hearing aid and 0.2% to 0.4% of Americans are functionally deaf (Wirth et al., 2023). Hearing loss may be caused by aging, disease, injury or trauma, genetics, medication side effects, and excessive noise exposure (Committee on Accessible and Affordable Hearing Health Care for Adults, 2016; Wirth et al., 2023). Of particular concern, 22% of Americans currently work in environments that involve unsafe noise levels (National Council on Aging [NCOA], 2023). In addition to the reduction in sensitivity to sound and ability to interpret auditory stimuli, individuals who are deaf or hard of hearing (D/HH) may experience communication barriers and mental health concerns (NCOA, 2023). Some functional limitations to consider are the inability to discriminate sounds or understand instructions, lack of balance and motor coordination, and difficulty in verbalizing and communicating with others. Depending on the age of onset, familial decisions, opportunities, and preferences, clients who are D/HH may use cochlear implants, hearing aids, or sign language to communicate with others. In addition, some clients who are D/HH may benefit from closed captioning services, written or electronic communication measures, and other assistive devices (such as visual alarms or alerting systems and speech-to-text software; Job Accommodation Network [JAN], n.d.).

CASE MANAGEMENT AND EMPLOYMENT PLANNING CONSIDERATIONS

Although not recipients of the same additional protections and programs as persons with B/LV, the Deaf population is commonly served in the general VR system by counselors through specialized caseloads (National Deaf Center [NDC], 2023). To support the working alliance and rapport building, direct counselor-to-client communication in the client's preferred communication style is best. Although not all D/HH clients converse through sign language, sign language fluency is generally a required skill for VR counselors with D/HH caseloads. Unfortunately, specialized caseloads for clients who are D/HH have decreased, and only about 2% of VR counselors are deaf themselves, resulting in a reduction of qualified and experienced professionals with familiarity of Deaf culture and a presence in the Deaf community (NDC, 2023). Extending to service providers, careful consideration should be employed when selecting external service providers for assessment activities and job placement/search services to ensure the usage of appropriately trained and skilled staff.

When not available internally, interpreting services can be provided through contractual agreements with outside entities. In the VR process, the infusion of an intermediary (such as an external interpreter or relay system) may increase client concerns over privacy, confidentiality, and lack of connection between service provider and client. However, if proper communication cannot be provided without the assistance of an interpreter, it is better to have the assistance than create a situation that will increase the odds of reduced or inaccurate communication and information exchanges. Remember, this could be a new experience for a D/HH client, as past appointments of a medical or sensitive nature may have been supported through interpreting provided by a family member or other trusted individual. Establishing expectations and providing information on the Code of Professional Conduct for interpreters through the Registry of Interpreters for the Deaf (2005) can be effective in reducing concerns and increasing communication. Ultimately, focus should remain on client comfortability and preference in communication modalities, services and service providers, and occupational choices.

Similar to communication, lack of self-advocacy skills may impact a client's ability to participate in services, seek employment, and maintain a position once acquired. As research encourages, the assessment and cultivation of self-advocacy skills should be interwoven into the VR process through intentional activities and encouragement (Schoffstall et al., 2015). In addition, transportation options and safety considerations should be explored in the assessment, planning, and transition into employment phases, as these dimensions will be very specific to the individual and work setting. In fact, transportation is positively associated with successful employment outcomes, as is assessment, counseling and guidance, diagnosis and treatment, maintenance, and rehabilitation technology (Cuevas et al., 2021). When exploring best practices and services for this population, the proper and consistent usage of assistive technologies to support communication and the delivery of other VR services is crucial (Cuevas et al., 2021; JAN, n.d.). Ultimately, as with any other population, each D/HH client is unique and requires individualized attention based on their preferences and needs.

SUMMARY

In conclusion, research demonstrates that some disability populations are particularly susceptible to disparities in service delivery and successful outcomes when compared to other VR populations. Targeted case management strategies that mitigate barriers and enhance services and goal attainment, as recommended, can foster more equitable treatment and improved results. In addition, specialized interventions and caseloads can support populations of interest related to their complicating nature or high prevalence within the VR system. This chapter took a deeper dive into a group of broad disability categories and offered unique insights, considerations, and recommendations for case management activities. With an understanding of potential additional challenges and contributing factors, rehabilitation practitioners can be better prepared to serve individuals intentionally and effectively through EBPs and case management strategies in an effort to increase client participation and improve case progression.

QUESTIONS FOR DISCUSSION

1. What case management issues may arise when working with individuals with dual diagnoses? What strategies should rehabilitation professionals consider employing to engage the individual, meet their complex needs, and fulfill their case manager roles?

2. What might be some case management benefits of specialized caseloads?

3. Which populations may be of particular interest to you? Please explain. What, if any, specialized skills, trainings, or credentials might you pursue to support service delivery to this population?

4. A client is seeking employment services. The individual has a history of depression and a moderate intellectual disability. The person is on an antidepressant prescribed by a primary physician yet is receiving no other services. Consider the following questions in reference to this person or a person with another combination of co-occurring disorders. What case management issues may arise when working with individuals with dual diagnoses? What strategies should rehabilitation professionals consider employing to engage the individual, meet their complex needs, and fulfill their case manager roles? What supports and resources are available in your local community to support this population? What inclusive and specialized transportation, housing, socialization and intervention services are available?

5. A client is seeking assistance with maintaining a job after sustaining a TBI. The individual has been experiencing employment difficulties due to new behavioral issues such as outbursts directed at supervisors and relationship conflicts with coworkers. Consider the following questions in reference to this person or a person with other limitations from a TBI. What case management issues may arise when working with individuals with TBIs? What strategies should rehabilitation professionals consider employing to engage the individual, meet their complex needs, and fulfill their case manager roles? What supports and resources are available in your local community to support this population? What inclusive and specialized transportation, housing, socialization, and intervention services are available?

6. A client is seeking self-employment assistance to start a kettle corn business. The individual has CP with some mobility and fine dexterity limitations. The individual also has a strong family support system. Consider the following questions in reference to this person or a person with another DD. What case management issues

may arise when working with individuals with DD? What strategies should rehabilitation professionals consider employing to engage the individual, meet their complex needs, and fulfill their case manager roles? What supports and resources are available in your local community to support this population? What inclusive and specialized transportation, housing, socialization and intervention services are available?

7. A client has requested assistance either maintaining their current job or finding a new job. The person has been an office building cleaner for 20+ years yet is experiencing difficulty keeping up with the work. The person is diagnosed with asthma, cardiovascular disease, and obesity. Consider the following questions in reference to this person or a person with other chronic illnesses. What case management issues may arise when working with individuals with chronic illnesses? What strategies should rehabilitation professionals consider employing to engage the individual, meet their complex needs, and fulfill their case manager roles? What supports and resources are available in your local community to support this population? What inclusive and specialized transportation, housing, socialization, and intervention services are available?

8. A veteran with posttraumatic stress disorder is seeking assistance with finding employment as a truck driver and securing a service animal. The individual has some old shrapnel lodged in a lower limb but reports no physical limitations. Consider the following questions in reference to this person or a person with another mental health disorder. What case management issues may arise when working with individuals with mental health disorders? What strategies should rehabilitation professionals consider employing to engage the individual, meet their complex needs, and fulfill their case manager roles? What supports and resources are available in your local community to support this population? What inclusive and specialized transportation, housing, socialization, and intervention services are available?

9. A client is seeking employment services. The individual has an SUD due to heroin use yet has not used any opiates for 4 months and faithfully participates in an outpatient treatment program. The client currently drinks alcohol and smokes cannabis occasionally (and within legal limits). Consider the following questions in reference to this person or a person with another SUD. What case management issues may arise when working with individuals with an SUD? What strategies should rehabilitation professionals consider employing to engage the individual, meet their complex needs, and fulfill their case manager roles? What supports and resources are available in your local community to support this population? What inclusive and specialized transportation, housing, socialization, and intervention services are available?

10. A client who is both deaf and has low vision is requesting assistance with finding a new job. The person had assistive technologies and natural supports in place at their current worksite, but the company is closing. The individual is anxious about the prospect of securing new employment with an employer who is as accommodating. Consider the following questions in reference to this person or a person with other sensory impairments. What case management issues may arise when working with individuals with a sensory impairment? What strategies should rehabilitation professionals consider employing to engage the individual, meet their complex needs, and fulfill their case manager roles? What supports and resources are available in your local community to support this population? What inclusive and specialized transportation, housing, socialization, and intervention services are available?

PUTTING IT INTO PRACTICE

Ask yourself these questions to target issues or concerns with rehabilitation management issues and special populations.

1. When working with individuals facing functional limitations that may affect their communication in meetings, self-advocacy, service participation, and task completion, what unique case management strategies do you employ? How do you address the specific implications relevant to special populations?

2. What issues and resources, both inclusive and specialized, are available to support employment-related needs, such as transportation, housing, socialization, and intervention or treatment providers?

3. Considering the global changes and the impact of the COVID-19 pandemic, as well as technological advancements leading to increased life spans, how can rehabilitation professionals prepare for the future? What transformations do you foresee in case and caseload management? Additionally, what skills will be necessary to effectively serve special populations that might emerge in tomorrow's society?

A robust set of instructor resources designed to supplement this text is located at **http://connect.springerpub.com/content/book/978-0-8261-5963-2.** Qualifying instructors may request access by emailing **textbook@springerpub.com.**

REFERENCES

ADA National Network. (2021a). *The ADA, addiction, recovery, and employment.* https://adata.org/factsheet/ada-addiction-recovery-and-employment

ADA National Network. (2021b). *The Americans with Disabilities Act, addiction, and recovery for State and Local Governments.* https://adata.org/factsheet/ada-addiction-and-recovery-and-government

Ahonle, Z. J., Barnes, M., Romero, S., Sorrells, A. M., & Brooks, G. I. (2020). State-federal vocational rehabilitation in traumatic brain injury: What predictors are associated with employment outcomes? *Rehabilitation Counseling Bulletin, 63*(3), 143–155. https://doi.org/10.1177/0034355219864684

Almalky, H. A. (2020). Employment outcomes for individuals with intellectual and developmental disabilities: A literature review. *Children and Youth Services Review, 109*, 104656. https://doi.org/10.1016/j.childyouth.2019.104656

American Psychiatric Association. (2013). *Diagnostic and statistical manual of mental disorders* (5th ed.). Author.

Amsalem, D., Hasson-Ohayon, I., Gothelf, D., & Roe, D. (2018). Subtle ways of stigmatization among professionals: The subjective experience of consumers and their family members. *Psychiatric Rehabilitation Journal, 41*(3), 163–168. https://doi.org/10.1037/prj0000310

Anderson, M. L., Ziedonis, D. M., & Najavits, L. M. (2014). Posttraumatic stress disorder and substance use disorder comorbidity among individuals with physical disabilities: Findings from the national comorbidity survey replication. *Journal of Traumatic Stress, 27*, 182–191. https://doi.org/10.1002/jts.21894

Andrew, J. D., & Andrew, M. J. (2017). *The disability handbook.* Aspen Professional Services.

Arthritis Foundation. (n.d.). *What triggers an arthritis flare?* https://www.arthritis.org/health-wellness/healthy-living/managing-pain/pain-relief-solutions/what-triggers-an-arthritis-flare

Beaulieu-Bonneau, S., St-Onge, F., Blackburn, M. C., Banville, A., Paradis-Giroux, A. A., & Ouellet, M. C. (2017). Alcohol and drug use before and during the first year after traumatic brain injury. *The Journal of Head Trauma Rehabilitation, 33*(3), 51–60. https://doi.org/10.1097/HTR.0000000000000341

Bhatt, N. V., & Gentile, J. P. (2021). Co-occurring intellectual disability and substance use disorders. *AIMS Public Health, 8*(3), 479–484. https://doi.org/10.3934/publichealth.2021037

Buckley, C. P., & Powers, B. F. (2022). Targeted motivational interviewing techniques assist the process of verbal de-escalation in vocational rehabilitation. *Journal of Vocational Rehabilitation, 56*, 217–222. https://doi.org/10.3233/JVR-221185

Cabán-Alemán, C., Iobst, S., Luna, A. M., & Foster, A. (2020). Addressing the poverty barrier in collaborative care for adults experiencing homelessness: A case-based report. *Community Mental Health Journal, 56*, 1–10. https://doi.org/10.1007/s10597-019-00526-1

Center for Managing Chronic Illness. (2011). *What is chronic disease?* https://cmcd.sph.umich.edu/about/about-chronic-disease/

Centers for Disease Control and Prevention. (2021). *Vision loss and mental health.* https://www.cdc.gov/visionhealth/resources/features/vision-loss-mental-health.html

Centers for Disease Control and Prevention. (2022a). *Developmental disabilities.* https://www.cdc.gov/ncbddd/developmentaldisabilities/

Centers for Disease Control and Prevention. (2022b). *What is cerebral palsy?* https://www.cdc.gov/ncbddd/cp/facts.html

Centers for Disease Control and Prevention. (2022c). *Prevalence estimates—vision loss and blindness.* https://www.cdc.gov/visionhealth/vehss/estimates/vision-loss-prevalence.html

Centers for Disease Control and Prevention. (2023a). *Report to congress: Traumatic brain injury in the United States.* https://www.cdc.gov/traumaticbraininjury/pubs/tbi_report_to_congress.html

Centers for Disease Control and Prevention. (2023b). *Facts about Down syndrome.* https://www.cdc.gov/ncbddd/birthdefects/downsyndrome.html

Centers for Disease Control and Prevention. (2023c). *National Center for Chronic Disease Prevention and Health Promotion (NCCDPHP).* https://www.cdc.gov/chronicdisease/index.htm

Chan, F., Tansey, T. N., Chronister, J., McMahon, B. T., Iwanaga, K., Wu, J. R., Chen, X., Lee, B., Bengtson, K., Umucu, E., Flowers, S., & Moser, E. (2017). Rehabilitation counseling practice in state vocational rehabilitation and the effect of the Workforce Innovation and Opportunity Act (WIOA). *Journal of Applied Rehabilitation Counseling, 48*(3), 20–28. https://doi.org/10.1891/0047-2220.48.3.20

Cimera, R. E. (2009). The outcomes and costs of public vocational rehabilitation consumers with mental illness. *Journal of Applied Rehabilitation Counseling, 40*(2), 28–33. https://doi.org/10.1891/0047-2220.40.2.28

Cimera, R. E., Rumrill, P. D., Chan, F., Kaya, C., & Bezyak, J. (2015). Vocational rehabilitation services and outcomes for transition-age youth with visual impairments and blindness. *Journal of Vocational Rehabilitation, 43*(2), 103–111. https://doi.org/10.3233/JVR-150760

Cleveland Clinic. (2022). *Fibromyalgia.* https://my.clevelandclinic.org/health/diseases/4832-fibromyalgia

Committee on Accessible and Affordable Hearing Health Care for Adults. (2016). Hearing loss: Extent, impact, and research needs. In D. G. Blazer, S. Domnitz, & C. T. Liverman (Eds.), *Hearing health care for adults: Priorities for improving access and affordability.* National Academies Press (US).

Cuevas, S., Hansmann, S., Rodrigo, H., Saladin, S. P., & Shoen, B. (2021). Factors contributing to successful employment outcomes for individuals who are hard-of-hearing. *Journal of Vocational Rehabilitation, 55*(1), 43–60. https://doi.org/10.3233/JVR-211145

Currier Kipping, K. R., Phillips, B. N., Whicker, J. J., McKnight, M., & Landon, T. J. (2021). Exploring the knowledge, perceptions and practice patterns of school counselors regarding vocational rehabilitation for transition age youth with disabilities. *Journal of Rehabilitation, 87*(4), 38–47.

Davis, M., Koroloff, N., Mizrahi, R., & Morrison, E. (2022). Collaboration between mental health and vocational rehabilitation programs for transition-age youth vocational outcomes. *Psychiatric Rehabilitation Journal, 45*(4), 303–313. https://doi.org/10.1037/prj0000539

De Dios Pérez, B., Radford, K., & das Nair, R. (2022). Experiences of people with multiple sclerosis at work: Towards the understanding of the needs for a job retention vocational rehabilitation intervention. *Work, 72*(1), 303–313. https://doi.org/10.3233/WOR-210012

Degeneffe, C. E., & Lee, G. (2015). Brain injury and the family: A guide for rehabilitation counselors. In M. Millington & I. Marini (Eds.), *Families in rehabilitation counseling: A community-based rehabilitation approach* (pp. 153–170). Springer.

Degeneffe, C. E., Tucker, M., & Ahonle, Z. J. (2023a). Brief report: Participation among transition-aged youth with traumatic brain injury in the state/federal vocational rehabilitation system. *Rehabilitation Counseling Bulletin, 65*(2), 161–165. https://doi.org/10.1177/0034355220967109

Degeneffe, C. E., Tucker, M., Ross, M., & Umucu, E. (2023b). The influence of state-level contextual factors on state/federal system vocational rehabilitation employment outcomes for persons with traumatic brain injury. *Rehabilitation Counseling Bulletin, 66*(2), 83–99. https://doi.org/10.1177/00343552211067576

Delin, B. S., Hartman, E. C., & Sell, C. W. (2012). The impact of work incentive benefits counseling on employment outcomes: Evidence form two return-to-work demonstrations. *Journal of Vocational Rehabilitation, 36*(2), 97–107. https://doi.org/10.3233/JVR-2012-0585

Dillahunt-Aspillaga, C., Nakase-Richardson, R., Hart, T., Powell-Cope, G., Dreer, L. E., Eapen, B. C. Barnett, S. D., Mellick, D., Haskin, A., & Silva, M. A. (2017). Predictors of employment outcomes in veterans with traumatic brain injury: A VA traumatic brain injury model systems study. *Journal of Head Trauma Rehabilitation, 32*(4), 271–282. https://doi.org/10.1097/HTR .0000000000000275

Drake, R. E. (2020). Introduction to the special issue on Individual Placement and Support (IPS) international. *Psychiatric Rehabilitation Journal, 43*(1), 1. https://doi.org/10.1037/prj0000401

Dreer, L. E., Ketchum, J. M., Novack, T. A., Bogner, J., Felix, E. R., Corrigan, J. D., Johnson-Greene, D., & Hammond, F. M. (2018). Obesity and overweight problems among individuals 1 to 25 years following acute rehabilitation for traumatic brain injury: A NIDILRR traumatic brain injury model systems study. *Journal of Head Trauma Rehabilitation, 33*(4), 246–256. http://doi.org/10.1097/ Htr.0000000000000408

Ebener, D. J., & Smedema, S. M. (2011). Physical disability and substance use disorders: A convergence of adaptation and recovery. *Rehabilitation Counseling Bulletin, 54*(3), 131–141. https://doi .org/10.1177/0034355210394873

Falvo, D. R., & Holland, B. E. (2018). *Medical and psychosocial aspects of chronic illness and disability* (6th ed.). Jones and Bartlett Publishers.

Fleming, A. R., Phillips, B. N., & Kline, K. M. (2014). Clients with chronic illness in VR agencies: How do they compare with other client populations. *Journal of Vocational Rehabilitation, 42*(2), 101–113. http://doi.org/10.3233/JVR-150728

Frain, M. P., Lee, J., Roland, M., & Tschopp, M. K. (2012) A rehabilitation counselor integration into the successful rehabilitation of veterans with disabilities. In P. J. Toriello, M. L. Bishop, & P. D. Rumrill (Eds.), *New directions in rehabilitation counseling: Creative responses to professional, clinical, and educational challenges* (pp. 255–281). Aspen Professional Services.

Friedman, C., & Rizzolo, M. C. (2017). "Get us real jobs:" Supported employment services for people with intellectual and developmental disabilities in Medicaid Home and Community Based Services Waivers. *Journal of Vocational Rehabilitation, 46*(1), 107–116. http://doi.org/10.3233/JVR-160847

Giesen, J. M., & Hierholzer, A. (2016). Vocational rehabilitation services and employment for SSDI beneficiaries with visual impairments. *Journal of Vocational Rehabilitation, 44*(2), 175–189. https://doi .org/10.3233/JVR-150789

Giesen, J. M., & Lang, A. H. (2018). Predictors of earnings enabling likely roll departure for SSDI beneficiaries with visual impairments in vocational rehabilitation. *Journal of Disability Policy Studies, 29*(3), 166–177. https://doi.org/10.1177/1044207318780363

Glenn, M. K., Huber, M. J., Keferl, J., Wright-Bell, A., & Lane, T. (n.d.). *Substance use disorders and vocational rehabilitation: VR Counselor's desk reference*. https://medicine.wright.edu/sites/medicine .wright.edu/files/page/attachments/VR_Desk_Reference.pdf

Glenn, M. K., & Keferl, J. (2008). An exploratory investigation of rehabilitation counselors' perceived readiness to undertake substance use disorder screening in vocational rehabilitation. *Journal of Applied Rehabilitation Counseling, 39*(2), 37–42. https://doi.org/10.1891/0047-2220.39.2.37

Hall, J. P., Kurth, N. K., & Hunt, S. L. (2013). Employment as a health determinant for working-age, dually-eligible people with disabilities. *Disability and Health Journal, 6*(2), 100–106. https://doi .org/10.1016/j.dhjo.2012.11.001

Heinemann, A. W., McAweeney, M., Lazowski, L. E., & Moore, D. (2008). Utilization of substance abuse screening by state vocational rehabilitation agencies. *Journal of Applied Rehabilitation Counseling, 39*(2), 5–11. https://doi.org/10.1891/0047-2220.39.2.5

Heinemann, A. W., Moore, D., Lazowski, L. E., Huber, M., & Semik, P. (2014). Benefits of substance use disorder screening on employment outcomes in state–federal vocational rehabilitation programs. *Rehabilitation Counseling Bulletin, 57*(3), 144–158. https://doi.org/10.1177/0034355213503908

Hill, J., Koch, L. C., & Rumrill, P. D. (2017). Ethical considerations for providing vocational rehabilitation services to individuals with chronic pain. *Journal of Vocational Rehabilitation, 48*(3), 321–330. https://doi.org/10.3233/JVR-180941

Honeycutt, T., Bardos, M., & McLeod, S. (2014). *Bridging the gap: A comparative assessment of vocational rehabilitation agency practices with transition-age youth*. Mathematica Policy Research.

Hoy, K. E., & Miner Holden, J. (2014). Licensed professional counselors' attitudes about and interest in providing services for clients with schizophrenia: Advocacy implications. *Journal of Counselor Leadership and Advocacy, 1*(1), 67–82. https://doi.org/10.1080/2326716X.2014.893214

Iwanaga, K., Chan, F., Tansey, T. N., Hoyt, W. T., & Berven, N. L. (2021). Evaluation of constructs based on self-determination theory and self-efficacy theory as predictors of vocational rehabilitation engagement for people with physical and sensory disabilities. *Rehabilitation Counseling Bulletin, 64*(3), 131–144. https://doi.org/10.1177/0034355220942301

Job Accommodation Network. (n.d.). *Deafness*. https://askjan.org/disabilities/Deafness.cfm

Johnson, J. E., Aref, F., Ward-Sutton, C., Moore, C. L., Washington, A. L., & Webb, K. (2020). National study of American Indian vocational rehabilitation program and Veterans Affairs interagency collaborations: An emerging conceptual framework for co-serving Native American and Alaskan Native veterans with disabilities. *Journal of Rehabilitation, 86*(4), 48–57. https://link.gale.com/apps/doc/A651085303/ITOF?u=durh55126&sid=summon&xid=2161bebe

Kaya, C., & Chan, F. (2017). Vocational rehabilitation services and outcomes for working age people with depression and other mood disorders. *Journal of Rehabilitation, 83*(3), 44–52. https://link.gale.com/apps/doc/A511384438/EAIM?u=anon~35fc6457&sid=sitemap&xid=0a78e5bd

Kim, J., Riesen, T., Inge, K., Keeton, B., Weathers, M., & Tansey, T. N. (2023). Customized employment as a pathway to competitive integrated employment: An analysis of RSA 911 data of state vocational rehabilitation agencies with the highest use of this intervention. *Journal of Vocational Rehabilitation, 58*(1), 89–98. https://doi.org/10.3233/JVR-221227

Koch, L. C., & Rumrill, P. D. (2017). *Rehabilitation counseling and emerging disabilities: Medical, psychological, and vocational aspects.* Springer Publishing Company.

Larsson, K., Liljestam Hurtigh, A., Andersén, A. M. V., & Anderzén, I. (2021). Vocational rehabilitation professionals' perceptions of facilitators and barriers to return to work: A qualitative descriptive study. *Rehabilitation Counseling Bulletin, 66*(1), 66–78. https://doi.org/10.1177/00343552211060013

Leahy, M. J., Del Valle, R. J., Landon, T. J., Iwanaga, K., Sherman, S. G., Reyes, A., & Chan, F. (2018). Promising and evidence-based practices in vocational rehabilitation: Results of a national Delphi study. *Journal of Vocational Rehabilitation, 48*(1), 37–48. https://psycnet.apa.org/doi/10.3233/JVR-170914

Linge, A. D., Jensen, C., Laake, P., & Bjørkly, S. K. (2021). Changes to body mass index, work self-efficacy, health-related quality of life, and work participation in people with obesity after vocational rehabilitation: A prospective observational study. *BMC Public Health, 21*(1), 936. https://doi.org/10.1186/s12889-021-10954-y

Lusk, S. L., Koch, L. C., & Paul, T. M. (2016). Recovery-oriented vocational rehabilitation services for individuals with co-occurring psychiatric disabilities and substance use disorders. *Rehabilitation Research, Policy, and Education, 30*(3), 243–258. https://doi.org/10.1891/2168-6653.30.3.243

Lusk, S. L., & Paul, T. M. (2017). Rehabilitation professionals' attitudes towards medicinal marijuana use: A pilot study. *Journal of Applied Rehabilitation Counseling, 48*(1), 25–30. https://doi.org/10.1891/0047-2220.48.1.25

Lusk, S. L., & Stipp, A. (2018). Opioid use disorders as an emerging disability. *Journal of Vocational Rehabilitation, 48*(3), 345–358. https://doi.org/10.3233/JVR-180943

Magura, S., & Marshall, T. (2020). The effectiveness of interventions intended to improve employment outcomes for persons with substance use disorder: An updated systematic review. *Substance Use & Misuse, 55*(13), 2230–2236. https://doi.org/10.1080/10826084.2020.1797810

Mayo Clinic. (2018). *Fetal alcohol syndrome.* https://www.mayoclinic.org/diseases-conditions/fetal-alcohol-syndrome/symptoms-causes/syc-20352901

Mazzotti, V., Rowe, D. A., Kwiatek, S., Weight, A., Chang, W., Fowler, C. H., Poppen, M., Sinclair, J., & Test, D. W. (2020). Secondary transition predictors of postschool success: An update to the research base. *Career Development and Transition for Exceptional Individuals, 44*(1), 1–18. https://doi.org/10.1177/2165143420959793

Moore, D., McAweeney, M., Keferl, J., Glenn, M., & Ford, J. A. (2008). Policy issues in vocational rehabilitation related to consumers with substance use disorders. *Journal of Applied Rehabilitation Counseling, 39*(2), 12–18, 47–48. https://doi.org/10.1891/0047-2220.39.2.12

Muller, V., Peebles, M. C., Chiu, C. Y., Iwanaga, K., Tang, X., Brooks, J., Eagle, D., & Chan, F. (2017). Association of employment and health and well-being in people with fibromyalgia. *Journal of Rehabilitation, 83*(3), 37–43.

Multiple Chronic Conditions Resource Center. (n.d.). *Multiple chronic conditions.* https://www.multiplechronicconditions.org/multiple-chronic-conditions/

Nash, A. J., Marcus, M. T., Cron, S., Scamp, N., Truitt, M., & McKenna, Z. (2017). Preparing nursing students to work with patients with alcohol or drug-related problems. *Journal of Addictions Nursing, 28*(3), 124–130. https://doi.org/10.1097/JAN.0000000000000175

National Council on Aging. (2023). *Hearing loss is more common than diabetes: Why aren't we addressing it?* https://www.ncoa.org/adviser/hearing-aids/hearing-loss-america/

National Deaf Center. (2023). *How will fewer VR counselors affect deaf people across the US?* https://nationaldeafcenter.org/news-items/how-will-fewer-vr-counselors-affect-deaf-people-across-the-us/

National Institute of Health. (2013). *The benefits of slumber.* https://newsinhealth.nih.gov/2013/04/benefits-slumber

National Institute of Mental Health. (2021a). *Chronic illness and mental health: Recognizing and treating depression.* https://www.nimh.nih.gov/health/publications/chronic-illness-mental-health

National Institute of Mental Health. (2021b). *Statistics: Mental illness.* https://www.nimh.nih.gov/health/statistics/mental-illness.shtml

National Institute of Neurological Disorders and Stroke. (n.d.). *What is a traumatic brain injury (TBI)?* https://www.ninds.nih.gov/health-information/disorders/traumatic-brain-injury-tbi

National Technical Assistance Center on Transition. (n.d.). *Pre-employment transition services.* https://transitionta.org/topics/pre-ets/

Nazarov, Z. E. (2013). *Can benefits and work incentives counseling be a path to future economic self-sufficiency for SSI/SSDI beneficiaries?* Boston College, Center for Retirement Research. https://www.semanticscholar.org/paper/Can-Benefits-and-Work-Incentives-Counseling-Be-a-to-Nazarov/4201c821dde6d7986b78ae636222c0c93c171823

Niemeier, J. P., Leininger, S. L., Whitney, M. P., Newman, M. A., Hirsch, M. A., Evans, S. L., Sing, R. F., Huynh, T. T., & Perrin, P. B. (2016). Does history of substance use disorder predict acute traumatic brain injury rehabilitation outcomes? *NeuroRehabilitation, 38*(4), 371–383. https://doi.org/10.3233/nre-161328

Office of Disability Employment Policy. (n.d.-a). *Employment first.* https://www.dol.gov/agencies/odep/initiatives/employment-first

Office of Disability Employment Policy. (n.d.-b). *Competitive integrated employment.* https://www.dol.gov/agencies/odep/featured/bbs

Olney, M. F., & Emery-Flores, D. S. (2017). "I Get My Therapy from Work": Wellness recovery action plan strategies that support employment success. *Rehabilitation Counseling Bulletin, 60*(3), 175–184. https://doi.org/10.1177/0034355216660059

Olney, M. F., Emery-Flores, D., Compton, C., Zuniga, R., & Tucker, M. (2014). It takes a village: Influences on former SSI/DI beneficiaries who transition to employment. *Journal of Rehabilitation, 80*(4), 28–41.

Olney, M. F., & Gill, K. J. (2016). Can psychiatric rehabilitation be core to CORE? *Rehabilitation Research, Policy, and Education, 30*(3), 204–214. http://doi.org/10.1891/2168-6653.30.3.204

Oswald, G. R., Flexer, R., Alderman, L. A., & Huber, M. (2016). Predictive value of personal characteristics and the employment of transition-aged youth in vocational rehabilitation. *Journal of Rehabilitation, 82*(4), 60–66.

Peterson, S. (2023). Facilitating a warm handoff in state vocational rehabilitation service delivery. *Journal of Applied Rehabilitation Counseling, 54*(1), 33–47. http://doi.org/10.1891/JARC-2021-0019

Peterson, S., Alkhadim, G., Davis, M., & Olney, M. (2021). Increasing successful employment outcomes for individuals with psychiatric disabilities with on-the-job training. *The Rehabilitation Professional, 29*(1), 21–36.

Peterson, S., & Olney, M. (2020). An examination of CACREP curriculum standards from a psychiatric rehabilitation recovery model perspective. *Rehabilitation Research, Policy, and Education, 34*(4), 222–234. https://doi.org/10.1891/RE-19-17

Peterson, S., & Olney, M. (2021). Disparities between individuals with and without psychiatric disabilities: State vocational rehabilitation services and employment outcomes. *Journal of Rehabilitation, 87*(3), 36–46.

Peterson, S., Saia, T., Maya Castellanos, A. D., & Olney, M. (2021). Promoting ethical individualized plan for employment (IPE) development with the wellness recovery action plan (WRAP). *Journal of Rehabilitation, 87*(4), 4–11.

Pickens, J. L., & Dymond, S. K. (2022). Keys to the employment services castle: Needed skills and experiences. *Journal of Vocational Rehabilitation, 56*(2), 165–175. https://doi.org/10.3233/JVR-221180

Pradeep, S., Saunders, K. W., & Von Korff, M. (2013). Prevalence and characteristics of flare-ups of chronic nonspecific back pain in primary care: A telephone survey. *The Clinical Journal of Pain, 28*(7), 573–580. https://doi.org/10.1097/ajp.0b013e31823ae173

Registry of Interpreters for the Deaf. (2005). *NAD-RID code of professional conduct.* https://acrobat.adobe.com/link/track?uri=urn%3Aaid%3Ascds%3AUS%3A154885ef-2f50-3664-ba5e-f9654c395ddf&viewer%21megaVerb=group-discover

Rehabilitation Services Administration. (n.d.). *State vocational rehabilitation agencies.* https://rsa.ed.gov/about/states

Reif, S., Karriker-Jaffe, K. J., Valentine, A., Patterson, D., Mericle, A. A., Sayko Adams, R., & Greenfield, T. K. (2022). Substance use and misuse patterns and disability status in the 2020 US National Alcohol Survey: A contributing role for chronic pain. *Disability and Health Journal, 15*(2), 1–9. https://doi.org/10.1016/j.dhjo.2022.101290

Roux, A. M., Rast, J. E., Anderson, K. A., Garfield, T., & Shattuck, P. T. (2021). Vocational rehabilitation service utilization and employment outcomes among secondary students on the autism spectrum. *Journal of Autism and Developmental Disorders, 51*, 212–226. https://doi.org/10.1007/s10803-020-04533-0

Rumrill, P. D., & Koch, L. C. (2020). Americans with traumatic brain injuries and the vocational rehabilitation process: Strategies for meeting the needs of emerging consumers. *Journal of Rehabilitation.* https://worksupport.com/research/documents/pdf/ContentServer.pdf

Salzer, M. S., Baron, R. C., Brusilovskiy, E., Lawer, L. J., & Mandell, D. S. (2011). Access and outcomes for persons with psychotic and affective disorders receiving vocational rehabilitation services. *Psychiatric Services, 62*(7), 796–799. https://doi.org/10.1176/ps.62.7.pss6207_0796

Schoffstall, S., Cawthon, S. W., Tarantolo-Leppo, R. H., & Wendel, E. (2015). Developing consumer and system-level readiness for effective self-advocacy: Perspectives from vocational rehabilitation counselors working with deaf and hard of hearing individuals in post-secondary settings. *Journal of Developmental and Physical Disabilities, 27,* 533–555. https://doi.org/10.1007/s10882-015-9435-3

Sevak, P., & Khan, S. (2017). Psychiatric versus physical disabilities: A comparison of barriers and facilitators to employment. *Psychiatric Rehabilitation Journal, 40*(2), 163. https://doi.org/10.1037/prj0000236

Smith, T. J., Dillahunt-Aspillaga, C., & Kenney, C. (2015). Integrating customized employment practices within the vocational rehabilitation system. *Journal of Vocational Rehabilitation, 42*(3), 201–208. https://doi.org/10.3233/JVR-150740

Social Security Administration. (2020). *Annual statistical report on the social security disability insurance program, 2019.* SSA publication (13-11826). https://www.ssa.gov/policy/docs/statcomps/di_asr/2019/di_asr19.pdf

Sprong, M. E., Dallas, B., Melvin, A., & Koch, D. S. (2014). Substance abuse and vocational rehabilitation: A survey of policies & procedures. *Journal of Rehabilitation, 80*(4), 4–9.

Substance Abuse and Mental Health Services Administration. (2020). *Key substance use and mental health indicators in the United States: Results from the 2019 national survey on drug use and health.* Center for behavioral health statistics and quality, substance abuse and mental health services administration. https://www.samhsa.gov/data/sites/default/files/reports/rpt29393/2019NSDUHFFRPDFWHTML/2019NSDUHFFR1PDFW090120.pdf

Substance Abuse and Mental Health Services Administration. (2022). *Highlights for the 2021 national survey on drug use and health.* https://www.samhsa.gov/data/sites/default/files/2022-12/2021NSDUHFFRHighlights092722.pdf

Taylor, J., & Seebeck, R. (2020). Preinjury psychological factors and case formulation in mild traumatic brain injury rehabilitation: A case report. *Rehabilitation Counseling Bulletin, 63*(3), 156–167. https://doi.org/10.1177/0034355219878500

Taylor, R. M., & Minkovitz, C. S. (2021). Warm handoffs for improving client receipt of services: A systematic review. *Maternal and Child Health Journal, 25*(4),1–14. https://doi.org/10.1007/s10995-020-03057-4

Topitzes, J., Mersky, J. P., Mueller, D. J., Bacalso, E., & Williams, C. (2019). Implementing Trauma Screening, Brief Intervention, and Referral to Treatment (T-SBIRT) within employment services: A feasibility trial. *American Journal of Community Psychology, 64*(3–4), 298–309. https://doi.org/10.1002/ajcp.12361

Tucker, M. S., & Degeneffe, C. E. (2017). Predictors of employment following postsecondary education for vocational rehabilitation participants with traumatic brain injury. *Rehabilitation Counseling Bulletin, 60*(4), 215–226. https://doi.org/10.1177/0034355216660279

Walker, E. R., & Druss, B. G. (2017). Cumulative burden of comorbid mental disorders, substance use disorders, chronic medical conditions, and poverty on health among adults in the U.S.A. *Psychology, Health & Medicine, 22*(6), 727–735. https://doi.org/10.1080/13548506.2016.1227855

Wang, G. S., Davies, S. D., Halmo, L. S., Sass, A., & Mistry, R. D. (2018). Impact of marijuana legalization in Colorado on adolescent emergency and urgent care visits. *Journal of Adolescent Health, 63*(2), 239–241. https://doi.org/10.1016/j.jadohealth.2017.12.010

Waynor, W. R., Reinhardt-Wood, D., & Taylor, E. (2018). The role of work-related self-efficacy in assertive community treatment. *Rehabilitation Research, Policy, and Education, 32*(4), 244–252. https://psycnet.apa.org/doi/10.1891/2168-6653.32.4.244

Wehman, P. (2012). Supported employment: What is it? *Journal of Vocational Rehabilitation, 37,* 139–142.

White, A. R. (2011). Characteristics of three consumer cohorts in vocational rehabilitation: A comparison of consumers with dual-diagnosis, psychiatric, or substance use related disorders. *Journal of Applied Rehabilitation Counseling, 42*(1), 15–24. https://psycnet.apa.org/doi/10.1891/0047-2220.42.1.15

Wirth, J., Hall, A., & Jorgensen, L. (June 27, 2023). *Deafness and hearing loss statistics.* Forbes Health. https://www.forbes.com/health/hearing-aids/deafness-statistics/

Workforce Innovation and Opportunity Act. (2014). *Public Law 113-128—July 22, 2014.* https://www.govinfo.gov/content/pkg/PLAW-113publ128/pdf/PLAW-113publ128.pdf

Xiao, Y., & O'Sullivan, D. (2019). Development of a rubric to assess state/federal vocational rehabilitation substance use disorders policies and procedures. *Journal of Rehabilitation, 85*(3), 55–63.

Xiao, Y., & Zhou, L. (2020). Connecting vocational rehabilitation policy and practice: A national study on substance use disorders. *Journal of Rehabilitation, 86*(1), 54–64.

Yang, L. H., Wong, L. Y., Grivel, M. M., & Hasin, D. S. (2017). Stigma and substance use disorders: An international phenomenon. *Current Opinion in Psychiatry, 30*(5), 378–388. https://doi.org/10.1097/YCO.0000000000000351

Yetman, D. (2022). Comorbidity: Causes and health implications. *Healthline.* https://www.healthline.com/health/comorbidity

Yi, H., Corrigan, J. D., Singichetti, B., Bogner, J. A., Manchester, K., Guo, J., & Yang, J. (2018). Lifetime history of traumatic brain injury and current disability among Ohio adults. *The Journal of Head Trauma Rehabilitation, 33*(4), E24–E32. https://doi.org/10.1097/htr.0000000000000352

Young, N. D., Mathews, B. L., Pan, A. Y., Herndon, J. L., Bleck, A. A., & Takala, C. R. (2020). Warm handoff, or cold shoulder? An analysis of handoffs for primary care behavioral health consultation on patient engagement and systems utilization. *Clinical Practice in Pediatric Psychology, 8*(3), 241–246. https://psycnet.apa.org/doi/10.1037/cpp0000360

Zhang, D., Li, Y., Roberts, E., Orsag, M., & Maddalozzo, R. (2023). An investigation of the collaborations between educators and vocational rehabilitation counselors in providing pre-employment transition services. *Inclusion, 11*(2), 135–146.

CHAPTER 15

Challenges and Visions for the Future of Professional Practice

---

LEARNING OBJECTIVES

By the end of this chapter, learners will be able to:

- Explain current challenges to the field of rehabilitation and their impact on everyday case and caseload management.
- Recognize potential future directions within rehabilitation.
- Appreciate opportunities that exist for the field that may sustain and improve supports and processes within case and caseload management.

INTRODUCTION

As in most professions, there are various **challenges** and **opportunities** that present themselves throughout the life span of an occupation. Some events prove pivotal in the evolution of an entire field, while others appear more like bumps in the road when reviewed in hindsight. Over the past several decades, the field of rehabilitation has faced **threats** to funding, service and outcome features, credentialing, curricular standards, and educational requirements for employment (Friedman, 2022: McClanahan & Sligar, 2015; McDonnall et al., 2022; Perry et al., 2018; Peterson, 2022). This erosion or, at the very least, test has left practitioners questioning the proliferation of the unique knowledge, skills, abilities, and identity of **rehabilitation** professionals (Friedman, 2022; McClanahan & Sligar, 2015 O'Brien & Graham, 2009). Little consensus, if any, has been found on the long-lasting impact of this assault on the profession or resulting practical trends in education and employment opportunities.

Through all of these experiences, one unifying mandate has remained: the absolute necessity to ensure the continuation of quality in the services and outcomes of individuals with disabilities and other life-altering experiences. Knowledge is power, and inaction will result in further instability and the chipping away of the rehabilitation field. Therefore, it is the responsibility of all professionals (practitioners, educators, and advocates) to be part of the solution, determining and following through with the required steps to safeguard the sustainability of this vocation and confirm a brighter future for the next generation. To that end, this chapter will explore current challenges to the field that have been percolating for years, or even decades, yet are now reaching an undeniable crisis level. In addition, a look into the future and potential areas of opportunity will be offered.

CHALLENGES

Rehabilitation is not unique to other professions in that there are various times and situations that create monumental challenges and long-felt adverse repercussions across the field. More specifically, many *helping* professions have experienced changing societal sentiments and threats to their validity over time (Feyereisen et al., 2021; Levine, 2022; Lingel et al., 2022; Samman, 2021). Professions have reformed or strengthened their positions through a formalized and unified strategy, often infused with **evidence-based practices** (EBPs), public informational campaigns, effective advocacy efforts, increasing educational requirements and professional competencies, and meaningful impact data (Cashin, 2018; Davenport, 2021; Dennis & Ramsay, 2019; Mikhly, 2014/2015; Moore, 2018; Torres, 2023). Many may argue that rehabilitation is currently experiencing one such crossroad. As national, state, and local challenges mount and pressure rolls down the proverbial hill from administrators to **case management** staff, policies and practices will evolve. In order for such adjustments within the system to be realistic and effective, all stakeholders must be involved (including but not limited to clients, client advocates and support networks, service providers, **caseload managers, vocational rehabilitation** [VR] counselors, administrators, educators, and legislators). All parties must be informed of the realities and solution-focused, compromising within reason and holding steadfast to what is sacred. For those discussions to occur and prove fruitful, exploring challenges is an appropriate first step.

Elevated Mental Health Concerns

Beyond formally diagnosed severe mental illness, 90% of Americans are concerned over the **mental health** of the general population in the United States (Lopes et al., 2022), highlighted through an increase in symptomatology (symptoms and their significance) and demand for mental health services for issues such as anxiety and depression, substance use and overdose, and suicidal ideation (Wagner, 2023). Additionally, recent research highlights the mental health impact of the COVID-19 pandemic on the general population, of which VR clients and staff alike were not immune (Armitage & Nellums, 2020; Galea et al., 2020; Godfrey, 2020; Lund et al., 2020). For instance, 12.4% of youth (aged 12–17) reported that the pandemic negatively affected their mental health either "quite a bit or a lot," and 15% of youth who had serious thoughts of suicide attributed those thoughts to the pandemic (Substance Abuse and Mental Health Services Administration [SAMHSA], 2020). Half of all adults reported they or a family member experienced a severe **mental health crisis** as a result of the pandemic (Lopes et al., 2022), including nearly 16% of adults who also had serious suicidal ideation (SAMHSA, 2021).

No matter the cause, the elevated concerns and demand for mental health services have not diminished and remain high. Americans may be less anxious about the pandemic, yet 70% remain anxious or extremely anxious about keeping safe (American Psychiatric Association [APA], 2023). In addition, 78% currently report being anxious about inflation, 70% over a potential recession, 67% due to gun violence, 66% over their health, and 65% related to paying bills or expenses. In fact, 37% reported feeling more anxiety in the current year than the year before (APA, 2023).

In 2021, 5 million youth aged 12 to 17 experienced a major depressive episode, with almost 15% experiencing severe impairment and 40% seeking treatment (SAMHSA, 2021). Almost 60 million adults reported any mental illness and 26.5 million sought services such as inpatient or outpatient mental health services, prescription medication for a mental health issue, or virtual (i.e., telehealth) services (SAMHSA, 2021). Of the 21 million adults who had a major depressive episode in the same year, 60% received treatment. Moreover, 14 million adults experienced a severe mental illness, with 65% seeking treatment and 50% reporting unmet mental health service needs.

A similar concerning pattern is evident when examining substance use, substance overuse, and suicidal ideation during the same time period. Almost 60% of Americans aged 12 and older reported being current users of tobacco, alcohol, or an illicit drug in the past month (SAMHSA, 2021). Binge drinking was present in 45% of alcohol users. Approximately 20% of the general population aged 12 and older currently use marijuana and over 3% misused opioids (including prescription pain relievers or heroin). Over 15% of the general population needed substance use treatment, with the rates of substance use disorders highly dispersed by age at 25.6% for individuals 18 to 25, 16% for people 26 and older, and 8.5% for 12- to 17-year-olds. Over 15% needed substance use treatment (SAMHSA, 2021). Suicidal ideation, planning, and attempts are another indicator of mental distress. For youth between 12 and 17 in 2021, 13% reported serious thoughts of suicide, while 6% developed a plan and 3.4% made an attempt. Among adults, almost 5% had serious thoughts of suicide, 1.4% created a plan, and 0.7% tried.

Such widespread prevalence within the general population has required rehabilitation staff to focus more heavily on the support needs associated with mental health conditions across their caseloads. Even in clients receiving services due to other disabilities, undiagnosed mental health issues and generalized anxiety may impede case progress. EBPs are emerging that can guide practitioners on how best to engage and empower individuals with diagnosed and undiagnosed mental health symptoms (i.e., Davis et al., 2022; Kaya, Iwanaga, et al., 2023; Peterson, 2023). In addition, **trauma-informed services** can support clients who have experienced various levels of traditional and unrecognized traumatic events (Chopp et al., 2023). Moreover, the implementation of appropriate EBPs and trauma-informed VR services universally across a caseload, as well as having a solid understanding of local resources and informal sources of support, may improve service delivery and outcomes without the need for excessive accommodations or strategy development. Finally, administrators and supervisors should be cognizant of and responsive to the mounting pressure experienced by their staff based on general mental health concerns, the pandemic, service delivery changes and reporting expectations, and the additional strain felt by clients that are then passed on to their counselors (Levine et al., 2022).

Pervasive Issues in Rural Communities

There are many benefits to living in rural communities. However, people with disabilities and rehabilitation professionals also face many challenges unique or amplified in rural environments that may contribute to the increased unemployment rate for this population (Adams et al., 2019; Erickson et al., 2018). Beyond basic environmental accessibility concerns and lack of resources (Isley & Low, 2022; McDaniels et al., 2018; National Rural Health Commissioner, 2020; Quilliam & Bourke 2020), pervasive issues specific to employment and the VR process are the lack of service providers, transportation options, and employment opportunities. As disability rates are higher in the most rural areas of the United States (Erickson et al., 2018; Leopold & Greiman, 2022), it will be important for rehabilitation professionals working in such settings to acknowledge the barriers while maintaining a solution-focused mindset.

VR agencies that support rural clients not only experience internal **staffing shortages** but also struggle with service provider availability (Association of People Supporting Employment First [APSE], 2020; Herbert et al., 2023). Many rural agencies exist within service deserts where few, if any, service providers are available. Moreover, agencies that do offer services are often overwhelmed by the demand for services and experience their own difficulties in recruiting and retaining highly qualified staff members (Osmani et al., 2023). Turnover is consistently high (Thompson & Nygren, 2020), resulting in persistent attention and effort required in the hiring and training process. These challenges can be mitigated through targeted actions aimed at recruiting additional providers to specific geographic areas, supporting providers in the hiring and **professional development** process of new employees, and assisting providers to navigate effective business models and multiple funding streams.

Service utilization and employment opportunities are contingent on available and reliable **transportation**. Unfortunately, transportation remains a barrier acutely felt for clients with disabilities seeking **rural rehabilitation services** (Arcury et al., 2005; Burkhardt et al., 2004; Gonzales et al., 2006; McDaniels et al., 2018; Myers et al., 2022). Creative solutions may be necessary when exploring transportation opportunities based on unique community features and resources. The first avenue often overlooked or dismissed out of hand is assisting the client to obtain a driver's license and reliable vehicle. Another option is to start a specific transportation system for people with disabilities through a voucher program (see the Toolkit for Operating a Rural Transportation Program developed by the Association of Programs for Rural Independent Living at https://www.umt.edu/rural -disability-research/resources/transp-voucher-prog/complete-transp-voucher-toolkit.pdf). Other opportunities to explore include ride sharing, faith-based organization-provided transportation, employer-provided transportation (because hiring one employee to drive around and pick up all of the other employees to ensure a reliable workforce makes a lot of business sense), and the development of a small transportation business to be owned and operated by an individual with a disability who may already have an entrepreneurial spirit and access to an accessible vehicle (possibility cultivating multiple successful vocational outcomes).

With transportation barriers addressed, clients will be ready to start the job search, which feeds directly into the final rural challenge to be addressed: the lack of overall and specific employment opportunities (Adams et al., 2019; Eades & Hughes, 2017; Pender et al., 2019). One recent EBP to consider is customized employment, which has proven effective for historically hard-to-place individuals (Kim et al., 2023). In addition, rural environments have several key characteristics that can be leveraged for the good of the VR population. One is social capital, or the positive product of one's social networks and interpersonal relationships (Kenton, 2022). A quick exercise to establish what social connections (family, friends, neighbors, organization membership and affiliations, farmers market conversations, etc.) exist through the rehabilitation professional and client may offer many opportunities for employment exploration. Furthermore, rural settings are offset with unique industries (such as the fishing, logging, and agricultural industries) and small businesses that can be engaged. In fact, 99.9% of all businesses in the United States are small and account for 63% of new job creation (U.S. Chamber of Commerce, 2023). Rehabilitation practitioners can leverage the nature of small businesses, including their greater flexibility, local decision-making powers, and less overarching corporate policies and procedures, to navigate in the hiring and job duty negotiations. However, it is important to remember that small businesses may need guidance and support, as they could lack practical knowledge in disability awareness, workplace inclusivity, accessibility and reasonable accommodations, and employer benefits such as tax credits and supports. In preparing to engage with and support small business owners, one resource to consider is the Small Business Steps to Success Toolkit available at https://steps.askearn.org/.

Anecdotally, rural communities often exude the growth mindset and inspire a natural incubation of **entrepreneurship**. Although entrepreneurship has skyrocketed in the United States over the past two decades, experiencing a 722% increase from 2000 to 2017 (Rothwell & Harlen, 2020), the use of **self-employment** reflected in VR outcomes remains low (Frain et al., 2023; Revell et al., 2009; Sánchez et al., 2023; Yamamoto & Alverson, 2017). Historically, individuals with disabilities outpace those without disabilities in self-employment rates (Frain et al., 2023) and benefit from being able to address health issues, set alternative hours, remain close to home, and side-step environmental barriers and preconceived notions regarding accommodation costs and employee limitations/abilities from potential employers (Boeri et al., 2020; Cook & Burke, 2002). However, rehabilitation counselors may view self-employment goals as a last resort due to the complicated nature of an individualized plan for self-employment and/or a lack of understanding in the process or confidence in the client's abilities to manage all tasks required of small business ownership (Frain et al., 2023; Moore & Cavenaugh, 2003). In fact, research demonstrates that self-employment is not only a viable option for individuals with disabilities (Ipsen & Swicegood, 2017: Revell et al., 2009) but that it is particularly helpful in rural settings and can lead to comparable employment wage outcomes (Conroy et al., 2019; Deller & Conroy, 2016; Ipsen & Swicegood, 2017). To that end, Frain et al. (2023) recommend four strategies to support entrepreneurship for VR clients: (a) inform and train stakeholders on entrepreneurialism, (b) realize entrepreneurship aligns with the rehabilitation philosophy, (c) suggest and cultivate supportive legislation and federal regulations, and (d) develop more researchers and experts in the field. A Vocational Rehabilitation Self-Employment Guide is also available at https://vrselfemploymentguide.org/home.

In addition to many great scholarly articles and books dedicated to serving clients with disabilities in rural settings, several online resources are available to rehabilitation professionals. Various resources offer illustrations of success stories, **best practices** and recommendations, professional development opportunities such as webinars and live events, and other technical assistance. For those interested in accessible farming, check out AgrAbility (http://www.agrability.org/). To learn how locals are engaging in some niche rural economies, explore Maine AgrAbility (https://extension.umaine.edu/agrability), Maine FishAbility (https://extension.umaine.edu/agrability/fishing-resources/), and Maine LogAbility (https://extension.umaine.edu/agrability/logging-resources/). Another great resource for targeted communities that often overlap with rural demographics is Project 3E: Educate, Empower, Employ (https://projecte3.com/). As well, the University of Montana currently houses the Rehabilitation Research and Training Center (RRTC) on Disability in Rural Communities (https://www.umt.edu/rural-disability-research/). Although not an exhaustive list, these resources will provide a jumping-off point for those seeking further information and guidance.

Remote Work

Case management has evolved over the past several decades to include and rely upon **technology** in ever-increasing ways to support communications and the documentation of information collected. Based on the changing nature of personal preferences and the world of work across the board, **remote work** opportunities are now commonplace in most industries. **Tele-rehabilitation**, similar to telehealth, is a promising practice that can offer various rehabilitative services to clients at a distance, via the internet, expanding the availability of services and convenience (Froehlich et al., 2023; Holmes & Reid, 2018; Leahy et al., 2018). Whether limited due to transportation issues, geographic distance, or disability-related challenges, **virtual services** can remove various barriers and increase **accessibility** and client engagement (Castillo & Cartwright, 2018; Embree et al., 2018). Conversely, rural clients may be at a disadvantage due to reduced broadband availability and internet access (Isley & Low, 2022). As service coordination and partnerships are integral to a holistic and person-centered case management approach, virtual meetings and electronic communications may be leveraged to streamline services and improve collaboration of various service providers and support networks when available. In addition, partial or total remote **working conditions** may improve **job satisfaction** for some rehabilitation professionals, resulting in less staff turnover or burnout (Herbert et al., 2023).

However, remote work and tele-rehabilitation will not be the most beneficial approach for some clients and do require different skillsets and competencies (Commission on Rehabilitation Counselor Certification [CRCC], 2023; Froehlich et al., 2023). When the client prefers or requests virtual services, it is important to assess each case for appropriateness to maintain high-quality services. Does the client have the technology and skillset to engage effectively in virtual services? If not, can those challenges be mitigated? If not, how might the case manager work with the client to increase awareness in the cost and benefits of both traditional in-person and virtual services so that the client can make an informed choice on service delivery?

As mentioned, providing high-quality tele-rehabilitation services requires practitioners to acquire and maintain a unique skillset (Froehlich et al., 2023). Skills and competencies for remote work and virtual services include but are not limited to time management; organization; work–life balance; dedicated time and a secure physical space for confidential meetings and paperwork; the ability to minimize and manage disruptions; general and specialized computer skills; technology troubleshooting to support their own work and the clients; hardware operations (such as computer/laptop, smartphones, printers, headsets, etc.); software usage (project management tools, shared electronic calendars, virtual meeting platforms, etc.); and knowledge of specific laws, rules, regulations, and ethical requirements related to virtual and remote work (Health Insurance Portability and Accountability Act of 1996, agency policies and procedures, Section K of the CRCC Code of Professional Ethics, etc.; Froehlich et al., 2023). Rehabilitation practitioners must also stay up to date on technological advances and internal and external threats to privacy and security (CRCC, 2023; Froehlich et al., 2023; Hill et al., 2023).

Although convenient and widely available in some locations, many clients will struggle with consistent internet service, secure and private meeting opportunities, technological hardware, assistive technologies to use technology effectively, and the proper skillset to manage all of this. Clients may rely on their service providers to support them in troubleshooting technological barriers and problems (Oswald et al., 2022). As the professional, teleservice providers need to recognize potential threats to privacy and confidentiality, as well as other external interference to the process, and be prepared to address them with the client (CRCC, 2023). Internet and computer usage in public places or shared spaces may be easy to access but not appropriate for certain conversations, assessment activities, or a whole host of services. Many ethical challenges will arise throughout the course of virtual service delivery, and rehabilitation practitioners need to be knowledgeable and vigilant in order to identify and problem-solve such issues or concerns (Froehlich et al., 2023; Hartley et al., 2023; Hill et al., 2023). As well, agency administration and those with supervisory responsibilities must also manage the impact of remote work on supporting and overseeing staff who may be working remotely and providing virtual services (Bernacchio et al., 2022; Hartley et al., 2023).

Staffing Shortages

A persistent challenge for the field is staffing shortages across rehabilitation work settings (Barrett et al., 1997; Frain et al., 2006; Herbert et al., 2023), especially in state VR agencies (Herbert et al., 2020). Beyond internal unmet staffing needs, community rehabilitation agencies that deliver critical services (such as assessment, job development, and coaching) to clients in the community are experiencing difficulties hiring and maintaining employment specialists (APSE, 2020; Osmani et al., 2023). These shortages can lead to increased caseload sizes, delayed service delivery, and the lack of availability of specific services (Herbert et al., 2023; Oswald et al., 2022). Combined, these experiences only amplify the conditions that fuel burnout, turnover, and further shortages.

The VR staffing crisis will take a multipronged approach to address. First, agencies should seek to address the underlying causes of the staffing shortage. As fewer students enter rehabilitation counseling graduate programs and even fewer elect to enter traditional rehabilitation employment opportunities (Smith et al., 2020), agencies and educators must collaborate to strengthen the pipeline of qualified applicants. Marketing and recruitment tactics of both educational programs and rehabilitation employment opportunities should be investigated and a strategic plan based on activities proven effective implemented. Second, agencies should make a concerted effort to understand the factors that result in VR staff leaving agency employment. Past research points to many contributing factors related to working conditions, job tasks, and lack of return on investment (Andrew et al, 2002; Herbert et al., 2020; Landon et al., 2023; Layne et al., 2004; Pitt et al., 2013; Zheng et al., 2017). What makes some stay and the rest move on to other opportunities? For those with competing priorities or needs, addressing barriers and increasing incentives for those who want to stay can reduce their likelihood of exiting the agency or field. Compensation, flexible working conditions, better relations between administration and staff, streamlining processes and compliance measures, promoting EBPs through professional development and support, and opportunities for advancement may increase practitioner job satisfaction and reduce turnover. Third, agencies need to plan accordingly, knowing that staff turnover will continue to occur yet the doors must remain open. Wishing and hoping are not helping. Succession planning should be a top priority for agency administrators. If not to demonstrate their understanding of the situation and respond compassionately to the negative impact it has on staff and clients alike, being proactive will mitigate the worst effects of staffing shortages on the provision of services and client outcomes.

As agencies attempt to recruit and maintain more qualified staff, they recognize the reality that there is not enough current staff to meet their service provision needs. Fixing the pipeline and job retention issues are more long-term fixes, while offices and regions need staff now. As hiring eligibility expands and employment qualifications shrink at all position levels, the knowledge and skills deficits surfacing in new hires at both state VR and service provider agencies must be addressed through effective and efficient professional development. Establishing knowledge and skills needs is an essential first step. From there, agencies can determine appropriate and targeted interventions such as disability, case management, and VR-focused college courses; webinars available through technical assistance centers and research institutes; professional organizations and conferences; and agency-driven professional development. Agencies may provide internal training through a formalized training unit or contracts with an external training entity. Activities may include formal trainings on targeted topics, technical assistance sessions, dedicated time at staff meetings for case reviews and knowledge translation, or book clubs. Agencies may also provide training to their fee-for-service providers on a voluntary or mandatory basis in an effort to standardize expectations and improve service provision across vendors. No matter the avenue taken, professional development offerings and mandates should be intentional and thoughtfully executed. Acknowledging competing time commitments, demanding work schedules, learner modality preferences, and the need for a healthy work–life balance and job satisfaction, every attempt should be made to provide high-impact and convenient professional development. While some learners benefit most from the experiential nature of in-person trainings, others may prefer or require virtual or on-demand opportunities to meet their working conditions and learning styles. On-demand may come in the form of prerecorded webinars or content available through professional journal articles and other print materials.

Looking to the future, rehabilitation educators need to focus on bringing their field experience into the classroom, igniting a passion for the work and awareness of the realities of working conditions. Graduate and undergraduate programs need to work with agencies to provide scholarships (Smith et al., 2020), short-term exposure (Oswald et al., 2017), and field experience opportunities (Huck et al., 2019) to students to assist them in their career exploration and employment decision-making. Serving on program advisory boards, guest speaking in classes, and offering paid internships are all excellent ways for agency personnel to connect with programs and recruit future hires with the requisite VR knowledge and skills (Oswald et al., 2018). In addition, cultivating new educational programming for direct-care providers is a new frontier to be explored. How can agencies connect with and support high schools, career and technical centers, and community colleges to build curriculum and credentials, facilitating the development of whole new pipelines to meet service provider staffing needs? Agencies also have an opportunity to actively promote from within those who have already made a commitment to the field. Encourage an administrative assistant or caseload support staff member to further their education through tuition remission programs and some flexibility in their work schedule. Cast your net a little wider and seek talent in promising service providers and individuals who have received services (such as clients of state or federal VR programs).

Compliance Versus Quality Services

In conjunction with the staffing crises, there has been a general negative perception of the impact of new Workforce Innovation and Opportunity Act (WIOA) requirements to the VR process (Sherman et al., 2019). The lack of understanding, confusion on requirements, and minimal process or system-oriented support have left staff feeling less like VR experts and more like data entry specialists (Oswald et al., 2022; Sherman et al., 2019). Does their mission remain to provide quality services to individuals with disabilities or meet **compliance** standards? Many staff yearn for more time to do traditional counseling and guidance. They dedicate ever-increasing amounts of face time with clients to completing documentation requirements and less on building the working alliance and supporting their individuals through the process. It is not that staff do not recognize the need for and benefits of case notes and recording the process, accountability, and compliance measures. They simply wish to have case management tools, agency policies and protocols, and clear direction that all align and streamline the process. Reducing paperwork and tasks to that which is essential and supporting staff in case and caseload management skills development can also assist practitioners in improving their efficiency and eliminating unnecessary or clunky steps.

Lack of Evidence-Based Practices and Best Practices

To be effective and efficient, case managers need to stay knowledgeable of evidence-based and **promising practices**. EBPs are interventions and services that are proven effective under specific conditions. EBPs have been empirically researched and demonstrate statistically significant results, based on criteria that correspond to various levels of strength and types of evidence. An evidence-based clinical practice has been defined as both (a) the integration of expert opinion, available information from scientific literature, and the client's perspective (American Speech-Language-Hearing Association, n.d.), and (b) holistic, quality care based on current research and knowledge, not traditional methods, advice from colleagues, or personal beliefs (American Nursing Association, n.d.). When selecting EBPs, rehabilitation practitioners should recognize the populations, environments, strategies, and fidelity measures used to establish the evidence and any potential limitations to generalizability. What works for one client group in one setting does not automatically mean it will translate or be just as successful for another group in another setting. It may, however, be an intervention to consider as a promising practice, a service and activity that has strong yet not sufficient evidence of effectiveness to support replicability or generalizability (Leahy et al., 2018). Overarching both categories, best practices represent evidence-based and promising practices that are recommended or encouraged within the field by local, state, or national experts or agencies.

Currently, there is little information available on EBPs implemented through individual state agencies and community service providers (Leahy et al., 2018). Unfortunately, the rehabilitation field is at a disadvantage in the development of EBPs. Because a basic premise of the rehabilitation philosophy is that all clients are unique, resulting in a common commitment to individualized services, it is very difficult to implement large-scale randomized experimental research projects to establish the highest level of *evidence* and generalizability (Oswald et al., 2015). More often, research is conducted through descriptive research and convenience sampling methods, which reduces the strength of the evidence and ability to generalize within specific and across diverse populations (Leahy et al., 2018; Oswald et al., 2015). Thus, rehabilitation researchers have amassed few EBPs and must continue to investigate promising and best practices currently employed in the field. **Table 15.1** outlines current evidence-based and promising VR practices and their descriptions based on recent research (Leahy et al., 2018).

As rehabilitation practitioners work in very diverse work settings and geographic locations with a wide range of client populations, more EBPs and promising practices are needed (Huber et al., 2017; Oswald et al., 2015). Researchers are encouraged to continue to partner with practitioners to build meaningful field-initiated research projects, establish user-friendly fidelity measures, and collect evidence of the effectiveness of their services and strategies (Oswald et al., 2015; Powers et al., 2022). As well, practitioners should remain informed of current practices and supporting research. Rehabilitation professionals interested in specific populations are encouraged to seek meta-analyses and research studies such as the work by Mazzotti and colleagues (2020) on transition-aged youth for information most reasonably generalizable to their practices. Helpful resources to consider include peer-reviewed journal articles on specific practices (i.e., Jones et al., 2020; Kaya et al., 2023; Torres et al., 2021), professional development opportunities through conferences and webinars, technical assistance centers such as the Vocational Rehabilitation Technical Assistance Center for Quality Employment (Tansey et al., 2023), and the National Clearinghouse of Rehabilitation Training Materials (https://ncrtm.ed.gov/).

Provider-Driven Versus Client-Driven Policies and Practices

Effective rehabilitation professionals understand that quality services are supported through the interplay of practitioner knowledge and skills, the use of EBPs, and available resources. Unfortunately, services and strategies may be limited, due to staffing shortages, geographic availability, and lack of resources. In these instances, it can be easy to fall into the trap of offering **provider-driven** practices. Provider-driven policies and services focus on what can be delivered, not what *should* be delivered. Plans and services are developed based on which providers are accepting referrals at the time and what they can commit to, instead of what the client needs or wants (see **Figure 15.1**). The ultimate goal is client compliance and adaptation to the dictated service plan (Rose & Moore, 1995).

In direct contrast, **client-driven** practices focus on the individual being served, both their strengths and needs (Greene & Uebel, 2007). Clients are active participants in the process, maintaining their autonomy and empowering self-advocacy (Rose & Moore, 1995). Services are explored and selected based on the client's ultimate aspirations and goals, strengths and competencies, confidence, opportunities, and totality of resources (including community and informal social networks; Greene & Uebel, 2007; Rose & Moore, 1995). The focus is on solutions and possibilities, as well as the development of self-efficacy and resiliency (Greene & Uebel, 2007). Rehabilitation practitioners need to be open to exploring all opportunities and resources, as well as committed to cultivating more options when required. Just because something is currently unavailable does not mean that it is not possible. It may just require extra effort to foster additional relationships and advocate for resources and service expansion.

TABLE 15.1 EVIDENCE-BASED AND PROMISING PRACTICES IN VOCATIONAL REHABILITATION

VR SERVICES	DESCRIPTION
Secondary Transition Services	A coordinated set of activities for a student with a disability designed to be a results-oriented process facilitating movement from the school to postsecondary activities and/or employment (e.g., early intervention, interagency collaboration, summer work experiences).
Assistive Technology	Application of rehabilitation engineering services and assistive technology services to meet the needs of and address the barrier confronted by individuals with disabilities.
IPS Model for Supported Employment	Supported employment strategies to help people with mental illness obtain employment (Dartmouth Model).
On-the-Job Training	Training in a specific job skill by a prospective employer, either paid or unpaid, to help an individual remain in the same or similar job upon successful completion of the training program.
Demand-Side Employment Strategies	Strategies focusing on the employer and work environment, emphasizing the preparation of people with disabilities for employment (e.g., diversity training, ADA, and job accommodation consultation).
Benefits Counseling	Benefits counseling program for consumers who receive SSI or SSDI.
Motivational Interviewing	Goal-directed counseling technique that seeks to help a client overcome ambivalence to change.
Customized Employment	Flexible process designed to personalize the employment relationship between a job candidate and an employer in a way that meets the needs of both. It is based on an individualized match between the strengths, conditions, and interests of a job candidate and the identified business needs of an employer.
Community-Based Work Program	On-site training program tailored to an employer's specific hiring needs. The training takes place in the actual work area in the workplace and may include a trained job coach located on-site to provide additional support in training.
Working Alliance	The affective relationship between the client and the counselor, which makes it possible for the client to work purposefully in the counseling relationship and for the counselor and client to agree on goals and tasks.
PCP	A process for planning and supporting an individual with a disability receiving services that builds upon the individual's capacity to engage in activities that promote community life, honoring preferences, choices, and abilities.
Soft Skills Training	Training programs with a standardized curriculum designed to change behavior and improve employability through an interactive training approach.

(continued)

TABLE 15.1 EVIDENCE-BASED AND PROMISING PRACTICES IN VOCATIONAL REHABILITATION (*CONTINUED*)

Dual Customer Approach	Both employers and clients are considered to be customers, with an approach of meeting business need through referral of qualified VR applicant.
Job Club	Formal behavioral support group for job seekers that assists participants with job hunting activities and helps with job search support and advice (Azerin Model).
Family Involvement and Support	Families, community groups, and individuals partnering to maximize resources and expertise in addressing client issues.
Social Skills Training	Systemically teaching new interpersonal skills through social learning strategies.
Cognitive Behavioral Therapy	Short-term therapeutic approach to problem-solving and modification of thinking and behavior.
ACT	Community team-based approach specializing in customized services and case management for people with mental illness.
Positive Psychology Interventions	Psychological interventions designed to facilitate positive emotions, well-being, growth, and happiness.
Project Search	Program that provides competitive employment opportunities for individuals with disabilities and places these individuals in internships at local businesses with the goal of securing nontraditional employment for persons with disabilities (transition service/supported employment for those with intellectual disabilities).
Solution-Focused Brief Therapy	Goal directed, collaborative counseling approach focusing on problem-solving and solutions leading to change.
Health Promotion Interventions	Interventions to manage disability and promote quality of life.
Person-Centered Therapy	Nondirective form of therapy based on counselor congruence, unconditional positive regard, and empathic understanding for the client.
Online Community of Practice	Exchanges information collaboratively and contributes solutions to identified challenges aimed at improving employment outcomes for people with disabilities.
Social Media	Use of media sites, often available to the public (e.g., LinkedIn, Facebook) where someone posts information and/or comments seeking employment opportunities and information.
Telehealth/ Tele-rehabilitation	The use of electronics information and telecommunications technologies (using the internet and mobile platforms) to support long-distance clinical healthcare, patient and professional health- related education, public health, and health administration.

ACT, assertive community treatment; ADA, Americans with Disabilities Act; IPS, individual placement and support; PCP, person-centered planning; SSI, Supplemental Security Income.

FIGURE 15.1 Decision-making flowchart for provider-driven services.

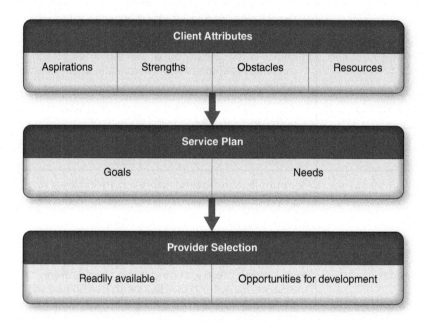

FIGURE 15.2 Client-driven plan and provider selection process.

As mentioned, a client-driven process begins with client attributes and needs that then direct the plan and provider selection (see **Figure 15.2**). This process is appropriate for all cases, yet is especially helpful for individuals with significant or complex needs. The benefits of such an approach are vast, including the development of a shared vision and goals, enhancement of assessment and planning activities, cultivation of working relationships between all stakeholders, coordination of services, assurance that supports tie directly to the goals, and the fostering of natural supports.

Questions to consider when developing a client-driven mindset include the following:

1. How am I engaging in deep listening with this person?
2. How do I ensure I understand their wishes and that they feel comfortable sharing with me?
3. What am I learning about who this individual is and what they would like their life to be like?
4. How can I explore and discover more about this individual?
5. How am I using what I learn about this person?
6. How am I empowering this individual to make their own decisions and advocate for their needs?
7. Am I setting low expectations or asking this person to accept something inferior because the alternative is harder for me to deliver?
8. Is there a discrepancy between what I want and what the client wants, and am I trying to persuade this individual to agree with me?

9. Am I willing to move out of my comfort zone and into uncharted territory?
10. What resources, interventions, and programs could I explore that will be new to me but potentially more appropriate for this individual?

None of this is possible, though, without the support of administrators and supervisors. Unless policies, guidelines, and practices are aligned with client-driven services, rehabilitation practitioners will experience a discrepancy between the client-centered philosophy or ideal (what they would like to do) and the realities of their work (what they are told to do). In addition to direct support through managers and policies, staff professional development and capacity to perform such services will enhance the likelihood and effectiveness of professional efforts to be client-driven.

SUMMARY

The concluding chapter to this book offered an exploration of current challenges, pervasive trends, and potential opportunities. As rehabilitation professionals move forward with the most pressing threats, those which were already present yet amplified by the COVID-19 pandemic, the field is again tasked with rising to the challenge and turning adversity into opportunity. Without hope and optimism, it is easy to wallow in the current frustrations and pressures bearing down on organizations and their staff. However, that does not give us enough credit nor pay appropriate homage to our unique rehabilitation mindset. We are strength-based, resilient, and master advocators! While the challenges may be clear, the direction the field must take requires further clarification. With a little grit, flexibility, and creativity, the field of rehabilitation will find a path forward and continue to ensure that individuals with disabilities are properly served and supported in their pursuit of optimal independence and autonomy.

QUESTIONS FOR DISCUSSION

1. What local challenges are your rehabilitation agencies facing? What, if any, evidence-based or best practices are offered within rehabilitation or related fields to address such challenges?

2. What mental health challenges are most pressing in your community and what resources, if any, are available to support those in crisis?

3. What, if still relevant, is the persistent impact of the COVID-19 pandemic on the general population, individuals with preexisting mental health conditions, and VR agencies and staff?

4. How can rehabilitation professionals remain responsive to client needs while promoting their own self-care and mental wellness?

5. How might agency administrators and those in supervisory roles support their staff?

6. What EBPs related to mental health support and trauma-informed practices may be implemented universally within case management services to support all clients?

7. What are specific self-case strategies that work for you to support a healthy work–life balance and overall mental wellness?

8. What are some unique industries and small businesses in your local community or state that could be explored for job creation and customized employment?

9. What do you need to know or have to feel confident in when supporting an individual to pursue self-employment and how can you get what you need?

10. How might you balance the need to meet compliance requirements and provide quality services?

11. Based on your rehabilitative interests, what evidence-based or promising practices are available and of potential benefit?

12. What specific strategies could you employ to develop and maintain a client-driven mindset?

PUTTING IT INTO PRACTICE

Ask yourself these questions to target issues or concerns with challenges and visions for professional practice.

1. How can you strike a balance between adhering to compliance requirements and delivering high-quality, client-centered services? What methods can you employ to continuously improve your practice while adhering to ethical standards?

2. What steps can you take to stay updated on the latest research and incorporate best practices into your interventions? How can you harness those best practices to foster a culture of innovation and continuous improvement within your professional setting?

3. What trends do you foresee shaping the future of rehabilitation, and how can you prepare for these changes? What untapped opportunities exist in your current practice that could elevate the quality of skills you offer?

 A robust set of instructor resources designed to supplement this text is located at http://connect.springerpub.com/content/book/978-0-8261-5963-2. Qualifying instructors may request access by emailing **textbook@springerpub.com**.

REFERENCES

Adams, C., Corbin, A., O'Hara, L., Park, M., Sheppard-Jones, K., Butler, L., Umeasiegbu, V., McDaniels, B., & Bishop, M. L. (2019). A qualitative analysis of the employment needs and barriers of individuals with intellectual and developmental disabilities in rural areas. *Journal of Applied Rehabilitation Counseling, 50*(3), 227–240. https://doi.org/10.1891/0047-2220.50.3.227

American Nursing Association. (n.d.). *What is evidence-based practice in nursing?* https://www.nursingworld.org/practice-policy/nursing-excellence/evidence-based-practice-in-nursing/

American Psychiatric Association. (2023, May 10). *Americans express worry over personal safety in annual anxiety and mental health poll.* https://www.psychiatry.org/News-room/News-Releases/Annual-Anxiety-and-Mental-Health-Poll-2023

American Speech-Language-Hearing Association. (n.d.). *Evidence-based practice (EBP).* https://www.asha.org/research/ebp/

Andrew, J. D., Faubian, C. W., & Palmer, C. D. (2002). The relationship between counselor satisfaction and extrinsic job factors in state rehabilitation agencies. *Rehabilitation Counseling Bulletin, 45,* 223–232. https://doi.org/10.1177/00343552020450040501

Arcury, T. A., Preisser, J. S., Gesler, W. M., & Powers, J. M. (2005). Access to transportation and health care utilization in a rural region. *The Journal of Rural Health, 21,* 31–38. https://doi.org/10.1111/j.1748-0361.2005.tb00059.x

Armitage, R., & Nellums, L. B. (2020). Protecting health workers' mental health during COVID-19. *Public Health (London), 185,* Article 18. https://doi.org/10.1016/j.puhe.2020.05.044

Association of People Supporting Employment First. (2020). *Impact of COVID-19 on disability employment services and outcomes.* https://apse.org/covid-19-impact-survey/

Barrett, K., Riggar, T. F., Flowers, C. R., Crimando, W. C., & Bailey, T. (1997). The turnover dilemma: A disease with solutions. *Journal of Rehabilitation, 63*(2), 36–42. https://link.gale.com/apps/doc/A56175561/HRCA?u=anon~4c99739f&sid=googleScholar&xid=a1a872b8

Bernacchio, C. P., Kuo, H. J., Schultz, J. C., Brink, E. A., & Soldner, J. L. (2022). A technology-assisted supervision option in rehabilitation counseling: Ethical considerations and best practices. *Journal of Rehabilitation, 88*(4), 4–12.

Boeri, T., Giupponi, C., Krueger, A. B., & Machin, S. (2020). Solo self-employment and alternative work arrangements: A cross-country perspective on the changing composition of jobs. *Journal of Economic Perspectives, 34*(1), 170–195. https://doi.org/10.1257/jep.34.1.170

Burkhardt J. E., Nelson, C. A., Murray, G., & Koffman, D. (2004). *Toolkit for rural community coordinated transportation services.* Transportation Research Board (TCRP No. 101). https://www.nap.edu/read/13751/chapter/1

Cashin, A. (2018). A scoping review of the progress of the evolution of the Doctor of Nursing Practice in the USA to inform consideration of future transformation of Nurse Practitioner education in Australia. *Collegian, 25*(1), 141–146. https://doi.org/10.1016/j.colegn.2017.05.001

Castillo, Y. A., & Cartwright, J. (2018). Telerehabilitation in rural areas: A qualitative investigation of pre-service rehabilitation professionals' perspectives. *Journal of Applied Rehabilitation Counseling, 49*(2), 6–13. https://doi.org/10.1891/0047-2220.49.2.6

Chopp, S., Topitzes, D., & Mersky, J. (2023). Trauma-responsive vocational rehabilitation services. *Behavioral Sciences, 13*(6), 511. https://doi.org/10.3390/bs13060511

Commission on Rehabilitation Counselor Certification. (2023). *Code of professional ethics for rehabilitation counselors.* https://crccertification.com/wp-content/uploads/2023/04/2023-Code-of-Ethics.pdf

Conroy, T., Deller, S., & Kures, M. (2019). Entrepreneurship in rural employment in the US. In S. Davidova, K. Thomson, & A. Mishra (Eds.), *Rural policies and employment* (pp. 93–108). World Scientific. https://doi.org/10.1142/9781786347091_0006

Cook, J. A., & Burke, J. (2002). Public policy and employment of people with disabilities: Exploring new paradigms. *Behavioral Sciences & the Law, 20*(6), 541–557. https://doi.org/10.1002/bsl.515

Davenport, S. J. (2021). Impact of occupational therapy in an integrated adult social care service: Audit of therapy outcome measure findings. *Journal of Integrated Care, 29*(4), 439–451. https://doi.org/10.1108/JICA-04-2021-0020

Davis, M., Koroloff, N., Mizrahi, R., & Morrison, E. (2022). Collaboration between mental health and vocational rehabilitation programs for transition-age youth vocational outcomes. *Psychiatric Rehabilitation, 45*(4), 303–313. https://doi.org/10.1037/prj0000539

Deller, S., & Conroy, T. (2016). Survival rates of rural businesses. *Choices, 31*(4), 1–5. https://www.choicesmagazine.org/UserFiles/file/cmsarticle_559.pdf

Dennis, H., & Ramsay, J. D. (2019). A roadmap to professionalism: Advancing occupational safety and health practice as a profession in the United States. *Safety Science, 118,* 168–180. https://doi.org/10.1016/j.ssci.2019.04.018

Eades, D. C., & Hughes, D. W. (2017). Too few skills for some, too many skills for others: Are future rural employment opportunities a poor match for the rural labor supply? *Career and Technical Education Research, 42*(2), 79–101. https://doi.org/10.5328/cter42.2.79

Embree, J. A., Huber, J. M., Kapp, V. A., & Wilson, J. F. (2018). Utilizing telerehabilitation to deliver rehabilitation services remotely as an alternative to traditional counseling. *Journal of Applied Rehabilitation Counseling, 49*(2), 40–47. https://doi.org/10.1891/0047-2220.49.2.40

Erickson, W. A., VanLooy, S., von Schrader, S., & Bruyere, S. M. (2018). Disability, income, and rural poverty. In D. A. Harley, N. A. Ysasi, M. L. Bishop, & A. R. Fleming (Eds.), *Disability and vocational rehabilitation in rural settings: Challenges to service delivery* (pp. 17–41). Springer Publishing Company.

Feyereisen, S., McConnell, W., Thomas, C., & Puro, N. (2021). Physician dominance in the 21st century: Examination of non-physician autonomy through prevailing theoretical lenses. *Sociology of Health & Illness, 43*(8), 1867–1886. https://doi.org/10.1111/1467-9566.13366

Frain, M., Bishop, M., Frain, J., Rohack, D., Shirley, G., & Sánchez, J. (2023). The time is ripe for entrepreneurship in vocational rehabilitation: A four-pronged approach. *Rehabilitation Counseling Bulletin, 66*(3), 215–222. https://doi.org/10.1177/00343552221116051

Frain, M., Ferrin, J. M., Rosenthal, D. A., & Wampold. B. (2006). A meta-analysis of rehabilitation outcomes based on education level of the counselor. *Journal of Rehabilitation, 72*(1), 10–18. https://link.gale.com/apps/doc/A144013047/HRCA?u=anon~4ad479ee&sid=googleScholar&xid=1a709f97

Friedman, K. B. (2022). Educator perspectives on rehabilitation counselor identity in the post-CACREP context. *Dissertation Abstracts International: Section B: The Sciences and Engineering, 83*(3-B).

Froehlich, R. J., Henry, J. S., Tichy, N., Hill, J. C., & Thompson, K. (2023). Rehabilitation counselors and technology, social media, and distance counseling: Contemporary considerations. *Rehabilitation Counseling Bulletin, 66*(4), 265–273. https://doi.org/10.1177/00343552221147219

Galea, S., Merchant, R. M., & Lurie, N. (2020). The mental health consequences of COVID-19 and physical distancing: The need for prevention and early intervention. *JAMA Internal Medicine, 180*(6), 817–818. https://doi.org/10.1001/jamainternmed.2020.1562

Godfrey, E. (2020, April 3). Americans with disabilities are terrified. *The Atlantic*. https://www.theatlantic .com/politics/archive/2020/04/people-disabilities-worry-they-wont-get-treatment/609355/

Gonzales, L., Stombaugh, D., Seekins, T., & Kasnitz, D. (2006). Accessible rural transportation: An evaluation of the traveler's cheque voucher program. *Community Development, 37*, 106–115. https://doi .org/10.1080/15575330.2006.10383112

Greene, R. R., & Uebel, M. (2007): Chapter 2. Intervention continued. *Journal of Human Behavior in the Social Environment, 14*(1-2), 31–50. https://doi.org/10.1300/J137v14n01_02

Hartley, M. T., Bourgeois, P., & Clarke, B. J. (2023). Ethics of technology practice: Beliefs and behaviors of certified rehabilitation counselors during the COVID-19 pandemic. *Rehabilitation Counseling Bulletin, 66*(4), 244–256. https://doi.org/10.1177/00343552221147216

Herbert, J. T., Joon Yoon, H., O'Shea, A., & Al Balushi, I. (2023). Recruitment and retention of state vocational rehabilitation counselors: A mixed methods analysis. *Journal of Rehabilitation, 89*(1), 61–71.

Herbert, J. T., Zhai, Y., & Coduti, W. A. (2020). Predictors of intent to leave current employment among rehabilitation counselors. *Journal of Rehabilitation, 86*(1), 32–40. https://link.gale.com/apps/doc/ A621689301/HRCA?u=anon~fa6e60c9&sid=googleScholar&xid=f137856b

Hill, J. C., Stokes, L. E., Froelich, R. J., Emmanuel, D., Landon, T., & Hicks, S. (2023). Ethical dilemmas: current and projected concerns reported by certified rehabilitation counselors. *Rehabilitation Counseling Bulletin, 66*(4), 231–243. https://doi.org/10.1177/00343552221146159

Holmes, C. M., & Reid, C. A. (2018). Ethics in telerehabilitation: Looking ahead. *Journal of Applied Rehabilitation Counseling, 49*(2), 14–23.

Huber, M. J., Oswald, G. R., Chan, F., Shaw, L. R., & Wilson, J. (2017). A call for a national evidence-based programs and practices registry in vocational rehabilitation. *Journal of Vocational Rehabilitation, 46*, 11–18. https://doi.org/10.3233/JVR-160838

Huck, G. E., Oswald, G. R., & Blake, J. (2019). Undergraduate rehabilitation students' perspectives and advice on strategies for successful field experiences. *Rehabilitation Research, Policy and Education, 33*(3), 184–197. https://doi.org/10.1891/2168-6653.33.3.184

Ipsen, C., & Swicegood, G. (2017). Rural and urban vocational rehabilitation self-employment outcomes. *Journal of Vocational Rehabilitation, 46*, 97–105. https://doi.org/10.3233/JVR-160846

Isley, C., & Low, S. A. (2022). Broadband adoption and availability: Impacts on rural employment during COVID-19. *Telecommunications Policy, 46*(7). https://doi.org/10.1016/j.telpol.2022.102310

Jones, K. T., Landon, T., Kipping, K. C., & McKnight-Lizotte, M. (2020). State vocational rehabilitation counselors' knowledge of the discovery process in customized employment. *Journal of Rehabilitation, 86*(2), 13–21.

Kaya, C., Bishop, M., & Torres, A. (2023). The impact of work incentives benefits counseling on employment outcomes: A national vocational rehabilitation study. *Journal of Occupational Rehabilitation, 33*, 538–549. https://doi.org/10.1007/s10926-022-10092-1

Kaya, C., Iwanaga, K., Hsu, S., Akpinar, E. N., Bezyak, J., Chen, X., & Chan, F. (2023). Demographic covariates, vocational rehabilitation services, and employment outcomes of working-age adults with anxiety disorders: A multivariate logistic regression analysis. *Journal of Occupational Rehabilitation, 32*, 742–752. https://doi.org/10.1007/s10926-022-10038-7

Kenton, W. (2022, November 27). What is social capital? Definition, types, and examples. *Investopedia*. https://www.investopedia.com/terms/s/socialcapital.asp

Kim, J., Riesen, T., Inge, K., Keeton, B., Weathers, M., & Tansey, T. N. (2023). Customized employment as a pathway to competitive integrated employment: An analysis of RSA 911 data of state vocational rehabilitation agencies with the highest use of this intervention. *Journal of Vocational Rehabilitation, 58*, 89–98.

Landon, T. J., Phillips, B. N., McKnight, M., Sabella, S. A., & Kline, K. M. (2023). The impact of organizational factors and professional identity on turn over intent in state vocational rehabilitation agencies. *Rehabilitation Counseling Bulletin*. https://doi.org/10.1177/00343552231155215

Layne, C. M., Hohenshil, T. H., & Singh, K. (2004). The relationship of occupational stress, psychological strain, and coping resources to the turnover intentions of rehabilitation counselors. *Rehabilitation Counseling Bulletin, 48*(1), 19–30. https://doi.org/10.1177/00343552040480010301

Leahy, M. J., Del Valle, R. J., Landon, T. J., Iwanaga, K., Sherman, S. G., Reyes, A., & Chan, F. (2018). Promising and evidence-based practices in vocational rehabilitation: Results of a national Delphi study. *Journal of Vocational Rehabilitation, 48*(1), 37–48. https://doi.org/10.3233/JVR-170914

Leopold, A., & Greiman, L. (2022, February). *America at a glance: An update on rural-urban differences in disability rates*. The University of Montana Rural Institute for Inclusive Communities. https:// scholarworks.umt.edu/ruralinst_independent_living_community_participation/80/

Levine, B. E. (2022). *A profession without reason: The crisis of contemporary psychiatry—untangled and solved by Spinoza, freethinking, and radical enlightenment*. AK Press.

Levine, A., Rumrill, P. D., Espinosa, C., & Sheppard-Jones, K. (2022). Vocational rehabilitation in the COVID-19 era: The importance of supervision. *Rehabilitation Counseling Bulletin.* https://doi .org/10.1177/00343552221087178

Lingel, J., Clark-Parsons, R., & Branciforte, K. (2022). More than handmaids: Nursing, labor activism and feminism. *Gender, Work & Organization, 29*(4), 1149–1163. https://doi.org/10.1111/gwao.12816

Lopes, L., Kirzinger, A., Sparks, G., Stokes, M., & Brodie, M. (2022). *KFF/CNN mental health in America survey.* https://www.kff.org/report-section/kff-cnn-mental-health-in-america-survey-findings/

Lund, E. M., Forber-Pratt, A. J., Wilson, C., & Mona, L. R. (2020). The COVID-19 pandemic, stress, and trauma in the disability community: A call to action. *Rehabilitation Psychology, 65*(4), 313–322. https://doi.org/10.1037/rep0000368

Mazzotti, V., Rowe, D. A., Kwiatek, S., Woggt, A., Chang, W., Fowler, C. H., Poppen, M., Sinclair, J., & Test, D. W. (2020). Secondary transition predictors of postschool success: An update to the research base. *Career Development and Transition for Exceptional Individuals, 44*(1), 47–64. https://doi .org/10.1177/2165143420959793

McClanahan, M. L., & Sligar, S. R. (2015). Adapting to WIOA 2014 minimum education requirements for vocational rehabilitation counselors. *Journal of Rehabilitation, 81*(3), 3–8. https://link.gale.com/ apps/doc/A432170448/AONE?u=anon~4f8df258&sid=googleScholar&xid=ab9b0b86

McDaniels, B. W., Harley, D. A., & Beach, D. T. (2018). Transportation, accessibility, and accommodation in rural communities. In D. A. Harley, I. N. Ysas, M. Bishop, & A. Fleming (Eds.), *Disability and vocational rehabilitation in rural settings* (pp. 43–57). Springer.

McDonnall, M. C., Cmar, J. L., & McKnight, Z. S. (2022). The impact of the Workforce Innovation and Opportunity Act on agency-level vocational rehabilitation outcomes for adults and youth with blindness and low vision. *Journal of Disability Policy Studies.* https://doi.org/10.1177/10442073221135811

Mikhly, M. (2014/2015). The role of the medical profession in swaying public policy: Exploring physician responsibility and advocacy. *Einstein Journal of Biology & Medicine, 30*(1/2), 2–5. https://www .einsteinmed.edu/uploadedFiles/Pulications/EJBM/Article1.pdf

Moore, J. (2018). Health professions regulation in the United States. *Revista de Direito Sanitário, 19*(2), 131–155. https://doi.org/10.11606/issn.2316-9044.v19i2p131-155

Moore, J. E., & Cavenaugh, B. S. (2003). Self-employment for persons who are blind. *Journal of Visual Impairment & Blindness, 97*(6), 366–369. https://doi.org/10.1177/0145482X0309700605

Myers, A., Ipsen, C., & Standley, K. (2022). Transportation patterns of adults with travel-limiting disabilities in rural and urban America. *Frontiers in Rehabilitation Sciences, 3.* https://doi.org/10.3389/ fresc.2022.877555

National Rural Health Commissioner. (2020). *Report for the Minister for Regional Health, Regional Communications and Local Government on the improvement of access, quality and distribution of allied health services in regional, rural and remote Australia 2020.* https://www.health.gov.au/sites/ default/files/documents/2021/04/final-report-improvement-of-access-quality-and-distribution-of-al lied-health-services-in-regional-rural-and-remote-australia.pdf

O'Brien, M., & Graham, M. (2009). Rehabilitation counseling in the state or federal program. Is there a future? *Rehabilitation Counseling Bulletin, 52,* 124–128. https://doi.org/10.1177/0034355208323948

Osmani, K. J., Oswald, G. R., Brooks, J., & McDowell, K. (2023). *2023 comprehensive state needs assessment for New York State adult career and continuing education services, vocational rehabilitation.* Cornell University.

Oswald, G., Accordino, M. P., Bernacchio, C., & Oswald, G. (2022, Fall). *The effects of the pandemic on state vocational rehabilitation service delivery: Preliminary findings from the NE.* Presentation at the National Council on Rehabilitation Education conference.

Oswald, G. R., Alderman, L., & Willmering, P. (2017). Short-term job shadowing experience benefits for undergraduate rehabilitation students. *The Australian Journal of Rehabilitation Counselling, 23*(2), 79–89. https://doi.org/10.1017/jrc.2017.2

Oswald, G. R., Huber, M. J., & Workman, J. R. (2015). A guide to developing evidence-based practices in rehabilitation counseling research. *Journal of Applied Rehabilitation Counseling, 46*(1), 34–39.

Oswald, G. R., Huck, G., & Duncan, J. C. (2018). The state of undergraduate rehabilitation education: Current program coordinator perspectives. *Rehabilitation Research, Policy, and Education, 32*(4), 253–261. https://doi.org/10.1891/2168-6653.32.4.253

Pender, J., Hertz, T., Cromartie, J., & Farrigan, T. (2019, November). *Rural America at a glance, 2019 edition.* EIB-212. U.S. Department of Agriculture, Economic Research Service. https://www.ers.usda .gov/publications/pub-details/?pubid=95340

Perry, D. C., Schiro-Geist, C., Marme, M., Duncan, J. C., Robertson, R., & Willmering, P. (2018). Undergraduate rehabilitation education and accreditation: The importance of being persistent. *Journal of Applied Rehabilitation Counseling, 49*(4), 34–41.

Peterson, S. (2022). CACREP and the rehabilitation counseling profession. *Rehabilitation Professional, 30*(2), 51–70.

Peterson, S. (2023). Facilitating a warm handoff in state vocational rehabilitation service delivery. *Journal of Applied Rehabilitation Counseling, 54*(1), 33–47. https://doi.org/10.1891/JARC-2021-0019

Pitt, J. S., Leahy, M. J., & Lewis, A. N. (2013). Turnover intent predictors among state vocational rehabilitation counselors. *Journal of Rehabilitation Administration, 37*(1), 5–18.

Powers, K., Clarke, S., Phillips, J. A., Cripps, R., Craven, K., Farrin, A., das Nair, R., & Radford, K. A. (2022). Developing an implementation fidelity checklist for a vocational rehabilitation intervention. *Pilot and Feasibility Studies, 8*, 234. https://doi.org/10.1186/s40814-022-01194-x

Quilliam, C., & Bourke, L. (2020). Rural Victorian service provider responses to the National Disability Insurance Scheme. *Australian Journal of Social Issues, 55*(4), 439–455. https://doi.org/10.1002/ajs4.107

Revell, G., Smith, F., & Inge, K. (2009). An analysis of self-employment outcomes within the federal/state vocational rehabilitation system. *Journal of Vocational Rehabilitation, 31*(1), 11–18. https://doi.org/10.3233/JVR-2009-0467

Rose, S. M., & Moore, V. L. (1995). Case management. In R. L. Edwards (Ed.-in-Chief), *Encyclopedia of social work* (19th ed., pp. 335–340). NASW Press.

Rothwell, J., & Harlen, J. (2020). 2019 gig economy and self-employment report. *Gallup.* https://quickbooks.intuit.com/content/dam/intuit/quickbooks/Gig-Economy-Self-Employment-Report-2019.pdf

Samman, E. (2021). The origins of incivility in nursing: How reconstruction-era policies and organizations impacted social behavior within the nursing profession. *Creative Nursing, 27*(1), 66–70. https://doi.org/10.1891/CRNR-D-20-00085

Sánchez, J., Frain, M. P., Shirley, G., Rohack, D., & Pan, D. (2023). Persons with disabilities in self-employment served by the federal/state vocational rehabilitation system: Differences between 2011-2013 and 2017-2019. *Rehabilitation Counseling Bulletin, 66*(3), 203–214. https://doi.org/10.1177/00343552221102396

Sherman, S. G., Schuster, R., Eischens, P., Limbrunner, L., Sanders M. P., Bloomberg, M., & Scroggs, L. B. (2019). Perceptions of vocational rehabilitation professionals regarding Workforce Innovation and Opportunity Act policy changes and employment outcomes. *Journal of Rehabilitation, 85*(4), 50–61.

Smith, T. J., Dillahunt-Aspillaga, C., Chou, C., Ching, D., & Weston, A. (2020). Rehabilitation scholarship program: A solution to personnel shortages in the vocational rehabilitation system. *Journal of Vocational Rehabilitation, 52*, 267–277. https://doi.org/10.3233/JVR-201076

Substance Abuse and Mental Health Services Administration. (2020). *Key substance use and mental health indicators in the United States: Results from the 2019 national survey on drug use and health. Center for behavioral health statistics and quality, substance abuse and mental health services administration.* https://www.samhsa.gov/data/sites/default/files/reports/rpt29393/2019NSDUHFFRPDFWHTML/2019NSDUHFFR1PDFW090120.pdf

Tansey, T. N., Bishop, M., Iwanaga, K., Zhou, K., & Chan, F. (2023). Vocational rehabilitation service delivery: Technical assistance needs of vocational rehabilitation professionals. *Journal of Vocational Rehabilitation, 58*, 49–62. https://doi.org/10.3233/JVR-221224

Thompson, J. R., & Nygren, M. A. (2020). COVID-19 and the field of intellectual and developmental disabilities: Where have we been? Where are we? Where do we go? *Intellectual and Developmental Disabilities, 8*(4), 257–261. https://doi.org/10.1352/1934-9556-58.4.257

Torres, A. (2023). The history of ethnic minority psychological associations in the United States. *North American Journal of Psychology, 25*(1), 87–98. https://link.gale.com/apps/doc/A739324886/HRCA?u=anon~ed329f74&sid=googleScholar&xid=12aca39b

Torres, A., Diaz, P., Breund, R., Baker, T. N., Baker, A. Z., & Peluso, P. (2021). Therapeutic alliance in vocational rehabilitation counseling: Assessing client factors and functioning. *Journal of Vocational Rehabilitation, 55*, 313–322.

U.S. Chamber of Commerce. (April 10, 2023). *The state of small business now: What you need to know about small business in American including the latest data on job creation, business starts, and more.* https://www.uschamber.com/small-business/state-of-small-business-now

Wagner, R. (July 26, 2023). *Estimated revenue of employer firms providing mental health services in selected industries grew to more than $100 billion in 2021.* https://www.census.gov/library/stories/2023/07/public-health-emergencies-and-mental-health.html?utm_campaign=20230726msacos1ccstors&utm_medium=email&utm_source=govdelivery

Yamamoto, S. H., & Alverson, C. Y. (2017). Individuals with disabilities in self-employment through vocational rehabilitation: Predictors of successful case closure from 2008 to 2012. *Journal of Career Assessment, 25*(3), 450–466. https://doi.org/10.1177/1069072716639862

Zheng, L. X., Talley, W. B., Faubion, C. W., & Lankford, G. M. (2017). The climate of job satisfaction: The relationship between extrinsic job factors and satisfaction among community rehabilitation program professionals. *Journal of Rehabilitation, 83*(1), 23–30. https://link.gale.com/apps/doc/A491582912/AONE?u=anon~8d7b83a0&sid=googleScholar&xid=b469b5d8

Index